Dong Ha
Camp Carroll
(Rock Pile)
DMZ
Quan
Hue (Camp Evans)
Khe Sanh
Phu Bai
Camp Eagle
Hamburger Hill
Da Nang (Marble Mountain)
Hoi An
A Shau Valley
Tam Ky
Americal Div
I CORP
An Hoa
Chu Lai
Kham Duc
Tra Bong
Dak Pek
Dak To
GI Plateau
Quang Ngai
Duc Pho
Ben Het
LZ English
Plei Kleng
An Loa Valley
Fire Base November
Happy
Valley
Bong Son
Kontum
Hammond
4th Inf Div
Phu Cat
An Khe
Qui Nhon
Camp Holloway
Pleiku
Rok Valley
Camp Enari
Van
Canh
Che Reo
LZ X-ray
173rd Abn Bde
Oasis
Phu Tuc
Dong Tre
Ban
Blech
Tuy Hoa
I Field Force
Cong Son
Phu Hiep
5th Special Forces Gp
Duc My
18th Engineer Bde
Ban Don
Khanh Duong
Ban Me Thuot
Nha Trang
Duc Phong
II
CORP
Dong Ba Thin
Song Be
Bu Dop
Nhon Co
Da Lat
Cam Ranh Bay
Quan Lei
1st Inf Div
Fish
Hook
Phan Rang
Nui Ba Den
(Black Virgin Mountain)
An Loc
Iron
Triangle
Bao Loc
Song Mao
Tanh Linh
Tay Ninh
Phu Loi
Vo Dat
Parrot's Beak
III
CORP
Xuan Loc
An Long
Moc
Hoa
Bien Hoa
Bear
Cat
Phan Thiet
Task Force South
Cu Chi
Ham Tan
(obile)
nf Div
Dong
Tam
My
Tho
Long Giao
Long Binh
Vung Tau
Inf Div
Vinh Long
Long Thinh
Rach Gia
Can
Tho
Mekong
Delta
SAIGON
Tan An
Phu Vinh
US Army, Vietnam
1st Logistical Command
1st Signal Bde
1st Aviation Bde
II Field Force
44th Medical Bde
18th Military Police Bde
199th Light Infantry Bde
11th Armored Cav Reg
20th Engineer Bde
U Minh
Forest
IV
CORP
3rd Bde, 82nd Abn Div
Soc Trang
Ca Mau
(Quon Long)

SOUTH VIETNAM

I'M READY TO TALK TWO

I'M READY TO TALK TWO

ROBERT O. BABCOCK

Deeds not Words!

Bob Babcock

DEEDS PUBLISHING | ATLANTA

Published by Deeds Publishing in Athens, GA
www.deedspublishing.com

Printed in The United States of America

Cover design and text layout by Mark Babcock

HARDCOVER ISBN 978-1-950794-66-9
PAPERBACK ISBN 978-1-950794-65-2

Books are available in quantity for promotional or premium use.

For information, email info@deedspublishing.com.

First Edition, 2022

10 9 8 7 6 5 4 3 2 1

This book is dedicated to all those who honorably answered our country's call to duty during the Vietnam War, and all other wars our nation has fought. It is also dedicated to the Family members and friends who lived the experience with us and who want to learn more from the point of view of those of us who participated in Vietnam and other wars—past, present, future.

And I especially want to dedicate this book to my fellow Atlanta Vietnam Veterans Business Association members who cared enough about their Family, their friends, their unit's history, and American history to take the time to write their stories to include in this book. It is a legacy we leave for future generations.

ACKNOWLEDGMENTS

First, I thank the Vietnam veterans and wives who have written their stories to include in this book. As the second book in our I'm Ready to Talk series, you who contributed to our first book once again came forward to preserve more of your stories. Plus, several who did not contribute to our first book realized you had missed an opportunity and stepped forward to be included. I remain impressed with the quality of the way you have expressed your honest memories of what, to most of us, is the most memorable time of our lives.

I thank my team at Deeds Publishing for making sure this book is as good as it can be. Jan quickly sold me on the title and cover picture (again), Mark used his design talents to make it into a cover that will catch anyone's eye, and Mark and Matt for their layout work.

My editors—Skip Bell, John Butler, Vince Corica, John Fraser, and Norman Zoller—teamed their editor's eyes with the experiences they had during the Vietnam war to make sure this book is as real and accurate as it can be.

And I thank all who encouraged me to make this project happen. This is a legacy that all who participated are leaving for generations of Americans to come. I've never had a person tell me they knew too much about the military service of their Family members. This is our gift to our Family, our military unit, and to American history—our legacy of telling our personal experiences from our time in Vietnam.

CONTENTS

PREFACE

BOB BABCOCK, PLATOON LEADER/XO, B/1-22 INFANTRY, 4TH INFANTRY DIVISION – JULY 1966 TO JULY 1967

Vietnam was not a sixteen-year war, it was a one-year war fought sixteen times by a different set of troops each year from 1959 to 1975. Unlike WWII, we were not in for the "duration". The war morphed continually. Each year was different and had its own list of good, bad, and ugly, just as have all wars since the beginning of time. Each of the veterans who served in Vietnam has stories to be preserved for posterity.

Our highest troop concentration was in the years 1965 to 1971, with the peak hitting in 1968 with almost 550,000 troops deployed. Earlier and later, we had fewer US troops engaged. But as my favorite quote from wartime explains, which came from a WWII vet, "Any battle is a big one … if you are in it." So, let's never think any year of the entire sixteen years of the war were any more or less life changing for those who were there.

No person can say, "This is how it was in Vietnam." He or she can only talk about his/her own experiences during the timeframe they were there. Some of the factors that make it impossible for anyone to describe anything more than individual experiences was **branch of service** (Army, Marines, Air Force, Navy, Coast Guard); **type of job** (combat arms, aviation, support); **rank** (private to general); **area of country served in** (I, II, III, IV Corps, Yankee Station, Thailand, or Philippines); **time period served** (advisor phase—1959-1964, buildup phase—1965-1967, Tet and major battles—1968-1969, withdrawal phase 1970-1972, Vietnamization advisory phase 1973-1975); **public opinion** (Ignorance and apathy to mild support, disillusionment, opposition, protests and riots, relief and indifference).

I speak from the viewpoint of being an Infantry lieutenant in the Army in the buildup phase (July 1966 to July 1967), in the central highlands (II Corps), when the American public was apathetic to mildly supportive. I also had the advantage of training my troops while at Fort Lewis, Washington and taking men that I knew to fight next to me.

Just as our fathers from World War II did, we came back from war and lived productive lives. We were mostly ignored until recent years, but random formal and informal polls of Vietnam veterans show that about 90% of us are proud we served in Vietnam and would do it again if called on. There must have been something "good" that causes such a high percentage to feel that way. Among the intangibles that is common among all who have been to war is the brotherhood with those who shared your experiences, whether in the same unit or simply because you fought in the same war.

I will always believe that there is no stronger bond in the world, except for a mother and her child, than that of combat veterans who have fought together. Our fellow veterans have experienced the good, the bad, and the ugly with us—and we focus on the total picture.

* * * * *

For anyone reading this who do not know a Vietnam veteran to talk to, let me suggest you go to **http://www.witnesstowar.org/** and watch video interviews of Vietnam veterans talking about their experiences. From these short (two to six minutes each) video clips, you can get a good view of what we Vietnam veterans think about our experiences in Vietnam. You will find nine separate video clips that Vietnam's best known war correspondent, Joe Galloway, did with me included there—and hundreds of clips of veterans from all branches and specialties and timeframes from the Vietnam War. The stories you will see give a different perspective—they cover the "good" as well as the "bad" and "ugly."

In this book, you will find 140+ stories from all years of the war, all branches, all ranks, and we tell it like it was for us…The Good, The Bad, The Ugly.

A COMMENT FROM THE AUTHOR

With roughly 70 authors contributing stories to this book, we (the editing team) have agreed to keep the basic style and voice of each author in his/her story. Thus, you will see inconsistencies in use of capitalization, abbreviations, military jargon, and style. We considered putting a glossary of military terms in the book, but it is already longer than we thought it would be. We were adamant that we preserved each author's story in their unique style and manner.

Therefore, don't be an English teacher critic if you find some things that don't suit you. Our focus is the story, not making it so vanilla and proper that the story's intent is lost.

If you want to understand a term we use, do like most people do, go to your computer and Google it—or, better yet, ask a veteran. We all speak the same language and would love to explain it to you, and maybe tell you another one of our stories because you showed an interest in us. Remember the title…after years of silence, I am Ready to Talk shows that we who contributed to this book are ready to tell our stories to anyone who cares about hearing them. That is why we titled this book, *I'm Ready to Talk (Book 2)*.

Show some interest, ask your favorite veteran a few questions, and I bet he or she will tell you more than you expected to hear.

Also, you will see some profanity sprinkled through the stories. That has been a way of life for all wars since the beginning of time. It's hard to express yourself with, "Gee whiz, that was bad…" Instead, it takes some profanity to best express yourself in these toughest and most memorable times of our lives. If you are offended, it is not our intent to offend but to tell our stories in the best way we know how.

Steadfast and Loyal — Deeds not Words!
Proud — Professional — Patriotic
Bob Babcock, Rifle Platoon Leader and XO
Bravo Company, 1-22 Infantry,
4th Infantry Division — Vietnam — July 1966 to July 1967

ADVISOR PHASE

(1959 TO 1964)

July 8, 1959 — First two Americans killed in Vietnam.

November 30, 1961 — President Kennedy expanded American involvement in Vietnam.

January 12, 1962 — Operation Ranch Hand Began (spraying of Agent Orange in Vietnam).

February 20, 1962 — John Glenn orbited the Earth.

October 14, 1962 — Cuban missile crisis began.

January 2, 1963 — Battle of Ap Bac (VC guerillas defeated a much larger South Vietnam force, American advisors were killed).

January 11, 1963 — Buddhist monk burned himself to death to protest President Diem.

August 28, 1963 — Reverend Martin Luther King, Jr. gave his "I Have a Dream" speech at Lincoln Monument in Washington, DC.

November 2, 1963 — President Diem, president of South Vietnam was assassinated.

November 22, 1963 — President Kennedy was assassinated.

March 24, 1964—COL Floyd Thompson captured by VC, longest held POW in American History.

July 2, 1964—Civil Rights Act was signed.

August 2, 1964—Gulf of Tonkin incident—the Gulf of Tonkin Resolution by Congress gave the President unprecedented power to commit US Forces without a declaration of war.

August 5, 1964—LT Everett Alvarez, US Navy, shot down—became first pilot detained in Vietnam, was released in 1973.

Source: www.vvmf.org

Unfortunately, no stories were submitted for inclusion from this time period of Vietnam veterans. Read on to read about actions from 1965 forward.

BUILDUP PHASE

(1965 TO 1967)

March 2, 1965 — Rolling Thunder bombing campaign of North Vietnam began.

March 8, 1965 — First brigade sized US force of Marines landed in Da Nang, first large-scale ground force deployed to Vietnam.

August 18, 1965 — Operation Starlite began, first major US battle of the war, 5,000 Marines against a stronghold of VC. Two Marines earned the Medal of Honor.

November 14, 1965 — Battle of Ia Drang Valley started, first major battle between US and NVA forces.

November 27, 1965 — March on Washington for Peace in Vietnam, 25,000 protestors.

March 8, 1966 — Australia sent first troops to Vietnam, one of five allies to send troops to fight alongside US.

August 6, 1966 — President Johnson increased troops deployed to 292,000, which would later peak at more than a half million deployed (Author's note: I landed in Vietnam on this date — will never forget it, as will all our vets remember when they arrived).

October 21, 1967 — Over 50,000 protestors marched on the Pentagon in protest against the war.

November 30, 1967—American deaths in Vietnam hit the 15,000 mark.

Source: www.vvmf.org/VietnamWar/Timeline

ROBERT O. "BOB" BABCOCK

US Army — Infantry Officer

Dates of Military Service (Active Duty and Reserves Combined): 1965 to 1974

Unit Served with in Vietnam: Bravo Company, 1st Battalion, 22nd Infantry Regiment, 4th Infantry Division

Dates Served in Vietnam: July 1966 to July 1967

Highest Rank Held: Captain (O-3)

Place and date of Birth: Heavener, OK — 1943

TRAINING AT FORT LEWIS, WA — NOV 1965 TO JUN 1966

"What in the hell happened to you, Sir?" First Sergeant Bob MacDonald growled as I hobbled into the Bravo Company orderly room. His tone of voice added to the gloom of that rainy, late November morning. Two days earlier, my wife and I had arrived at our new duty station, Fort Lewis, Washington. Those first two days had been spent checking into post housing and doing the seemingly endless processing that comes with any new post assignment. Now I was ready for duty with my new unit, Bravo Company, 1st Battalion, 22nd Infantry Regiment of the 4th Infantry Division.

"I broke my leg in AIRBORNE School, First Sergeant," was my reply. He shook his head with a look of disgust on his face and motioned to a chair. "Have a seat, Sir. The Old Man will be with you in a minute," he said as he disappeared into the Company Commander's office. Soon he reappeared and said, "Lieutenant Fiacco will see you now."

I got up, hobbled into the CO's office, and gave my best salute as I stood at attention in front of the "Old Man's" desk. Lieutenant Fiacco was a slender, sandy haired, athletic looking first lieutenant. He left me standing at attention as he eyed me up and down. I stood as tall and as rigidly as my six-foot two-inch frame would hold me. With a very stern look on his face he asked, "What in the hell happened to your leg,

2 | ROBERT O. BABCOCK

Babcock?" Once again, I responded with how my leg had been broken. He replied, "I don't need a lieutenant with a broken leg, what good are you to me?"

In my best military voice, still braced firmly at attention I responded, "Sir, I can walk on my walking cast, I will put a plastic bag over it to keep it dry and will do everything I can to do my job over the next month as my leg heals. I will not let you down, Sir."

Still staring sternly at me, he responded, "Have a seat, Lieutenant." I sat on the front edge of my chair as he started my orientation to the company. "The company is terribly under strength. In fact, we only have 40 of our authorized 180 men assigned. With all the things that have to be done around here, we are lucky to be able to muster enough men from the entire battalion to do any decent training."

Lieutenant Fiacco continued, "There is a strong rumor going around we are scheduled to get a large group of replacements right after the first of the year. That should really keep us busy.

"Babcock, you are going to be the platoon leader of the third rifle platoon. Your authorized strength is 43 men but there are only eight now. Sergeant Roath has been running the platoon for the past six months." He continued, "Sergeant Roath is good, you can learn a lot from him. He is a combat veteran and was a prisoner of war in the Korean War. He will stay in the platoon and be your platoon sergeant. One word of caution, he does not like second lieutenants. I want you to learn from him and not get in there and screw things up. Any questions?"

After I had asked all the questions I knew to ask, he called First Sergeant MacDonald back in. "Get Sergeant Roath down here so he can take Lieutenant Babcock upstairs to his platoon area." Sergeant Roath soon appeared in the CO's office. He was blond with the ruddy complexion of a man who spent a lot of time in the elements. He stood about the same height as Lieutenant Fiacco; 5'9" was my guess. My uneasiness was multiplied as I looked at his "Indian Head" Second Infantry Division patch on his right sleeve and his Combat Infantryman's Badge (CIB) above his left fatigue shirt breast pocket. (A unit patch is worn on the right sleeve only when you have served in combat with that unit. CIB's were a rarity in those days since it had been over twelve years since the end of our last war).

He had an obvious look of scorn on his face as he sized me up and focused on the cast on my right leg. For the third time in less than an hour I got the same opening comment, "What in the hell happened to your leg, Sir?"

We walked in silence from Lieutenant Fiacco's office and up the stairs toward our platoon area. He finally broke the silence with, "Lieutenant, if you get any of my men killed in combat, I'll kill you."

And "that" was the beginning of my first day with Bravo Company, First Battalion, Twenty Second Infantry Regiment of the Fourth Infantry Division. My name and "hell" had been mentioned three times in the same sentence and I had an offer to be killed. Having heard enough stories about how new, green second lieutenants are treated when they join their first unit, I was not devastated by their treatment, but I sure was uncomfortable and apprehensive about what lay ahead.

By the end of January 1966, my leg had healed, and I was back at full strength. The rumor Lieutenant Fiacco had heard was true and my platoon was filled, overnight, with 48 men, most of them fresh out of basic training and ready for Advanced Individual Training (AIT). Our entire brigade was filled with troops to "train and retain." Even though it was unofficial, we all felt certain we would be in Vietnam before the summer was over.

AIT consisted of weapons training with the M60 machine gun, .45 caliber pistol, 81mm mortar, M79 grenade launcher, M90 rocket launcher, hand grenades, and other specialized weapons. We also did extensive training on small unit tactics at the fire team and squad levels. Many other subjects, such as map and compass reading, radio procedures, first aid, land navigation, escape and evasion, artillery fire adjustment, and other skills infantrymen needed to survive and perform their mission in combat rounded out the eight weeks of AIT.

Most of the teaching load fell on the four platoon leaders. We tried to share the load as best we could. Even at that, for one week, I was the primary instructor for eighty hours of live fire day and night squad attack exercises. At the end of the week, I was physically and mentally exhausted. The intense lecture load was tough but that was nothing compared to the responsibility of teaching troops how to work together under combat conditions, with live ammunition, without shooting each other. And I was still a rookie myself.

After successfully completing the eight weeks of AIT, capped off by a graduation ceremony with all the military pomp and circumstance, we took a deep breath over the weekend, and went into our platoon and company training phase. It was during that two-month period we really learned to work together as a unit. Feeling certain we would be going into combat together, the leaders made special efforts to learn everything we could about the individual men — their strengths and weaknesses, their quirks, and other important idiosyncrasies.

Every day we learned something new and valuable. During hand grenade training, we learned one man could not master the skill of throwing one. Despite repeated attempts at teaching him with dummy grenades, we had to dive for cover behind the protection of the concrete bunkers every time he threw a live grenade and it landed only a few feet in front of his position. We made sure he did not carry hand grenades when we got to Vietnam.

Two men in my platoon showed unique skills at pathfinding. Ernie Redin and Mark Petrino had grown up playing in the woods of their native Connecticut. They possessed keen skills of observation, alertness, and selecting the best path through the forest. They became the two men I alternated as point man in critical times. Point man was a dangerous and extremely important job — a skilled point man was priceless. He kept the unit from walking into an ambush as well as leading them to their objective. Because of the skills Ernie and Mark demonstrated, I am certain they saved more lives in Vietnam than we will ever know.

A quirk I learned was Mark would follow a compass azimuth heading as straight as an arrow. Ernie would always drift five degrees to the right. Knowing that, I could compensate for the drift when I gave Ernie a heading to follow. It was learning quirks such as this that was invaluable.

Too many men went into combat without knowing the capabilities of the Soldiers they were depending on to do the job. By training together as a unit, we gained an advantage far too few men in Vietnam had. I have always been thankful we had the advantage of five months training together before we saw actual combat.

Some leaders are born, others have to be trained. We were successful in training some outstanding small unit leaders during those long, rainy days at Fort Lewis. Each day we gave our men the opportunity to show their leadership skills. Soon we had an outstanding group of young leaders, not just in my platoon but across the entire company. Again, we had the advantage of building a team before we came under enemy fire.

Physical conditioning was another element of training Lieutenant Fiacco led by example. Before we completed our training day, he led us in daily five mile runs around the back roads of the training areas. This was in marked contrast to the other companies who sat back and poked fun at us as we ran by. Our men complained, but we knew Bravo Company was better prepared than most for what lay ahead of us.

Towards the end of company training, we got the official word. We were shipping overseas to USARPAC—United States Army, Pacific. Vietnam was not mentioned in the orders, but we all knew beyond a shadow of a doubt what our destination was to be.

* * * * *

The first of June was the beginning of our final training before we left the States—a fourteen-day Brigade Field Training Exercise (FTX). After two days of intensive preparation, we were up long before daylight on the first day of the FTX. Our brigade was to attack a mythical southeast Asian objective, pacify the natives, and wait for further orders. Our battalion was to lead the attack, Bravo Company led the battalion, and my third platoon had the lead for our company and thus led the brigade into the FTX.

We had a spring in our step as we entered this "final exam" stage of our training. Soon after we left the line of departure, we came upon a river. A sign reading 'Bridge Blown Out' attached to a roadblock kept us from crossing the bridge. Several umpires stood by to insure we followed the rules of the FTX.

Not to be slowed down, we quickly found a spot to ford. Our teeth chattered as the freezing cold water from the spring thaw raced by us on its way from the Cascade mountains to nearby Puget Sound. We had barely reached the opposite bank after wading through the chest deep water when the "aggressors" opened fire. We spread out and returned fire, forgetting how cold we were.

The radio quickly crackled to life as Lieutenant Fiacco called, "Do you want an air strike?" Without hesitation, I replied, "Affirmative!" as I tried to assess the situation in the confusion of the gunfire. He told me, "Mark your position with smoke." In less than a minute after I threw out a yellow smoke grenade, two F-4 Phantom jets came screaming out of the sky toward us. The noise was deafening as they came to the bottom of their bomb run and turned their nose back skyward and hit their afterburners to make a quick getaway.

I had frequently called for an air strike during our training. Everything was always simulated, and no real airplanes ever appeared. You can imagine the shocked look on all our faces when real airplanes responded to our call. That really brought it home to me, we were about to finish training and go on to the real thing. (The "real thing", we found out, was much more spectacular and awesome than this.)

Fortunately, the planes did not drop real bombs, or they would have gotten us. We learned from that experience to respect the power of an air strike and to hug the earth and use whatever terrain features were available for protection when we called one in.

The FTX was a success but it strongly pointed out to us the confusion and chaos that can reign when so many men are involved in an operation. We saw which leaders responded well under pressure, which ones did stupid things, and the true meaning of SNAFU — Situation Normal, All Fouled Up. We were all sobered with the knowledge our next operation would be for real and mistakes would be paid for in American lives — potentially our own.

Our five months of training at Fort Lewis were very eventful. I was transformed from a green, broken legged "shave tail" to a qualified, confident infantry leader. During that time, I also gained the confidence and respect of Sergeant Roath. He was always true to his tradition of looking down his nose at second lieutenants, never failing to point out he was a "senior" NCO and I was a "junior" officer, only slightly more intelligent than dirt. But he showed me in subtle ways he thought I was doing okay.

This story is extracted from *What Now, Lieutenant?* by Robert O. Babcock, available from **www.deedspublishing.com** or **www.amazon.com**.

RICHARD GOOD
U.S. Army — Commanding Officer EOD Detachment
Dates of Military Service (Active and Reserves): 17 June 1967 to 1 June 1969.
Unit Served with in Vietnam: 42nd Ordnance Detachment (EOD)
Dates Served in Vietnam: 20 September 1965 to 21 September 1966.
High Rank Held: Captain (O-3)
Place of Birth and Year: San Francisco, CA — 1940

BUSINESS WAS BOOMING — HOW VIETNAM CHANGED EOD

On the morning of 8 March 1965, my 42nd EOD (Explosive Ordnance Disposal) team got a call that an infantry unit had found a Viet Cong claymore mine that had apparently misfired. They requested EOD assistance for disposal. Unlike the U.S. claymore, a defensive weapon, the VC version was designed for offense. A pie-shaped metal casing attached to a tripod with a sight on top, the weapon consisted of a concave thin metal face which covered a claylike material containing a hundred or more inch-long pieces of steel rebar backed with a 2-inch-thick layer of high explosive — usually obtained from one of our unexploded artillery projectiles or aerial bombs.

These deadly weapons were usually set up to face down a road or trail and command detonated electronically when our guys showed up. On more than one occasion, we were called to investigate the scene where one of our vehicles was hit by a VC claymore, usually causing multiple KIAs. The vehicles always looked like they had been hit multiple times by a heavy machine gun. Specialist 6 Fred Pollard and I caught a ride from Bien Hoa Air Base to a 1st Infantry Division firebase at Xuan Loc in a C-123 loaded with 175mm artillery projectiles. We BIPed (blow in place) the claymore.

This was a typical incident which we handled multiple times daily during our tour. It was not to be the reason March 8, 1965, stands out in my memory. While waiting for an air ride back to Bien Hoa, we got a radio call that a Huey was on the way to fly us further north to the Song Be Special Forces camp where we needed to deal with an unexploded 500 lb. bomb.

Landing at Song Be, we were greeted by an SF Captain who led us to the "500 lb." bomb. What we found lying about 50 feet away from a small rural hospital wasn't a 500 pounder. The hospital had already been evacuated to a half mile or so. The bomb was 1,000 pounds of steel casing stuffed with Trinitrotoluene. Obviously, this was not going to be a BIP, but a classic, old-time (see WWII Battle of Britain) EOD RSP (Render Safe Procedure).

The first order of business was to remove the bomb's "teeth"—the nose and tail fuses. Before removal we had to determine the types of fuses. Because the VC acquired most of their HE (High Explosives) from our unexploded ordnance, we had begun attempting to discourage them by using long delay fuses in some of our bombs. These fuses included anti withdrawal devices designed to detonate the bomb.

A few months before we set up shop at Bien Hoa, a mortar attack on the base hit close to several bombs fused with our chemical long delay fuses, jarring them enough to trigger the delay mechanism. The names of three Air Force EOD techs are on the EOD Memorial Wall at Eglin AFB as a result of attempting to render those bombs safe with a rather complicated and slow process, a procedure which was replaced after this event by a faster, emergency RSP which we trained to perform before leaving the States.

We determined that both fuses were the conventional impact variety. I threaded the nose fuse out by hand. Both fuses were a little scuffed and muddied up by the impact, so we decided to use a remote, spring-loaded impact wrench on the tail fuse in case of a misidentification or a mechanical hang up and the previously mentioned anti withdrawal trigger. Remote is relative. When dealing with a 1,000 lb. general purpose bomb, 50 feet ain't remote enough.

Sending my partner to a safe distance, I hunkered down in a small depression, the only cover available given the limited length of cord on the "remote" wrench. I started tugging on the line. The wrench worked as advertised and after several clunks, that fuse spun right out of the threads in the tail fuse well. The SF team had a "deuce-and-a-half" truck equipped with a small crane which was able to load that monster onto the truck's cargo platform for a trip several miles out into the scrub jungle outside Song Be. We found a several acre clearing and set the bomb down in the middle. I packed the tail fuse well with C4 plastic explosive, measured about a half hour piece of time fuse, and crimped a blasting cap onto the fuse.

While pushing the cap into the C4, the SF Captain said, "Aren't you going to double it?" I had probably primed close to a hundred shots by that time during my tour, many of which were executed in unsecured areas like this one where time was not to be wasted. Never had a misfire. So, I pulled the pin on the igniter, we loaded up in the truck and jeep, and "di di'd" (Vietnamese slang for scram quickly) to a safe spot about a half mile away. And then we waited…and waited…30 minutes, 45 minutes.

As some wise man once said, haste makes waste. After about an hour, I hopped into the captain's jeep and set out by myself with TWO strings of time fuse and two caps. I'm sure the SF guys were wagering on whether I, or the jeep, would ever be found. While driving back to that bomb, my mind was racing from one bad outcome to another. Had I mismeasured the time fuse, was the fuse defective, but still smoldering, had a VC observed us from the surrounding jungle and pulled out my cap, replacing it with his own wired detonator?

As I approached the bomb, I could see the charred time fuse protruding from the bomb's fuse well. I stopped the jeep about 50 feet from the biggest firecracker I had ever played with and sprinted toward that charred fuse, grabbing it, and jerking it out of the C4. I don't think I took a breath of air over those fifty feet. After a loud exhale, I gulped some air and stuffed in both caps. I lit the fuses and jumped back into the jeep, heading for our safe spot.

Thirty minutes later we got a very large, and very beautiful, high order detonation. The crater that bomb made was an instant farm pond, if only there had been a little creek flowing in. I slept sitting up in the Huey "slick" during the ride back to Bien Hoa. Needless to say, I double primed all the big shots during the remainder of my tour.

EOD was a special military discipline developed during the Battle of

Britain when Hitler tried to bomb the Brits into submission by breaking their will to resist with millions of tons of bombs, dropped mostly on the civilian population. Those bombs were often equipped with long delay fuses which included anti withdrawal devices and trembler switches. Many of the British EOD techs were wounded and maimed soldiers who could no longer serve in combat roles, and a large percentage of them died attempting to RSP (Render Safe Procedure) those bombs and trying to protect civilians.

U.S. EOD also began during WWII, patterned after the British model as mostly a rear echelon function. The guerilla warfare in the early stages of the Vietnam war changed EOD. Our main mission was to deny the enemy access to their primary source of high explosives—our dud projectiles and bombs, ranging from 60mm mortar rounds and CBU (Cluster Bomb Units) bomblets to 1,000-pound blockbusters. The CBU bomblets were a Cong favorite. When one of our air support planes had damage or mechanical problems, they would jettison their ordnance, including CBU dispensers. Those little anti-personnel bomblets were easily converted into small, and easily concealed, anti-personnel mines which maimed a lot of our soldiers and which we were clearing and destroying frequently. The rule of thumb then, and it probably still applies, is that 10 percent of all explosive ordnance malfunctions.

So, when you're projecting and dropping millions of tons of explosive ordnance on a relatively small piece of global real estate, 10 percent of which are duds, which the enemy was using against us, explosive ordnance reconnaissance by the infantry, and disposal by EOD, became a high priority. For a handful of EOD guys "in country"—business was booming.

On the flight back to Bien Hoa, while I wasn't dozing, I was thinking, "How in God's great and sovereign name, did I get here, doing what I was doing?" Like most of my Oregon State fraternity brothers, I had volunteered to take two more years of ROTC, after completing two required years, to get a U.S. Army commission. During the summer of my senior year at OSU, I attended summer camp training at Ft. Gordon, GA, near Augusta.

Right off the bat came the physical. My level of myopia was over the line for a combat arm, so I would later be assigned to the Ordnance Corps which gave me four MOS choices: Maintenance officer (never liked fooling with old cars as a teen) — boring; Supply officer — super boring; Nike Missile Battery officer (they were getting warmer). Or I could extend my three — year commitment by one year and go to EOD school at Indianhead, MD, an all-service school run by the Navy.

As a kid I loved fooling with firecrackers and their larger kin — Cherry and "TNT" bombs. It was a no brainer. Little did I know how those childhood fun and games would be drastically fulfilled. At the time, Vietnam was a back page story involving a handful of Army Special Forces soldiers trying to help the locals defeat a Communist insurrection in a little known, far off corner of our planet. I never gave handling unexploded ordnance daily in a combat zone a second thought.

Now back to a few of my more harrowing days "in country." The 42nd Ordnance Detachment (or the "fighting 42nd" as my senior NCO, SGM Dick Staude, who earned a CIB in Korea, liked to call us), was based at Ft. Monmouth, N.J. when I arrived fresh from EOD school. The unit, which consisted of 10 men (nine EOD qualified techs and a clerk), embarked from Oakland, CA, Army Terminal (just across San Francisco Bay from where I grew up) on September 20, 1965, aboard the USS Mann, with elements of the 1st Infantry Division, the "Big Red One." I was leaving behind my young bride of three years, Linda, and my first-born daughter, four-month-old Tracy. Linda has seen three men in her life leave for war. Her dad, Maj. Carl Carlson, a medical doctor, served in North Africa and Italy for three years in the Medical Corps. And her son-in-law, COL John Dyke, 5th Special Forces, served six tours in Iraq and Afghanistan.

The 42nd EOD unit arrived about two weeks later at Vung Tau and transferred to an LST (Landing Ship, Tank) which took us on a "cruise" up the Saigon River to Saigon. After a couple of days, we were reunited with our vehicles and equipment and moved to Long Binh, a few miles north of Saigon, and then to Bien Hoa Air Base where we set up shop in an old warehouse for the duration of our 12-month tour. Strategically,

Bien Hoa was perfect for our mission. To do our job we needed ready access to air transport and Bien Hoa had big Huey base adjacent and was alive with C130s, C123s, and other aircraft which moved ammo, supplies, and us daily to the units we supported (I flew in 10 different aircraft during my Vietnam tour).

I also believe we were there to lend backup to the Air Force team which had suffered the aforementioned EOD KIAs following a mortar attack. Our first few months were spent primarily supporting the 1st Infantry Division, headquartered at Di An a few miles southwest of Bien Hoa, and the 173rd Airborne Brigade which was positioned on the north side of the base to provide security while also conducting offensive operations in III Corps. We also had occasional forays into the Mekong Delta. As the year progressed, and the buildup continued, the 25th Infantry Division arrived and moved into a village northwest of Saigon—Cu Chi—a notorious stronghold for the Victor Charlies.

Apparently, the populace of Cu Chi believed Karl Marx knew better how to run a railroad than the leaders of South Vietnam's fledgling Republic. So, our mission was to provide EOD support to all U.S. units (and allies) in III Corps. We had many EOD incidents, some 500-plus during our tour, with the ROKs (Republic of Korea), Aussies, and New Zealanders. The major change in the EOD mission became obvious very quickly. We needed to support tens of thousands of soldiers who were finding tons of unexploded ordnance daily.

We immediately set up three sub teams, each with three EOD techs. As CO, I led one team, my first sergeant (Dick Staude, who was promoted to SGM halfway through our tour) led another, and SFC Harold Osbourne led the third. During our tour, two of our teams were usually deployed at forward infantry bases, with the third on call at Bien Hoa, rotating all three weekly. So, our little band of EOD men, made up of a CO who was assigned to the Ordnance Corps due to a high degree of near sightedness (I wore contacts and luckily never lost one) and eight NCOs and Specialists who were aging, mostly overweight and out of shape, running around in the boonies with very fit infantrymen. The need for EOD qualified AND combat qualified EOD teams became obvious in Vietnam and, I believe, remained the case in most of our military efforts in subsequent conflicts.

I ran into a young soldier in the Atlanta Airport a few years ago who was deploying to the Middle East. He had an EOD emblem on his duffle bag, and he was young and very fit and looked ready for Ranger School. The Army obviously had wisely changed the requirements for the EOD troopers.

That new mission led us into the field with infantry units for the majority of our work. On February 1, 1966, for example, when the 25th ID set up shop in Cu Chi, we flew to an LZ a few clicks outside of the village. First order of business was to dress properly for the occasion. My flak jacket tailor disappointed me. Instead of pulling out a tape measure to size my chest and hat size, he rudely thrust a flak jacket and steel pot at me and said, "Put these on." I carried an M16 for most of the tour, even though my assigned weapon was a .45 cal. pistol. I had qualified with the sidearm before deployment but would just as soon throw rocks.

Our first day in Cu Chi was interesting. Lots of sniper fire kept us ducking and weaving from time to time as our guys squirted flame throwers into tunnel entrances. We collected a large cache of small arms ammo, grenades of Russian and/or Chinese origin, and mines, including an antitank mine that I RSPed, first probing under it for a possible boo-by trap and then removing the pressure plate with detonator attached. Cu Chi had a huge network of tunnels, so I briefly turned into a "tunnel rat" by pushing some of the recovered enemy ordnance, along with a lengthy plastic tube filled with an ammonium nitrate/diesel fuel mix, into one of the tunnels.

I primed it with a block of C4, cleared the area and sang my best rendition of "fire in the hole." We pulled back 50 yards and watched the detonation create an amazing spectacle. The tunnel we had primed collapsed, along with a huge spread of connecting tunnels, not unlike watching an elaborate array of dominoes collapsing. My diary entry for that day recorded that we were shot at a lot and that I lost five pounds of sweat off an already very boney body, running across open areas and diving into holes.

A few weeks later, on the 17th of March, my team flew by Huey into a War Zone D clearing in heavy jungle with elements of the 173rd Airborne which had just engaged a large force of NVA regulars in and around what we later learned was called LZ Zulu Zulu. A few weeks later, I learned from an article in Time Magazine that this engagement was one of the first major battles with NVA troops in III Corps. There were lots of dud munitions, ranging from 40mm grenade launcher rounds and Russian RPGs to mortar projectiles—theirs and ours, scattered among NVA bodies. With occasional sniper fire, we gathered and destroyed stuff until we ran out of explosives. It was a very hot, steamy day and the evacuation slick I boarded didn't have sufficient lift to clear the jungle canopy, so we came back down to Zulu Zulu. I volunteered to hop off and the next Huey I boarded made it out. I had undoubtedly perspired sufficiently.

On August 1, 1966, nearing the end of our 12-month tour (short time status), my sub team and I flew to a little village called Loc Ninh, which earlier had been an SF A team camp. It was located in one of a number of old Michelin rubber plantations. We also spent a lot of time in the Lai Khe plantation with the 1st ID. I loved those rubber trees because it always seemed to be 10 degrees cooler in their shade. But I digress. A battalion of the 1st ID was taking over the camp and setting up a fire base. The Special Forces A Team that was being replaced by the battalion from the 1st ID was constantly under threat of attack by many times larger enemy units, and they had put a lot of time and effort into setting up defenses.

When the camp was abandoned in favor of the 1st ID, the defense apparatus was still in place. The SF guys had set up a dozen or so Fougasses around their perimeter. A Fougasse consisted of a 55-gallon drum full of homemade napalm (gasoline thickened with Ivory soap flakes I was told), set at about a 45-degree angle facing out toward the perimeter. At the base of the drum was a quarter pound block of TNT with a white phosphorous (Willie Peter) grenade duct taped to the TNT as both a propellant and igniter for the napalm. The detonator was a blasting cap inserted into the TNT block and connected to command detonation wire. An easy RSP—we cleared the area and began hooking the wires to our own hand-held blasting generators. After successfully lighting up the rubber trees with several of the Fougasses, one of them malfunctioned (remember the 10 percent rule).

The TNT popped, but the Willie Peter grenade did not, spreading jellied gasoline over about a 30 yard by 50 yard deep "field of potential fire." I decided we needed to find that grenade. I headed out into the gasoline reeking stretch of rubber plantation with all the low vegetation dripping with napalm, and fumes visibly rising from the ground ahead. About 10 yards into my search my foot caught on a vine. Looking down to free my boot I discovered it wasn't a vine. A trip wire, connected to a trip flare, was stretched across the laces of my boot. Oops! And pucker. My boots and fatigues were dripping with napalm and looking a little more carefully at my surroundings I realized the whole area was crisscrossed with trip wires connected to trip more flares. It probably, or seemed to take me, half an hour to gingerly tiptoe out of the BBQ zone without tripping. I attached a lengthy line to one of the trip wires and gave it a yank, lighting up the dim rubber grove. Unfortunately, we didn't have any Graham Crackers, marshmallows, or Hershey bars.

These are just a few examples of the incidents my sub team and I carried out. The other two teams had every bit as many incidents as we did. My detachment of nine EOD pros received four Purple Hearts and the men recruited to conduct RSPs in combat zones were changed, during our '65-'66 tour, forever. EOD's mission and modus operandi and the men who accomplish those tasks had changed and continues today as long as our country is involved in unconventional conflicts where IEDs are a serious risk to our soldiers.

ROBERT L. "BOB" HOPKINS

US Army— Infantry Officer

Dates of Military Service: Aug 1965 to Jun 1968

Unit Served with in Vietnam: Bravo Company, 1st Bn, 39th Inf Regt, 9th Inf Division

Dates in Vietnam: Dec 1966 to Dec 1967

Highest Rank Held: First Lieutenant

Place of Birth and Year: Baltimore, MD—1943

UPSIDE-DOWN JEEP

The question is how did the jeep get upside-down?

It was one of those rare quiet evenings when Bravo Company, 2nd Battalion, 39th Infantry was not tramping through the boonies looking for "Charlie." Tonight, we would be at Bearcat and would have the opportunity to soundly sleep on a cot. There would be no mosquitos or leeches to worry about, and we were well protected by the berm guards. To kill time in the evening, we were watching television on the Armed Forces TV Network, while playing cards, and imbibing in multiple cans of San Miguel beer.

Our quiet time was disturbed by a distant crash. A minute later, Lieutenant Strickland stuck his head under the side tent flap and, giving us the sheepish look of an inebriated happy drunk, said, "I wrecked the jeep." Not knowing how wrecked the jeep was, we went to inspect the damage. There in the bottom of a four-feet deep drainage ditch was an upside-down jeep. As to how Lieutenant Strickland survived the plunge can only be attributed to his inebriated condition.

Of course, the fact the jeep was wrecked, and Lieutenant Strickland was the sole culprit, if caught, he would be in for some punishment by the battalion commander. But the band of brothers stuck together. We arranged for the warrant officer who ran the maintenance platoon to get a wrecker to retrieve the jeep. Success! The incident was squashed, and Lieutenant Strickland continued to serve with distinction.

Lieutenant Strickland was a character. Always happy. He was a graduate of the University of Florida, receiving his commission through ROTC. He had been with the 9th Infantry Division since its formation at Fort Riley, Kansas in January 1966. He led the newly drafted troops in a basic training course and was on the ship that took them to Vietnam in December. He was fortunate to get a battalion staff position to finish his Vietnam tour.

Everyone has a person they fondly remember from Vietnam; Lieutenant Strickland is someone I will never forget.

RAYMOND L. COLLINS

US Marine Corps — Combat Logistics Officer

Dates of Military Service: 1960 — 1980, a lifer

Unit Served with in Vietnam: 1st Tour: FLSC-A, FLC, IIIMAF; 2nd Tour: HQ IIIMAF

Dates in Vietnam: 1st Tour: Aug 1968 to Nov 1969; 2nd Tour: Jan 1971 to Apr 1971

Highest Rank Held: Lt Colonel (O-5)

Place of Birth and Year: Kinston, NC — 1938

As has been repeated many times herein, our Vietnam experience was a montage of mixed memories: some good and some bad, some humorous and some sad.

THE INFAMOUS YELLOW FOOTPRINTS

In the fall of 1965, troop buildup in the US to support the Vietnam War effort became a big deal. In the Marine Corps, recruits from east of the Mississippi River were trained at the MCRD at Parris Island, SC (PISC) whereas those from west of the river were trained in San Diego ... the *Hollywood Marines*. The Marine Corps reacted by shortening the basic training period at MCRDs and implementing a 'full court press' for recruiting.

I arrived at PISC in August 1965 as a very disappointed young Captain; I had hoped my next assignment would be Vietnam. The previous year I had decided on a Marine Corps career and was afraid the war would end before I could get there as I knew that a combat tour would benefit my career.

I had just completed a tour of sea-duty as the Executive Officer Marine Detachment aboard the US Albany CG-10, a guided missile cruiser and flag ship for COMCRUDESFLOT-Eight in the US Navy Second Fleet (Atlanta). In those days, Sea-Going Marines had a multi-faceted mission: Ship's Landing Party (nucleus), Ship's Security, Operate Ship's Brig, Manning the 5-inch Guns and Providing Honors for Visiting Dignitaries & VIPs. On the Albany we guarded the nuclear weapons spaces with 'a-round-in-the-chamber'; it was serious business.

So…when I reported for duty at PISC, I was told that the Commanding General (a two-star-Major General) wanted to meet with me. General Masters wasted little time in telling me that PISC was in the midst of making some major changes (because of Vietnam and the troop build-up). The legendary Recruit Reception Center at the Yamasee SC railhead some 25 miles west of Beaufort and PISC had just been closed for reasons stated elsewhere; new recruits were now being flown-in commercially to Charleston and Savannah and then commercially bused from there to PISC.

The General had just approved conversion of one of the old WWII barracks into a Recruit Receiving Barracks (RRB)…where the buses would deliver new recruits. Since this barracks would be the first-place new recruits would experience at PISC, he wanted it to make a very positive, memorable impression. He knew it needed a lot of repairs and TLC to make it a showplace. Since I was coming from sea-duty where spit and polish was commonplace if not routine, he was assigning me as the first OIC of Recruit Receiving Barracks. He made it very clear that I would be administratively assigned to the Recruit Training Regiment (RTR) but in reality, I was working for him.

I was to let his Staff Secretary know of any problems and when I needed something: paint, lumber, tools, polish, etc. He wanted everything that could be shined to shine with lots of motivational signage and fanfare. I could have my pick of 12 of the top Drill Instructors (DI) at PISC to handle the recruit in-processing and an administrative team of seven Marines to begin setting up a Service Record Book (SRB) for each recruit. We were allowed to use recruit labor on a very limited basis to perform work on the barracks, so my DIs were continuously alert for painters, carpenters, landscapers, etc. We would try to get 3-4 days of labor out of them before assigning them to a platoon.

In essence, RRB's mission was to receive, in-process, and build new recruit platoons ready for training and hand-off to the various Recruit Training Battalions (RTB) and a team of permanently assigned DIs. The in-processing ritual included: contraband inspection, haircuts, medical exam, issuance of utility uniforms & boots, mailing of civilian clothes home, issuance of personal equipment (782 gear), issuance of dog tags & military ID cards. Upon completion of the in-processing, RRB DIs would call the receiving RTB to send their DI team to pickup their new platoon. This was essentially a 24-hour operation done expeditiously with minimum time at the RRB as we were limited in the number of recruits we could house overnight.

So, you ask...What does all this have to do with yellow footprints. Too much time has elapsed to remember the exact date, but one night in October 1965, we had *nine* busloads of recruits to arrive within a few hours of one another; we literally had recruits coming out of our ears. They had just completed the bus ride from either Charleston or Savannah and were ready to get off the buses, to use the head (toilet), etc. *CONTROL* was a major problem as we could ill afford having recruits roam around without supervision.

The next morning, I huddled with my DI staff, and we came up with the plan of painting the footprints in platoon formation on the pavement adjacent to where the buses parked for off-loading. I called the General's office and quickly got trial approval. We obtained yellow paint and brushes from the Base Maintenance Department while a couple of DIs constructed footprint templates from cardboard boxes. The first night we had two platoons of footprints ready, and they worked beautifully. Problem solved! We eventually painted five or six sets of platoon footprints. In short order, the Hollywood Marines at MCRD San Diego copied our footprint prototype. The rest is history.

BRUCE BURGEE GEIBEL

US Navy — Seabees and Civil Engineer Corps Officer
Dates of Military Service (Active and Reserve): 1962 to 1991
Unit Served with in Vietnam: Naval Mobile Construction Battalion ELEVEN
(NMCB-11)
Dates in Vietnam: Jun 1966 to Sep 1968 (three tours to Vietnam/Thailand)
Highest Rank Held: Naval Captain (0-6)
Place of Birth and Year: Washington, DC — 1942

THE WAR STORY OF SEABEE TEAM 1104 — DONG XOAI, VIETNAM — JUNE 1965

Many military people in the Navy establishment had ideas about how to fight brushfire wars like the Army (Green Beret) and Navy (SEAL) Teams that were established to match up with what President John F. Kennedy said we should have in the United States Armed Forces. The objective was to have a balanced military force to handle so-called "brushfires" and "Wars of National Liberation" and to take care of rising military threats like we were experiencing in Korea and our early days of Vietnam. The Kennedy administration, in their budget address to the 87th Congress in 1961, concluded that specially trained American military units might be needed "…to combat the enemy's political-military offensive measures."

After the Army established the Special Forces Green Beret and the Navy Special Warfare Group established the Navy SEALS (Sea, Air and Land Force), the Navy's Civil Engineer Corps (CEC) in 1961 had their own ideas on how to fight brushfire wars. They said: "Why should we fight these wars if they could be prevented?" The U.S. Navy was asked by the Chilean government to send a small detachment of Navy Seabees to provide technical assistance and training to help Chile repair their earthquake damaged Naval Shipyard. "Technical Assistance" and "Training" seemed to jump to the forefront of their thinking at that time. The idea of a Seabee Team (early called a Seabee Technical Assistance Team or STAT) equipped to provide both engineering and construction services and assistance while at the same time training the local populace in building trades was born.

Thirteen (13) man Seabee Teams were established with one junior engineer officer, one chief petty officer, one Navy corpsman and ten men from the construction trades — two equipment operators, two construction mechanics, two builders, one steelworker, one utilitiesman, one engineering aid and one electrician as the complement of each team. Each team would provide technical assistance on any engineering and construction problems to emerging nations as well as established nations, assist in construction of a wide range of civil action and socioeconomic projects, teach construction and mechanical trades to host country public works and rural citizens, and provide limited medical assistance to nations that become victims of disasters such as earthquakes and floods.

During the period 1963 to 1968, there were 60 Seabee Teams deployed to Vietnam, 22 teams deployed to Thailand and 13 teams in training in the United States (that would later deploy to Vietnam and Thailand). Teams would continue to deploy to Vietnam and Thailand until about 1970. These were 13-man specialized construction teams that helped rural Vietnamese and Thais construct infrastructure in their respective countries, fought alongside Special Forces troops in Vietnam, and assisted Thai paramilitary Border Patrol Police (BPP) Teams in their defense against infiltration of hostile forces from abroad during the Vietnam War, while also helping Thai rural community villages improve their roads and infrastructure.

This is the story of one team, Seabee Team 1104, from Naval Mobile Construction Battalion ELEVEN (NMCB-11), and their fateful but heroic deployment to Vietnam in 1965. The Seabee Team officer-in-charge was Lieutenant (Junior Grade) Frank A. Peterlin, CEC, USNR. They first deployed to Ben Soi in Tay Ninh Province, Vietnam, in February 1965, to support a U.S. Army Special Forces "A" team construct their campsite. With that mission completed on June 3, 1965, they moved to Dong Xoai, Vietnam to support another Special Forces "A" team, Detachment A342, 5th Special Forces Group (Airborne). At the latter site they were close to the Cambodian border doing work with the Green

Beret team at a Vietnamese Civilian Irregular Defense Group (CIDG) outpost adjacent to their joint campsite. The CIDG force was a quasi-military unit made up of minority Vietnamese civilians. The campsite was astride one of the main Ho Chi Minh Trail supply routes that the North Vietnamese were using to support the Viet Cong (VC) forces in South Vietnam. The mission of Seabee Team 1104 at Dong Xoai was to build a new Special Forces camp and airstrip in support of the assigned CIDG force structure and their village.

Two companies of Vietnamese CIDG troops were at Dong Xoai and were highly regarded by the Army Special Forces commander, Capt. William N. Stokes, III, U.S. Army. His assistant team commander was First Lieutenant Charles Williams, U.S. Army. They lead their team of nine other Special Forces "A Detachment" troops.

THE HEROIC WAR STORY OF SEABEE TEAM 1104 – DONG XOAI, VIETNAM.

The Seabees of Team 1104 arrived on site on/about June 5, 1965, to begin construction of their team site. They occupied several existing Vietnamese buildings in the camp site. "The quiet serenity of a rainy night in a small Vietnamese military compound quickly turned into a nightmare of death and suffering for nine members of Seabee Team 1109 on June 9, 1965." Four other members of the 13-man Seabee team were not on site: two members were on R&R (CE3 Richard S. Supzak and EA2 Frederick J. Alexander, Jr.) and two other members (EO2 Jack L. Allen and EO2 John C. Klepfer) remained at their previous site loading up the remainder of the team's equipment and gear for transport to their new site. All members of the Team are listed at the end of this article. Also on site were 11 members of the Army Special Forces "A" Team. The nine Navy Seabee Team members and 11 Army Special Forces team members on site were trapped in one of the bloodiest and hardest fought battles of the Vietnam war up to that date. They were to stand against overwhelming odds of men and arms for the next 14 hours. All the Americans were to feel the searing pain of shrapnel fragments entering their bodies and the deafening roar of battle. Two of the Seabees and one of the Special Force troopers were to die. All others were wounded in action.

The bizarre sequence of events started when a lookout reported "...Viet Cong were all over the airfield." The battle opened with a 200-round barrage of 60mm mortars at 1145 hours and was immediately followed by "human wave" assaults on the perimeter walls of the compound. Intense close-range combat continued until 0230 hours the next day when the CIDG defenses were breached, and surviving U.S. troops made their way to the adjacent District Headquarters. They were quickly surrounded there by the Viet Cong who were employing flame throwers, machine guns, recoilless rifles, and small arms against the allied fortifications.

A jury-rigged radio put together by a Special Forces sergeant was a life saver according to Seabee CM1 James D. Wilson after the action. That radio enabled the U.S. teams to communicate with command headquarters in Saigon. When daybreak approached, the Second Air Division and Vietnamese Air Force aircraft began hitting the Viet Cong positions around the camp site.

Early in the morning of June 10, the Viet Cong swept over the north ramparts, hurling grenades, firing small arms, and using flame throwers. They were supported by a couple of Viet Cong machine gun positions menacing the American defenders and District Headquarters building. But, when the light broke the morning of June 10th, Army Lt. Charles Williams, who had relieved Capt. Stokes as commander of the Special Forces team when he was severely wounded in action overnight, and Seabee Petty Officer (CM3) Marvin Glenn Shields, who had also been wounded in action, teamed up to man a 3.5-inch rocket launcher and headed outside to get a better firing position on the enemy machine guns. Having no prior experience with a rocket launcher, Shields assisted Lt. Wilson to aim and load the launcher. Coming close but with no success on two rounds, the third round hit one of the machine guns spot on and silenced the deadly gun and its operators. Retreating from their location to a safer location, machine gun fire from the other enemy gunner stuck Shield's right leg, nearly tearing it off. Somehow, he crawled back towards the Headquarters building. A Seabee and two Special Forces men came out and rescued him, carrying him back to safety where the team corpsman rendered medical aid. Throughout the rest of the morning, Shields was instrumental in keeping the spirit of the defenders up with his laughter and small jokes.

Finally, the site was taken under close air support by fixed wing aircraft, which permitted elements of the 118th Aviation Company to evacuate the wounded and dead from the compound with three helicopters. Critically injured Seabee Shields was placed on one of the helicopters for removal to a hospital. He died in route during the flight to Saigon. Shortly thereafter, an ARVN (Army of the Republic of Vietnam) Ranger relief force of 300 men arrived by air and recaptured the Headquarters compound while capturing numerous Viet Cong weapons in the process. Sporadic gunfire continued throughout the second night, but the Rangers moved out and recaptured large areas around Dong Xoai.

Eyewitness accounts of the battle area described the bodies of civilian and military Vietnamese strewn throughout the town. Many members of the two companies of Vietnamese CIDG troops were killed as well as hundreds of the Viet Cong aggressors. It was later confirmed that the attacking Viet Cong force numbered close to 2,000 troops—a full regiment.

Of the 20 American Special Forces and Navy Seabees in the compound, two Seabees—CM3 Marvin Glenn Shields and SW2 William C. Hoover—and one Special Forces soldier (unknown) were killed in action and the remaining 17 Americans all suffered wounds. Both 1st Lieutenant Charles Williams and Construction Mechanic 3rd Class Marvin G. Shields were subsequently awarded the Congressional Medal of Honor, America's highest award for valor in combat, for their heroic action in manning the 3.5-in rocket launcher to destroy one of the enemy machine gun positions firing on their compound. CM3 Marvin G. Shields received the MOH posthumously. He was the first Navy man to receive the Medal of Honor in Vietnam and the only Navy Seabee who has ever been awarded this medal.

In presenting the Medal of Honor to Shield's widow, Joan, and daughter, Barbara, at the White House in Washington, DC on September 13, 1966, President Lyndon B. Johnson pointed out that Shields in his deeds exemplified the spirit of the Seabees. The president continued by saying Shields was typical of a "…new kind of fighting man, forged and tempered in a new kind of war…men fighting with one hand and building with the other."

Members of Seabee Team 1109—Medals for Combat in Vietnam: Ltjg. Frank Peterlin, CEC, USNR (Silver Star Medal & Purple Heart); EOC Johnny McCully (Silver Star Medal & Purple Heart); CM3 Marvin G. Shields (MOH & Purple Heart, Posthumous); SW2 William C. Hoover (Bronze Star Medal & Purple Heart, Posthumous); BU1 Dale B. Brakken, UT2 Lawrence W. Eyman, BU2 Douglas M. Mattick, CE3 Richard S. Supzak, and CM1 James D. Wilson (all—Bronze Star Medals and Purple Hearts); EO2 John Klepfer, HM2 James M, Keenan and CM2 James D. Wilson (all—Purple Hearts). Seabee Team 1104 was also awarded the Navy Meritorious Unit Commendation (MUC) for their actions at Dong Xoai, Vietnam—"On the night of 9 June 1965…Seabee Team 1104 through their fortitude and indomitable fighting spirit of each of its members in the face of overwhelming odds, upheld the highest traditions of the United States Naval Service." Paul H. Nitze, Secretary of the Navy.

Sources: Seabee Teams in Vietnam, 1963-68, Reprint by Kenneth E. Bingham, 2013; and Family of 11th Seabee Battalion, Bruce B. Geibel, 2005.

CHARLES "CHUCK" BAYLESS

US Army—Armor officer, UH-1 Helicopter pilot
Dates of Military Service: November 1964 through May 1968
Dates Served in Vietnam: July 1966 to July 1967
Units Served with In Vietnam:
July 1966 to Jan 1967 Troop C, 1/9th Recon Squadron, 1st Cav Div.
Jan 1967 to July 1967 48th Assault Helicopter Co.
Highest Rank Held: Captain (O-3)
Place of Birth: Cleveland, OH—1942

GOOD MEN LOST, WITHOUT A SHOT FIRED

Over dinner a few years ago, out of the blue, my young nephew Chris asked me, "Charles

(he was always formal with me), what was the war really like?"

Seeing an opportunity that doesn't happen often, I puffed out my chest and was about to launch into, "Well, you see, Chris, it was this way...", but I pulled myself up short. Would he and my other relatives at the table really understand?

Sure, there are many events I could regale them with about my Vietnam tour, but how could they ever understand what my stick buddies (helicopter cyclic stick for steering) and I went through? And besides, my brother-in-law, sitting at the same table, was an Air Force LT who served during the same period but was nowhere near Southeast Asia. Knowing him, I thought he would probably get a little prickly about any commentary I made.

Yet, deep down I would really like to tell them about some of the unglamorous parts of the war, such as that hellish night of August 8, 1966. It would probably be cathartic for me and surely enlighten them. If I did tell them, I'd start it this way:

Just five weeks out of flight school and upon arriving in Saigon, South Vietnam, July 1966, I was assigned as a helicopter co-pilot to Troop C, 1/9th Reconnaissance Squadron, 1st Cavalry Div., based in An Khe, in the Central Highlands. It was probably good then that I didn't know this was a 24/7, 365 day/year assignment in Hell. From my second day with this unit, living in tents (sometimes even sleeping!), I was always flying in and out of battlefields. Every day, except for bad weather (which our commanding officer didn't know existed), our mission was to find and engage the VC/NVA soldiers. It was constant stress. I saw lots of death on both sides. I saw brave attempts and dumb accidents that resulted in death for our air crews and the infantry "Blue Platoon" that was an integral part of our Troop C.

In one incident, on August 8, 1966, in the Central Highland's area, our XO, a major who was the aircraft commander and me, were flying our Huey gunship in a "chase ship" role. Our unit Standard Operating Procedure was to always fly in two ship missions. We served as the chase ship for our new CO, Major Oliver Simons, just in-country a matter of three weeks, and his co-pilot, 1st LT Richard W. Meehan. In addition to aircraft commander and co-pilot, each of our ships had two more men, a crew chief and a door gunner. It was dusk and we had just left a briefing at the Turkey Farm, our squadron's headquarters near Pleiku. We were en route back to our Troop C encampment at LZ Oasis, about twenty miles away. Both ships were flying low level due to the ominous low cloud cover.

The XO and I had kept close tabs on our CO's helicopter but suddenly they were gone, apparently in a fog bank. We made an immediate sharp bank to the left to avoid entering this area ourselves. We were too low to fly on instruments. As we started our turn, I began radioing our CO's ship to let them know our actions. We received no response. I continued calling every sixty seconds as we flew back to squadron headquarters, at this point the safest place to land in this fast-lowering ceiling. Still no response.

Our starboard side door gunner said he thought he had seen a flash of light just before we had started our turn back. From my seat on the same side, I thought I had seen the same. To think back now, I saw our commander and his co-pilot, my friend Dick Meehan, killed before my eyes. At that moment all of us in our crew were filled with trepidation as to what had happened. We were expecting the worse. And we were desperate to get back to the squadron headquarters as our weather window was closing quickly.

I continued the radio calls to our commander's ship until we landed, but their radio remained silent.

It was now dark and misting steadily as we entered the squadron operations tent to brief the squadron CO and his operations staff. Using the area we had pinpointed, they immediately sent out a "firefly light ship" (a search and rescue type Huey aircraft with a bank of powerful headlights mounted in the side door that can be aimed at the ground to pick up any nighttime activity). Knowing the weather and the terrain we had just come through, I wondered if this was a good idea, but I was so new in-country that I probably didn't have a right to an opinion on this. The operations officer then ordered an infantry company camped in that area to begin looking for a possibly downed ship, our commander's.

With the weather deteriorating and flying conditions poor, we listened in the operations tent to the amplified radio net as the light ship pilots tried to do their job and then became disoriented in the fog. They were panic stricken and arguing over who had command of the aircraft, both the aircraft commander and his co-pilot each thought they could handle it, all the while we could picture them plunging to the ground. This seemed to last only seconds before one of the infantry platoons radioed back that the light ship had just crashed. (All four crewmen were killed instantly.)

Immediately rage and frustration broke out among the squadron officers present. There was yelling and literally "gnashing of teeth." It was haunting to see these senior officers listening to the evolving events and they not be able to control it. Everyone's emotions were stretched to the breaking point.

From that moment on, I seemed to be operating on "auto pilot," not fully cognizant of what was transpiring minute to minute. I had seen our commander and his co-pilot, my friend Dick Meehan, killed before my eyes. Dick had been my tent-mate since I arrived at Troop C. All of us looked up to him as one of our most skilled pilots.

We remained at squadron headquarters and then at first light the next morning we flew back over that dreadful area. The skies were now clear, and we found both crash sites. The ground was littered with only white "ash", from the burned metal helicopter hulls. There were no aircraft parts large enough to identify. By then the infantry platoon had recovered the bodies and taken them to the squadron morgue.

It was the responsibility of our XO and me to identify the bodies. When the corpsman unzipped those body bags, it was a very gruesome sight. It became imprinted on my mind. I'll never forget the look of shock on each dead man's face with their arms outstretched and locked in a defensive posture as if to instinctively protect themselves from the impending crash. I could hardly identify the crew chief and door gunner because of their mangled skull and torso; the crew chief's head misaligned and cracked down the middle from forehead to chin.

Later that morning, our XO and I flew back to our troop encampment at LZ Oasis. Upon our return, I was spent. I'll never forget our guys in the troop looking at us survivors like we were the walking dead. I remember going to the water trailer and soaking my face, as if to wash away the events of the last 20 hours. Then, wandering into the chow line with my face dripping wet, I think everyone thought I was weeping. No, not then, but little did they know that I had done plenty of that the preceding night when there was no way I could fall asleep. During that night, I kept seeing those body bags and what had been real people, skilled people, people just doing their job.

I stumbled through the next several weeks, including an endless string of interviews with the accident investigators. Many sleepless nights followed. A few months later, a captain joined our unit as a replacement pilot. When he learned our former CO was Major Simons, he told us he had been at the Ft. Rucker swimming pool the day the post chaplain came looking for Mrs. Simons to give her the bad news. He said she screamed at his sight and broke down sobbing uncontrollably.

We lost eight dedicated, extremely professional service members that evening due primarily to poor weather conditions, and not a shot fired. Part of why it has been so difficult for me to accept this episode is that it was not the result of the usual firefights we were accustomed to. It was a situation that evolved over a number of nerve-racking hours. It was not a quick, "seconds only" type of event as many deaths were in Vietnam. I was there but it was as if I had been sleep walking through those hours.

Looking back, fortunately our aircraft commander, the XO, had the wisdom and experience to know that we as the chase ship had to avoid that fog bank and get the hell out of there ASAP, or else it would have been 12 lost souls that night.

It was a harrowing experience, one that I repeat in my mind frequently. As a young lieutenant and pilot, it seemed like it didn't have to happen, but it did, and it will haunt me for the rest of my life. I often think of Major Simons' family, I know he had children and I wonder what his tragic demise did to their lives. Sure, they were young, and we all move ahead, but just the same, I imagine they had some very difficult days, and years, for that matter.

So, there you have it, nephew Chris, this is war you can only experience if you've been there. Eight good lives wiped out in minutes, in helicopter accidents, in a war zone without a VC shot fired. I've had nightmares about that deadly night ever since. It's always overcast, alternating misting and rain. Once the drama starts in my mind, I've been unable to stamp it out until it runs its course.

For years, I've been suppressing this episode. Like so many of my comrades, I didn't believe the VA was there to help Vietnam Vets, only the old guys of World War I and II. Now I know better. There are great healing benefits in the camaraderie found at our local Vet Center and even more so in groups like the Atlanta Vietnam Veterans Business Association and the Georgia Chapter of the Vietnam Helicopter Pilots Association. God bless them all!

Oh, and Chris, there is one redeeming aspect of this whole episode. Years later I was able to explain to fellow Atlanta Vietnam Veterans Business Association member George Murray what had taken the life of his flight school classmate and friend, LT Richard "Dick" Meehan. For all of us who made it back, it's always comforting in a way that only pilots would understand to know the rest of the story, that is, how our former classmates and unit buddies sacrificed their lives.

PHILIP H. ENSLOW, JR.

United States Army, Signal Corps Officer

Dates of Military Service: 1951 to 1975

Units served in in Vietnam: Headquarters, 1st Signal Brigade; Headquarters, Regional Communications Group (Apr 1967 to Nov 1967); 173rd Airborne Brigade (Separate) (Nov 1967 to Apr 1968)

Highest Ranks Held: Lt. Colonel (O-5)

Place of Birth and Year: Richmond, VA — 1933

A "STATE-SIDER" INSPECTS A COMBAT SIGNAL UNIT

When I arrived in Vietnam, I was first assigned to the Operations Section in the Headquarters of the 1st Signal Brigade. The first day, the Commanding General of the Brigade told me that I was going with him on an inspection trip the next day. [The Brigade Commanding General was General Robert Terry. I first met him when I was a cadet at West Point, and he was the Executive Officer of the Department of Electricity.] General Terry pointed out that that trip would be a great opportunity to be introduced to the operations going on within the Signal Brigade. That was certainly true, but here I was going out to inspect a combat unit and my fatigues still had stateside starch in them. Although I had no experience in country, a lot of the things to be inspected were common, not specific to Vietnam. An earlier commanding officer had pointed out that I was very good at "taking names and kicking butts!"

For those of us working in the operations section, our working hours were set by the Commanding General's hours. There was a big difference in our travel between the Brigade Headquarters and the hotel where I was temporarily billeted compared to the CG's transfer with his sedan and driver. Of course, we rode the bus. Since we had to be at the Brigade Headquarters earlier, and later, than the General, we had to leave earlier than him to get there on time and depart after he had left. A rough schedule, but a great opportunity to learn what was really going on.

My assignment to the Signal Brigade Headquarters was not very long, but it was an extremely valuable introduction to communications operations in South Vietnam. After just over two weeks, I was off to the Headquarters of the Regional Communications Group. The RCG was responsible for long lines communications in South Vietnam, and I was to be responsible for the activation of the very high-capacity system being installed to cover all of South Vietnam. This new communication system was known as the "Integrated Wideband Communications System," the "IWCS."

ACTIVATING THE IWCS

When we first deployed troops into Vietnam, the long-distance communications available was what the troops brought with them, their tactical communications systems, and what little long-distance communications that had existed prior to our entry. As we remained in Vietnam longer, it was decided to install a much larger, high-capacity communication system similar to what is used by telephone companies back in the United States. That new system was known as the Integrated Wideband Communications System, the "IWCS."

After a short tour at the 1st Signal Brigade Headquarters, in the Operations Section, I was transferred to the Regional Communications Group (RCG) Headquarters, which was also in Saigon. My primary job in the RCG was to orchestrate and control the activation of the IWCS. I would have that assignment for about six months before being transferred to the 173rd Airborne Brigade as the Brigade Signal Officer.

The IWCS was very different from our tactical communication systems. Tactical systems were totally focused on single, voice channels that could be combined into groups of 12 or 24 channels. The IWCS provided much wider usable bandwidth with many more channels possible. It was now possible to have systems with many more than 24 channels. Another, much more important difference in the IWCS was the distance that could exist between repeaters.

For the tactical systems, this distance was usually 25 miles or less. For the IWCS, the separation between repeaters could be much greater. The advantage of this was that we did not have to have as many repeater stations out in the jungle, often on isolated peaks, that had to be defended. To provide that defense, the RCG, which operated the IWCS, Included a number of Infantry troops. Another important difference between the tactical systems and the IWCS, was the inclusion in the IWCS of "Over The Horizon" operation, also known as "Tropo or Tropospheric Scatter." A good example of the use of this mode of operation was communication between the islands in the Caribbean. OTH operation enabled much longer distances between the repeater locations.

A major obstacle in activating the WCS was the training of the troops to operate it. There were many major differences between the operation and control of the IWCS and the tactical systems for which the troops had been trained. The equipment and its operation were also quite different. We had to set up a special training program to prepare our troops to operate the IWCS. Training material had to be developed for these courses. My previous experience as an instructor was put to very good use in setting up this training program. I collected together instructional material from the manufacturers of the IWCS equipment to prepare the instructional material for our classes. I also contacted the Signal School, back in the States, so that they could include our requirements into their training programs.

I had a very difficult time with my periodic briefings on our progress in activating the IWCS—that is, getting traffic onto the IWCS comm channels, "How many of the existing comm channels were we able to transfer to IWCS channels during the previous week(s)." I had to give numbers on our progress, and one of the major critics of our progress was the J6. He, as well as many others in the briefings, did not fully understand what we were doing and what our problems were. I had to go into detail on the differences between tactical equipment and the IWCS. The attendees at these briefings, if they knew anything about communications equipment, were familiar with combat systems where activating channels was the simple operation of connecting two wires together.

For the IWCS channel activation, a number of pieces of specialized equipment had to be interconnected at each intermediate point. This involved a large number of physical connections that had to be made.

Sometimes as many as 16 connections had to be soldered and then tested at each intermediate point—very time consuming. Fortunately, I had very strong support at these briefings from the Commanding General of the Signal Brigade,

Among other problems I had were complaints from the Commanding General of the Marines in Vietnam about the quality of the Armed Forces Radio Network (AFRN) signal when it arrived up north where his troops were located. The signal that arrived at Danang to be broadcast over the local AFRN station was so weak and noisy that the programs were often unintelligible. This was a problem with music programs, but much more important was the very poor quality of baseball and football programs. The cause of this problem I was easy to identify. At each intermediate IWCS node that the AFRN program signal went through, the operators there would connect a loudspeaker for the entertainment of the personnel at that location.

Of course, each of these "illegal taps" weakened the signal while the noise continued to increase. Once the problem had been identified, the solution was pretty simple. We rerouted the AFRN signal over the undersea cable that went from Vung Tao direct to Da Nang with no immediate stations where the operators could tap into the signal and lower its quality while increasing the noise.

To say the least, I was happy that the Marines were satisfied with the quality of their program. By the way, we left the original signal path unchanged so the system operators would continue to listen to it and not go looking for the new signal path and damaging its quality.

COMMUNICATIONS FOR "MR. MCNAMARA'S ELECTRONIC WALL"

Under Mr. McNamara's influence, our operations in Vietnam became a "high tech war." An example of this was—to control and attack the Ho Chi Minh Trail, microphones, mounted on a rod shaped like a javelin, were emplaced at locations along the trail, i.e., shot into the jungle alongside the trail by low flying aircraft. These locations were recorded and sent to the control center at NKP, the U.S. Air Force base at Naknon

Phenom, NKP, in Thailand. Sounds heard on the trail were then radioed back to NKP.

There were control planes, as well as fighters, orbiting over the area where it was expected to hear activity on the trail. After analysis of the sounds at NKP, instructions were radioed to the planes with location information. The activity on the trail was then attacked with bombs and gunfire to destroy the troops coming down the trail and the supplies they were transporting. Then, of course, the microphone and radio "javelin" had to be replaced.

Another example of the "high tech war" was using technology to assist in protecting our fire bases. Microphones were installed along the perimeter wire. We had been using, and continued to use, tin cans tied to the wire to alert us when NVA infiltrators were attempting to get through the wire. Now we had microphones alerting us when there was any noise in the wire.

In order for these "high tech" systems, as well as others, to function properly, there had to be good communications. An important job I had was providing communications between Vietnam and NKP. To make sure that the communications were working properly end-to-end, I had to visit Thailand and NKP. Not too surprising, any travel from Vietnam to Thailand had to be approved by a general officer. In my case, that was the G2 of ARVN.

One day some problems arose, and I had to get to Thailand immediately. I gave my orders to my driver and sent him to Long Bien to have the G2 sign them. When he returned, his description of his "adventure" was very interesting! When he went to the G2's office, he was directed to talk to the G2's Aide. The Aide told my driver, "Give me the orders and I will get them signed." My driver then did as he was instructed and told the General's Aide, probably a major or lieutenant colonel, that he had strict instructions to give those orders to no one other than the G2 himself.

Very reluctantly, the Aide escorted my driver into the General's office and told the General that, "This man has something that he has been instructed to hand to you personally." My driver gave the orders to the

General, who opened them, read my note which identified the reason for my trip, signed the orders, gave them back to my driver, and placed all the other correspondence into his "burn basket." My driver told me that he was then escorted back into the front office by a very angry Aide and told to "Get out!"

Under the category of "This is a small world," I ran into two people I knew very well in the hotel in Bangkok. The first was my roommate from West Point, George Burkhart. I was in the hotel lobby talking to him, when a very attractive young woman came over, called me by name, and started talking like we were old friends. In fact, we were old friends. She was Jill Hallett, the daughter of a very good friend of my wife's family. Her father was working for the "Agency" in Thailand, and she was at the hotel as a model in a hairstylist competition. "It truly is a small world."

When I returned from my second trip to Thailand, the Commander of the Regional Communications Group, a full colonel, asked in a somewhat joking manner "Did I need any help on my trips to Thailand?" I am sure he knew what I was doing, so I told him I was sorry, but I did not need any more help.

I will leave it to others to evaluate the effectiveness of "Mr. Mc-Namara's Electronic Wall" and the other "High Tech" toys. I can proudly say that I received no complaints about the communications.

When I returned from Thailand after what turned out to be my last trip, I received a telephone call from General Terry, the Signal Brigade CG. General Terry asked me if I was "jump qualified." Any good soldier would hesitate to answer such a question coming out of the blue like that. Not receiving a reply, General Terry then said, "It does not matter. You are now the Signal Officer of the 173rd Airborne Brigade." {See my stories in the first volume of "*I Am Ready To Talk*."]

ROBERT L. "BOB" HOPKINS

US Army— Infantry Officer

Dates of Military Service: Aug 1965 to Jun 1968

Unit Served with in Vietnam: Bravo Company, 1st Bn, 39th Inf Regt, 9th Inf Division

Dates in Vietnam: Dec 1966 to Dec 1967

Highest Rank Held: First Lieutenant

Place of Birth and Year: Baltimore, MD— 1943

THE TUNNEL

During the Vietnam War, our opponent was quit adept at constructing complex underground tunnel systems, giving them an advantage in infiltrating, often unbeknown, to our forces. One of the largest of these tunnel complexes was near the U.S. base camp at Cu Chi, the base camp for the 25th Infantry Division. It is interesting to note that today the Cu Chi tunnel is a tourist attraction and can be toured for a nominal fee of approximately $17.00.

The Cu Chi complex is northwest of Saigon and is 45 miles long, which at the height of the war stretched from Saigon all the way to the Cambodian border. The tunnels were narrow and generally only navigable by the smallest of US soldiers. Those who went into the tunnels were nicknamed "tunnel rats." The "rats" would go into the tunnel with a small caliber handgun and a flashlight. They were ever so cautious of booby traps set by the Viet Cong to discourage entry. The tunnel entrances were often well hidden under food storage bins or animal barns. During the war, the tunnels were noted for their escape holes, their use for underground food and supply storage, medical needs, kitchens, areas for rest, and headquarters centers.

The tunnel discovered by my platoon, first platoon, Bravo Company, 2nd Battalion/39th Infantry, of the 9th Infantry Division is in the Hat Dich Secret Zone (the Hat Dich area is noted for the city of Vung Tau, (now a resort area reachable from Saigon by hydrofoil and the location of several luxury resort hotels) in southeastern Bien Hoa Province where the unit was involved in Operation Akron. It was in late June 1967. First Platoon was transported by our usual mode of transportation, the versatile Huey helicopter from our basecamp called Bearcat, following south along highway 15 to join the Akron Operation.

The platoon was on a routine search and destroy patrol in our area of operation (AO) when we discovered the Viet Cong tunnel complex. It was a sophisticated five-level complex, containing enough medical supplies to treat a regimental-size force. The multi-tiered underground system, with some compartments 60 feet below topsoil, was discovered in the jungle maze of Phouc Tuy Province, 40 kilometers east of Saigon.

Inside was a dental chair with the drill powered by bicycle pedaling. The power for lighting was also provided by someone using the bicycle pedals to power a small generator. Along with plaster for casts, ether, alcohol, gauze, and glucose to treat casualties, there was a typewriter and numerous medical records. The medical records were given to the S2 (Intelligence) section of the Division and were useful in determining the type of wounds the Viet Cong were sustaining from our weaponry. Additionally, hand-grenades and supplies of ammunition were confiscated.

The estimated size of the tunnel was 700 by 300 meters. The tunnel had been hastily abandoned a few days before discovery, since this area had been pounded by pre-planned air strikes. Much of the jungle cover had been stripped away. It was not easy to discover the entrances to the complex since they were concealed in empty shacks and huts. Underground in the kitchen area, fresh rice and fish had been left behind. Bedding made from leaves was still green and fresh.

The tunnel was discovered late in the afternoon. After reporting to my company commander and giving an assessment of the tunnel discovery, the platoon was ordered to remain at the location for the night. We bivouacked, setting up a circular defense with listening posts in two directions. Since we were isolated in a known Viet Cong stronghold, we wanted to have some preplanned defensive concentrations (def-cons) around our position. Not being that proficient in adjusting artillery, I had to do my best adjusting. Also, the artillery support unit mentioned they had run out of marking rounds and had to use HE on the deck. I cautioned all my troops to take cover when a round was incoming. The pucker factor became intense! But we did survive.

The tunnel discovery caught the attention of division commanders. After my platoon's "tunnel rats" cleared the underground complex, Major General George G. O'Connor, division commander, and Brigadier General Morgan G. Roseborough, assistant division commander, wanted a tour. Since there was no clear landing zone to get the division commanders to the location, we had to use a lot of C4 explosive to blow down trees for the LZ. With support from an engineer unit, we successfully cleared a small landing zone.

It was awesome to witness a skilled Huey pilot corkscrew his bird into that tight LZ we created. The Division wanted to get as much favorable publicity as possible from the tunnel discovery and visit by the "brass," so a photographer from the Signal battalion accompanied the generals. The photographer was afraid to enter the tunnel for pictures, so my platoon sergeant and I went into the tunnel to snap the memorable photographs.

Also, to maximize the favorable publicity from the discovery, a full-page article was published in the July 5, 1967, edition of the division newspaper, *The Old Reliable*. My hometown newspaper in Middletown, New Jersey received a press release from the division's public relations office.

As a result of me being the platoon leader, I was awarded an Army Commendation Medal for the tunnel work.

ARTHUR "ART" KATZ

US Coast Guard— Captain of CG Cutter, Point Cypress
Dates of Military Service (Active Duty and Reserves): 1959 to 1967
Unit Served with in Vietnam: Coast Guard Squadron Zone, Division 13, patrolling the Mekong River Delta and Coastal III Corps, South Vietnam
Dates in Vietnam: Jan 1966 to Oct 1966
Highest Rank Held: Lieutenant (O-3)
Place of Birth and Year: New York, NY — 1942

SEMPER PARATUS (ALWAYS READY)

The US Coast Guard's role (USCG) in the Vietnam (VN) War is not widely known. As the AVVBA's only USCG Officer member, I will do my best to shed some light on USCG involvement.

The USCG and its predecessor agencies began serving our nation in 1790 as the Revenue Cutter Service, conceived and initiated by then Secretary of the Treasury, Alexander Hamilton. Since WWI, the CG has played a vital combat role in every US foreign armed conflict. During WWII, for instance, the USCG had the highest number, per capita, of WIA/KIA. In VN, the CG responsibility included a coastal blockade, port security, explosives handling (loading and unloading), aids to navigation, gunfire support, aviation supply and Merchant Marine advisory services.

The CG involvement in VN began in 1965 and continued through 1975. It turns out that prior to 1965, the Viet Cong (VC) were receiving most of their military supplies by sea via North Vietnamese (NV) steel hulled disguised fishing trawlers. The trawlers were in the 100-120 foot long range, and capable of carrying in excess of 100 tons of weapons and ammunition (to provide another perspective, one trawler carried as much materiel in a one week sailing as 4,000 people could carry in a two-month overland Ho Chi Minh trail journey).

In February 1965, a trawler was discovered unloading arms and munitions in Vung Ro Bay, South Vietnam. As a result, the Navy recognized the need for an inshore coastal blockage to stop the illicit flow by sea.

Operation Market Time was initiated, anchored by 25 CG 82-foot cutters, comprising the newly formed Coast Guard Squadron 1. The coast of South Viet Nam was divided into nine large patrol areas approximately 40x100 miles each, and then each area was subdivided. The US Navy maintained an outer blockade approximately 20 miles offshore, and subsequently also formed an inshore capacity with 50 foot long Swift Boats.

During the existence of Market Time, the 82-foot-long Point Class (all named Point xxx) severely disrupted the seaborne supply efforts of the NVA, intercepting, capturing, and sinking multiple trawlers. Subsequent intelligence reports determined that prior to early 1966, almost 75% of military supplies sent to the VC by NVA were done by sea. One year later, that number had dwindled to a mere 10%, forcing the VC and NVA to change their means of supply from the sea to the Ho Chi Minh trail.

I trust that the above provides suitable background regarding the CG in VN. With this in mind, I will shift my focus from the CG in VN in general to my personal command, the USCGC Point Cypress, as a logical next step.

Carol and I were married four days after I graduated from US Coast Guard Academy. During the next two years I took on increasing responsibility, first as Operations Officer of a CG Cutter based in Portsmouth, VA, and then as Executive Officer of another Cutter based at Staten Island, on the shores of New York Harbor. In early October 1965, at age 23, I received orders promoting me to Commanding Officer of USCGC Point Cypress, directing me to report to the CG Base in Alameda, CA as an intermediate stop en route to VN. (Carol and I had less than two weeks' notice and had just learned of her pregnancy).

A great deal was happening very quickly between October and December 1965, as the CG rushed to war. In Alameda we met our 12-man crews (none of us had ever known another member), and we went through physical fitness training, damage control training (what to do to remain afloat if your boat is hit by enemy fire), survival training (how to avoid capture by the enemy, how to behave if captured, how to treat wounds, time in a "POW" camp experience, etc.) Since the only survival training school in operation in the US at the time was 12,000 feet up in the Sierra Nevada Mountains at the Marine Corps Mountain Warfare Training Center, initial survival training was in sub-freezing temperatures surrounded by 10+ feet of snow.

During this same period, our peacetime-configured Patrol Boats were loaded on large freighters, and shipped to the US Naval Base, Subic Bay, Philippines. It was there that they were outfitted with weapons, wartime communications systems, etc., and then tested and retested. We trained as a crew operating under "wartime conditions." It was very intense — our lives would subsequently depend on how well we performed. We also experienced jungle survival training, and in less than one month, we sailed the 1200+ miles to VN. Upon arrival in February 1966, we were briefed on current circumstances, given our specific missions, assigned patrol areas, and were deployed.

Each Cutter was responsible for patrolling a specific area along the coast, including the rivers that flowed into the sea, if navigable. We were one to two weeks at sea, refueling at sea, and then two days in port. Through the months it was never cold, and often sweltering, and the three-month monsoon of never-ending wind, rain, and waves meant little sleep and great discomfort.

In March, Cypress was assigned to patrol the Soi Rap River, which bordered the west side of the VC controlled mangrove swamp area named the Rung Sat Special Zone (RSSZ). The east side was bordered by the Saigon River, on which most of the allied war supplies for the southern half of south Vietnam were shipped. Thus, containing and minimizing the VC fighting capability in the RSSZ was extremely vital. Since there was no drinkable water or food supply in the RSSZ, preventing any personnel, food, and water, or weaponry from exit or entry into the zone would eventually starve out the VC.

On the night of March 24, 1966, after dark, Cypress stealthily navigated well upriver to a point where we could maintain radar surveillance of a very long stretch of the riverbanks. After several hours, we noted movement at the mouth of one of the creeks flowing into the Soi Rap.

After a couple of repetitions of poking its nose out into the main river, looking around and then pulling back into the creek, a large sampan headed for the far shore. We waited at general quarters in total darkness and silence until the sampan reached an intercept point of no return. We then approached at full speed, illuminated the target, and were immediately fired upon. We opened fire, killing at least seven, wounding and capturing three, including a VC colonel, along with arms, ammunition, and valuable intelligence papers. During this firefight, and to this day, I remember the sound of a bullet zipping just past my left ear, so close that I felt the air move for the briefest of moments.

The captured Colonel was seriously wounded, and I performed my first, and fortunately only, battlefield wound treatment, packing and bandaging his wound, and administering morphine. Although Cypress took many bullet hits, we sustained only minor damage and no WIA/KIA.

More routine patrols followed, until the night of May 6, 1966, when the USCGC Point Grey intercepted a NVA trawler and sustained considerable damage and wounded crewmen as the trawler made a run for the river mouth, supported by a small army of VC on the beach. Cypress was the nearest patrol unit when Grey first encountered the trawler and headed to the scene at flank speed. Grey had lost all but handheld radio capability, and with multiple wounded, had very limited fighting capacity.

Cypress assumed on scene communications, awaiting additional Navy support, and continued strafing of the trawler and beach, while receiving heavy return fire. The goal was to prevent any material from being offloaded to the VC on the beach, and this was achieved. By daybreak, the USS Brister was on scene, other units were en route, and phantom jets literally blew up the entire beach where the VC had been dug in. Tons of communist Chinese weapons and munitions were recovered.

Cypress returned to normal duties, and often patrolled the Mekong River Delta area, a VC hotbed by night. The Mekong is one of the mightiest rivers in the world, flowing south 2,700 miles from the Himalayan Mountains to the South China Sea. As it approaches the sea, it splits into five smaller, but still very large rivers, as part of the Mekong River

Delta. This area of more than 16,000 square miles, is flat and swampy, and interlaced with a very substantial network of creeks and canals. Near the sea, the 12-foot tide impacts this network dramatically. Transportation is primarily by water. The area contained major VC groups and is agriculturally very rich.

During May and early June, I became aware of intelligence reports that the VC were using very large, motorized junks to transport substantial volumes of personnel and munitions via the network of canals. They used the darkest nights of the lunar cycle to avoid detection. I requested and was granted permission (Duh, isn't there a saying about not volunteering?) to undertake a night patrol in order to interdict the flow of supplies. My plan was to enter the river at low tide. We had no idea what we might encounter once a few miles upriver.

The challenge was to safely navigate through the treacherous and uncharted river mouth, with its constantly changing currents and shifting sand bars. In addition to these considerations, the area was heavily studded with numerous permanent fishing nets strung between telephone pole sized timbers. The good news was that it would be reasonable to assume that Cypress could make a much faster departure from the area due to the quickly rising tide.

June 16 was a moonless night, with low tide occurring at dusk. Admittedly, it was slow and testy going, but Cypress made it through the hazards. We proceeded upriver a few miles in pitch darkness, and essentially total silence. We dropped anchor at a well-positioned radar surveillance location. After a few hours, we detected three large, motorized junks emerging from one of the larger canals, and heading across the river. We waited to lift the anchor so that once floating free, the river current would carry us to an intercept point near mid-river, giving the junks minimal opportunity to escape into one of the canals. Stealth was on our side, and our prior training in total darkness proved to be an invaluable asset.

The three junks were traveling in a triangular pattern. We started the engines and proceeded at full speed into the triangle from the rear. This allowed us to open fire at close range on all three junks simultaneously, utilizing all five .50 caliber machine guns. The withering fire caused one junk to explode in a huge fireball, lighting up the black sky as bodies and debris flew in all directions. A second junk was sunk, disappearing off radar. The third junk also received devastating fire from Cypress, but in the darkness and super-heightened battle action, we were unable to report, with certainty, on the third junk's sinking. Without delay, and with more comfortable water depth, Cypress hastened out of the area in complete darkness. Daylight post battle inspection revealed numerous hits from enemy fire, but no serious damage. The VC never knew what hit them. Mission accomplished!

As a note of interest, 11 days later, very near that same Mekong River mouth location, I learned from Carol that our first child, Lisa, was born.

I remained the Commanding Officer (CO) of the Point Cypress until September 1966. During my eight months as CO, Cypress cruised 17,848 miles, detected 1,413 junks and sampans, inspected or boarded 1,084, and engaged in seven gunfire support missions. Without question, our greatest accomplishment was to be able to report zero WIA/KIA. It is the highest tribute I could give to my crew.

Upon leaving Cypress, I was transferred to Da Nang. There I assumed the sad responsibility of overseeing the repair and return to battle readiness of the Point Welcome, which was badly damaged by friendly fire, on August 11. During that encounter, my classmate and friend, David Brostrom, was killed, and several of his crew badly wounded.

I returned to the States, was promoted to full Lieutenant, and served as Assistant Chief, Search and Rescue for the Third Coast Guard District, based in New York, until I resigned from the CG in July 1967. My pride in serving my country remains unfailing, and like many of my fellow wartime warriors, I remain convinced that we won the war, but sadly, and tragically for so many, lost the political battle.

JOHN "MARK" WALKER

United States Navy— Supply Officer

Dates of Military Service (Active and Reserve): 1963 to 1992

Unit Served with in Vietnam: USS Wrangell (AE-12)

Dates Served in Vietnam: Nov 1965 to May 1966

Highest Rank Held: Captain (O-6)

Place and Date of Birth: Memphis, TN— 1941

HOW NOT TO LEAD

We recently discovered some letters that I had written my parents while our Navy ship, the USS Wrangell (AE-12), was serving off the coast of Vietnam. I did not realize, or even remember, how I felt about my job as the ship's Supply Officer at that time. The phrase that hit me hard was, "I hate my job!"

Most likely the reason I felt that way at the time was the terrible relationship I had with the ship's Executive Officer or XO. I was an O-2 (LTJG) and he was an O-4 (LCDR). He hated me, and never missed an opportunity to make me look bad. At the tender age of 23, I certainly needed some serious coaching. But never in the more than 12 months we served together, did the XO ever offer me any counseling or coaching on how to be a better officer. By the way, one of an XO's primary jobs is the training of his junior officers.

At one point during our six-month service time in the Vietnam theater, our ship's Captain, an O-6 (CAPT) was trying to help an acquaintance, who was the Commanding Officer of an aircraft carrier we were scheduled to rearm in a few days. The carrier was low on fresh water, possibly due to an equipment failure. (Navy ships make their own fresh water from seawater using "evaporators.") Our CO agreed to save our water and transfer it to them while we were re-arming them. So, the order went out, "No showers until the water transfer is complete." The objective was for us to have the maximum amount of fresh water to give the carrier. We endured four days of no showers in the heat of the South China Sea.

I was standing Bridge Watches at that time and had just completed a "mid-watch" from midnight to 0400 hours (4:00 AM). My face was greasy and sweaty, so I ran a basin of water (which was permitted) and washed my face before taking a nap and starting the workday. My stateroom was next to the XO's stateroom. He likely heard the water running for the 15 or 20 seconds it took to fill the sink.

It was customary on our ship for each of the four department heads or their duty officers to meet with the XO or his representative every evening at 2000 (called "eight o'clock reports") as a group and report that everything was okay in their division or give a situation report (SITREP) if there were problems. So that evening I was standing with the other department heads who were all former enlisted senior leaders who had been commissioned and had O-3 rank, or LT. As the junior department head, I reported last, and the XO said, "LTJG Walker, you are in hack!" (That meant that I was not to leave the ship for liberty the next time we were in port.) I asked, "May I ask why, sir?" The XO said, "Because you took a shower last night against the Captain's orders." I was mortified and said, "I beg your pardon, sir, I most certainly did not! I ran water into the sink to wash my face. That was it!" He was adamant that I had showered. I just dropped it and when we were next in port, I ignored his "hack" order. He never said another word about it.

Now I was not the most agreeable junior officer on that ship. Working for that XO, I just wanted to serve my time and get out when my active-duty obligation of three years was complete. But one thing I remembered from the Officer Candidate "Leadership" course was "Praise in public and reprimand in private." Standing with the other department heads, all of whom were senior to me, the XO had completely surprised me with that public reprimand. Plus, I was innocent! Had he called me aside during the day and told me about his view of my "shower," we might have worked it out with neither of us being embarrassed. Looking back on it, I should have requested a meeting with the Captain and the XO together and discussed the obvious rancor the XO was expressing in our relationship. It would have probably helped him and would have certainly helped me feel better!

When it came time to transfer the fresh water, no one had ever thought to figure out how we could transfer several thousand gallons of water to the Carrier in an hour or less while steaming through the ocean. When our engineers tried to perform the water transfer, our two-inch transfer hose was just too small to provide any meaningful contribution to their water needs. We endured four days of no showers for NOTH-ING! At least we tried!

When it came time a few months later to discuss my future in the Navy, I had absolutely no interest in remaining on active duty. I understood that one's Navy career could depend on working for a poor leader like our XO and could be the end of one's career dreams. I wanted nothing to do with that. Thus, I left the Navy and got a job.

After a few months of living on a tight budget in the Washington, DC area, I got a call from the Commanding Officer of a Navy Reserve unit who asked if I would be interested in affiliating with his Reserve Unit. As I talked with him, he pointed out that after 20 years (I already had almost four) I would retire with full medical benefits that would kick in *with pay* at age 60. Plus, I needed the extra monthly income at that time! So, I checked it out.

While my active-duty experience was not very positive, I loved the people and the work as an Active Reservist. When we moved to Atlanta, I continued my Reserve career, had some excellent assignments, and was able to retire as an O-6, a Navy Captain. Imagine how surprised my former XO would be if he knew about that!

ROBERT O. "BOB" BABCOCK

US Army—Infantry Officer
Dates of Military Service (Active Duty and Reserves): 1965 to 1974
Unit Served with in Vietnam: Bravo Company, 1st Battalion, 22nd Infantry
Regiment, 4th Infantry Division
Dates Served in Vietnam: July 1966 to July 1967
Highest Rank Held: Captain (O-3)
Place and Date of Birth: Heavener, OK—1943

"WHAT NOW, LIEUTENANT?"

In late August 1966, we had been in Vietnam less than a month and had just flown to Tuy Hoa from our base camp at Pleiku. Our battalion was "op-con" or under the operational control of the 101st Airborne Division's First Brigade.

The second day in Tuy Hoa, word came down that a platoon was needed to secure an engineer unit clearing mines from a road west of Tuy Hoa. The road had last been cleared by the French before their defeat in 1954. Since we were the best company in the battalion, we were selected for this first "real" mission since our arrival in country. I was both pleased and apprehensive when Lieutenant Fiacco told me my platoon had the mission.

We were to be picked up by "deuce and a half" (two and a half ton) trucks early the next morning and taken out to join the engineers on the road. I found out the engineer unit we were supporting had been with Captain Bill Carpenter, the famous "Lonesome End" from West Point, when he had called an air strike in on his own position when he had been overrun less than three months earlier. I vividly remembered having read about Captain Carpenter's experiences while we were still at Fort Lewis.

We were up bright and early, checking our equipment and weapons thoroughly, making sure we had plenty of ammo, testing our radios to be sure they worked right, and just generally feeling nervous, very green, and inexperienced.

The big green trucks picked us up on schedule. Soon we were speeding west through Tuy Hoa, watching the people closely. Regardless of what people told us about the towns being relatively safe, we did not trust anyone. Sticking to our training, we kept our weapons at the ready, ready to pounce from the truck and respond to any hostile action.

A few miles outside Tuy Hoa, we saw a unit of American troops laying at ease alongside the road. A lump came up in my throat as I realized this was it. We had to get off the trucks and do what we were sent over here to do.

As I climbed down from the truck, I scanned the troops looking for someone with captain's bars. When I could not find him, I asked one of the men where the captain was and he said, "That's me."

I really felt like a green rookie after looking at him. He had no rank insignia, his uniform was well worn, in marked contrast to my still new jungle fatigues. Knowing he had been almost overrun with Captain Carpenter put me more in awe — for the first time I was on a genuine combat mission with real combat veterans.

"Glad to have you, Lieutenant Babcock," he said. "I want you to patrol out in front of us and make sure we don't run into any ambushes. Stay at least a quarter mile in front, work both sides of the road, but stay off the road. It is heavily mined. Any questions?"

My concept of combat engineers was they went first and cleared the road, and we would follow along and be available as a quick reaction force if they ran into anything. I quickly remembered the Infantry's job is out in front, not behind anyone else.

"No sir, no questions. Are you ready for us to move out now?"

"The sooner you can get out there the sooner we can get on with our work." I overcame my instinct to salute as I turned and headed back for my platoon.

Walking back to my platoon, which Sergeant Roath had formed into a loose perimeter along the road, I took off my helmet, took the gold lieutenant's bar off my camouflage cover, and tossed it into the muddy water filled ditch alongside the road. I sure did not want to bring attention to my rank if that experienced captain was not going to show his.

My troops listened closely as I briefed them on our mission. We saddled up and moved past the engineers and along either side of the road, careful not to set foot on the road. Stepping on a land mine was not in our plans that day.

The morning sun beat down on us unmercifully as we moved along uneventfully. Soon we approached a valley cutting off the right side of the road and forming a box canyon at the foot of steep mountains about 400 yards from the road.

The engineer captain called me on the radio, "Oscar 61, check out that valley to your right flank. Someone shot at a helicopter from in there yesterday." With that information, I was not too excited about the next phase of our mission. "Wilco," (Army lingo for "understand and will comply") was my reply as I stopped our movement and prepared to move into the valley.

Since caution is the better part of valor, I remembered my training and decided to prep the area with an artillery barrage. Frequently, I had simulated calling in artillery fire, but this was my first time to call real fire on a real target.

Charlie Battery, 4th Battalion, 42nd Field Artillery responded quickly as I called in and adjusted several 105mm artillery shells. As the shells crashed into the box canyon, I felt comfortable I had the artillery aimed at the right target if we needed it. (Many times after this, the same artillery battery responded like the true professionals they were when we called for fire support).

While I adjusted the artillery fire, Sergeant Roath set up a machine gun crew and a rifle squad along the road, ready to support us with fire. With a knot in my stomach, I moved into the valley with my other two squads, one on either side of the valley. We made sure we stayed close to the foot of the mountains and not out in the open where we would be easy targets.

Our finely honed senses soaked in everything as we worked our way up the valley to the end of the box canyon, ready to fire on the first thing that moved. An Army tactics instructor would have been proud of us—each man crouched low, keeping the proper distance from the man to his front, and constantly searching for signs of movement. No sign of activity was seen as we came to the end of the canyon.

With the same caution, we searched every potential hiding place in the canyon and on the surrounding mountains as we returned to the road. Still nothing. Breathing a sigh of relief, I radioed back our negative report and started moving down alongside the road again, wondering what our next challenge would be.

As we moved, loud explosions pierced the quiet as the engineers periodically found mines and blew them up. The day continued to get hotter, and the sun continued to beat down. Despite the heat, we were too keyed up to let our guard down. My next opportunity came from our left flank, about 100 yards off the road.

"Sir, come over here—I've found some mortar shells," came from one of my men. When I moved over to check it out, I saw several 82mm mortar shells concealed by brush in a shallow hole. I radioed our find back to the engineer captain. He responded, "Good job, blow them up and move on."

Since we did not have any plastic explosive (C4), I had to use the only thing available to me—a hand grenade. I moved the platoon into a perimeter, behind cover, out of range of the grenade.

Taking a grenade off my belt, I straightened the safety pin so it would come out easily and tied a 50-foot piece of string to the pin. Having been indoctrinated on the dangers of booby traps, I was very careful not to move any of the shells as I searched for a hole to slip the grenade into. I found a small hole and slipped the grenade down among the mortar shells.

Sergeant Roath and Sergeant Benge, my third squad leader, stayed close and found a little ridge of dirt, about 50 yards away, to hide behind. Pleased with how in control I was, I sent them to cover, walked to the end of the string, yanked it, and ran like hell. Covering the distance in no time, I dived over the ridge and slammed myself onto the ground. I hunkered down, trying to "make myself one with Mother Earth" and waited for the massive explosion. We waited and nothing happened.

I started to notice the sweat and the heat seemed more intense. All eyes were on me as my platoon peered out from their positions, wondering what had gone wrong. The piece of string was still clutched in my hand. I pulled it in and, sure enough, the safety pin was firmly attached. We either had a dud grenade or something else had gone wrong.

Sergeant Roath looked at me, grinned, and said, "What you gonna do now, Lieutenant?" More sweat started to roll down my face as I contemplated my next move. I knew I had only one choice, go see what was wrong. With my entire platoon watching me, I cautiously crawled back to the cache. Expecting an explosion at any minute, I slowly closed in on the mortar shells.

As I rose on a knee to see what the problem was, I could see the safety lever on the grenade. It had partially flipped away but had hit one of the mortar shells and stopped, not allowing the firing pin to hit the fuse. Here I was with a live grenade, safety lever barely in place, and a pile of enemy mortar shells I had to assume were booby trapped. To say I was concerned is an understatement.

I knew I was the only one who could do anything. To back away now was to show my platoon their platoon leader was a coward. Sweat continued to roll down my face and back as I eased up closer to the mortar shells. Carefully, I slipped my hand down through the hole I had dropped the grenade through and firmly grasped the safety lever against the body of the grenade. As I started to pull my hand back out the hole, it would not come out. My hand with the grenade in it was too large for the hole. Now I was really in a predicament!

I had a live grenade in my hand with no safety pin. If I let it go again, chances were good the safety lever would fly off and let it explode in five seconds—and I was pretty sure I could not make the fifty yards to cover from my crouched down position in that length of time (world class sprinters are barely that fast and I did not think my adrenalin would make me into one in five seconds). If I moved the mortar shells to get my hand and the grenade out, I would have set off any booby trap that might have been set.

I lay there for what seemed like an eternity with more sweat rolling down the back of my neck. My mind whirled as I looked around the perimeter at my men, each watching me intently. Sergeant Roath eased up toward me and with another grin said, "What you gonna do now, Lieutenant?"

"Get back, Sergeant Roath, no sense in both of us being in this mess," was my reply.

Finally, I decided to take a chance on the booby trap and jerked my hand, and the grenade, out of the hole. When I did, several of the shells moved—but, fortunately, nothing exploded. My next decision was an easy one. Getting up, I walked over to a rice paddy, and threw the hand grenade as far as I could. It exploded with a roar, shooting a spray of water high into the air.

I radioed the engineer captain, "I will mark the location of the shells. You can blow them with C4 when you get to this point. I am moving out. Out."

We continued our mission along the road. About a half hour later, a tremendous explosion shook the area as the engineers set off the captured mortar shells. Suddenly, I felt very tired. I wanted to sit down and rest but could not. We continued to patrol. We had expected to be finished and back at base camp before dark, but such was not the case. As darkness engulfed the area, the engineer captain finally decided to quit for the day.

The trucks, which had been following the engineers all day, pulled up to take us back to Tuy Hoa. We now had to ride back down the road we had just spent the day walking.

Expecting to be ambushed at any time, we were ready to fire at anything as we sped through the small villages with our lights out. The Vietnamese families, squatting in their huts, eating rice, were oblivious to our concerns. Fortunately, none of them came out of their houses or we might have blown them away.

It was nearly ten o'clock when we finally made it back to base camp. Sergeant Angulo, our mess sergeant, had saved hot chow which the troops quickly devoured. Lieutenant Fiacco met us at the gate and took me to Colonel Morley to debrief our day's actions. I could tell both had been worried about our not returning until so late. When

I finally got back to my tent and lay down on my canvas cot, I slept well.

It had been a hard and exciting day. My first real combat patrol was under my belt and, more importantly, I had earned my keep in the eyes of my platoon.

ROBERT L. "BOB" HOPKINS

US Army— Infantry Officer
Dates of Military Service: Aug 1965 to Jun 1968
Unit Served with in Vietnam: Bravo Company, 1st Bn, 39th Inf Regt, 9th Inf
Division
Dates in Vietnam: Dec 1966 to Dec 1967
Highest Rank Held: First Lieutenant
Place of Birth and Year: Baltimore, MD—1943

BOOBY TRAP

Elections were always contentious in South Vietnam, especially with the Viet Cong trying their best to disrupt them. On 3 September 1967, election day, there was a slate of five presidential contenders vying for the top job. The race was won by Nguyen Van Thieu who garnered 34.8% of the vote. Considering the turmoil the country was in, participation was an amazing 83%.

At the time, my unit, Bravo Company, 2nd Battalion, 39th Infantry of the 9th Infantry Division was on a pacification mission at the small village of Ap Binh Song. The village was surrounded by a Michelin rubber plantation, had a villa for the overseer, and was along a small stream, which we used as a recreational swimming hole.

On election day we were tasked by higher headquarters to be sure to support the election effort. The day started off quiet, but there was something troubling the company commander as he observed the villagers drive their loaded three wheeled Izetta's in the direction of the district headquarters to vote. Surprisingly, the Izetta's would turn around and head back to the village.

I was ordered by my company commander to take my platoon and scout the road to determine what was causing the villagers to turn back. A platoon-sized patrol was formed, and we proceeded along the road leading to the District Headquarters. Not far from the village of Ap Binh Song, we came across a brush barricade across the road with a sign in Vietnamese, cautioning the villagers about voting. There was also a Viet Cong flag strung between two rubber trees (I brought the flag home as a trophy of my service, and it has been donated to the Atlanta History Center to support the Vietnam history project.).

Being quite apprehensive about what might lie ahead, the platoon "reconned" by fire (firing our M16s into the brush ahead to provoke return fire). The firing was to trigger an ambush if the Vietcong were planning to spring one.

When we got up to the barricade, we looked it over carefully for booby traps and wanted to tear it apart to allow the villagers the opportunity to vote. Our very careful inspection did not disclose danger, and we began to tear the barricade apart. But our careful inspection was not good enough, because there it was just in front of me, carefully hidden in the growth, a US type hand-grenade wired with a trip wire. The grenade was in a C-ration can with the trip wire running through the brush. The VC were experts in hiding their booby traps.

It was very close to me and if it had not been discovered, I would not be here today. The Lord was with me that day and saved my life for what was to become a productive life. I often think of the 58,320 men and women whose names are on the Wall who did not have the opportunities I have had. It makes me cry. I came back unscathed, without any wounds, both physical and psychological.

It is for that reason I do so much volunteering for veterans' causes. I often volunteer at the Atlanta Airport working at the USO, welcoming home troops and cooking hotdogs for those just out of basic training. This is just my little way of giving back and giving thanks that I made it.

MILTON JONES

US Marine Corps—Telecommunications Cryptographic Technician
Dates of Military Service: 1964 to 1970
Unit Served with in Vietnam: HQ Co., Regimental Landing Team 26 (Forward), 3rd Marine Division
Dates in Vietnam: Aug 1967 to Dec 1967
Highest Rank Held: Sergeant (E-5)
Place of Birth and Year: Augusta, GA—1946

HOME AGAIN

I left Khe Sanh on Christmas Eve, 1967, headed home. My 13-month WestPac tour was up. We were surrounded at the Khe Sanh Combat Base by large numbers of NVA regular troops, but the "Siege of Khe Sanh" had not yet begun. I'm sure I said some goodbyes, but I don't remember any.

A chopper to Da Nang and then, a Continental Airlines charter back to Okinawa. Two weeks later, I boarded the Freedom Bird from Kadena AFB to make my grand swoop back to the World! Another Continental Airlines charter with flight attendants; the whole kit and caboodle. Again, I'm traveling individually. I don't know any of these guys. We land at Travis Air Force Base.

After the Transpacific flight, we get off the plane. We are so thankful to be back in the World—the good old US of A! We kneel down and kiss the runway. I'm home. I'm back in the World! Proud to have answered my Country's call to arms. Everything is going to be great!

A few hours later, after processing out, we walk off the base and along comes a hippie bus. They throw crap, feces, whatever else out on us, call us all sorts of names—"baby killers," "murderers." I'm thinking "how can I fit this experience into the warm feelings of pride, excitement, and exuberance I was just expressing?" I couldn't. I just couldn't.

As I headed home, I realized that something must be wrong with me. If I sat on a bench at the airport, all of a sudden people just got up and vanished. So, I get back home. I've got just under three months left in the

Corps and I'm reporting back into my old unit at Marine Corps Air Station Beaufort—Marine Air Base Squadron 31, Marine Aircraft Group 31. I've got leave, so I come home. We marry one week after my return. Two weeks after my return, Khe Sanh is emblazoned on the front pages; on the six o'clock news; in magazines— *Time* Magazine—wherever.

I'm looking at this stuff, and my first impulse is, "Man! Thank God! I'm out of there!" I'm back in the World. I'm not dealing with that. Then, my next thought is, "I wonder if anybody heard me thinking that?" I'm supposed to be back there with the troops; with my brothers. Does anybody know how I'm feeling about getting out of there? What a cowardly thought. What would they think of me if they knew I was back home rejoicing about being out of there?

And this thing—the Siege of Khe Sanh—was just constantly in the news. Will Khe Sanh become another Dien Bien Phu where French Army forces were defeated by the Viet Minh (Vietnamese Communist forces) a dozen years before? Even the President was expressing concern and had a scale model of the Khe Sanh Combat Base and surroundings installed in the White House. I was silently ashamed.

Meantime, I'm trying to get situated for a civilian career. No. Career wasn't even a thought. A job! A civilian job. While still at Khe Sanh, I came across an old magazine— *Ebony*—that happened to have one of these little coupon recruiting ads. "People with whatever skills, electronic maintenance skills, complete this." I sent the thing back into IBM Corporation.

Turned out it was IBM in Atlanta. And literally, I got a response from them while I was still at Khe Sanh. Years ago, we found the letter with some old papers, and I still have it. At Khe Sanh, I kept the letter folded up in my pocket, thinking, "This is my ticket when I get back." Naturally, I got Khe Sanh mud on it. You know, red mud.

This would have been October-ish of '67 when I communicated with IBM. Actually, the letter dates just days before a C-130 aircraft crashed and burned on the air strip at Khe Sanh. All but one member of the crew was killed. I have no memory of the C-130 crash. I do have the letter as evidence of the memory of communicating with IBM.

Now, I'm trying to rationalize what's happening in our country. Essentially, I've been out of primary society during a period of its greatest change. And out of the country for the last year plus. The Civil Rights Act of 1964, the Voting Rights Act of 1965, and all of this. I had grown up in the rigidly-segregated South of the late 1940s, the '50s, and '60s. American society had since undergone a sea change that I now needed to meld into—a delicate balance. Also, there was so much anger about the war and much more. So confusing.

I'm trying to fit all of this into my head. Meantime, here is this never-ending barrage of information about Khe Sanh—the Marines under siege. I believe that self-preservation required me to get this thing—my Khe Sanh conflict—locked off someplace so that I could operate. Meanwhile, this is the first quarter of 1968.

Back at Khe Sanh, I do remember multiple occasions of making it to a bunker during relatively infrequent incoming. We would take in rockets, a little mortar, a little artillery here and there while I was there. Now, as soon as I left, they were sustaining incoming at the rate of 1,000 to 1,500 rounds a day coming into the base. So, I'm reading this, and I'm seeing this, and it was just more than I was prepared for. Looking back, I think it was an overload, psychologically, and I just kind of pushed it off.

I didn't really deal with the experiences I was having. I realized that it was not in vogue to be even associated with the military. And the thought of being in Vietnam, you definitely didn't want anybody to know that. This all contributed to my Khe Sanh experiences being locked away—or, at least, no memories. I still have no real memories there.

It's interesting. I got that letter from IBM and I was holding on to that thing like, "This is my ticket!" So, I come home. We're living in Augusta, Georgia, my hometown. I'm stationed at Beaufort, South Carolina, 110 miles away. I contact IBM and my new bride and I drive to Atlanta. I come into the IBM office wearing my green service "A" uniform. I asked for this fellow, Mr. Lovett, Bill Lovett, with whom I'd called for an appointment. He wasn't there at the moment, so I sort of stood around.

In those days, 1968, many business offices had a glass front area and a big imposing reception desk where the receptionist could sort of look over at you. They also had a glass door to the back office. So, you've got this Vietnam guy out here in the lobby. They told me, "Well, we're going to see if we can't get an appointment for you, and if you'd like to call back..." I said, "No, you don't understand. I need to see someone today." So, one manager comes out. He actually takes me back and interviews me. And he's got favorable words, "Good to have you here. Good interview. I'm sure we'll be in touch."

He's patting me on the back while ushering me towards the door. I'm not going anywhere. I'm spit shined. My barracks hat is under my left elbow. Its visor is gleaming after a spit-shine. Likewise, my shoes are like mirrors. I'm all squared away.

So, he goes off into the back office. I'm still around. I can see people coming and looking out into the lobby where I was. "Is that crazy guy still out there?" The manager comes back out again. I have a couple of more interviews. Finally, I tell him, "You don't understand. I need to know if I've got the job." He says, "Well, this is highly unusual. Our practice is to let you know by letter what our next steps are." I said, "I'm getting out of the Corps in a month or two. I've got a brand-new wife. I need to know if I've got the job." He vanishes off again.

In the meantime, this is becoming kind of a soap opera in the back, because other people are coming along and looking out through the glass. So, he finally comes back and says, "This is highly irregular. I'm not authorized to tell you what the salary might be, but I can say that you will be getting an offer." I didn't hear anything else!

Doesn't matter to me what the salary is going to be! I don't have an appreciation for civilian money anyway. Boom! So, I'm out of there. Sure enough, the next week or so I get a letter from IBM with an offer to go to work, literally the day after I get out. I'm getting out on April Fools' Day of 1968, and they want me to start on April 2nd. I call them and ask for some time to get moved, so I started on April 8th.

Actually, going to IBM was just what the "doctor ordered" for my situation. Essentially, I traded my Marine Corps uniform for an IBM dark suit with white shirt. You could wear any color shirt you wanted to, as long as it was white. And a drab tie. I traded my Marine Corps uniform for the IBM uniform, and I traded my hard metal Marine Corps tool kit for a nice, disguised like a briefcase, IBM tool kit. I came to an organization, IBM of the sixties, which was very regimented. Very hierarchical in its organizational structure. I knew exactly where I fit in the organization; what my role was; what my contributions could be. I had a great time with IBM. I retired after thirty-three years there, during which I worked and led in virtually all phases of the Information Technology and Training businesses.

As a veteran after getting out of the Corps, I spent years staying under the radar. Not talking about it. "Just keep your head down. Don't engage if the military or Vietnam were likely to come up." I never would have been caught with veterans' caps, insignias, or pins. I got rid of everything I had that was military related. I kept only one field jacket. All the old uniforms—gone. "Travel incognito. Don't let anybody know." Not that they wouldn't have known, anyway. But I hid the fact that I was a veteran, and it was that way for years.

I started college again at Georgia State while working full-time, but I just didn't get too close to anybody because of the atmosphere toward the military. I went that way until the mid-eighties, over fifteen years. Then, I read a newspaper article about the Moving Wall coming to Atlanta. This was a traveling version of the Vietnam War Memorial. I was compelled to pick up the phone, called home and said to Barbara, "Gee, let's keep the girls out of school that day. I want to go see this thing." When I went down there it was like BOOM! An awakening, or whatever.

I think it was such a potent moment for us—even for our daughters. Years later, when our older daughter went off to college, her birthday gift to me was a print. It's a pretty popular and common print ("Reflections" by Lee Teter). A print of a businessman standing at the Wall with his briefcase down. He's standing with his hand against the Wall, and there are comrades, fallen soldiers reaching out from within the Wall. Our daughter must have been in middle-school when we went to see the Moving Wall, so it clearly had been impactful for her. But for me, it was just like…things just opened up. I just…I mean I was in tears.

Even then, though, I had not yet reached the point where I wanted to talk about the military, and certainly not publicly acknowledge that I had something to do with the military or Vietnam. Slowly, after my awakening, I began to acknowledge that the US Marine Corps, including my Vietnam service, is a significant part of who I am. Thankfully, my wife, Barbara, my family, and friends provided a wonderful support structure to help keep me balanced throughout all this. Years later, Barbara noted that I eventually stopped gritting my teeth during my sleep.

More and more, I began to "come out" as a Vietnam Veteran over the following 15 years or so until the time of my retirement from IBM in early 2001. Since then, I've been trying to re-construct my experience, and it's been very cathartic for me to try and rebuild my service — especially my time on Okinawa, and in Vietnam.

I found the Khe Sanh Veterans Association online and joined. However, I didn't initially engage much with anyone in the organization. I periodically perused the website and the membership directory. I always looked forward to the Red Clay magazine which I immediately devoured whenever I received a new issue. Our youngest daughter started regularly telling me, "Dad, you need to go to a reunion." I didn't think so. But when I finally did make a reunion, it was really like *coming home again*! Since then, I look forward expectantly to our annual reunions with my Khe Sanh family, several of whom I engage with throughout the year.

NOTE: "Home Again" is excerpted and edited from Milton Jones Interview, October 5, 2015, Atlanta History Center, Veterans History Project.

JAY PRYOR

U.S. Naval Reserve—Communications Officer
Dates of Military Service: 1967 to 1970
Unit Served with in Vietnam: USS Hissem (DER-400) & Commander Destroyer
Squadron 29
Dates in Vietnam: Three deployments in period of 1967 to early 1970
Highest Rank Held: Lieutenant (Junior Grade) (O-2)
Place of Birth and Year: Albany, GA—1944

THE BLUE WATER WAR

Fortunately, there was a fire escape outside my hotel room window. I was on the 12th floor and the fire escape was a vertical ladder with hoops around the outside. As I descended the ladder, rung by rung, the only thing between me and the ground was gravity.

My senior year at The University of Georgia was 1967, and I knew that as soon as I was graduated, Uncle Sam was going to claim me and send me to the jungles of Vietnam. I thought that for me the better option was the U.S. Navy. The decision to join the Navy led to lessons I learned in responsibility, a sea chest of "war stories" and abundant pride in the fact that I did my part to the best of my ability to serve my country in a time of war.

It was in that senior year at UGA that I took the exam administered by the Naval Recruiter in Athens, was fortunate enough to go to Officer Candidate School in Newport, Rhode Island, and from there went to Communications Officer School in San Diego, California.

Next up was the trip from San Diego to find my assigned ship, the USS Hissem (DER-400), which was somewhere in the Western Pacific (WestPac). I had one night to see the sights of San Francisco before making my way to Travis AFB and on to WestPac.

It was near midnight when I returned to my hotel room for the night. At 3 a.m. I woke to what sounded like flowerpots being thrown against a nearby wall. I smelled smoke. Next, I discovered the hallway was filled with smoke. I opened my window and put all my belongings on the fire escape landing, then made the descent to the alley below.

The next morning, I went to Travis AFB and soon was on a flight to WestPac. It turned out that the hotel fire was not the only adventure I experienced as I made my way to the USS Hissem. I learned the ship was on Taiwan Patrol duty, showing the flag, going up and down the Taiwan Straits to show the Chinese Communists that the U.S. was ready to defend the Republic of China on Taiwan. I was in Taipei, Taiwan, on the north end of the island and learned my ship was in the south, in Kaohsiung Harbor.

The Army shuttle aircraft had space available, and I gathered my gear, much more gear than I needed, and got onboard. The plane landed and I disembarked, got all that gear together, and asked the first taxi driver I saw to take me to the Kaohsiung Harbor. He refused. He spoke little English and didn't give me a reason, so I went to the next driver. Same story. After asking several taxi drivers to take me to the harbor, one agreed.

More than five hours later we arrived in Kaohsiung. The pilot of the plane neglected to mention that we would be making a stop roughly halfway between Taipei and Kaohsiung. But I must admit it was one of the best $20 I've ever spent. I saw aspects of Taiwanese life that I never would have seen otherwise. And the taxi driver's English was much better than my Taiwanese. When I asked him how he learned to speak English so well, he told me he had fought in the Philippines with the U.S. Army in WWII.

I found my ship and soon assumed the duties of Communications Officer, having responsibility of all external communications for the ship. The ship's duties off the coast of Vietnam were Market Time and providing Naval Gunfire Support. Market Time was a program to prevent the North Vietnamese from using sea lanes to supply their troops in the south. When we were called on for gunfire support, it seemed that we were more directly involved in the War. It was particularly gratifying when our relatively small 3"/50 guns caused secondary explosions.

Soon I became accustomed to wartime life aboard a destroyer, or in my case a destroyer escort. First was the ever-present routine of standing watch, whether on the bridge or in the ship's nerve-center, the Combat

Information Center. The watch consisted of a four-hour period of duty followed by eight or twelve hours off, depending on the number of watch sections. Sleep was a precious commodity. At first it was a hindrance, but it became somewhat soothing to go to sleep hearing the sloshing of the fresh water being held in the tanks under the deck of the junior officers' quarters.

As we patrolled the coastal waters, we were resupplied by underway replenishment (UNREP) ships. The UNREP ships steamed up and down the coast providing supplies to the smaller ships such as destroyers, destroyer escorts, and others. It was from the UNREP ships that we received not only supplies needed by the ship but also movies and most important for morale, our mail. It usually took five days for a letter postmarked from Atlanta to reach our ship off the coast of Vietnam.

Being in the combat zone provided some benefits. There was the $65 per month of extra pay and no federal income tax for every month in/offshore Vietnam. And when writing a letter home, all one had to do for postage was write "free" where the stamp would ordinarily go.

I was one of 14 officers on the Hissem and had 24 men and two chiefs reporting to me. With that came responsibility. One of the infrequent assignments given the Hissem was the task of "SOPA Admin" for Hong Kong. SOPA is Navy-speak for Senior Officer Present Afloat. With this assignment we would spend three weeks in Hong Kong harbor, and we would handle all administrative paperwork for the men and women on R&R from Vietnam.

My first time in Hong Kong I was standing on the Hissem quarterdeck looking forward to going ashore. While waiting, a small boat approached our ship. As it got closer, I could see that one of the men in the boat was a leading petty officer in my division, a man with years of Naval experience—and he was in handcuffs. He had gotten into a fight in a Hong Kong bar, and since he was in my division, he was turned over to me. We went to a secluded area of the ship, and I asked him what was going on. In tears, he told me no one liked him. That was one of several times that I encountered a situation not covered at Officer Candidate School (OCS)!

Following one of our month-long assignments off the Vietnam coast, we were assigned Taiwan Patrol. We headed to Kaohsiung and on arrival we were nested outboard of two destroyers. That is, there were two destroyers already tied up next to one another and we tied up next to the second ship. There were a number of things routinely done when we docked following sea duty. One of those was to swab down, or mop, the bridge area. On this occasion, one of the most squared away sailors on the ship had that duty. He was doing his usual excellent job, swiping the mop back and forth, when his elbow hit the ship's general quarters alarm.

Immediately the klaxon horn sound was broadcast throughout our ship—and the whole area. Men were running to their general quarters, not only on our ship but on the two ships next to us, while at the same time wondering what would cause us to go to general quarters while docked in Kaohsiung! Another situation not covered at OCS.

When I reported onboard the Hissem, it was only a month after the Pueblo incident, in which the USS Pueblo (AGER-2) was taken over by North Korea. To prevent boarders from taking over the Hissem, we held "repel boarders" drills. My station, since I was the Communications Officer, was in the crypto room (more like a closet) and I was issued a sawed-off shotgun. I'm not sure that the shotgun was Navy-issued equipment, but I know that in all my time on the ship, the shotgun was never fired.

There was one time when our Captain's dedication to preparedness didn't go as well as everyone would have hoped. One of the "escort" duties of a destroyer escort was protecting other ships from submarines. Hissem carried on her fantail (the back end of the ship) two structures made for dropping depth charges. Our Captain thought it would be a good idea for the Hissem to drop a depth charge as an exercise in preparedness. You can't drop a depth charge just anywhere, and you must let it be known you're going to drop one so that there are no friendly, or for that matter unfriendly, submarines in the area.

I don't know how far up the chain of command it went, but I know that we had to get permission from a number of senior Naval officers. Finally, we received permission and we arrived at the designated drop area. I don't remember the depth at which our captain wanted the depth charge to explode, but our senior sonarman didn't think it was deep enough. Thankfully our Captain listened to the sonarman and added 100' to the explosion depth. We dropped the depth charge, it went off at the deeper depth, and the resulting explosion blew a hole in our hull. For a few hours we were taking on 25 gallons of water per minute.

Compared to the foot soldiers who faced death and disease in the jungles of Vietnam, I had it easy. But the ships I served on, first as Communications Officer for the USS Hissem (DER-400), and then as Communications Officer for the six ships of Destroyer Squadron 29, all played a part. I like to think we helped the troops on the ground with the gunfire support we provided, and there is no question that with Market Time Patrol we at the very least made it much more difficult for the North Vietnamese to get supplies to their troops in the South.

The older I get, the prouder I am of my Vietnam service in the U.S. Navy.

ROBERT L. "BOB" HOPKINS

US Army— Infantry Officer

Dates of Military Service: Aug 1965 to Jun 1968

Unit Served with in Vietnam: Bravo Company, 1st Bn, 39th Inf Regt, 9th Inf Division

Dates in Vietnam: Dec 1966 to Dec 1967

Highest Rank Held: First Lieutenant

Place of Birth and Year: Baltimore, MD— 1943

THE LONGEST PATROL

During the year when first platoon of Bravo Company, 2nd Battalion, 39th Infantry was in Vietnam, we participated in company size operations. There would be a base camp with the company commander and the support elements, such as our artillery forward observer, remaining in place while the three rifle platoons would patrol out from the base in a clover leaf pattern. The weapons platoon would remain with the mortars and provide security for the headquarters. While away from the command section, each platoon operated independently.

"The longest patrol" was a relatively rare mission for the first platoon, since under my command we were being sent out alone. We left our base camp at Bear Cat and were ferried in a "deuce-and-a-half" truck to our starting point. Using trucks as our mode of transportation was unusual. We normally were transported by Huey helicopter, especially over a great distance.

Because the mission was expected to last for two days, we were heavily burdened with C-rations and extra ammunition. It was our practice to carry the rations in a sock suspended from our web gear. The socks would remain relatively dry and giving us an extra change if needed. The rucksack frame many of us slung over our shoulders made it convenient to carry an air mattress and a poncho liner, along with a sack for toiletries. Many of us carried three or four canteens of water. Also, since we were expected to be a distance from a base camp, headquarters ordered us to take a two-niner-two antenna, giving us greater range on our radios. We had two PRC25 radios, the standard issue for an Army ground combat unit, and spare batteries.

The starting point was northwest of Bien Hoa, approximately twenty "klicks" from Bear Cat, along Route 20. The instructions from the chain of command were to walk back and observe any Viet Cong activity. Using a Lensatic compass to give us direction and a pacer counting steps to give us distance, first platoon plunged into the jungle.

The first night was extraordinary. We had not yet set our camp site when the thunderstorm struck. There was heavy rain and lightning, and we were experiencing the beginning of a typical tropical monsoon. The rainy season had begun. Because of the storm, we lost radio contact with headquarters. To help get greater broadcast range from our radios, we dug the two-niner-two antenna out of its sack, assembled it and tried to achieve contact with headquarters at Bearcat. No luck. The rain was so heavy our signal never went through. For one night, first platoon was out of contact and thought to be lost in the jungle.

The night was miserable. We could not stay dry because of the deluge of rain and the howling wind. We did not worry about "Charlie," he would have been too smart to not remain sheltered from the storm, so for one miserable night first platoon was out of contact.

Day two began sunny and bright. As we dried ourselves out, we prepared to trudge on. An interesting situation happened as we were crossing a relatively clear area of tall grass. I spotted a lone individual about 20 meters distant. He was a young man dressed in what appeared to be a plaid sport shirt. I did not see any weapon. This man was in an area where anyone like him would be considered a Viet Cong and a threat. But a strange thing happened, he did not fire at us, and we did not fire at him. I guess neither had an argument with the other. Everyone proceeded on their merry way!

With the heavy rain the previous night, a stream marked on our map as "intermittent" was a raging torrent. We had to cross that stream. No longer a trickle, the stream was six feet wide and flowing wildly. No one was carrying any rope. The only usable line was the coaxial cable that was in the antenna's bag. One brave soul volunteered to cross to the other side. He jumped in the stream and after fighting the intense water flow was successful in crossing. We were able to flip the cable to him and now could set up a way to give us support to cross the stream. The cable was secured to trees and became a lifeline.

Now this is where I did something stupid. Remember...I was the platoon commander, the leader who was to bring his troops safely back to Bearcat. I decided to be the one who carried the two-niner-two across the stream. So, I threw this heavy bag over my shoulder, plunged into the stream, and was forced to hang on for dear life as the surging water tried to rip me away. If the cable snapped, the knots slipped, or the trees uprooted, I would have been swept away. The coaxial cable held, it may have stretched a little, and the knots were strong. I made it across, but I learned my lesson about flowing water, it can be powerful.

After crossing the stream, Bearcat was just a klick away. Knowing a hot meal waited us, we hurried on home.

Was our mission a success? We did not find any Viet Cong, nor any bunkers or tunnels. We did cover a lot of distant territory around the ammo dump at Long Binh and discovered no threat. Our mission was a success.

GEORGE MURRAY

US Army—Armor Officer / Aviator

Dates of Military Service: 1964—1968

Unit Served with in Vietnam: A/82d Airmobile Light, re-designated
335thAssault Helicopter Company

Dates in Vietnam: Feb 1966 to Feb 1967

Highest Rank Held: Captain (O-3)

Place of Birth and Year: Grenada, MS—1942

MEDAL OF HONOR—CHAPLAIN CHARLES J. WATTERS—173RD AIRBORNE BRIGADE

The Medal of Honor was presented posthumously to CHARLES J. WATTERS for actions with 2d/503 Parachute Battalion of the 173d Airborne Brigade. The action took place near Dak To, Kontum Province, RVN November 19, 1967.

My connection to Chaplain Waters is only a "maybe." In the summer of 1966, I was flying utility helicopters, aka Huey slicks, for the 335th AHC serving the 173d Airborne, including the 2d/503d. Our unit was resupplying the Brigade combat units with ammo, C—rats, water, and anything else the S-4 deemed necessary (sometimes, ice cream or beer and lots of mail).

We got a mission to fly only ammo to a small unit in contact with a strong Viet Cong unit. Of course, being a 23-year-old aircraft commander of a D-model Huey, this was what we were all about. My crew and had been to the landing zone and knew it was small with high trees on all sides. On a hot summer Vietnam day, our aircraft power was always an issue, so we were careful to be sure stuff put in the cargo area was only what the "grunts" needed to kick ass.

As we were in the loading zone, rotors turning and listening to radio traffic from the action, my crew chief told me over intercom that we had a passenger. I told him to throw the passenger off, only ammo and water.

Suddenly a "grunt" in field gear leaned between the pilot seats and flashed the Major leaf on his shirt collar, then he flashed his other collar displaying a CROSS.

Yelling over the sounds of a running helicopter "My kids are getting hit, I am a Chaplain, they need me." My Southern Baptist upbringing took over, and I respectfully replied, "OK, Sir, if you are crazy enough to go, have a seat."

I have no way to confirm that this chaplain was WATTERS, but the display of dedication of this chaplain has gone with me all these years as an example of Medal of Honor courage.

Chaplain Watters performing his duties to the troops in the Vietnam environment.

The President of the United States in the name of The Congress takes pleasure in presenting the Medal of Honor to:

MAJOR CHARLES JOSEPH WATTERS

United States Army

For conspicuous gallantry and intrepidity in action at the risk of his life above and beyond the call of duty. Chaplain Watters distinguished himself during an assault in the vicinity of Dak To. Chaplain Watters was moving with one of the companies when it engaged a heavily armed enemy battalion. As the battle raged and the casualties mounted, Chaplain Watters, with complete disregard for his safety, rushed forward to the line of contact. Unarmed and completely exposed, he moved among, as well as in front of the advancing troops, giving aid to the wounded, assisting in their evacuation, giving words of encouragement, and administering the last rites to the dying. When a wounded paratrooper was standing in shock in front of the assaulting forces, Chaplain Watters ran forward, picked the man up on his shoulders and carried him to safety. As the troopers battled to the first enemy entrenchment, Chaplain Watters ran through the intense enemy fire to the front of the entrenchment to aid a fallen comrade. A short time later, the paratroopers pulled back in preparation for a second assault. Chaplain Watters exposed himself to both friendly and enemy fire between the two forces in order to recover two wounded soldiers. Later, when the battalion was forced to pull back into a perimeter, Chaplain Watters noticed that several wounded soldiers were lying outside the newly formed perimeter. Without hesitation and ignoring attempts to restrain him, Chaplain Watters left the perimeter three times in the face of small arms, automatic weapons, and mortar fire to assist the injured troopers to safety. Satisfied that all the wounded were inside the perimeter, he began aiding the medics…applying field bandages to open wounds, obtaining and serving food and water, giving spiritual and mental strength and comfort. During his ministering, he moved out to the perimeter from position-to-position redistributing food and water and tending to the needs of his men. Chaplain Watters was giving aid to the wounded when he himself was mortally wounded. Chaplain Watters' unyielding perseverance and selfless devotion to his comrades was in keeping with the highest traditions of the U.S. Army.

ROBERT O. "BOB" BABCOCK

US Army — Infantry Officer

Dates of Military Service (Active and Reserves): 1965 to 1974

Unit Served with in Vietnam: Bravo Company, 1st Battalion, 22nd Infantry
Regiment, 4th Infantry Division

Dates Served in Vietnam: July 1966 to July 1967

Highest Rank Held: Captain (O-3)

Place and Date of Birth: Heavener, OK — 1943

"HOBOES"

Our trained reaction to the first crack of a rifle shot brought us all to the ground. The sound was followed by intense gunfire as we immediately responded to the enemy fire with our own. My heart was pounding. Adrenalin pumped through my body at an ear-throbbing rate. I had tried to overcome the initial mass confusion, assess the situation, and determine what to do next. ("What you gonna do now, Lieutenant?")

We had found a number of abandoned enemy bunkers earlier in the afternoon. As I observed where the gunfire had started, it appeared there was another line of bunkers on the small rise in front of us. From where we were, it was impossible to tell how many there were and how many people were occupying them. The sound of the radio interrupted my thoughts. "Oscar 61, this is Oscar 6. What is the situation? Over."

"We have a bunker line in front of us and have received fire. We need a fire mission, over." It took no time to get our supporting 105mm howitzers from Charlie Battery, 4-42 Field Artillery called into action. The jungle soon shook from the exploding artillery blasts.

As we lay watching the area and continued to direct our rifle and machine gun fire at the bunker line, we got a radio call. "Oscar 6, this is Birddog 19. I have a flight of Hoboes on station. Do you need them? Over." "Hobo" was the radio call sign for the 1950's vintage, propeller driven, Douglas A1E Skyraiders stationed at Pleiku Air Force Base. "Birddog 19" was the Air Force Forward Air Controller (FAC) whose job it was to direct the fire of all the airplanes in the area.

"Roger," was my reply. "We will shift the artillery and you can come in on target." As soon as I called to adjust the artillery fire to the rear of the target area, we could hear the first Hobo screaming toward us from right to left.

The FAC had marked the target with a white phosphorus marking rocket and the A1E released his bomb load right on target. His bombs were Cluster Bomb Units (CBUs) that exploded before they hit the ground, throwing thousands of tiny BB size projectiles across the target area. Our position was scarcely 100 yards from where the CBUs were hitting.

The shrapnel was ricocheting through the trees above us as well as on the target area. The sound of the metal ripping through the trees gave the saying, "Make myself one with Mother Earth" new meaning.

The first Hobo was followed closely by a second and then a third as they saturated the bunker line with their CBUs. I had never heard anything like the clatter made as the projectiles ricocheted through the trees.

As quickly as they came, they were gone. As we were getting up to move across the bunker line, we got another call from Birddog 19. "The Hoboes have some 20mm cannons they can help you with. Do you want them to strafe the area before you go in? Over."

Again, "Roger," was my reply. (No one ever accused me of not using all the firepower I had at my disposal).

This time the Hoboes came from our rear and flew directly overhead as they peppered the area to our front with their 20mm cannons. Another reality of war hit me as a hail of spent 20mm cartridge hulls came raining down on our heads. Training had never included getting pelted with the four-inch-long brass cartridge hulls which fell through the trees as the Hoboes flew over. I pulled my steel helmet down tightly. Those things would have hurt if they had hit you directly on the head. Not only that; they were still hot as hell.

As the third Hobo completed his strafing run, we got up and quickly swept across the bunker line, firing into each bunker as we advanced. We moved through without stopping and took up defensive positions fifty yards past the bunkers, waiting for the rest of the company to join us.

As was so frequently the case, all we found were blood trails leading away from the bunker complex. We never knew whether we had killed any of the NVA. Fortunately, none of us were hurt.

We gained a better appreciation for the Hoboes. We knew they were usually on station to come to our aid when we needed them. They were slow and ugly in comparison to the sleek jets, but they had more staying power and could fly in much nastier weather.

When I went on R&R a couple of months later, I met one of the Hobo pilots, "Hobo 23" from Pleiku. While sitting at the Cam Ranh Bay officer's club waiting for our R&R flight, I bought all his drinks. It was a small way to thank him for the close support which gave us infantrymen so much peace of mind as we walked through the jungle.

BRUCE BURGEE GEIBEL

U.S. Navy—Seabees and Civil Engineer Corps
Dates of Military Service (Active and Reserve): 1962 to 1991
Unit Served with in Vietnam: Naval Mobile Construction Battalion ELEVEN
(NMCB-11)
Dates in Vietnam: June 1966 to September 1968 (three tours to Vietnam/
Thailand)
Highest Rank Held: Navy Captain (O-6)
Place of Birth and Year: Washington, DC—1942

I'M AN OFFICER IN CHARGE OF SOMETHING – SEABEES – DANANG, VIETNAM – 1966

I deployed for my first tour of duty in Vietnam on June 24,1966, from Travis AFB, CA, via Hawaii, Wake Island, and Clark Air Base in the Philippines. I arrived at Danang Air Base on June 26th via C-130 aircraft. I had never been so hot or experienced such unrelenting humidity in the summer anywhere before. And the stench of burning feces from military outhouses, local sewer lines in the streets, garbage dumps, and Vietnam smells was something else. I was dripping wet when I got to our cantonment area at Camp Adenir, next to the NSA Fleet Hospital, and across from MAG-16 and the Army Forces Special Forces Camp on China Beach, Danang East, Vietnam.

I was assigned as the Assistant Operations Officer (S-3A) in charge of surveying, drafting and design, and operation of the Command Management Information System (CMIS). We used the CMIS for reporting projects assigned, work in place, and manpower and construction efforts undertaken. Most formal command in-house and external briefings were centered around the information which measured the progress of construction projects and work in place (WIP) which was most important to the Brass (higher ups) in and out of our chain of command.

As a young Ensign in the U.S. Navy Civil Engineer Corps, one of my first projects was to design the III MAF (Marine Amphibious Force) China Beach R&R Center. The facility was situated on China Beach on the South China Sea between Monkey Mountain and Marble Hill, Danang East, in the Marble Mountain Military Complex. Prior to going to Navy Officer Candidate School in 1965, I worked for a civilian architectural engineering firm in my hometown of Columbia, SC, as a graduate architect. In that firm I was responsible only for doing tracing drawings for registered architects, looking up specifications for working drawings, and nothing more. No one worked for me, and I worked for everybody else; I was told what to do, how to do it, and when to do it.

Now I was in charge of the surveying and design of all battalion projects that we didn't contract out or receive from higher ups. Wow! I was actually *in charge* of something, and that kept me motivated beyond belief as a young naval officer.

The III MAF R&R camp was situated in a beach area that was 540' x 1,380' in size. It consisted of the following infrastructure for which I did the design and the plans and specifications with the help of two draftsmen: eight 20' x 48' wooden berthing barracks; a 20' x 40' chapel with wooden cross over the entrance; a 20' x 40' library and reading room building; a 480-man outdoor amphitheater with seats and sitting areas with enclosed 27' x 41' stage and plywood movie screen; men's and women's dressing rooms behind the theater stage; a 20' x 40' gang shower and associated toilet facilities for the troops; two gear-issue sheds; an NCO club; an EM Club pavilion and secondary pavilion; tennis courts, badminton court, volleyball court and horseshoe pits; a septic tank and leeching field; three 100-barrel platform water tanks; 3 picnic table areas; several bunkers and fighting positions; perimeter barbed-wire fencing around the cantonment area; a large generator shed; and supporting utilities. We also expanded an existing mess hall and its kitchen facilities. This China Beach facility eventually became the idea behind the movie "China Beach" on TV screens at home.

Our battalion also did work for U.S. Navy and Marine Corps units, the Army Special Forces Detachment, the NSA Field Hospital, the MAG-16 airfield and POL infrastructure, the US Air Force at the Danang Air Base, and Vietnamese and Korean units assigned in our area of responsibility. We did work at Camp Tin Shaw, NSA Transportation and Maintenance (T&M) site, 3rd Battalion, 9th Marines Cantonment Site, the Tourane River Bridge south of Danang, the China Beach PX, and the PX Covered Storage sites. We also did lots of road work and construction on Monkey Mountain for the LAAM Missile Units on the hill, as well as other commands with sensitive operations also located on the hill. We housed and messed Bravo Company, 1st Marine Military Police Battalion in our cantonment area. They provided tank and ON-TOS support, and (along with our Seabees) helped maintain security on our perimeter.

So, there you have it, some of the work the Navy Seabees, and in particular our battalion, Naval Mobile Construction Battalion ELEVEN (NMCB-11), did during four tours of duty (1966-69) in Vietnam. We served in Danang, and later Hue-Phu Bai and other areas in I-Corps, including Dong Ha, Khe Sanh, Cua Viet, Camp Carroll, the Rock Pile, and Quang Tri.

Having the opportunity to be in charge of surveying, design, and specifications, and overseeing major construction projects in Vietnam as a young officer in the Seabees for 27 months led me into a 26-year career in the Civil Engineer Corps of the U.S. Navy. I retired in September 1991 as a Navy Captain. I never looked back with any regrets about my service or contributions to the Navy or my Country. God Bless the USA.

MAJOR GENERAL DAVID BOCKEL (FORMER 2ND LT)

US Army — Materiel Readiness Officer
Dates of Military Service: 1966 to 2003 (37 Years)
Unit Served with in Vietnam: Co A, 25th Supply and Trans Bn, 25th Inf
Div — Dec 1966 to Jun 1967; Co B, 7th Combat Spt Bn, 199th Light Inf
` Bde — Jun 1967 to Dec 1967
Dates in Vietnam: Dec 1966 to Dec 1967
Highest Rank Held: Major General
Place of Birth and Year: Dallas, Texas — 1944

MEMORIES OF A PROUD R.E.M.F*

I consider myself fortunate to have been introduced to the Vietnam Veterans Business Association by good friends and fellow Vietnam vets. There are many Vietnam vets that I know who are not members of this really great organization. They have their own memories, good and bad, that they could share with AVBBA members and find a missed degree of fellowship by joining this fine organization.

I wrote this "glossary," for lack of a better term, to remind you of a few experiences we share, but I added my own descriptions and memories of these terms that I know you will be familiar with. Perhaps you can add some of your own humorous memories. Note that I went out of my way not to recall bad memories, but memories that might bring a smile or two.

So, here we go ...

BA MU'O'I BA

Brand name of a Vietnamese beer (I didn't know it was spelled that way. I thought it was just "ba mi ba" or Vietnamese battery acid. The first time I ever drank one was at a Vietnamese restaurant in Doraville. Not bad. I still preferred Hamms which was one of the brands which always seemed to be available in the little PX's.

BEANS AND DICKS

Military C-ration hot dogs and beans. I think it was a favorite that you could eat cold or heat up (if you had a heater?)

BEANS AND MOTHERF**KERS

Military C-ration lima beans and ham (who knew?) Who comes up with these names, anyway?

BEEHIVE ROUND

An explosive artillery shell which delivered thousands of small projectiles, "like nails with fins," instead of shrapnel. (I have a friend who commanded a 105 mm-artillery battery and they were about to be overrun. He ordered the guns to be leveled and fired beehive into the attackers. Was worth a Silver Star for his action and protecting his gun crews.)

BIG MAX

Maximum security section of Long Binh Stockade, fashioned out of conex containers. There was one small hole in each side for light and air; in the sun they grew quite hot. Prisoners were allowed out twice a day to use the bathroom and exercise. More to follow...

BREAKING SQUELCH

Disrupting the natural static of a radio by depressing the transmit bar on another radio set to the same frequency. A lot of folks broke squelch when they probably shouldn't have and gave away their position.

C-123

Medium size two engine cargo airplane. About half the size of a C-130.

I think we ended up giving them back to the Canadians. I think they may also have been a delivery system for Agent Orange.

CARIBOU C-7A

Smaller twin engine transport plane for moving men and material. (Flew out of Tay Ninh in one. Pretty short take off roll—less than a football field. As soon as the wheels left the ground the airplane was almost vertical with the rear ramp wide open! I think we had to give them to the Air Force because of the "Key West Accords" which prohibited the Army from having certain winged aircraft).

CHOI OI

Exclamation of surprise—sort of like "holy shit! If you added the word "duc" between "choi" and "oi" it made it twice the surprise. Sort of like "Choi Oi! What in the hell was that?!

CIAO

Hello or goodbye, depending upon the context. Maybe the Italians spent time in Vietnam?

CLAYMORE

An antipersonnel mine carried by the infantry which, when detonated, propelled small steel cubes in a 60-degree fan-shaped pattern to a maximum distance of 100 meters. If you ever had to place them, you made sure you took the charging handle with you and pointed the mine to face the enemy. Oh wait! Didn't it say that on the front of the mine? Apparently, Mr. Claymore knew what he was doing when he invented them.

DEROS

Date of Expected Return from OverSeas. Or as I knew it "date eligible to return from overseas." The day all American soldiers in Vietnam were waiting for from the day after they arrived in-country. Maybe the first entry on your "short timers calendar."

DI

Go (never heard that word said by itself)

DIDI MAU

Slang Vietnamese for "go quickly" That was usually reserved for emergency situations such as "we need to get the f**k out of here."

DINKY DAU

To be crazy (One of my personal favorites!) I knew a lot of those and I'm sure you did too!

DUST-OFF

Medical evacuation by helicopter flown by **a special kind of hero.**

EAGLE FLIGHTS

Large air assault by several helicopters. Very awe-inspiring and very noisy!

EARLY-OUTS

A drop or reduction in time in service. A soldier with 150 days or less remaining on his active-duty commitment when he DEROSed from

Vietnam also was discharged from the army under the Early Out program. A ticket to get on a "Freedom Bird" ahead of time! In many cases you did not have much to do other than pack your stuff. However, some senior officers thought you needed to work until the last minute. That's why another lieutenant who was an artillery forward observer just in from the boonies and I were made to inventory the brigade finance section before we could go to the 90th Replacement Battalion to get our flight home. We had to inventory "greenbacks," military payment certificates, and Vietnamese money. We were told that all the books had to balance before we could head out. The other lieutenant and I agreed that we would make up any shortages out of our own pockets. Looking back, it was just "busy work," so we didn't leave too soon!

FNG

F**king new guy. Been there. Done that. Got a medal and a short timer calendar.

H&I

Harassment and Interdiction. Artillery bombardments used to deny the enemy terrain which they might find beneficial; general rather than specific, confirmed military targets; random artillery fire. I had the pleasure of having my hooch next to a combined 8" and 175 mm artillery battery that fired H&I at 2200 and again at 0500. My reward was loss of hearing in one ear.

HONEY-DIPPERS

People responsible for burning human excrement. I never knew what those soldiers did to deserve that dubious duty. I don't think they gave a medal for that. Was particularly troublesome on the day after the malaria pills were passed out. More to follow …

LBJ

"Long Binh Jail"—The Long Binh Stockade, a military stockade on Long Binh post (Whatever happened to M. O. Johnson? If you know him don't tell him where I am. I served as a "trial counsel" on a special court martial and got him put in LBJ for a 6-month sentence. That was considered "bad time" and got added to his tour. I was told and then told him when I served him with the results of the court martial, I was sure he would get an "early drop." He may still be there, or he may be living nearby and wondering where I am!)

MARS

Military Affiliate Radio Station. Used by soldiers to call home via Signal Corps and ham radio equipment through civilian HAM radio operators in the US. (Did you try it? *"over"* How did it work for you? *"over"* How many times did the radio operators hear these words: *"I love you—over"?*)

MPC

Military Payment Currency. (Also known as military payment certificates). The scrip U.S. soldiers were paid in. Just like "Monopoly money" but worth more at the little PX. For more information see "Early Outs."

NUOC-MAM

Fermented fish sauce used by the Vietnamese as a condiment. No, I never ate any. Recalling the smell, I could not bring myself to eat it!

PBR

Patrol Boat, River. Navy designation for the fast, heavily armed boats used for safeguarding the major canals and rivers and their tributaries in South

Vietnam. I think a certain well-known current politician thinks he should have received the Congressional Medal of Honor for his "experience" serving on one of these. I think the clerk he was trying to convince to write it up for a recommendation suddenly forgot how to use a typewriter.

PISS-TUBE

A vertical tube buried two-thirds in the ground for urinating into. Another example of GI ingenuity in finding a use for the metal tubes that artillery rounds came in.

PONCHO LINER (AKA "WOOBIE")

Nylon insert to the military rain poncho, used as a blanket. Probably one of the best inventions of personal military gear. In addition to serving as a sort of blanket, it also kept the laterite dust from getting on your sheets and pillows. What was "laterite" you ask? Try driving on a laterite road that has been coated with diesel fuel just after a rainstorm.

R&R

Rest and Recreation. A three to seven-day vacation from the war for a soldier. Also known as I & I for "Intoxication and Intercourse." Depending on where you went on your R & R and who you were meeting, you might have gotten a good dose of both I & I. (And maybe came back needing a penicillin shot).

REPO DEPO

Replacement detachment. The ones I knew best were "Camp Alpha" at Tan Son Nhut and the 90th Replacement Battalion in Long Binh. You could tell by either the look of stark terror on the guy who just got off the plane and the guy having a beer waiting for his name to be called to head to Bien Hoa for his "Freedom Bird" flight.

ROTATE

To return to the U.S. at the end of a year's tour in Vietnam. One of the first terms you learn soon after you arrive in country.

SHIT BURNING

The sanitization of latrines by kerosene incineration of excrement. Same thing as "honey dippers." You could see the pyres of black smoke beginning early in the morning until later in the day. Another good use for diesel fuel and the smell probably cut down on the mosquito population.

SPOOKY

A large propeller-driven aircraft with a Minigun mounted in the door. Capable of firing 6,000 rounds per minute. As I recall, these, also known as "Puff the Magic Dragons" were WWII era DC3's with mini guns on both sides that did a wonderful job during the dark of night blasting suspected VC positions. Later in the war, the DC3's were replaced with the AC-130, and the name Spooky remained forever.

STARLIGHT SCOPE

An image intensifier using reflected light to identify targets at night. It was a highly classified device that most of us had never heard of until we arrived in country and were checking the perimeter when we had duty officer. The night vision devices in use today are much lighter and much better.

TET OFFENSIVE

A major uprising of the National Liberation Front, their sympathizers, and NVA, characterized by a series of coordinated attacks against military installations and provincial capitals throughout Vietnam. It occurred during the lunar New Year at the end of January 1968. I had my DEROS at the end of December '67. I was replaced (this is true) by my college roommate who was transferred to take my place after having served in the Big Red One! To this day he never discusses it with me.

THREE-QUARTER

A three-quarter ton truck. The most uncomfortable, most reliable small truck in the Army. There are still a few of those relics existing on some rural farms.

I think this just about covers all the memories I thought you would want me to share with you. Note that I only included those that should not cause any really bad memories. What you have read are pretty much the memories of an Army lieutenant in '66 and '67. I imagine there are some of you who have some of the same memories.

POST SCRIPTS:

"GOOD MORNING VIETNAM!"—Depending on when you were there, you might have heard that wakeup call on the radio at 0600 every morning spoken by:

- **Adrian Cronauer**—1965—66 (the real guy portrayed in the movie by Robin Williams)
- **Cramer Haas**—1966—1967 (later a disc jockey on a Fort Lauderdale radio station)
- **Pat Sajak** (yes, the "Wheel of Fortune" host) 1968-1969

CHRIS NOEL—Who doesn't remember the sultry voice of Chris Noel at 2100 hours each evening on Armed Forces Radio? You had to tune in precisely at 2100 hours to hear her start each night's program with "Hi, Love..." and stay until 2159 hours to hear her end it with "Bye,

Love…" In between those highlights was lots of popular music and listening to a beautiful American woman's voice talking to you.

GARY McKEE—Many of us remember Gray McKee when he was a disc jockey on WQXI-AM radio in Atlanta back in the 80's. Gary was also a Vietnam veteran and every Veteran's Day he dedicated his radio show to all military veterans. I will always remember a quote he made during one of those shows: "You couldn't give me a million dollars for the experience of being in Vietnam. And you couldn't give me ten million dollars to go back." Well said, Gary!

*"REMF"—I didn't know I was one until it was pointed out to me many years later by one of my 25th ID buddies who served in the 3/4 Cav. I was officially proclaimed a "Rear Echelon Mother F**ker." To an extent that was true, but I didn't always stay in the base camp. I served in the forward support base for Operation Junction City for three months and I served as an "MRE" (Military Readiness Expediter) in the 199th Light Infantry Brigade spending every day on the road between Long Binh and the 506th Field Depot in Saigon. Every command had an MRE. The supply system was so bad that they needed us to identify everything in the depot that they didn't know they had on hand that were mission-essential for all of our combat units. A fringe benefit was where do you think all those steaks and lobster tails came from?

So much for your trip down "Memory Lane." I hope it brought back memories that are not too painful. It is just interesting to look back almost 60 years and remember things that you probably should have forgotten. I do sort of enjoy looking at old photos that I took with my $25 half-frame Fujica camera (which I still have). Most of those photos were slides and I no longer have a slide projector, so they have all been transferred to computer photos. I also have some regular photos taken with a Polaroid camera I bought for $25 from my battalion commander as he was heading back to the mainland. He also left me with a big supply of film. Those photos are all faded now.

I'm proud of my service and proud that I have the opportunity to belong to an organization with a group of heroes that I can share stories and humor with.

Submitted with pride for having served with you!

TIM BOONE

U.S. Army – Special Forces Officer

Dates of military service (Active and Reserve): Oct 1965 to Nov 1976

Unit(s) you served with in Vietnam: 5th Special Forces Group (Also 46th Special Forces Company – Thailand)

Dates served in Vietnam – Aug 1967 to Aug 1968 (Thailand), Aug 1969 to Aug 1970 (Vietnam)

Highest Rank – Captain (O-3)

Place and date born: Watsonville, CA – 1945

CAMP HUNKY – THAILAND – 1967-68

"The Original Good Deal" — That's what the business cards we received said when we arrived at 46th Special Forces Company (Abn) in Lopburi, Thailand, in August 1967! For a rookie 2LT, wearing 1LT insignia for PR purposes, that sounded great to me.

While based in Thailand, we were part of the U.S. Army Support Command, Thailand. These Army units fulfilled direct or indirect support functions related to the Vietnam conflict to the extent that most received Vietnam service credit to recognize our supporting role. Under U.S. Military Assistance Command Thailand (MACTHAI), our public mission was to train the Royal Thai Volunteer Regiment (Queen's Cobras) and then the Royal Thai Army Expeditionary Division (*Black Panthers*) for service in Vietnam.

About 40,000 Thai military personnel would serve in South Vietnam, with 351 killed in action and with 1,358 wounded. Other Missions were to **assist Thai forces in resisting communist guerrilla activity** along the Laotian border and in the south on the Malay Peninsula.

The 46th S.F. Co. deployed at several Thai Army training locations around the country. I served my first six months as S3 for a B-Team at Camp Nam Pung Dam, Sakon Nakhon Province, along the Laotian border in Northeastern Thailand. It was a typical jungle camp with cleared and concertina wired perimeter with napalm fougasse and claymore mines on expected avenues of advance. However, we still had some trees, and we were on the shore of a beautiful lake.

We were responsible, along with our Thai Special Forces Counterparts, to conduct a week-long field training exercise every few weeks to culminate pre-deployment training for Thai infantry companies. Unfortunately, given a local Communist Terrorist Battalion operating in the province, these exercises often became live fire!

I have many memories of my time at Camp Hunky, as it was affectionately known. I will share a few here…

The first evening I was at Camp Hunky, wearing my boots, as Thai SF warned us that tiny Russell's Vipers found their way into the camp, I walked down to the main gate. I was amazed to see a giant cobra peering at me over the top of the 8-foot high gate! "Original Good Deal!" like hell! What had I gotten myself into?? It turns out Thailand has more venomous snakes than any other country in the world.

General Richard Stillwell, commander of USARSUPTHAI, visited the camp, and because of our location on the lake, he had a boat and outboard motor sent to us. It was for recovering us when we made parachute jumps into the lake. However, the real motto of Special Forces is "You don't have to practice being miserable—work-by-work and play-by-play." So, we had someone send us water skis. Our camp became an attraction for U.S. Air Force crews from NKP. And they paid well with bartered goods that the Air Force always seemed to have and the Army didn't, like air conditioners and refrigerators, etc. If you could stay away from the snakes, it was a nice place. Most of the time!

CONTESTED TERRITORY

A few weeks after arriving at Camp Hunky, we heard that Communist Terrorists (CTs) had attacked a local village and attempted to ambush our civilian engineers. We rushed out and made contact with the CTs and drove them from the village. During this small skirmish (my first time under fire), I suddenly realized that SGM Fred Davis had hold of my jungle fatigues and told me what to do to remain safe and lead the attack. Thank God for great experienced NCOs!

When we entered the village, we found several wounded. The CTs had targeted the village leaders.

I found the schoolteacher with a severe wound to his upper arm. As the medics were busy with others, it fell to me to stop the bleeding with a tourniquet and start an IV of blood expander through a "cut-down" on his leg. I was very thankful for the medical pre-mission training we received at Ft Bragg. We asked the Air Force for help, and they sent a helicopter to take the wounded to the Thai hospital in Sakhon Nakorn. Suddenly I wasn't so sure about the "Original Good Deal" brand…We weren't in a Combat Zone, after all! No CIBs, No Purple Hearts.

ENGAGING WITH LOCALS

We shared the camp with the Thai Special Forces. The Thai Major, the camp commander, lived in the same 8-person "Hooch" as I did. He was a terrific warrior and philosopher. He took me with him to luncheons and celebrations in Thai villages nearby. The subsistence farming locals would use everything they had to feed us and show appreciation. The Major would always bring along a few sacks of rice and a pig or two in the back of our truck. When everyone was at the party, a couple of the locals would unload the food and put it in the village storage area at the temple (Wat). He made it a mission to teach all the American officers to view the Thai people with respect and honor by treating them that way himself.

We held traditional Thai celebrations at the camp and invited the locals. The young women were timid, and the culture strongly frowned on consorting with men of any kind! The older women, however!! They cut their hair in flattop buzz cuts and wore traditional Thai costumes. And they were highly provocative teasers of all the young American men! They could make you blush.

UP COUNTRY CUISINE

We bought our groceries in Bangkok and flew them in every two weeks by Caribou that could land on our 2000 ft laterite airstrip next to the lake. We bought ribeye steaks by the case, and on Sundays, we had "Cook your own steak" days on the grill. I think I became addicted to them there!! We had Thai/Lao cooks in our mess hall who didn't seem to know how to cook anything that didn't have fiery hot Thai peppers in it. Even in the omelets at breakfast! We used to watch the Detachment Commander and the Sergeant Major eat them every morning, and we swore you could see the steam coming out of their ears!

FLYING HIGH

We conducted a Jumpmaster School for the U.S. and Thai SF personnel and made jumps into the lake and Landing Zones around the area that we had to secure with patrols before the jump. For security reasons, we made sure not to advertise when these jumps would take place. In every case, though, the local kids would find out and descend on us to collect our parachutes for us and then charge us a Baht (US$.05)

A squadron of U-10 Heliocourier, short-takeoff-and-landing planes used for Psyops missions flew out of Nakon Phanom AFB. These single-engine planes had castered landing gear allowing landing and take-off in a crosswind. They could land and take off in the length of a football field. They flew a regular route around Northeast Thailand. They delivered our mail, as well as taking us in and out for a variety of reasons. The Detachment Commander flew me to Bangkok many times and, in the process, taught me to fly and land the plane. He was a brave soul. He would pick me up in the morning, confirm we had the correct TACAN settings for navigation, and then pull his hat down and take a nap while I took off and flew the trip!

On New Year's Eve, we held a big party in the camp, and U.S. and Thai people came from all around. The USAF Colonel flew the two of us to NKP at midnight, and we conducted a tear gas attack on the New

Years' Eve Party in the Officer's Club there! The next day a colossal CH-53 Jolly Green Giant helicopter from NKP came to our camp and hovered down. The chopper blew everything everywhere! Everything got coated with red dust. Payback certainly was hell. And, I was in serious trouble with everyone!

ART

One piece of Art came directly from our experience at Camp Hunky. A C-123 overran the airstrip while landing and stopped with its front wheels stuck in the mud of the lake bottom! A local farmer brought a team of Water Buffalo and hitched them to the plane. He was able to pull the aircraft out of the lake, much to the crew's relief! One of the senior U.S. NCOs drew an excellent pencil cartoon of the event. We made sure that the cartoon appeared in every Officer's Club on every Air Force Base in Thailand!

Camp Hunky was on the Air Force map. It was a good deal. Great experience with highly qualified people and the opportunity to work very closely with the tremendous Royal Thai Special Forces. It was excellent training for my next overseas tour, which would be in Vietnam in 1969 and 70.

JOHN FRASER

US Army—Chaplain

Dates served: 1953—1983 Texas National Guard (Enlisted) 1953-1956; Army
Ready Reserve (Enlisted) 1956-1960; Army Active Duty(Commissioned) 1963-
1983.

Units Served with in Vietnam: 2/14 Inf and 1/27 Inf, 25th Inf Div; 8 RRFS.

Dates Served in Vietnam: Apr 1966 to Apr 1967; Nov 1969 to Nov 1970

Highest Rank Held: Lt. Colonel (O-5)

Place of Birth and Year: Greenville, TX—1936

THIS JUST DIDN'T WORK OUT WELL

This is a story about how good people, with good intentions, who are trying to do something good, may watch things go to hell in a hand basket.

I was the chaplain for the 2/14 Inf, 1st Brigade, 25th Inf Division in Vietnam. The battalion had just recently returned from the field after a very usual operation. I was expecting to be sought out by a larger number of soldiers than usual because we were just in from the field. It always seemed strange to me that soldiers in the field didn't have nearly as many personal problems as did the same soldiers when we were back in base camp.

One of these soldiers was SP/4 Martin (we'll use that fictitious name), a medic in one of our rifle companies. He was a little unusual because he was a conscientious objector. His religious convictions would not permit him to shoot at anyone, so he became a medic when he was drafted. Most of the enlisted medics had no problem with using a weapon, and I was somewhat amused at how many conscientious objectors decided that they weren't as opposed to weapons as they thought they were after they had been in combat. But Martin was not one of those. He had spent time in combat and still had no desire to pick up a weapon.

SP/4 Martin came to my tent and asked if I could spend some time with him. I asked what was on his mind. He reminded me that he was a conscientious objector, that he had been in a lot of combat, and would like to be transferred to the medical battalion in in division rear where he would seldom come under fire. We talked for a while about his experiences in Vietnam and his ambitions back home. In the final parts of the conversation, I had to tell him that he was known as a good medic, that he was no more tired of combat than anyone else, and that if being tired of getting shot at was a reason to get out of an infantry battalion, we would all be gone. He understood that, but he asked if it was okay if he went to the brigade chaplain to see if he could help. I assured him that he was welcome to do that.

A few days later the brigade chaplain and I met at his tent at brigade headquarters. Among other things he told me that a young medic named Martin had talked with him about getting moved to division rear because he was tired of combat. I asked if he was going to help Martin get a transfer. No, he wasn't because if being tired of combat was a reason to leave an infantry battalion, no one would still be there. That sounded familiar.

A few weeks went by. I had been careful to drop by the battalion aid station where Martin worked just to spend some time with him and his fellow medics. Then one day the word reached me that Martin was in trouble because he had let a Viet Cong prisoner escape. That didn't make any sense at all! I couldn't wait to hear the rest of that story! Martin had been the medic with a squad sized patrol. They had stumbled upon a Viet Cong and taken him prisoner. The patrol was bringing the prisoner back to company headquarters, but they had stopped to rest. They had been up all night and part of the previous day. Martin was told to be sure to stay awake and watch that prisoner. The other soldiers drifted off into a light nap. Martin, who had no weapon, watched the prisoner. He watched the prisoner stand up and walk away while the others slept!

I thought, "How in thunder can a leader tell a conscientious objector to watch a prisoner? What in blazes will that company commander do to Martin?" So, I walked over to the company commander's tent. We had known each other for several months, and nearly every day saw each other at the battalion commander's staff meeting. I was so pleased that I was not going to confront a stranger. The company commander saw me coming and he spoke first. "I'll bet you're here about Martin. I'm not going to do anything with him. But why in hell would anyone tell a conscientious objector to watch a prisoner?" Both of us mused for a while about that. I told him I appreciated his decision not to discipline Martin. He replied, "Why would I do that—he's a good medic!"

A few days later, the brigade chaplain dropped by my tent. "That medic, Martin, that we were talking about: he went to see the division chaplain. Martin is being transferred to the med battalion."

Now fast forward three or four weeks. Martin has been gone for a while, and I haven't even thought about him since he was sent to division rear. But I was pleased that the division chaplain had suggested to someone that it would be a good idea to move Martin. I was with the brigade chaplain again, who asked, "John, have you heard about Martin?"

Me: "No, has he lost another prisoner?"

Bde Chaplin: "No, he's dead."

Me: "What happened? I thought he went to the rear!"

Bde Chaplin: "He did. He spent some of his time being a medic and part of his time filling sandbags for the medical battalion. He didn't like filling sandbags and volunteered to go back to an infantry battalion. A Chicom claymore got him."

I still wonder what would have happened if he had stayed with my battalion. Martin got exactly what he wanted—a safer place in the rear. But he would rather take care of soldiers in the field than fill sandbags. If he had stayed with the 2/14 Infantry, he would have been appreciated and would have received more consideration about his duties. He might have gone home to his family. But no, we gave him exactly what he wanted—and it killed him.

FRANK COX

US Marine Corps – Artillery Officer

Dates Served (Active and Reserve): August 1964 to July 1967

Unit Served with in Vietnam: Forward Observer, Fox Company, 2nd Battalion, 9th Marines

Years Served in Vietnam: 1966

Highest Rank Held: Lieutenant (O-2)

Place and Date of Birth: San Antonio, TX – 1941

FLASHBACK

March 18, 1966...1730 hours

Heat consumed the Marine rifle company. The air was thick, hard to suck in. Sweat streams dumped salt into our eyes. We were humping a search and kill operation in an enemy infested area south of Danang. On the move for six hours, we combed through villages, waded across streams, crossed dried rice paddies and crop fields, sliced through sharp hedgerows and thick tree lines. The three platoons moved south in one long column.

We encountered a few snipers we quickly ran off. The villagers, old, crinkled women, and younger women with babies clenched tightly, stared solemnly, emotionless. Twice we were forced to loudly announce our presence when we summoned choppers to evacuate healthy 19-year-old Marines suffering heat stroke. It had been another mundane day for Fox Company, 2nd Bn., 9th Marines, as we neared our final objective for the day, the north bank of the Song La Tho River. I was the artillery Forward Observer for the company.

At 1730 hours, the unit of 140 Marines entered the trap. Instantly and unexpectedly, mortar rounds whistled in, exploding into the first platoon. We were exposed, out in the open. Tree lines to our left and right erupted with interlocked AK-47 and automatic weapons fire. Rocket-propelled grenades whizzed into our ranks.

The Main force Vietcong R-20 Doc Lap Battalion trapped us in a classic ambush. We were vastly outnumbered and outgunned. But Marines race to the sound of guns.

The second platoon reacted and frontally assaulted the tree line to our left. The third platoon attacked the right tree line. Marines fell on the brown soil of the hard panned potato field. My radio operator and I raced to the first platoon. We hoisted my scout observer into the first medevac chopper that roared in. Shards of shrapnel had raked across his back. Five more wounded were shoved in. He smiled at me through his pain while the chopper lifted off.

I requested fire missions on the left tree line, and across the river where the mortar tubes were. Quickly, our heavy metal howitzer rounds exploded on target. The company regrouped in a heavily wooded area nearby.

God had smiled upon us. Trench lines over four feet deep and three feet wide had been dug by Viet Cong soldiers years before. The Marines set up in a 360-degree perimeter. The company commander and I slid into a trench in the middle of the circle.

He ordered me to call in artillery nonstop as close as possible. We created a ring of fire. The sun sank and there was no moonlight. Our killed were gently placed nearby while our wounded moaned. We were surrounded. The fight had just begun.

Throughout the endless night I steered in hundreds of 105 mm and 155 mm high explosive and white phosphorous shells on enemy targets. Meanwhile, the enemy dropped in hundreds of 82 mm and 60 mm mortar shells on us for endless hours. Their shells shrieked in, exploding like thunderclaps. We burrowed deeply into our trenches. VC probed our lines. A chopper braved the fire, coming in with water and ammo, ready to ferry to safety some of our wounded. It was slammed by an RPG round, flipped, and smashed into a nearby paddy dyke, 20 yards from our perimeter. VC green tracers streamed through the nearby bamboo, fired from inside our perimeter. At 0425 mortar rounds slammed on the ground just outside our trench. There were no casualties. Young Marines soothed their wounded friends and fought like savages.

MAY 30, 2021 ... 0230

AK rounds snap through the tall, thick bamboo. Another of endless mortar barrages crashes in our midst. The night sky flickers white, then shifts back to a black umbrella.

We cannot call in close air support. The enemy is too close. My captain turns to me and suggests the unthinkable. "Frank, better prepare and plot a big one right on top of us if the worst happens." I have already done that. Our batteries will deliver a fire mission directly on our position if I send the request. The enemy has penetrated our perimeter of beleaguered Marines.

I have been in this green hell of Vietnam for nine months. Finally, I pray ... *Holy Mary, Mother of God, pray for us sinners, now and at the hour of our death. Amen.*

I jerk. Miller, the white Lhasa Apso, crosses over my feet. I groan. My woman, Lynne, traces her fingers softly across my forehead. She whispers comfort. I am perspiring, short of breath. But so happy. To be alive. To enjoy life.

JUNE 28, 2021

Events gallop through his lifetime. Love, children, triumph, disaster. Common experiences for American men.

But, for a few there is a difference. Deep-buried memories spring to life from the subconscious of the Vietnam War combat veteran. They come to haunt, in the middle of the night, unbidden.

We Vietnam survivors know full well the warning the Eagles issued in *Hotel California*. "You can check out, but you can never leave."

Franklin Cox is the author of the award-winning book *Lullabies for Lieutenants*.

GLENN PEYTON CARR

US Army—Aviator

Dates of Military Service: 1958 to 1986

Unit Served with in Vietnam: 213th Assault Support Helicopter Company
(Chinook); B Troop 7th Squadron 17th Cavalry Regiment (Air)

Dates Served in Vietnam: XO & CO 213th May 1967 to May 1968; CO B Troop
7/17, XO 52nd Combat Aviation Battalion 1971

Highest Rank Held: Lt. Colonel (O-5)

Place of Birth: Shawnee, OK—1934

MY FIRST NIGHT AND WEEK IN VIETNAM

I had just returned to Fort Sill, OK from pre-deployment leave. After having the nail on my left big toe removed, the Flight Surgeon gave me a final check. This was the third time since my high school days that it had been removed. It was still swollen and sore, but it was sufficiently healed for him to release me for deployment.

The next evening, 25 May 1967, the 205th Assault Support Helicopter Company Chinook boarded buses to Tinker Air Force Base, Oklahoma, to start our flight to Vietnam.

We all stood in the deployment formation then boarded the commercial jet bound for Vietnam. That was a sobering thought. Walking around in combat boots, my foot was getting very uncomfortable. Upon getting seated on the plane, I took off my boot and propped my foot up on the seat in front of me. That was very comfortable. I continued that posture all the way to 'Nam.

We refueled at Travis AFB near Sacramento, CA then on to Honolulu. Oh boy, we get to see Hawaii—at 2:30 in the morning. Big deal! No Hula dancers, no leis, no nothing except a coke and junk food. Then off to some other Pacific wonderland. I think it was the Philippine Islands.

After landing at Cam Ranh Bay late in the evening, we were told we would be bussed over to a village named Dong Ba Tinh. The local troops called it Dong Number Ten for a very good reason. I was about to learn why.

On the bus ride, I had received several mosquito bites. Being a very senior Captain, I was given a single room with one GI bunk with a mosquito net. I was very ready for some prone sleeping. Once inside I immediately shed my uniform and boots. First big mistake! I was now slapping two mosquitos with one hand and scratching three more bites with the other hand. I had not used a mosquito net since ROTC summer camp in 1956 at Ft Hood, TX.

I got in the bunk and reached up to pull the tie straps and the net came rolling down. Second big mistake! I trapped a squadron of mosquitos inside. I would not survive another five minutes of this attack. So, out of the bunk I flew. I quickly decided I could survive the hot muggy weather fully dressed rather than being eaten alive. I taped my socks to my pant legs with 300-mile per hour tape. Somewhere along the line I had made off with a roll of that so named tape because it was used to patch bullet holes in aircraft that would go 300 MPH.

All openings in my uniform were taped. I then folded the netting under three sides of the mattress and crawled in. It was a drill to fold the fourth side of the net under the mattress with me laying on it. I then used my bath towel to cover my head. Success! I did get a few hours sleep, even though one or two mosquitos continued to probe my lifeless body.

Next morning, I returned myself to a normal uniformed soldier. Walking to the mess hall, I needed at least six hands to accomplish all the necessary scratching. I had more red skin than white. At that moment, I realized I did not have enough blood to feed these bastards for the next 364 days.

At the morning formation, things began to happen fast. All the pilots were being farmed out to in-country Chinook units for in-country orientation. I was assigned to Lane Army Heliport near Quin Nhon. I ask what unit. It was the 196th. I almost shouted with glee. I knew all the folks in that unit as I had helped them prepare for deployment about three months earlier at Fort Sill. Lane was about 15—20 miles inland.

NO MOSQUITOS!! I was welcomed to the 196th by my good friend D.R. Martin. We were neighbors some years back at Fort Knox and we worked together at Fort Sill. On the way to Lane, I sat on the jump seat and my orientation began as we pulled pitch taking off at Dong Number Ten.

The next morning, D.R. and I were on the number one aircraft. The first mission was to haul 32 Korean Troops on a combat insertion. Landing in the brush up hill, the troops left the Chinook before I could look back to watch. I was impressed. D.R. picked up and turned right where I could see the landing site. Not a soldier in site, nothing. I was very impressed. Later, I learned they were part of the most elite unit in the Republic of Korea Army. Thus finished my first combat mission. No shots fired; that would change.

After the orientation week was completed, I was flown to rejoin the 205th which had been assigned to Phu Loi about 15 miles north of Saigon—very far from mosquito country. Combat is looking better.

I found my Platoon Leader doing paperwork on his bunk. Asking what he wanted me to do. He asked to get a box for him to write on. Off I went, returning about two hours later with five rocket boxes and some hand tools. He gave me a quizzical look saying, "What the Hell you gonna do with those?"

"Build you a desk," I answered.

Late that afternoon, I had finished the desk and about three quarters of the chair when a stranger appeared asking for Captain Carr. I waved him over, introducing myself. He said, "I'm Maj Adamson. You are coming with me." I asked, "Where to?" Maj Adamson said, "I'm the CO of the 213 Chinook right across the big ditch, and I selected you to infuse."

Infusion was a process whereby new units with one year to serve were mixed up with in-country unit personnel who had varying dates to return to the US. Well, I put up a polite fight while he listened. Then he smiled and said, "Come on, Captain. It's been approved by the Battalion Commander and reluctantly by your Commanding Officer. You see, he has seven Majors and with your seniority, you could be the eighth." So, off I went to my new unit—the 213th Chinook. It turned out to be one of the best moves of my career.

In two weeks, I was a Platoon commander and two months later was the company Executive Officer. The following week I was called to the Battalion Commanders office and surprisingly promoted to Major. When I looked at my promotion orders, I found out I had been a Major since five days before getting on the deployment aircraft at Tinker Field. Wonder if that would have made any difference to those damn mosquitos.

On the flight from Tinker Air Force Base to Vietnam, three senior captains were seated together. Carr, Gorday, and Chambliss. One year to the day later, I was the designated troop commander for the flight home. I was first to board. I told Gorday and Chambliss I would hold seats for them. So, the three Captains who sat together going to Nam returned to the US seated the same way as Majors. If memory serves me correctly, we were in the same seat numbers.

BRUCE BURGEE GEIBEL

US Navy — Seabees and Civil Engineer Corps Officer
Dates of Military Service (Active and Reserve): 1962 to 1991
Unit Served with in Vietnam: Naval Mobile Construction Battalion ELEVEN (NMCB-11)
Dates in Vietnam: Jun 1966 to Sep 1968 (three tours to Vietnam/Thailand)
Highest Rank Held: Naval Captain (O-6)
Place of Birth and Year: Washington, DC — 1942

NAVY SEABEE TEAM 1109: DEPLOYED TO CHIANG KHAM, THAILAND
April — November 1967

I was the Officer-in-Charge of a 13-man Seabee Team 1109 deployed to Chiang Kham, Thailand, in April 1967. We were a detachment from Naval Mobile Construction Battalion ELEVEN (NMCB-11) deployed to Dong Ha, Vietnam. We were one of three teams serving in Thailand at that time. We spent a week in Bangkok receiving briefings by personnel from United States Operations Mission (USOM) Thailand, the U.S. Embassy, Air America CIA Operations, and the Thai Border Patrol Police (BPP) Headquarters prior to deploying to our team site in Thailand.

Seabee Team effort in Thailand began in June 1963 at the request of the Royal Thai Government and was under the sponsorship of the United States Operations Mission (USOM) to Thailand. USOM was the military wing of the U.S. Embassy in Thailand and provided Seabee teams with military and logistical support. In the process, local villagers were trained on site on specific projects by Seabee/BPP teams to enable them to accomplish similar work for themselves after the teams left the area.

A little-known fact was that Seabee teams in Thailand were part of the U.S. military's larger counter-insurgency force. They worked with their counterpart 15-man BPP team, a para-military force, to pioneer and develop a series of connecting roads to ease travel of the paramilitary forces into the remote hill tribe regions of Thailand and allow the villagers access to larger cities to sell their wares.

The Thai and U.S. governments were working with their own intelligence gathering forces in various counter-insurgency operations in Thailand along the Laos border. This was an attempt to thwart Communist infiltration into Thailand and shift hill tribes from growing opium to other types of domestic crops. Seabee teams in Thailand were supported by Air America, a subsidiary airline of the CIA, in traveling to and from the many remote villages where the Seabees were conducting civic action work and pioneering roads and short-takeoff-and-landing (STOL) airstrips in support of U.S. and Thai military remote jungle operations.

An article published in the Bangkok Times in 1967 offers an unsettling view of Communist threats to military forces and Seabee counter-insurgency teams serving in Thailand: "N.E. Red Document Revealing Rewards offered to Kill U.S. Soldiers." Official translations of the Red document captured from foreign agents indicated to a news agency the price of "…500 U.S. dollars for killing 'foreign soldiers." The document was signed by a group calling itself "Thais who love the nation." Another warning showed killing prices of "…200 U.S. dollars for flying officers, 100 dollars for ground officers and 50 dollars for enlisted men." A local interpreter in Chiang Kham indicated these threats also included Navy Seabees in Thailand. There were then about 37,000 American military personnel in Thailand, about 27,000 of whom were participating and supporting United States bombing raids over North Vietnam.

Each Seabee team consisted of 13 members: one junior naval engineering officer; one chief petty officer; two builders, two equipment operators; two construction mechanics; one utilities man; one engineering aid; one construction electrician; one steelworker; and one hospital corpsman. We went through 16 weeks of formal military and construction training in the United States and cross-trained in various ratings to enable each of us to perform all team maintenance and construction functions, which was an added benefit.

This comprehensive training resulted in a compact, self-contained, expertly trained, highly mobile, air-transportable, construction and civic action team capable of deploying overseas on short notice in support of

United States counter-insurgency efforts. For long-range programming at the State Department level, the Seabee Team could:

1. Furnish technical assistance on any engineering and construction problems to emerging as well as established nations;
2. Assist in the construction of a wide range of both civic action and socioeconomic projects; and,
3. Provide engineering, construction and limited medical assistance to nations that that become victims of disasters such as earthquakes and floods.

Our team site was located in the northern most region of Thailand known as the "Golden Triangle." It is the area where Thailand, Burma (now Myanmar) and Laos borders meet. During the team's deployment there in 1967 it was known as a major center for the production of opium from poppies grown by the hill tribes of the region. Seabee teams deployed there to assist the U.S. and Thai governments construct and/or improve roads and infrastructure to enable hill tribes to cultivate other crops that could be brought to the marketplace in larger towns for sale.

We rented two Thai houses in Chiang Kham from a Thai landlord who lived in our neighborhood. Our shop and Thai BPP team headquarters and billeting buildings were located at the opposite end of town at the Chiang Kham Airport, which could only handle helicopters, Caribou and other short-take-off-and-landing (STOL) aircraft on its short dirt/grass airfield.

One of the Seabee team's houses had office space with radio communications to the rest of the world, our dining room, kitchen, a safe for our defensive weapons, shower, and restroom facilities. The facilities were supported by a water storage tank filled by a pump from a hand-dug well system adjacent to the team quarters. A hot water heater provided hot water for shaving and bathing. The second floor served as a berthing area (beds with mosquito nets) for half of the team.

The second house contained a storage area in the center of the stilts on which the second floor rested. The upper level consisted of team quarters for the second half of our team. Neither of the houses had windows or screens. Team members slept in bunks with mosquito nets. When it rained, the wooden shutters on both sides of the windows were able to be closed to keep the rainwater from blowing on us inside our houses. Although better than tents, it was open-air living to the extreme but way better than living in tents in the sand in Vietnam.

A portable generator powered the stove, hot-water heater, fans, lights, and electrical connections in the houses after hours when the local utility company shut down village power during the late evening and early morning. We had a short-wave radio to listen to the BBC and monitor North Vietnamese communist propaganda sites and a reel-to-reel tape system to listen to music tapes from the USA.

We had a 4' x 8' piece of plywood, painted white, on the side of one house to show movies on that we got monthly from USOM Thailand. Sometimes our Thai neighbors and an American missionary family watched our movies with us. The local Thai movie theater owner authorized our team to build an enclosed glass front booth seating 8 people on the balcony level of the theater where the owner could pipe in the English language in speakers for us to see local movies and hear the English language.

Our cooks and housekeepers were a Thai family, mom and pop, and their five children ranging in age from 2 to 12 years old. They did the cooking, housekeeping, shopping for local meats and vegetables, and the laundry as well. Pop and mom spoke some English and helped us communicate with surrounding neighbors and shop owners in town.

A visit to the local Chiang Kham Whiskey factory was almost a monthly occasion. Somehow, the team members never tired of the visit since free samples of the products were given out during each visit.

We purchased water bottles for our shop and work sites from the U.S. Air Force Commissary in Bangkok, along with our primary team foods and drinks, on a monthly basis. We also returned movies seen the previous month and picked up new movies for the following month. Our outgoing and incoming mail was exchanged during the Bangkok trips. Sometimes we were able to bring our foods and other stuff back on-board U.S. or Thai Caribou aircraft but most times the two Seabees we sent to Bangkok every month for that purpose and had to return by truck with our foods on a long two-day overnight non-stop trip on dirt and gravel roads. That 3–5-day trip to Bangkok for the grocery run sufficed as our in-county R&R since we were not eligible for official R&R in Thailand.

There were several restaurants in town including a Chinese restaurant. One had to be careful what was ordered to eat since sometimes they might get cooked dog, snake, mountain oysters, or a chicken's head with the open eyes looking back at you from your plate. Sometimes you just didn't ask what it was and ate it anyway. Eating the brains from the chicken's head was considered a delicacy and an honored tradition by the owner or village chief if they shared food with us. I just couldn't pick and eat that, and the hosts understood that. Living and eating in Chiang Kham wasn't too bad as long as you watched what you ate and drank. Local Thai Singha beer came in quart-sized bottles and therefore a bottle of beer was a big cold thing to drink.

Several of the Seabees purchased motorcycles in Thailand to ride out to their job sites or for recreation during our time off on the weekends. I had a Red Honda-90 motorcycle provided by USOM Thailand. The Seabees hit the road resembling "Hells Angels" on the weekends driving through and exploring the local countryside. On one occasion, a team member accidentally hit and killed a water buffalo on the highway. The team had to pay the 'life-cycle' cost of the buffalo to the owner—a couple hundred dollars.

Our Thai counterpart BPP team(s) consisted of 15 Thai paramilitary police members assigned to protect the Seabee team and work beside us in civic action and village pacification programs. Several interpreters were assigned to each team to aid in communication between the two teams and with local villagers. At one time we had two BPP teams working with us. We had our own defensive weapons on site, but they were never taken out in the open and kept under lock and key in our quarters.

One CIA mission was delivering POL fuel to a remote site in Laos. Our Seabee Team Chief Petty Officer EOC Henry M. "Hank" Knowles was on board one flight. Approaching the small remote airfield in Laos their aircraft came under fire from the ground with a bullet coming through the seat injuring the co-pilot. Chief Knowles rendered first aid to the co-pilot until they returned to our base camp in Chiang Kham where our corpsman rendered first aid and applied a tourniquet until he was medevacked to a hospital for further treatment. It was one of those operations we weren't supposed to talk about during our time in Thailand.

A brief summary of our work is provided here: upgrading and pioneering 43 miles of roads (sometimes trails) to the border with Laos; overseeing hand-digging of 12 water wells in local villages; repairing or construction of 34 timber vehicle bridges and 4 swinging personnel bridges across rivers and streams; improving or constructing 6 earthen dams; helping with construction or providing some construction materials for several Thai military infrastructure projects, 22 schools and 12 Buddhist Temples; clearing and/or expanding 4 short-takeoff-and-landing (STOL) airfields including our own Chiang Kham airfield. In terms of medical assistance, our team corpsman and his BPP counterparts, along with other members of our respective teams, treated some 13,000 patients in 110 different villages during our deployment.

Thus, you have a bit of history of Seabee teams deployed to Thailand. It was both challenging and enjoyable work for our team in Thailand in 1967. Our BPP counterpart team was impressive as to their security for our Seabee team and the civic action and medical treatment actions that they worked with us on during our time there. Thailand was another place the Seabees worked with other countries services supporting the Vietnam War.

We were relieved by another Seabee team in Chiang Kham, Thailand, in November 1967 with two members on their team who had been with the team we relieved on site the previous May 1967. The work at that site went on with other Seabee teams relieving each other every 7-1/2 to 8 months until 1970.

It was a great time in Thailand and another reason I elected to complete 26 years of active duty with the U.S. Navy after three years in the naval reserve Seabee force. "Construimus, Batuimus—We Build, We Fight—for peace with freedom around the world." We are the "Can Do" Navy Seabees and we have done and continue to do construction around the world.

CHARLES "CHUCK" BAYLESS

US Army—Armor officer, UH-1 Helicopter pilot
Dates of Military Service: November 1964 through May 1968
Dates Served in Vietnam: July 1966 to July 1967
Units Served with In Vietnam:
July 1966 to Jan 1967 Troop C, 1/9th Recon Squadron, 1st Cav Div.
Jan 1967 to July 1967 48th Assault Helicopter Co.
Highest Rank Held: Captain (O-3)
Place of Birth: Cleveland, OH—1942

LANDING A BOEING 707-320 AIRLINER AT LZ HAMMOND (PIECE OF CAKE)

Since I was a kid, I was fascinated with commercial airliners landing at the Buffalo, NY, international airport, which happens to be my hometown. My parents and I, and later my future wife, Diane, would go out to the airport with me on the weekends. We would park along a remote runway fence. I was mesmerized by the sounds and sights; the roar as the pilot reversed the engines to slow the great bird down and the grace of the great beast as it smoothly landed on the runaway.

Fast forward to Vietnam, my first assignment after flight school in 1966, where I had the rare opportunity to emulate those super birds of the sky. I was assigned to Troop C, 1/9th Reconnaissance Squadron, 1st Cav Div., at this particular time based at LZ (landing zone for those non-military readers) Hammond in the Central Highlands. I say at this time because our squadron was very restless, we moved every month. It was often suggested before most missions that we ought to take along our air mattress, shave kit, and a change of underwear as we were never sure we'd return to this landing zone.

One evening, nigh on to twilight, my gun platoon leader, CPT Lynn Schrader, the best West Point grad in all of Vietnam, asked me to refuel 095 (Huey gunship). I grabbed SGT Debose, one of our best crew chiefs and we lifted off for the fuel depot on the other side of the LZ. Our refueling went like clockwork and soon SGT Debose and I were back in the air.

I began to think about how the last few months this LZ had expanded twenty-fold, becoming a major jumping off point for flight and infantry operations. We had a first class, upgraded runway with C-130's landing every fifteen minutes and a real tower operation. No more seat of the pants flying here, we had all the protocols of an active airfield.

It kind of made me think of those big planes at the big city airfields back home. (That was a bad mistake.) It was really a delightful fall evening, clear sky, warm air, and sun just going behind the mountains to our north. I suggested to SGT Debose that we fly a little farther east of the LZ, then make a nice lazy, long landing (just like I had seen those airliners perform in my youth). The SGT said, "OK, whatever," (I believe they said this in the 60s, too). I knew he wanted to get back for the two beers we were allocated nightly. Believe me, the Cav was very strict!

After banking into a long final approach, it was time to make a call to the tower. "Hello LZ Hammond Tower, this is American Spirit Five Zero Niner, Boeing Heavy Lift 707-320B, descending out of 18,000, 15 miles out, on glide slope for Runway 27Romeo, what's your weather?" (Actually, my Huey was two miles out at 1500 feet.)

Then I had to go through my landing checklist. Wish I had a stewardess (that's what we called them in the 60s) to help me. "Let's see, flaps set, throttles at the ready—no auto pilot," this was going to be the real McCoy. Those quad Pratt & Whitney JT4A turbojet engines were roaring, well they should be, they were completing 5,000 nautical miles, (9,300 km), our max range for this aircraft.

Those engines probably realized this beast could be converted soon to a Boeing "E-3 Sentry" airborne reconnaissance platform—that's like putting a thoroughbred out for kiddie rides at the county fair. "Hope our 141 passengers are buckled in and comfortable." "OK, water bottle, Bayer aspirin, Tums, Jack Daniels flask," we were whipping through this checklist.

Now we've got the landing zone in sight. It should be a piece of cake. We were moving along, quite low, but we had a beautiful, smooth approach underway. SGT Debose was looking uncomfortable, pointing to objects on the ground during our approach. Our landing pad is right ahead of us. Ease up on those Pratt & Whitney turbo jet engines, slide this 707 right onto the runway numbers, then ease it to a rolling stop, set the brakes, Ah-h-h, listen to the applause from our passengers. Thrust two thumbs in the air and shout, "We did it!"

I was basking so much in the glow of that technically perfect and beautiful landing of my 707 that I hardly felt the taps on my shoulder from SGT Debose as I filled out the logbook. Then the intensity of his taps grew to where it was almost hurting me. I glanced back at him, and he was pointing to an officer from the infantry encampment just off the apron of our landing pad.

This wasn't any ordinary officer, this was a fuming major, jumping up and down, yelling, cursing, and frantically waving me over. I thought he must be upset about something. Wow, I swear there was smoke coming out of his ears and fire out of his mouth. He was really upset. Then SGT Debose sheepishly pointed to what was lying next to the major, a two-man latrine, completely upside down. My first thought was it hadn't been that windy when I made my phenomenal landing.

This on-fire major kept waving me over and pointing to the latrine. Then it hit me, Lord, the rotor wash on my apparently too low approach had blown over the latrine! Had he been in it? I saw my military career going down the drain, rapidly!

Approaching the major warily because I thought he was going to punch me out, he was using words I had never heard before, and I was a tenement city kid. He threatened me with court martial or even worse, a black mark in my Personnel File. Oh man, it was over, so long to my hopes of someday becoming a general, or now, even a private!

Next, I had to go before my platoon leader, CPT Schrader, in front of the whole platoon. I thought he stifled a little laugh at one point, but I was probably wrong. The punishment he doled out was to write a 20-page thesis on how to land a HUEY. Twenty pages—where did that come from? Several of the captains in our platoon (we had dozens of them), offered to help me. They were good guys and maybe a little sympathetic. I appreciated this.

Well, after a week of writing, sometimes from the quiet recesses of our platoon latrine, I produced a 20-page treatise on landing a UH-1 helicopter in a congested area. The Bell Helicopter management in Texas would have been proud. Then our 1st Sergeant sent it from the field to be typed up for my eventual presentation to our company commander, Major Richey.

Do you know there were no military clerk typists in all of Vietnam in 1966? I don't know how far my valuable package was sent to get typed, possibly to Okinawa. Anyway, after many weeks, I received the typed manuscript. It took me a few hours to gather up all the gumption I could summon to then present it to Major Richey.

He took a cursory look at it, then bellowed, "Good, now get your low flying ass in gear and get to the flight line. We've got an air crew that's overdue 60 minutes and we don't know their whereabouts. We need aircraft in the air to conduct a search, ASAP!" The subject of this turned out to be our maintenance officer, 1st LT Albert J. McAuliffe, a flight school classmate of AVVBA member George Murray. The search didn't turn out well, but that's another story.

Moral of this story: If you are going to make a low approach & landing with a Boeing 707-320 Airliner, make sure there's no one in a latrine-like building under your engine turbulence. It could be a harrowing movement for them to remember!

ED FELL

US Army— Armor Officer, Aviator (Huey Pilot)
Dates of Military Service: 1965 to 1968
Unit Served with in Vietnam: 68th Assault Helicopter Cosmpany
Dates in Vietnam: Nov 1966 to Nov 1967
Highest Rank Held: Captain (O-3)
Place of Birth and Year: Stockport, OH— 1943

A STORY ABOUT A BEAUTIFUL YOUNG WOMAN

This is story about a beautiful young woman. Her name was Barbara Ober-hansly. She was affectionately known as "Bobbie" and she aired daily weather forecasts from Saigon on the Armed Forces TV channel. Every soldier within broadcast range of the TV station knew who Bobbie was and would drop everything they were doing to see her evening telecasts. We really didn't care much about the weather; we just wanted to look at Bobbie.

About half-way into my Vietnam tour, I chose to go to Japan on R & R. Well guess who was on my flight to Tokyo; you guessed it— Bobbie! We sat next to each other, got acquainted, and became friends. For the next week we hung out together shopping, eating, and seeing the sites. Bobbie couldn't have been nicer. On the flight back to Saigon, I told her that no one in my unit would believe me when I told them that I had spent the week with THE Bobbie Oberhansly and asked her if she would mind saying "Hi" to me and the Top Tigers of the 68th Assault Helicopter Company on her next broadcast.

Upon landing in Saigon, we said our goodbyes and I hitched a ride back to Bien Hoa where I was stationed. Sure enough, when I related my story about hanging out with Bobbie to the guys, they gave me the "Oh, sure you did" routine. No one believed that I could have been so lucky. So, the next evening we were all gathered around the TV in the Officer's Club to watch Bobbie. And sure enough, at the end of her telecast, she said, "And in closing I want to send out hugs and kisses to Ed Fell and all of the Top Tigers." Well, the place erupted in cheers, and I never had to buy a drink the rest of the evening!

Bobbie Oberhansly was a wonderful human being. She was a West Coast girl who had a wonderful life in the States but who felt a patriotic calling. She joined the Red Cross and volunteered to go to Vietnam to help out in any way she could. She was beautiful, charming, and fun to be around. Unfortunately, Bobbie passed away after returning to the States in 1968. She was only 24 years old. I think of her often and remember how much joy she brought to the troops when "We Were Soldiers Once and Young."

ROBERT O. "BOB" BABCOCK

US Army — Infantry Officer

Dates of Military Service (Active and Reserves): 1965 to 1974

Unit Served with in Vietnam: Bravo Company, 1st Battalion, 22nd Infantry Regiment, 4th Infantry Division

Dates Served in Vietnam: July 1966 to July 1967

Highest Rank Held: Captain (O-3)

Place and Date of Birth: Heavener, OK — 1943

(From letter to my wife) 16 Mar 67 — Sorry I have not written the last couple of days, but I have been pretty busy. In fact, the past two days have been unforgettable to say the least! By now I am sure you have heard about the Second Brigade, Fourth Infantry Division forward base camp being mortared. Man, it sure was!

On the night of 13 March, a little before 11:00, I had just gone to bed when I heard something whiz over my tent and then mortar rounds started landing all over the place...

MORTAR ATTACK ON PLEI DJERENG

"Those NVA mortars are lined up out there like piss tubes," joked the GIs sitting around the supply tent listening to the Chris Noel show on Armed Forces Radio. We had gotten another Army intelligence report that the NVA were going to mortar our forward base camp that night.

After Chris Noel had bid us farewell with her sultry, "Bye, love" to close out her nightly show, I headed back to my tent to write a letter before turning in. By 10:45 I had turned off the lantern, tucked the mosquito netting in around me, and was drifting off to sleep. The sound of an NVA B-40 rocket screaming over the top of my tent and exploding less than fifty yards away woke me in a flash! We had heard the intelligence reports so often we totally ignored the warning. Intelligence reports were like the little boy who cried, 'wolf', we did not believe them since they had always been wrong.

My instincts were running full speed as I rolled off my cot, tearing the mosquito netting down as I fell to the floor. I instinctively grabbed for my steel helmet and rifle as I heard the explosions of 82mm mortar rounds walking across the large helicopter landing pad and toward my tent.

I huddled close to the floor, praying we did not get a direct hit. Sandbags protected the bottom two or three feet of the tent. As long as I stayed close to the ground and we did not take a direct hit, I felt as safe as you can under those circumstances.

I was pulling my pants on as we waited for a break in the explosions so we could make a run for our bunker. Sergeant George Wilhelm, my tent partner, was busy pulling his boots on, without pants. (It is funny what you consider important in a situation such as that, we really did not need either our pants or our boots.) When the rounds quit falling, we jumped up and scrambled out of the tent in a low crouch, George with no pants and me with no boots.

Several men had already made it to the bunker. As they counted noses and saw we were missing, they had assumed we had been hit. When the rounds stopped, they shined a bright flashlight from the entrance to the bunker, scanning the area trying to find us. All it did was blind me as I tried to find the door of the bunker. "Turn out that damn light!" I shouted. "Do you want the NVA to know exactly where you are?!"

With the light out, I could see the outline of the bunker entrance and dived head-first into its safety as the mortar rounds started peppering the area again. George had tripped on his bootlace and twisted his knee but quickly got up and tumbled in on top of me, cursing every step he took.

The mortar fire was much more accurate this time as the rounds pounded our area. A round hit scarcely three yards from our bunker, exploding with an ear shattering blast. We were shaken by that blast but not nearly as much as by the one that hit a few seconds later, squarely on top of our bunker. The noise and concussion were deafening. Dirt and dust, along with the acrid smell of burning gunpowder, engulfed us, causing us all to start choking and coughing.

Fortunately, we always constructed good, strong bunkers and this one took the explosion without crumbling down on us. With tears streaming down our faces from the dust and gunpowder fumes, we were all shaking as we waited to see what would happen next. Even though we wanted to hug the bottom of the bunker, we knew we had to be ready to repel any sappers who might have broken through the perimeter. The last thing we wanted was to have a satchel charge thrown in on top of us.

It was a sweet sound when we heard return fire going out from our artillery and mortar positions. Soon after our artillery started firing, the NVA mortar positions went silent. But we felt far from safe. It was pitch black, there was no moon to light up the night, and we had no idea whether any of the NVA had breached the perimeter. I posted a man on each side of the bunker to make sure no one sneaked up on us. I climbed on top so I could get a better view all around. We waited and watched, but nothing happened.

Soon "Spooky" flew over dropping flares, lighting up the area like daylight. We quickly scanned the shadows and found no NVA had made it through the barbed wire perimeter, at least not in our area.

We breathed a sigh of relief and started filling sandbags to reinforce our bunker. It had taken one direct hit; we wanted it to be even stronger in case of another one. While filling sandbags, we became a cheering section as a flight of Air Force jets started working over the likely NVA mortar firing position. Each time a bomb or napalm canister exploded a cheer went up from the GIs.

In less than half an hour, the planes had departed, the flares had burned out, and darkness crept back across the camp. It was an uneasy bunch of GIs that headed back for their tents to try to sleep through the rest of the night. I slept with one eye open and jumped every time I heard one of our howitzers fire their random H&I (Harassing and Interdicting) fires. It was an extremely uncomfortable feeling to lay there and hope the NVA did not come back to visit.

As daylight returned, we were up surveying the damage. Amazingly, the damage had been very slight. Except for small shrapnel holes in all the tents, the heaviest damage had been to the Charlie Company supply tent. It had taken a direct hit and supplies were strewn all around, but no one had been hurt. After surveying our tent area, I walked to the battalion motor pool to see if any of our vehicles had been damaged. They, too, had escaped with minor damage.

As we stood in the motor pool and marveled at the small amount of damage, we heard a sound we never expected to hear in the daylight. From just outside the perimeter, we heard the unmistakable "whump whump whump whump whump..." of mortar rounds being fired at us. I counted twelve "whumps" as we all screamed, "Incoming!" and dived for the nearest bunker. I scrambled into the motor pool bunker and found it already crammed with men who had reacted at the first "whump" and had not waited to count the rounds before finding shelter.

The NVA were deadly accurate. All twelve rounds landed inside the motor pool. I was barely inside the bunker and could plainly see and feel the explosions that shook the area. One round landed on top of a "deuce and a half" (two and one-half ton cargo capacity) truck loaded with 4.2-inch mortar rounds scheduled to be carried out to the forward fire base early that morning. The truck started to burn.

I knew all hell was about to break loose. Not only was that truck loaded with mortar rounds, the one parked next to it was loaded with 81mm mortar rounds. For a brief second, I said to myself, "Babcock, if you want to earn a Silver Star for certain, go get in that truck and drive it out of the motor pool." Fortunately, my sane self took command before I made any move to do such an insane thing.

Suddenly, the mortar rounds started blowing. It sounded like high intensity popcorn as round after round exploded. Pieces of truck were hurled through the air like toys. When the truck with the 81mm mortar rounds started to explode, I decided it was time to get the hell out of that motor pool and find a bunker that was sturdier and further away from the raging inferno.

Taking a deep breath, I pulled my helmet down tight on my head and ran like a sprinter to put distance between the motor pool and me. My company bunker was about fifty yards away and the distance was covered in record time. For the second time in less than twelve hours, I dived through the entrance to the bunker as mortar explosions and pieces of truck flew through the air. Once again, several others tumbled in on top of me in a heap. They had followed my lead and had also decided to get the hell out of the motor pool area.

For the next hour, we sat in the bunker and listened to the American mortar rounds explode. As I looked out the door, I vividly remember seeing an entire truck fender hurtling through the air fifty feet above the ground. We sat in the bunker for several minutes after the last explosion, waiting to make sure nothing else was going to blow.

Once again, we ventured out to survey the damage. The vehicles in the motor pool were in shambles. There were no identifiable pieces left of the two "deuce and a half" trucks containing the mortar rounds. Every vehicle was damaged beyond repair, except for my jeep. Surprisingly, the only damage to it was a dent in the front wire catcher and a flat spare tire. The jeeps parked on either side were destroyed.

The rest of the day we worked trying to put some order back into the chaos the NVA had brought. After the twelve early morning rounds, nothing more was heard from the NVA mortars. We suspected they had fired and then run before we could zero in on them. They were probably back on some hill congratulating themselves for the great job they had done. They had gotten our attention.

We spent much of the day filling sandbags to reinforce the bunker that had saved our lives. By the time we were through reinforcing it, that bunker would have taken a direct hit from a 500-pound bomb and held up. We were a nervous bunch of soldiers as night descended on us again. Chris Noel did not have us in her radio audience that night, we were hanging around the bunker keeping our eyes and ears alert for anything out of the ordinary.

Despite our tired and sleepy state, none of us made any attempt to go into our tents to sleep. All of us stayed close to the bunker and drifted in and out of an uneasy sleep lying around or in the bunker. The night passed slowly but uneventfully.

The next morning, we received orders to move back to Artillery Hill near Pleiku. We made record time packing our equipment and belongings into borrowed trucks. We were extremely happy to see Plei Djereng disappear over our shoulder as we slowly wound our way back toward relative safety.

16 Mar 67 (Cont'd)—The trip was uneventful. We are now setup just north of Pleiku. We can sleep a lot better here than out at Plei Djereng. Also, we have grass and very little dust. We will be here about a month before we make another move…

PHILLIP (PHIL) CRENSHAW

U.S. Army—Military Police group operations clerk

Dates of Military Service: 11 Aug. 1964 – 10 Aug 1970

Unit Served with in Vietnam: 615th Military Police Company (STRAC); 716th Military Police Battalion; 89th Military Police Group; Saigon area

Dates Served in Vietnam: 8 Aug. 1965 to 5 Aug. 1966

Highest Rank Held: Sp4 (E-4)

Date of Birth: 13 May 1942

TRAVEL TO VIETNAM EXTREME EXPERIENCES

Our company in Ft. Hood, Texas, all volunteered for duty in Vietnam. Our commander, Capt. Lawrence Wolmering, organized travelling together. We were picked up early July 1965 by a troop train which started in New Jersey and arrived in San Diego, after various troop pickups on the way. We were to load onto a huge ship a train full of an unknown number of troops. We never saw the front or end of the ship or the train. The train blocked roads in the city for more than a day or two; anti-war demonstrators threw things at the train; some troops jumped off, beat them up, and left when the train moved, to continue loading on ship.

An unbelievable amount of men were jammed into a high level of canvas bunks, maybe ten high, maybe two feet between, sleeping with duffel bags. We stopped in Manila with, I believe, more troops added, I do not remember the time. We were introduced up close to a huge aircraft carrier. Overall, it was a smooth ocean passage. First stop: Cam Ranh Bay at a huge dock and deep water at the side toward the ocean. It took about a day to disembark troops destined there. Then on to Saigon to deliver the rest of us, total voyage time was probably three weeks.

At Saigon, the ship anchored out away from land, because of the lack of deep water going up the Saigon River to the port. We disembarked using many landing craft with heavy metal sheets welded on to extend the sides up for small arms fire protection from the sides of the river; fortunately, we did not receive any small arms fire on our trip. The Saigon port was on the other side of the river. A huge amount of delivered military equipment for various units was clogging the area, plus all troops coming off the ship.

The port perimeter and outgoing traffic was part of our MP assignment. The Navy handled town patrol. The Army provided multiple conveys through the city for our company and battalion to our destination at the airport area. Part of our company/battalion was immediately assigned traffic control to guide troops and their materials to their destination. The port commander provided maps.

OUR CAMP SITE REQUIRED INGENUITY

Upon arrival, we found that the engineers had set up a large amount of squad tents for us in the middle of a large area bordered by a golf course, with a golf club house about one quarter mile away. Next to the golf course was a row of about thirty cottages (2 story 2 BR/1B, over storage & car port), all being empty when we arrived, except one used by a major and a captain, a top sergeant, and two E3s. Our group commander, Colonel Charles Helderman, moved into the cottage next door. On the other side was underbrush and trees and a road to the airport with constant traffic, both military and civilian. It was unbelievable to be camped in the city.

Captain Wolmering directed me to report to Colonel Helderman and he assigned me the duty of setting up reporting and records retention according to regulations, and preparation of the Group SOP, Standard Operating Procedures. During my tenure, I was assigned various publications and reports which I completed and circulated as required.

THE SWAMP AND SOLUTION

A month or two after our arrival, heavy daily rains permeated everything, including under our tents. The ground was so wet that our bed frames were sinking into the ground like a swamp. Drainage was nonexistent. Everything on the ground ended up on our beds. Col. Helderman directed me to assemble a team to go back to the port to see if we could find anything not being used that we could bring back to solve our drainage problem. The port was storing lots of empty/used pallets, of various condition and which could be used as floorboards for our whole swamp area. We took a truckload. We obtained a second truck, sent three more men back to the port to pick up more pallets, while we unloaded and started installing the pallets from the first truck load in and around our tents.

The system was to keep the trucks moving so we could take all the pallets until we accomplished a complete "flooring" of our area. If anyone requested our authority, we referred them to Colonel Helderman. Apparently, no one had the nerve to call him (he was always available on his radio phone). We worked some very long days to accomplish this mission, and the port accomplished disposing of troublesome waste.

The cottages had electricity, water, and sewer service. Colonel Helderman observed I was starting a study of Vietnamese and talking with non-English speakers. Some electrical issues developed, and he directed me to practice speaking with the electricians for necessary repairs, which I did, and the repairs were accomplished.

LANGUAGE AND BILINGUAL BOOKLET CREATION

Immediately after arrival, Colonel Helderman directed me to organize preparing and publishing a bilingual manual, of common words, phrases, and popular statements similar to what travel agents give to international travelers. I requested various men of all jobs to assist using their work experience to collaborate in what everyone needed in this manual. We also contacted Vietnamese troops we were working with. All contributed. We submitted the manual to various Vietnamese for complete translations. Transcribers with Vietnamese typewriters finalized the draft and publication was accomplished in approximately six weeks. The pamphlet was quite usable according to some men using it. I could not find my copy in things I shipped home.

YEARLY TARGET RANGE TRAINING WAS ALMOST NOT BORING

When we as a company went to the range for weapon qualification, the range had been attacked by enemy troops. The group using the facility ahead of us responded and drove away the attackers without casualties, they thought. They and we inspected the entire area and found no enemy troops.

NEGATIVE IMPACT OF CIVILIAN POLITICS

When we initially arrived in the area, the troops in the one cottage on the golf course told us we were part of the buildup, including preparing to invade North Vietnam. They said the objective was to bring the country back together, and to not make the mistake that was made in Korea when General MacArthur was brought back from their border with China. In the year I was there, I did meet Vietnamese joining the army to be involved in the invasion. We know our politicians wasted that opportunity.

I met unrelated US troops who worked on the Cambodia and Vietnam border and lost their Commanding General to D.C. politicians because of prisoner questioning techniques. These techniques supposedly provided much accurate information. The story was reported in a French magazine by a field reporter named Sean Flynn. He was Errol Flynn's son, who lived with his mother in the summer in Palm Beach. I knew her.

The soldier who told me this story and the men in his company determined Sean's article, circulated in a popular magazine in France, was 100% responsible for their General being recalled for investigation of his command's "illegal" procedures. The replacement was not as aggressive, decreasing information and causing avoidable casualties. He indicated Sean was out of the country when we talked (early 1966). He expected if Sean ever returned to Vietnam, he would not survive to leave the country. In 1971 or 1972, I was working in West Palm Beach and observed a small article in a Florida newspaper that "the well-known war reporter" Sean Flynn had been lost in Vietnam.

TET AND MAJOR BATTLES PHASE

(1968 TO 1969)

January 21, 1968 — Siege of Khe Sanh began. The isolated Marine outpost was under siege into April 1968. 205 Americans died related to the battle.

January 30, 1968 — Tet Offensive began by the North Vietnamese and Viet Cong. Over 100 military and civilian installations across South Vietnam were struck in coordinated and surprise attacks on the first day of the Lunar New Year. This caused news anchor Walter Cronkite to announce that the US could not win in Vietnam, even though each of the attacks of the Tet offensive resulted in military victories for the South Vietnamese and Americans. The real impact was on American popular opinion at home and the will of American political leaders.

March 31, 1968 — President Johnson announces he will not seek re-election. His announcement was, "I shall not seek, and I will not accept, the nomination of my party for another term as your President."

April 4, 1968 — Reverend Martin Luther King, Jr. was assassinated in Memphis, TN. Riots erupted in the streets of every major US city. Many Americans thought the country was being torn apart by divisions over race, equality, and the war in Vietnam.

June 5, 1968 — Senator Robert Kennedy, presidential candidate, was assassinated in Los Angeles, CA. Brother of slain President John F. Kennedy, Robert was a source of hope that he could start healing our country.

August 26, 1968 — Riots broke out at the Democratic National Convention in Chicago, IL. The National Guard was mobilized the help the Chicago police in quelling the riots and restoring order.

November 5, 1968 — Richard Nixon elected President of the United States, running on a platform of withdrawal from Vietnam. His plan was called "Vietnamization" with a plan to equip South Vietnamese military and withdraw American troops.

December 31, 1968 — American deaths in Vietnam reached 30,000. By all accounts, 1968 was the most tumultuous year in American history. The number of Americans killed in Vietnam had doubled in a single year and the damage to American popular support was something that would not be recovered for the rest of the war.

April 15, 1969 — Woodstock…more than 400,000 people gathered in Bethel, NY for the Woodstock Music Festival. It is considered a definitive moment for the counterculture generation.

April 30, 1969 — American troop strength in Vietnam peaks at 543,282 in-country.

May 10, 1969 — Battle of Hamburger Hill in Vietnam's A Shau Valley. With over 70 killed in action, it sparked public debate of America's strategy in the war. Reacting to public and political pressure, GEN Creighton Abrams altered US strategy from "maximum pressure" to "protective reaction" in an effort to lower casualties.

July 20, 1969 — Neil Armstrong becomes first person to set foot on the moon.

September 3, 1969 — North Vietnam leader Ho Chi Minh dies at age 79.

November 12, 1969 — News of My Lai Massacre in South Vietnam reaches the US. The massacre was the mass killing of Vietnam citizens by US Army soldiers. Despite the atrocities, a US helicopter pilot tried to stop the killings and rescued civilians.

Source: www.vvmf.org/VietnamWar/Timeline

THE HONORABLE COLIN LUTHER POWELL: A REMEMBRANCE
April 5, 1937 – October 18, 2021

In recounting the many stories contained in this volume, we respectfully pause to recall and honor the service to the military and our Nation by Colin Powell: diplomat, statesman, and four-star general, including tours of duty in Vietnam. Powell was the 65th Secretary of State (2001-2005), the 16th National Security Advisor (1987-1989), and the 12th Chairman of the Joint Chiefs of Staff (1989-1993).

During his first tour in Vietnam (1962-1963) and while on patrol as an advisor to the South Vietnamese Army, (then Captain) Powell was wounded by stepping on a punji stake for which he received the Purple Heart Medal. Powell returned to Vietnam in 1968 as a major and was assistant chief of staff for operations with the 23rd Infantry (Americal) Division. During this second tour he was awarded the Soldier's Medal for bravery after he survived a helicopter crash and singled-handedly rescued three others including Major General Charles Gettys from the burning wreckage.

Of note and during his formative years, Powell wrote: "It was only once I was in college, about six months into college when I found something that I liked, and that was ROTC, Reserve Officer Training Corps in the military. And I not only liked it, but I was pretty good at it. That's what you really have to look for in life, something that you like, and something that you think you're pretty good at. And if you can put those two things together, then you're on the right track, and just drive on."

Colin Luther Powell: a life well-lived; courageous follower and servant leader extraordinaire.

(Thanks to Norman Zoller for recommending and writing this inclusion in our book).

CLINTON E. DAY

US Army— Signal Corps Officer

Dates of Military Service (Active Duty and Reserves): 1965 to 1971

Units Served with in Vietnam: MACV, 36th Combat Signal Battalion and 972nd Sig Bn (attached)

Dates in Vietnam: Feb 1966 to Feb 1967; Nov 1970 to May 1971

Highest Rank Held: Captain (O-3)

Place of Birth: San Francisco, CA—1942

Editor's Note: Vietnam Veteran and great American Max Cleland died on November 9, 2021, just before this book was finalized. It is only appropriate that the following story from his buddy, Clint Day, be included here. Max was a member of AVVBA.

MY BUDDY MAX CLELAND

We all experience special people through our life journey. The most unforgettable person I met was from Army service during Vietnam. Young signal corps officers from all over the U. S. were sent to Fort Gordon, Georgia in the fall of 1965. It was a time when things were heating-up in Vietnam as President Johnson started to commit ground troops.

About 32 officers seated nine weeks alphabetically gathered at Ft. Gordon outside Augusta, GA for the Signal Corps Officers Basic Course. There were a couple of graduate degrees, but most were 4-year college grads who had taken ROTC. They were from Boston, Indiana, Texas, New York, and California, and the heaviest accent I ever heard was one from rural Maine.

A couple of us stood out, one being Max Cleland from Atlanta who had spent his summer in D. C. as a staffer to a Senate committee. We had our own officers club annex called, appropriately, the "Dot Dash" where off-duty hours allowed us to get to know one another. Because I sat next alphabetically to Cleland as Day, a few of us accompanied Max home to suburban Atlanta once or twice. Max knew the night spots, and would arrive at the clubs with us, but spent his time on the dance floor with different ladies the entire evening.

The Army was preparing us for war, and most signal grads went on to Fort Monmouth, NJ for the advanced course. Olin Linke and I, both business majors, went on to Fort Lee, VA to supply school, and we lost track of Max for the time being. He became a General's aide at Fort Monmouth and could have stayed there in the position for a long time. However, his desire to be in the center of the action, a life-long trait, compelled him to volunteer for service in Vietnam.

Many know what happened next. Regrettably, Max was seriously wounded by a grenade explosion while jumping from a hovering helicopter. Only immediate surgery saved his life, but doctors had to remove both legs and one arm. Max was flown back to the States and spent months recovering at Walter Reed Army Hospital. As he says in his book, *The Heart of a Patriot*, "It is a journey to the dark places of life — terror, fear, pain, death, wounding, loss, grief, despair, and hopelessness. We have been traumatized physically, mentally, emotionally, and spiritually. I've found in my own life that I had to exude positive energy into the world in order not to be overwhelmed with sadness and grief over what I had lost. I found solace in attempting to "turn my pain into somebody else's gain" by immersing myself in politics and public service."

Public service he did. Serving with Jimmy Carter in the Georgia State Senate, he became Carter's Secretary of Veterans Affairs, returned home to become Georgia Secretary of State for 14 years during which he designed the country's model for stocks regulation, served as U. S. Senator after Sam Nunn's retirement, and was defeated in one of the dirtiest campaigns in history. Not deterred, although the defeat spun Max into PTSD late in life, he went on to serve on the Board of the Export-Import Bank, taught at American University, and became the Secretary of the American Battle Monuments Commission.

It was my good fortune to spend most of my commercial insurance career in Atlanta, GA and stay in touch with such a dear, inspirational friend. My wife and I met Evander Holyfield, Brenda Lee, and other luminaries at fund-raising events and enjoyed Max's jokes many times.

One quality all close friends will readily attest is Max Cleland's enormous heart for helping others. Countless Georgians were assisted, supported, and given a hand-up by his caring. He simply was the most unforgettable person I have ever met, and I love the man!

THOMAS A. "TOM" ROSS

US Army—Special Forces
Dates of Military Service (Active and Reserve): 1966 to 1992
Unit Served with in Vietnam: Detachment A-502, 5th Special Forces Group
Dates in Vietnam: Jan 1968 to Dec 1968
Highest Rank Held: Major (O-4)
Place of Birth and Year: Huntington, WV—1945

THE FIRST DAY

EVERY AMERICAN WHO BECAME a part of the Vietnam War can probably recall his or her first day "in country" with little difficulty. The following account is how I remember my first day after being dropped off at the Nha Trang Air Base by a helicopter shuttle from Cam Rahn Bay...

A jeep roared and stopped beside me. A young Special Forces soldier was at the wheel. He had the face of a high school student but was wearing a .45-caliber sidearm and had an M-16 lying across his lap. He eyed my name tag, offered a crisp salute, then queried, "Lieutenant Ross?"

"Yes," I said, returning his salute.

"I'm Spec 4 Daily. I've been sent by 5th Group to take you back to collect your orders and draw equipment. Welcome to Nam, sir."

"Thank you, Daily," I responded, amused by his welcome to war.

I threw my duffel bag in the back of the jeep, mounted the passenger seat, and Daily quickly sped away toward 5th Group Headquarters.

As we drove along the busy runway, aircraft roared overhead, and I again surveyed my environs. Passing a line of obviously departing soldiers, I noticed a hand-scrawled sign on the pack of one. It read, "FOLLOW ME BACK TO THE USA." Daily and I made eye contact and we both smiled—this soldier was clearly ready to go home.

Farther down the runway, we passed an Army aviation headquarters building with the unit's crest prominently displayed. "Intruders" was emblazoned diagonally across the red-and-white-on-blue painted crest. Across the bottom of the crest was the unit's motto, "Hell from Above."

"Sound like guys to have as friends," I commented, regarding the crest.

"Absolutely. That's the 281st AHC (Assault Helicopter Company), some of the most fearless men in Nam. They fly the Delta missions."

"Impressive. Everyone in SF knows about Delta's missions and reputation," I said, having learned about Delta back at Fort Bragg.

"Right, but the 281st doesn't just fly for Delta, sir. They fly for you too."

Confused, I asked, "What do you mean?"

"They also fly for Detachment A-502. The Ops (Operations) officer who sent me, said that's where you're headed. I'm taking you there after you pick up your orders and gear."

With that, Daily turned, drove through the gate, and off the base.

* * * * *

At that moment, like so many other things, I had no real understanding of the 281st's role in the war—or any thought that men of this unit would one day risk their lives to save mine. But what I did know was that helicopters were the workhorses of the Vietnam War. They were the primary means of delivering troops and supplies to the battlefield. The derring-do of U.S. helicopter pilots and crews was already well documented—even legendary. They were professional airmen from whom you could expect selfless and courageous actions on a routine basis.

During the year ahead, I would be amazed and proud to discover that a person's job description was no indicator of anyone's level of personal courage. Especially, for those holding what seemed to be routine and often mundane non-combat positions.

As we drove along a base perimeter road, I quizzed Daily. "So, what do you know about 502?"

"Well, I know it's the largest A-Team ever formed. Rather than the standard 12 men, 502 has over 50."

"You're kidding."

"No, sir. They've got a really big job. 5th Group has given them the responsibility for the defense of Nha Trang City and the Northern approach to Cam Rahn Bay."

"You're right. That sounds like a huge job."

As we entered the city, Daily told me that our ride to 5th Group Headquarters was taking longer than usual. The reason was obvious. Barricades had been erected and placed in strategic locations to restrict rapid movement through the city. We were driving past heavily combat-scarred shops and buildings of Nha Trang's once charming inner city. Residents and shopkeepers were busy trying to restore a small measure of normalcy by clearing debris and repairing the damage.

"Looks like it was a hell of a battle," I commented on what I was seeing.

"TET, sir! We had a hell of a battle here the other night. They say at least two battalions hit us. The Cong were running around everywhere, so our guys put these things in the road in case they tried to roll in with heavier stuff."

The "Cong" Daily referred to were Viet Cong, South Vietnamese who sympathized with our North Vietnamese enemies. They fought against the South and its allies, which, of course, included the United States.

"Looks like they did enough damage with what they had," I muttered, noting the damage caused by the recent battle.

"Yes, sir. They did—and they came out of the damn woodwork like roaches. They were everywhere!"

I had arrived in Vietnam in the middle of the 1968 Tet Offensive, a major surprise attack mounted by almost seventy thousand North Vietnamese and Viet Cong soldiers. The attack, launched during Tet, the lunar New Year, violated a holiday truce and occurred virtually simultaneously all over the country. In a single night, the war moved from the jungle and rural villages to the heart of over a hundred Vietnamese cities and towns, some previously thought to be impregnable. Nha Trang had been one of the first coastal cities hit as its inhabitants prepared to celebrate the New Year, the Year of the Monkey.

According to superstition, the monkey is considered a harbinger of bad luck. Certainly, in this case, it was. During the Tet Offensive, South Vietnam and its allies lost thousands of troops, hundreds of American soldiers among them. However, the Viet Cong and North Vietnamese who launched the attack lost thousands more.

While dissension had been growing regarding the war in Vietnam, the Tet Offensive would dramatically change public opinion in the United States and around the world. Events surrounding this offensive would cause antiwar resistance to intensify significantly. On that note, my tour of duty began.

As we wound our way through the narrow streets, I began to be concerned about our safety and eyed the M-16 lying across Daily's lap. Not having been issued a weapon yet—I was unarmed.

"Are we okay riding through here?" I asked.

"Yes, sir," he said. "We should be fine. Not much has happened during the past couple of days, but they're still active and probe us at night. So, they're still around."

Daily's words proved prophetic. We rounded the next corner and "Pow! Pow! Pow!" The street ahead erupted with explosive gunfire. Red and green tracers blazed back and forth across the road.

The enemy soldiers were the source of the green tracers, and they were far outnumbered by the red ones being fired by the friendly ARVN troops. That was the first and only time I ever saw green tracers. And, for the few minutes they ricocheted around me, that was enough.

Daily jammed on the brakes, the M-16 flew off his lap, tires screeched, gravel flew, and we skidded to an abrupt sideways stop. A cloud of dust boiled up and quickly enveloped our jeep.

In front of us, a 2 1/2-ton troop transport truck blocked the road. From behind a low wall, South Vietnamese soldiers were shooting into an abandoned building where enemy soldiers were hiding. The enemy fiercely returned fire.

Suddenly, the windshield of our jeep was shattered by enemy gunfire, glass chards flew everywhere. Daily grabbed his M-16 off the floorboard and rolled out onto the street. I quickly followed and moved around to the protected side of the jeep with Daily. I peeked over the back of the jeep and watched a furious exchange of gunfire.

"This is crazy!" I said. "I haven't been here for fifteen minutes, and I'm not ready to be shot!"

Daily, clutching his M-16 was crouched behind the front tire of the jeep and shouted to me, "You're in the middle of it now, LT!"

LT was an abbreviation for lieutenant and was pronounced just as it appears, ell tee. This was a common way that enlisted men addressed lieutenants.

"Yeah, and I'm unarmed!" I answered — feeling very helpless.

Daily responded immediately. He reached down, drew his .45 pistol, and tossed it to me.

I nodded thanks and again peeked over the jeep. Through gun smoke and settling dust, I was shocked by what I saw. At the rear corner of the truck, an attractive American brunette in her mid-20s was standing at the center of the shoot-out. She was wearing green Army fatigues and was holding a long lens camera.

"What is she doing out there?" I said, astounded by the sight.

Daily peeked over the hood of the jeep.

"I don't know who she is, but I've seen her around. I think she's a reporter or something like that.

Bullets ripped the road from the truck to the jeep.

She's gonna get herself killed out there, I thought.

As I watched, the brunette leaned out and snapped pictures, documenting the action. As she moved around, presumably to get a better angle on her subject, I was completely awestruck by her tenacity.

Concerned that we were exposed to fire from the upper windows of the building, I shouted to Daily, "Let's get off the street!"

"I'm with you, sir."

"Okay, let's go."

We jumped up and ran toward the doorway of a nearby building about half the distance to where the brunette was busy, still snapping pictures. I wasn't sure what I could do for her, but I felt better just being closer to her.

Inside an alcove, Daily and I stood shoulder to shoulder with our backs pressed against the wall. Gunfire continued to crack and echo along the street.

After the South Vietnamese troops fired M-79 grenades into the building, the gunfire stopped, and yelling came from inside the abandoned structure. Shortly, three bloodied men with their hands raised high in the air appeared in the upper windows. When ordered out, they emerged tentatively from the building. The men, who were either VC (Viet Cong) or NVA (North Vietnamese Army), seemed extremely concerned about the reception they would receive once outside. Their reluctance to come out was not without sound reason. The South Vietnamese soldiers began imposing street justice, jumping on them, and beating them violently.

With things seemingly under control again, Daily and I remounted the jeep and pulled out. I had Daily stop near the brunette. She was still taking pictures of the action. As she moved to another position she looked up and we made eye contact. *Pleasantly attractive... and bold!* I thought.

"You want a ride outta here?" I asked.

"What?! No, I'm working! I'm a war correspondent. This is my job," she snapped, obviously annoyed by my question.

"Okay, then we'll be on our way. Take care of yourself," I said.

Over her shoulder, as she walked away, "Always do."

She hadn't gone far when she stopped and turned to face me.

"Thanks for stopping," she said and showed me a warm smile. Then, she quickly turned and hurried away to document the capture. I turned and looked at Daily, a huge grin covered his face.

"You've been here less than fifteen minutes and caught a girlfriend, LT," he teased.

"I don't think so. Let's go. She doesn't need us."

"Maybe not, but she sure is easy to look at," Daily observed.

When Daily pulled away, I savored a parting view of the attractive bold brunette in the side mirror. I would love to have stayed.

As we continued to make our way through the city, it occurred to me that both Daily and I had reacted to the young female journalist in a typically male fashion. We had observed and commented on her physical appearance rather than the more serious consideration of what she was doing, which was covering a war, a serious and clearly dangerous job. While I had noted the boldness in her effort to document the capture of the enemy soldiers, there was more to consider in assessing her actions. She was the only woman on the street, and she was unarmed. While, other than me for a few minutes—and not by choice, every male on the street was armed, some heavily.

Many, many lessons were to be learned in Vietnam, a war brought into American living rooms by journalists similar to the one I had just encountered. My arrival in Nha Trang constituted the first day of class; my first instructor had been the female journalist, whose lesson covered well the courage of women. That day, I learned a woman can be every bit as brave as any man I ever met. And, before I returned home, others would reinforce her lesson.

RICK WHITE

US Army— Infantry Officer

Dates of Military Service: 1966 to 1997

Unit Served with in Vietnam:1st Tour: 3rd Platoon, C Company & Recon Platoon, 2nd Bn, 35th Inf Regt, 4th Inf Div; 2nd Tour: B Company, 503rd Abn Inf Regt, 173rd Abn Bde

Dates in Vietnam: Dec 1967 to Dec 1968; Jan 1970 to Dec 1970

Highest Rank Held: Colonel (O-6)

Place of Birth and Year: Atlanta, GA— 1947

IT FELT LIKE WE WERE WALKING INTO "THE VALLEY OF THE SHADOW OF DEATH" – WE WERE, EXCEPT IT WAS IN THE MOUNTAINS!

On the morning of Tuesday, 27 February 1968, I, 20-year-old Second Lieutenant (2LT) Rick White from Norcross, Georgia was leading my Infantry Rifle Platoon in the mountainous and triple-canopy jungle in Quang Nam Province, Central Highlands, South Vietnam. This platoon, 3rd Platoon, and the rest of C Company, 2nd Battalion, 35th Infantry Regiment ("Blue Cacti"), 3rd Brigade, 4th Infantry Division, along with the attached Battalion Recon Platoon, were slowly, very slowly, moving up a narrow and steep trail. Of the four platoons, 3rd Platoon was last and responsible for rear security.

On this same day, I sadly found out later, Walter Cronkite had made his infamous and demoralizing pronouncement that, *"This war is un-winnable...."* Thanks Walt, we *really* appreciated your boost of confidence!

As we moved up the mountain trail with flank security extended left and right, I noticed everything was eerily quiet. There were no sounds of nature, no birds singing, no insects buzzing, just the constant grunt and groan of tired young Soldiers placing one sore foot in front of another while bent over, far over, under a heavily loaded rucksack of ammo, precious water, C-Rations, Claymore Mines, extra machine-gun (MG) ammunition, grenades of many varieties, poncho (our bed), steel pot, personal or crew-served weapon, and a few personal items. The weight ranged from 60 to 80 pounds, depending on how long it had been since our weekly resupply or the last engagement with the enemy (each day = less food to carry or enemy contact = less ammo to carry).

The steep trail grade plus the temperature and humidity made breathing laborious. Sweat drained out of every pore. There was no "fat" to be found on anyone's body, we were all skinny. We found that one could "exist" on one C-Ration meal a day because to eat more meant to carry more and our rucks and backs were already maxed-out. During lulls, small talk seemed to always eventually circle back to the longing of ice-cold milk, ice cream, and delicious meals that would be ladened with lots of meat and carbs. We were young, hungry, perhaps still growing physically, and *always* hungry.

Every other night a platoon would be on "trail ambush" duty with the requirement of no sleep. The next night, that platoon would be on company perimeter guard duty with the much-interrupted sleep totaling about five to six hours per enlisted man while the Platoon Leader and Platoon Sergeant would get about four to five hours of likewise much-interrupted sleep due to constantly checking the perimeter's many defensive fighting positions. Needless to say, we were all very "sleep deprived."

The description of these day-by-day conditions is by no means meant to be a "gripe," but simply provided as a reference and a connection to the life of all combat Infantrymen, regardless of the war or country, past to present. So far, "technology" can only do so much when it comes to lighter loads, adequate rest, and sufficient amounts of food and water.

Thus was the physical condition of the 120 or so men that were dutifully trudging up an unnamed mountain somewhere in Southeast Asia on a hot, thick humidity, non-monsoon morning.

Like most of these men, all my senses were acute and on high alert. Although the enemy was unseen, we could all "smell" them, as I am sure they could smell us. We could just simply "feel" him. Little did we know that we were about to "tangle" with a large element of the well-trained and well-equipped Second Division of the North Vietnamese Army.

At approximately 1000 hours, the two lead platoons were subjected to a deafening barrage of enemy MG fire from well camouflaged and, thus, undetected positions. They / we had walked into a three-MG gun "Kill Zone" (KZ). This initial fusillade lasted only seconds, but resulted in many friendly wounded, dying, and dead.

The Company Commander, extremely brave and highly decorated (already two Silver Stars, two Purple Hearts, etc.) First Lieutenant (1LT) Homer Kraut from Virginia was in his fifteenth month of jungle combat. He was an all-business leader and was well respected by everyone that knew him.

After directing a base of fire toward the enemy guns he radioed me:

"Charlie 36 this is Charlie 6, what is your status, over?"

"Charlie 6 this is Charlie 36, we have no casualties and are ready to move, over."

"Charlie 36, you are to maneuver to my left flank and behind the enemy positions and take them out. Once you do that, start getting the WIAs and KIAs out of the kill zone and keep your ass down, over."

"Roger!"

As we moved through the thickly vegetated jungle toward the enemy, the point man, who was just ahead of me, tripped a camouflaged booby-trapped Chicom grenade which mortally wounded our platoon medic who was an arm's length from me. Twenty-two-year-old Specialist Dennis Wayne Jacobs from San Diego died within a few seconds in my arms. He was the first man, of too many, that I lost in 24 months in Vietnam. We kept moving.

"Taking out the enemy machine guns" proved to be a job best suited for artillery, mortars, and gunships. Thus, the men of 3rd Platoon were directed to our second mission of crawling as low as possible into the KZ, moving up next to a WIA or KIA, getting them on our backs and then "clawing" our way out of the KZ as MG fire whizzed close-by, overhead.

Each Christmas, I receive a heart-felt, handwritten card from one of the men that I had the privilege of hauling out that day, Specialist Tom O'Conner from New York City. At one of our 35th Infantry Regiment reunions, I told Tom that I got to wear his blood on the back of my jungle fatigue shirt until sweat and rain eventually washed it off. Without missing a beat, Tom said that, therefore, we are literally "Blood Brothers!"

One of the WIAs that day that we got out was a sucking chest wound causality, a great man and leader, the recon platoon leader, 1LT Henry. The next day, I was paid the humbling honor by the Battalion Commander of taking command of the recon platoon, which I did my best to lead for the remaining months of my first tour in South Vietnam. It was the best job that I had in 31 years of active duty in both war and peace.

"Yea, though I walk through the valley of the shadow of death, I will fear no evil, for Thou art with me."

— *Psalm 23: 4a*

God Bless the USA and our Selfless, "Defenders of Freedom."
Respectfully,
Richard H. White, Colonel (Retired) United States Army
Director & Chairman of the Board
Georgia Military Veterans' Hall of Fame

Isaiah 6:8 / John 15:13

ROBERT REESE

US Army— Infantryman
Dates of Military Service: 1968 to 1971
Unit Served with in Vietnam: B Company, 1st Battalion, 26th Infantry, 1st
Infantry Division
Dates Served in Vietnam: Dec 1968 to Nov 1971 (two tours)
Highest Rank Held: Sergeant (E-5)
Place and Date of Birth: Atlanta, GA—1949

'TIL DEATH DO US PART

The reader may remember a monthly feature of the old Reader's Digest magazine—"My Most Unforgettable Character." A different author would write a story each edition about a person they met in life who could truly be termed memorable, for whatever reason.

I met two of my most memorable people in December 1968. Each was remarkable in their own unique way. One of them I was privileged to know for only a few short weeks. The other I didn't see again for 50 years. The two were intimately intertwined with each other as they were husband and wife when I first encountered them in the small, fortified town of Lai Khe in Binh Duong Province, about 50 miles north of Saigon.

I had just arrived in Vietnam the first week of December 1968. After a couple of weeks in a transit unit in Long Binh, I was assigned to Company B, 1-26th Infantry, First Infantry Division as an infantry rifleman. I remember thinking how happy I was to get sent to the 1st Division whose headquarters were "only" 50 or so miles north of Saigon. After all, I wouldn't be going to 101st on the DMZ or the 9th Division in the Mekong Delta, for example. I mean I would be less than 100 miles from bustling, glittering Saigon with all its enticements.

I thought—couldn't be too bad, could it? Wrong again, GI!

It would be 45 years before I got to make that trip to downtown Saigon.

As I was later to learn, the Big Red One's area of operations encompassed the Iron Triangle, the infamous Highway 13 aka "Thunder

Road", the equally dangerous and evil Michelin Rubber Plantation, and stretched all the way past An Loc to the Cambodian frontier 175 miles from Saigon. It was an area which had never been under the complete control of French nor the South Vietnamese government since the Japanese had been ousted from the country after World War II. The whole region had been controlled by the communists since 1945.

My misconceptions as to my "lucky" assignment to the 1st Infantry Division would be dispelled in quick order. In the meantime, I was ferried by Chinook helicopter to Fire Base El Paso deep in the remote countryside of the province. It was there I first met Captain Russ Reinel, CO of Bravo Company, 1-26th Infantry—my new boss.

Captain Reinel was a 22-year-old company commander from Columbus, Georgia, not too far from my own hometown of Smyrna. He was a good-looking young man, movie star handsome I'd say. From the first I was impressed with Reinel. He spoke briefly with us new guys, assuring us we were welcomed and needed by the unit. He came across as being genuinely interested in us as newly arrived individuals. When you were a new guy in Vietnam you were usually not considered a full—fledged person. You had to earn some measure of respect by simply surviving for a few weeks. Then you had passed the test and were eligible to be considered as a friend and a brother in arms.

I remember CPT Reinel giving the company an informal motivational talk a couple of weeks later at a two day stand down at the battalion headquarters in Lai Khe. He told us that one of his goals was to make sure we all returned home safely. I knew when he said it that he could not make good on a commitment like that, but I appreciated the sentiment. He was an officer that truly did have his men's welfare at heart.

There was another individual present at this bunker side chat from Reinel. His wife—Lt. Patty Reinel. Yes, an infantry company's commanding officer was pulling a combat tour in Vietnam joined by his wife. Patty was a US Army nurse assigned to the surgical unit at base headquarters there in Lai Khe.

Now I suppose of all the 2.5 million men who served in Vietnam, maybe there was nothing new under the sun. But I must believe that a husband and wife serving together in a combat zone must have been very, very rare, if not unique to Russ and Patty.

The backstory was that they had met and been married while in the service. Russ was the first to post to an overseas assignment—executive officer of an infantry company in Korea, not Vietnam. Subsequently, Patty received her orders for Vietnam. This induced Russ to ask for a 1049 (request for transfer) to Vietnam himself.

Even after the Army agreed to have them both in-country, it's still hard to believe they would have had the good fortune not only to be stationed in some proximity to each other, but to actually be stationed in the same location. This does not sound like something the Army that I knew would do on purpose—made too much sense! Russ' father was a retired Army doctor so possibly he pulled some strings to pull off this astounding personnel coup.

Be that as it may, there the young newlyweds found themselves living in (separate) Quonset hooches set in an old French rubber plantation in far off Indochina. Truly they were uniquely fortunate in that respect. One has to wonder whether it was tougher for Patty to be close to where Russ had to perform his extremely dangerous professional duties than it would have been if she were posted in say, California. Subsequent events would test that question in the strongest possible way.

Thirty days to the day after being in-country, I earned a Purple Heart. It gave me pause for thought. Since I already had acquired the award after only thirty days, it was natural to wonder how many more I'd collect during the next 11 months! (The answer was zero.) Once I returned to the field after a short two week stay in the medical compound in Lai Khe, I was faced with what was a virtually certainty for incoming new guys—I was assigned to walk point for my platoon. I'd have to continue doing that for a few weeks until the next unlucky new guy arrived from the States—if I lasted that long of course.

The three platoons in Bravo Company rotated each day as the point element of company, so that meant every third day I had to perform my new duty leading the column through the day's march. As a point man,

I had many occasions to observe CPT Reinel's leadership style up close. He spent a lot of time at the front of the column, talking to my platoon leader, squad leader, and me. He was determined to observe things firsthand—checking out trail junctions or evidence of enemy activity personally.

On several occasions, I saw him don an unauthorized boonie hat, step out onto the trail, and beckon to an enemy soldier in the distance. Reinel was dark complexioned and slight of build so I think he must have been trying to trick the enemy personnel that he himself was one of them or perhaps he was just offering the enemy soldier a chance to go *chieu hoi*, that is, desert to the other side. While impressed with his hands-on style of leadership, I felt like sometimes he might have been pushing the envelope a bit too far in endangering himself unnecessarily—performing actions that would have been better left to one of his subordinates or me. In the final analysis, his proactive style did lead to his undoing.

On the fateful day, I was walking point along the edge of a rubber tree grove where it abutted thick, impenetrable scrub woods. He told me to be on the lookout for a particular trail juncture. Now walking along a trail is in itself not recommended practice as it's a very good place for the enemy to spring an ambush or rig a booby trap. So I was on high alert and was at an even more elevated level of concentration than usual. When I came across the juncture of the two trails, I stopped and Reinel came to the head of the column to take a look for himself.

He studied his map for a minute then told me to take a break. Reinel, one of the platoon leaders, and his RTO proceeded to press forward along the trail then quickly were lost to sight. Ten minutes later, the platoon leader and RTO returned. CPT Reinel had lagged behind to recheck his position or some other reason unknown.

The quietness of the morning was suddenly shattered by a loud explosion from the direction Reinel had gone. We pressed quickly ahead and discovered him dead on the trail, the victim of a booby trap. Whether it was a command detonated mine or rigged to be tripped by an unwary GI we never found out.

Patty Reinel of course must have been notified in short order since she was only five or six miles away in Lai Khe. I never saw her again—in Vietnam anyway.

Forty years later, I was shocked to find out that Patty had been interviewed on CBS's 60 Minutes weekly news program. This particular one focused on five nurses' experience in Vietnam. She was interviewed and among other things asked about how she found out about her husband's death.

She said had had stopped by the small PX in Lai Khe to pick up a few things. An orderly from the medical unit found her and told her that the chaplain needed to see her right away. As she articulated in the interview, "It's not good when the chaplain needs to talk to you urgently."

"They would not let me see the body. I was told his head had been blown off by an explosion," she told Morley Safer, the interviewer. I can confirm that for once somebody in the Army made a good decision in preventing her from seeing his remains.

Years later I reached out to Patty across the internet, and we became friends 40 years after I first saw her sitting on a bunker in Lai Khe. She left the service after Vietnam but had a career helping veterans in civilian life. She was remarried (to a Vietnam vet). We met in person at a Bravo Company reunion in 2008. I had the pleasure of being picked to present an award to her in honor of our much-respected fallen leader.

Patty Reinel now lives in New Jersey and is on her third marriage (to yet another Vietnam vet).

Captain Russell Reinel is on The Wall—Panel W33, line 68. He is buried at Ft. Benning post cemetery in his hometown of Columbus, Georgia, next to his mother and father. He was 22 years old.

Russ and Patty lived a storybook romance for a short time. It turned out to be a tragedy in the end. Two most unforgettable people and it was my privilege to know and serve with them both.

PHILIP H. ENSLOW, JR.

United States Army, Signal Corps Officer
Dates of Military Service: 1951 to 1975
Units served in in Vietnam: Headquarters, 1st Signal Brigade; Headquarters, Regional Communications Group [Apr 1967 to Nov 1967]; 173rd Airborne Brigade (Separate) [Nov 1967 to Apr 1968]
Highest Ranks Held: Lt. Colonel (O-5)
Place of Birth and Year: Richmond, VA – 1933

TET OFFENSIVE 1968

In January 1968, I was the Brigade Signal Officer for the 173rd Airborne Brigade, and I had to go to Saigon to take care of some communications issues in the 173rd. I needed some place to stay, so I decided to visit my old unit, the Regional Communications Group, Headquarters. Just my luck! The night I was in Saigon, January 30, 1968, was the night that the Viet Cong decided to launch their very large "Tet Offensive."

That night was the most frightening night that I had in Vietnam. There were rear area types shooting at anything and everything! Who gave those people ammunition? Even with all our "friendly fire," I did not hear of any of the Viet Cong being killed. Also, luckily, I did not hear of any "friendly casualties from our friendly fire."

I had been shot at a number of times in my helicopter. After we landed following one mission, I noticed that there was a hole in the body of the chopper just three feet from my head, but, even with that, I was never as scared as I was during this night of wild shooting in downtown Saigon. Actually, I was very happy to get back up to the real combat zone at Dak To. So much for visiting the "big city of Saigon."

JAMES DAVID ELY

US Army — Signal Corps Officer
Dates of Military Service (Active and Reserves): 1966 to 1972
Unit Served with in Vietnam: 69th Signal Battalion, Tan Son Nhut Air Base
Dates in Vietnam: Sep 1967 to Aug 1968
Highest Rank Held: Captain (O-3)
Place of Birth and Year: Caledonia, NY — 1945

MEMORIES OF A YEAR IN SAIGON

As I write this, I realize how blessed I am to be 76 years old and in relatively good health. I never dreamed that breathing the air in Vietnam would cause so many health issues for so many of us. I also find it more and more challenging to remember many of the exact details of my eleven and a half months in Vietnam. I will do my best to pass on some of my memories as I recall them.

In college, I was informed by my draft board that I would be drafted when I graduated in June of 1966. I had two options — enter as a private or as a 2nd Lieutenant. I chose the latter and enrolled in the ROTC program at my school. I was never really "gung ho." Well, I made it! One of my life's high points was when my dad — a WWII tank driver, got to pin on my shiny gold 2nd Lieutenant's bars. He was so proud!

My college degree was in Business Administration, specializing in the foodservice industry. So, of course, the Army in its infinite wisdom placed me into the Signal Corps specializing in microwave radios. After short tours for training at Ft. Gordon, GA, Ft. Monmouth, NJ, and Ft. Huachuca, AZ, I received orders for Vietnam.

A 21-hour flight from Oakland, CA landed me at Bien Hoa airbase just north of Saigon. As the plane descended through the clouds, it seemed as if every person on board reached up to see where the A/C had gone. This was a sign of the HOT weather to come. One of my first memories in country was the song by "The Animals" — "We got to get out of this place, if it's the last thing we ever do..."

I was very fortunate to be quartered in a hotel in Saigon called the

Kai Minh. I have come to realize a hot shower every day with a pressed, starched uniform were a real luxury, especially now that I have many friends in AVVBA who lived in the bush and seldom received either.

Every day I was bussed to Tan Son Nhut AFB to work. On one occasion, I looked out the window of the bus and there was an old mama-san buck naked taking a shower under a gushing fire hydrant. Finishing, she put on her black silk pajamas, flip flops, and went on her way. Just part of a new culture to adapt to.

There were many perks to living in Saigon, including its many restaurants, night clubs, and one very special prize, the Cholon PX located in the Chinese district. There you could get all kinds of electronics and other goodies to send home. One negative aspect of living in Saigon was that snipers were everywhere. They enjoyed picking off U.S. officers while they ate at a roof top restaurant or riding in a Pedicab to the PX. An interesting story I recall is my men would ride to work in the back of a deuce and a half truck. Every day, a small boy would run up and throw them three loaves of freshly baked French bread. They would toss him piastre to pay for the bread. One day the loaves felt a bit heavy. They immediately threw them back where they exploded because hand grenades had been baked into them.

I had several roommates, but one in particular stood out as "special." He was a good bit older and a real "country boy" from Tennessee. His name was John Benson. John and I sat on a court martial board which issued one of the first marijuana convictions in country. Marijuana and opium were rampant and easily obtained.

I also vividly remember monsoon season where it rained torrents daily for six months. I got used to letting my uniform dry on my body. Dry season was just the opposite six months where there was no rain and dust everywhere!

The TET offensive changed everything in Saigon. The enemy was everywhere, intertwined among us. It's said for six months prior to TET there wasn't a funeral in Saigon that didn't have weapons buried with it. The Viet Cong had dug a tunnel network joining all of Saigon's cemeteries. Needless to say, it was very chaotic and dangerous.

Some others of my most vivid memories of the war:

Mail call was always special. It was good to hear from home.

The music of the times played everywhere. Two songs I remember are "For What It's Worth" by Buffalo Springfield and "Fortunate Son" by Credence Clearwater Revival.

When it came time for me to leave Vietnam, I had to clear a hand receipt on which I was signed for over a million dollars' worth of equipment! Much to my dismay I was missing a jeep! My First Sargent encouraged me not to worry! He had a jeep flown in from up country over night and I was able to clear the hand receipt and come home!

The evil, heartbreaking, sad side of war for all sides. I heard of many of the atrocities but, fortunately, I didn't experience any.

Bob Hope inspired me!

Jane Fonda angered me!

My Ft. Monmouth roommate Rodney Alfano from Providence, RI was killed by a rocket attack. His name is on "The Wall."

Every Saturday evening, we would join a recording of Kate Smith singing "God bless America." Tears still well up as I think of it!

After returning home from the war, I attended the premier of the movie, "Platoon." As I watched veterans leave the theatre, some crying, I had a desire to run up and say to them, "Tell me your story."

In summary, as a Patriotic American Veteran, I realize how our total Armed Forces who fought in the Vietnam War operated as a balanced team. A team which *always* looked out for each other's back, from the Marines to the Army, Air Force, Navy, and yes, even the Coast Guard. We were a team! If our government had not let us down by interfering politically, I believe we would have ended that war much, much sooner with fewer casualties. Soldiers are trained to win.

As I left Vietnam out of Tan Son Nhut Air Base, I looked out the window of the plane and there was machine gun tracer fire in the jungle below. What an appropriate way to close this chapter of my life.

We won! Welcome Home! God bless the United States of America!

SONNY DELLINGER

Army — Medical Service Corp — Field Medical Assistant
Years of Military Service (Active and Reserve): August 1967 — August 1973
Unit Served with in Vietnam: HHC 1/503 Infantry — 173rd Airborne Brigade
Dates of Service in Vietnam: August 1968 — August 1969
Highest Rank Held: 1st LT
Place of Birth and Date: Annapolis, MD — 1945

COMBAT MEDICS — 68 "WHISKEY"

The name might be Farmer, Sturkie, Purvis, Gonzales, Swinson, Rainey, Vreeland, or Smith but from the moment you got the MOS 68W, you are "Doc." During my tour as a Medical Service Officer in Vietnam, Doc is "technically" assigned to the Medical Platoon, HQ Company, 1st Battalion 503rd Infantry, 173rd Airborne Brigade (Separate). In reality, Doc identifies himself as part of "Alpha," "Bravo," "Charlie," or "Delta," Company. That is where he spends the majority of the year in country.

It's Doc's job to treat the blisters, cuts, and bruises as he humps through the "boonies" with his Infantry Company. He also makes sure his men are taking their malaria prevention pills and trying to help maintain their general health. When it "hits the fan," at some point, Doc is there to treat wounded. He gets them stabilized so they can be picked up by a Medevac, sent to the Battalion Aid Station, and then on to the Hospital in Qui Nhon if required.

As Medical Platoon Leader for the 1/503rd, I was "technically" in charge of Doc, whether he was with the Infantry Company or back at LZ Uplift at the Battalion Aid Station. All of the Docs in my platoon were well-trained, including a number of them with Special Forces medical training.

As a general rule, as soon as the Medics got in-country they would be sent to the 173rd Brigade HQ, then on to one of the four Battalions like the 1/503rd at LZ Uplift. A week or so later, they would be assigned to an Infantry Company, depending on where they were needed. They would then spend about six months in and out of the field with the Infantry before they were brought back to the Battalion Aid Station at LZ Uplift for the balance of their tour.

Daily life at the Aid Station started with "sick call" for all the troops at the LZ. The medics assisted the doctor (the "real" one that actually had a medical degree) with any necessary treatments, shots, etc. Our doctor was a great guy from Arkansas and the man that had the final decisions when it came to medical issues. After sick call, the rest of the day was taken up with checking health concerns at the LZ and waiting for the next Medevac (Dust-Off) mission to bring casualties to the Aid Station.

We also met up with our Battalion Infantry companies in the field to conduct MEDCAPs (Medical Civilian Aid Program) — sick call for civilians in the local villages.

I recently read "Walk in My Combat Boots" by James Patterson and Matt Eversmann. Here's an excerpt from one of the stories told by a combat medic in Iraq: "Dealing with trauma on the battlefield, seeing limbs blown off by an IED, the amount of carnage and blood ... it's more than anything from a movie. Two Army soldiers have been torn apart by a blast. One is dead....

"The other is still alive. He's on his back, blinking up at the harsh Iraqi sun. I drop to my knees and begin to apply a tourniquet around the stump of his missing leg.

"His name, he tells me his name is ... and he says, 'I need to level with you, Doc.' He licks his lips, his eyes sliding to mine. 'Is my junk still there?'

"Gallows humor. It's the only thing that keeps us sane. 'Still there,' I tell him."

Oddly enough, I heard this question asked a number of times — in Vietnam — from casualties that came to our Aid Station with various wounds that might affect their manhood. GIs are still the same.

"Docs" that served in the 1/503rd were awarded a number of Bronze Stars and one Silver Star during my tour in Vietnam, plus each who worked in an Infantry unit on the ground earned a Combat Medic Badge. It is worn with the same proudness that Infantry Soldiers wear their Combat Infantryman Badge. Undoubtedly, they saved many lives back then and continue to do so in today's military.

THE COMBAT INFANTRYMAN BADGE

By Bob Babcock, B/1-22 Infantry, 4th Infantry Division

Following the excellent story above about the Combat Medic Badge, I am taking my prerogative as author of this book to explain the importance and prestige of the Combat Infantryman Badge. All branches of the military have medals, ribbons, and badges they award to their personnel. All of these are important to the individual who earned them. I respect them all, as do most military personnel.

With that said, there is one badge that stands above the others — worn on the uniform above all ribbons. That is the Combat Infantryman Badge. In my opinion as an Infantryman who has earned the CIB, the second most prestigious award behind the CIB is the Combat Medic Badge (CMB), per the previous story. The medics are living in the same conditions and are called on to treat sick and wounded while the Infantry is accomplishing its mission against enemy forces trying to destroy our Soldiers.

The Infantry Branch is the maneuver branch with the **mission to close with and destroy the enemy by means of fire and movement to defeat or capture him,** or repel his assault by fire, close combat, and counterattack. The Infantry is the only branch specifically designed to engage the enemy in direct ground combat.

The CIB and its non-combat contemporary, the Expert Infantryman Badge (EIB), were created in November 1943 during World War II to boost morale and increase the prestige of service in the Infantry. Specifically, it recognizes the inherent sacrifices of all infantrymen, and that they face a greater risk of being wounded or killed in action than any other military occupational specialties.

After the United States' declaration of war in 1941, the War Department had difficulty in recruiting soldiers into the Infantry branch in the case when men were given the opportunity to choose their branch of assignment. The morale of soldiers in the Infantry Branch remained low, namely because "of all Soldiers, it was recognized that the infantryman continuously operated under the worst conditions and performed a mission that was not assigned to any other Soldier or unit…the infantry, a small portion of the total Armed Forces, was suffering the most casualties while receiving the least public recognition."

On 27 October 1943, the War Department formally established the Combat Infantryman Badge (CIB) and the Expert Infantryman Badge (EIB) awards in Section I, War Department Circular 269:

The present war has demonstrated the importance of highly proficient, tough, hard, and aggressive infantry, which can be obtained only by developing a high degree of individual all-around proficiency on the part of every infantryman. As a means of attaining the high standards desired and to foster esprit de corps in infantry units; the Expert Infantryman and the Combat Infantryman badges are established for infantry personnel.

MOREOVER, WAR DEPARTMENT CIRCULAR 269 STIPULATED:

"…only one of these badges will be worn at one time" and "the Combat Infantryman badge is the highest award"; the awarding of the CIB was officially authorized with an executive order dated 15 November 1943; later, on 30 June 1944, the U.S. Congress approved an extra ten dollars in monthly pay to every infantryman awarded the CIB—excepting commissioned officers.

The World War II regulations did not formally prescribe a specific combat service period establishing the infantryman's eligibility for being awarded a Combat Infantryman Badge, thus, in 1947, the U.S. government implemented a policy authorizing the retroactive awarding of the Bronze Star Medal to World War II veteran soldiers who had been awarded the Combat Infantryman Badge, because the CIB was awarded only to soldiers who had borne combat duties befitting the recognition conferred by a Bronze Star Medal. Both awards required a commander's recommendation and a citation in the pertinent orders. General Marshall initiated this after Medal of Honor recipient Major Charles W.

Davis noted to him that: "It would be wonderful if someone could design a badge for every infantryman who faces the enemy, every day and every night, with so little recognition."

War Department Circular 105, dated 13 March 1944 amended WD Circular 269. Page 2, paragraph IV. BADGE — Section 1, Circular No. 269 War Department, 1943, is amended by adding paragraph 8 as follows:

8. Retroactive award of Expert and Combat Infantryman badges may be awarded to any infantryman who, on or after 6 December 1941, has established eligibility and been recommended for such award under the provisions of paragraph 2b or paragraph 3b. The Expert Infantryman badge may be awarded under paragraph 2a, only to those infantrymen who have established eligibility and been recommended for such award on or after 27 October 1943.

From the beginning, Army leaders have taken care to retain the badge for the unique purpose for which it was established, and to prevent the adoption of any other badge that would lower its prestige. At the close of World War II, the largest war in which armor and artillery played key roles in the ground campaigns, a review was conducted of the CIB criteria with consideration being given to creating either additional badges or authorizing the badge to cavalry and armor units. The review noted that any change in policy would detract from the prestige of the badge.

A soldier must meet the following requirements to be awarded the Combat Infantryman Badge:

Be an infantryman satisfactorily performing infantry duties

Assigned to an infantry unit during such time as the unit is engaged in active ground combat

Actively participate in such ground combat

In developing the CIB, the War Department did not dismiss out of hand or ignore the contributions of other branches. Their vital contributions to the overall war effort were certainly noted, but it was decided that other awards and decorations were sufficient to recognize their contributions. From the beginning, Army leaders have taken care to retain the badge for the unique purpose for which it was established and to prevent adoption of any other badge which would lower its prestige.

Keith Nightingale (Colonel, retired) in his book *A Soldier Looks Back: Memories and Reflections of a Combat Veteran from Normandy to Afghanistan* gives his thoughts on those who have earned the CIB:

"Within a relatively small community of those that have been shot at on behalf of our nation, the Combat Infantry Badge (CIB) may rank as the most prestigious award. The valor awards are fine but the people who have been engaged in warfare know that the award is a matter of luck, timing, and good writing. The one award that bears no vicarious aspects is the CIB. Those that wear it are truly in a brotherhood of shared deprivation, danger, and service to a cause greater than any single person. It is a badge of honor and recognized by all as the signification that the wearer has seen the tiger, endured the unendurable, and been part of something greater than himself. It is the ultimate personal and associative honor among those who lay their lives on the line for this Nation."

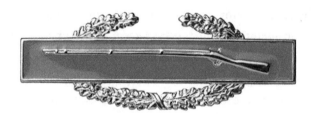

GLENN PEYTON CARR

US Army—Aviator

Dates of Military Service: 1958 to 1986

Unit Served with in Vietnam: 213th Assault Support Helicopter Company
(Chinook); B Troop 7th Squadron 17th Cavalry Regiment (Air)

Dates Served in Vietnam: XO & CO 213th May 1967 to May 1968; CO B Troop
7/17, XO 52nd Combat Aviation Battalion 1971

Highest Rank Held: Lt. Colonel (O-5)

Place and Date of Birth: Shawnee, OK—1934

MY MOST TERRIFYING THIRTY MINUTES IN TWO YEARS OF COMBAT

I think this occurred in the last weeks of TET '68. The 213th Chinook
Company had been moving a lot of artillery around in the 1st Infantry
Division area. We had finished a long day's mission around 9:30 in the
evening. After refueling at Loc Ninh, we took off for what we thought
would be an easy and enjoyable night flight back to home base at Phu Loi.

Heading down Highway 19, which in this case barely meets the
description of a dirt road, there were infantry units securing the road,
and the forced landing areas are better than in the jungle. About fifteen
minutes into the flight, my copilot (Peter Pilot) said, "Sir it's snowing." I
responded, "Can't be, It's too hot." I thought, being well above 3000 feet,
"Just what is the temperature?" It was showing 15 degrees on the OAT
(outside air temperature). I reconfirmed the gage was in Celsius so that
would mean about 60F outside. That settled the snow problem.

I took my glove off and captured a few of the flakes. My God! This is
aluminum shavings! I called for the Crew Chief to come forward to confirm my diagnosis. Which he did. We were just west of Quan Loi about
eight miles. I told Peter Pilot to make a very slow turn into Quan Loi.
Make no abrupt control inputs, especially with the thrust lever. We have
something coming apart up there, and I didn't want to aggravate the
situation with abrupt or unnecessary loads. I got on the radio to Quan
Loi tower and declared an emergency and requested a running landing
so we could stop in the large staging area at the far end of the runway.

I told the tower that we had aluminum shavings coming from the forward head, which could mean anything up to the possibility of blade dephasing, and personnel should not be anywhere near the aircraft until the blades stopped turning. Tell the fire crews to approach as close as needed but stay in or behind their equipment until the blades are safe.

With that taken care of, I began to monitor all the gauges to see if I could determine any trend—all was OK. If the transmission was not the problem, what else could it be? Could it be the drive shaft that powers the forward transmission and keeps the blades in phase? That's when stark terror set in. If that shaft failed, those blades would definitely dephase. They would literally throw a scrap-iron fit and it would all be over. We would be a gigantic aluminum beer can with 2,000 lbs. of fuel on board falling back to earth.

To my knowledge, in the early development of the Chinook, several dephasings occurred. No one has survived a dephasing at altitude. I believe some have survived dephasing on the ground.

After that chilling thought process, we are now on very short final to Quan Loi. Upon touch down, that's where I, the aircraft commander, takes over the brakes and power steering and thrust for the roll out. Peter Pilot holds the cyclic flight control and operates the radio. We did an emergency shutdown and quickly left the aircraft.

When the rotors came to a stop, we climbed on the front transmission and began pulling panels. As soon as the Crew chief pulled up the first section on the tunnel cover, exposing the drive shaft, there it was. A bright shinny groove in the drive shaft about six inches from the U joint at the transmission. The groove was about 5/16 inch wide and 1/16 inch deep. Between the shaft and the tunnel floor was a 9/16-inch box end wrench wedged against the shaft. Looking thru the U joint you could see inside the shaft where the wrench had deformed the shaft inward. There was total silence and trembling at what catastrophe had *almost* happened.

I would note here that the maintenance manual says for the first eighteen inches on each end of the drive shaft that scratches, dents, cuts, and nicks will not exceed five thousandth of an inch in depth. That's

.005." The *Almighty* was not in the copilot's seat. He was on the jump seat with his hands on both pilots' shoulders!!!

The next morning, our maintenance aircraft arrived with parts needed and an expert, the Boeing Technical Representative that was stationed with us. When viewing the drive shaft, the Rep was astonished beyond words. He couldn't believe it held together fifteen to eighteen minutes after discovering the aluminum flakes. He later said, "To say it almost failed is a bit misleading. It should have failed maybe an hour before you landed." He had the shaft boxed to send back to Boeing for analysis. We later found that the wrench had been in the tunnel all day. Most likely and thankfully not against the drive shaft.

My Crew Chief had his 9/16 wrench, but it was found that a mechanic who worked on the aircraft the night before was missing his 9/16" wrench. He became so distraught and suicidal over the situation that the Flight Surgeon had him hospitalized for therapy for about a month. He later became OK and returned to duty.

Obviously, our maintenance officer reviewed and strengthened our tool control procedures as well as designating a final person to review the work area after the work was signed off.

Had it not been for the *Almighty* and the *Almost* I would not be here writing this.

TERRY GARLOCK

Army — Helicopter Pilot
Dates of Military Service (Active and Reserve): Jun 1968 to Dec 1971
Unit Served with in Vietnam: 334th Attack Helicopter Company — Bien Hoa
Dates Served in Vietnam: 1969
Highest Rank: Warrant Officer — W2

LIFESAVERS REMEMBERED

A few years ago, I took my daughter's car to the annual inspection station. In a short line of cars, I noticed on the rear window of the truck in front of me a sticker saying, "Combat Medic."

Since we had a little time to wait, I walked up and tapped on his driver window. When he lowered his window, I saw a man much younger than me in Army camos and I boldly asked with a smile, "Are you a real combat medic?" He said yes.

I told him, "There's something you should know." He asked what I meant, and I told him the short version, "The guys you patched up in combat will think about you with gratitude for the rest of their life. Some of them will wish they could find you to shake your hand."

He asked if I had been in combat and I told him I was old enough to be his Dad which was too kind to myself, that I flew Cobra helicopters in the Vietnam War, that some of my missions were flying gun cover for Dustoff picking up wounded, and when I was shot down, in a turnabout, Dustoff came to rescue me.

I told him I knew many other guys who wish they could find the Medic who kept them alive, or the Dustoff crew that picked them up, or the hospital staff that treated them, to thank them personally for getting them through the meat grinder.

Nick Donvito from Syracuse, NY was shot up bad in thick jungle near Nui Ba Din and presumed dead at first. Nick says his tour in Vietnam will never be complete until he finds the Dustoff crew that hovered not far from the firefight still in process and pulled him up through the jungle trees in a basket on a hoist wire.

Nick asked me to help him search for his Dustoff crew, so I posted a message on the Dustoff Association website. At the same time, I posted details of my own shootdown in the Iron Triangle, not far from Cu Chi. I got no response on Nick, but I did get a response from Pete Atack in Rhode Island, who said he was flying the Huey guns Fire Team that covered Dustoff picking me up that day, and that he took 22 hits in his own firefight keeping the enemy off us while Ron Hefner and I were loaded on the Dustoff. Our crash was hard, and I guess a pile of Cobra wreckage was memorable, especially since Pete had the task of destroying the remains to keep ammo, weapons, and radios out of enemy hands.

Finding a particular Dustoff crew from Vietnam is close to impossible since they flew so many missions, too busy keeping their brothers alive to keep detailed records. But every day, a number of our wounded think about them, wishing they could find them to buy them a beer.

It wasn't just the Medics and Dustoff crews. Search and Rescue (SAR) crews like Sandy A-1E's and Jolly Greens, who risked everything to find and pick up downed pilots, many in Laos, will never be able to buy their own drinks around pilots who flew bombing missions to the North.

Scattered around South Vietnam, doctors and nurses and orderlies in hospitals worked feverishly every day to physical and emotional exhaustion to keep a steady stream of wounded alive. I doubt they realize how much their patients think of them with gratitude even into old age, and I know the same thing happened in Iraq and continues now in Afghanistan.

RJ Del Vecchio in North Carolina was a Marine combat photographer. In his first hump in the steep mountain jungles of Vietnam, in the sudden violence of his first firefight, he found out up close how Medics do their frantic work under the worst of conditions when they hear the shout, "Medic!" and dash into the inferno to do their job, no matter how much they want to dig a hole and hide. Del set aside his camera to help a Medic work on a Marine with a sucking chest wound, and he will never forget how hard they tried, or how the Medic beat the ground with his fists when the young Marine died, and how a man seemed to become heavier when dead as they switched off carrying his body in the steep hills.

Wayne Franz lived next door to me in Peachtree City, GA. He was trained as a Medic at Fort Sam Houston Texas. When he arrived in Vietnam and was sent to a Dustoff unit, he expected some orientation and training. The Sergeant he reported to in the Orderly Room told him to drop his duffle bag in the corner, pointed to a helicopter running up on a pad and told Wayne to hustle out there because they had a mission and were waiting on a Medic. Wayne ran to jump aboard with apprehension since he had never been on a helicopter, and with no handholds feared he would fall out as it jerked off the pad and made tight turns at treetop level to avoid enemy fire, then after a little while suddenly flared to a stop and touchdown in an LZ where ground troops ran out to push aboard two of their wounded on litters.

Wayne didn't have more than a couple seconds to wonder what to do when the aircraft leapt off the ground to get out of there, zigging and zagging then popping up just over the trees, while in the back Wayne applied bandages and pressure to stop bleeding, trying to remember his training on IVs and pleading with God not to let either of these men die before they made it to the hospital.

He was so busy, before he knew it, they were on the hospital pad and the ground crew took the litters to rush the wounded to the ER. Wayne stepped off the helicopter with blood dripping off him, wondering what the hell just happened. That was his first mission, and they usually flew 3-4-5 a day unless it was urgent enough to fly more.

Norm McDonald grew up in Utah. When he was a young hippie who wanted nothing to do with war, he was drafted and found himself a machine gunner in Vietnam since he was big and could easily carry the heavy M-60. Near the end of his tour, Norm took a large and very sharp mortar shrapnel fragment deep into his foot through his boot. In the dirty, warm humidity, his treated wound turned to gangrene and he was shipped to a hospital.

They cut out the infected tissue, left the wound open to heal, and changed the minimal dressing daily. Norm said there was one nurse who was so pretty he couldn't help staring, and while changing the dressing on his foot one day, when she tugged to loosen it, a small artery tore and he had a tiny fountain of blood spurting out of his foot with each heartbeat. The nurse freaked and called over a doctor, who worked on Norm's foot in what he said was a painful repair. An orderly cleaned up the blood splatter all over his bed and the floor, then the pretty nurse came back, hugging him and holding on for a while, tearfully telling him she was so sorry. The pain had subsided by then and Norm thought, "Well, that was worth it!"

Norm said there was also a nurse from Utah, and they talked some about home. One evening down near the nurse station she was with doctors struggling to stabilize a new patient when Norm dozed off. When he woke in the middle of the night, that bed was gone. He figured that patient had died, and he could hear the nurse quietly crying. Norm worked himself into his wheelchair, grabbed the guitar someone kept in the ward and wheeled down to check on her. He parked himself next to her, she leaned her head on his shoulder and they didn't speak a word while he played some rifts and chords and pieces of melodies for her until she stood up to get back to work.

Donna Rowe lives in Marietta, GA. She was an Army Captain at 3rd Field Hospital in Vietnam, in charge of the triage unit. Donna is not very tall, but she is a very large bundle of dynamite, and she ran a tight ship. She is proud of her record of never losing a patient while they were in the care of her triage unit. She says a patient might have died on the helicopter before they arrived, they might have died in surgery or from complications later, but her staff moved heaven and earth to keep them alive and they never lost a single one during her year.

Many years ago, there was a TV program on PBS about American women in Vietnam. One nurse spoke about the daily strain of working on "beautiful, torn up young men," and she could have been talking about any war. She said the disappointing part was when she went home at the end of her tour, nobody cared or wanted to hear what she had been through because the American public had learned Vietnam was a dirty word, a subject not discussed in polite company. She said she tried to talk about it with her parents, but even her own mother didn't want to hear about her experience and changed the subject to cookies or the church social as if she were still a child.

She said with tears streaming down her face, "So thanks for asking, for having this forum to talk about it, because every one of us was deeply changed by what we did. It was important and we should talk about it."

For me it was 50+ years ago. My hard crash crushed lumbar vertebrae, and besides terrible pain in my guts, my legs and a few other things didn't work. Dustoff took me to a small hospital nearby at Lai Khe where their quick exam and X-rays told them to send me by helicopter to the big hospital at Long Binh for surgery. I remember the surgeon, taking a moment from his habitual hurried walk, to stoop down to my litter level to tell me with a touch of compassion that they would do their best to fix me up, and I remember a nurse sitting with me while holding my hand when the pain was really bad, but it was too soon to give me another pain shot.

They put me back together and over time helped me learn to walk again.

As the years pass and hair turns grey, these memories seem to become even more important. I am just one of many thousands who remember with gratitude and an occasional fantasy of finding those in the life-saving business who touched us in a way we will never forget.

STEVE MOSIER

USAF: Fighter Pilot, Squadron Commander, Chief Checkmate Group, HQ
USAF
Dates of Military Service – Active Duty: September 1966 to July 1993
Unit Served with in Vietnam: 433rd Tactical Fighter Squadron, 8th Tactical
Fighter Wing, Ubon Royal Thai Air Base, Thailand
Dates you were in Vietnam: August 1968 – August 1969
Highest Rank Held: Colonel (O-6)
Place of Birth and Year: Kansas City, Missouri – 1943

HOOT GIBSON – THE SONS OF SATAN'S ANGELS

Not a senior officer, nor a strategist of note, Colonel Ralph D. "Hoot"
Gibson deserves serious consideration for inclusion in any discussion
of the air war in Southeast Asia. Hoot was my first operational squadron commander, leading the 433rd Tactical Fighter Squadron, Satan's
Angels, out of Ubon, Thailand. As background, the 433rd was one of
the premier squadrons in the Southeast Asia operation. Flying first C
models and finishing with the F-4D it was a multi-role operation. Air
to Air kills—the Angels had 12 MiG Kills, including ones by Robin
Olds and Bill Kirk. It was one of the first to employ "smart" weapons,
including the Walleye glide bomb and the Paveway Laser Guided Bomb
(LGB), dropping over 1,600 two-thousand-pound bombs—a majority
hitting within 10' of their target—often bridges, bulldozers, and AAA
sites—as a guy, said, "Not bad for pig iron and tritonal."

The Angels flew day and night, delivering bombs, CBUs (Cluster
Bomb Units), rockets, and napalm against high value targets (and sadly
some targets of no value at all—but designated by powers that were in
Saigon, Hawaii, and Washington (if you've read Catch 22—and we all
had—you know what I mean—"Men, I want a good pattern") in Laos
and North Vietnam, and supported the Wolf Fast Fac Mission with
aircrews and jets. It wasn't always pretty—losses tallied 31 to SAMS,
MiGs, AAA, and just plain flying into the ground over nearly eight years
of continuous combat with weather, treacherous terrain, and an enemy

that was deadly, and given some significant advantages due to the political tomfoolery in the seats of power in Washington.

I'll always remember Hoot, with a cigar clenched in his teeth and shooter glasses on, taking charge of any and every situation. Joining the AF in 1943, he didn't see combat in WWII but was one of America's first Jet Aces in Korea, scoring five kills on his ninety missions. Later he led the USAF Thunderbirds, showing off Airpower to thousands of kids that later became fighter pilots—I was one. In the air over Vietnam and Laos, he was a fearless leader, always taking care of his wingmen, using his Phantom to its fullest capability. On the ground he was a mentor and teacher in all things. I remember Hoot admonishing a young pilot offering a light for *the* cigar, "A man always lights his own stogie."

These were the days before Tom Cruise and Top Gun, where everyone has a call-sign/nick name. We had ones that were earned by exposure of habits and performance—there was Padre, Evil, Phineas, Mr. Earl, Hoss, Fast Eddy, Ghost, Horney Billy—all earned in the air, in the squadron, or perhaps through exposure to the local Ville. In the air, radio calls were disciplined and serious—no chatting, taunting, or criticism—that came later in the debrief or at the bar, perhaps during a sockey game—a hybrid sport where a crushed beer can on a watered-down floor was used as a playing field by grown men willing to get bruised, sprained, and required to pay for damages to the bar furniture before the break of dawn.

The "Angels" were full of talent and energy. Hoot controlled it in the air and on the ground—often stepping in with senior leaders to defend his young warriors, at the same time disciplining them in the best way possible—off the schedule and on the duty desk—thinking about things. Effective and not career threatening. I count at least seven of his "guys' that made stars, and at least a score having very successful careers as colonels in the fighter community. As a young aviator, I really didn't appreciate Hoot's style and his impact on careers—in combat and for years later. I didn't know how fortunate I was to have been "one of old Hoot Gibson's boys, mean as he could be" until later. I learned few commanders were remembered in ballads. Hoot built skilled leaders, kept young guys alive, and seeded the Air Force with talent for years to come. I was lucky. He was one of a few that matter, and many prospered in the art of fighter aviation because of Hoot. He deserves to be remembered.

(Credit to Dick Jonas for the ballad, one among many about the Robin's Wolf-pack and Satan's Angels)

BILL HACKETT

USMC—Combat Engineer Officer

Dates of Military Service (Active and Reserve): 1968 to 1988

Units Served with in Vietnam: 1st Engineer Bn, 1st Marine Div; 9th MAB, 1st Marine Div.

Date in Vietnam: April 1969 to May 1970; April to May 1975

Highest Rank Held: Lt. Colonel (O-5)

Place of Birth and Year: Griffin, GA—1946

MEMORIES OF A MARINE COMBAT ENGINEER OFFICER

After completion of two summers of Marine Corps Platoon Leaders Class training and completion of my senior year at North Georgia College, I graduated, was commissioned, got married, and commenced my Marine Corps career. First, TBS (The Basic School) which all Marine Officers attend, then Engineer School and Vietnam Advisors School, after which I finally received my orders to Vietnam.

I traveled to Travis Air Force Base and then on to Vietnam. First stop, Okinawa. Very soon we found out that an attack by the VC on a major ammo dump near Da Nang caused all flights into Da Nang to be cancelled. Ordnance was scattered all over the area. We were stranded in Okinawa before we even got started.

My best friend was Tom Hayes. Tom's father was an Air Force Colonel and CO of the only squadron of SR 71 Blackbird aircraft. Tom found out his dad would be flying the C-141 chase bird accompanying a Blackbird flight to Okinawa. So here we are, two LTs at Kadena Air Base, getting picked up by an Air Force Captain in a staff car and taken onto the runway to observe the SR-71 landing and Tom's dad landing the C-141.

We followed the SR-71 taxiing to a standalone hanger. Doors immediately went down. We got up close to the Blackbird inside the hangar. It seemed like everyone had special identification badges except us. We just had silly grins. It still amazes me to this day how special that was. It was 1969 and the SR-71 was Top Secret. It was an unforgettable experience, and it gave us a thrill before our departure to RVN.

After six days, we finally got manifested and departed from Okinawa. We landed in Da Nang, Vietnam. My battalion headquarters was located near the Marble Mountain Marine Corps Air Facility and adjacent to the NSA hospital. I joined my platoon at Cau Do, about five miles south of the Battalion. My platoon had been without a Lieutenant for about five months and had a staff Sergeant running it. It took a few days to turn a few things around.

Easing my way into being their leader was quite a shock, but they looked like a good team. I was really glad to hit the ground running. The funny thing was what occurred the second day. I was informed by one of my squad leaders I had to pass an "engineer test" of my hand and eye coordination. The engineer test involved me getting on my knees, removing my finely starched USMC cover, blindfolding me, and handed me a hatchet and a block of wood.

Blindfolded, I had to prove I had good hand-eye coordination. To prepare I reached out and felt where the block of wood was. I was to hit it five times. I felt like I had it lined up just right and they gave me the go ahead. I was so confident and felt like I had hit it all five times. They said, "Well, you passed, Lieutenant." I took the blindfold off and looked down. They had put my perfectly starched cover in the place of the block of wood and I had chopped it to pieces. They acted like that was the funniest thing ever seen. Anyway, it was good way to break the ice and step in.

I quickly got into the daily routine of leading every morning with two road sweeps, each going 2-4 miles away from our home base. We met up with another sweep team from our company, always altering the meetup location; we never met at the same place. We did not find mines every day but frequently enough to keep the sweep team on alert. We were also under frequent sniper fire.

The two mine sweep teams were very deliberate. The man with the mine detector was called the "ear." The backup man with a bayonet to probe a hit was called the "finger." The third man carried the C-4. You were doing your job when you got a hit from the mine detector and found something in the road that could be blown up with a quarter pound block of C-4. A small hole was sufficient if nothing substantial was found, but if a large mine was detonated, it required engineer equipment to come out to patch the road. That was how we started our day, every day, for about 5-6 months for me.

After that daily task, we began construction projects throughout our AO. We built a lot of bunkers in different locations around the division AO. We built five connected 16 by 32 bunkers for a triage area at the First Medical Battalion. My platoon also operated the water point and the shower unit for the Infantry Battalion, 2nd Bn, 1st Marine Regiment, which we supported.

It was fairly routine work until we participated on a combat operation called Pipestone Canyon that was conducted south of Da Nang. An area called Go Noi Island, an 'island' created where the river forked and circulated on both sides of this body of land. We route marched for two days to get to our objective. The Air Force conducted numerous arc light strikes on Go Noi for several days prior. To feel the ground shake that way under your feet...what an awesome amount of power and destruction!

Another thing I remember about this operation was crossing Route 4 on the way to Go Noi Island. We bivouacked at night with defensive positions and security. We were moving as a battalion of four companies plus headquarters. Around midnight, we heard the loudest screaming you've ever heard in your life. It was a foreign voice but we couldn't make out the language. All hands were on high alert.

The next morning as we got on the move again, we came upon a ROK (Republic of Korea) Marine compound. They were occupying a four-sided compound with two-man fighting positions and a bunker at each corner and lookout tower in the center. Every four hours, the OD for the ROKs would go up in the tower and yell down to each post asking if "all secure." It was all in Korean language and we didn't know what was going on. The Koreans didn't even have protective wire. I think they were confident that the VC weren't going to mess with them.

On Go Noi Island, our battalion mission was to provide security for a joint-service land clearing company. Their mission was to clear cut the entire landscape. Large trees as well as lots of bunkers that needed to be taken down. When unexploded ordnance was found, a flare would notify one of my engineers. He would blow the item in place. One memorable task I received was when my Battalion CO summoned me to the CP one night. There were several wet areas that the bulldozers couldn't get to without getting bogged down, leaving many trees standing. The CO asked me if I could get my engineers with chainsaws to clear those trees. I laughed to myself because I knew in the entire country we probably didn't have a single chainsaw that would run, but I told him we would take care of it.

With one of my sergeants, we came up with a plan to get some Bangalore torpedoes and daisy-chain connect them with C-4 det cord, and then we could blow a charge and become basically like a weed-eater taking the trees down. We ordered four cases of Bangalore torpedoes—each case had 10 pieces, each 5 feet long. We had plenty of raw material to get this job done. When the helicopter brought an external load, we discovered it was a full pallet load of Bangalores instead of four cases; the load delivered was 40 cases.

I went to the S4 and asked, "Can you put these on the logistics track?" We had two amtracs move along with the command track and a logistics track had the beans, bullets, and bandages. He looked at me like I was crazy and said, "No way do I have space for the excess." We used 10 cases and exploded the rest as we had no way to take them with us.

I participated in another op named Operation Durham Peak in the Que Son Mountains. Our Battalion hadn't been operating in the mountains. It was a new environment, but we adapted quickly. All resupply was by helo. A CH-46 Sea Knight with an external load of 81mm mortar ammo dropped it before making it to the drop zone. I did not see the load drop, but other people had. Estimates were "probably 2+ miles away 'line-of-sight,' in the mountains."

Observers thought they had pinpointed the site and the Weapons Platoon began shooting rounds from a 106mm Recoilless rifle, attempting to achieve detonation. After no success, I was tasked to take a patrol to locate the ammo and blow it in place. It became a futile two-day search following a line-of-sight route through the mountains. We never found any of the ammo. I am sure these mortar rounds, even though probably damaged, were used against us as booby traps.

After my seven-month tour as 2nd Platoon commander, I rotated back to my Company CP and took over duties as Company XO. Even though I had attended the Army Vietnam Advisor school, I never had an opportunity to use that training.

One day our Battalion Chaplain asked me to build some wooden cribs using pallets. It was an unusual request for sure. So, I asked him the purpose. He had visited the China Beach PX and the PX manager found out he was from an engineer unit.

The PX manager told him that he needed the containers for beer and soda. Most of our supplies came through there, including tons of pallets of beer and soda. Back in those days they came in metal cans and when left out the rain, the cardboard wrapping would disintegrate. The loose cans then lay on the ground and became rusty and dented. He wanted those cribs so that Vietnamese workers could cull the bad ones that were rusted or dented. He could not sell them.

For giving him the wooden cribs, the manager would give us the damaged goods. It was a no-brainer, as we used scrap material. We delivered them in a dump truck. Each time we made a drop-off, we left with a five-ton dump truck loaded with loose cans of beer and soda, with some dents and small parts of rust, but totally intact. We would give them to the troops. One day I remember we were driving down to our base camp and came to a tank unit guarding a bridge.

We used to bring a company out of the bush, thereby giving them a break and assigned them to guard a strategic bridge. These troops were glad to be getting a break from the bush, but the worst part of it was they were bored. The second part was they were dusty and dirty. We would pull up and say, "Hey guys, want some beer?" Their reaction would be priceless. They looked at us like we had stepped off the moon. My troops would throw sandbags full of beer and soda to them. The troops would put the sandbags in the river just to get a slight chill. They were incredibly happy to get that surprise, which was sort of fun for us. I wish I had photos of that experience.

Near the end of my thirteen-month tour, I got notified by my Battalion XO to pack, as I was going home early. He said I got a great job for you to embark a company back to the States. We were downsizing and sending some units back and this unit was from the 5th Marine Division. There was a small amount of equipment and gear going back. I was a CO of a company that embarked aboard ship to the States.

The ship we boarded was the USS New Orleans. In addition to units on board, there was a draft of Marines also going home that way. Leaving 'Nam early was good, but looking at a nineteen-day voyage was not encouraging. Logistically, I was not in good shape. I had always been told to never part with your pay record when you're in transit from one location to another. Officers could hand carry their pay record. I went to the dispersing office with my orders to draw my pay record. There I found out my record was pulled with the draft and shipped back to the States.

I had very little money (Military Payment Certificates which I converted) and I couldn't draw partial pay without my pay record. The New Orleans was an LPH (landing platform helicopter) craft, with an open flight deck (no helos and just a few vehicles) and an open hangar deck so it was perfect for taking a load of troops back to the world. Spending the time cruising home provided us a great opportunity to decompress. The Navy provided movies and bingo games for the troops. The ship did not have perfect communication with the States back then, but we did find out the air traffic controllers were on strike and many airlines were down. Some of us became friends on the ship and made plans to rent cars in California to drive to the east coast.

When a deployed Navy ship comes home, it is an exciting experience. I knew full well that no one was going be waiting for me on the dock at North Island. But as we arrived, the Navy really does it right as they had bands, balloons, and fire ships shooting water up in the air. All hands were standing on the on the deck waiting to get off the ship.

After disembarking, we made it to a "cattle car." We had a very good Marine driver, but you can imagine that being on a ship for 19 days and then hitting the ground and then getting on a cattle car going through

San Diego traffic up to Camp Pendleton (Las Pulgas) was an unforgettable, crazy trip. Since we were arriving on orders as a deployed unit, I had to process the equipment, transfer the troops, sign over the equipment, and deactivate the unit.

Initially I was told it would take 30 days to get all that accomplished, but this mustang Captain was able to get all the paperwork done and I was able to get out of there within about 12 hours and caught a plane to Atlanta.

I had a good tour with some interesting episodes to remember. Thanks for letting me share them. Semper Fidelis and God Bless the ones who did not return.

LTJG JIM DICKSON

U.S. Navy — Operations Intelligence Division Officer (Combat Information Center) — Officer of the Deck Underway

Dates of Military Service (Active and Reserves): 1967 to 1977

Unit Served with in Vietnam: USS Ticonderoga (CVA-14)

Dates in Vietnam: Jan 1968 to Aug 1968; Jan 1969 to Jul 1969

Highest Rank Held: Lieutenant (O-3)

Place of Birth and Year: Lancaster, PA — 1944

YANKEE STATION — VIETNAM WAR — PART 2

Editor's Note: Yankee Station — Vietnam War — Part 1 is included in the first I'm Ready to Talk book.

I served aboard the aircraft carrier USS Ticonderoga (CVA—14) for both the 1968 and 1969 deployments to Yankee Station during the Vietnam War as Operations Intelligence Division Officer for about 60 men who worked in Combat Information Center (CIC)—the operations center on most navy ships—and Officer of the Deck Underway.

There were normally three attack aircraft carriers on Yankee Station called Task Force 77 that conducted air operations for twelve hours each day—one from noon to midnight, another from midnight to noon, and another one during daylight hours from 0600 to 1800 which provided 24-hour coverage and additional effort during daylight hours when sorties were most effective.

Many records were made during the 1968 deployment, including the launch of over 16,500 planes from the two catapults and more than 9,000 tons of ordnance dropped on enemy targets. On one occasion, there were 20 A-4 Skyhawk jet planes launched in seven minutes and 45 seconds—an average of one every 24 seconds and six seconds faster than what the Navy considers outstanding. On two occasions, more than 170 aircraft were launched in one day, including the record of 175 on April 5, 1968.

The only Russian MiG encountered by pilots from the USS Ticonderoga (CVA-14) during five deployments to Yankee Station during the Vietnam War was shot down over North Vietnam by Lieutenant Commander John B. Nichols III on July 9, 1968. His request to do a high speed—low level fly by with his F-8 Crusader upon return to the ship was approved by the Commanding Officer Captain Norman K. McInnis and was done very low and upside down just off the port side of the flight deck to the loud cheers of many shipmates.

There were regular underway replenishments called UNREPS from different types of ships for different supplies—oil and aviation fuel, ammunition, and food supplies. The 1968 deployment involved 183 days at sea and 147 UNREPS—another record. Ammunition was brought aboard at an average rate of 141.2 tons per hour—the fastest rate was 255 tons per hour. The UNREPS would be on a preset course called Romeo Corpen after approaching the supply ship from astern (behind) and be done at a speed of 10—12 knots, a distance of about 120—150 feet, and last about 90 minutes on average. The supply ships would always be located to our starboard or right side and our ship to their port or left side.

During the 1969 deployment, the UNREPS were done less frequently with the availability of larger replenishment ships that carried all types of supplies. Sometimes during UNREPS, individuals would be transferred between ships on the boatswain chair—often the person would get wet as the chair hit the ocean waves caused by slack in the transfer line from the bank suction that would tend to move the ships slightly closer together—not the best way to come aboard.

The number 14 was the order of the day on May 14, 1968 when the USS Firedrake (AE-14) provided simultaneous replenishment for the USS Ticonderoga (CVA-14) located off her port side and the guided missile destroyer USS Buchanan (DDG-14) located off her starboard side. The first line went over at 14:14 hours and the aerial photographer was in his 14th year of service.

Something highly unusual happened one day during the 1968 deployment in the middle of flight operations—a sailor decided to jump overboard for no particular reason. Everything was ordered to stop while the rescue helicopter that was always airborne during flight operations quickly retrieved the sailor. He was immediately brought up to the bridge dripping wet to see Captain McInnis for a 10 second conversation that ended with his being sent to the brig for 30 days to reflect on why he jumped overboard after not knowing the answer to that question.

While life aboard an attack aircraft carrier during time of war was very serious, there were some lighter moments, and this article ends with a few stories about them.

After the midnight watch was over each night about 0400 hours, officers from departments throughout the ship would usually have breakfast in the wardroom and then go to their quarters. Many went to the Junior Officers Bunkroom where alcoholic libations were sometimes discretely served, even though against U.S. Navy regulations.

One early morning during nonflying hours after the midnight watch and some libations, it was decided to have a football game on the flight deck. LTJG Howard Mackay was a former lineman for the famous football coach Bo Schembechler. He appointed himself quarterback for one of the teams and on the very first play of the game widely overthrew the receiver—the ball went into the ocean to promptly end the game.

The trip to Vietnam involved going from Pearl Harbor in Hawaii after training exercises near there to Yokosuka Naval Base not far from Tokyo. During this long part of the trip across the Pacific Ocean, we would always encounter a Russian plane called the "Bear"—a large four—engine turboprop powered bomber. Intelligence information would be received in Combat Information Center when the plane departed from somewhere in Siberia—and the course of the Russian "Bear" was plotted on the large scrub board for aircraft. There would be two F-8 Crusader fighter jets launched to intercept the "Bear" and escort the Russian bomber that would always circle our ship to the waves and loud greetings of many sailors before returning home.

During the 1969 deployment, there were photos taken of one of the F-8 Crusader pilots tipping the Russian "Bear" pilots with a can of Budweiser—and another photo of him giving them the finger—official U.S. Navy photos!

One day in early January 1968, during the training exercises near Hawaii, involved making scenes for the epic movie—Tora! Tora! Tora!—a film later released in 1970 about the infamous attack of Pearl Harbor on December 7, 1941. It was somewhat strange to see the takeoff and landing of Japanese Zero airplanes from our U.S. Navy aircraft carrier.

One of the most colorful individuals aboard for both deployments was Commander G.W. Govan—head of Strike Operations. When the ship periodically returned to Subic Bay in the Philippines, he would keep up his required hours as a pilot by flying Filipino stewards from nearby Naval Air Station Cubi Point to their homes throughout the country. The stewards provided a variety of hospitality services for officers at the time such as food, laundry, and bed preparation. As a result of his flying many stewards to their homes, Commander Govan had what amounted to his own entourage of private servants—nothing was too good for him, and his service was impeccable.

Each time we departed Yankee Station for rest and relaxation somewhere, there were so-called Zoning Inspections after the clean-up of department spaces throughout the ship, followed by reports at a meeting of the officers who conducted the inspections. Commander Govan would always give the report for the ON space or Operations Nuclear where nuclear bombs were stored—an area so classified that it was always just referred to with the letters O and N and could only be entered by three individuals on the ship: the Captain, Commander Govan, and a designated Chief Petty Officer.

His report was always the same: he was pleased to report that ON space was immaculate since nobody had been to the space since he conducted the last inspection and was very confident it would be immaculate when he conducted the next inspection—comments that always generated considerable laughter. Many veterans of the Vietnam War remember both their serious experiences and lighter moments as if they were yesterday.

JAMES J. "JIM" HOOGERWERF

US Air Force — C-130 Pilot

Dates of military service — 1966 — 1973

Dates served in Vietnam: May 1968 — May 1970 (not inclusive)

Units served with in Vietnam: Based offshore in the Philippines at Clark Air Base 773rd TAS, 463rd TAW, In-country TDY to 834 Air Division, Det. 1 TSN; Det. 2 CRB

Highest rank held: Captain (O-3)

Place and date born: Detroit, MI — 1943

THE "DUTY GUNNER" AT KATUM SPECIAL FORCES CAMP

Katum was a Special Forces camp in the Parrot Beak of RVN, only four kilometers from Cambodia. Without secure road access, the camp relied on fixed and rotary winged aircraft for support. Airmen supplying the base expected to be shot at, mortared, or attacked. My friend Bob Choate experienced a mortar attack at Kontum, a similar outpost, during a resupply mission. He described it as follows:

> "The next thing we knew there was a series of mortar explosions walking up the runway and coming directly toward us. Major Sheehan turned the aircraft around and taxied to the far end of the runway in order to put some distance between us and the mortars while I ran the before takeoff checklist. This turned out to be a critical step because the flaps needed to be reset for takeoff in order to become airborne at our weight with the artillery shells on board. After we turned around, all we could see was the dust from our propellers. We didn't know if the mortars were still coming toward us or not. As we began to apply takeoff power, the other C-130 started to appear through the dissipating dust as it taxied toward us. We were obviously stuck there until he spun around and took off. When he started to roll, we were enveloped in a solid cloud of brown dust from his propellers. I hacked the clock and we waited for his dust to clear. After 15 seconds we released brakes and were delighted to see him climb above the dust. We returned to Bien Hoa with the cargo. We received some superficial fragment damage behind the right paratroop door."

For C-130 Hercules pilots, landing on Katum's 2900' North-South runway was challenging. Assault landings were flown at less than minimum control speed if an engine quit; the touchdowns were within 100-300' from the threshold; and to stop, the props were reversed. But, if a prop failed to reverse and immediate corrective action was not taken, the aircraft would depart the runway. Ground time was kept to a minimum. But, what really set Katum apart was the "duty gunner." We never knew if he was 'on duty.'

The gunner used a quad .51 cal. Russian made crew-served antiaircraft gun, shooting down or damaging C-130s and helicopters – one that I am personally aware of was a Huey Cobra (more on that later). Despite listening posts, search patrols, and Air Force B-52 ARC light missions, the duty gunner tallied up his score to the consternation of airmen and Special Forces.

25 June 1968: An "E" model Lockheed C-130 from CCK (Ching Chuan Kang), Taiwan, got hit in the left wing on takeoff. The number one engine burst into flames, but was put out by discharging both fire extinguishing bottles. However, a fire on the outer wing burned uncontrollably, damaging the wing structure. 1st Lt. Pat Hatch, on his first in-country rotation as a new aircraft commander, and his crew managed to nurse the stricken aircraft to a crash landing at Tay Ninh, about 40 kilometers distant. Touching down with only the nose and left main landing gear extended, the C-130 swerved off the runway in flames and was destroyed. The crew survived by exiting through the cockpit overhead escape hatch.

18 Aug. 1968: The Vietcong 5th Sapper Battalion attacked the base. The battle raged for ten hours but was beaten back. During August and through September, Katum was subjected to constant artillery and mortar bombardment, challenging its re-supply.

25 Sept. 1968: In the morning, after a mortar and rocket barrage, the Vietcong attacked, but were again defeated at a cost of 14 Civilian Irregular Defense Group (CIDG), 61 Vietcong killed, and 10 Vietcong captured.

6 Mar. 1969: I flew from Tan Son Nhut (TSN) to Katum and back. We had to hold for about forty minutes as only one aircraft was permitted on the ground at a time. Our ground time from touchdown to liftoff was a mere five minutes. We returned to TSN without incident. Apparently, the gunner was not on duty, or he fired and missed.

9 Mar. 1969: Three days later, I flew another mission to Katum. Flying time back-and-forth to TSN was a mere twenty-five minutes each way, but the ground time was a long fifteen minutes – lots of time for a mortar crew to lob a few rounds if they were so inclined. Picture the scene: Low lying sandbagged bunkers all around and a C-130 with its 40' tail sticking up as a tempting target. It was our lucky day; apparently the gunner was off duty (maybe on R&R?)

27 May 1969: A C-130A Herk from Naha, Okinawa (21st TAS, 374th TAW), commanded by Maj. A. M. Moore, took rounds in the left wing while on approach with a load of construction equipment. Apparently unaware of being hit, when the props were reversed on landing, leaking fuel was sucked into the engines and ignited. The crew survived but the aircraft was damaged beyond repair.

23 June 1969: Capt. Gary Brunner, from my squadron (773rd TAS, 463rd TAW), like Pat Hatch about a year earlier, was on his first in-country rotation as an aircraft commander from Clark Air Base, Philippines. The six-man crew were in-bound to Katum with a load of 105mm artillery shells. Flying at 3,000', they were hit in the right wing by a quad fifty radar-directed anti-aircraft gun. With the right engine and wing on fire, the aircraft stalled and spun into the ground. All crew members perished. Bodies of four were recovered, but it was not until the site was excavated in 1994 by a joint US/Vietnamese team that the remains of the other two were recovered and identified.

7 Nov. 1969: This must have been a unit move as I made two trips to Katum from Phu Loi. Air Force combat control teams were directing air traffic, which meant a big movement was underway. At Katum, we had the option to request suppressing fire and were warned of ground fire SE of the runway. Our ground time was :35 and :50 minutes respectively – too long for comfort.

8 Nov. 1969: The next day, apparently this was a continuation of the previous day's missions. The enemy was still threatening as we were required to have F-100 fighter cover. However, as we approached, the fighters advised they were bingo on fuel and left. It would be a while for another flight to show up so we weren't supposed to land. However, two Huey Cobras were on the ground and said they could cover for us. They lifted off and we proceeded to land. While we were loading, one of the Cobras was hit and went down. The other gunship went to provide cover. There was nothing we could do and heard no more of the situation except that the downed pilot was okay.

24 May 1970: A medevac helicopter was shot down on approach to Katum. Sgt. First Class Louis R. Rocco, a passenger, evacuated the wounded, an action for which he was awarded the Medal of Honor. The citation reads: "On May 24, 1970, Rocco volunteered to accompany a medical evacuation team on an urgent mission to pick up eight critically wounded Army of the Republic of Vietnam (ARVN) soldiers near Katum Camp. The helicopter in which the team was riding came under heavy fire as it approached the landing zone. The pilot was shot in the leg and the helicopter crashed into a field. Under intense fire, Rocco was able to carry each of the unconscious crash survivors to the ARVN perimeter. Despite having suffered a fractured wrist and hip and a severely bruised back, he was able to help administer first aid to his wounded comrades before collapsing and losing consciousness."

I do not know of the "duty gunner's" ultimate fate. It is still a mystery, but he had our attention!

THE "DRAGON'S JAW" BRIDGE

The Ham Rong, "Dragon's Jaw," rail bridge in North Vietnam crossed the Song Ma river near the city of Thanh Hoa. Funneling men and equipment to the Ho Chi Minh trail, it was a strategic and heavily defended target. Year after year United States airmen braved withering antiaircraft fire to rain missiles and bombs on its two narrow steel truss spans. Anchored by heavy concrete abutments and supported by a huge concrete central pillar, the Dragon's Jaw defied destruction.

The Air Force hatched an audacious plan to knock out the bridge once and for all. Code named, operation "Carolina Moon," donut shaped mines, dropped upstream by Lockheed C-130 transports, would float downstream, carried by the current. Magnetic sensors then triggered shaped charges, directing a powerful blast upward to blow the bridge from below. Two C-130 air crews attacked separately on consecutive nights. The first mission went off as planned but failed to destroy the bridge. The second mission never returned. Fighter pilots on a diversionary strike reported a large explosion in the area, but not on the bridge. Ultimately the Dragon's Jaw succumbed to new precision "smart" weapons.

I first heard of the attack while flying C-130 missions in South Vietnam; the full story only emerged after the war. Reflecting on the courage and persistence of American airmen to destroy the bridge, I wrote this poem in their honor using the bridge as a metaphor.

The Legend of the Dragon's Jaw

Children　　　　　　　　　*There is a dragon?*
Gather 'round
Listen　　　　　　　　　　*It roams the earth*
To the message　　　　　　*Moving from*
Of this tale　　　　　　　 *Place to place*
　　　　　　　　　　　　　　To wrack its havoc
Do you know　　　　　　　*Upon humanity*

In a time
Not too long past
The dragon haunted
The north country
Of a distant land
Across a wide ocean

There
Languishing near
The city Thanh Hoa
It stretched
With feet of concrete
And skeleton of steel
'cross the Song Ma

Spanning
The wide river
The dragon's jaw
Fed its appetite
For conquering
Lands and peoples

Brave men
Your fathers
Journeyed afar
To answer the plea
Of strangers in need

On swift wings
From great heights
They dove at the dragon
Unleashing
Powerful weapons

But
The dragon defied
Destruction

Flight after flight
Year after year
Again, and again
They faced the dragon's
Fiery breath

Still
The dragon
Fought back

Aircraft were lost
Some men died
Some were captured
To endure
Incredible hardship

In time
Smart weapons
Were devised
To breach
the dragon's armor
Leaving it
To collapse
Of its own weight

Now you may think
The dragon gone

But
Be cautious

Be wary
For the dragon
Still exists
In dark caverns
Of soulless men
To reemerge
At any time

If you should
Face the dragon
Stand tall
To the challenge
For the dragon
Must be defeated
Again, and again

And again.

©1988 J. Hoogerwerf

JEFF HOFFMAN

Army — Infantry Officer, Platoon Leader
Dates of Service: February 1968 to March 1998
Unit Served with In Vietnam: C/3-7 IN, 199th INF BDE (LT, SEP)
Dates in Vietnam: January 1969 to January 1970
Highest Rank Held: Colonel (O-6)
Place of Birth/Year: Akron, OH 1945

EXPERIENCES WITH THE FLORA AND FAUNA OF VIETNAM

There aren't any stories of intense combat with VC or NVA in the paragraphs to follow. But, I suggest there might be an interesting narrative of engagements with the flora and fauna of Vietnam, speaking as a Biology major in college. They deal with personal contact, not necessarily in order of importance or chronology.

Red Hooker Ants. Usually found near riverbanks. They were on you before you realized you were standing on a well camouflaged mound, biting with intense ferocity and tenacity while standing on their heads. Hard to dislodge, the most effective remedy was to hit them with the Army issued bug juice. Care had to be taken not to hit anything plastic (like a watchband) or it would start to dissolve before the ants were killed.

Leeches. Found in the backwaters of the many streams encountered multiple times in daily patrols west of Saigon. SOP after exiting these areas was to perform a leech check up to the level where water had covered your body. When found, the expedient solution, again, was to douse them with the Army issued bug juice while avoiding sensitive parts (that the leeches had invaded). If found on or near sensitive parts ... well, we won't go there.

Scorpions. Our company C/3-7 IN, had been redeployed from the area mentioned above to an AO east of Bien Hoa, extending to Xuan Loc. Much different terrain. Not much water encountered, but had some rubber trees and lots of dense, thorny vegetation. While taking a break in our more or less non-tactical movement, I foolishly took off my fatigue jacket and laid it on the ground. Unfamiliar with this kind of creature's habitat, putting my jacket back on proved to be interesting, because a scorpion had taken refuge in it, became greatly disturbed and went into the attack mode, stinging me three times before I could get the jacket off. An unceremonious evacuation by jeep was initiated, an exam performed at Bien Hoa, was treated with topical anesthetic and released with no effects from the attack.

Hornets. While on patrol in some fairly thick brush, I was knocked to the ground by something that hit my head, hearing nothing. After cautiously feeling for blood and not hearing calls from my platoon, I soon determined that I was not shot, but several hornets still flying around were identified as the source of the attack. Alerted now to the threat, we moved more cautiously, and even more so when a CHICOM grenade booby trap was discharged a short distance away. As we learned later, it had slightly wounded an Advisor for the VN unit patrolling with us, but the hornets had given us a good reason to slow down earlier.

Cobras. Mostly a low-level concern but gave us cause to maintain an awareness of their possible presence when patrolling around the many small "villes" in the AO. The Vietnamese sighted them quicker than we did and dispatched them quickly.

F**K YOU lizards. Not a hazard but amusing, particularly to the Newbies.

Bamboo. Besides being hard to move through (reference thorny vegetation earlier), it was lethal to plastic two-quart canteens and unprotected poncho liners. No fix for the canteens, so we had to go back to the plastic one quarts; poncho liners had to be placed *in* the ruck, not *on* the ruck.

Nippapalm. No real issues here besides providing cover for VC using the streams to maneuver and resupply. When too close to the "villes" to use Agent Orange, thickened contaminated fuel (homemade napalm) was dropped in by helo, which we repositioned for max effect and detonated it. Fun mission, good times.

Elephant Grass. Found along the many waterways in the Delta. Tall, thick, and everywhere. Not a good place to be when taking fire.

I found much of Vietnam to be beautiful country, at least the II Field Force AO in and around Saigon, from the far west, near south, and west to Xuan Loc. The Delta, though, not so much. Tough to get around in all the water. It was interesting working off the Navy riverboats and hitting "wet" LZ's in helos. Using the term "wet" LZ's is used to describe exiting the helo from about two feet above the water level. Not sure the Navy guys were ever able to figure out the tides that affected the rivers and streams far up in the Delta, but it made for some anxious moments getting picked up at night.

That's my story, and when I can dig out some pictures, I know I have stored in an unknown location, I may be able to recall more stories to tell the kids and old buddies.

MAJOR GENERAL JAMES E. LIVINGSTON, USMC

US Marine Corps – Infantry Officer

Dates of Service: June 1962 to September 1995

Unit Served with in Vietnam: 1st tour – Platoon Commander, 3rd Battalion, 3rd Marines, 3rd Marine Division; 2nd tour – Company Commander, Company E, 2nd Battalion, 4th Marines; 3rd tour – Operations officer, 4th Marines, 3rd Marine Division (RVN Evacuation and Operation Frequent Wind)

Dates in Vietnam: 1964; 1967 to 1968; 1974 to 1975

Highest Rank Held: Major General

Place and Date of Birth: Towns, GA – 1940

REFLECTIONS FROM A MARINE MEDAL OF HONOR RECIPIENT

I come from a small place called Towns, Georgia. I was not from a military family, we were farmers, and my dad had exemptions as a result of the family business. After high school I attended North Georgia College and then Auburn University. I received my draft notice in 1961, since we still had mandatory military service. I did not know much about the military and even less about the Marine Corps. I did know that the Marines had the reputation for getting involved in any threats to our country before anyone else. They also had a history of getting the job done.

Dodging the draft was never a consideration. I did not want to act like my college peers and avoid the draft by staying in college, and I decided that if I was going to serve, I wanted to be with the most aggressive and direct contact branch we had. So, for me, joining the Corps was not that difficult a decision. After completing all my required schools and a tour at Quantico, I was a newly minted second lieutenant, an "Officer and a Gentleman" by an act of Congress.

Later I did sea duty assigned as a platoon leader in Lima Company, 2nd Battalion 5th Marines, which was a sixteen — month tour which placed us off the coast of Vietnam as a combat service support group and security and observers at the airfield in Da Nang. I was able to go ashore there and observe operations against the VC. Following a stint at Parris Island, I requested combat duty.

My request was approved in September 1967, and I arrived in Da Nang at 3rd Marine Division Headquarters in Quang Tri Province. I became CO of Echo Company 2nd Battalion 4th Marine Regiment in Dong Ha. We were known as the "Magnificent Bastards."

We had a few engagements that tested us, but we were up to the task. Most of our fights through December 1967 were against the Viet Cong. Next, we were assigned as security for Quang Tri airfield. Then we relocated to Phu Bai as a battalion-sized reaction force, until we were ordered to undergo training and refit in the Philippines, and we left for Subic Bay two to three days before the attack on Hue.

We returned from Subic Bay and were the ground element for Special Landing Task Force Alpha and placed on ships as part of the Amphibious Ready Group. We landed at the Cua Viet River at a point that became known as Camp Big John, east of Jones Creek. The battalion set in and we replaced 3/1 which had been in a major fight north of the Cua Viet River.

Our first action was to send Foxtrot Company north toward Lam Xuan, supported by Hotel Company. Foxtrot was ambushed, losing 14 Marines who were left in the battle area. The next day we were ordered to embark on amtracs, cross Jones Creek near Lam Xuan, seize the area, and recover the bodies. We were supported by Hotel to our east, they were south of the village. However, the amtracs could not climb the east bank, so we withdrew to reduce casualties. The next day we attacked Lam Xuan up the east side of Jones Creek and arrived in the village without any contact. It was a bad scene with the bodies in bad shape, but we recovered our Marines.

After that we moved farther north to Nhi-Ha, again without contact and were joined by Hotel who were engaged. They lost several Marines. Hotel then returned to Camp Big John and we occupied Nhi-Ha to interdict enemy flow south at Jones Creek on the east and were joined by Golf Company to the west side of Jones Creek.

There was activity north of Cua Viet at Highway 1, as the ARVN unit had major contact. Golf also made contact as they were moving into position, crossing paths with an NVA company also on the move. The sharp firefight that followed resulted in Marines being wounded, including Golf C.O. Captain Bob Mastrion. All were evacuated when HMM-362 (known as "The Ugly Angels") flew into a very hot LZ to evacuate the wounded and take them to the *USS Iwo Jima*. Captain Jay Vargas then took over as Golf Co. Commander. It was at that time Echo successfully returned to Nhi-Ha.

Operation Night Owl was our April 27-28, 1968, night attack, including sweeping the abandoned hamlet of An My. We thought it contained a battalion from the 320th NVA Division that had just moved over the DMZ. After passing through the ARVN position at ALPHA 1, we surrounded An My and attacked but had no contact as the enemy had left.

We had unknowingly stumbled across elements of the NVA 320th Division. On April 29, Task Force Robbie launched an attack which included 1/9 with tanks to intercept the NVA that had hammered the 2nd ARVN Regiment and were ambushed and almost wiped out. Echo Company had already departed Nhi-Ha (replaced there by Golf, also securing Lam Xuan West) and assigned to 3rd Marine Division securing the Dong Ha Bridge straddling the Cua Viet and Bo Dieu Rivers. They secured that area as well as Highway 1, which ran north and south, and Highway 9, which ran east to west. The next day, on April 30, the NVA fired upon a Navy LCU, killing a sailor and injuring several others.

Hotel attacked an enemy force and seized Dong Huan and the CO, Captain Jim Williams, was wounded, so 1LT Scotty Prescott took command. Foxtrot was sent in to assist, but both companies were pinned down by the enemy. Foxtrot later reached Dai Do, Hotel was in Dong Huan, Golf commanded by Captain Jay R. Vargas moved by boats to An Lac to attack Dai Do.

The entire time I had been listening to the radio. On May 1, our Battalion Commander, LTC Bill Weise, secured Echo's release from 3rd Division, as Golf, Hotel, and Bravo Co. 1/3 needed help. I told my men to abandon their steak dinner and get moving. Like great Marines, they did not even flinch. Our brothers were in trouble.

The next morning Weise called me into the CP and told me to plan an attack. The next morning, at 0500 on my 180 Marines fixed bayonets. We joined battalion headquarters and linked up with Bravo 1/3 at An Lac which was in bad shape. They had lost all of their leadership, so I reorganized them into a defense. The next day, on May 2, Echo moved on to Dai Do 500 meters away from An Lac. We attacked across open rice paddies, two platoons in the attack and the reserve platoon, with me in the middle following, supported by fire from Golf. Then we saw that Dai Do was fortified by hundreds of bunkers.

My two forward platoons were bogged down by intense enemy fire, so I took the reserve platoon and company headquarters and assaulted. Golf attacked from the south to the rear, Hotel followed. My XO, Dave Jones, was wounded, so Sergeant James Rogers took over his platoon. We penetrated their defensive lines, cleared bunkers at close quarters, then pushed on and rolled them up, killing hundreds as they withdrew. As we advanced farther, my RTO Frank Valdez and I were hit by grenades. Then I launched my reserve platoon.

Our Marines continued knocking out bunker after bunker, hand-to-hand fighting, finally neutralizing about a hundred bunkers. Golf skipper Jay Vargas was remarkable. He also earned the Medal of Honor for his actions, and well-deserved. We had secured Dai Do and pushed the NVA north and out. The regimental CO, COL Milton Hull, ordered Weise and 2/4 to push north to Dinh To and finish the job. I had about 30 out of 180 Marines with whom I started still able to fight. Hotel, with only 70 Marines, attacked by moving west of us, and 200 yards into the village they were surrounded. The remaining Marines and sailors from Echo joined me and we linked up with Hotel.

The fighting was just as intense as Dai Do. Then the NVA launched wave after wave at us, and we had air and indirect fire support, but we still pushed. That was when I was hit by heavy machine gun fire, shattering my thigh. It was over for me, and Lieutenant Cecil took over, but I still wanted my wounded evacuated and the dead collected. I was ordering the wounded to be taken care of when two black Marines came and got me, which probably saved my life.

They took me to the collection point near the river. I was placed with the others and shot full of morphine. Then I agreed to be evacuated to the ship after I was assured that all my Marines were secured at Dai Do. Even though I was out of the fight, as were several others, the Marines pressed on and it was effectively over the next day. We had won. We secured the area, protected the province and our bases, and maintained our control over the rivers and supply routes.

We collected our dead and wounded and the 3rd Engineer Battalion brought bulldozers to dig graves for the enemy dead. There were approximately 2,500 enemy dead, because one engineer said that one trench alone contained about 1,000 bodies. We had no idea of the enemy strength, but these guys were pros. They knew their business and somehow, they managed to build dozens of underground bunkers and pillboxes, unobserved and completely camouflaged. They were undetectable in the area around the villages of Dinh To, Nhi Ha, Dai Do and other smaller hamlets.

It was only in the 1990s, after meeting our former enemy division commander, that we learned just how massive our enemy was, and why they fought so hard. Retired BG Bill Weise (who received the Navy Cross) believed that since the 2nd ARVN regiment was responsible for An Lac, Dong Huan, Dai Do, and Dinh To that there was collusion with the NVA. That allowed them the time to build those fortifications. Many of us agree.

I later returned in 1974 for a third tour and organized the April 1975 evacuation of Saigon with COL Alfred M. Gray, who later became a general and Commandant of the Marine Corps. We managed to get the last of the embassy staff and Marines out, as well as evacuate the embassy in Phnom Penh, Cambodia. These were successful, but then we had the SS Mayageuz incident. We sent Marines in to secure the ship and crew, and despite some tragic losses among the rescue team of Marines, we were successful with the crew being released.

Upon reflection regarding Dai Do, we learned decades later that our 653 Marines and Navy corpsmen had engaged about 10,000 NVA, and we were within 250 to 300 yards of the enemy's division CP, which explained their furious resistance. If we had succeeded in pushing them out into the open, our artillery and air assets would have finished them off. They knew it, and we did not, which explained why they fought like hell. No quarter was asked nor given, and a major victory was ours, against all the odds.

Our action was the result of a series of incidental contacts that developed into a major battle. Our efforts prevented the enemy from taking all of Quang Tri piece by piece. The NVA objective was to take the Cua Viet and Bo Dieu rivers and the surrounding villages, Dong Ha Bridge, the combat base, Quang Tri airfield, and secure the province, cutting our supply lines. That would have been the greatest and only combat loss in Vietnam and ended the war much sooner with great loss of life.

DONALD H. NAU

U S Army—Armor/Infantry Officer

Time in Military (Active Duty and Reserves): 1967-1974

Unit Served with in Vietnam: HQ Co, 3rd Combat Brigade, 25th Infantry
Division

Dates in Vietnam: Aug 1969 to Aug 1970

Highest Rank Held: 1LT

Place of Birth and Year: East Cleveland, Ohio—1944

THE JOHN DEERE LETTER

Isn't it true, humor gets you through the tough times? Humor was difficult in Vietnam—it took very strange courses. There was Bob Hope,
when introduced in December 1969 at the 25th Infantry Christmas
show, said, "It's great to be back in Cu Chi—that's Cu Chi by the
Sea—pause—The V-C." And the troops went crazy! Cu Chi is about
100 miles from the South China Sea.

Mr. Hope wasn't the only one who left us laughing. The time I
worked out a swap with an Air Force pilot buddy who needed eggs
and we (Army) needed paint. Somehow our different service branches
were able to acquire items the others could not. So, he brought back
two 5-gallon cans of red and blue paint placed between his legs on an
OV-10 FAC plane. I was able to take a gross of eggs by Jeep to the AF
compound. Both Colonels were pleased and, of course, didn't ask. We received no commendation—don't know how it would have been worded.
Anyway, we laughed trying to determine how we would have explained
that particular ribbon—which would have been red, yellow and blue.
Later, the pilot, a great friend, was shot down. I am still in contact with
his daughters—trying to smile about something.

And laugh we did when Special Services would provide a worldly
band to play and sing "We Gotta Get Outta This Place", followed by the
"Green Green Grass of Home" and ending with "Let the Sunshine In."
To this day, I do not know any of the other words to those songs.

Other attempts were ones such as: Did you hear about the Iowa farm boy who joined the Army and six months later got a John Deere letter?

After the laughter subsides, you realize that joke is based on real human situations in war, but with a gag-line.

One evening, my perimeter wire sector guards and I were readying for all night duty. Free-fire was on. That was a time to test weapons; to fire at imaginary targets, kick up mud, dirt, or puddles—but leave the water buffalo alone! Machine guns poured out the ammo as did the rifles and occasional pistols from the officers—me in this case. It is very, very, very, very loud!

Suddenly, from the sector on my left, a grenade exploded. This was unusual as grenades don't lend themselves to practice or aiming adjustments (ever hear of close enough for horseshoes or hand grenades?) Was it enemy incoming? Possible, but too early. All went silent.

Radio traffic started and shortly MPs arrived and soon came a 25th Infantry ambulance. Dust-off Hueys and Cobra gunships circled—just in case.

Soon, the all-clear sounded—we went back to "facing outward" again. Within an hour, the word came to me: A soldier had received a letter from his girl back home. She had met someone else—wished him luck—and just knew he would be fine when he got back.

He sat on the edge of the foxhole—pulled the pin and dropped the grenade into the pit. He blew his legs off—but was alive. The 25th Medical team saved his life. After a couple of days of stabilization, he was flown out. I have no further knowledge of him—a write your own ending.

There doesn't seem to be one word for the opposite of humor—tragedy may be the closest. It certainly is not "bad times"—but the opposite of tragedy is not humor. I can only hope he was fine—as she said.

In the end—there was nothing damn funny about the War.

ROBERT REESE

US Army—Infantryman
Dates of Military Service: 1968 to 1971
Unit Served with in Vietnam: B Company, 1st Battalion, 26th Infantry, 1st Infantry Division
Dates Served in Vietnam: Dec 1968 to Nov 1971 (two tours)
Highest Rank Held: Sergeant (E-5)
Place and Date of Birth: Atlanta, GA—1949

ROLLIN' ON THE RIVER

Infantrymen love to ride on things.

Since time immemorial, the foot soldier, by definition, walks everywhere. He carries his weapon, food, water, and other gear he needs to take on the enemy. The infantryman is the very essence of what war is all about, boiled down to the basics. You have to take control of territory, and to do that, you have to inhabit and control the battlefield at the personal level.

Walking is hard physical work for the individual foot soldier. A large portion of your training and work in combat situations is walking, marching, trekking over distances carrying those weapons and gear. I walked over south Georgia during basic training at Ft. Benning and the northern Alabama Mountains during advanced infantry training at Ft. McClellan. You get trained to the point where you can just switch to auto pilot and keep on walking.

"Humping" is what you do — your lot in life. On occasion though — on occasion — Providence shines on you for a short time. There's a truck, a helicopter, or an airplane to haul your butt somewhere. Whereupon you get out and walk — again.

You learn to savor those brief moments when something moves you around besides your own two legs.

My first experience in life with my feet off the ground of Mother Earth was a 10-minute training ride in a Huey at Ft. McClellan. My second experience was a Boeing 727 flight a couple of weeks later from

Atlanta to San Francisco with orders to report to Oakland Army Base for transport to the Republic of South Vietnam. The third leg of my initial flying experience was departing from Travis AFB for Bien Hoa, South Vietnam via Honolulu, Wake Island, and Yokota AFB in Japan aboard Flying Tiger Airlines!

This was followed in due course by numerous air assaults during my time with the First Infantry Division in III Corps in 1968-1969.

All combat veterans acknowledge the horrors, the tragedy, and yes, oft times the boredom of war. That said, there are many instances of exhilaration and high excitement during your time spent in a combat zone. I must say, the experience of zooming through the skies aboard a helicopter is something quite unique. Riding along at fifteen hundred feet, with no seat belt and your legs hanging out the door, the cool breeze blowing across your face, observing the exotic war-torn countryside spread out below—it's a unique thrill that's difficult to appreciate for those who've never experienced it.

Of course, that experience of your reality changes dramatically after your ten-minute ride and you are summarily deposited in a remote hostile environment in the back of beyond. The sight of your Huey now rapidly vanishing into the distance rapidly closes out the brief exhilaration of your aerial joy ride.

A different kind of ride I looked forward to was to be transported through the Vietnamese landscape on an armored personnel carrier (APC), or better yet, a Patton tank or Sheridan fighting vehicle. How cool would it be to perch on an invulnerable armored vehicle while crushing the brush and vegetation beneath your grinding treads! All topped off with the luxury of not having to lug your gear on your own back—how sweet it would be!

Well, when we performed combined operations with armored units, I quickly found out the life of a mechanized soldier is not at all what I had envisioned. Firstly, armor makes a great deal of noise. This is not optimal for trying to move quietly through hostile country. The enemy has plenty of advance notice you are paying a call on him—plenty of time to prepare his reception with all his best high-powered ordinance, specifically the B40 shoulder fired rocket, aka the RPG. After an encounter with the business end of a B40 on my 30th day in country, I spent two weeks in a Lai Khe hospital re-evaluating my views of a longed-for transfer to an armored outfit.

I got my one and only joy ride on an M-48 Patton tank after performing a mine clearing operation outside the town of Ben Cat one morning. Upon completion of the mission (which entailed walking on the side of a dirt road pulling security for the minesweeping personnel), we were ordered to climb aboard the M-48 for a ride back to the firebase. Great — another opportunity to avoid humping 50 pounds of my gear in the hot morning sun. What a treat. Wrong again, GI!

After clambering up behind the turret, I discovered that sitting on the exterior of a tank after it's spent two hours in the tropical sun is roughly equivalent to resting your posterior on a hot cast iron griddle. Moreover this 50-ton frying pan is hauling ass down a bumpy dirt road at 35 mile per hour. This results in huge clouds of red Vietnamese dust boiling over you, so thick that it is nearly impossible to see or breathe. Top all this off with a tank driver whose one and only thought is to fly down that road as fast as he can to hopefully avoid any unpleasant encounter with enemy forces. You hang on for dear life and pray that you don't get thrown off this steel mega-bronco ride directly into the path of its twin brother following along immediately behind.

Some infantry units were mechanized — meaning that the soldiers normally moved around the countryside on top of an armored personnel carrier. Then, except for the driver and the vehicle commander, the soldiers dismounted for combat and fought on foot. We'd sometimes operate in cooperation with these outfits, so you become familiar with how their daily existence is different from a straight "leg" company.

The chief thing you learn straight away — unlike the vision of the engineers who designed the APC — nobody normally rides inside, except the driver. Two reasons. Firstly, the hollowed-out interior of the vehicle is packed to capacity with C-rations and more importantly, ammunition for the .50 caliber and M-60 machine guns that make up the armament. Secondly, the "armor" of an APC is not steel but mostly reinforced aluminum. That means the sides of the vehicle, when struck by a B-40 rocket at the right angle, have roughly the stopping power of cardboard. The B-40 anti-tank round can penetrate several inches of *steel*, whereupon it explodes inside the vehicle after exiting the armor plating, filling the interior with molten steel fragments. That makes the interior of an APC not a place you'd want to be in such an event. The detonation of a land mine would similarly have a deadly effect on anyone inside the vehicle.

So, the unit soldiers ride on the top of the APC, completely vulnerable to small arms fire or explosive devices rigged in trees designed to rake the top of the carrier.

So no…APC's were not something I wanted to ride on. I tip my helmet to the mechanized infantrymen for the unique dangers they lived with each day and for the assistance they often provided to us straight legs.

The most unique ride I experienced during my combat experiences was the result of a combined operation we undertook with the so-called brown water navy. The brown water navy was made up of US Navy personnel who manned a wide variety of boats/ships designed to ply and fight on the vast river networks of the Mekong Delta in the southern most region of South Vietnam.

The First Infantry Division's area of operations (AO) did not include the Mekong Delta. We had no knowledge of riverine fighting and indeed had no thought of ever experiencing anything like it. However, the western border of our AO was the Saigon River, a fair-sized river not connected with the huge Mekong waterway. During our normal patrols and missions, we sometimes worked near the river and had a passing familiarity with it from a geographical standpoint. But weighing anchor, launching ourselves upon its murky waters, and reinventing ourselves as brown-water sailors was something we never dreamed of.

Nevertheless, in the spring of 1969, we were ordered to proceed by truck (another ride!) from divisional headquarters at Lai Khe to the town of Phu Cuong on the river, just a few short miles away. There my company would board a US navy aggregation of vessels of various types for a mission up the Saigon. Anchors aweigh, Bravo Company!

There was a fair-sized bridge across the river at Phu Cuong. Naturally it was heavily guarded against saboteurs (I think there were more destroyed bridges than functional bridges in Vietnam when I was there). One of the security measures was to generate a huge electrical shock charge in the water underneath the bridge at night at unscheduled intervals to discourage underwater tinkering by some of the locals. Yeah, that would do it for me. The only other bridge was a smaller one thirty miles upstream at Dau Tieng. The method there was more primitive as those on guard duty would simply drop bricks of C-4 explosives into the surrounding water to provide a similar disincentive.

The US Navy squadron we linked up with was a hodge podge of vessels of various types. Each of the three platoons in our company embarked on a landing craft, very similar to the ones you see in WW II movies. They had a hinged door on the front that was lowered once the craft approached shore, then you tumble out just like John Wayne in *The Sands of Iwo Jima*. The boat had an awning to protect the passengers from the tropical sun as you leisurely made your way up stream. Additionally, there were two or three heavily armored craft that formed the real striking power of the squadron.

They resembled the Monitors you see in pictures of American Civil War river warfare. There were turrets with a small howitzer plus .50 caliber machine guns and 20mm automatic cannons. Lastly, there were several small "speedboats" that could be used for squad sized forays up side streams or canals connected to the main body of the river. A riverine veteran told me fifty years later that the boats in my pictures were old French boats (paid for by the US Government), that had been used in the first Indochina War.

We had a multi-day mission to proceed up the Saigon to a small village and cooperate with some ARVN forces to surround it in order to try to trap enemy forces thought to be operating there. Other than that main mission, the idea seemed to be to maneuver our ship up the channel and attempt to draw fire from the bank. Whereupon we, the infantry, would storm the shore and dispense with the bad guys. One envisions the little ducks in a fairground shooting gallery that steamed back and forth for the amusement of the armed patrons.

Though we did encounter contact over the week we spent on the river, it was not as intense as I would have guessed. I learned decades later that there had been no vessels operating that far upriver for several years. I think we probably caught the enemy a bit off guard on this operation. There was a second operation over the same waters later where we were not as fortunate and took some serious casualties.

At night, each platoon would be carried to a different crossing point on the river and set up a night ambush position. In a way, I felt it was similar to operating with armor since the Communist forces must have been pretty much aware of where we were due to the noise and of course the visibility of large boats traveling up and down the river.

The crew of the squadron were made up of some US Navy personnel but also a number of Vietnamese deck hands, mostly teenage boys. I recall one quiet evening, one of the kids produced an acoustic guitar and serenaded us with a couple of Beatles ballads. It was surrealistic, enjoying a quiet tune from home even if for just a few brief moments during the tropical sunset.

Since being clean was a rarity for us, we took advantage of the river on occasion to take a quick swim when the boat stopped for a break in the operation. It felt great jumping into the deep, slow moving waters. A rare treat indeed. Of course, one squad stands guard with automatic weapons while the other squad enjoys the water. Not quite standard operation procedure to go for a swim on combat patrol, I guess, but sometimes you take your chances for such a luxury to get rid of the dirt and stink, even for only a few hours.

We reached the objective village and assisted in setting up the cordon. I don't think there was much found and there was a very unfortunate incident where two ARVN Hueys collided, killing all the Vietnamese passenger soldiers and crews. A microcosm of the war—people killed, a fortune spent on machinery, fuel, ammo—for some purpose unknown. All of which was done before and would be repeated again at some future point by the next set of guys.

Nearby was another more famous village, Ben Suc, that had gained some notoriety a couple of years previously when a combined US/ARVN operation uprooted the entire population and moved them to a new village in another province. One can image how that must have gone over with the families that were uprooted in such a fashion.

Anyway, that previous operation is sometimes said to be the origin of the well know quote "we had to destroy the village in order to save it." The quote has been attributed to other places and times during the war. The interesting thing is no one has ever been able to document who, if anyone, ever actually said it. There's some speculation that it was made up by a reporter as a cool quote to capture the futility of the war. Peter Arnett, who later made a name for himself reporting on the Gulf War, was said to be the possible origin.

Some forty odd years later, I traveled up the old dirt road with my two teen-age kids, a road now paved. It meandered along the riverbank from Phu Cuong to the same village we surrounded back in 1969. At one deserted point on the road, there was a huge modern bridge that had been built across the river. There was no habitation visible on either side. The Viet friend with me told me that the locals termed it "The Bridge to Nowhere", constructed as a thank you to the local populace that supported the Communists during the war. Seems politicians operate in much the same fashion on both sides of the Pacific.

Nearby, and a mile or so away from one of my old fire bases, we were fortunate to be introduced to an elderly gentleman who was a resident of the area for many years. He invited us to his home where we were welcomed by his wife. Through my interpreter, the man told me he had fought the Japanese, the French, and the Americans over the years in that local community. He told me that the single shot rifle he used against the Japanese was longer than he was tall!

It's a shame we couldn't have had a conversation back in 1969 and tried to figure out why we couldn't just stop trying to kill each other. But such is war. Sometimes the soldier doesn't really understand why he is there. The reasons are all forgotten…if they were ever known. You just fight against the other person without realizing in some alternative universe you would just go fishing together, drink a little rice liquor, and be good pals. Where have all the flowers gone…etc.

Those are far off days, all finished now. But whenever I hear a Creedence Clearwater Revival oldie, I think of my adventures long ago, rollin' on the Saigon River.

DAN BENNETT

US Air Force — Flight Engineer

Dates of military service (Active and Reserve): 1967 to 1975

Units served with in Vietnam: 4th Special Operations Squadron, Da Nang AB and 18thSOS, Nha Trang AB

Dates in Vietnam: 1967 to 1968; 1972 to 1973

Highest Rank Held: Tech Sergeant (E-6)

Place of Birth: Atlanta, GA — 1947

"SPOOKY"

March 1968, our AC-47 was performing close ground support for ground troops near Binh Thuy, South Vietnam. Several ground units had made contact with the enemy and requested Air Force assistance. Spooky obliged. We arrived on station (2500 feet AGL) at or near midnight March 11th and began providing suppressing fire. This action brought badly needed relief to the guys on the ground. We flew several sorties that night that required landing for fuel and ammo between each mission. Binh Thuy AB was the nearest location for what we needed.

At or near 4 am that morning, March 12, 1968, contact between the ground troops and the NVA ceased, and our aerial presence was no longer required. We went back to Binh Thuy AB and our Captain suggested that we get some hot chow.

We had just sat down for a hot breakfast when we began hearing the thump of in-coming explosions. It sounded like they were in the direction of the flight line. The warning horn began blaring and anyone who has experienced in-coming mortars/artillery/rockets knows full well what it's like to have your balls in your throat. Especially when the rounds begin falling near where you are located.

Mr. Charles (NVA) had worked over the flight line pretty hard. The mortars caused a lot of damage to aircraft and equipment, plus a lot of buildings and hangers were hit, with some burning.

The thump of explosions quickly began coming closer and closer to the barracks area. This is where the chow hall is located. While sitting at a table, the corner of the chow hall was hit, and the hall quickly emptied with each person fleeing towards cover. We made a mad dash outside and found cover in a Benjo ditch just outside the front door. Mortars began falling all around us. It was horrible. The Benjo ditch was filled with stagnant water and slime, but we didn't mind! The chow hall and several barracks' buildings were completely destroyed. I remember feeling the concussion shake my entire body, causing my ears to pop each time a round fell close. No one in our crew suffered any injuries. We were soaked to the bone with water, slime, and mud.

After the all-clear was given, we climbed out of our hiding place and counted four fairly large craters within 15 feet (we measured) of where we were hiding. That is too close for comfort.

We caught a ride back to the flight line to check on our aircraft. We were sadly disappointed since we found it with most of its left wing up to the engine root missing and the left side of the aircraft was peppered with holes from exploding shells. I was somewhat surprised the aircraft didn't burn, since the fuel tanks were topped off with 800 gallons of 115/145 octane AVGAS. The aircraft was a total loss.

March 12, 1968 was probably the most exhausting and "nerve-racking" night I had in Vietnam. I have no idea how many casualties we suffered, but I know it was too many. I thanked God that I wasn't one of them.

JAMES "JIM" TORBERT

US Army—Aviator
Dates of Military Service: July 1967 to July 1970
Unit Served with in Vietnam: 281st Assault Helicopter
Company
Dates in Vietnam: Nov 1968 to Nov 1969
Highest Rank Held: Captain (O-3)
Place of Birth and Year: St. Louis, MO—1944

DATE NIGHT

I was a helicopter pilot in Vietnam and flew for the 281st Assault Helicopter Company based in Nha Trang. Our mission was air support for the 5th Special Forces Group. We regularly flew missions from Nha Trang to the different Special Forces camps located throughout Vietnam. We also flew in support of the Recondo School, which was an in-country school for all branches of service which techniques of long-range reconnaissance patrolling, ambush, and escape and evasion (E&E) were taught. Most of our flying time was in support of Project Delta. Delta force had missions assigned as what were called "Special Ops" and covert missions all over Southeast Asia.

All Special Forces operations in Southeast Asia were based at their Headquarters in Nha Trang. We lived with them at their base which was located on the south side of the main airfield at Nha Trang. Also located at the airfield was a unit of the South Vietnam Rangers, the U.S. Air Force, an Army field hospital, and the Headquarter of the 17th Combat Air Group. The American Red Cross and the USO also had operations at the airfield. To live in Nha Trang was perhaps the best assigned location in all South Vietnam.

However, our mission to support Delta took us all over the country. Depending on their mission we would set up a base camp in remote locations to be near to where they were going to operate. These missions would routinely last from four to eight weeks long. We would miss all the comforts and pleasantries of being in Nha Trang. It made ending the mission and returning to Nha Trang as a highly anticipated event.

It was great to be able to return to Nha Trang and look forward to a little rest and down time before we had to go back to the field. It also gave us a chance to party a little bit and make up for being in the field for so long

I turned 25 years old during my year in Vietnam. I was single and did not have a promised girlfriend back in the States. This was a year missed of being able to date and look forward to beginning a long and lasting relationship. I did have three or four young ladies who would occasionally send a letter, but nothing so established as to make my Mom happy, who was eagerly awaiting with the anticipation of grandchildren. I was thinking that 1969 was pretty much a waste of any dating or relationship building time.

On one of our Delta Operations, I became friends with one of the Special Forces Officers. He was single, like me, and in our long talks at night he would tell me about the parties that he would host back in Nha Trang. He told me about the ladies from the Red Cross, known as "Donut Dollies" and the nurses from the Hospital that he would invite to come and party as his "hootch." I asked him how he did that, and he said that he would just call on the radio over to their location and whoever answered the radio he would invite them to a party.

This sounded pretty easy to me, and I decided that when we got back to Nha Trang that I might try this out. Now communication while we were in Vietnam was not anything like what we have today. Trying to call someone in a different unit was not easy at all. You had to get patched in from one switchboard to another and most of the time that was not an easy task.

We were back in Nha Trang, and it looked like we were going to be there for at least a couple of weeks. So, one afternoon I went and saw our Company Commander and asked for a day off. I told him I meant the whole day. We worked every day in Vietnam and a request for a day off was kind of unique. He said of course I could take a day, but I was not sure he knew what was on my mind.

I then went down to the operations shack where there was a small room with a phone. I started my mission to get through to the nurse BOQ at the hospital. After several tries, I got a ringing at the BOQ. A Captain answered and she asked me what I needed. I explained to her that I was a Captain, a helicopter pilot, single, and that I had the day off the next day and was there by chance anyone there who was off tomorrow who wanted to go to the beach.

I heard her yell down the hall for anyone who was off tomorrow and wanted to go to the beach with some Captain. After what seemed like a really long time, a voice on the radio said, "Hello." It sure was nice to hear a woman's voice. We talked for several minutes. She had been in country for about four months, and this was her first day off. She thought it would be great to go to the beach. She said she would make lunch, and I could bring the drinks. I told her that I had a jeep and would pick her up at noon.

The USO maintained a secure beach on the ocean in Downtown Nha Trang. It was there for all services to use. Of course, it was beautiful white sand and the clear blue water of the ocean. What a perfect setting for a first date, and a first date in six months.

We had a wonderful time talking, eating, and drinking, and taking a plunge into the warm water every now and then. Before we knew it, the sun was going down and we had to get back to beat curfew. On the way back she mentioned that the nurses were having a going away party the next week and they were going to have a steak cookout and would I like to come. YES! I would be there.

I do not know how many guys were lucky enough to have any chance to talk to a young lady while they were in country. I would guess there were very few that got to have a date while they were there. It was a great experience to be able to forget the war and all the things we saw and heard and had to deal with at that time and to have a chance to be able to be like normal young people in the real world at the time. I will remember her, and I guess she remembers me also, wherever she may be. "Thanks for the memories."

THOMAS A. "TOM" ROSS

US Army— Special Forces
Dates of Military Service (Active and Reserve): 1966 to 1992
Unit Served with in Vietnam: Detachment A-502, 5th Special Forces Group
Dates in Vietnam: Jan 1968 to Dec 1968
Highest Rank Held: Major (O-4)
Place of Birth and Year: Huntington, WV— 1945

HAVE I KILLED MY FRIEND?

GENERAL WILLIAM TECUMSEH SHERMAN is credited by
historians with first using the phrase "War is hell." While there is some
question about exactly when he uttered the phase, I have no doubt about
its accuracy. One night in 1968, I found the doors to hell wide open, and
without a choice, I walked right through them.

Not far from the location of a recent supply train ambush, there was a
village we suspected to be a safe haven for NVA soldiers who lived in the
Dong Bo Mountains. In fact, we suspected that those who had attacked
the train might have used the village as a staging area for the ambush.
During an after-action discussion of the train derailment, Major Ngoc,
our Vietnamese Camp Commander, and I agreed that we should set up an
ambush at a point between the village and the mountains.

My friend, 1st Lieutenant Bill Phalen, was scheduled for ambush duty
the night of the village mission. Sequence for ambush duty was determined
by a rotation schedule, and it was Bill's turn. He would serve as the senior
U.S. Adviser to his Vietnamese counterpart and a platoon-size unit (twenty-five to thirty-five men) from CIDG (Civilian Irregular Defense Group)
Company 555.

Bill and his wife, Lisa, had been very kind to me when we were stationed at Fort Bragg. They lived off-post and, on several occasions, had
invited me to dinner at their home. So, when Bill's call for help came the
night of the ambush, I would unleash a hellish artillery barrage in an aggressive and desperate attempt to save his life. While using every artillery
direction skill taught to me since entering the service, ultimately, it would

be unseen artillerymen who would have to help me deliver the firepower that would either save — or kill my friend.

I had been asleep for about two or three hours on the night I will never forget when one of our radiomen, SPC 4 (Specialist Fourth Class) James Miller, burst into my room.

"Lieutenant Ross! Wake up! Lieutenant Phalen is in contact!"

For non-military readers, that meant that Bill's unit had triggered their ambush and at that moment they were probably in a blazing gunfight with the enemy.

Instantly awakened by Miller's loud intrusion, I responded, "Let's go!" exploding from my bed.

On my feet, I bounced off the walls of the hallway on my way to the radio room.

"Where is he?" I asked, trying to focus my eyes on the map in the bright light of the radio room.

I knew where the original ambush site was located, but I wasn't sure whether they had moved from that position.

Miller put his finger on the map.

"He's right there, sir."

I picked up the radio handset and immediately tried to reach Bill to determine his status.

"Blue Bandit Zero Six, this is Bunkhouse Zero Two. Over."

When the radio remained silent and there was no response, I tried again. "Blue Bandit Zero Six, this is Bunkhouse Zero Two. Over."

Miller and I just looked at each other while the radio remained silent. "You know," I said, "they're not that far away. Go to the door and see what you can hear."

Unless there was heavy rain, we could almost always hear the intensity of a firefight from camp. Miller came running back to the radio room. "It sounds like a hell of a fight out there, sir."

"Okay, get the rest of the team up and make sure the Vietnamese know what's happening and are getting reinforcements ready to roll."

I tried again to make radio contact with my friend, whom I knew might have already been down and hurt — or worse. Knowing the fighting must be fierce and loud, my call was louder this time. "Blue Bandit Zero Six, this is Bunkhouse Zero Two. Over!"

Finally, the first response came. Initially, there was no voice, just the sound of gunfire. Someone had squeezed the button on the handset but hadn't said or wasn't able to say—anything.

The possibilities of what might be going on out there raced through my mind. *Is he hurt and unable to talk? Has an enemy soldier picked up the radio?*

Then came the familiar sound of Bill's voice. Instantly upon hearing it, I knew his situation was extremely serious. Over the sound of hammering gunfire, his voice was unemotional but matter-of-factly urgent. "Tom, we're not going to make it outta here!"

As he spoke, the speakers pounded with the background sound of exploding rockets and grenades. The ear-piercing clatter of gunfire filled any void between the sound of rockets and grenades.

Bill was a skilled, confident military man, but when his response came in the clear, using my name and no call signs, I knew he was in serious trouble. I was sure he believed what he had just said to me—he expected to be killed.

"Bill, reinforcements are on the way," I tried to reassure my friend.

"They won't make it, Tom. We've ambushed a whole damn company (perhaps 75 to 150 men), and they are going to roll right over us. In fifteen minutes, there won't be anyone left to reinforce."

With Bill advising a unit of no more than 35 men and the enemy company having 75 to 150 or more, Bill's unit was vastly outnumbered.

"All right!" I said. Then, I asked, "Have you moved since you set up?"

"No, we're still here. They're all over the place and might be trying to surround us."

"Okay, stay near your radio and listen for me to call back."

I drew an X over Bill's position, then drew lines on three sides around him, drawing a box around his position with one side open. Then, I asked Miller to plot the three-line positions. Artillery would be fired along these three sets of coordinates. Hopefully, a wall of fire would separate Bill from his enemy.

"Give them to me in this order," I said, pointing to the sequence we would use.

While Miller was writing down the line positions, I picked up one of the other radio handsets and set the frequency to the Korean artillery battery.

"White Horse, White Horse, this is Bunkhouse. Over."

The response of the Korean voice was quick and professional. "Roger, Bunkhouse, this is White Horse. Over."

We had often entertained Colonel Chang, the commander of the ROK unit to our north, at Trung Dung. I was sure they would help unless they were already firing a mission for one of their own units.

"White Horse, we have a fire mission. We have a unit in contact and need your assistance. Over."

"Roger, Bunkhouse. We will help. At what coordinates do you want us to fire? Over?"

"Wait one, White Horse."

"White Horse, Bunkhouse. Use these coordinates," I said, and immediately gave them to him. "Wait for my command to fire. Then, fire all rounds HE (high explosive). Over."

"Roger, Bunkhouse. You don't want smoke first? Over?"

"No, we have no time. Over."

"Roger, we are ready. We wait for your command. Over."

"Roger, White Horse. Bunkhouse — out."

Normally, smoke rounds are fired first as marking rounds, to ensure that the high-explosive rounds don't kill friendly troops in case the coordinates were calculated or reported incorrectly. However, as I had told the Korean radioman, we had no time to take that precaution. Bill and his unit might all be killed even before we fired.

Miller changed the frequency on a third radio as I took the handset and called Trip Hammer, the artillery battery in Nha Trang. As soon as they answered, I repeated the same instructions given to the ROKs, using the second set of coordinates.

"Bunkhouse, this is Trip Hammer. Confirm ... no marking round."

"Trip Hammer, this is Bunkhouse. No smoke, HE first rounds. Wait for my command to fire. Out."

Then, quickly changing the frequency to reach the big guns in Ninh

Hoa, several kilometers/miles away, fire mission directions were given using the third and final set of coordinates.

As with the other two artillery units, they questioned the request for HE rounds first. The HE confirmation with these guns was critical and more important. They were firing 175-mm shells from miles away, and any one of them could kill or injure many of our own troops if they went off target.

The direction to Ninh Hoa was confirmed and in fewer than five minutes all guns were now ready to fire.

I called Bill to tell him what was about to happen.

"Blue Bandit Zero Six, Bunkhouse. Over."

"Go, Two."

"Bill, we've built a wall of artillery around you and are ready to fire. Over."

"Roger, Fire!" he yelled.

"Bill, there's no smoke."

"Roger, understand, no smoke. Fire!!"

"Roger. Bill, after impact, run north and into the village. Give me a mark every hundred meters, and we'll follow you. Get down! Over!"

"Roger, understand! We're down! Fire the damn things!"

At that point, I had a handset in each hand. I quickly dropped the one Bill was on and picked up another one, on which one artillery battery was waiting. All sets of guns were waiting, and two handsets were now open.

As I moved them close to my mouth, I looked at the X over Bill's position on the map and into both handsets gave the command to fire simultaneously.

"This is Bunkhouse. Fire! Fire! Fire!"

Then, quickly, Miller rolled the frequency dial around to the third set of guns, and the "Fire! Fire! Fire!" command was given once more.

Again, focused on the map and the X that indicated my friend's location, I could do nothing more for him—other than pray. I had made marks on a map with a grease pencil and reported them to the artillery batteries just as I had been trained to do. The effort to save Bill and his unit now fell to men at those various batteries.

The "Fire!" command had barely passed my lips when we heard multiple distant booms. All three artillery batteries were pouring ordinance into the night sky. All we could do was wait and hope to hear Bill's "Mark" after he began to move.

When the artillery rounds began to impact, we could feel tremors in the radio room. As the big ones impacted, they boomed like thunder. I prayed they had been on target.

While the first rounds were still impacting, each of the artillery batteries was called and given directions for shifting their next volley of rounds. When we received Bill's "Mark", they would shift fire to cover his disengagement and withdrawal as he and his unit made their way to a nearby village which was home for some of our soldiers.

While we waited to hear from Bill, one of our teammates ran in and told me the trucks with reinforcements were on their way. Several of our American advisers were with them. Those of us gathered around the radio wanted to believe they were going to make it in time to help.

Time seemed challenged to pass as we waited for Bill to call with the signal indicating he was still alive, had been able to disengage, and move a hundred meters north. I began to wonder if the call would even come.

Maybe I've killed him, I thought. *How ironic and terrible it would be if he has been killed by a friend, rather than by the enemy. And, how will I ever explain to Lisa?*

As the sound of impacting artillery rounds continued to thunder in the distance, Miller, who I'm sure didn't want to make anyone feel worse, voiced his concern.

"Sir, that's an awful lot of ordnance hitting the ground out there. I hope he's still there."

Then, visualizing my friend out in the dark in a fight for his life, and even though he couldn't hear me, I began to encourage him.

"Come on, Bill…come on. Call! I know you're out there somewhere. Call me!"

I rubbed my forehead, looked at my watch, folded my arms, and leaned back against the radio room wall.

Then, finally—the call came!

"Bunkhouse, this is Blue Bandit! MARK! MARK! MARK!"

Without a moment's delay, the order was given to the three sets of guns that were providing Bill's lifesaving wall of protection.

"Shift and fire!" to all three sets of guns.

Then, without knowing anything about the emergency situation to which they had been asked to respond, and without being able to see their target, the gunners at three artillery batteries once again lit the black Vietnamese sky with huge bright orange muzzle flashes. More high-explosive rounds were on their way to shield Bill and his men from enemy pursuit.

After giving my command to the guns, I again urged Bill and his unit on. "Run, damn it, run!"

While we knew that he was still in danger, we were encouraged that Bill's unit had moved the first hundred meters successfully. With artillerymen now firing a second volley of rounds, I plotted and called the battery with the next set of shift directions. Then, once again, we waited for Blue Bandit's next call.

While we were waiting for the next "Mark!", Lieutenant Colonel Allan Baer, an Air Force FAC (Forward Air Controller) had gotten his 0-1 Bird Dog observation plane airborne. He had heard what was happening from his headquarters at the Nha Trang Air Base and was headed our way. He checked in with an offer to help, one I quickly accepted.

Colonel Baer had been adopted by A-502 after Major Lee, our team commander, convinced 5th Special Forces Group Headquarters that a runway would give us greater mobility. While it was only about twelve hundred feet long, it gave us the ability to stage and launch missions quickly. Major Lee and Major Ngoc named the airstrip "Baer Field" in honor of the colonel who was the first pilot to land on it.

"Bunkhouse Zero Two, this is Walt Three Zero. Over."

With Bill due to signal at any second, I wanted to keep the frequency clear. My response to Walt Three Zero was brief. "Roger, Walt Three Zero. This is Zero Two. Try to determine Blue Bandit's location and stand by. Out."

When the word "over" is used on the radio, a response is expected.

When the word "out" is used, it means the transmission is complete and no response is required. Just as the button on the handset was released, Bill's signal came.

"Bunkhouse, this is Blue Bandit! MARK! MARK! MARK!"

Once more, the guns were called with the direction to "Shift and fire!" As before, battery gunners sent rounds streaking on their way to a point between Bill and anyone foolish enough to still be pursuing him.

For the first time since the situation had begun, everyone began to relax a bit.

They're going to make it, I thought. Miller and others who had gathered around the radio room were also confident that Bill and his unit had successfully disengaged.

Comments like, "They're good!" and "Yes!" could be heard from more than one person. I hoped they were right.

After the third set of artillery fire hit the ground, Colonel Baer called to report. Knowing the situation, his transmission was concise.

"Zero Two, Walt Three Zero. Assuming they're on the north side of your fire, I have your men, over."

"Great! Please stick with them. We may need you. Out."

"Roger. Will do—out."

Then, as twice before, a new set of shift directions were given to the guns and, one more time, we waited to hear from our teammate who was quite literally running for his life.

Finally, after his last "Mark!" and after the last volley of rounds hit the ground, Bill radioed that he and his unit had made it into the village.

When that call came, more cheers of "All right!" once again burst from the small brotherhood of American advisers collected around the radio room.

Bill and his unit had reached cover from which they could more effectively defend against the much larger unit they had ambushed. They waited, and we waited, to see if the battle would continue.

After a few minutes, Bill called to say that there was no sign of the enemy, pursuit had ended. He said they were moving through the village to the north side, where they would set up defensive positions and wait for reinforcements.

The reinforcing unit called in on Bill's frequency to say they were off-loading from trucks and would soon be approaching the village from the north. I called Bill to make sure he had heard the transmission, so he and his men wouldn't open fire on the reinforcements.

With the battle over and the artillery now silent, the night was once again quiet. Finally, I could relax. But, during the time I feared that I may have killed my friend or worried that the enemy would kill him if I hadn't—General Sherman's three words echoed in my mind. The flames of hell couldn't have been more painful. My experience that night is one I will never forget.

STEVE MOSIER

USAF: Fighter Pilot, Squadron Commander, Chief Checkmate Group, HQ
USAF

Dates of Military Service — Active Duty: September 1966 to July 1993

Unit Served with in Vietnam: 433rd Tactical Fighter Squadron, 8th Tactical
Fighter Wing, Ubon Royal Thai Air Base, Thailand

Dates you were in Vietnam: August 1968 — August 1969

Highest Rank Held: Colonel (O-6)

Place of Birth and Year: Kansas City, Missouri — 1943

THE NIGHT SHIFT

Every big organization operating on a 24-hour basis has a *night shift*.
The United States Air Force is a big organization and in the days of the
Vietnam War was clearly operating a *night shift*—-around the world
to plan for and support allied forces engaged with the enemy in various
parts of Southeast Asia. I spent some time on the *night shift* while I was
stationed at Ubon Royal Thai Air Force Base (RTAFB) located in the
eastern central part of Thailand. Part of that was flying with the 433rd
Tactical Fighter Squadron on F-4D strike missions in Laos and North
Vietnam. This was the exciting part of the *night shift*— flying mostly two
ship sorties looking for trucks and other vehicles on the Ho Chi Minh
Trail after dark or supporting gunships and special forces teams as they
conducted similar missions to interdict the flow of supplies (from USSR
and China) down the Trail to North Vietnam Army and Viet Cong
units in the south.

One of the mundane tasks of the *night shift* involved manning the
"*FRAG* Shop" from 1100 to 0700 (we used the term *0-dark thirty* long
before the media began to throw it around over the past two or three
years) where a small group of aviators, intel personnel, and some maintenance folks — all pretty much of the Lieutenant variety — were responsible for taking the *Fragmentary Order* aka *FRAG* from 7Th Air Force in
Saigon and parsing the information to provide instructions: to the flight
line as to how many sorties (aircraft) we would fly; what ordnance they

would be loaded with; whether or not air refueling would be needed; and where and when the flights would join their tankers; which squadrons would fly specific missions and; what and where the targets were.

Once this information was digested, it would be provided to the four F-4 squadrons where call signs would be assigned, and specific pilots would be assigned by position (leader and wingmen). Along the way, the Frag team would do a logic check to see that weapons were appropriate for the target, review the threats in the area of operation (types, numbers and best estimate of the location of anti-aircraft systems in the area—guns, SAMS, and disposition of MiGs), the tanker FRAG married up with the fighter tasking, perform several other quality control scrubs of the product Higher Headquarters had given the wing for the next flying day.

Mostly breaking the FRAG was a time constrained process that always had a late minute change causing a rework of the product and scurrying by Lieutenants to get a product out before the aircrews and day shift began to show up for mission prep and preflight actions—which was normally around 0330 to make ready for pre-dawn launch of 25th TFS Assam Dragons on their mission supporting the McNamara Wall with sensor drops monitoring and targeting movement on the Trail.

But all was never routine—special missions, emergency searches for downed pilots, support for Special Ops teams operating routinely in all parts of Laos and North Vietnam—all parts, change in weather, threats, tanker availability, and the whimsy of higher headquarters were frequently sand in a well-oiled FRAG operation, causing lots of changes to be jammed in up to the time the aircrews actually stepped to their jets, nominally 45 minutes or so before takeoff.

I easily remember one night for its special nature. LTs Mosier and Mulder, with the expert help of Staff Sergeant "Radar" were taking a break with Royal Crown Cola, our drink of choice—because there was no Pepsi or Coke—RC *was* the choice—when we got a hot line call from the command post, "head's up, the ADO (Assistant Deputy Commander for Operations) and a VIP are headed to the *FRAG* Shop!" We tidied up a bit and prepared for a short show and tell. The ADO and a

Congressman (whose name I don't think I ever got, and certainly don't remember) came in the Main Briefing room where all of the crew briefs took place, and all the annotated maps and photographs were displayed on boards around the room.

Now it is to be noted that ADOs are never with much to do, neither do they routinely have great responsibility, but in fact are hoping to be elevated to DO status if things go well for their Boss. This one was no different. He did want to give the impression he was alert, informed, and on top of his game to the Congressman, and asked us to describe the night's missions. I grabbed the *FRAG* and Mulder went, with pointer, to the map. I described the missions on the Board, with, "Sir, Dipper is working with Mk36s near Mu Gia Pass, Pintail has a mission with Covey 43 working a truck park just east of Tchepone, and Banyan is escorting Spectre 06 working Route 7 where it enters Laos from Pack 1 — they have flares and CBUs" — pretty good I thought, especially since Mulder was right with me with the pointer.

Well, I was WRONG. The ADO bristled, and addressed me very sharply, "Lieutenant, in my wing we don't do anything that lacks precision — I didn't expect a brief sketch of the activity — I wanted exactness! Let's try again the Wolf Pack way!" He glanced knowingly at the Congressman and apologized for having his time wasted by my casual discussion of important information. I know he wanted to strike me with a glove — like Patton — to emphasize the gravity of my lack of appreciation for the situation — regrettably he had no glove!

We rewound the tape: 'Sir, Pintail is a flight of two F-4Ds. Each has six Mark 36 Destructor 500 pound bombs with delayed fuses. Each is carrying a SUU-23 20mm cannon pod on the centerline. They will be placing their bombs on a section of road recently successfully cut with Laser Guided bombs by the 433d TFS in an attempt to keep the NVA road crews from repairing the road and moving supplies in this segment of the Trail tonight. The DMPI is WE336433 (these are map coordinates used to precisely reference a target location, common to ground troops and pilots, used before precision of GPS came into the routine use of today, and these aren't the actual coordinates for these targets — for you detail monsters, I am too lazy to find my old maps and give you the real coordinates—but the ADO and the congressman got the real ones in 6-digit accuracy).”

"Much better," the ADO replied, "now just where is WE366433?" Mulder, with a deft move of the pointer, replied, "Right here, near Mu Gia Pass, sir"—pretty much where the pointer was moments ago—no, not pretty much—exactly where Mulder had placed it two minutes earlier. We proceeded to review the details of the remaining sorties with exhausting depth and enjoyed a similar opportunity for the ADO to demonstrate his mastery of Lieutenants.

After some other discussion highlighting limited knowledge and actual interest in doing anything other than talking in front of the congressman, he allowed us to come to attention as they departed for another adventure in the workings of a Fighter Wing at night. Our RC Colas were warm by now, but we finished them anyway and prepared to turn over our work to the Day Shift and headed to the club for the world-famous Chili Cheese Omelet, proud that we had played even a bit part in keeping our leadership happy and a VIP even slightly entertained on his Oriental shopping trip. And, into crew rest, so we could get back on the flight schedule for the good gig on the *night shift*!

Note: This ADO was actually a FADO, and I don't make any reference to Portuguese music, rather to the four-letter prefix applied to ADOs with little promise of ever rising higher in responsibility or rank. Our Colonels in the 8TFW were WW II Aces, Thunderbirds, Test Pilots of Century Series aircraft and competent aviators and leaders. They made sure FADOs got their combat tours, never actually harmed anyone's livelihood or career, and quietly faded in to jobs they deserved.

HUBERT "HUGH" BELL, JR.

US Army — Aviator

Dates Served (Active and Reserve): 1966 to 1996

Dates and Units in Vietnam: 1967-1968 Co. A, 25th Avn Bn;

1971-1972 73d Survl Apln Co, 1st Avn Bde

Highest Rank Held: Lieutenant Colonel (O-5)

Place of Birth and Year: Elberton, GA — 1942

CLOSEST BRUSH WITH DEATH

In February 1968 during the Tet Offensive, we had, of course, an increased tempo of operations. One day after about nine hours of continuous flying, hot refueling, we returned to the Cu Chi base after dark. We had just refueled the helicopter and taken off to enter closed traffic to land at the airfield and secure the aircraft.

My pilot had the controls — I think it was CW2 Carl Muckle; he was my regular pilot for about six months. The runway lights were out, and Carl lined up on a long dark strip which he took to be the runway. As he descended on final approach, I turned on the landing light just to help him out. I saw immediately ahead of us a cable stretched between two utility poles. I grabbed the controls: full up collective, aft cyclic. We popped over the cable with about one millisecond to spare.

I took over and swerved to the right to land on the runway. I was so shaken and unnerved that I radioed maintenance ops for another pilot to hover the aircraft into the revetment.

My legs were so wobbly when I got out of the aircraft that I could hardly walk, by pure blind luck we had avoided what would have been the most spectacular helicopter crash fireball ever at Cu Chi. I am glad I was not the star of *that* show.

JOHN FRASER

US Army—Chaplain

Dates served: 1953—1983 Texas National Guard (Enlisted) 1953-1956; Army Ready Reserve (Enlisted) 1956-1960; Army Active Duty (Commissioned) 1963-1983.

Units Served with in Vietnam: 2/14 Inf and 1/27 Inf, 25th Inf Div; 8 RRFS.

Dates Served in Vietnam: Apr 1966 to Apr 1967; Nov 1969 to Nov 1970

Highest Rank Held: Lt. Colonel (O-5)

Place of Birth and Year: Greenville, TX—1936

THE STATIONARY MERRY-GO-ROUND

In late November 1969, I arrived at the 8th Radio Research Field Station at Camp Eagle, Vietnam. What a surprise that was! My first tour in Vietnam was with an infantry battalion where life was either all too boring or all too exciting. Someone said that life with the infantry in combat will alternately bore you to death or scare you to death. There was no doubt in my military mind that when I arrived in Vietnam for my second tour, I would be assigned as an infantry brigade chaplain because my entire first tour had been with infantry at battalion level, and I was especially qualified to move to brigade level because I had worked out well at battalion level.

It never occurred to me that the two and a half years that I spent as the post chaplain at an Army Security Agency Field Station an hour west of Washington D.C. might keep me out of an infantry unit on my second tour in Vietnam, but that's exactly what happened. The ASA was a military intelligence organization where nearly everyone had a top-secret clearance. So of course, I had been investigated and granted the top-secret clearance also. Thus, I was assigned to Radio Research on the second Vietnam tour. When I arrived at the 8RRFS, a signal corps organization, I was met by several longtime friends with whom I had just recently served at the ASA post. It was almost like coming home!

The 8RRFS was surrounded by Camp Eagle, but we had our own perimeter within Camp Eagle. Our field station had been a small French garrison before the French army left Vietnam, so we had several small permanent buildings to which had been added a few small American built semi-permanent buildings. The chapel was one of the old French buildings. It was a drab place, two or three small pews for a small (all male) choir, and probably fifty or sixty chairs for the congregation. But we had a Wurlitzer electric organ! I was amazed! Who ever heard of an Army chapel in an infantry division base camp in Vietnam that had an electric organ!

The Christian season of Advent begins four Sundays before Christmas. Most churches start decorating the sanctuaries for Christmas very near the beginning of Advent, so it was time to try to brighten that drab chapel for Advent and Christmas. I didn't have a clue how we would do that without decorations. So, the way to solve that problem was to assign someone to go scrounging. I called in a chaplain assistant (an enlisted man who is trained to run the usual administrative affairs of a chapel, who is the driver of the chaplain's jeep, and who carries a rifle to defend himself and the chaplain because the chaplain isn't supposed to shoot back).

"Frank, we need to decorate the chapel for Christmas. Go find something to decorate the chapel. I don't care where you look for decorations. If you need to spend a few dollars, I'll reimburse you. The decorations don't have to be the usual Christmas things. I'm not going to ask where you found the decorations. Just don't look anywhere for anything that's so good that I won't be able to get you out of any trouble that you might get into because you might be a little too enterprising."

A day or two later, he announced that he had found some donations—and was I astonished! Not only had he found a fair supply of Christmas decorations, but several things that could be turned into bright Yuletide trimmings. There was an especially abundant supply of brightly colored crepe paper. Frank had performed admirably, and he assured me that he hadn't had to buy anything.

So we announced on Sunday morning that on Wednesday evening we would decorate the chapel. Anyone wanting to help with the decorating would be welcome.

Wednesday evening came. Probably a dozen or maybe fifteen soldiers showed up for decorating. I didn't much care how they decorated the place, as long as they made it bright. Maybe I should have used better judgment, but I told them to decorate the way they wanted to, but remember that it was for Christmas, and I'd be back later that night to see what they had done after I left.

I got back a little later than I intended to. I walked into the chapel, turned on the lights, and gasped! The place had been decorated to a fare-thee-well! Crepe paper nearly papered the place. Even the outside of the confessional had been decorated! All three confessional doors had been gaily trimmed! And the center confessional door (for the Army chaplain who came by each Sunday for confession and mass) was given special attention. The whole interior of the chapel was reminiscent of a merry-go-round without horses!

I didn't sleep very well that night. What in the world had I caused to be created! This was an ecclesiastical monstrosity! But those soldiers had done exactly what I had asked them to do! They had made that drab chapel become bright!

The next morning at the daily staff meeting I announced that the chapel would look a little different until Advent and all twelve days of Christmas had passed, and I described what had been done. When Sunday morning came, I met the Catholic chaplain at the door, and said, "Before you go in, you need to know that the chapel looks a little different this week." We entered, and he got a good laugh out of the decorations. Then when he opened the center door of the confessional, he looked surprised and exclaimed, "Oh my God!" And broke into laughter. Even the inside of the confessional had been decorated! I assured him that all decorations would come down by Epiphany. The priest was very gracious and said that would work out well, and that it was refreshing to see something that had a lot of color.

Anyway, attendance at both Catholic mass and my Protestant service increased. And when we made the decorations go away for Epiphany, a good many people said they thought that maybe we should have left the Christmas decorations up.

CARL H. "SKIP" BELL, III

U.S. Army—Armored Cavalry Officer, Aviator

Dates of Military Service (Active and Reserve): 1967 to 1998

Units Served with In Vietnam: A Troop, HHT, B Troop, 1st Squadron, 4th Cav,
1st Inf Div (First Tour); C Troop, 3rd Squadron, 17th Air Cav; 18th Corps Aviation Co; G3, HQ 1st Aviation BDE (Second Tour)

Dates in Vietnam: Feb 1969 to Feb 1970; Feb 1972 to Feb 1973

Highest Rank Held: Colonel (O-6)

Place of Birth and Year: Decatur, GA—1945

THE DEATH OF LT PHILIPS, NOVEMBER 24, 1969

I don't remember precisely what we were doing when the radio call came
in. I do remember that we were several kilometers east-southeast of Lai
Khe basecamp, that we were not moving for some reason, and that we
were on a reconnaissance-in-force (RIF) mission. I was commanding B
Troop, 1/4 Cav. The time of day was late morning, November 24, 1969.

I don't recall what I was thinking about, either, though given the date,
I was probably considering how we'd handle the upcoming Thanksgiving
observance—whether we'd get a maintenance stand-down day in the
field that day, how we'd handle the feeding of the Thanksgiving meal, etc.
It didn't feel like the normal Thanksgiving season back home in Georgia.
By this time of year, the air would most likely be crisp and cold (or at
least cool). Here in Vietnam, it was another hot, humid, tropical day.

I was sitting on the left rear portion of my command track (B66),
monitoring the two VRC-46 FM radios mounted inside. I had one on
the Troop frequency and one on the Squadron frequency and used an
A-B switch to allow me to transmit on the frequency on which I wished
to talk. That arrangement allowed me to stay in constant contact with
both my Troop and my next-higher HQ.

Suddenly, a transmission came over the Squadron Command Net
that caused my knees to become weak and a cold feeling of dread to
permeate my chest and stomach.

"We ... have been ... hit ... we ... " (gurgling sound, then nothing).

I didn't recognize the voice, but I knew instinctively that whoever made that transmission was dying. The voice was high-pitched and in obvious agony. I'll remember that radio transmission as long as I live.

Immediately, the other stations on the net (me included) started transmitting things like, "Last station calling, say again call sign and location," or other similar messages. It was highly unusual for us to make contact in the area in which we were working during the daylight, and this added to the confusion. One of the RTO's from the Squadron TOC finally broke in and said for everyone to stay off the net until they could figure out where that transmission came from.

They began calling each station in turn that was supposed to be monitoring the command net, in an effort to identify the station that had transmitted that message. After what seemed like a long time, someone finally deduced that the transmission came from Rat 6, who had gone out on a patrol that morning to reconnoiter potential ambush sites in the daylight.

Rat 6 was 1LT Burton K. (Burt) Philips. Until recently, Philips had been a platoon leader in C Troop. He was a fine officer and platoon leader. When the Squadron had been directed by Division to establish a "Rat Patrol," Philips had answered the call for volunteers, and had become its leader. The Rat Patrol was named after a TV show that was popular in the States at that time. The show was about commandos in the North African desert in World War II who drove around in gun jeeps raiding behind German lines. Each maneuver battalion in the First Infantry Division had been directed to establish and employ a Rat Patrol after a Sergeant-Major in one of the infantry battalions had organized several HQ clerks into a Rat Patrol and had gone out and killed several VC.

In its constant quest for "body count," the Division Command Group decided that this was a viable way to kill more bad guys, and directed that each maneuver unit establish a Rat Patrol. Maneuver units in the First Division consisted of the infantry battalions and the cavalry squadron.

I thought it was a dumb idea at the time for several reasons. We were already mounted in vehicles (and those vehicles could take a mine or booby-trap a lot better than a jeep); it seemed superfluous to me for the cavalry squadron to set up a unit like that. The second (and more important) reason was that Charlie was not a fool—it wouldn't (and didn't) take him long to figure out what was going on, and to take appropriate measures. The third reason was that a lot of the folks who volunteered (or were dragooned into "volunteering") for the Rat Patrol had very little training as combat soldiers—many were clerks or had other non-combat MOS's like supply or transportation. There were some combat soldiers in the various battalion/squadron Rat Patrols, but not all were by any means.

My personal feeling about the formation of that unit was that it was an accident waiting to happen. Unfortunately, this was a not un-typical move by Division HQ. These are the same guys who allowed the Division Long Range Reconnaissance Patrol (LRRP) unit to go out on ambushes (!?!). They had nine infantry battalions and a cavalry squadron who were organized and equipped to do this, and they sent the LRRPs (who by definition were to gather intelligence without being detected, and who went out in six-man teams) out with orders to ambush if the situation permitted it.

Again, in my opinion, the all-mighty body count got in the way of clear, professional thinking. Sometimes I marvel that the First Infantry Division remained as fine a unit as it was, given some of the decisions that were made by the Division Command Group. We were fortunate to have some excellent junior leaders and soldiers who got the job done in spite of those questionable decisions.

Once the determination was made that the transmission had come from Rat 6, the next problem was to figure out where he was. He had gone out with two gun-jeeps earlier that day and was going to look at several places where the Rats might set up ambushes in the near future. The problem was that nobody knew specifically which site he was visiting when he was hit.

A LOH was launched, and a frantic search ensued. I'm not sure how, but they found the vehicles after about an hour. They were in a small draw to the west of the road that ran between Ben Cat and Lai Khe.

This draw was one of several "tributary" draws leading into a larger draw formed by a stream. They had hit a Chicom claymore mine that was set up in a tree overlooking the path they were following. Once they were found, I'm not sure how they were extracted from that place. Philips was KIA, and the three other members of the patrol were wounded. The word was put out over the Squadron Command Net about Philips. It was a sad day. He was a popular officer (well thought of by subordinates, peers, and superiors).

The next question became, "What are we going to do about it?" The answer was not long in coming. Shortly after 1300, B Troop received the mission to go clear the place where the Rat Patrol was ambushed. The plan was to put in an airstrike and then for us to move in and clear it. We would then check out the main draw along the stream and other tributary draws if they showed sign of enemy activity. The operation would have to be done on foot, since the tributary draw where Philips got ambushed was not wide enough to get tracked vehicles into, and the walls of the main draw where the stream was located were too steep for tracked vehicles to descend.

My plan was to move to an area south of the draw, bring the unit up online, and await the air strike. Then we would move forward in assault formation to the edges of the draw and, using the vehicles in overwatch positions, put dismounted patrols down into the area, starting with the place where the ambush occurred. Since we didn't know if the Chicom claymore was set off by a trip wire, or was command detonated, we weren't sure of the enemy situation (whether the area was still occupied, etc.). My suspicion was that it probably wasn't, given the amount of time between when the ambush was initiated and when the reaction force got on the scene.

Nonetheless, we could not let the ambush go unanswered, so we put troops on the ground to verify that the enemy had left the area, and to see if we could find what they were trying to protect with the Chicom claymore.

We came up online near a cemetery that was located approximately 600 meters from the draw, and we waited for the airstrike to go in. There were several aircraft in the strike (F4's, I think), and they dropped high explosive and napalm into the draw. Since we were going to be walking into that place later in the day, I hoped that the bombs and napalm detonated (or at least destroyed the trip wires for) any more booby traps that might be in the area.

When the airstrike ended and we were cleared forward, we moved to the edge of the draw. I had one of the tanks move to the near end and fire a canister round down the long axis of the draw (down the path where the ambush had occurred). The objective was to try to knock out any booby traps that had survived the airstrike. We then dismounted several Troopers (I believe from 2nd Platoon) and went into the draw.

It appeared to be a small base area. I went with them and discovered a tunnel entrance that had been uncovered in the bombing. We also found the remains of several booby-traps that had been placed there. I went into the tunnel. It didn't go back very far and was empty. It appeared that whatever had been in there had been recently removed.

As I was emerging from the tunnel, the Squadron Commander, LTC Murchison, nearly stepped on my hand. As was his custom, he admonished me that my job was not to go in tunnels, and (as was my custom), I answered that I felt like I should lead from the front. He walked off shaking his head, and we continued to search the area. As I had figured, we found nothing of significance. The bad guys had been there, but they were long gone by the time we arrived. Fortunately, none of the Bravo Troopers were hurt in the operation.

As we were getting everyone back together and getting ready to go find a place to spend the night, a LOH pilot (probably 1LT Dwight Cheek from the Division Aviation Battalion) came up on my troop command frequency and said that he had as passengers the two USAF Forward Air Controllers (FACs) who had put in the airstrike earlier. They wanted to see the results of their efforts from the ground. I told them that we'd be happy to show them around, and the LOH landed.

One of the FACs was a Lt. Col., the other was a Capt. (rank abbreviations are the way the USAF does it). I gave them a tour of the site, and we even let them fire a canister round from one of the tank's main guns. I was glad to do this because it meant now those guys knew us and might go a little further than they would otherwise if we got into trouble. We weren't just voices on the radio anymore, we were real people (and so were they). Sometimes things like that made the difference between surviving and not surviving.

Of course, that also meant that if one of them was shot down and we could do anything to help, we would go that much harder to get to them. They spent approximately 30 minutes on the ground with us, and then they left.

We packed up and moved to that day's night defensive position (I can't recall where it was). I remember being frustrated that we hadn't done more damage to the bad guys, and relieved that none of my troopers were hurt in the operation. But the thing I remember most of all about that day was hearing Burt Philips die on the radio. That really hit all of us who heard it hard. He was a fine, brave cavalry officer and his passing was a great loss.

Shortly after that, the Rat Patrol was disbanded. It's a shame that it took the death of Burt Philips, and the wounding of three other fine young cavalry troopers to prove what a stupid idea that whole thing was to begin with.

TIM BOONE

U.S. Army — Special Forces

Dates of military service (Active and Reserve): Oct 1965 to Nov 1976

Unit(s) you served with in Vietnam: 5th Special Forces Group (Also 46th Special Forces Company — Thailand)

Dates served in Vietnam: Aug 1967 to Aug 1968 (Thailand), Aug 1967 to Aug 1970 (Vietnam)

Highest Rank: CPT (O-3)

Place and date born: Watsonville, CA — 1945

"LIFE ON THE BEACH"

August 4, 1969. I arrived at HQ 5th Special Forces Group (Abn) in Nha Trang, RVN, to begin my second tour in SE Asia. As I was processing in, LTC "Pappy" Lamar" approached me and told me that he had injured his foot and had been reassigned from Project Sigma to command the Nha Trang Installation Defense Command (IDC). He said that he needed an S2 (Intel and Security) officer. I knew Pappy was a renowned combat leader in SF and that working with him would be a great experience…but, I was unsure about being in Nha Trang right at the 5th Group HQ. So Pappy said, "Come with me, California Boy," and we went in his jeep over to the Nha Trang IDC Bunker…get this!! A 3,000 square feet reinforced concrete bunker…On the Beach!!…Beautiful beach, palm trees, white sands, the water was aqua blue.

We could enjoy the beach, go snorkeling and catch 5-8 lb lobsters by hand, walk half a mile and be in downtown Nha Trang and enjoy 4 Star restaurants!! Who would even cook our lobsters for us! Well…

IDC was a joint HQ representing forces from the US, Vietnam, and South Korea (ROK), based in and around the city. As the S2, I was responsible for overseeing security for the whole complex and developing and reporting local intelligence from 21 different agencies to the 5th Group Commander daily. Our Tactical Operations Center also commanded and coordinated all combat operations supporting the Nha Trang Complex, including the HQ for II Field Force (II Corps).

August 5, 1969, I was assigned as S2 Nha Trang Installation Command!! It Looked good to me!!

Pappy introduced me to my S2 NCOs and my Vietnamese and ROK counterparts and then showed me to my standard metal government-issue desk adjacent to a wall covered with a Nha Trang Area of Operations map. Next, one of the lieutenants in the S3 section gave me a tour. The highlight was the rooftop lounge area and sunbathing deck!! Nothing fancy, just a flat roof and folding chairs, etc. We had a beautiful view of Hon Tre Island in the center of Nha Trang Bay. It was easy to see what a lovely resort area this would be if it weren't for the war. The fishing boats were all over the bay at night with lanterns hanging from a small mast, creating a fairyland of lights.

Of course, NVA underwater sappers were also swimming in the waters, and sinking ships moored in the harbor. We had a US Navy Detachment that patrolled the harbor and tossed three-pound depth charges over the side periodically to make it a little more challenging for the NVA. They also produced quite a fish kill which we gathered up and donated in the fishing villages. I got to tour and have dinner with the skipper of a wooden-bottomed minesweeper that my sailor brother had served on in the Tonkin Gulf!

The second day I was at work in the IDC bunker, several other officers invited me to lunch with them. As we got ready to leave the bunker, one of them told me to take all my pencils and paper and paperclips and any other office supplies I had and put them in a box and lock them in the closet. It seems that our Korean counterparts were also known as "slicky boys." They would clean a desk out if left unattended...so we learned to carry everything in a pouch and store nothing in the desks.

The Koreans also had early warning whenever new shipments of TVs, or air conditioners, or cameras and other electronics arrived at the Post Exchange. They would have a whole convoy of 2 and ½ ton trucks lined up at the door and buy the store out in a couple of hours. The merchandise was then taken directly to Korean ships and sent home to Korea. The ROKs had a reputation as brutally effective soldiers, but they had their way of interacting with everyone else. They were respected, but not much liked. I did get to take daily Taekwondo classes with the Koreans at IDC. Pretty good exercise. Several of the ROK officers and NCOs became good friends.

As part of my job, I made inspection tours of the entire perimeter of the Nha Trang complex and reviewed reaction/security plans for all units. It was challenging to get many logistics units to take local security seriously as things had been relatively quiet since Tet of 1968. A mortar or rocket or two every couple of days, but no ground attacks. Bunkers needed maintenance, and perimeter wire needed weeding. A little like herding cats. And of course, I was a Captain, and all these units were led by Colonels.

One of the most exciting things I did was fly "Sniffer Missions" twice a week. The four to eight-hour missions consisted of four helicopters — two slicks with door gunners only and two gunships armed with miniguns and rockets. The "hole ship" flew at treetop level at 75-80 knots around mountains and across the wind if possible, with me sitting in the back with a sniffer machine and its sensor hanging out the open door. We were sniffing for smoke from enemy campfires. I sat in the door with an M16 loaded with magazines full of tracer ammunition. If I got a reading on the sniffer, I would call it out over the radio, and my senior NCO riding in the "high ship" about 1500-2000 feet above and behind me would plot the reading on his map. A vector would sometimes then appear on the map based on these readings.

These sniffer readings pointed us to where the enemy bases were. Sometimes the NVA would be foolish and shoot at me in the "hole ship." I would return fire and mark their location with the tracers. Momentarily, rockets and minigun fire from the gunships would converge on the target. Amazing firepower. I included all of these actions as part of my daily intel briefing to the 5th Group Commander, Col. "Iron Mike" Healey.

On September 29, 1969, I was airborne with a sniffer team. I received a call that one of our Special Forces/ Civilian Irregular Defense Group (CIDG), companies, was engaged in a firefight. A company of NVA on the Dong Bo Mountain just outside of Nha Trang had ambushed them.

One American had suffered a sucking chest wound, and one CIDG had been impaled in the abdomen by a large splinter from a tree blown up by NVA mortar fire. I diverted my helicopters to support the troops on the ground. The gunships made passes until they had expended their ammunition and then returned to NHA Trang, refueled and rearmed as fast as possible, and returned.

The Dong Bo is a steep range of mountains that, in many ways, are like a pile of rocks the size of city buses. The ROKS had sealed many caves among these boulders, but there was still plenty of cover. Medevac helicopters did not want to try to land on the boulders in such a vulnerable place.... In hindsight, they were incredibly wise. On the other hand, I asked my pilot to take us through the canyon with the gunships trailing us. We took no fire and so circled back to touch the nose of the skids down on one of the immense boulders while we tried to load the wounded...Eight NVA stood up about 20 meters from us and proceeded to punch what later turned out to be 66 holes in the chopper. One went through my thigh. Three others went through my jungle fatigues without touching me! We returned fire, and the pilot pulled us out with every alarm in the ship going off. He managed to get us over the mountain and the five kilometers to the 8th Field Hospital pad at Nha Trang. He set the chopper down with no power and disabled it for future flying. That was one skillful crew!

So I ended up in the hospital for ten days. Now I had heard that in Army hospitals, you have to make your bed. So, the first morning when an orderly came through and dropped sheets on my bedside table, I climbed out of bed and started to remake it. Suddenly, I felt a heavy tapping on my shoulder. I turned, and an Army Nurse Corp Major was standing there. She was about six feet, three inches tall, and had eyes of flint. Her comment was, "Captain, we have people here who can make these beds. Now get your ass back in that bed before I put it there!" I said, "Yes, Ma'am!" and complied immediately.

One of the sergeants I worked with smuggled me in a bottle of vodka, which I shared with my ward mates each evening by liberally lacing orange drink from the hospital snack bar. There were six of us. Five were wounded, and one had kidney stones. He was the one suffering the most pain, so we took turns distracting him and helping him with his needs. During those days in the hospital, I had a severe confrontation with my mortality. Of course, being shot will get your attention.

After ten days, I was discharged to light-duty and returned to the SFOB and work at IDC … no more sniffer missions for about six weeks. I was given the "opportunity" to fill a 250-gallon tank of Agent Orange in the back of a helicopter outfitted with spray booms every day for two weeks. We flew out into known VC/NVA food production areas and sprayed their fields to kill all the vegetation and deny them the food they needed. No one had any idea that Agent Orange was contaminated with dioxin and that we were putting ourselves and the Vietnamese at risk of terrible diseases.

We celebrated Christmas at the Officers club on the Air Base. It was our regular hang out when not on duty. Usually, it was just a lot of good fun and lots of alcohol. A group of Australian SAS officers were there. They got into an argument, and fisticuffs ensued, as did flying beer mugs. They had an excellent time for about 20 minutes, and then all went off together to the Bachelor Officer Quarters. All had a Merry Christmas.

One of the Lieutenants in the S2 shop played poker late every evening at the club. He never drank alcohol. Not surprisingly, he was able to send $1,000.00 poker winnings home to his wife every week. The fact that others would get inebriated and play against him more than once was surprising.

Life on the beach in Nha Trang was an eye-opening experience. Not at all what I thought the Vietnam war should be. In January 1970, all changed as I was assigned as S3 to Detachment B55, 5th Mobile Strike Force (a brigade-sized, country-wide reaction force) supporting SF Camps throughout the country. But that's another story.

RAYMOND L. COLLINS

US Marine Corps — Combat Logistics Officer

Dates of Military Service: 1960 — 1980, a lifer

Unit Served with in Vietnam: 1st Tour: FLSC-A, FLC, IIIMAF; 2nd Tour: HQ III MAF

Dates in Vietnam: 1st Tour: Aug 1968 to Nov 1969; 2nd Tour: Jan 1971 to Apr 1971

Highest Rank Held: Lt Colonel (O-5)

Place of Birth and Year: Kinston, NC — 1938

GUARDSMEN INVASION

In the latter part of November 1968, I was serving as the S-4 of FLSG-Alpha in Phu Bai just west of Hue. We were in the midst of flip-flopping mission assignments with FLSG-Bravo which was moving north to the Dong Ha-Quang Tri area to support the 3rd MARDIV. The plan called for Alpha to consolidate and move south to Camp Books at Red Beach near Da Nang to assume responsibility for providing logistical support to the fire support bases (Chu Lai, Hill 55, An Hoa, Hill 327, Hoi An, & others) occupied by 1st MARDIV throughout the southern portion of I Corps.

A few days before Thanksgiving, we were invaded by a convoy of Army vehicles loaded with what appeared to be American civilians. They were dressed in civilian clothing with greenbacks in their pockets and had no weapons or personal equipment. As I recall there were about 100+ of them. As it turns out, they were Army National Guardsmen who had just arrived from the States following an injunction denial by a US Court. The Army reacted immediately by getting them airborne and en route to Vietnam.

Back home, the unpopularity of the Vietnam war prompted an increase in draft evasion and there were many instances where the draft system itself was being challenged in the US Courts; even some National Guardsmen and Reservists were petitioning for an injunction to block their being sent to Vietnam.

Our unit was one of many tasked to temporarily in-process the new arrivals: house, feed, collect their greenbacks, and provide jungle uniforms and boots for these soldiers. We erected a tent complex with cots and brought in a shipment of jungle utilities and boots from Da Nang. Our Paymaster converted their US dollars (greenbacks) to MPC and the mess hall extended feed times to accommodate and handle the influx. As I recall, they were with us for about 10 days before they were transported to their permanent unit assignments. This episode added to the growing legend among the troops "that many strange things happened beneath the Vietnamese sun."

As a footnote, most of the National Guardsmen who were called to active duty around the country did their jobs as well or better than others in Vietnam, but as with any organization, there was the small percentage who fought the system.

RICHARD H. MOUSHEGIAN

Army — Quartermaster Corps, Logistical Officer

Dates of Military Service (Active Duty and Reserves Combined): 1968-1993

Unit Served with in Vietnam: HHC, Ling Binh Post, USARV (US Army Vietnam)

Dates you were in Vietnam: Oct 1968-Oct 1969

Highest Rank Held: Lt. Colonel (O-5)

Place of Birth and Year: Camp Wheeler (deactivated after WWII) near Macon, GA — 1943

MEMORIES OF A QUARTERMASTER OFFICER

Background: As a Quartermaster Captain in the Army while in Vietnam (1968-69), I was the Logistics Officer (supply and maintenance) for a 40-unit club system in Long Binh (near Saigon) for American officers, Senior NCOs, and enlisted troops. The clubs provided a friendly environment for the troops after their duty hours to purchase and consume adult beverages and food items such as pizzas, hamburgers, packaged snack items, and cigarettes. The majority of the clubs were located in the sprawling Army post of Long Binh with a few clubs at the nearby Air Force base at Tan Son Nhut. I have two observations and a flight experience while serving in that capacity.

As the Supply and Maintenance Officer of the club system, I was responsible for maintaining the five reefers (in this case, the reefers were walk-in freezers) at the main office to store frozen goods not yet distributed to the individual clubs. Additionally, the club system had a fleet of civilian vehicles that were used exclusively by the club personnel (small, Japanese Daihatsu pickup trucks) and larger delivery vehicles (Ford F-350 trucks) used by my supply personnel to pick-up and deliver goods primarily from the PX system.

We had a maintenance contract with a civilian Korean company that maintained the refrigeration units and vehicle maintenance. As you would expect, they seriously overcharged us for parts, and they had a high hourly-rate for work performed. Fortunately, my (military) boss asked me to review the charges before the bill was paid, and I noticed a 20% profit at the end of all the detailed charges. When I deleted the surcharge, the Korean supervisor didn't even put up a fight, nor did he ask for a reduced percentage. That is when I realized that he had already sufficiently padded the account to make a handsome profit. My situation confirmed what I had heard during and after the Vietnam War, that many people were making lots of money related to the US military's war effort.

Another observation from the club system was the edict from highly placed senior officers that they did not want experienced senior NCOs running the clubs (even with a club specialty MOS—military occupation specialty) because they would know how to "game the system" and make lots of "pocket money" that would be untraceable. Hence, the club system was forced to place 19-22 year old servicemen (Specialists grades 4 and 5) to run the clubs!

Now, I ask you to think about what the effect is of placing an immature man with limited business and worldly experiences in a situation where he is managing liquor, money, and female (Vietnamese) waitresses. For the booze situation, frequently the very young club manager was found in bed at the club with a hangover the next morning while we were trying to deliver supplies to his club. (Can you imagine him not being tempted to grab a drink here and there during the evening with his buddies?) For the money situation, short-changing the register is a temptation with youngsters who don't think about the consequences.

However, the interesting problem was with the female waitresses. The most cunning and quickest of the females would latch onto the young club manager and make sure that all of the other girls knew that SHE was the girlfriend. Next, she would promote herself from working waitress to cashier behind a cage to accomplish two goals: sit on her rump during the entire evening making money transactions (making change for the troops and paying bar tabs?—I am not exactly sure), but, more importantly, she took charge of the entire female staff! If you visited the club in the evening, she usually had a scowl on her face!

Of course, by taking charge of the female staff by reason of "the manager's girlfriend," the girl barked orders from the cage with the effect of making all the other waitresses unhappy. Do you think the young club manager could correct the situation when she satisfied all his worldly needs? (If you doubt me, think again.) After first-hand witnessing the downside risks of inexperienced, young club managers, I thought that the senior military commanders were short-sighted in their guidance.

To my way of thinking, it would have been more important to run the clubs efficiently with experienced club-managers (senior NCOs) with well-functioning staffs and well-served troops. The military management could closely watch the NCO-managers and threaten to fire them and place adverse comments in their military records if their club was seriously short in supplies (including liquor) or cash during an un-announced-inventory!

The other experience was based on the fact that my brother, 1LT Stephen Moushegian, was in-country at the same time, and I was able to get him assigned nearby. He was assigned to the 25th Aviation Company in which their mission was to transport high-ranking officers and civilians (or VIPs — Very Important Persons) around Vietnam within 1-2 hours of Long Binh Post. Sundays were my days off because we employed foreign nationals in our front office in the club system, and they did not work on Sundays. On those days, I would fly with him or his pilot buddies (with the full knowledge of flight operations) for something to do (instead of drinking) by relieving the door gunner (enlisted) on the Huey helicopter (UH-1) until my brother transitioned into the Loaches (OH-6A).

While in uniform, I was just considered a "door gunner" or a passenger. I didn't care where the destinations were because the 25th Aviation Company always returned to the same helipad after the mission. (That arrangement continued for about three months until my brother requested and received a transfer to the 11th Armored Cavalry Regiment (ACR) as an aerial scout flying a Loach with a "real mission" according to him.[1])

However, that situation was re-evaluated after one trip on a weekend

---

1. For his 11th ACR assignment, he was highly decorated for valor and was interred (in-ground) in Arlington National Cemetery on August 7, 2020 in the company of other warriors.

when one of the pilots asked if I would like to fly with them for a night flight. An artillery Lieutenant Colonel (LTC) wanted to observe/supervise a TOT, time on target, in which artillery would be concentrated on a specific target for a brief amount of time to neutralize the target. It should be spectacular with tracers and explosions. I agreed and came back at dusk.

I assumed the door-gunner position and was outfitted with headphones with intercom. We lifted off in a Huey with the LTC. Nightfall arrived shortly into the flight. I was staring over the M-60 into the dark abyss. There were NO lights of any kind to be seen. No starlight, no village lights, no streetlights, no vehicle lights — nothing. We were about 45 minutes into the flight, and the aircraft started banking. I still saw nothing, for I was on the wrong side of the aircraft to observe the artillery barrage. Then, the PIC (pilot in command) announced that we were headed back home. Up to that point I was fine.

The next thing I heard on the intercom was the PIC telling the co-pilot to take over the controls and fly the aircraft back to the helipad. The inexperienced co-pilot protested by saying, "No, wait! I don't know where we are. I don't want to do that! Where are we?"

PIC: "Just calm down. Take a look around you and see if you can get your bearings. By the way, what should our bearing (magnetic compass heading) be on the return flight?"

Co-Pilot: "I don't want to fly the return trip. Just take over."

PIC: "No, you need to figure out where we are and select our bearing for the flight back home."

There was silence on the intercom, so I hoped that the co-pilot was checking his maps for the flight path and bearing that he MUST have made during his pre-flight preparation. (The PIC must have been understandably disappointed in his co-pilot.)

Me (on the intercom): "What are all the fires on the ground? (To me it looked like "Dante's Inferno", as there were fires in all directions. However, I did not add that commentary to the tense situation in the cockpit.)

PIC: "Those are fires started by artillery ammunition."

At that point, I started to re-evaluate my position in the dark in a he-licopter somewhere in Vietnam that could possibly have a forced landing (polite term for "crash"):

I had no side arm/weapon (pistol) for I was not in a combat assign-ment at Long Binh Post.

I had my hands on an M-60 that was bolted to the aircraft and no knowledge on how to release it and carry the ammunition—let alone fire it.

I had no knowledge of our location and no knowledge what direction it was to the "friendlies."

If this aircraft goes down in the dark and in a fire started by artillery ammunition, the situation would be even more grave.

If this aircraft goes down, I was *****. (Use your own terminology; you get the idea.)

However, I rapidly came to a conclusion: IF WE MAKE IT BACK TO THE HELIPAD TONIGHT, I AM *NEVER, EVER* GOING TO MAKE ANOTHER NIGHT FLIGHT IN VIETNAM!

EPILOGUE:

I never made another night flight in Vietnam, even when offered.

I have since acquired a civilian pilot's license after retiring from the military. It is a Sport license (FAA issued; airplane, single engine, land—among other restrictions). One of the restrictions is that it re-quires the holder to only fly VFR (Visual Flight Rules) meaning NO NIGHT FLIGHTS!

STEVE MOSIER

USAF: Fighter Pilot, Squadron Commander, Chief Checkmate Group, HQ
USAF

Dates of Military Service – Active Duty: September 1966 to July 1993

Unit Served with in Vietnam: 433rd Tactical Fighter Squadron, 8th Tactical
Fighter Wing, Ubon Royal Thai Air Base, Thailand

Dates you were in Vietnam: August 1968 – August 1969

Highest Rank Held: Colonel (O-6)

Place of Birth and Year: Kansas City, Missouri – 1943

THE NIGHT THE LIGHTS WENT OUT IN ROUTE PACK II

We had four fighter squadrons at Ubon in '68-'69. The 497th, the Night
Owls, flew almost exclusively after dark. The bellies of their Phantoms
were painted black, and their cockpits were taped over in a unique way to
protect night vision, requiring a very close collaboration between the AC
and the GIB for spatial orientation. The 25th Assam Dragons had the
Igloo White mission for the main, taking off before sunrise, delivering
their sensors from unique dispensers and pods with the precision their
LORAN equipped D models allowed. The 433rd Satan's Angels had
mostly day missions and was the pioneer of LGB (Laser Guided Bombs)
operations with the Zot system, also having 4-8 sorties on the early night
schedule. Then there was the 435th. No one knew what they really did,
and no one really cared.

For a period of several months in 1968 I flew night missions in the
433rd. We were a pretty small group working this mission. We called
ourselves the "Sewer Doers" and had a special patch showing a scrawny
rat peeking out of a sewer main, graphically depicting what we felt about
mucking about in bad weather, after dark, in Laos and North Vietnam.
Our weapons loads consisted of CBU-24/49s, MK82s with and without
fuse extenders, and in most cases, one bird in a two-ship had SUU-25
flare dispensers. We worked with O-2 Nail FACs and C-130 Blind Bats
that used starlight scopes to pick out "lucrative targets" along the trails.
Sometimes we had pre-fragged targets (targets selected before the frag

orders came down from higher HQ) that we sought out and bombed on our own, using visual cues illuminated by the moon or by our own flares. If it was a good night, we hit some trucks, fuel and POL dumps and aroused the gunners creating other targets of the 23mm, 37mm, 57mm, and sometimes 85mm sort.

Some nights we just moved dirt and trees. DJ, one of the Night Owls, and a pilot training classmate sent a "suggestion" to 7AF that we fill our external tanks and all of the napalm cans with wet concrete, and drop them in the choke points at Mu Gia and Ban Kari, noting that concrete was harder to move than bomb craters were to fill, and at the end of the day we'd have some neat pedestals to install war memorials on—funny we never heard back. I remember one special evening. Hal, one of the Sewer Doers, had contacts in 7AF and a penchant for doing his own target assessment. Using these two factors he divined that there was an area on the Ho Chi Min trail just north of Mu Gia Pass in Route Pack (RP) II, one of the areas allocated to the Navy, but beyond the combat radius of their strike force on the carriers in Yankee station. It was Hal's bet that the NVA were using this sanctuary to marshal supplies before the push into Laos and through Steel Tiger on to South Viet Nam.

I was never sure whether we had permission to go into RPII, but we checked in with Moonbeam and pressed on to the area we were going to check out. We made low passes with varying angles and offsets, and were pretty sure we saw supplies, including POL pipes along the road. At first we drew no reaction from the NVA. So, the flare bird dropped a string across the road—holy s—t—there was s—t everywhere! I vaguely remember that one of our Phantoms had CBU-2 on this sortie, but maybe I am mistaken. In any case, we dropped everything we had on several passes and the fires we started were massive. So was the AAA in response.

Winchester, (code word for all ammunition/ordnance expended), we climbed out and checked back to see blazes at least a couple of hundred feet high, secondaries, and lots of visual AAA. We called Moonbeam and informed them that there were some REAL lucrative targets and gave coordinates. There was a pause to check the coordinates of the location ("set Elizabeth over Richard ...") again — it was maybe, just maybe, somewhere we should not have been.

Regardless, 'Beam diverted the night's action to where we had just departed, and they kept the pot stirred for the day go, which continued to pound the area with great success for another twelve hours or so. Checking out with Bruce on Moonbeam, he congratulated us on "good work." (If you'd have flown in Laos in '68-'69 you'd know who Bruce was — a distinctive and familiar voice for the night fighters). It *was* good work — and we were proud of Hal for being the best intel/targeteer we knew, and happy the A-4s from the carriers left us a sweet spot for that one night. Beer at 2230, chili cheese omelets in the Club dining room, in the rack by 0130 and out till the next afternoon and another trip to the Sewer.

THOMAS A. "TOM" ROSS

US Army— Special Forces

Dates of Military Service (Active and Reserve): 1966 to 1992

Unit Served with in Vietnam: Detachment A-502, 5th Special Forces Group

Dates in Vietnam: Jan 1968 to Dec 1968

Highest Rank Held: Major (O-4)

Place of Birth and Year: Huntington, WV—1945

MY GUARDIAN ANGEL

When most people think of a guardian angel, they think of a powerful winged being that has come from somewhere in a place most of us hope to go one day—to watch over and protect us. These heavenly protectors have sometimes been described as gloriously dressed in flowing white robes with a golden aura surrounding them. Certainly, this would be an awe-inspiring vision to behold.

Surprisingly, I was once fortunate enough to have an encounter with a guardian angel and he wasn't the vision one might expect of such a being. He didn't appear powerful, had no wings or golden aura, and he wasn't dressed in white robes—but he may have indeed been sent from Heaven.

My guardian angel was barely five feet tall, was dressed in camouflaged combat fatigues, and he wore combat boots! He also often wore a huge smile and always carried a carbine rifle. His name was Ahat (pronounced "Ah-ott").

In 1968, I was serving with the 5th Special Forces Group in the Republic of South Vietnam as a military advisor with Special Forces Detachment A-502 in Khanh Hoa Province. I was a young lieutenant and had been assigned as 502's Intelligence (S2) and Operations (S3) Officer.

As a Special Forces advisor, we were typically not with a large American unit when we went out into the field on a mission. Usually, two of our American advisors would be assigned to one of the South Vietnamese CIDG (Civilian Irregular Defense Group) units we were training and advising when they went to the field on a combat mission. Because our intelligence told us that as many as fifteen percent of those troops could also be VC (Viet Cong) and/or NVA (North Vietnamese Army) sympathizers, being in the field with them was almost as hazardous as being out there with the enemy. As a result of this reality, Special Forces often employed and trained body guards to accompany American advisors.

To protect themselves from the constant threat of assassination, some of the first Special Forces advisors to arrive in Vietnam turned to the Montagnards as a solution. Montagnard means "mountain dweller" in French and the name was given to the indigenous tribesmen living in the Central Highlands of Vietnam by the French when they occupied the country. Having been tipped off to their loyalty by the French, American Special Forces advisors quickly developed a trusting relationship with the tribesmen. Both were tough, versatile, and accustomed to living and working in rugged mountain and jungle conditions—it was a perfect match.

The Montagnards, nicknamed "Yards" by Americans, were treated with distain by the Vietnamese who viewed them as little more than primitive. So, it was easy for the Montagnards to develop an affinity for the Americans who treated them extremely well and offered them training and friendship, something the Vietnamese weren't interested in offering them.

Even before I went to Vietnam, I had learned about the Montagnards and their extremely important role with our teams there. So, when I eventually arrived in country, I looked forward to meeting those who worked with A-502.

When I was first introduced to Ahat, I was a bit surprised. He appeared more Polynesian than Asian to me. He was small, looked like he could be about sixteen years old, and his handshake was weak—almost timid. And, Ahat had a huge ingratiating smile that made me think of him as the little brother I never had. He looked like someone who might need to be taken care of rather than someone who would be the guardian and protector. However, demonstrating how wrong first impressions can be, during the next year, Ahat would prove himself to be as fearless as any guardian angel and, when it came to my safety, his vigilance was very close and constant. His watchfulness over me almost became a game.

Occasionally, I would look around to see where he was. And, when he caught me, which was nearly every time, he would show me his big smile as if to say, "No worries Trung uy (Vietnamese for Lieutenant). I've got your back." And he did—always.

At least twice during our time together, Ahat leapt between me and a perceived threat like a leopard from a tree. Once, it was near dark when one of our Vietnamese CIDG troops had his knife out and was within only steps of me. Ahat jumped from I don't know where and jammed the barrel of his carbine up into the soldier's ribcage. As it turned out, the soldier was only going to cut a piece of fruit that was hanging in a tree over my head. At least, that was his story.

After that incident, the soldier would never come near me when Ahat was around. That amused Ahat, who would smile and chuckle when he saw the soldier taking the long way around to his destination.

Another time, it was very late at night when we were on a mission in the Dong Bo Mountains, a very dangerous Mountain complex that was crawling with both VC and NVA soldiers. We had a captured NVA soldier with us to act as guide to an enemy basecamp. He was tied up several feet away from me and under guard by a South Vietnamese soldier. I was in my hammock making a radio check with my back to the enemy soldier when the Vietnamese either fell asleep or became distracted.

Suddenly, there was a loud "Thud!" behind me. I dropped the radio handset, grabbing my M-16 as I quickly jumped to my feet, and leveled my M-16. It was Ahat! He had jumped out of the darkness from a rock above me to a position between me and the enemy soldier.

When I asked what had happened, Ahat quickly explained that the Vietnamese soldier guarding the prisoner had fallen asleep and not long after he did, and even though his hands and feet were tied, he picked up a rock and had started to crawl toward me. That was when Ahat once again leapt into action.

While the Vietnamese soldier guarding the prisoner claimed that he had only become distracted—he was never clear about exactly what had distracted him.

I rarely, if ever, slept when I was in the field. But, for the brief few minutes when I did, I slept well, knowing that my guardian angel was awake and watching over me. And, he had come from a place on high. Ahat had been born in the jungle of the Vietnamese mountain highlands—not quite heaven, but close enough.

If you enjoyed this chapter, you can read more about Ahat and some of my other experiences in Vietnam in my book, Along the Way, published in December, 2020.

HUBERT "HUGH" BELL, JR.

US Army—Aviator

Dates Served in Military (Active and Reserves): 1966 to 1996

Dates served in Vietnam: 1967 to 1968, 1971-1972

Unit Served with in Vietnam: 1967-1968 Co.A, 25th Avn Bn; 1971-1972 73d

Surveillance Airplane Co, 1st Avn Bdeß

Highest Rank Held: Lieutenant Colonel (O-5)

Place and Date Born: Elberton, GA—1942

SENIOR OFFICER ROLE MODELS

I was very fortunate to have the opportunity to work during my two tours in SEA with some outstanding military officers who went on to positions of greater responsibility. I've learned from their abilities and the way they carried out their commands and other responsibilities.

I was a Command and Control helicopter pilot for a while, sharing that assignment with another lieutenant, for Colonel Marvin Fuller, commander of the 2d Brigade, 25th Infantry Division, Cu Chi, Vietnam. I also flew combat assault, resupply, and ash & trash missions. Colonel Fuller was an energetic, thoughtful, analytical, and decisive commander. He was also considerate of his junior officers, including me. The aircraft had a communication console mounted behind the pilots' seats to enable COL Fuller to communicate with his battalions and his headquarters. We served as his airborne command post overseeing each of the three infantry battalions. He later reached LTG and commanded Fort Hood and III Corps.

I also was the Command and Control aircraft pilot for COL Fuller's replacement as Brigade Commander, COL Wallace Emerson. COL Emerson employed me not only as his C&C pilot but also as his de facto aide. For example, when he issued a warning order to one of his battalions, he asked me to go to the battalion headquarters in the field and brief the battalion commander on the upcoming operation.

I was the pilot for COL Emerson for several months. I exceeded the 140 hours maximum flying time every month. Therefore, I was required to get three days' downtime. Each time I was grounded for three days, COL Emerson contacted my aviation battalion commander and requested that I be allowed to go to Vung Tau on the southeastern coast of South Vietnam, a French resort town known as Cap St. Jacques for in-country R&R. Of course, my commander agreed that I could spend three days on R&R at Vung Tau. The lesson takeaway was good commanders take care of loyal troops.

No matter how considerate COL Emerson was, his brigade operations officer (S3), MAJ Pawlak, was a real jerk. For example, when the Bob Hope Christmas show came to Cu Chi in 1967, he sent me and my crew on a bogus mission just to prevent us from attending any of the Bob Hope show.

The first mission for my temporary replacement C&C aircraft commander was to take me to Vung Tau. On the third day he was directed to pick me up.

One day in late 1967, I was piloting the aircraft with COL Emerson and some of his staff officers west of Cu Chi. The commander, LTC Glenn Otis, of the 3rd Squadron, 4th Armored Cavalry Regiment was in contact with COL Emerson. They needed to discuss an immediate upcoming operation, so I landed in a huge rice paddy, several hundred acres. LTC Otis landed in his helicopter near us in the field. He and COL Emerson and the staff spread maps on the ground and were planning this immediate offensive operation.

After a few minutes, we began to receive mortar fire from the VC. Everyone scrambled back aboard their respective aircraft and we took off to escape the fire. I enjoyed working occasionally with LTC Otis and his squadron. He was an aggressive commander who knew how to employ his air and armored cavalry. LTC Otis went on to gain four stars and became the Supreme Allied Commander, Europe (SACEUR).

On my second tour in 1971, I was transferred for TDY at Udorn Royal Thai Air Force Base in Thailand. I was given command of an Army OV-1 Mohawk airplane surveillance unit. Its mission was to conduct electronic surveillance in Laos, primarily the Plaine des Jarres region in western Laos. My first task was to renegotiate the Interservice Support Agreement with the Air Force. The former commander of the unit apparently did not get along with the commander of the 432d Tactical Reconnaissance Wing which provided logistical and avionics support for my unit.

I met with the Wing Commander, COL Charles Gabriel. We had a cordial discussion and a few other meetings, unlike his experience with the previous commander of my unit. He was courteous, professional, engaging, and direct, so we had no difficulty in renegotiating the Agreement. Thereafter, we received superb support from his Wing units. COL Gabriel went on through successive assignments and promotions to become the Chief of Staff of the Air Force.

After my return from my second tour in Vietnam, I had the privilege of working with other outstanding officers who were destined for high command. Norman Schwartzkopf was promoted to four stars and commanded all the allied forces in Operation Desert Storm to drive Saddam Hussein's Revolutionary Guard and other army elements from Kuwait.

Likewise, when I was the Assistant Division Aviation officer (ADAO) of the 9th Infantry Division I worked with LTC John Shalikashvili on a joint service task force to develop military doctrine for command and control of the tactical battle airspace. This was a thorny problem because that airspace might at times include Army, Air Force, and Marine aircraft, artillery, and naval gunfire. We spent many days in Fort Lewis, Bergstrom AFB in Texas, and White Sands Missile Range in New Mexico to try to develop an interservice protocol to manage the airspace to permit nearly simultaneous use. Shalikashvili went on to four stars and Chairman of the Joint Chiefs of Staff.

The defining characteristics of these officers were professional competence, high intelligence, and modest courtesy. I observed that no one who was a jerk reached flag rank.

JEFF 'BIC' BICKERTON

US Army — U-1A 'Otter' — Crew Chief

Dates of Military Service: 1966 — 1969

Unit Served with in Vietnam: 18th Aviation Company, 223rd Combat Avn Bn, 1st Aviation Brigade

Dates Served in Vietnam: February 1, 1968 to April 24, 1969

Highest Rank Held: SP5 — Crew Chief on Otter 'Reliable 713'

Place and Date of Birth: Queens, LI, NY — 1946

GOODBYE, FAREWELL AND ... HELLO

Goodbye: My father (David Lloyd Bickerton) took me to JFK Airport to board a flight to Vietnam late January 1968. My Dad was a WWII Veteran (from 1939 NCO to field promoted 1st Lt by 1943). He had a son, my older Brother (Steve-22), who was drafted into the Marines and was already in VN. He was scheduled to be returning as I was leaving the USA (Steve did make it home). Dad knew about War, but we had never really talked about it. At JFK, he tried to say a few things about being careful and making it home, but at this point, I can't remember what he said. I was in the 'don't-worry-about-me' phase of life (21) and his words did not sink-in to my thick skull. But something did — a look he had. After we hugged at the gate, I looked into his eyes and I will always believe I saw them telling me that this was to be our last hug. I stared at him and my eyes welled-up. We hugged again. I boarded the plane.

Farewell: In VN, after my assignment to the 18th Aviation Co in Qui Nhon, I was sent to Pleiku to learn how to 'Crew' an Army U-1A Otter. I was stationed there for about three weeks and in-country about five weeks. The '68 Tet Offensive was over and things were getting back to normal as normal could be in the VN highlands. One evening, I was called into my Commanding Officer's (CO) tent. I remember pulling back the flap and seeing two Officers sitting at a table in the CO's quarters. One was a chaplain, and one was our CO (who I did not know very well). The CO told me that my Dad had died (of his 1st Heart attack) and that they were sending me home for 30 days to get thing settled on the home front. We had lost my mother about 2½ years earlier from her long battle with Polio related disabilities. Her poor polio-ravaged lungs could not fight the pneumonia she caught in 1965. Gloria Rita Bickerton was a Saint (I swear it). I went home to the 'world' and took care of family business. Also, got to know my future wife, Teri Macek, who I had met only one week before I left for VN in January. After my 30 days leave, I went back to VN and was assigned my own ship to 'Crew'. It was good-old Otter 'Reliable 713', which started the rest of my 14-month tour in VN.

Hello: Some 44 years after I left VN, the 18th Aviation Co. had its 1st Reunion in Branson, MO. Of the 1,750 guys in the 18th over the ten years they were in VN, 19 guys showed up. Of the 19 guys there was a guy named John Heathcock who was a Captain with the 18th. John lived in the Atlanta area about 16 Klicks (10 mi.) from my home in Marietta, GA. We decided to meet once we got back to Atlanta and talk further about our experiences in VN. We met at an IHOP in Roswell, GA and started reviewing our time in Nam with the 18th. I got to the part when I was in Pleiku at the end of Tet '68 and was called into the CO's tent and told my father had died.

John looked at me, cocked his head and said, "Bic, I just realized that I was that Captain that told you about your Dad, and sent you home. It only happened once to me in VN, and I was the CO in Pleiku in February '68." **Hello! Say what?** Of the 1,750 men in our company and the 19 guys that came to the Reunion, I am sitting in front of The Captain, my CO in Pleiku in Feb 1968, again some 44 years later. It's a crazy and amazing world. John and his wife, Jan, are still living in Alpharetta, GA and they belong to our 18th Avn. Unit Association. Life is fun. Glad I am living it.

RUBBER TREE PLANTATION

One day in '68, we picked-up a fully equipped 'A' team of Special Forces (Green Beret) guys in Pleiku. We flew them south to a Rubber Tree Planation somewhere between Lai Khe and Loc Ninh (NW of Saigon about 70 Kliks (Kilometers) or 44 Miles. It could have been one of the Michelin Plantations, but I don't remember. We radioed in, circled and dropped down below the 90-110 feet rubber trees onto a dirt road in the Plantation itself. The STOL U-1A Otter could do that. There was another 'A' team there waiting for us.

As we off-loaded and started to reload the plane, we heard helicopters coming, which wasn't a bad thing, but it sounded strange and very close. All of a sudden, out from under the trees, just above the dirt crossroad, came two Army OH-6A 'Loaches', one after the other. Again, they came out from under the trees. Instead of climbing up and out of the clearing where we were, they disappeared back under the trees, still following the crossing road. I could not believe what I saw. I turned to one of the SF guys and said, "Did I just see that?" He said, "Yes you did. That is how they break-in the new guys. They're Cowboys."

We loaded up. Getting out of that Plantation took everything we had to clear those tall trees, but 'Otter' horsepower worked again. I never forget those 'Cowboys' and their guts and gumption.

BIG JOHN

During my tour, I knew another 18th Aviation Crew Chief. His name was **Jon S. 'Stew' Stewart** from the Denver CO area. A wonderful guy you just wanted to have as a friend. He flew out of our 2nd Platoon based at Camp Holloway Army Airfield in Pleiku (Central Highlands). We would meet at different 'A' Camps out near the Cambodian border, talk of home and better times. Since I crewed a 'floater' plane, my plane and I would sometimes be assigned to cover planes from the different Platoons that had to go down to our Qui Nhon Maintenance Base for repair or hourly-based inspections. So, Jon and I got to know each other while

I was covering for another Pleiku based Crew Chief. Jon was a High School football player and a big, strong and likeable guy.

Later in my tour, Jon and I did a 'remain-overnight' (RON) in Qui Nhon, our main base and our HQ, on the same evening. Of course, we went to the NCO Club for some entertainment and a beer or two. While there we sat at a table with a few company clerks from the 18th Aviation Co. One guy was named Louis. He was a smallish, black guy that always had a smile. I always liked him. At the next table was some 'thick fore-headed' Corporal that started giving Louis some lip and they had a few words. It got worse the longer we stayed at the club. I had an early flight the next morning, so I told the guys at our table I was walking back to the 18th and hitting the rack. The 18th was a quarter mile down the runway side-road. Louis said he would walk back with me.

It was dark except for the runway lights and some lights across the airfield. We got 3/4 of the way back to our area and three of the four guys from the next table came running up from behind and started jawing at Louis and me. The 'Forehead' was a strong looking guy and was ready to fight (I don't remember what it was all about). 'Forehead' was pushing Louis around and the others were his wingmen.

A punch was thrown at Louis that knocked him down (but not out) and Forehead was standing over him and his 'boys' were in my face. A 'deuce & a half' truck was coming up the road behind us from the NCO direction. Just as Forehead was screaming at Louis to get up, a body came darting past me and powered into the Foreheads chest, knocking him off his feet. The Forehead crashed 10'-15' feet backwards onto the ground, hitting his head and was out. I mean out (the booze might have helped but he was not getting up). The other two started backing off, turned, and walked away. It was over that fast.

It was **'Big Jon' Stewart** standing over the Forehead with his fists clinched. He had jumped on the passenger sideboard of the 2½ ton Truck in order to catch up with us. He knew when the Forehead and friends had left the club, they were coming after us and he was going to back us up. Once he reached us, using the trucks momentum, he jumped off, did an Olympic style run-jump-&-skip (I can only imagine). He used his HS football abilities to spring into the Forehead's chest with his full weight and his forearms (like a blocker). The impact was amazing. 'Stew' became 'Big Jon' forever after that night.

We remained friends after VN. After his VN tour, he went to Germany and finished up with the Army. 'Big Jon' married his Colorado hometown girlfriend (Diane) and they had two great kids (Bonnie & Jack). He went on to work for Eastern Airlines as an A&P mechanic in the Atlanta area. Jon died in 2013 from Agent Orange related causes. He is missed. One of the 'great' guys in my life. His family and I remain in touch and good friends.

LUCKIEST 'OTTER' LANDING

The 18th Aviation Co had some unscheduled landings caused by inflight incidents. Yes, some were 'shoot-downs', but most were caused by some form of engine failures. These engine failures seemed to be happening mostly from mid-'67 into '69. They were engines sent to the 18th by the 'low-bid' engine rebuilder in the US. Not a good thing when flying over some of the densest mountainous jungles in the world. Thankfully, my 'Reliable 713' Otter never had an engine failure.

One incident happened to a crew on take-off from Phan Thiết Special Forces camp. The engine failed on climb-out and the crew quickly dropped the aircraft's nose and turned sharply back to the strip. The plane had just enough airspeed to reach the end of the threshold before stalling and dropping onto the dirt strip. It hit hard on the landing gear which collapsed backward and took out one of the wing struts. The Otter veered off the strip, down an embankment and into an ammo dump containing crates of mortar rounds. The plane crashed ahead, and the not-spinning prop pushed, not cut through the crates. No explosion.

The Otter engine was pushing into the firewall and into the laps of the Flight Crew, WO 'Chuck' Whigham and Captain 'ER' Hunt. Both had leg injuries from the crash that lasted for years but both flew again for the Army. They survived the war and later retired as senior Officers. The Crew Chief and all the five passengers survived the crash and walked away. It could have had a completely different outcome, as you can imagine. They were the luckiest Otter Crew to ever land in a Vietnam Ammo Dump.

The 18th Aviation Co. flew the DeHavilland 'Otter' all over Vietnam between 1961 and 1971. We lost many good men. We remember them and their sacrifice. I made it back to the 'world' and left the Army in 1969 in time for the moon landing, married Teri Macek and we drove off to College in Melbourne, FL. I became a Commercial Pilot and worked in the ever-expanding Air Cargo Industry the rest of my career. In 1998, I married my now loving wife, Margaret, and live in Canton GA. I have lived a long, wonderful life. 'Bic'

CARL H. "SKIP" BELL, III

U.S. Army—Armored Cavalry Officer, Aviator

Dates of Military Service (Active and Reserve): 1967 to 1998

Units Served with In Vietnam: A Troop, HHT, B Troop, 1st Squadron, 4th Cav, 1st Inf Div (First Tour); C Troop, 3rd Squadron, 17th Air Cav; 18th Corps Aviation Co; G3, HQ 1st Aviation BDE (Second Tour)

Dates in Vietnam: Feb 1969 to Feb 1970; Feb 1972 to Feb 1973

Highest Rank Held: Colonel (O-6)

Place of Birth and Year: Decatur, GA—1945

AVLB INCIDENT

In mid-to-late April 1969, my unit (1st Squadron, 4th Cavalry, 1st Infantry Division) received a mission to seal a village on the Saigon River called Ap Ben Chua. It had a years' long history of being a Viet Cong stronghold and had been the scene of numerous firefights over the years that the 1st Infantry Division had been in Vietnam. The 1st Squadron, 4th Cavalry (known as either the Quarter Horse or the Quarter Cav (1/4 Cav)) was based out of Lai Khe, a rubber plantation turned Infantry Division Forward Headquarters that was located several miles east of Ap Ben Chua.

For reasons based on decisions that were made way above my pay grade, the Squadron was to road march from Lai Khe south to Phu Cuong and then west through the area of operations of the 25th Infantry Division to vicinity of Dau Tieng (another 1st Infantry Division Brigade Headquarters Base Camp located just south of a large Michelin Rubber Plantation and several miles northwest of Ap Ben Chua). My guess is that we were to advance on Ap Ben Chua from the west to take them by surprise (since they would be expecting us to approach them from the east where our basecamp was located). In any case, we made the long road march from Lai Khe to Dau Tieng over the course of one day and spent the night in an ad hoc night defensive position a kilometer or so east of Dau Tieng.

We started out bright and early the next morning moving down a highway (dirt road) called LTL-14. The road paralleled the Saigon River and crossed over several streams that flowed into the Saigon River. In order to cross these streams with armored vehicles, the Squadron brought along a couple of Armored Vehicle-Launched Bridges (AVLB), which were scissors bridges that were approximately 40 feet long, could bear the weight of a medium tank (50 tons), and which could be quickly laid in place and retrieved by its launch vehicle (a tank chassis without the turret specially modified to carry and launch/retrieve the bridge).

I was a platoon leader in A Troop, which was the lead Armored Cavalry Troop in the Squadron's advance down LTL-14. My platoon was the lead platoon in the Troop that day. We had to move cautiously because the road was known to be heavily mined (in fact, we moved parallel to the road, off to one side or the other, whenever we could). At places where the terrain or thick jungle forced us to use the road, we would put mine sweep teams with mine detectors ahead of our vehicles. Of course, this slowed our advance to the speed of an individual walking slowly sweeping for mines, so we tried to only use the road where we absolutely had to. The objective was to get to the town of Ap Ben Chua before the Viet Cong had time to leave the village and move to their basecamps in the jungle.

Things went well until we got to the site of a blown bridge over a creek that fed into the Saigon River. The banks of the stream were seven to ten feet high on either side of the stream and the stream itself was about 20 feet wide and about two to three feet deep. As we approached the bridge, I halted my platoon and took a dismounted patrol forward to the near-side bridge abutment. We mine-swept the road leading to the abutment and mine-swept the abutment. We then waded across the stream, mine-swept the far side abutment and the road leading away from the abutment for approximately 100 meters.

We set up security on the far side of the blown bridge and I called back to my boss (the Troop Commander, CPT Bill Newell) and asked that one of the AVLB's be sent forward to span where the old bridge had been. That was done and I brought my platoon's vehicles across the bridge (one vehicle at a time) and we set up in a semi-circle on the other side of the bridge to provide security for the remainder of the Squadron to cross. Once my platoon's vehicles were in position, I climbed back on my Armored Cavalry Assault Vehicle (ACAV) and was watching to the front. We were approximately 50 meters from the bridge.

The second tank of the second platoon in the line of march was on the bridge when there was a TREMENDOUS explosion. The blast literally took my combat vehicle crewman helmet (a football helmet-like head gear worn by armored vehicle crewmen that had a set of headphones inside and a microphone attached) off my head. As I looked around, I saw the AVLB flying out toward the Saigon River — it reminded me of a boomerang — and the 50-ton tank that had been on the bridge was lying on its side in the creek. Evidently, the Viet Cong had planted either a 250 lb. or a 500 lb. USAF bomb under that bridge. I had walked right over it when we had waded the creek earlier that day.

I immediately advised my platoon to be looking out for a ground attack from the jungle to our front — we were by ourselves on one side of that creek and the rest of the Squadron was on the other side of the creek. Fortunately, no ground attack followed. Also fortunately, the Squadron had another AVLB which was quickly brought up and put in place and the remainder of the Squadron was able to cross the bridge without further incident. Sadly, one of the tank crewmen (the tank commander, I think) was killed and the other tank crewmen were all injured.

Also injured was one of the Troop cooks (a man from Louisiana whose last name was Terrebone). He had wanted to ride on a tank and was allowed to do so. He was sitting on one of the sponson boxes on the side of the tank dangling his legs over the side when the explosion occurred. It took both of his legs off at the knees. We MEDEVAC'd the injured Soldiers and continued to move toward Ap Ben Chua (which was three-four more miles down the road). Of course, any surprise we thought we might achieve disappeared with that explosion, which we believe was command-detonated by people assigned to watch that bridge site.

We got to Ap Ben Chua several hours later and put the seal in place. This involved moving our vehicles into a large semi-circle on the north side of the village (which sat on the banks of the Saigon River). We had vehicles starting at the river's edge on the west side of the village and going to the river's edge on the east side of the village. Our vehicles were approximately 100—150 meters from the edge of the village, and we alternated facing the vehicles so that one vehicle faced the village and the next one faced the jungle to our rear. We did this because we were concerned that we might be hit from the jungle as easily as we might be hit from the village.

After the seal was in place (late in the afternoon) an ARVN (Army of the Republic of Vietnam) infantry unit was sent into the village to clear it. We stayed in position around the village all night and were subject to sporadic sniper fire and several RPG's fired from the village toward our vehicles. That was the first time I had seen an RPG fired at night and noted that there were two different rocket initiations—one blast took the rocket out of the tube and the second rocket ignited and sent it toward its target. It was a long night.

The next morning while we were still sealing the village there was an Arclight (B-52 strike) about three kilometers north of the village into a huge basecamp that was located there. The ground literally shook when those bombs hit the ground. Shortly after that, we broke our seal and moved out to the enemy basecamp where that B-52 strike had been delivered (and where, presumably, the Viet Cong Soldiers that had been in the village had gone to hide). We stayed in that base camp for over a week, finding bunker after bunker of supplies, weapons, rice, etc. Once we had destroyed as many bunkers as we could and either burned or removed the rice, weapons, and other supplies, we went back east across country to our basecamp at Lai Khe.

NORMAN E. ZOLLER

US Army – Field Artillery Officer (later Judge Advocate General Corps Officer)
Dates of Military Service (Active and Reserve): 1962-69; 1978-93
Units Served with in Vietnam: Detachment B-130, US Special Forces; 3d Brigade, 82nd Airborne Division
Dates in Vietnam: Sep 1964 to Mar 1965; Mar 1968 to Feb 1969
Highest Rank Held: Lt. Colonel (O-5)
Place and Date of Birth: Cincinnati, OH – 1940

DUTY WITH THE THIRD BRIGADE OF THE 82D AIRBORNE DIVISION

Shortly before my first tour in Vietnam with Special Forces in 1964-65, I became engaged to Harriet and then in June 1965, we married. Five months after the birth of our first son in October 1967, my second tour began in March 1968 with the Third Brigade of the 82nd Airborne Division at Phu Bai, about ten miles south of Hue. It concluded in late February 1969. The Tet Offensive, which has been compared to WWII's *Battle of the Bulge* in 1944, began January 30, 1968. Over the 22 months the Third Brigade was in combat, we suffered more than 1,100 wounded and 227 of our members were killed in action.

While in-country, I wrote a letter to Harriet almost every day during that 12-month tour. She still has them. Like some of our fellow vets, I missed our child's first steps, his first words, and his early development. Harriet told me that son David thought his daddy was an 8" x 10" photograph. Fortunately and happily, however, I did return from that tour of duty to resume family life; but sadly, too many of our comrades did not.

This story contains excerpts of a few of my letters juxtaposed against what the Brigade was doing and experiencing on the ground as extracted from several historical references**. Below is an early letter and thereafter several succeeding letters. (When I arrived in Vietnam, I was a captain and was promoted to major shortly before my second tour concluded.)
**NOTE: The several texts about the Brigade's experiences and exploits are extracted from the uncopyrighted book, *Vietnam, 3d Brigade, 82nd Airborne Division, February 1968 to March 1969*, authored by Captains

William R. Porter and Thomas M. Fairfull, both of blessed memory; published and produced by Image Public Relations of Toronto and Tokyo.

AND SO, FIRST LETTERS FROM A SOLDIER AFAR...
15 March 1968

Hi Honey,

You are no doubt surprised by my return address (3d Bde, 82d Abn Div, APO S.F. 96325). So am I. I'm not there yet and really, I hadn't intended to write until I did get to my duty station and had an assignment. The assignment I still do not have, and I'm not yet with the 82nd. Let me start back a couple of days ago.

We left on time from S.F. at 2100 and got to Honolulu at 0045. We were on the ground about 20 minutes, so I didn't even have time for a mai tai. We then spent the next 11 hours and 20 minutes in the air to Clark ... a long, long time. We didn't go on to Kadena (Okinawa) as I had earlier told you. Don't know why not as it was posted on the schedule. An hour at Clark and then 2 ½ hours to Bien Hoa, where we landed. It went to 95 degrees that day and since we got in at 1030, we didn't have much time to acclimate. I still haven't. We then bussed to the 90th Replacement Battalion (BN) at Long Binh (about four or five miles).

Long Binh post is now the largest Army installation in VN and as you may recall, it's where LTC Wilkinson (aside: my boss during an earlier tour on Okinawa) is stationed. We turned in our records and were told we would be notified in a day or so of an assignment. That afternoon I did get to call LTC W—and he sent his jeep to pick me up. (I didn't know until later that new arrivals are restricted and aren't supposed to leave the replacement compound.) Colonel Wilkinson showed me around his place; I was really impressed. He asked if I had an assignment yet. Coincidently, he was looking for an adjutant. He then proceeded to make several phone calls in an effort to have me assigned to his BN, but to no avail. There is a shortage of airborne soldiers here. I am staying now at the 101st where about 30% are not air-

borne qualified. At any rate, Colonel Wilkinson learned I was being assigned not to the 25th (Inf Div, under my previous orders), but to the 3d Bde, 82nd Abn Div which is currently at Phu Bai. Phu Bai is where General (Creighton) Abrams is currently located in I Corps. It's about 14 km south of Hue.

That may be somewhat alarming, but I believe the 82nd is providing most of the security for General Abrams, and I further learned today there is strong speculation they (the 82nd) will be returning to the States soon. Don't get your hopes too high ... I'm almost assured of being ... here ... about five months and will then be located in a job of my choosing. In fact, I ran into a fellow yesterday on seven days TDY doing nothing but looking for a new job. The 82nd reportedly has 21 captain vacancies—14 at Bde level. I also have been told tactical units prefer to work new arrivals about three months in a staff assignment then four to six months in a command-type job, then the remaining time in a non-essential staff job (club officer, PIO, replacement unit, etc.) ...

Back to the chronological sequence. I stayed with Colonel Wilkinson about an hour and a half, and he confided in me some of the feelings he has about the situation here ... and reiterated his possibly retiring as soon as he can. I was very tired and while he asked me to stay for dinner, appreciated my asking for rain check—I was bushed.

On the way back to my barracks, he showed me some of the waste he told me about earlier—I saw stacks of rotting tires and probably enough snow fencing to run the entire distance of I-70 in Kansas. He and I couldn't figure out what the Army intends to do in Vietnam with snow fencing. Got any ideas?

Yesterday I spent the day waiting. I learned late in the afternoon I would be coming to the 101st over at Bien Hoa, probably in the morning. This morning I did come over here, processed some, but won't complete it until I get up north. I'm supposed to leave tomorrow afternoon.

I think it'll be all right to go ahead and use the 96325 APO. It may change but include my serial number for a while, and I think all the letters will eventually find me. I need one now.

Oh yes, one more thing—current return dates to the States are about 10 days earlier than one's arrival date. So, I should be back about 3 Mar 69.

One more thing… 1st Special Forces Group, the 101st, 173d, and the 82nd are all drawing jump pay, but there is no jumping. That's all for tonight. I'll write again tomorrow or Sunday.

Love always, N–

MEANWHILE… WHY WAS IT THAT A BRIGADE (I.E., A SELF-SUPPORTING 4,000-SOLDIER UNIT) OF THE 82ND AIRBORNE DIVISION WAS DEPLOYED 9,000 MILES FROM ITS BASE IN NORTH CAROLINA TO SOUTHEAST ASIA?

As previously reported, attacking 13 cities simultaneously in central Vietnam, one of which was Hue on the Perfume River, the Tet Offensive initiated by the Viet Cong began January 30, 1968, and continued until September 23, 1968. During the battle of Hue alone, it was estimated that 216 Americans, 452 South Vietnamese soldiers, and a roughly estimated 2,800 to 6,000 civilians were killed. On the Viet Cong side, an estimated 5,000 were killed, mostly by artillery and air strikes. By mid-February into the Tet Offensive, enemy casualties had risen to about 39,000, including 33,000 killed. Allied casualties amounted to 3,470 killed and 12,062 wounded, almost half of whom were Americans.

It was against this backdrop that General William Westmoreland requested additional combat forces to be deployed immediately from the United States. He specified that a portion of these units be airborne troops, reflecting his confidence in the proven ability and reputation of these soldiers. As it turned out, the only stateside unit from which such soldiers could be drawn was the 82nd Airborne Division, about which General Westmoreland already knew.

And so after an alert and within 24 hours, under leadership of 82nd Airborne Division Commanding General Major General Richard J. Seitz (later promoted to LTG), an advance party of the 3d Brigade of the 82nd under command of Colonel Alexander R. Bolling, Jr. deployed from Fort Bragg to Chu Lai on 12 February 1968, with remaining elements of the Brigade arriving in late February and early March at Phu Bai, south of Hue.

On the morning of 3 March, the first convoy pulled out of Chu Lai and, despite heavy rains the night before, reached the safety of Da Nang at 1830 hours with no incidents. That night, however, the enemy slammed rockets into Da Nang, but the overhead cover in the serial bivouac prevented casualties.

It was a wartime and dangerous environment at and near Hue with offensive and defensive combat operations expanding apace. And more was to come in the months ahead until the principal attacks were quelled by mid-September. By that time, there were more than 500,000 American service members in-country.

As noted in my letter above and subsequent ones thereafter to Harriet, I had been diverted from my initial orders to the 25th Infantry Division at Cu Chi. Indeed, I was joining the 3/82 in Phu Bai and all that was to entail.

MEANWHILE... GENERAL WESTMORELAND VISITS PHU BAI AND MORE...

3 April

Hi Honey,

I'm exactly one full day on my (new) work. We received word last night that General Westmoreland would visit us today at 1215. Well, that put a lot of people into complete orbit. He came today and stayed about an hour. I didn't talk to him, but I understand he was generally impressed so I guess our late hours last night were worth the effort...

Today I received three letters. Happiness. One was postmarked the 22d and two on the 23d. So I suspect now that all of them with the old APO have caught up.

I think your idea about having a get together between (Cincinnati's) waiting wives and LBJ (is good). Don't know if he'll oblige but it's worth a try. I also enjoyed hearing about David's further exploits with a cup and his Jello.

I figured that I'd be hearing about the snow emergency in Cincy. The sports section had a picture of Crosley Field with 9", and I also saw the same picture in the Stars and Stripes several days ago.

… We're improving here all the time and while I don't now have comparable facilities to either Can Tho or Long Xuyen (aside: my first tour was in the Mekong Delta area with Special Forces), it could be worse. I could be on a steady diet of 'Cs' and no showers at all for instance. My morale is pretty good really.

There's not much I can do about laundry. I don't have either the time or the facilities to do it myself so the soap wouldn't help too much. One of our (fellows) has supposedly found a new laundry so maybe things'll improve. How about some chocolate chip cookies in a coffee can? The tent I used to work in and live in I've moved from (to a nice bunker I told you about the other night.)

… Colonel Bolling is very nice, (and)… has an XO (who's my [OER] endorser) who takes names and kicks rears. So we're in good shape. I've been fortunate in my dealings with him. I hope to keep it that way. (Aside: Alexander R. "Bud" Bolling, Jr. was promoted in October 1968 to brigadier general; he was destined for increased responsibilities, including Corps Chief of Staff and later promotion to major general.)

Love always, N–

MEANWHILE, THE BRIGADE CONTINUES TO ENCOUNTER THE VC…

On 5 April, Company B, 1-505 Infantry moved out on a reconnaissance in force into the area of the previous ARVN contact. The location was five kilometers northwest of Hue, near five bends of the Song Bo River which formed the shape of a lazy "W."

Moving east along the northern arm of the river-shaped "W", the company approached a stream crossing. The second platoon of the command group and half of the first platoon had crossed the bridge when the air exploded with enemy fire. A B40 rocket slammed into the area, wounding six troopers, including Captain Elmo Tyner, the

Company Commander. Artillery and air strikes were called in while the third platoon maneuvered to positions on the far bank to place suppressive fire on the enemy and cover the withdrawal of the other elements across the bridge. With this maneuver completed, an even heavier concentration of artillery fire rained down on the North Vietnamese Army (NVA). Lieutenant Charles Posey assumed command, established a night defensive position, and posted several ambushes. Those early operations were to become an integral part of (then) Colonel Bolling's principles established at Phu Bai to "take the night away from Charlie."

Company B resumed the attack on 6 April following the same route. A company of ARVN troops also attacked with Company B, forming a "V", the apex pointing toward the enemy hamlet. Company B, 1-501 Infantry crossed the river beyond the hamlet and set up a blocking position to stop any NVA escape. Major Joseph Cincotti the Battalion S3, came in to coordinate the three attacking elements.

...Many acts of individual courage marked the day's fight. Major Cincotti moving back and forth on the ground to coordinate the combined attacks, encountered several NVA troops in trenches. He killed all he saw but was seriously wounded by an exploding B40 rocket and was evacuated. (He later received the Silver Star and the Purple Heart Medals for his actions that day.) First Sergeant Louis Pigeon was also wounded while assisting in evacuating wounded men from Company B. (For their actions that day both Lieutenant Posey and First Sergeant Pigeon were later awarded the Bronze Star Medal with "V" Device.)

MEANWHILE, PERSONALLY FROM PHU BAI VIA BIEN HOA TO PHU LOI...
6 October

Hi Honey,

Tomorrow I'm going to Phu Loi to live ... you've probably never even heard of the place. It's not too far from here (Bien Hoa); it's northwest and I

282 | ROBERT O. BABCOCK

hope to drive up there and look around. It's not as nice as Bien Hoa, but we won't be living in tents.

By the time you get this David'll almost be a year old (aside: he was born 13 Oct 67). That's a hallmark. I like your idea to have David's picture taken for Grandma's birthday present. I'd like a small copy. With the Nikomat, we'll get some good ones henceforth. Nikon lenses are excellent for portraits. Love always, N–

MEANWHILE, THE BRIGADE APPROACHES ITS FIRST YEAR IN RVN…

During January and February (1969), the elements of the Brigade in the Saigon area continued to defend the western approaches to the city and conduct pacification operations.

Pacification was directed at eliminating the VC infrastructure and establishing firm government control in the hamlets and villages. Saturation patrolling, resource control check points, and "snatch" operations rounded up many of the VC cell members who worked against the South Vietnamese government. Night operations and ambushes prevented their movement. Another asset in detecting Viet Cong hiding places was added to the Brigade when the 37th Scout Dog Platoon was assigned to its ranks. Led by Lieutenant Robert Crowder the dog and handler teams went to work with the field units to hunt out VC concealed in spider holes and tunnels.

Security against Viet Cong terrorism was a main concern in pacification. At night, ambush squads pre-empted enemy movement and concentration. In daylight, detailed searches uncovered VC weapons caches, and hide-outs. Constant probing kept the enemy off balance and poorly supplied…

MEANWHILE, GETTING CLOSE TO ROTATION…

22 February (which was the last letter I wrote prior to my return on 27 Feb to CONUS, arriving on 28 Feb).

Hi Honey,

I agree with you—it's hard to find anything to talk about except Thursday (or Friday). (As) I leave … I'm going to start throwing things away (and) my dirty clothes as I use them. You cannot imagine how I've looked forward to doing that. I'll have enough to last me through Saturday and a couple pairs of socks. Hope the weather isn't too cool later this week stateside. While I really don't care, I have nothing to keep half-warm except my field jacket. And it's cooler in N.J. than in California.

Love always, N–

23 Feb (added text in same letter)

Hi again,

Finis arrived today—I laid around today and got a plague shot. Tomorrow I'm going to lay around some more and pack tomorrow evening. I don't know how long I'll stay at the 90th. Although I may leave Thursday on that flight to Dix, if they want to send me earlier—like Tuesday afternoon—I'll go. I'm ready.

Love always, N–

AN EPILOGUE AND MEANWHILE …

Soldiers of the Brigade continued to be forcefully engaged maneuvering, attacking, defending, extracting, and experiencing casualties. But also, many were positioned in the jungles, at fire bases, and other largely fixed locations: planning combat operations, maintaining and repairing vehicles and aircraft, providing food and other logistical and administrative support. And all these soldiers were exposed and at risk for enemy small arms fire, rockets, and sappers attempting to over-run and destroy our fire bases, compounds, and inflict injury and death to American soldiers.

As this partial history was written in early 1969, the 3rd Brigade sustained the defense of Saigon. Over a year had passed since that day at Pope Air Force Base when troop carriers rumbled down the runway and lifted into the air. For the Brigade, it had been a year of great achievements. The final test of any combat unit's capability is trial by fire. The Brigade had met the challenge and added a new page to the chronicles of the US Army. The troopers of the Brigade wrote the names of Highway 547, Chau Chu, the Lazy "W", Nui Ke, and all the rest in blood and sweat on the page beside Sainte Mere-Eglise and Nijmegen. It had proved its mettle. The Airborne spirit prevailed. The Brigade could reflect on the past with pride. But memories of the first year will always be shaded with sadness for the troopers who fell.

If past is prologue, the All Americans will continue to excel. As long as there is a job to be done, a mission to fulfill, the men of the 3rd Brigade, 82nd Airborne Division will perform it with skill and enthusiasm, never slacking, never resting until they have gone "All the Way!"

Concluding Thoughts: In re-reading my letters to Harriet, which I had not done since they were written more than 50 years ago (with the exception of my reading a few of them in early 2017), I was struck, but not surprised, by how sanitized they were. They were admittedly personal (between a husband and wife who care for one another then and now), largely newsie, upbeat, factual, and purposely not alarming or disquieting.

As with my first tour in Vietnam (1964-65) with Special Forces, I am humbled and proud to have served with the 3d Brigade of the 82nd Airborne Division, which was deployed in direct response to the 1968 Tet Offensive. The Third Brigade was to become widely known as *The Golden Brigade* for the reported reason that former 82nd Airborne Division commander, Major General John Throckmorton, once told Colonel Bolling, "Bud, everything your brigade touches turns to gold."

We respect and remember these highly skilled, intrepid, and courageous soldiers.

Finally, following my discharge after nearly seven years of active duty, I attended graduate and then law school and subsequently returned to military duty for 15 more years in the National Guard and Army Reserves as a Judge Advocate General Corps officer. That military service partially over-lapped with my civilian work for 37 years as a public administrator in state and in federal courts. Thereafter, I helped to create and then worked almost nine years for the State Bar of Georgia coordinating a volunteer lawyer program, which continues to this day, benefitting service members and veterans needing legal help, many of whom have been Vietnam veterans.

HARRIET ZOLLER
Wife of Norman Zoller

A WAITING WIFE JOINS WAITING WIVES

I'm a joiner. So when Norm returned to Vietnam for his second tour, it was only natural for me to seek out other women in the proverbial "same boat."

During his first tour (TDY with 1st Special Forces), Norm and I were already engaged to be married and I was a busy student, hurrying to finish college in three years so we could get married, and I could join him in Okinawa. His second tour coincided with the start of the Tet Offensive, and by then I was a young wife and new mom. David Ethan had been born five months earlier, on Friday, October 13, 1967, at Fort Carson, Colorado.

In early 1968, David and I settled into the apartment in Cincinnati that would be home during Norm's year-long deployment. Joiner that I am, I immediately sought out the "local chapter" of the informally constituted Vietnam Waiting Wives group that became my community.

With opposition to the war growing, it was comfortable and reassuring to know other young wives who understood what I was going through: who knew the sinking feeling of the empty mailbox, the anxiety of dealing alone with a sick infant, the excited anticipation of R&R in Hawaii, the shared joy when a husband safely returned. By summer, Waiting Wives had become my extended family. We were a group of new friends who hailed from all over the U.S., who had lived all over the world, and who were joined by an existential bond that typically lasted only as long as our husband's tour.

In March, I learned that President Johnson would be in town July 23 to address the governors of the 50 states who would be gathering in Cincinnati for their annual meeting. It seemed appropriate to me that the Waiting Wives should meet their husbands' Commander-in-Chief. I immediately decided to try and make that happen.

Of course, I wrote Norm about it, and in reply to one of my daily missives, he wrote back: "I think your idea about having a get-together between the Waiting Wives and LBJ is good. Don't know if he'll oblige, but it's worth a try."

I was lucky enough to find someone in the National Governors' Conference planning hierarchy who agreed it was a good idea. Indeed, our Waiting Wives group was assured a table for 10 at what was dubbed the Grand Ball, to be held at the Cincinnati Convention-Exposition Center.

When the 10 of us arrived, we found our table at the edge of the dance floor identified for "Waiting Wives." There was a bit of a problem, however, because the wives of some conference staffers (all men in those days, of course) thought *they* were the "Waiting Wives," and they really objected to giving up their premium seats. Ultimately, the military waiting wives, the *real* Waiting Wives, were seated nearby.

As it turned out, Norm was right: the Commander-in-Chief (who, on April 1, 1968, had declared his intention *not* to run again for President) really wasn't interested in meeting the spouses of the troops serving in Vietnam. His loss.

Lots of the Governors did want to meet us, though. And many greeted us warmly. One, I recall, was particularly gracious. It was, after all, from Travis Air Force Base in California that most of our husbands departed for their assignments. And the then-California Governor, Ronald Reagan, greeted each of us with a warm smile, kind words, and a hug.

Among the Ohio notables present that night was Cincinnati's Mayor Eugene Ruehlmann, whom I did not know. When Norm returned from Vietnam, having finally secured release from his Regular Army commission, he went on to get his Master's in Public Administration and then his law degree. While earning his Master's, he worked as the Administrative Assistant to the Mayor of Cincinnati, Eugene Ruehlmann. Life takes us on winding paths.

GLENN PEYTON CARR

US Army—Aviator

Dates of Military Service: 1958 to 1986

Unit Served with in Vietnam: 213th Assault Support Helicopter Company (Chinook); B Troop 7th Squadron 17th Cavalry Regiment (Air)

Dates Served in Vietnam: XO & CO 213th May 1967 to May 1968; CO B Troop 7/17, XO 52nd Combat Aviation Battalion 1971

Highest Rank Held: Lt. Colonel (O-5)

Place of Birth: Shawnee, OK—1934

A SERVICE MISSION...OR SO I THOUGHT

I don't remember the date, except it was late in my first tour '67-'68, flying Chinooks. We had several artillery enlisted men to fly to Cam Rahn Bay northeast of us on the South China Sea for a training session on sling load netting and webbing along with some of their own webbing as training aids. It was a small load, passenger run, milk run, or "boondoggle" as they were commonly called.

The weather to the coast from Saigon was 1,000-foot ceiling with occasional light rain, but good visibility. Okay, but we would like to cruise at or above 3,000 feet to avoid small arms fire. Off we go, straight east from Saigon to Phan Thiet on the coast and then follow the coast north to Cam Rahn Bay.

There are three prominent mountains in the III Corps area, Nui Ba Den in the west, Song Bae in the north, and Gia Rae in the east. We crossed Gia Rae on the south side. Flying just under the clouds, we were probably 600-800 feet from the ground. NOT ENOUGH! Just as we passed abeam the mountain, BLAP BLAP!! We took two rounds! The master caution light came on, which tells the pilot in no uncertain terms that he has a problem and to immediately check the caution segment panel, which contains about twenty segments, telling you what you don't want to know. The crew chief had just confirmed that the back of the aircraft was okay. No hydraulic line ruptures, no fire, engines running normal.

We calmed down a little bit, trying to contemplate what had happened to our "office." All caution segments were illuminated, and I mean every damn one of them, and all gauges were at zero except the air speed and altimeter, which are not electrically operated. Essentially with the rest of that non-display, the aircraft should be falling out of the sky! We then noticed that the forward head extension gauge was still showing the head extended.

An explanation is due here. As you transition from hover flight to forward flight, the forward head begins to tip forward to give forward thrust while maintaining its share of the vertical load. As you slow up to land, the head retracts to lessen the forward speed while maintaining the vertical lift. Lesson complete. Unfortunately, the head switch also appeared to be inoperative.

If the head remained forward upon landing, how would this affect our landing on a wet PSP runway? PSP is pierced steel plank. It gets very slick when wet and with no power steering, God only knows where you'll end up! Peter pilot Captain Hyneck (I can't remember his first name) and I discussed this at great length, even trying to experiment with manually retracting the head and reducing the airspeed, but nothing worked, and the head remained forward.

Nearing Phan Thiet, we chose to go out over the water a few hundred yards to shoot a long, slow approach. I was very pleased with the approach so far, and as we touched down I was on the power steering. All of a sudden, all hell broke loose! The back of the aircraft bounced, shuddered, and made the loudest "everything's coming apart" noise I have ever heard.

The crew chief announced we had taken a third and fourth round in the right rear landing gear, the steerable one. Both tires went to pieces upon touchdown. Now we had no steering control. We only had two aluminum rims on the steel PSP ramp. That was about as **not** good as you could get! Captain Hyneck pulled up as we were heading off the runway; and seeing a large rain-soaked red clay (laterite) mud hole to the left, plopped the aircraft into that slop hole. The three and a half remaining landing gear were enough drag to stop the aircraft's forward motion. Thank God for small favors!

The crew chief was inspecting the aircraft for bullet holes when he noticed an artilleryman rubbing his lower left leg. We found he had almost taken a bullet. It had cut several of the laces out of his boot. The crew chief inspecting the sound blanket behind and above him found an oblong hole. Apparently, the bullet had begun to tumble, making it a bit more destructive. The crew chief had a gleam in his eyes as he removed the sound blanket saying "Ah-Hah!" exposing a 2" diameter bundle of wires. At first glance it looked as if all wires were severed. That made this mission an overnight trip. As it turned out, only 43 wires were severed!

Captain Hyneck and I, having a clearer picture of what we were up against, left the aircraft to check with the local unit. We found their operations shack with a radio but no personnel. After about twenty minutes, we found an NCO who got us to an advisor who had decent long-range communications. They were able to get a message through several units that we were down safe and would return in the morning as soon as the wiring problem was solved.

When I returned to the aircraft, the crew chief proudly announced, "Sir, the wires are patched up and we are ready to go!" "Well, wait just a minute, chief, just what kind of magic wand did you wave over this situation?" I asked. He quickly responded, "Sir, you know all the wires are serial numbered so there was no problem matching each pair so we taped them up with all the band-aids from our eight first aid kits on board!"

I checked the work and found it to be very professional. We did an electrical check and found all the gauges were giving proper static readings. The only thing I wanted to do now was to get the aircraft out of the mud hole and wash the mud off the gear and brake systems. With that accomplished, we adjourned to our host unit B Troop, 7th Squadron, 17th Cavalry (Air) for beer and a movie. I had explained earlier that I was not going to fly this helicopter into a major airdrome without power steering. Hovering this behemoth in close quarters would be disastrous, and I certainly don't relish flying across Gia Rae Mountain at night with low clouds and crappy weather. They certainly understood the latter, so we stayed the night.

It is interesting to note that two years later, on my second tour, I would be selected to command this unit, B Troop, 7th Squadron, 17th Cavalry (Air) after it had been moved to Pleiku in the central highlands. While having a beer that evening watching my crew intermingle with the Cav troops swapping war stories, I began to think how lucky we were to have a company full of such talented can-do soldiers—super, super, super soldiers. Where else would you find soldiers who would use medical first aid kits to patch up a wounded helicopter?

RICHARD H. MOUSHEGIAN

Army—Quartermaster Corps, Logistical Officer

Dates of Military Service (Active and Reserves): 1968-1993

Unit Served with in Vietnam: HHC, Ling Binh Post, USARV (US Army Vietnam)

Dates you were in Vietnam: Oct 1968-Oct 1969

Highest Rank Held: Lt. Colonel (O-5)

Place of Birth and Year: Camp Wheeler (deactivated after WWII) near Macon, GA—1943

CHOICE TO LIVE IN CHAOS WITH COMRADES OR LIVE ALONE IN PEACE

When I was first assigned as the Supply and Maintenance Officer to the club system, I was offered the choice to bunk in the company area in private, officer quarters of Headquarters and Headquarters Company (HHC), Long Binh Post, or live in a semi-private area separate from HHC with a few other officers in the club system.

I quickly chose to live in the company area with a larger collection of fellow officers with all the friendly chaos that 50-60 people can generate, but with one common goal: to survive together the unaccompanied tour in Vietnam by doing your job, supporting each other, and staying out of trouble with companionship as a substitution for boredom.

Contrast that with living with only a handful of officers in a separate, private area where daily drinking of alcoholic beverages without boundaries would be the apparent solution for boredom. (My family history of alcohol abuse going back three generations was not in my favor, so I was always very careful and respectful of personal, alcohol consumption.) My billeting choice was wise; but challenging.

The first two days of the assignment consisted of me getting settled in the company area and going to the main office of the club system to learn the expectations of supporting a 40-club system with supplies and maintenance. On the third day, I decided to meet the personnel in charge of each club on their jobsite to understand what type problems that they were handling. A crusty old WO-2 (Warrant Officer, Grade 2), a Food Service Specialist, was my escort. He knew the locations of each job site throughout the sprawling post and the personnel since he was responsible for the sanitation standards.

We visited about four sites in the morning by interviewing the person in charge and inspecting the kitchen area, storerooms, refrigeration units, and general layout of the building. We continued the visits until mid-afternoon when the WO announced to the club manager after the visit, "Set the Captain up with a drink."

I reluctantly selected a rum and coke, and the WO helped himself to a free drink as well. We visited the next jobsite, and, at the conclusion of the visit, the WO made the same demand and helped himself to a drink, as well. Being a young officer, I went with the flow of things with the experienced WO, thinking that this was how they conducted business. The next visit played out the same way, and we called it a day. As a result, we had visited eight units in a day, I had one drink on the last three visits, and I was feeling somewhat tipsy.

At that point, the WO went back to his private "hooch" (building) in the club-billeting area, and I headed to the officer's mess hall (dining facility) for supper with the headquarters personnel who had no access to drinks during their duty hours. This situation could turn out to be disastrous starting with drinking during duty hours, in a combat zone, in the midst of other officers who were sober as a judge for the last 8-10 hours, and in the presence of someone who was probably my boss's boss who could write a disastrous endorsement on my efficiency report. Hence, I decided to keep my mouth shut, act "soberly," and sit alone since I was so new.

The next day we visited eight more clubs. About mid-afternoon, the WO asked the club manager to set us up with drinks for the conclusion of that visit. The same thing transpired for the next two clubs, and the WO went back to his private hooch to continue drinking in private, while I went back to the sober headquarters! Again, I kept my mouth shut, acted "soberly," and sat alone.

On the third day, we visited eight more units, and I firmly declined all (free) drink offers. That day I returned to the same mess hall and started greeting the people in the headquarters and making friends outside of the club system. As a result of that billeting choice, I gained several, memorable experiences:

Since Long Binh Post was a large, American, army post, it was susceptible to harassment by Viet Cong, unguided rockets—usually at night. As a result, the hooches had several horizontal, conduit pipes (about 5' to 6' in diameter) scattered around the area. The pipes were sandbagged on all sides but allowed a protected entrance at each end, making them bunkers. The bunkers were primarily designed as personnel protection during rocket attacks.

At that time, our uniform was olive-drab over-shirts, trousers, and boot sox, and Vietnam boots. We wore our own white underwear—shirts and shorts. (A few months later, we were issued olive-drab undershirts.) In the headquarters company, we were issued our olive-drab, load-bearing web-gear, and steel helmet with liner. We kept all our web gear and helmet with liner in our hooch. The first rocket attack occurred within the first week that I was assigned to the headquarters company, and it occurred in the middle of the night. As a quartermaster officer, I knew that the goal was to get into the bunker *as quickly as possible.*

Since I slept in my underwear and was not thinking too clearly, I jumped into my boots without really tying them, put on the web gear and helmet, and ran the 15 feet to the bunker. As I looked around at all of us sitting on opposing benches in the bunker, I noticed that everyone was in olive-drab clothing, and I was the only one with white underwear showing. They said nothing. I volunteered, "I thought we were supposed to get out here as quickly as possible!" They just smiled. That did not happen, again. On the next rocket attack, I was fully dressed and ready for any action that was required.

Since I was the newest member in the headquarters, I was "volunteered from the audience" to participate in a slapstick, comedy routine in the club next to our headquarters. The routine was hilarious, and I looked like a fool. It was all in good fun.

Since the headquarters people knew me, I was "selected" to perform a Report of Survey for a missing piece of equipment. When I met with the property officer, he mentioned that the survey was needed for a missing typewriter. I challenged him: "Are you kidding me! You are worried about a missing typewriter *in a combat zone*? Why not use me for investigating a missing truck or a jeep?"

His answer with a smirk: "The typewriter is listed on the Property Book. I need a Report of Survey from you before I can legally drop it from the book." As a Quartermaster officer, I knew that he was correct, but for a missing *typewriter*?

The next day I was on my way to Saigon where the supply officer's files showed that the item had been turned-in to a civilian business for repair. The kind, Vietnamese businessman greeted me, mentioned that he had all the necessary records, and asked me to sit down.

Vietnamese businessman: "How about a mixed drink?"

Me: "No, thanks. I cannot do that. I am in uniform and am on-duty."

Vietnamese businessman as he looked around: "As you can see, no one else is around. How about a coke (soft drink)?"

Me: "OK."

Vietnamese businessman: "How about a coke-deluxe?" (This guy was an expert with people.)

OK, so I had *one* coke-deluxe. Then, the businessman showed me from his books that the typewriter with that serial number had been declared as unrepairable and had been disposed as unsalvageable. That was the conclusion, and I could finalize the report upon my return.

While on the same trip to Saigon after the meeting with the businessman, I had my camera and wanted to take some pictures of how the Vietnamese people celebrated their new year. While standing on the sidewalk looking at nothing in particular and trying to decide where to go to take some interesting pictures of the area and people, I noticed a Vietnamese man who was in his early 30's roll out his motorbike from his apartment to the sidewalk. He was nicely dressed in a collared shirt, dark trousers, and black shoes. He momentarily disappeared but returned with a helium-filled balloon on a string that tied to the back of his cycle.

Then, out came his very attractive wife dressed in a beautiful, light-colored, cotton, native dress (that I cannot spell) that was high-collared, tightly tailored, long dress with high splits up both sides to the waist forming front and back panels of material. (Don't let your imagination run wild; this is Vietnam, not Paris!) She wore tailored, white slacks underneath the dress and was carrying an infant child. The husband started the cycle, his wife sat behind him with the infant sandwiched between them, and they took off down the street with the balloon trailing them in the air.

That is the moment when I realized I had just witnessed a family celebrating the Vietnamese New Year. I snatched the camera, turned it on, focused, made lighting adjustments, and took a picture of them. I was the proud owner of a developed, 3" x 5" picture of a beautiful family on a motor bike, from the back, whose image was as large as a half-used, pencil eraser.

While living in the company area, there was a chapel a few buildings away. On Sundays, I attended the services for many reasons. During one such service, the chaplain asked if anyone could play the electric Hammond organ since the chaplain's assistant was returning to the states in five weeks, and no one else was available to play for the services after his departure. I ignored the request since, out of the entire congregation of officers and enlisted, someone always volunteered. For the next two Sundays, I heard the same plea, but more urgently each time. At the end of the third week, I approached the chaplain.

Me: "OK, I don't play the organ, but I have played the piano since childhood. If your assistant will show me the differences between the two instruments, I will do it."

Chaplain: "Thank you. You have no idea how much you will be helping. I hated to think that I would be leading in the singing of hymns, a cappella [without a supporting musical instrument]."

As agreed, the chaplain's assistant showed me the differences in techniques. The techniques were easy enough that simply took a little time to perfect. However, the item of most interest to me was the pedals: a large keyboard at the feet of, at least, two octaves! Those pedals made the entire project a great musical challenge. As a result, I volunteered to play in the military chapels the rest of my tour in Vietnam and on and off military posts for 12 years.

One day in the headquarters billeting area, I saw the captain who arranged for maid service for the officers. (Each officer paid about $12 per month for daily cleaning of our sleeping area, uniform washing and ironing, and "spit-shining" of our combat boots!) However, there was one such maid who was probably in her 30's and was generously endowed with a pectoral development that we were not supposed to notice and that was very uncharacteristic of the slender, Vietnamese women. (She must have had some recent, French ancestors.)

As a result, some of the officers teased her to the effect that all of her assets weren't real and that she used extra clothing-material to fill-out her tight shirt. One day she snapped and decided to immediately stop the teasing. She stormed directly to the office of the American Captain who was charge of the maids in the headquarters company and confronted him.

Maid: "You[r] Dai Uy (meaning Captain, pronounced "die we"; she used the term in the plural) say this is not me. I show YOU. This is me. YOU tell them!"

Then, she proceeded to disrobe and completely bare her chest to him to prove her point(s).

The day that I saw the captain in the company area, he had a big grin on his face and looked startled. I asked what was going on. He relayed this event to me that had happened earlier in the day. His final comment to me was three words: "They were real!"

I was glad to have chosen to live in the company headquarters area with a large number of men working in a combat zone and spending leisure time, together. I would have missed it all if I had chosen to live like a hermit. The friendships were real, the time passed quickly, and we all stayed out of trouble.

JOHN GALT

U.S. Army – Signal and Transportation Corps – Platoon Leader, Operations
Officer, XO
Years of Service (Active and Reserve): 15 April 1967 to 1989
Dates in Vietnam: 4 July 1968 – 4 July 1969
Unit Served with in Vietnam: 176th Assault Helicopter Company
Highest Rank Held: Colonel (O-6)
Place and Date of Birth: Montgomery, AL – 1944

SEBASTIAN CABOT – VIETNAM HELICOPTER PILOT

How do you write a story about your time in Vietnam if you never really
did anything exceptional, but were surrounded by guys that did? My tour
of duty started on July 4, 1968, when I landed at Cam Rhan Bay and
ended rather uneventfully when I landed in Seattle, Washington on July
4, 1969. As an ROTC Signal Corps officer, I got assigned as the Avionics Platoon leader for the 176th Assault Helicopter Company, 14th
Combat Aviation Battalion, Chu Lai, RVN.

Like all aviators, I was eager to build my skills as a helicopter pilot
and spent the first couple of months in country gaining flight time and
valuable experience. However, my ability to write a complete sentence
and type seemed to trump the need to fill the pilot's seat. I was assigned
more and more administrative duties. Many hours were spent editing
and re-writing awards.

It seemed that several times a week one of my fellow pilots would do
something above and beyond the call of duty that was worthy of sending
up the chain of command for recognition with an award. So, more and
more flight time was administrative in nature as opposed to missions in
direct support of the battalions that we were tasked to support. I spent
November travelling to Saigon to escort a "Project 100,000" soldier back
from Camp LBJ in Saigon. Each month the paperwork responsibilities
increased, and the flight time decreased.

As I look at the few souvenirs that remind me of my tour of duty, I move the

Chicom mortar tail fin that I retrieved from our flight line from the top of my "Pandora" box and dare to look inside and fondle the souvenirs, shuffle through the pictures, and trifle with the memories. I rub the 7.62 mm bullet that was my "cherry", the first time the aircraft I was flying in took hits. I remember we had holes in the tail section and rotor blades where we took six or eight hits but, this bullet lodged in the engine compartment at head level, but about 10 feet behind my position in the right hand (copilot) seat. But it does not bring back a searing memory etched in my mind forever. After all, no one was hit or injured. The aircraft was not shot down and returned to the ramp safely when the mission was done. It was just "routine."

I don't display my souvenir as I am not proud that my door gunner was closer to the place it hit and extracted it from the engine compartment. But I felt I had a right to it since it was the first time I was flying when we took hits.

In other words, I pulled rank as a 1LT, but as a retired O6, I view it differently and am not proud of my decision at the time. I probably share those feelings with most soldiers, since most of us have moments when we do the right thing at the right time and take pride in our actions and there are instances in which we thought we took actions for which we are later convinced that we did not do the right thing.

Then there is the old black and white picture of Mac (WO1 Angus W. McAllister. Jr.) with his unforgettable smile. And next I pause on the picture of Sebastian Cabot in the right-hand pilot seat where I am supposed to be sitting. Maybe that is a story worth telling…

I was serving as operations officer but was scheduled for my annual check ride in February 1969 when the call came in from Division Headquarters asking if we had an aircraft available for a VIP mission. Captain Terry Bryant lead our maintenance platoon and took pride in maintaining one of the highest availabilities and flight time levels of any AHC in Vietnam, which was well known at Division. We were fortunate to have highly skilled NCO's and qualified technical inspectors and, on many occasions, accomplished maintenance tasks that were supposed to be performed at the Direct Support level.

Sending an aircraft to Direct Support took a lot of time and meant the aircraft was not available for missions for an extended period of time. All our available aircraft had departed on missions, although the Huey assigned to the company HQ was being used by the unit Instructor pilot WO1 Wyatt for check rides, and I was scheduled for my annual check ride.

We accepted the mission. It turned out that the mission was to fly the actor Sebastian Cabot from Division HQ at Chu Lai down to the Duc Pho area to visit a couple of units and back to Chu Lai.

The pickup at Division HQ helipad was typical and Sebastian Cabot, his escort officer, and public affairs entourage were quickly on board with the assistance of the crew chief. We flew about an hour to the south and landed at a Signal Battalion Headquarters that overlooked the South China Sea. Sebastian Cabot began making the rounds to meet and greet soldiers who were going about their daily tasks.

I ran across the following description of Sebastian Cabot's personality and gift for engaging the troops written by a public affairs officer, Eric L., who encountered him on this same tour in 1969 and posted the following blog comment. I found his comments online on www.franklarosa.com Frank's Vinyl Museum commenting on Sebastian Cabot's album of Bob Dylan's poetry.

"Sebastian Cabot, Actor"
Actor Sebastian Cabot performing 'dramatic readings' of Bob Dylan songs

"Eric L. says: Assigned to the Information Office at Cam Ranh Bay, I spent a day with Sebastian Cabot as he visited with patients at the hospital there one-on-one and met with other troops. A lot of celebrities deserve a tremendous amount of credit for the work they did in Vietnam during the war, but none impressed me quite as much as Sebastian Cabot. He reached out to EVERYONE, regardless of rank and was tremendously effective at cheering people up and making them laugh and feel good.

"At the hospital, he headed straight for the intensive care ward where many patients were in horrible shape and beyond hope, and he spent several minutes with each and every one. It absolutely blew me away. In the hospital and elsewhere, he gave everyone he met his undivided attention. He was a huge talent, but he was as down-to-earth and sincerely nice as they come. I asked him why he was there in the middle of a war, and he said he felt he owed it to his adopted country and to those who were fighting to preserve his freedom. As far as I know, he got nothing in the way of publicity or any other kind of compensation for being there, and for my part, he impressed me as being one of the friendliest and most decent men who ever walked on the face of this planet. *(06-19-2006)*"

That was the Sebastian Cabot that started begging us to let him fly the helicopter. Sebastian Cabot was very persuasive with his marvelous British accent and his desire to support the troops. I did a bit of rationalization that it would be okay to let him fly right seat back to Chu Lai since WO1 Wyatt was the unit Instructor Pilot. I took the photo of him in the pilot's seat and climbed into the passenger compartment with his escort officer (who was apoplectic), and his public affairs entourage.

Just getting Sebastian Cabot into the right seat was challenging since he was only about 5' 4" tall and must have weighed at least 250 pounds. I used my right shoulder to boost him into the seat and helped him adjust the seat all the way forward so he could barely reach the control pedals. Fortunately, the flight from the Signal Unit south of Duc Pho back to Chu Lai was relatively uneventful and WO1 Wyatt let Sebastian Cabot get some stick time so he could truthfully say he flew a helicopter in Vietnam. In return he agreed to come to our unit that evening after his dinner at Division Headquarters.

True to his reputation, Sebastian Cabot had ditched his protesting escort officer and entourage and was waiting for his ride at Americal Division Headquarters when WO1 Ken Fritz arrived around 9:00 pm to bring him to the 176th AHC after his dinner with MG Gettys, the 23rd "Americal" Division Commander. Major Ron Metcalfe, commanding officer of the 176 AHC relied on Ken as his "go to" guy for tasks that typically fell outside of the normal duties. During the time our paths crossed, he was the guy that arranged for the Seabees to install a fresh water well shower point for our unit and arranged for a periodic case of filets for the unit commander.

Ken delivered Sebastian Cabot to a crowd of fellow aviators who had gathered in the 14th Aviation Battalion Officer's Club to meet "Mr. French" of "Family Affair" fame, drink a few beers, and celebrate his first flight at the controls of a helicopter in Vietnam. The few beers turned to many beers as Cabot took on all challengers to a chugging contest and emerged victorious. He was truly a down to earth celebrity who reached out to use his God given gifts to cheer up the men who were serving in Vietnam.

Hence my picture of Mac with his broad smile since he and WO1 Butler (Merle Floyd Butler, II) joined in the Sebastian Cabot party. As I recall, they did not stay to the bitter end around 2:00 A.M. since they had mission responsibilities the next day. About a week later, on 24 Feb 1969, their aircraft took a hit from a 51-caliber machine gun and they and SP4 Jon Bailey and SP5 Richard Wayne Ford gave their lives for their country. Sebastian Cabot probably gave them the last moments of lighthearted diversion and happiness in their shortened lives.

I was somewhat surprised to learn through my research for this article that Sebastian Cabot had performed a similar role in WWII through the USO in support of troops in the European theater. I learned this through Sebastian Cabot's obituary published in the New York Times on August 24, 1977. I found it interesting, but not at all surprising, that the NY Times would note Sebastian Cabot's service as a USO celebrity in WWII but not mention his outreach in Vietnam.

Perhaps that was a relief to his children in 1977 when the antiwar sentiment was at its height. After all, they were residents of Vancouver, Canada, a country that welcomed America's minority of draft dodging youth with open arms. Sebastian is buried in West Hollywood with his fellow theatre professionals as he had adopted the USA. He had also adopted the American Soldier and I for one would have recommended that he be interred in Arlington near his fellow helicopter pilots.

RAYMOND L. COLLINS

US Marine Corps – Combat Logistics Officer

Dates of Military Service: 1960 – 1980, a lifer

Unit Served with in Vietnam: 1st Tour: FLSC-A, FLC, IIIMAF; 2nd Tour: HQ IIIMAF

Dates in Vietnam: 1st Tour: Aug 1968 to Nov 1969; 2nd Tour: Jan 1971 to Apr 1971

Highest Rank Held: Lt Colonel (O-5)

Place of Birth and Year: Kinston, NC – 1938

NIGHT SAPPER ATTACK

After moving from Phu Bai-Hue in early 1969, FLSG-Alpha was head-quartered and housed in the old 7th Motors cantonment inside Camp Books where FLC was headquartered near Red Beach. The road to our cantonment ran parallel to the perimeter fence, about a mile and a half from FLC and passed a complex of warehouses filled with critical supplies and materials controlled by the Central Control Point (CCP). FLC was responsible for the resupply, maintenance, POL, ammo, EOD, repair parts, etc.; in essence *all classes of supply*, all logistics support for III MAF units in I Corps.

It was considered a critical, strategic organization and its resources were a prime target for rocket, mortar, and sapper attacks almost daily. To make the security situation worse, FLC units employed a large number of indigenous personnel; no doubt many of whom became VC at night and/or were sympathetic to the VC cause. It was not unusual to catch them pacing between buildings and/or sketching drawings showing the location of key facilities.

One night in June 1969, a VC sapper team cut through the perimeter fence to gain entry to Camp Books and blew up and damaged several CCP warehouses. Fortunately, there were no casualties, just a great deal of physical damage. In the days that followed, the Red Beach Seabee unit was tasked to repair the perimeter fence and road that had been breached. When they finished the project, they erected a yellow diamond shaped sign next to the road that read "Caution-VC Cross-ing."

HITCH-HIKE DEPARTURE

In late October 1969 (I don't remember the exact date), my first tour ended. I was scheduled to catch the big commercial bird at the airbase in Da Nang and fly to Kadena AFB in Okinawa, Japan.

Note: all Marines serving in Vietnam were required to go through Camp Hansen Okinawa where they were medically checked, primarily for shots, and to stow their personal gear and service uniforms in a footlocker that they were not taking in-country. When your tour was completed, you went home via Okinawa to retrieve your gear and get a physical examination. The processing, going and coming, usually took two or three days, depending on flight schedules.

On or about 20 October, I left my unit at Red Beach and reported to the Transient Center at the airbase for my flight to Okinawa. Unfortunately, the flight was delayed until the following day because of bad weather, so I was assigned a billet for the evening. During the night we had a major rocket attack and incurred several casualties. In addition, the officers' billeting building was fragged with grenades by some US dope heads. So, I was anxious to depart the following day.

But Murphy's Law was still busy. We were told the flight was delayed again so we had to endure another night of rockets and fragging. At daylight I was approached by two Marine Captains, one was an aviator (I had been promoted to Major in Nov '68). They suggested we attempt to find a military flight, a hop that would get us out of Vietnam and eventually to Okinawa. We grabbed our gear and flagged down a jeep and convinced the driver to take us to the military side of the runway where all the services had their flight operations centers.

We began approaching each Flight Ops and got lucky on the third attempt with the Navy. They had a flight scheduled to leave within the hour to take some Admiral to Taiwan for R&R and then proceed to Futema MCAS on Okinawa to pick up some repair parts. The flight chief helped us load our gear and we were off. *Oki, here we come!* When we arrived at Futema around midnight, I grabbed a scosh cab who took me to Camp Hansen where I checked in with the Duty NCO at the BOQ for the night.

The next morning, I got really lucky; the coincidence amazes me even today 50 some years later. The Sergeant of the Guard was a Marine who had served with me on sea duty aboard the USS Albany back in 1965. After I explained my situation, he had my footlocker retrieved from storage, got me medically checked, got my PCS orders endorsed, and got me booked on a flight to Hawaii later that very same day. The next morning, I arrived at Honolulu International airport where my wife and family were waiting. I had literally hitch-hiked out of Vietnam.

THOMAS A. "TOM" ROSS

US Army—Special Forces

Dates of Military Service (Active and Reserve): 1966 to 1992

Unit Served with in Vietnam: Detachment A-502, 5th Special Forces Group

Dates in Vietnam: Jan 1968 to Dec 1968

Highest Rank Held: Major (O-4)

Place of Birth and Year: Huntington, WV—1945

TAKE THEM ALIVE

AS I WATCHED OUR MEDICS treat some of the local village children, one of our radiomen called out to me, "Lieutenant Ross, Walt Three Zero is on the horn for you."

"Okay. Tell him I'm on the way."

When I arrived at the radio room and called Walt Three Zero, he seemed fairly excited. "Zero Two, I've got two VC suspects in the open. Can you get out here?"

"Where are you?"

When he gave me coordinates for his location, I realized it was going to take a chopper to get to the area he was circling. Because of the demand for them, it could be difficult to obtain a chopper unless it had been previously scheduled. However, the 281st AHC always seemed to come through for us. They had a chopper available and dispatched it immediately.

The men of the 281st, whose company designation was "Intruders" and whose motto was "Hell from Above," were divided into three platoons. "Rat Pack" and "Bandits" were lift platoons, which means they were used primarily to deliver troops to a battlefield. "Wolf Pack" was a gunship platoon, which means they were primarily used to cover the lift platoons during troop insertions and extractions. They were also called upon to provide cover and/or support for ground units. They were like having a big brother, and I was always more comfortable when the Wolf Pack was nearby.

The pilots and crews of these UH-1 helicopters sat exposed to any and every danger on the battlefield as they entered and exited. The pilot and copilot sat in a cockpit surrounded by little more than Plexiglas, clearly visible to any enemy gunner who might be on or near their LZ. While they had small, armored shields on both sides and under their seats, it was always my opinion that they provided little more than psychological protection. On the lift platoon choppers, the two crew members who served as crew chief and door gunner sat on each side of the helicopter manning machine guns, fully exposed with no protection beyond the flak vests they wore.

The pilots and crew of these extremely vulnerable aircraft were supremely courageous men who never failed to respond to A-502's calls for support or help. Their bold and frequent intrusions into dangerous situations confirmed the appropriateness of their "Intruders" designation. But their response to our most recent call for assistance would demonstrate that they weren't just bold, they were skilled, intelligent, and compassionate.

With the 281st inbound, I sent a message to our Vietnamese Camp Commander asking that he have four members of his Vietnamese Special Forces Eagle Team, his quick response unit, meet me at the chopper pad. Our A-502 radio operator called Walt Three Zero and advised him that we would be airborne shortly.

It only took our ride about ten minutes to reach us and about the same to reach the place where Colonel Baer was circling in his 01 "Bird Dog" aircraft.

On the way out, I told the pilot we needed to capture the VC alive, if possible. It had been a while since we had received any fresh intelligence information, and this offered us a great opportunity to learn what was going on in Charlie's (slang for the enemy) head out west.

"Just show us where they are," the pilot said.

"They ought to be somewhere under that 01," I told him, then checked in with Colonel Baer.

"Walt Three Zero, this is Bunkhouse Zero Two. We're coming in on you from the east. Can you see us? Over."

"Roger, I've got you."

"Do you still have your targets?" I asked.

"Roger, I just chased them into that abandoned village directly beneath me. They ran into one of those houses down there."

"Okay," said the chopper pilot. "Let's go find 'em."

Then, he swooped down toward the village like an eagle after a fish near the surface of the water. My insides felt as though they had stayed somewhere a few hundred feet above us as we continued our steep dive toward the village.

"Let me know when you see our targets," the pilot told his crew as he finally leveled off and swooped low over the village.

After making about three passes over the village at around fifty feet, one of the door gunners spotted the two men.

"I've got 'em at five o'clock running between two small houses," he said.

The gunner had barely gotten "five o'clock" out of his mouth before the pilot pushed the chopper up around to the right and back down. It felt as though we had gone from one direction to the exact opposite instantaneously, and I wasn't sure exactly where my insides were that time. We all just hung on as the pilot maneuvered to locate and lock in on our prey.

We were still coming out of our U-turn when the copilot said, "Yeah, I've got 'em. They just ran behind that house with the blown-out roof."

"Be alert," the pilot said to his door gunners. "We're going to rock around behind that house."

That's exactly what we did. The nose of the chopper continued to point directly at the house as its tail started to swing around. In just a few seconds we were looking at the backside of the house and the two VC suspects. When they turned to run, we could see they were in civilian clothes, but it was similar to clothing we had seen on VC before. Because they were turning, our view was obscured. We couldn't tell what kind of weapons the men were carrying.

Obviously, they were trying to elude us and bolted for the corner of the house. Darting around the corner and along the side of the dwelling, they crossed an open area and ran toward yet another vacant house. But this time they were in full view as they made their crossing. The door gunner swung his M-60 machine gun around and had the two in the center of his sites the entire way. I watched the face of the young door gunner, whose focus on the men was intense. He had a tight grip on his M-60 and he was clearly ready to fire. I wanted the men alive and was concerned he might open up on them. One or two bursts from his weapon and the chase would have been over. The two men weren't very fast on their feet and would have been very easy targets if the gunner had intended to kill. Despite the intensity of the situation, the gunner never opened fire and simply kept his weapon trained on the two men as they ran into a house.

"Were those carbines they were carrying?" the pilot asked.

"Yeah, I think so," the copilot responded. "We could have nailed them," he added.

The pilot circled the house to make sure his quarry hadn't run out the back door. When he saw there was no back door, he said, "We've got 'em." Then, he moved back around to the front side of the house and hovered in a position that, once again, gave the left door gunner an ideal firing position. Immediately, three Eagle Team members moved with their M-16s to the chopper door to provide backup for the door gunner.

The pilot was hovering little more than twenty-five feet off the ground, dust was blowing everywhere. The door gunner had his M-60 machine gun trained on the front of the house to cover the door and two open windows.

In our low hovering position, our chopper was an easy target for the two men inside the house if they chose to duel. We waited to see either the men or their weapons. Then, finally, we saw their faces looking up at us.

When I waved and yelled for them to come out, they backed out of sight. When they appeared at one of the windows again, I waved and yelled once more for them to come out. But, as they had done before, they simply backed out of sight. That went on one or two more times. Then, the pilot very calmly said, "I'll run 'em out for you."

The pilot's next action was unorthodox and, frankly, amusing to me. He moved the chopper directly over the house and set it down on the roof. Then, he bounced on it a couple of times. When he roosted on the roof the next time, it started to collapse under the weight of the chopper, and the two men burst out of the house, unarmed, with their hands in the air. The pilot then quickly moved off the house and set the chopper down in front of it.

As soon as the chopper's skids hit the ground, three members of the Eagle Team and I jumped out to retrieve the two men. Without a gunship for covering protection, we didn't hang around. As quickly as everyone was back on board, the pilot lifted off with the quarry bagged and uninjured.

The two men that the pilot and his crew had skillfully captured could have been killed by either door gunner or crew chief, who also manned an M-60, on multiple occasions. But, given the challenging mission of capturing the two alive, that's exactly what they had done.

Even Colonel Baer who had stayed close at hand and seen the capture called with compliments for the chopper's pilot and crew.

"Zero Two, Walt Three Zero. Over."

"Roger, go ahead Walt Three Zero."

"Tell your pilot that was some mighty fancy flying. I especially enjoyed the rooftop landing. Ask him if he learned that at flight school. Over."

The pilot, who was monitoring the frequency, grinned as he listened to Baer's remarks and replied, "No, that one came out of my hat."

"Walt Three Zero, this is Zero Two. Seems that one wasn't in the book."

After thanking Colonel Baer for his tip on the two VC suspects, who were now prisoners, our communications were ended. But, with shared feelings of satisfaction, the Air Force 0-1 Bird Dog and Army UH-1 Huey flew together back toward Trung Dung.

It had been another good day that started with healing and ended with mercy—an unusual and welcomed event in Vietnam.

DAVID G. BEASLEY

U.S. Navy, Aviation Electronics Technician, Flight Deck Troubleshooter
Dates of Military Service (Active Duty and Reserves): 1967 to 1992
Dates Served in Vietnam: August to November 1968
Unit Served with in Vietnam: Helicopter Antisubmarine Squadron Eight (HS-8) onboard USS Bennington (CVS-20), Yankee & Dixie Station
Highest Rank Held: Command Chief Petty Officer (E-7)
Place and Date of Birth: Newport, AR — 1947

IN THE BEGINNING THERE WAS NTC/RTC SAN DIEGO

First off, I would like to acknowledge what an honor and privilege it is to be a member of the Atlanta Vietnam Veterans Business Association (AVVBA). It is so humbling to be a part of an organization in which there are so many individuals that are so deserving because of their service in the Vietnam War.

I entered military service in June of 1967 after flunking out at Arkansas State College (ASC). I really didn't know what I wanted to study in college after graduating high school in 1965 and had very little guidance. Someone suggested I should try an Economics major, so that is where I started. After one semester and one course in Economics, I decided that wasn't for me.

I switched my major to Political Science which was more to my liking since I enjoyed politics and loved history. Regardless, because of being young, unguided, and a host of other problems, including health, I was dismissed due to poor grades.

The one course that I did exceptionally well at was Military Science…Army ROTC. My grandfather Franklin Beasley was in the Army prior to WWI and was shot through the leg when some of Pancho Villa's men assaulted the Army truck he was driving outside of Brownsville, TX. My father was a WWII Navy veteran, as was my paternal uncle, both of whom were Seabees. As a child, I couldn't keep myself out of the scrapbooks of photos that my dad brought back from his Pacific Islands adventures.

After flunking out at ASC, I knew the draft was going to get me, so I went to the Army Recruitment Office to get things going. The Army was the logical choice for me since I had two years of Army ROTC behind me.

As I sat waiting for the Army recruiter to get back to his office, I noticed his secretary checking me out (or so I thought). Finally, she asked "Are you David Beasley?" I told her that I was, and she reminded me we had gone to school together at one time, then she asked me why I was there. I told her the story about flunking out of college and that I thought I would get ahead of the draft board and go ahead and enlist. Then, surprisingly, she asked me if I wanted to get training to which I replied that I would, so she told me to go see the Navy recruiter.

Chief Petty Officer (CPO) Stockton was the Navy recruiter in West Memphis, AR at the time. I went into his office and told him my story. After listening carefully, he then began talking about the training possibilities for which I might qualify, including Aviation Electronics Technician (ATA) school at Millington, TN.

I went home and told my mother I had enlisted in the Navy, expecting that she would be relieved that I wasn't joining the Army which was fighting a war in Vietnam. To my surprise she asked me why I didn't join the Army. I asked her why she would prefer me to join the Army over the relative safety of the Navy to which she replied, "Any fool knows you can walk farther than you can swim." Still scratching my head over that one.

A-SCHOOL TO VIETNAM

I enlisted through the delayed entry program, so although my official enlistment date is June 1967, I didn't leave for NTC/RTC San Diego until after my 20th birthday in September. Thirteen weeks later, I was graduated from Recruit Training Company 549 (one Battalion graduation behind Kelly Hope who is the adopted son of Bob Hope). I was assigned to the Outgoing Unit and worked around the Base until a slot opened for me at the Naval Air Technical Training Center (NATTC), Millington, TN.

Jumping ahead, a year later I had finished AFUN(P) school, AVA school and ATA school and was designated an Aviation Electronic Technician Radar with the rank of Airman (ATRAN). It was time to put training behind me and transition to "The Fleet" where I would put that training to use. When I filled out my first Duty Preference (DREAM) Sheet, I asked for the following:

HOME CITY: Memphis, TN
HOME PORT: San Diego, CA
TYPE SQUADRON: Helicopter
OVERSEAS DUTY: Japan
VIETNAM: Volunteered

My Detailer's idea of humor was to give me almost everything for which I asked. I got a helicopter squadron out of San Diego (Reem Field, Imperial Beach, CA), caught up with the squadron in Japan and left Sasebo, Japan two weeks later onboard USS Bennington (CVS-20) for Yankee Station off the coast of North Vietnam.

When I received my orders from NATTC Millington, I was told my route to Helicopter Antisubmarine Squadron Eight (HS-8) would take me to Okinawa where I would check on board USS Bennington. I flew to Dallas' Love Airport and then on to San Francisco International where I caught a shuttle bus to Travis AFB. At 2259 hours when I arrived at the US Navy ATCO at Travis the terminal was chock full of people (military and civilian) transiting to Japan and Vietnam. Lieutenant S. K. Jones, the OOD at the Navy desk read my orders, then told me I had a seat on a flight to Yakota AFB in Japan. I told him, "No, I'm going to Okinawa." He said no you're going to Yakota, I told him I was going to Okinawa to which he replied, "Listen boy, you're going to Yakota." I went to Yakota.

I flew from Travis AFB in the middle seat of a Braniff Airways aircraft in my dress blue uniform for 10 hours to Yakota AFB, Japan. No inflight entertainment. The only thing that broke the boredom of the flight was the crying of dependent children who were apparently as miserable as I was.

A bus took us from Yakota to Tachikawa AFB where we waited for a C-130 to fly us to Itazuke AFB. Unfortunately, our flight was cancelled, and we spent the night at the Yamada Ammunition Depot. What I recall vividly from the terminal at Tachikawa were the soldiers/Marines on leave from their units in Vietnam waiting for a space available flight. This was my first face-to-face encounter with military personnel who had served in-country. I was saddened by the lost time they spent just waiting for an empty seat.

Finally, I was on the next leg of my adventure, flying from Tachikawa to Itazuke on a C-130 military aircraft for the first time. Checking in at Itazuke AFB, we were given a room assignment in a barracks, given our bedding, and told we wouldn't be leaving until the next day. No sooner had I made my rack (bed), someone came in and announced the bus to Sasebo was there for us.

The trip to Sasebo was about three hours long with a meal stop along the way. I was logged onboard USS Bennington at 1900 hours 11 August 1968 by TMC Balderman. USS Bennington would remain moored at Naval Base Sasebo, Japan until 20 August when the ship's log reports USS Bennington steaming for Yankee Station. Typhoon Shirley delayed our arrival on station by one day, causing us to arrive 24 August instead of 23 August.

THE DRUNK WATCH AND THE LANDING SAFETY OFFICER (LSO)

My first full day onboard USS Bennington after checking in with the various squadron departments, I was assigned to the Master at Arms Division of Helicopter Antisubmarine Squadron Eight (HS-8), where for two weeks I would be responsible, along with some others, for the cleanliness of the compartments in which we lived. Our berthing area was immediately aft of the forecastle and between the two five-inch-guns mounted on the side of the ship just aft of the bow. Occasionally, the gunners would fire the five—inchers which caused an acoustic wave so strong to blow through our living spaces that it would cause curtains separating the berthing areas to blow straight out.

I had been on the ship a couple of days when, while taking a cigarette break in the port gun tub, one of my shipmates gave me a hard time telling me that I would be hanging my head over the rail puking my guts out when we left port. Days later when the ship departed, I did get a little queasy from the motion of the ship as we began our trek to Vietnam, but I felt nothing like my jokester shipmate who had his head over the rail heaving until he had nothing left in his stomach.

During our stay in Sasebo, I occasionally drew the Hanger Deck Integrity Watch from 2000 hours to 2200 hours (for Marines, that would be 8PM to 10PM). It's affectionately referred to as the "Drunk Watch" as this is the time many of the crew are arriving back onboard ship from drinking in the bars downtown. It was my favorite Watch as I observed sailors walking onto the hanger deck, stopping to get their bearings, picking a hatch to go through and a ladder to ascend/descend to their quarters and watching carefully for them to come back through the hatch onto the hanger deck a few minutes later and pick another hatch they hoped would lead to their berth.

After finishing my two-week compartment cleaning assignment, I was assigned to the Avionics Shop/Work Center 210 where I would perform routine maintenance and troubleshooting on SH-3 helicopters. Part of the time was spent in my shop which was at the fantail of the ship, one deck above the hanger deck. The rest of the time I was topside on the flight deck, most often tuning the Voyager radar to its maximum 16-mile range.

Life onboard ship is very routine and very boring for the most part. Finding my way around the ship was difficult at first with all the hatches and passageways, but there seemed at first as if there was a new space on the ship to discover every day. I loved to take my breaks standing on the fantail and just staring at the ocean and the wake the ship made as it glided through it. Life was good, but boring.

Then, one day I heard an announcement over the Ship's 1MC system as follows: "Now hear this, now hear this, away the helo salvage team…" I had no idea what that meant until one of my shipmates yelled excitedly that one of our helicopters had crashed and he called for me to follow him as he dashed out of the shop. My heart was pounding as I followed him as we sprinted toward the aft port guntub.

Running blindly behind my shipmate into the guntub, I was startled by the sudden appearance of a body tumbling down the safety net between the flight deck and the guntub. Quickly getting his feet under him, the Landing Safety Officer (LSO) quickly determined there were a few individuals in his vicinity who didn't belong and proceeded to show us a side of the LSO that enlisted personnel rarely get to see. Except for maybe Boot Camp in which the Company Commander is always in one's face screaming at us, I've never had a more intense butt chewing.

LIGHT ATTACK SQUADRON FOUR (VAL-4) YELLOW JACKETS

Someone is going to try to correct me and say the Navy didn't have OV-10 Broncos or they will try to challenge me and say the VAL-4 insignia was the Black Ponies and not the Yellow Jackets, but truth is VAL-4's insignia was the Yellow Jackets from 7 March 1969 until 14 July 1971.

After returning from our WestPac Cruise November of 1968, Helicopter Antisubmarine Squadron Eight (HS-8) disembarked at Long Beach for our home base at NAS Reem Field, Imperial Beach, CA. Shortly thereafter the squadron began the process of decommissioning. Likewise, USS Bennington (CVS-20) having just completed a WestPac Cruise and duty on Yankee Station in the Gulf of Tonkin was being decommissioned as well. The Benny Maru (or Big Ben) as it was affectionately called was an Essex-class carrier commissioned during World War II and served in combat during WWII, Korea, and Vietnam.

From HS-8, I received orders to NAS North Island, CA for training and further transfer to Carrier Antisubmarine Squadron Thirty Eight Red Griffins. While serving with VS-38, I made a Carrier Qual onboard USS Hornet (CVS-12) and was expecting to make another WestPac onboard Hornet, but because of medical reasons, I received orders to shore duty with Carrier Antisubmarine Squadron Forty One (VS-41) Shamrocks. Forty One was the training squadron for all West Coast S-2 Tracker squadrons.

September 1968, VS-41 officially was assigned additional responsibility for training personnel scheduled for assignment to VAL-4. VS-41 received its first OV-10A Broncos October 1968. January 1969, VAL-4 was established with the mission of conducting surveillance and offensive operations in support of river patrol craft, as well as providing air support for SEALS and combined U.S. Army, Navy and South Vietnamese operations.

While assigned to VS-41, my duties consisted of maintaining, troubleshooting and repairing the S-2 Tracker avionics systems. Although I never received any training on the OV-10, until their own maintenance personnel could be trained, I was assigned additional responsibility for OV-10 avionics systems along with some of my VS-41 shipmates. We maintained all the aircraft systems until VAL-4 personnel completed training and assumed responsibility for maintaining their aircraft.

March 1969, VAL-4 was permanently based at the Naval Support Activity Detachment Airfield, Binh Thuy, South Vietnam, for combat operations. The squadron had two detachments, Det A assigned to Vietnamese Air Force Base, Binh Thuy and Det B at the Vung Tau, Army Airfield. On 19 April 1969, the squadron began its first combat operations, flying air support of the Naval River Forces in the Mekong Delta of South Vietnam. The missions included normal patrol, overhead air cover, scramble alert and gunfire/artillery spotting.

I don't claim to ever have been assigned to this squadron, but I am proud of the role that I played in maintaining the aircraft for the flight crews until maintenance personnel arrived and I feel that I am a part of the history of VAL-4.

I HEARD THE DEAD: CYCLONE

USS Bennington arrived Hong Kong 23 September 1968 (my 21st birthday) where she was anchored until 27 September when we departed for Subic Bay, PI. Enroute, we encountered a cyclone (hurricane). I don't remember the name of the cyclone, which USS Bennington skirted, but I remember it to be a very scary experience.

Helicopter Antisubmarine Squadron Eight's Avionics shop was one deck higher than the hanger deck just forward of the fantail. We could look out the Work Center 210 shop forward all the way to the very front of the hanger deck. At times it looked as though the ship was flexing down the length of the hanger deck in two different directions. The storm was so bad, the screws (propellers), I was told, were breaking the surface of the water and causing a tremendous vibration that shook gear off the aft bulkhead (wall) of our shop. I never got sick, but I did get very queasy. All flight operations were suspended.

Unfortunately, I drew the 0000-0400 hours (midnight to 4AM for Marines) Flight Deck Integrity Watch while we were underway to the PI skirting the cyclone. It was scary enough being on the flight deck at night under any circumstances, but this was particularly scary because of the darkness, the rain, and the wind. There was the constant danger of being thrown overboard by the motion of the ship which was pitching and rolling with the wind and waves.

Nobody else was on the flight deck…no other *living* person that is! I had been told the story of the 103 crewmembers (mostly senior Petty Officers) who had been killed on USS Bennington in 1954 off the Eastern seaboard of the USA in a fire that broke out after a fluid leak from a catapult was ignited by a jet exhaust. I kept trying to tell myself that the sounds I was hearing was just the howls of the wind as it blew around and over the helicopters and aircraft which were tied down on deck, but my knees trembled at what sounded like the howls of the dead calling to me.

You cannot believe the relief I felt hearing the announcement over the 1MC to secure the flight deck integrity watch having only completed two hours of the four-hour watch. Someone had finally decided that it was far too dangerous to have anyone on the flight deck in those conditions. If I had been blown overboard, there was no chance for me to be recovered, alive or dead. The only signaling devices I had to use were a flashlight I carried in my hand and a small light attached to the life vest I was wearing.

I retired to my berth, climbed into my rack, but I wasn't alone. All those ghosts from the flight deck accompanied me to my compartment and wouldn't leave until morning.

05 October 1968, USS Bennington departed Subic Bay to return to Yankee Station.

ED HERMOYIAN

Army — Field Artillery

Unit Served with in Vietnam: 1st Bn 21st Field Artillery, 1st Air Cavalry Division — Assistant S/3, Battalion Liaison Officer, Battery Commander

Dates served in Vietnam: Sep 1969 — Sep 1970

Highest Rank Held: Lieutenant Colonel (O-5)

Place and Date Born: Pontiac, Michigan — 1944

BRINGING REALITY TO BROTHERHOOD

Beginning with the earliest days following my commission in the Regular Army Field Artillery in 1966, I was always conscious of our mission
of supporting the ground gaining arms. Prior to Vietnam, I had commanded a direct support battery in Korea and a general support battery
in Germany. I honestly preached our mission to my troops daily. However, in Korea the troops we supported were on the DMZ and it was only
on occasion that we interacted face to face. As a general support 8-inch
battery in Germany, my interaction with the Armor and Infantry was
even less.

In RVN, I was initially assigned as Assistant Battalion S3 and on
occasion interacted with those in the Infantry Brigade we supported.
After a short time (partly out of boredom), I volunteered to coordinate
fire support at the BuDop Special Forces Camp near the Cambodian
Border. Working daily face to face with the resident A Team and some
of their indigenous troops, our support mission became a reality. After a
month of being the target for every enemy mortar and rocketeer in the
area, I had developed a true relationship with my brothers at the camp.
This was a great warm up for my next job as Liaison Officer to the 1st
Battalion 7th Cavalry, GARRY OWEN!

My Battalion Commander picked me up at BuDop, flew me to the
1/7 Firebase and introduced me to the Commander 1/7, LTC Robert
L. Drudik. LTC Drudik was a true warrior and leader, and his radio
call sign was Red Baron 6. After my Battalion Commander left, LTC
Drudik put his arm around my shoulder and told me in no uncertain

terms, "Your heart may belong to mama, but your ass belongs to the Red Baron." Little did I know that at that moment a relationship began that I cherish even to this day.

My Battalion Commander was a great commander, but 24/7 I became a part of the 1/7 Cav. I got to know the Company Commanders, most of the Platoon Leaders and Platoon Sergeants, as well as many of the troops when they pulled firebase security. The respect I had for them became true reality.

Accompanying LTC Drudik on the Command-and-Control chopper, planning artillery fires with the 1/7 staff and commanders, and taking part in all operations planning was rewarding beyond words. I experienced firsthand their days of sadness and their days of joy (and an occasional drink). I was not forgotten by my unit but felt a major part of the 1/7 family. The 1/7 Sergeant Major would always bring me a carton of Marlboros and goodies from the SP Packs they received, to share with my Recon Sergeant. He and LTC Drudik always asked me what if anything I needed and were sincere in their concerns. To this day, I still have and cherish the card they gave me as a member of the 1/7.

In truth, this experience made our mission "real." They were truly my brothers. A few months later, I was given command of A Battery 1st Battalion 21st Artillery. I carried this same respect and relationship to my new job supporting the 2/5 Cav. In so many ways, my experience with 1/7 Cav made me a better battery commander. To this day, I consider these fine men to be a part of my family. GARRY OWEN!

JAY "DOC" COHEN

US Navy — Corpsman
Dates Served in Vietnam: March 1969 to April 1970
Unit Served with in Vietnam: Mobile Construction Battalion 1/3rd Marines — DaNang, Phu Bai, Hue, DMZ Vietnam
Highest Rank Held: Petty Officer 2nd Class
Place and Date Born: Philadelphia, PA — 1947

NAVY CORPSMAN WITH THE MARINES

I was an only child. I attended Olney High School and then Drexel University, where I received an engineering degree in 1972 — a bachelor's degree in construction science technology — but I didn't like hard core engineering.

I was in college and my rating for the draft with Selective Service came up, and I enlisted in the Navy Reserve in late 1967, hoping to avoid the draft. That didn't do any good because three months after I enlisted, my Navy Reserve Unit was called to active duty. That led me to spend just under four years on active duty.

After boot camp, I served aboard a destroyer escort, JD Blackwood (DE 219) as a seaman. For thirty days I became an expert at how to paint and chip paint. Then I received orders to A School — Hospital Corpsman Schools in Great Lakes, Illinois. After A School, I served as a Corpsman HM aboard the aircraft carrier USS Essex (CVS-9) and in Helicopter Squadron HS-9 out of Quonset Point, Rhode Island.

We spent six months in the Caribbean, of which three months were flight training for Navy pilots out of Pensacola, Florida. The Essex was going to be decommissioned, and I was assigned as part of the decommissioning crew in sick bay. Shortly after that, I received orders to B School — Field Medical Training run by Marines at Camp Lejeune, North Carolina. When I completed Field Training, I then had to go through Marine Corps boot camp. That was in late 1968.

Then I received orders to a Mobile Construction Battalion (MCB1) a Seabee Battalion, which was in Davisville, Rhode Island, which was right next to where the Essex was docked. The Essex was like home to me, and I found out that the Navy had decided to sell it for scrap to the Gillette Razor Company. Shortly after I arrived at MCB1, we got orders to ship out to Vietnam, in March 1969. We flew for 19 hours straight and arrived at 4:30 AM at Naval Air Base in DaNang.

When I reached the door to get out of the plane, the extreme heat and smell hit me like a two by four. Every morning at 5:00 AM the Air Base was rocketed. It was the VCs greeting and Welcome to Vietnam. After the rocket attack, I was helicoptered to Phu Bai, just south of Hue (part of the major TET Offensive in 1968), and I was assigned to a rifle squad that was a mixture of Navy Seabees from MCB1 and Marines from 3rd Marine Division that shared the base in Phu Bai. For the next six months, I became a Bush Corpsman assigned to a rifle squad.

I ended up in a rifle squad going out at night and setting up night ambushes. My first night out, we were to set up an ambush and came under fire. During the firefight, several Marines were wounded, and I heard the words "**Corpsman up.**" I ran to the first Marine. There was nothing I could do for him, he was dead. I hesitated a little bit, and then remember something the Chief had told me: *that I was the first line of defense,* and it was my job to take care of these Marines out here and get them patched up or evacuated to the battalion aid station, if need be.

We were in several other firefights that week and I hated to hear the words "**Corpsman up**" because that meant a Marine had been wounded. Being a Navy Corpsman, my obligation was to do first aid and triage on the wounded comrades. I would just go into a mode of not paying attention to what was going on around me. I would treat and bandage then up and make sure there were no other wounds; sometimes I would give a morphine shot, and in the worst cases there was nothing I could do because the Marine was dead. Then I would go to the next wounded Marine. This routine went on for a six—month period that I was in the bush.

We would go out on ambushes every other night. We would go out at dusk and stay until daylight. The ambushes could be things from rife firefight to full rocket attacks and grenades being used. Some nights there was no contact at all. It was always a relief to see the morning star because daylight was coming soon, and I knew we made it through another night.

Every man had two grenades, including myself. The Geneva Convention calls for Corpsman to only carry a .45 caliber pistol, even thou I qualified "expert" with both my .45 pistol and M-16 rifle.

After a firefight, we would go and collect the weapons, papers, pictures, and those types of things the VC had. There were times when there would be dead bodies everywhere and there was no way to know who killed who.

We were out on an ambush one night, and I had gone to urinate. I heard noise and saw a shadow of a VC in the distance, but I couldn't fire at him or give our position away. I stood frozen, holding my private parts and my breath, watching the VC, and hoping he wouldn't see me. Finally, the rest of the unit moved up and we opened fire. I ran back to my position. It was a hell of a night.

I think I had a clean uniform twice in the six months I was in the bush. My uniforms were always muddy, wet, and torn from the elephant grass. When we were in the jungle, we carried our food and, unable to have fires, we always ate cold food. It was enough to keep us going, but I lost about 40 pounds while I was there. During the monsoon season you stayed wet and sometimes even soaked boots and socks. I carried extra socks in my pack, but they would get wet too.

My main concern was for disease in the jungle, such as jungle rot and trench foot. I tried to check the water we were drinking coming out of rivers, creeks, and streams. Agent Orange would wash into the water we were drinking. We had pills to put into the water to purify it for drinking. The real problem was they were spraying Agent Orange, which was getting into the water, and it would cause lots of problems for the Marines and soldiers later. We were provided salt pills and required the Marines to take them because of the extreme temperatures, well over 100 degrees most of the time. We all were constantly sweating.

During my six months in the bush, I was scared. I treated the wounded and injured Marines. I also treated some of the Marines who set off booby traps and had their legs and arms torn off. **And then there were Marines that were dead.** My goal was never get wounded or hurt and just get out of there as soon as I could. After my six months in the bush were over, I came back to MCB1 in Da Nang and was assigned to the sick bay and was promoted to HM2. I became the rheumatoid hematologist, taking blood from soldiers that didn't feel good or were sick.

Most of my other patients were American civilians working in Vietnam. I was basically treating them for venereal disease. Once a month the Corpsman would have the Vietnamese prostitutes come in for a physical examination and give them antibiotics as needed to attempt to control the disease as much as possible.

Being back in Danang was pretty good because we ate real food, not cold C-rations. I really enjoyed the food and got a real good suntan. I played softball on Sunday and waited to finish my time and go home.

I came home after 13 months in Vietnam. We landed at NAS Quonset Point, Rhode Island on Easter Sunday 1970. We all marched in formation when we got off the plane and I marched past my mother, and she didn't recognize me. I lost 40 pounds and had a handlebar mustache and this golden look about me. When I came over to her, she had to stare at me for a minute before she realized it was me. 90 days later I got an early release from Active duty and spent my remaining days in Naval Reserve and was Honorably Discharged in June 1972.

I got married in February 1973 to my wife Susan and have been married for 48 years. We raised two daughters and have three granddaughters. I retired from 43 years in Project and Contract Management and am now live in Cumming, GA. I belong to American Legion Post 307, Veterans of Foreign Wars Post 9143, Atlanta Vietnam Veterans Business Association, Vietnam Veterans of America Chapter 1037, Johns Creek Veterans Association, National Foundation to Navy Corpsman, American Association of Navy Hospital Corpsman and Medal of Honor Foundation.

Once a Corpsman and always a Corpsman; I am a Veteran Volunteer to Season Hospice, and through my Veteran's Organizations I am active with Veterans like myself who have PTSD.

TONY HILLIARD

US Marine Corps— Combat Engineer Officer

Dates of Military Service: 1965 to 1992

Units Served with in Vietnam: 7th Engineer Bn, 1st Marine Div, III Marine
Amphibious Force

Dates Served in Vietnam: Jan 1968 to Jan 1969

Highest Rank Held: Lt. Colonel (O-5)

Place of Birth and Date: Philadelphia, PA—1944

BOOM!

It was the end of August 1968 and I had been with A Company at Camp
Love, near Danang for two months. I was told to pack my gear quickly
and prepare to move to B Company. I did not have a clear understanding of what was going on or why I was headed to Bravo. I got my gear
together and met the driver at the S-1's office in the early afternoon. Off
we went. Bravo Company was located South of Danang at Hill 10, about
6 km southwest of the Danang Air Base. I had never been there before,
so I was prepared for another RVN adventure. As we drove through the
city, we encountered the normal hustle and bustle of traffic in Danang,
but as we drove closer to the southern side, we began to see more and
more people coming toward us. I thought that was unusual.

The closer we got to the South side of town, the greater the crowd
heading toward us. I became a little apprehensive because it looked like
a stream of refugees heading into the city. Then as we got close to the
Cam Le Bridge, just south of the Danang Air Base, I saw a wounded
Marine among the people streaming by and the pucker factor increased
significantly. Our route to Bravo caused us to turn off the highway and
head southeast out of town before we got to the Song Cau Do River and
the Cam Le Bridge. We were heading into the rural area outside the city.
Once we got out of the built-up area, we were able to move pretty fast.

We got to Hill 10 late in the afternoon. I met the CO, Captain Mike
Esposito, as he was out in the company area directing the construction
of an enhanced defensive perimeter around the compound. There were

I'M READY TO TALK TWO | 327

bull dozers moving dirt to create high berms inside the wire, to make it difficult for anyone to get into the area. He indicated that VC/NVA units had assaulted the Cam Le Bridge during the previous night and that the battle was still going on. There was a lot of enemy activity in the area. There was a 175-artillery battery co-located with B Company and it was unclear whether the compound would be a target. I found out that the enemy activity was known as the "Third Offensive." The VC/NVA plan was to infiltrate the city and take over some of the key facilities in order to create a favorable impression at the Paris peace talks and to call for a general uprising by South Vietnamese political and military officials. I would like to have known what was going on before I left Camp Love.

I don't remember anything happening around Bravo's compound that night. There were lots of flares and a great deal of air recon activity during the hours of darkness. We were up all night and on edge. The next day we sat tight and waited to see what would happen.

I was assigned as the XO of the company. We had 6 officers assigned and were in good shape. I suspect this was due to the recent activity. Steve Anderson had transferred to Bravo earlier and there were two new guys who had been in country less than a month. Bravo Company's responsibilities were generally the same as Delta's. Road sweeps to keep the lines of communication open, mainly Route 1 south of the city, and also construction and repair jobs in the area of responsibility. The roads near Danang were hard surfaced, two lane thoroughfares that were in good condition. The roads we were responsible for were further South along Route 1, where they had not been maintained and had deteriorated, or were not improved.

Things got back into full swing pretty quickly. After I had been there only a few days, we got a radio message that one of the sweep teams had several casualties as the result of a booby trap. Information was very scarce. The message indicated that the casualties were officers. Since some of the officers were new in country, they were assigned to a platoon with a more experienced platoon leader to learn the ropes. With only sketchy information, the skipper told me to grab my gear and come with him. We got in his jeep and took off for the medical facility we thought the wounded were being taken to.

I don't remember whether it was NSA or Charlie Med, but they were not there when we arrived. The CO was persistent and got someone to find out where they had been taken. They had been flown out to the hospital ship in Danang harbor. I don't remember whether it was the USS Sanctuary or the Repose. Captain Esposito then got us over to the harbor area and we tried to find a boat going out to the ship. We managed to get a ride out there and were able to find one of the enlisted Marines who had been injured in the incident. He did not have life threatening injuries and was able to fill us in. It seems the sweep team came upon a container of some sort on the road. One of the Lt's picked it up and was examining it as another officer came over to see what was going on. A hand grenade fell out of the container and detonated, injuring both officers and the enlisted man.

The officers, Anderson and I believe Lee, were more seriously injured and were not available at the time. I don't remember if they were on the Repose or were taken somewhere else. I believe they were medevac'd out of country shortly thereafter. They all survived the incident. We were able to get a helicopter ride back to shore, hooked up with the driver and went back to Hill 10. Because of the booby trap incident, I was once again out on the road as a platoon leader with Bravo 1.

A short time later, our platoon was assigned to accompany another unit while it did its sweep on Route 1 south. We were to continue on to a Korean Marine Brigade compound near Hoi An for a minor construction job after the other platoon finished the sweep. The ride out to the sweep area was miserable. There was a cold, light rain and I was in back of the truck with my guys and the sweep team, getting wet. The other Lt had earlier called "shotgun" and was up in the cab with the driver. It was cold and rain was running down our necks. No one was happy. The truck reached the point where the road sweep was to start and the sweep team dismounted and got out in front of the truck. My guys and I stayed in the truck while the sweep team did their job. There was no one around. The truck followed slowly at some distance behind the sweep team.

I saw the opportunity to go up front and get in the dry cab with the driver, but I was too miserable to move from where I was. A few minutes into the sweep, the miserable, gray day got very dark, and I remember the sensation of being up in the air looking down at my guys below me. There was no sound. We were all moving up and then down, and we landed in a pile in the bed of the truck. The darkness was due to black smoke from the detonation of a mine in the road. Our adrenalin kicked in and everybody was up and jumping off the truck. I looked forward while I was still in the truck and noted that the left front of the truck was gone. The corpsman that was with us was lying on the ground and his legs were in terrible shape. He had been sitting with his legs over the front of the truck bed and caught the full effect of the blast below his knees.

An ARVN medic had reached him immediately and began working on him. Some of our guys got around to the front and were pulling the driver from the cab. I could see he had some very bad head injuries. I started to jump off the truck and saw Master Sergeant "Ski" lying out in a paddy about 20 yards from the road. I jumped off the truck and ran over to him. He lay there motionless. He could talk and said he couldn't move his limbs. I checked him over and could find no bleeding wounds. I tried to unbutton his flak vest but I couldn't get the snaps to open. I drew my big 'fighting knife" and was trying to cut his vest off, when his eyes got very big and he said "Lt, please put the knife away." I think he was afraid I would cut him. He started to recover feeling in his limbs and I was able to get him up and walking back to the truck. The situation was very bad.

The sweep platoon had run back to the truck and they were trying to help with the wounded. An emergency medevac was called and was inbound. The driver had severe injuries to his head and lower body. A corpsman from a CAP unit nearby was not able to do much for him and he passed away shortly after the explosion. Our corpsman's legs were in bad shape. He had to get to surgery fast. We had one KIA, two emergency medevacs, and two routines. Top Ski was banged up but not seriously injured. We got all those people out on the helo. The rest of us just had bumps and bruises. We had been very lucky that the explosion occurred where it did. The incident took place about 100 yards south of a Combined Action Platoon (CAP) outpost. These were compounds manned by both US Marines and ARVN soldiers to provide joint security in rural areas. The corpsmen attached to the CAP unit were on the scene very quickly and were able to treat the wounded. Things would have been much worse because the corpsman with us had been wounded in the blast and could not render medical aid to the other injured Marines.

We had to stay at the site until a wrecker could come out and pick up the damaged vehicle and get another truck to take us and the sweep team on to our respective next stops. The sweep team continued on their clearing mission and we stayed with the vehicle until the area was cleared up. The sweep team platoon leader and his people were feeling a great deal of guilt about what had happened. There wasn't much we could say to them. Consolation would have to come with time. Civilian traffic through the area had been at a standstill because of all the military activity and it was now flowing freely around and past us and the damaged vehicle. The faces on the people passing the scene were full of apprehension and sadness.

The new truck arrived and took us to the Korean Marine compound where we spent the night. The sweep team returned to Bravo. A heavy pall hung over the platoon. We didn't do any work that day and I believe we were recalled back to the company area the following day without working on the project. It was now the end of September and I had been in country for 9 months. I still had four months to go.

TOYS

Steve Anderson was a recently arrived LT. He had managed to buy a Thompson submachine gun from someone, somewhere. It was really cool. He had not been able to fire the weapon since he bought it, so the "Skipper" got a few of us together and we went out to an abandoned ARVN rifle range to test it. Since it was Steve's weapon, he got to shoot first. He stepped forward, aimed down range, and squeezed the trigger.

The Thompson started firing .45 cal rounds down range and wouldn't stop. Steve was having trouble keeping the muzzle of the gun pointed down range. Everyone who was there jumped over the jeep and took cover. Steve managed to hold the gun downrange until the magazine emptied. We found out later that the sear in the firing mechanism was broken. After the firing stopped, we heard yelling and obscenities directed at us from off to our left, down range. An EOD technician was in the process of preparing to destroy some artillery shells and other ordnance items when we started firing. We did not see him because he was down in a ditch that had been dug to contain the blast. He didn't care about what we had to say, he was pissed.

We offered many, many apologies, but he still didn't care. We left the area quickly and went home.

A BIG SURPRISE

It was about mid-September 1968, and the weather was not too bad. The stifling heat had passed, and the temperatures had moderated. The platoon was assigned a job to replace a large culvert under Highway 1 where it passed through the center of a small village. The culvert was about 36 or 48 inches in diameter and had to be bolted together before it was installed. It was about 30 feet long and had to go under the road and out beyond the shoulders. We had a small backhoe assigned to do the earthwork. The problem was that we were ordered to install only half of the culvert at one time. Civilian homes bordered the road and there was no way around the worksite.

Highway 1 could not be shut down because men, materials, and civilian commerce had to keep moving without interruption. This was not a good deal. We got ½ of the culvert in place and were ready to cover it up and then dig up the other side of the road the next day to repeat the process. Traffic was able to go around the work site by using the side of the highway that had not yet been dug up. We became concerned about having to leave the job half-finished and coming back the next day with the possibility of booby traps being planted overnight. I called the CO on the radio and asked if we could just continue the job and get it done that day. Definitely a NEGATIVE! Traffic must be able to pass at all times.

There was still a lot of daylight left and I believed we could get the job finished that day with only minor delays to traffic. Using my junior officer initiative, we started to dig up the second half of the road and were about 45 minutes into the work when the skipper called me. He wanted to know what was going on. Other people have radios also and they had called their units about the delay on Route 1. I got a reaming and we had to fill the section that we had dug on the second half and cover up the section of culvert that had been placed earlier, quickly. Traffic was free to move after about another 45 minutes. We left the job site and returned to Bravo where I was "counseled." I explained what and why, but the Boss was not a happy camper. I went back to the officers' hooch and hid for the rest of the day.

Next day we were back out at the site as early as we could get there. We checked the area thoroughly for booby traps, mines, and anything out of the ordinary. It looked safe, so the backhoe dug out the half of the road we needed to work on. Some of the platoon had to get down in the ditch to shape the hole for the culvert and to level it up with the piece that had been installed the prior day. I was standing at the top of the ditch when someone shouted, "Holy Shit." LCpl Friend was standing at the bottom of the ditch with a shovel full of dirt and a 105 artillery round sitting on his shovel. There were wires curling off the round's fuse, disappearing into the dirt. Somewhere on the other end was a person with an electric detonating device.

The first inclination is to run! Some did, it was scary. I pretty much became immobile. When my control returned a few seconds later, I knew I had to stay with Friend. His eyeballs were the size of golf balls. I told him to stay calm and not to move. I called for someone to get a pair of wire cutters from the tool kit. One of the other Marines did, jumped into the ditch and cut the wires from the fuse. LCpl Friend could not move for a few minutes because he was in a state of shock. He got out of the ditch and sat down and tried to recover.

The platoon went back into the hole and did a very thorough inspection of the area. The artillery round was taken out to one of the paddies behind the 'ville and detonated. We were very lucky. I called the incident in, and we got the installation completed a few hours later. We were glad to be gone from there.

DANIEL O. HYDRICK

US Army — Infantry NCO

Dates of military service (active duty and reserves): 1969 — 1975

Unit(s) served with in Vietnam: Americal Division — 23rd Infantry (196th / 198th), 26th Combat Engineers, 3rd Marine Division

Dates served in Vietnam: Jan 1969 to Dec 1970

Highest rank held: Sergeant (E-5)

Place and date of birth: Wynne, Arkansas — 1951

TOO SHORT FOR NAM!

BASIC TRAINING:

When I went into the Army, I was a strong, 5-foot 6 inch (ish) 135-pound high schooler, give or take a few pounds. I thought nothing of my height and size, and I figured neither did the Army at that time. I was healthy, athletic, with a size 11.5 boot. Built like a HOBBIT so to speak, big hands, big feet, wide shoulders, and a short frame.

All throughout basic training I excelled at PT (Physical Training). I actually didn't mind the physical part of the training and my body took shape fairly quickly. Arms, legs, back, and my wind were coming along nicely.

PT was daily and I could manage the 40-yard low crawl like a spider and The Run, Dodge and Jump course was a breeze, as was the horizontal ladder with 76 rotating rungs; I just had to jump to reach the start.

It was the 150-yard man-carry and the mile run that was my wall. It was my height and my short legs. I could carry the weight of my buddy for 150 yards just fine, but like the mile run, it was the clocked times they gave us to meet that was my downfall.

My thick, short legs were the problem. I was built for short, fast distances, not long runs, so I struggled. However, being Irish and from Arkansas, I was stubborn enough to be able to meet the standards and the times, just enough to win entrance into the 450 PT Club.

The PT course was designed to train you for combat. Points were given to each soldier for his best time throughout the course, with so many points per event. The run, dodge, and jump, the horizontal ladder, 40-yard low crawl under barbed wire, the 150-yard man carry, and then the dreaded 1-mile run, all timed, back-to-back events. It was your marker to beat each time the test was given.

The 450 club was designed for competition between men and platoons. The reward for an individual soldier who scored over 450 points was that you were recognized as an achiever AND, most importantly, you were able to go to the front of the chow Line and eat first; at every meal! Because the Army has strict rules to what and when you could eat, this was my goal. I loved to eat. It was work, but I made it in all four trials.

ON TO VIETNAM.

We were all issued Ruck Sacks (back packs with metal frames) to carry everything you needed into the bush. From socks, ammo, food, medical gear, water (lots of water), poncho liners, and everything in between. I realized the ruck sacks we were issued were not built for short soldiers. The fit was very awkward, too long of a body frame and too wide. The Army operates under the ideology of "one size fits all" so they weren't adjustable.

As all good soldiers do, you adapt and overcome ... meaning I cut the frame to fit me. Not regulation, but then again, I had to carry all that weight, so I made it work for me. I cut the tubing and had a guy weld the pieces to fit me. A carton of Kool cigarettes later and my pack was a perfect fit.

I won't get into our military issued uniforms much, but to say the "one size fits all" still applied. Yep, long legged pants and long trunk body shirts. I looked like you would imagine. The Army also does not approve of rolled up pant legs and sleeves. You either cut and trim or roll the excess under. I learned how to sew. It wasn't pretty.

As you might not know, replenished or replacement clothing, or re-fits, as we called them, were sometimes dropped off in the field. Again,

336 | ROBERT O. BABCOCK

with the idea in mind, they should fit. This time however, in my AO (Area of Operation) there was a local village lady that was usually happy to help me. Food was the best form of payment, however later on it was "smokes."

NOW INTO THE BUSH:

As most of you know, many things come up that you were never trained for, and you are called upon to just get it done. So, my first month on the line I was told to walk point for the platoon.

Being short in tall rice fields, elephant grass, thick jungle; short people can't see over tall things very well, and as the day went on, I felt very lost. I made my way best I could and let it be known that booby traps were not a problem, because being close to the ground I could see them, but distance was an issue. Asking me to see far, or to have a wider angle of view on things was just physically not happening.

I realized the consequences if I could not walk point and lead the guys safely, so I had to begin to make adjustments in my field of view, terrain, compass, and map reading. This was to become, for me, a curse and blessing at the same time.

I saw things in the bush that most didn't. I saw movement at low levels but missed things higher up. This was kind of like a deer that walks under a deer stand without noticing the stand in the trees. It was to my fortune that the VC (Victor Charlie) were like me, short, and weren't inclined to climb as much in our AO (area of operations), thank God.

However, the VC were very adept at digging tunnels. Yes, tunnels. They were everywhere and they had to be investigated. Usually by the shortest, most agile soldier in the units. I got so used to the LT (Lieutenant) looking around and sizing up the guys when we found a tunnel, that I used to stand on rocks, stumps etc., to look tall. This didn't work much of the time.

Needless to say, into the holes I would go. I am not a trained Tunnel Rat, nor did I accept the name, if ever called it. I would get pissed if someone looked my way and said, "Corporal Hydrick is a RAT!" Sometimes this would lead into a stressful situation for those thinking my size was a sign of weakness if you get my drift.

However, the holes were a lot cooler, direction of fire was pretty defined, and most of the time, thank God, uneventful. If I did find things it meant we would be hanging around awhile to either explore more or set up to blow the holes. This would allow us to rest for a while longer.

On occasion, things would get a bit hairy, and I would find myself with unexpected company (the enemy) and would use my size and speed to great advantage. Like the 40-yard low crawl I was taught in basic training, my spider speed came in handy. I believe in one or two occasions my aggressor was quite amazed at my ability to move.

Tunnels are a bit unnerving, as they should be, but from my days in Arkansas where caves were fun to explore (spelunking) I didn't mind it. Better me than someone else. I was indeed the right size, sometimes. If I couldn't get into the hole when called upon to do so, then it seemed the decision was made easier. We would just blow it!

This didn't change with rank. As I made Sergeant, the curse was on me. I felt bad sending someone else down the hole, so most of the time I went. UNTIL Shorty showed up. Yep, you guessed it. He was shorter than me and just as crazy. He volunteered to assist me or go it alone. I loved that guy as anyone would that has ever ventured down a hole.

CHOPPERS (HELICOPTERS):

This Stallions of the Air were our ride most of the time. I have no complaints, because it always beat walking and it was like having air conditioning in the sky. Sometimes too cool, but no complaints, except one.

Most of you know climbing in and out of a Chopper doesn't take a lot of skill, unless you are in a hurry to get on or off, the effort is usually done without notice. Other brothers would grab your Ruck or throw out their hand and help you on.

I did say unless you weren't in a hurry to get on or get off the Chopper, didn't I? Well, for many reasons, Choppers don't like staying on the ground for extended periods of time. VC, NVA, or enemy of the state just love to see them just sitting. This would be grounds for them to use them for target practice with mortars, RPG's (Rocket Propelled Grenade's), automatic weapon fire, and just about anything they can throw at them.

Hot LZ's (coming in under fire—Landing Zone) were the worst for short soldiers such as myself. You see, getting off the Chopper coming into a hot LZ was a trick and solely depended upon your pilot, the terrain, and the amount of enemy fire, he was about to set down in…OR NOT!

So first of all, if you can't LAND the Chopper, meaning putting your skids on the ground, the pilot would let us know about 15 seconds prior that he was going to hover and you were to un-ass his bird—expeditiously, meaning JUMP. Yes, jump, while carrying your ruck, weapon, ammo, etc. from a distance only determined by the pilot's discretion. Two feet, four feet, six feet, eight feet and sometimes higher. Gravity, your weight, and the terrain took care of the rest.

If you are not sitting at the door (a trick I learned later would be good and bad, as you can imagine) you could get an idea as to the drop you were about to have. If you were not sitting at the door, well just pray and slide on out.

In the beginning, my trick was to slide out and touch the skid on the chopper with my boot. Now this is where the military's one size fits all, again comes in to play. If you have short legs, you are literally out of the Chopper before your feet touch the skids. If you were lucky and didn't slip, you had a chance at a good jump and landing. If not, well, just imagine the kind of positions you were exiting the Chopper from. In the end, it was just easier to jump and bypass the skid technique.

The distance to the ground, your overall weight, and the terrain would decide your fate. I have had many soft landings in tall grass and some not so soft on cleared LZ's. To tell the story better, as we were coming into a hot LZ, guys were exiting the Choppers any way they could. As our Chopper passed over an earlier squad that had to jump, we could see that they looked like turtles laying on their backs, kicking and throwing their arms to get to their feet. The terrain they jumped into was on a slope and you can imagine how fast the ground slipped away as they jumped.

MONSOON SEASON:

Any time we crossed a riverbed, stream, or water of any kind made being short and first interesting. When walking point you directed the crossing. It was your primary job to walk out first. So, you just waded out and faced the music. At least I was a good swimmer if things got hairy.

I envied the tall guys forging any water event. They just stepped off and made their way, looking at me, and also often commenting, "Hey, need a 'LEG UP'?" You had to be there to see the humor. I just know that one day I would step down and never come up, especially if the water was swift.

Monsoon season made crossing any water element even more challenging for short folks, because the water was always moving swiftly. The rains never let up, so you were always, in one form or another, neck deep in water. That even meant being more careful where you stepped, slept, and forged. The hard part is keeping your weapon dry and being ready to ditch your ruck if the current was too swift.

Being back at the LZ wasn't any safer during monsoon season. I can tell you we even had to swim out of our bunker back at camp. The rains started one evening and by dawn, or what we could tell was dawn (because darkness was the norm during Monsoon season), the six of us were having to wade out of our underground bunker. I had to swim for it.

To add insult to injury, walking in general left me up to my knees in mud and muck. It was not uncommon to have someone else pull you out by your rifle. The tall guys had their troubles as well but not like the "vertically challenged."

We would all sink in and the more you struggled the deeper you went. Sometimes beyond your knees. So, you can only imagine the short guy's depth of muck. It just kept adding insult to injury.

Vietnam was unkind in so many ways. I know all of us have our stories of trials we faced, however, if you were tall, now you know the advantages you had. We were all brothers and the ribbing we took for not having the height only pushed us to be taller, sorta.

Time passed and Vietnam became just memories. However, my best buddy from Nam's wife called and wanted to surprise him with me coming out to his son's graduation party. I was so excited, and the secret was going to be the best.

When I met his family, they had told my buddy to wait while they went to get me. I was just in the distance waiting. I walked up to my brother of so many years and stuck out our unit patch and said, "I think you dropped this." He turned and we immediately hugged each other for the longest time. Many of you know the feeling.

The next thing out of his mouth was, "What the hell? How did you get so tall?" Yep, I come from a family of late bloomers; I was now 5'11." My best brother in the bush had not grown an inch. We were young once and shorter. But I still love him and will never call him short, not in our world.

DONALD H. NAU

U S Army — Armor/Infantry Officer

Time in Military (Active Duty and Reserves): 1967-1974

Unit Served with in Vietnam: HQ Co, 3rd Combat Brigade, 25th Infantry Division

Dates in Vietnam: Aug 1969 to Aug 1970

Highest Rank Held: 1LT

Place of Birth and Year: East Cleveland, Ohio — 1944

ALL CAME RUNNING

Who can forget the opening scene of MASH on TV? Alright — to the one who has never seen the show — a quick explanation.

Radar (the company clerk) SCREAMS, before anyone else heard them, "CHOPPERS!!!" Other than those in the middle of a surgery, *everything* stops — for less than a second — and then ALL run to the chopper pad. ALL means ALL! The Doctors, Nurses, Medical Staff and, yes, the Colonel.

CWO2 Pilot Howard and I were on a "last light" mission. At dusk — near dark — we flew the length of the perimeter defense wire of the 25th Infantry Division's Cu Chi base camp. This was the time of day when Charlie would start to come out of the tunnels for their night operations. Our role was to identify the specific tunnel openings for our perimeter guards. There were many tunnel openings — some were even inside the wire — remember, they were here first. NOTE: Mr. Howard went on to serve three tours during which he received multiple Distinguished Flying Crosses and Purple Hearts. Upon retiring, he worked at Brooke Army Hospital identifying pieces of metal, which at one time were whole combat helicopters, recovered from a location of a missing pilot and crew. This effort moved many from the MIA list to the KIA list — of which the families were grateful. An ironic "job well done!" reward. He did this for years. He knew some of the downed pilots.

Through the chopper's headphones, Mr. Howard hollered "Charlie at 9 o'clock"! I saw an image go into a tunnel and fired a grenade at the opening. Sidenote: I might add at this point that I was well acquainted with the Army's M79 Grenade Launcher. This was a rifle-like gun with a single round (smooth grenade) in a 1 ½ inch barrel. One evening, at the start of being the night perimeter sector duty officer, a soldier asked if I could hit a dead tree outside of the wire with the M79. I fired a round up into the air, reloaded and then fired a 2nd round directly at the tree—both hit the tree at almost exactly the same time with just enough difference to know there were two. BOOM—BOOM. The word got around.

I looked toward 9 o'clock and fired toward the hole. As the tunnel's entrances were booby-trapped, the round exploded and caused a secondary explosion—it looked like my "demo."

The chopper rocked—I looked at Mr. Howard and his face was all blood coming from his forehead—I kept wiping the blood so he could see—He radioed to clear air traffic, and we headed to the 12th Evacuation Hospital pad. As we approached, I saw them ALL running as fast as they could—to us. Mr. Howard, thinking we had landed, shut down the chopper about six feet off the ground—hard landing!

The medical team yanked us both from the chopper. On the litter, they were cutting away my jungle fatigues as, by now, I was covered in blood. It turned out, I was not hit by the shrapnel. The blood was all Mr. Howard's. This was Mr. Howard's first Purple Heart. The chopper sustained many, many tears and holes—still don't know why I didn't.

I, also, don't know how Charlie, or anyone else in that tunnel, could have survived that double blast. I have thought about that every day since. To be clear, the "Tunnels of Cu Chi" were there for a reason—to hide during the day, come out at night and kill the French, and now the Americans. At that moment, I was there to stop that.

It *was* a War—For All of us!

GLENN PEYTON CARR

US Army—Aviator

Dates of Military Service: 1958 to 1986

Unit Served with in Vietnam: 213th Assault Support Helicopter Company (Chinook); B Troop 7th Squadron 17th Cavalry Regiment (Air)

Dates Served in Vietnam: XO & CO 213th May 1967 to May 1968; CO B Troop 7/17, XO 52nd Combat Aviation Battalion 1971

Highest Rank Held: Lt. Colonel (O-5)

Place of Birth: Shawnee, OK—1934

IT WAS NOT AN INSTRUMENT LANDING SYSTEM (ILS) APPROACH. IT WAS A FLARE LANDING (FL) APPROACH!

The time was TET '68 and the date January 30, 1968. TET is the Lunar New Year celebration which lasts four to five days. During the Vietnam Conflict, the South Vietnamese and the opposing warring elements had a gentleman's agreement to observe an annual cease fire for the celebration period. However, this year the Vietcong and other fellows from the North decided to do otherwise and instead conduct massive surprise attacks countrywide, starting at 12:01 AM. By mid-morning on the 30th, nearly all, if not all, the provincial capitals were on fire. Saigon airport was also under heavy attack. I was the executive officer of the 213th Assault Support Helicopter Company; that's the long name for a CH-47 Chinook company based at Phu Loi RVN about 15 miles north of Saigon.

Now back to 02:30 AM that morning. As the company executive officer, I had appointed myself (the previous evening) as aircraft commander of aircraft #1, thinking the first day of TET would be relatively quiet, e.g. no combat, no ground fire, maybe only bacon and beans loads, a few troops to go in for showers, etc. A really laid-back day of flying with a relatively new copilot otherwise generally referred to as a "Peter Pilot." This was supposed to be a good day to train a newbie copilot. Boy was I in for a surprise!!

The #1 aircraft always performed a preflight the evening before to

ensure it was ready to fly in case a tactical emergency (TAC-E) was ordered. Sure enough, at 02:30 AM in the morning the operations runner
nudged me out of a deep sleep saying, "Sir, we have a TAC-E." I quickly
dressed and trotted to operations and surveyed the skies to make a quick
weather check—NOT GOOD—low ceilings, very low! Of course, I
could not determine the heights of the clouds until I got the weather
briefing from the Air Force weatherman.

We got our TAC-E and weather briefings from our operations sergeant while we put on all our gear, including flight helmet, emergency
vest, personal weapon, bullet proof chest plate (referred to as the "chicken
plate"), plus any other item we deemed appropriate, and quickly moved
out to the aircraft. The enlisted crew was at the aircraft performing a
quick once-over of the critical areas of the aircraft and mounting the
machine guns.

Here is where I need to compliment the mission planner. He must
have known of the crappy weather, so rather than making me fly 15 miles
southwest to the division rear and attempting to land in a built-up area
in crappy weather, he ordered the cavalry (Cav) squadron at the west end
of our runway to prepare the load. His planning saved me from trying to
execute a practically impossible mission, which now gave me nearly flat
country all the way to the embattled Infantry unit that was requesting
assistance.

Peter pilot taxied down the runway, sighting the Cav trooper standing on the load ready to hook up. He picked up, hovered over the load,
and got a "load is hooked, tighten the sling" from our crew chief. All this
time, I was on the radio talking to Saigon radar. The aviator lingo went
something like this: "Paris control this is Black Cat 5 on the west end of
Papa Lima runway, I have a TAC-E requesting Pigeons to map coordinates to ABC XYZ, Angels 3, advise stormy weather, and stay with me
for a return vector."

A translation of this diatribe would be something like this: Paris
control is Saigon radar, Black Cat 5 is my call sign for the aircraft, Pigeons to map coordinates means give me a vector (direction) straight to
the map coordinates, Angels 3 means I want 3,000 feet en route altitude,

advise stormy weather means let me know when I approach within a half mile of the Cambodian border, and lastly stay with me for a return vector means keep me on your radar scope for assistance back to Phu Loi.

As we hovered over the load and were tightening the sling, the crew chief said, "Sir, do you know our aft rotor is in the clouds?" I responded, "That figures, as the forward rotor is dusting off the bottom of the clouds." I instructed the peter pilot to lift the load and for the crew chief to check the load by looking through the "Hell Hole", which is a three-foot square hole in the center of the aircraft floor directly over the load hook. This allows the crew chief to view the load and instruct the pilot to go up, down, forward, backward, left or right to position the aircraft for either hook-up or release of the load.

Amusingly, that is the only situation I know of where an enlisted man can legally tell an officer or warrant officer where to go! Once we were satisfied with the load, I took control since I was the only one rated for instrument flying, which means not seeing anything outside due to the weather and relying completely on the instruments on our front panel for flight and navigation. We went into the clouds immediately as peter pilot told Paris control we were airborne. Paris replied, "No contact yet…" and a few minutes later Paris said radar contact had been made and to turn right for a positive identification. At this point, Paris put us back on the course to the infantry's location. Climbing to 3,000 feet we broke out on top of the clouds at about 1,000 feet to a clear, starlit night.

Making contact with the receiving infantry unit, I determined they were in the same location as the last time I delivered a load to them. That was a blessing as I now know the landing area is in an oblong field. I asked the infantry ground contact, Dogface 95, to give me a magnetic bearing to the long axis of the field so I could utilize the longest open area for landing. I then set up a standard aviation maneuver known as a holding pattern, which is basically a racetrack in the sky with standard rate 180 degree turns at each end and for this situation I chose one-minute legs between each turn. Paris placed me directly over the map coordinates in the direction of the long axis of the field.

I started my racetrack so the end of the inbound leg would put me over the Infantry unit. I performed two racetrack patterns to establish our holding pattern and each time Dogface 95 confirmed we were right over his location when and where we should have been. I had asked Dogface 95 if he had a hand-held flare. My plan here was to get Dogface 95 right on the spot where he wanted the load, and then hold the flare straight up and wait for my command to fire it.

Forty-five seconds into the third inbound leg, I commanded him to fire the flare. I was amazed to see that flare come right up and in-line with the center post of my windshield about 200-300 yards forward of our location. I bottomed the thrust lever (that's collective pitch to you Huey drivers) and started a steep approach before the flare burned out. The flare came back to earth about 10 feet from the soldier that fired it. I told Dogface 95 that he better kick the smoldering flare to the side of the field so I wouldn't set the load of ammo on top of it. That would certainly ruin our day!

Once the load was on the ground and off my hook, I asked Dogface 95 the usual question, "Were there any wounded or other back-hauls I can do for you?" He responded, "Not yet Black Cat 5. That was an excellent job, and we owe you a chicken dinner. The next time we have dead bird I'll give you a call to see if you can slip in here and eat with us."

Before I could answer, Dogface 6 came on the radio saying, "Excellent job, Black Cat 5, I'll see that your group and battalion commanders know of this excellent performance." Dogface 6 was Lieutenant Colonel Richard E. Cavazos, the battalion commander and later a four-star general. He was a magnificent leader of men. He passed away October 29, 2017.

Back to the TAC-E site and with the mission accomplished, the Infantry had their desperately needed ammo resupply.

As we lifted off, Paris control gave us a vector back to Phu Loi and I shot a GCA (ground-controlled approach) to our runway. While the crew refueled the aircraft, peter pilot and I went to operations to get the days "normal" missions. That's when we found we were up to our ears in combat all over Vietnam. That day ended with about 16.5 hours of flight time. I swear that day I moved every 105 Howitzer that the US Army owned! The first day of TET-68 was now in the history books, but it was a far cry from the lollipop day I had envisioned 24 hours beforehand.

BOB LANZOTTI

US Army — Aviator
Total Time in Military: 1960 to 1985
Unit Served with in Vietnam: 1st Avn Bde, 1st Cav Div
Dates in Vietnam: 1967 to 1968; 1969 to 1970
Highest Rank Held: Lt. Colonel (O-5)
Place of Birth: Taylorville, IL — 1937

CREW CAMARADERIE OF THE THIRD KIND

It was my good fortune to command a Chinook company in the 1st Air Cav Division during 1969/70. Initially, I wasn't at all thrilled with the unit's name, Crimson Tide, since I was on the Fighting Illini football squad during my University of Illinois college days. But then, the commander of the Alabama Crimson Tide, Bear Bryant, had led his teams to twenty-four straight bowl appearances and eight National Championships. Everybody loves a winner and I quickly got to love my call sign, Tide 6. While Bear Bryant didn't win a National Championship in 1969, Charlie Company, 228 ASHB, was the Crimson Tide Champion in '69, albeit in Vietnam. We had a great unit, and this is a story about one of our outstanding pilots and his crew that occurred during that championship season.

While Charley company pilots flew all of our unit's sixteen aircraft, flight engineers, crew chiefs, and gunners worked on assigned aircraft as teams. There were exceptions, particularly with gunners. A gunner was generally an Infantry 11 Bravo (Rifleman) who came from one of the Division's Infantry or Cavalry field units. One gunner, Private Doolittle, would not fly with anybody except CW3 Harry Stevens, a New Englander, and a particularly popular officer among the enlisted crews, and our entire unit for that matter.

Whenever Harry went up, Doolittle went with him — no arguments were ever attempted. That's just the way it was. You would have thought Private Doolittle was Harry's aide-de-camp as he was constantly in the presence of Harry. The gunner on a Chinook mans an M60 7.62mm machine gun on a swivel and is stationed on the left side of the fuse-lage, directly behind the aircraft commander's seat. A firewall separates the two. The aircraft commander and co-pilot change FM frequencies constantly and UHF frequencies less frequently, but there is always on-board intercom between crew members.

On one mission, CW3 Stevens and his crew were flying supplies to a non-divisional unit, the 11th Armored Cavalry Regiment (11 ACR) which was attached to the 1st Air Cavalry Division and assigned a screening and reconnaissance role. The season was dry, and landings in a Chinook could sometimes be hazardous because of the blowing dust and debris from the rotor wash. Harry made his approach into one of the few areas of the 11 ACR encampment where he could release his sling load of ammo and supplies. He also had some internal cargo and needed to land from a hover.

During this process, Harry's aircraft was creating a huge dust storm, and that didn't bode well with one 11th ACR trooper who had been sunning himself on the top of an Armored Personnel Carrier (APC). He jumped off his APC and ran toward the Chinook. He then attempted to punch Harry through the open cockpit window. He had to literally jump off the ground to deliver his blows to his target, Harry's head, which was a good seven or eight feet off the ground. The blows, even if they found their mark, could not have inflicted pain as Harry was wearing his flight helmet, every bit as protective as a football helmet. Harry had just transmitted over the intercom something to the effect of, "Look at this crazy SOB!"

Private Doolittle, with his gun trained on the deranged soldier, trans-mitted over the intercom to his aircraft commander, "Sir, do you want me to blow his S**T away?" Harry's immediate reply was, "No, don't shoot!" There could be no doubt that if Harry's command had been to the affirmative, there would certainly be one more name inscribed on the Vietnam Memorial Wall today.

Bob Lanzotti
Tide 6

DANIEL O. HYDRICK

US Army — Infantry NCO

Dates of military service (active duty and reserves): 1969 – 1975

Unit(s) served with in Vietnam: American Division — 23rd Infantry (196th / 198th), 26th Combat Engineers, 3rd Marine Division

Dates served in Vietnam: Jan 1969 to Dec 1970

Highest rank held: Sergeant (E-5)

Place and date of birth: Wynne, Arkansas — 1951

ALL IN A DAY

Somewhere south of Quang Nai Province, Vietnam

LZ Wrong Hole: (LZ Knight)

Most of my Vietnam brothers are quick to tell their story of first arriving in country and then leaving. Many choose not to remember the middle of the longest year in their young lives. Yes, my first day in country was eventful, terrifying, hot as hell, and my leaving was a little more painful, but that story is for another time.

This is just a memory that came to me while speaking to my son one day when he asked me, "What was a typical day in Vietnam? Were the days long? What started a day? When did it end?" This is now my answer to my son many years later.

I believe the location makes all the difference in time in NAM. Although sent out on various support operations, for me, being in the jungle on a small isolated NDP (Night Defense Perimeter) was home away from home for much of my time. We were an outpost in old western terminology. Patrols, ambushes, intel gathering, etc.

We were in a high traffic AO (a unit area of operation). Being a small unit in the bush like this always made for an easy target for visitors and a popular stop-over for any group of Viet Cong (Victor Charlie) who wanted to pay their respects.

Being isolated made some days longer than others, and as our little compound grew into a bonified LZ, (company size) the days became more active and longer.

As all days run together with moments of mind-numbing quietness, to sheer terror, I thought about a day that was clearer than others, and quite frankly easier to tell. A day as most of you understand should have been 24hrs long, 1440 minutes or 86,400 seconds, but who is counting?...we all did.

All the times I am giving you, by the clock, in this moment of my memory, are clearly estimated. I didn't care for time on a watch. You see I had six months left in country or 179 days and a wake up. You don't get to think about time or going home until you become a "two-digit-midget" (99 days and a wake-up left in country).

You have to understand the daily life on this small LZ, was simple. You were always filling sandbags, digging defense positions, checking the wire for holes, resetting claymores, details of one order or another, checking on the health of my guys, sending out and setting up LP's (Listening Post or Observation Post), basically tired, always hungry, checking ammo, and rotating guard duty. It was that way each day as a routine.

On this day, we were already very busy with new intel of Victor Charlie in the area. No contact by our teams, just signs. No need to walk you through it; just note that with suspected movement, everyone is busy getting ready for "something" in the night. Chuck (Viet Cong) owned the night.

So, my squad was sent out last to cover some ground and set up an ambush before dark. After about 1.5 clicks (kilometers) out, we were ordered to bring it back in. We now received other intel of "heavy' movement heading our way. All hands were needed inside the perimeter.

NOW THE DAY BEGINS

00:00 — A new day begins It gets pretty busy when Command gets spooked. Hard to see out, it's very dark inside the compound. Fire protocol, no fires, not cigarettes burning except in the holes. Everyone re-checking ammo, rethinking zones of fire, squad leaders talking it over with the guys, and then waiting.

0100 Everybody's ready for whatever is coming, we hoped. I got back to my digs (foxhole, parka covering hole) around 0100 after the last briefing. I checked how many grenades I had because I love me some grenades.

0145 Automatic weapons fire opened up from my corner bunker. The M-60 (machine gun) was talking (firing) to someone. It's proper for automatic weapons to fire to solicit a response. Suspected Victor Charlies in the wire, all hands on the berm. Everyone was returning fire, no matter what you don't see. (Suppression fire).

0200 All clear, no answer came back (VC didn't return fire). Quiet again—checked with Star Lights and hung lanterns (Mortar fired illumination rounds). No evidence of VC. Corporal "Arty Arty ", our corner M-60-bunker man was just a little jumpy, hence the name, (Arty Arty, short for Artillery shell). He was caught out in the open when the order was given to fire for effect on an artillery assault. This will tend to make you forever a "little jumpy."

Arty Atry thought he saw movement just outside the wire. So did I, to tell the truth. You kind of see things if you look too hard into the night. We reported that there was no contact.

SMOKE BREAK IN YOUR HOLE, TO CLEAR OUR HEADS.

0245 Back to my hole to shake off the craziness, and tried to remember what I saw, if anything. Promised myself I wouldn't do it again, maybe. Reloaded my magazines, calmed my thoughts and went back to looking for movement, this time changing my line of sight more often.

0320—I heard thumping sounds out in the distance. Here we go, incoming. Charlie (VC) was walking mortar rounds into the compound. I heard three thumps, one after the other, in the distance; three rounds, accurate, the ground was shaking, lot of shrapnel flying around. One mortar round outside the wire, two inside the compound, maybe 60mm's (size of mortar round). Everyone on the berm was up and firing.

0345 The firing slowed, no more incoming and we were told to stand down. All eyes over the berm as our watch continued to 0430

0430 A lot of us were up and moving, checking on guys and looking for causalities, policing ammo, checking damage, getting and giving instructions. Needed to do some night repairs on the wire, big hole.

0515 Incoming!! Second round of mortars, two of them. They fell inside the compound. Seems as though Charlie had a favorite spot. This time they were followed by small arms and an automatic weapon fire, concentrated on our corner M-60's positions. Maybe Arty Arty did see something. No direct attack, heaviest fire coming from thick jungle just outside the LZ...then quiet with a few smaller arms fire, then back to automatic fire. Roman was our grenadier on the thumper (M-79). He was working the thick jungle with HE's (High Explosives). Now all three 60's up and working the KZ (kill zone) / grenades out...then quiet again.

0730 A lot of movement inside the compound. Seems Charlie hit a few of us with the mortars. We check everyone for wounds, other damage, ammo check, and move some weapons around for next time. Heard the call go out for a Medivac for the wounded and we were told they were not considered critical enough for Dust off. It seems our new medic said wrong things about the wounded, so after an hour or so the word came back to us that we would walk'em out.

SMOKE BREAK TO CLEAR YOUR HEAD!

1000 Top (First Sergeant) says to gear up to mine sweep the road and walk out the wounded. We packed them in a previously commandeered jeep and ¾ ton truck and headed out to QL 1 and maybe an early Medivac along the way.

1045 Slow and steady walk behind two sweepers, with others taking turns digging up whatever they heard.

1100 Sniper fire along the way. Our squad was sent out to find the little fellow, who was either an incredibly bad shot or some of us were very lucky. VC doe this sometimes to slow your moment, but that's not a good sign either.

1130 Squad got moving and right away spotted movement and started chasing suspected VC in an open paddy. This little fellow could move. We fired at him while running in knee deep paddy mud. Little guy was fast. I decided to pull the squad off so as not to get too far out. We walked back to the road to rejoin the unit.

SMOKE BREAK TO CLEAR YOUR HEAD.

1230 We got word that a Medivac coming in early and to hold in place. We set up defensive position to protect the Chopper. It was an easy in and out, as they took out the wounded short of QL1. We began the long walk back to the LZ.

1345 ON the way back, we spotted several children standing along the roadside. They were perfectly still, scared faces, wanting G.I. to buy the unexploded rounds that were strapped to them by "someone." The children were often used to bring in the ordinance that we had advertised them to do. Well, not them but adults. You see, they were answering a US leaflet campaign that said that G.I. would "pay the villagers for unexploded rounds." The parents and others used the children to bring the rounds in for fear of something bad happening to the adult walking in with an explosive on them. We all needed to move slow now.

SMOKE BREAK TO CLEAR YOUR HEAD.

1530 We cleared the rounds and detonated them. This little girl was holding an unexploded 60 mm, like the one shot at us last night. She might have been all of 8-years-old. We took it from her and paid her in C-Rats. (food). After paying up, the little girl and I had a long talk with what might have been her aunt. I mean a long talk.

SMOKE BREAK TO CLEAR MY HEAD

1730 A lot of clouds coming in and it looks like rain coming. It was getting on to dusk and remember, Victor Charlie owns the night, time to pick up pace.

SMOKE BREAK TO, WELL, JUST SMOK'EM IF YOU GOT EM.

1830 We made it back LZ, hot, tired, and ready to stop moving. We dropped off the equipment, checked and got more ammo and reported into Top and let him know it was a delightful stroll. Squad leaders met up to review assignments for the night watch and OH YEAH, someone said to grab some C-rats for dinner, but eat it cold, no fires again tonight. I had to find some food; I forgot I gave mine to the kid.

SMOKE BREAK TO CLEAR MY HEAD!

2130 Victor Charley was always watching. We determined he had watched us come back into the LZ and decided to make sure we were not back our holes (foxholes), so he walked in a few mortars to bust up our rest break. The corner M-60's opened up, HE's (M-79's) flew out, teams put out suppression fire into the kill zone (KZ) and then quiet. NO, I didn't' get my food yet because it was too dark and I was just too tired to hunt for it.

SMOKE BREAK TO CLEAR MY HEAD!

2300 We were given the all clear, no wounded, nothing important hit because we had moved things around from the last event. Victor Charlie was able to hit two 55-gallon drum halves that we used for our latrine buckets. It made for a lovely smell inside the compound with no wind to move it out.

DOWN IN YOUR HOLE FOR, YOU KNOW, SMOKE BREAK TO CLEAR MY HEAD.

No more signs of our friends in the dark, so we checked our ammo and set up guard rotation assignments. LP's and OP's were checking in, all clear. Finally, back in my hole for some peace and quiet.

ONE LAST SMOKE TO CLEAR MY HEAD.

Time 0100 the next day.

Oh yeah, did I tell you I didn't smoke … not until I got here … **All in a day … or two.**

THOMAS A. "TOM" ROSS

US Army— Special Forces

Dates of Military Service (Active and Reserve): 1966 to 1992

Unit Served with in Vietnam: Detachment A-502, 5th Special Forces Group

Dates in Vietnam: Jan 1968 to Dec 1968

Highest Rank Held: Major (O-4)

Place of Birth and Year: Huntington, WV— 1945

WHO CALLED?

DURING MY TOUR OF duty, one of my most surprising experiences didn't occur in the jungles of Vietnam. It occurred within the relative security of my Special Forces compound and was so unexpected that I still find it difficult to believe.

I was in the Operations office working on plans for a rescue mission of a tribe of mountain villagers when I was interrupted. One of our radiomen poked his head in the office door and said, "LT, there's some guy from the Red Cross on the radio and he wants to speak to you."

"Okay, I'll be right there."

As I got up and headed to the radio room, my thoughts immediately turned to home. *Something has happened to someone at home*, I thought, I feared.

When a serviceman was killed in Vietnam, the family back home could be notified one of two ways. They could receive a very impersonal Western-Union telegram or by a more personal in-person visit from a member of the service, a chaplain when possible. Even though more considerate, that knock on the door was one no family welcomed. The use of the distasteful and the much-dreaded telegram was eventually discontinued.

In the reverse, it was the Red Cross that often made the notification to service members of the injury or death of a loved one back home. So, it was with serious concern that I entered the radio room.

When I acknowledged the call, an ominously calm voice on the other end of the radio identified himself by name and said he was with the

American Red Cross. Then he asked, "Is this Lieutenant Thomas A. Ross of Pensacola, Florida?"

After saying, "Yes, it is," I prepared myself for whatever bad news he was about to deliver.

"First," he said, "I want you to know that everyone back home is just fine." Then, he told me why he was contacting me.

I couldn't believe what he said. So, to confirm what I had just heard, I asked, "Who called?"

"Your mother. I just hung up from speaking with her."

"What?"

"Yes, she called the office here in Saigon. This is a combat zone and civilian calls are not supposed to be routed here."

"Yes, I'm sure," I replied. "Unless it's my mother on the other end of the line. She's a very persuasive and determined woman."

"I know, she said someone in Washington had given her our phone number. She wanted me to put her through to you at A-502, but I told her I couldn't do that."

After laughing out loud, I asked, "So, what did my mother want?"

"She said she hadn't received mail from you in two weeks and wanted to know that you were okay."

Before the rescue developed, I had been out on a 10-day long-range patrol west of Trung Dung. I had written a letter home the day after we returned, but it hadn't had time to reach home yet.

Continuing, the man from the Red Cross said, "Your mother told me that she wouldn't hang up until I promised to call her back after confirming that you were okay. So, I did."

"Well, you are very kind. Please tell my mother that you spoke to me directly. That will give her comfort. Then, please tell her that I said I am just fine and that I love her very much. Oh, tell her that I asked about my Dad, my sister, Polly, and my dog, Bingo. That will confirm that you spoke to me, and that news should make you her hero."

He laughed, then said, "I will. I'm going to call her right now."

I thought about whether or not to submit this story for the book, but how could it be left out? Families experienced the war right along with those of us who fought it. And, maybe even more so…imagining all the terrible things that might be happening to us.

WITHDRAWAL PHASE

(1970 TO 1972)

May 4, 1970 — Kent State shooting. Students were protesting government policies in the Vietnam war when National Guardsmen fired on them. Four were killed and nine wounded.

June 24, 1970 — United States Senate votes to repeal the Gulf of Tonkin resolution.

June 13, 1971 — Pentagon Papers were first published by the New York Times. They revealed broadened its scope of the war but had failed to tell the American people or news media about the decision. This deepened the distrust between the American people and their government.

June 22, 1971 — President Nixon signs the 26th Amendment, lowering the voting age to 18.

March 30, 1972 — Easter Offensive launched by North Vietnamese on South Vietnam.

May 8, 1972 — President Nixon launches Operation Linebacker I, which includes massive bombing of enemy forces in South Vietnam, resuming bombing of North Vietnam, and mining of Haiphong Harbor.

December 18, 1972 — President Nixon orders Operation Linebacker II, a massive new bombing of North Vietnam to force Hanoi back to the bargaining table and to impress the South Vietnam government with American resolve.

Source: www.vvmf.org/VietnamWar/Timeline

R. BRUCE AVERY

U.S. Navy, Communications Officer

Dates of military service (Active and Reserve): June 1, 1970 – June 1, 1976

Unit in Vietnam: USS Westchester County (LST 1167)

Dates served in Vietnam: August 1970 – October 1971

Highest rank: Lieutenant (O-3)

Place and date of birth: Tarrytown, NY – 1948

GOING TO SEE THE ELEPHANT

On June 1, 1970, I received a BA degree from Brown University and a commission as an Ensign from the US Navy. I had some choice in my first duty station and decided to volunteer for Vietnam. (A popular phrase from the Civil War described someone going off to the war as "going to see the elephant"). A couple weeks later, I was in San Diego, California for some brief training and, finally, in late July, was on my way westward to the Far East and my ship the USS Westchester County (LST 1167), or the WESCO as referred to by the crew.

The WESCO was a Landing Ship, Tank (LST) and was originally designed to deliver fully loaded vehicles and tanks directly onto an invasion beach. The LST could be run up on the beach where its clam-shell bow doors opened, a ramp dropped, and then the vehicles were driven off the ship without soldiers and Marines getting their feet wet. In South Vietnam, the LST was ideal for going into the country's shallow rivers that were full of uncharted shoals because the ship could be easily extricated if it ran aground. With these capabilities, the 370-foot WESCO provided mooring for Swift PCF (Patrol Craft, Fast) and PBR (Patrol Boat, River) patrol boats, utilizing the main deck as a flight deck for HAL (Helicopter Attack (Light)) 3 Seawolves gunships, and command facilities for US and South Vietnamese military. We refueled and re-armed boats and helicopters and provided "hotel" services (mess decks, sleeping quarters, ship's store, laundry, etc,) for their crews.

My trip to the WESCO in South Vietnam was not what I had envisioned as I set off "to see the elephant." My contract-commercial air flight lasted for nearly 18 hours, stopping at practically every American island between the Air Force base at Fairfield, California and our destination Atsugi Naval Air Station in Japan. After three or four days waiting around, I was headed out to Saigon's Tan Son Nhut military airport where standard procedure was for pilots to approach the runway with a very steep dive to avoid potential surface-to-air missile attacks on incoming flights. After this white-knuckle experience, passengers unceremoniously deplaned, collected our luggage, and changed all our American greenbacks into colorful military script.

I then headed to the "reception/information" desk and learned that the Air Force airman in charge had no idea where my ship was or how I should get to it but did suggest I check into the Annapolis Bachelor Officer Quarters (BOQ) "up the street." Thanking him for the guidance, I asked how to get there. He told me to go out the front door and catch the military "blue line" bus. I dragged my gear out the door across a bulldozed yard and waited.

After about an hour with no bus in sight, a little US Postal truck pulled up and a First Class petty officer (E-6) got out and asked me what I was waiting for. He informed me that the "blue line" bus didn't run anymore and that I and my luggage were in an area that had been mortared some weeks before (hence the bulldozing). However, he was very kind to the new Ensign and slung my gear into the truck while I grabbed the jump seat in front of the truck, and we proceeded up the street.

The Annapolis came into sight, a four-story building covered by curved metal bars from ground to roof (to fend off thrown or rocket-propelled grenades) and a front entrance surrounded by sandbagged machine gun emplacements. I thanked my ride and checked in at the front desk where I asked about getting to the WESCO. Of course, I received the by now familiar reply, "We don't know where your ship is, but don't worry, we'll get you there."

I would spend several more days waiting for the front desk to find the WESCO. I did use the hours to explore, via military buses, the city and immediate surrounding area. Others could do a better job of describing war-time Saigon, but I was immediately struck by the mixed Asian/French architecture and the beautiful Vietnamese people.

One afternoon I returned to the Annapolis and was pleased to meet the WESCO'S Supply Officer (affectionately know as the "Pork Chop" or "Chop" in the Navy), who was returning from emergency leave. I'd been found! He obviously had a better idea of what was going on than anyone else I'd met because a day or two later we were awakened before dawn and hustled onto a bus (with no breakfast), and headed to Tan Son Nhut MACV(Military Assistance Command Vietnam) air station. Once there, we stood around, hungry, thirsty and baking in the sweltering sun, and more hours passed. Eventually the well-fed, refreshed air crew arrived, and without further ado, we boarded the CH-46 Admin helicopter, and rose into the sky headed south.

My seat was next to the open door where an air crewman alertly manned a machine gun. En route, we landed in a lonely field, empty except for 50-gallon drums of aviation fuel. The gunner jumped down and proceeded to refuel the twin-engine helo. As he deplaned, he pointed at me and then at his gun and indicated that I was to take his place. (Oh this is rich ... I thought. Being a poor shot, I would do better throwing a .45 pistol at the target than trying to shoot it, and he wants me to guard the aircraft!) Fortunately, he finished fueling before General Giap and the entire North Vietnamese Army showed up; we resumed our trip.

At some point, we picked up the Cua Lon River and arrived at Sea Float/Solid Anchor. Sea Float was a floating base comprised of nine large barges tied together and anchored against an eight-knot current. Swift boats were based there as well as Seawolves gunship helicopters and SEAL detachments. Seabees (Naval Construction Battalion) were busily building a permanent shore base named Solid Anchor on the site of what had once been Nam Can City. However, we were dropped off with the mail bags on some pieces of aircraft matting at the edge of the river and across from the relative safety of the Sea Float barges. Just another stop in what seemed like an interminable journey to my ship!

The Chop, being senior, elected to head off to the construction site to radio over to Sea Float for a boat ride. So, I sat alone on the mail at the edge of the jungle. Suddenly there was some noise and the vegetation began moving. While the Viet Cong no longer held sway in the area, the regular North Vietnamese were active. As I watched the tall grass parting and wondered if I would be a casualty before I even arrived at my ship, a Seabee on roving patrol emerged. He was fully armed with an M-16, grenades, and the biggest boom box I had ever seen riding on his shoulder. I guess it was his idea of psychological warfare to scare the enemy away by blasting American rock and roll at top volume. Thankfully, he also had a small radio with him, and with the return of the Pork Chop, he called across to Sea Float for a boat, which showed up fairly quickly. Whatever vessel I could have imagined, our water taxi was not it. It was a Boston Whaler with a badly fire damaged and mostly missing bow.

But it did float, and we loaded our luggage, the mail, and ourselves onboard and the cocky young SEAL helmsman started across the choppy water. He pulled alongside the barges in a sloppy maneuver that caused the practically non-existent bow to dip, enabling brown river water to join us in the boat. As water rose up my leg, and I watched all my earthly goods and the mail float down the river, a voice above me said, "Ensign, give me your hand."

No, it was not a heavenly messenger, but an "angel" in the form of a Master Chief (E-9) who hauled me up on board Sea Float. He escorted me to the BOQ hooch and then went to check on my goods. The young SEAL who had created our "wreck at sea" must have had a really interesting, i.e. blistering conversation with the Chief because he brought me my sodden luggage and offered a sincere apology. I simply thanked him and did not add any other comments, as I was sure the Chief had covered the topic in depth.

After a few days, the Chop found me and announced that he had arranged for a Seawolves helo to make a special trip out to the WESCO to deliver us and the mail. They were not happy at first as they reviewed the over-weight load presented by the two of us, our luggage, and mail. However, as the Pork Chop was THE source of their beer, they rethought their decision and decided to make the trip.

We rose in the hot humid air and hovered for a moment to ensure that we were in fact airborne before heading off down the river. As we flew, we saw some enemy tracers, but our door-gunners ignored them as they did not represent an immediate danger. The pilots were focused on getting out to the ship and with the heavy load were not going to fool around. Finally, the gunner pointed out the door and there on the Bo De River sat the grey, rust-streaked WESCO with a group of patrol boats hugging close like chicks to a mother duck. We landed and the first man to the door, the man who would eventually be my boss, grabbed my hand and said, "Welcome aboard." After weeks of travel from California, I had finally arrived "home" at my duty station.

DANIEL O. HYDRICK

US Army — Infantry NCO

Dates of military service (active duty and reserves): 1969 – 1975

Unit(s) served with in Vietnam: Americal Division – 23rd Infantry (196th /
198th), 26th Combat Engineers, 3rd Marine Division

Dates served in Vietnam: Jan 1969 to Dec 1970

Highest rank held: Sergeant (E-5)

Place and date of birth: Wynne, Arkansas – 1951

GOING HOME!

While convalescing from wounds received, President Nixon offered me a deal. EARLY OUT!!! It was called a Phase Down program and I took it like a thief in the night.

I first thought it was a mistake or that the Army felt I was no longer useful. You see, after all, I didn't know of any other NCO's that had received such orders, but hell, who cared at that point; I just wanted to get my ass out of here.

My orders were set and as a "Two Diget Midget" (under a hundred days in country) I did not care. My brother was with the 101st and he extended his tour and it almost cost him his life. I, on the other hand, was "wheels up" in seven days.

My orders were to chopper down to Cam Ranh Bay and catch the Freedom Bird out of this "land that God forgot." I could not pack fast enough.

My CO (Commanding Officer) asked if my wounds were going to be a problem. I simply said, "Sir, you know I am all in here for you guys and I will miss my brothers badly, but you see I come from a family of 10 and my mom needs her boy's back to help out and well, I am sick of this place, to tell you the truth, so, if I were missing a leg, I would walk out of here if you said I could."

One last amazing drunk with the team, we told all the lies we could tell and made all the promises about catching up on each other when we were back in the "World," and then I was gone at dawn.

The chopper ride was nice. The chopper pilot, Tony, said he would take me straight away and softly set me down, IF I would call his wife back in the world and tell her he was still madly in love with her. I promised and I even asked if he wanted me to visit her on my way home. He simply replied, "You want a safe ride out of here or not?"

I landed and was told to visit the staging area, meaning take a shower and change out of those nasty clothes. The supply Sergeant said, "Nobody wants to see your nasty ass looking like that." So I got a set of new dress greens that looked and smelled great. I was not going to let anything slow my exit.

Next, I was on to the paperwork. I was asked by the clerk if my injuries were severe enough to take the medical plane out or could I make it on my own? I was told the medical plane wouldn't be leaving for a few more days, but I would have medical care on the way home. My answer was, "What injuries? I'm fine and I can go out with the others if you are ok with that." It was the longest pause on the planet. The Remington Raider (what we called clerks) looked me over several times before he, reluctantly, stamped my papers. His parting comment was, "Don't blame me if something happens." My reply was, "Oh, I won't," I said with the biggest smile I could muster.

The hardest thing I remember was turning in my weapon and gear. They had been with me through it all and I reluctantly said goodbye. Strange enough, there was a moment that I couldn't let go. I remember being asked if I wanted to keep it and if so, I could head back out to the bush. I didn't reply, I just quietly said my goodbyes.

Showered, shaved, new uniform, and man I was "styling." Now we waited as always. Delays came and went, more brothers showed up with the same look on their faces, disbelief. The distrust was written all over their faces. I watched them say goodbye to their weapons and packs as I did, almost with a reverence, as if to say, "I feel you, brother, but I'm GOING HOME!"

The word came down, that we were on the next bird out. The roar was electric! Laughter, hugs, fist bumps, and just a grand over all relief. So many words like, "We are going home, right? No more WAR, right?

To the land of the big PX (grocery store) right? This is real, right?" Just a lot of stupid, excited comments and it was all just wonderful. Young soldiers, older now, worn out and happy. We did our job, now get us the hell out of here, please.

Out of the hanger we filed, up the steps to the Freedom Bird and through the plane door, into the silence we went. All of a sudden, the chatter stopped, the cool breeze of the AC hit you in the face. Oh man, what a feeling. We grabbed a seat, any seat, and for a moment just sat there, not moving, not talking, just hoping, please God let it get off the ground.

There was very little talking, more whispers, as if not to be heard for fear of stopping the process. I looked around, some soldiers were just sitting there staring straight ahead, some were praying, some had a nervous twitch, and I felt their fear as I rubbed my Saint Christopher, given to me by my brother who I left behind.

We had served a straight twelve months, eighteen months and more, walking in this hell hole and it had taken its toll. We fought hard, we cried hard, we laughed hard, and through it all, here we were, pieces of our former selves. We hoped those that we knew back in the World would still love us and see past what we had become, older and harder.

The pilot came on and everyone went stiff. He said something about being honored to get us home and other stuff that I really didn't hear. What we all heard was the engines winding up and the movement to the runway.

Now no one was moving or talking. We weren't scared; after all, we had seen way too much to be scared. We were frozen in that moment between absolute panic and joy. As I watched, I can't remember breathing or how hard I held onto the armrest. The engines now at full force, we were moving and that's all I cared about.

There was a saying, "You would never leave the "NAM", because it will suck you back in," and this was on all their faces, meaning, will Nam let us go in peace? Then the captain came on the speakers with the words of life, "Ladies and Gentlemen, We are AIRBORNE!"

You literally could not hear yourself think over the ROAR of all the voices. "F***K Vietnam" was the chant, over and over and over we yelled. Then for some weird reason, it went silent. I mean nothing, not a peep. I know what we were all thinking! "What if NAM heard us?"

We slept on the flight back, a sleep of the dead. There was some quiet, nervous talk and ideal conversation. Then you would have thought we all had won the lottery, we landed in the UNITED STATES OF AMER-ICA. At that moment the second loudest roar ever heard, "HOME! HOME! HOME!"

I couldn't wait to get off that plane. I grabbed my gear and headed out of O'Hara Airport, excited to see my brothers and sisters and my mom and dad. They didn't come. They were all working, as I knew they would be, and rightfully so. I told them not to take me to the airport going out and that I would see them back at the house someday soon.

I was greeted warmly, however, by the Hare Krishna's. They hugged me and gave me stuff and they smelled really nice. They were all talking at once, however, I heard one of them say, "I bet you are glad to be out of that Bullshit war huh?" The thought of them thinking that way about the war made me sad and a little angry. They didn't know, how could they, and how could I explain, so I just turned and walked.

I watched others in the airport looking at me in a strange way. Maybe because I was using a cane to walk, so I tried to walk without it, but I only stumbled. It didn't work out so well, so I ignored their looks of pity, or maybe it was anger.

I ducked into a bar along the way and hoped I wouldn't get carded, because after all I was only 19 now. The bartender was kind and didn't ask. He did say I should probably change into civilian clothes because some folks aren't happy about the war around here.

As I sat there drinking the most delicious beer ever, the business-man next to me started staring. He turned to me and without thinking he poked my Americal patch and said without hesitation, "Baby killers huh?" The shock of what he said hit me in the worst way, so I returned the favor and took my cane and poked him back. Unfortunately, because he was drunk, it knocked him off his stool. The altercation that followed led to someone calling the SP's (Shore Patrol).

Two Navy SP's (Shore Patrol) came in and separated us. After the bartender told them what had happened, he turned to me and said, "Why don't you get out of here and let me handle this?" I noticed he was missing a finger and had a few scars on his face. He was wearing a Purple Heart ribbon and a Vietnam service medal. I told him I was grateful and left.

I decided that it wasn't my day, so I headed out of the airport and onto the bus to head for Rockford, Illinois, and home. Once off the bus, I grabbed a cab. As we approached my street, I became sad as I thought of leaving my brothers behind, but, so excited to be home that the thought passed quickly.

The cab driver turned to me and said he wouldn't accept my fare and welcomed me home. Yep, home. The words rang in my ears as I stepped from the cab. I grabbed my duffel bag and stepped out. The air was clean, cool, and the smells hit me like a brick. It was dinner time, and the neighborhood was cooking all the foods that I remembered as a kid.

Standing in my front yard looking up and down the street I noticed the stillness, the sounds, and then it hit it.

I was after all .... HOME!

BOB LANZOTTI

US Army Aviator

Total Time in Military: 1960 to 1985

Unit Served with in Vietnam: 1st Avn Bde, 1st Cav Div

Dates in Vietnam: 1967 to 1968; 1969 to 1970

Highest Rank Held: Lt. Colonel (O-5)

Place of Birth: Taylorville, IL—1937

ABOVE THE BEST

A Tactical Emergency or "Tac E" is an unscheduled mission that takes priority over all aerial missions. In the First Cavalry Division, a Tac E would only be made if the declarer was indeed under attack and resupply was necessary to repress the attacker. My unit, a Chinook company, received an inordinate number of Tac E missions during the Cambodian campaign. The attack typically began with a rocket and/or mortar barrage, followed by an infantry or sapper assault on the fire support base perimeter. Typically, our operations got the Tac E sometime between midnight to one o'clock in the morning, and we always scheduled stand-by pilots to eliminate confusion in the middle of the night.

Around midnight on June 24, 1970, our operations received a call from the Division TOC stating that TAC E had been declared at Fire Support Base Bronco. Beehive artillery rounds, already rigged in a sling load, were being carried to our flight line to expedite delivery.

Subsequent sorties if required, would be picked up and delivered from Song Be. The designated aircraft commander for this mission was CWO Larry Covey. Larry was a CW1 but well experienced. He, along with other W1s, namely Steve Lindholm and John Dearing, were considered among the best aircraft commanders in our company.

The weather that night was abysmal. It was, in fact, zero-zero weather...as in a ceiling down to the deck and zilch for visibility. I watched CWO Covey during his briefing in operations, and he appeared as calm as if he were missioned for a routine ash and trash milk run. We talked about use of the transponder and getting a radar-vector but finding FSB

Bronco was going to be the challenge. If the weather at Bronco was as bad as it was at Phuoc Vinh, our home base, then it would be difficult at best.

The transmission of the Tac E did use words like "breaching the perimeter" and "expending last available," so this was a true Tac E and our effort could save lives. Our takeoff was, in fact, delayed because the truck delivering the sling load of ammunition got sidetracked and missed a turn because of poor visibility. I went with the flight crew to the flight line and waited for the delivery of the ammo. The ammo was off-loaded right in front of the revetment so that CWO Covey could taxi forward, lift to a hover, hook up, and go. I will never forget that takeoff. The grimes light on the Chinook disappeared in the overcast and fog almost immediately.

Our Tac E sortie was underway, and it would be about a thirty-minute flight to FSB Bronco. That would get him in the grid square. Getting down to terra firma would be the problem. The terrain around Bronco was not flat like most of III Corps. There were plateaus and hills, and that would present a problem when descending into Bronco, most likely under IFR conditions. Then too, besides the weather, if Bronco was still under attack, he could expect enemy fire upon his approach to landing.

CWO Covey and his crew arrived in the vicinity of Bronco but was still flying totally on instruments with no visual contact with anything but the instruments in his cockpit. We could not pick up the ground FM radio traffic at Bronco but could hear some of Covey's radio transmissions as he was attempting to find the firebase. It was evident that Bronco was still under attack, and they were using flares to illuminate the perimeter. Covey could not see the flares, so resorted to using a FM homing instrument unique within the Chinook's array of navigational equipment. The vertical indicator would deviate right or left in the direction of the keyed FM mike on the ground. We knew he was using this navigational method because we heard him continually directing the ground radio operator to key his mike. We called it a poor man's ILS, but it found a lot of LZs during periods of low visibility when popped smoke was useless. It worked that night for CWO Covey.

We heard him transmit that he had flares in sight and was descending toward Bronco. We cheered in our operations for his success and his balls. What we did not know was that he successfully delivered his load under fire and received some battle damage, although the bullet holes in the aircraft would not be detected until the aircraft returned to Phuoc Vinh. On the way to Song Be to pick up another load of artillery ammunition, CWO Covey heard a distress call from an AH-1G Cobra pilot who was above the overcast, hopelessly lost, and running low on fuel. CWO Covey located the AH-G, flew to it, then led the Cobra safely to Song Be. When he returned to Bronco, the attack had been repelled, and after releasing his load, he and his crew returned to Phuoc Vinh.

What CWO Covey and his crew had accomplished was phenomenal. He had delivered needed ammunition to a fire base under attack and in the absolute worst weather imaginable. He may have saved the day for Bronco, and he certainly saved the day for a Cobra pilot. For his heroism while participating in aerial flight, CW1 Lawrence Covey was awarded the Distinguished Flying Cross. Tragically, Larry Covey would be killed in a civilian helicopter accident in Medford, Oregon almost 18 years later.

ALAN C. GRAVEL

US Air Force — Pilot

Dates of Military Service: 1969 to 1974

Unit Served with in Vietnam: 536th Tactical Airlift Squadron of the 483rd Tactical Airlift Wing; 4102nd Aerial Refueling Squadron

Dates in Vietnam: Sep 1970 to Sep 1971; May 1972 to Dec 1972

Highest Rank Held: Captain (O-3)

Place of Birth: Alexandria, LA — 1945

OOPS! — WRONG RUNWAY

Shortly after I arrived in-country in September of 1970, the C-7A Caribou squadron at Phu Cat was shut down, so for the year I was there, all four active squadrons operated out of Cam Ranh Bay (CRB). We had two regular temporary duty locations in Bien Hoa and Can Tho.

For Bien Hoa, we would fly out of CRB (with clothes and personal gear for a week) in the morning, fly a full day of missions, and recover in Bien Hoa. We would then fly two days out of Bien Hoa, have a day off, and then two more days. On the seventh day, we would launch out of Bien Hoa (with our personal gear on board), fly a full day of missions, and recover in CRB. We called it the "seven-day stage." A number of Caribou crews would be in Bien Hoa at the same time, so we had quarters designated for our use.

For Can Tho, we had a similar routine, but it was only three days and no day off. Predictably, we called it the "three-day stage." We lived in a civilian hotel downtown while there. The best meal I had in Vietnam was chateaubriand with avocado salad and strawberry shortcake at a small French restaurant down the street from our hotel in Can Tho.

Although these TDYs took us away from our permanent quarters and our personal stuff, they were a nice break in the routine. Cam Rahn City was closed to us. On our day off at Bien Hoa, we could take a taxi to Saigon to go shopping, eat at the Continental Hotel, and use the MARS phone at the USO to call home. In Can Tho we usually had a few hours in the evening to walk the streets, have a nice meal, and have a drink or two.

Can Tho and Binh Thuy were about four miles apart on the southwest bank of the Mekong River. The Can Tho runway was 08-26 and the Binh Thuy runway was 06-24 so the compass orientation was only 20 degrees different. Can Tho was 3,400 feet long and 60 feet wide with a pierced steel plate (PSP) surface. Binh Thuy was 6,000 feet long and 100 feet wide with an asphalt surface.

I did not witness this incident so what follows is my recollection of what we were told at the time.

In late 1970 or early 1971, a Georgia Air Reserve C-124 landed at Can Tho by mistake; they were supposed to land at Binh Thuy. They evidently realized their mistake too late to execute a go-around, so they stood on the brakes to stop the thing on the short runway. The PSP panels started folding up accordion-style in front of the wheels. Ironically, this might have assisted them in stopping before reaching the end of the runway.

The runway was closed to all traffic. They unloaded all the cargo and removed all non-essential equipment and trucked it over to Binh Thuy. We guessed that any extra fuel left on the plane was also removed. Somehow, they managed to take off from what was left of the Can Tho runway, no doubt assisted by the fact that in one direction it was only a short distance to the river where they could level off to gain airspeed. They flew over to Binh Thuy where the plane was restored to its normal configuration before leaving to return to Georgia.

The runway at Can Tho was seriously damaged. For the rest of my time in-country, we took off and landed on one end of the runway while the other half was repaired.

Landing at the wrong runway happened at least one other time during my year in-country. In the other case, a Lieutenant Colonel aircraft commander landed a Caribou at the wrong runway somewhere in the Parrot's Beak area. I seem to remember that the actual landing base was closed and therefore insecure. At the end of his landing roll, he began a turn into the ramp area, evidently intending to turn around and

378 | ROBERT O. BABCOCK

take back off. Had he succeeded in that, there would be no story to tell. Unfortunately, he turned too sharply into the ramp area and drove one of the main landing gear into a ditch, damaging the landing gear and disabling the airplane.

The story we heard was that they removed the wings (including engines) and tried to lift the fuselage with a Skycrane helicopter. Something happened with the rigging and the fuselage was dropped and "Class 26'ed" (totaled). I am told by Caribou historians that there is no record of the loss of this airplane in that manner, but that is the story that circulated amongst the troops at the time.

The lack of a record could be because it didn't happen that way or (more likely) because the paperwork was deep-sixed due to the identity of the aircraft commander.

BILL MCRAE

US Army — Armor Officer, CH-47 Helicopter Pilot
Dates of Military Service: Aug 1969 thru Aug 1973
Unit Served with in Vietnam: 132nd ASHC, 14th CAB, 16th CAG, American Division
Dates Served in Vietnam: Oct 1970 thru Oct 1971
Highest Rank Held: Captain (O-3)
Place of Birth: Gainesville, GA — 1947

GOD BLESS THAT CHIP DETECTOR

Back in 1971, I was assigned to the 132nd Assault Support Helicopter Company (ASHC) at Chu Lai in the Republic of Vietnam. Chu Lai was on the coast in southern I Corps, about 53 miles southeast of Da Nang. We flew support for units within the Americal Division. Our area of operation (AO) was from Da Nang south to the border with II Corps.

On 20 May 1971, we received a mission to furnish four CH-47 Chinooks to insert a new Army of Vietnam (ARVN) artillery battery of 105mm howitzers, ammo, water, and other supplies on a hilltop south and west of Tien Phuoc. Tien Phuoc was an old remote Special Forces camp, about thirty miles northwest of Chu Lai. It was almost due west of Tam Ky. It had a short hard surface airstrip, with the camp sitting at the far end of the runway. At the time of this mission, I think it had already been turned over to the ARVN's. The airfield also had a refueling point for aircraft on the far end next to the encampment.

The mission called for us to stage out of Tien Phuoc, with the external loads located adjacent to the runway. Two Charlie Model Huey gunship fire teams, from the 71st Assault Helicopter Company "Firebirds" would be on station to escort us to and from the LZ and to provide security in the area, as necessary. The new fire base would be within the artillery coverage range from both LZ Maryann and LZ Siberia. It was a free fire zone out there, as there were no friendly folks in that area.

The mission was delayed due to low clouds out in the mountains, so we started a little later than planned. I think we were Chalk #3 in the flight of four, in a loose delayed trail formation. Our Flight Lead set 90 knots as the max air speed, so the gunships could keep up with us. We departed Tien Phuoc at about ten-minute intervals to allow plenty of time for the crew ahead of us to deposit their load and maybe re-position it if necessary. There were ARVN troops on the ground when we got to the LZ. I'm guessing they were inserted the day before to secure the area.

On our second load, we were outbound for about five minutes with a load of 105mm ammo, when we got a warning light on our console. It was a chip detector warning light. The Chinook has five transmissions. A magnetic sensor in the sump of each transmission will attract any small metal bits and fragments from the grinding of the gears in that transmission. All the chip detectors are wired into a common warning light up front. Since they were all wired together, we had no way of knowing which transmission was a potential problem, but it was a serious problem that had to be investigated. For this situation, the Operating Manual says to make a Pre-Cautionary Landing as soon as possible, shut down the engines, and start pulling chip detector plugs, until the cause of the warning light is determined. The Flight Engineer and the Aircraft Commander (AC) will then evaluate the metal debris found on the detector, to see if it's a sign of a major problem, or if it's just normal wear and tear. But, before we could do anything, we had to return to Tien Phuoc and drop our load, so we can land, shut down, and check out the problem.

Chalk #4 (67-18452) moved up in the rotation and picked up the load we had just returned. The AC in 452 was one of our senior Instructor Pilots (IP) named Nate, with an FNG flying as Pilot named Frank. Frank was a 1st LT. and new in country. This was his first flight, and it was also his in-country check ride with an IP, so he could be evaluated and released to fly on a regular basis. Frank picked up the load of ammo and headed toward the LZ. They had already been once, so he knew the way. On short final approach to the hilltop, they received numerous hits from small arms fire. All sorts of alarms and lights started going off in the cockpit. It really scared the hell out of Frank. Nate grabbed the controls, punched off the load, and crash landed the aircraft on the hilltop LZ. They landed on a slope, which put the forward blades closer to the ground than normal. Nate shut down the engines, and everybody got out of the aircraft. Luckily, they did not land on anything or hit anybody with their front blades, and the aircraft did not catch fire. The Crew Chief was wounded in his right arm by either a bullet or bullet fragment. Nate and the crew evaluated the damages and counted more than twenty bullet holes in the bottom, with numerous bullet strikes to the blades.

Back at Tien Phuoc we had shut down to check out our chip warning light. That meant we were off the radios and oblivious to anything that was happening at the LZ. We located the problem chip detector and decided it was normal very fine shards of metal. The Crew Chief was to check it again the next time we shut down. So, we did not hear about 452 until we cranked and got ready to resume the mission. We learned the LZ was closed to further loads, and we were instructed to return to our ramp on Chu Lai East.

That afternoon our Maintenance Officer, CPT Sines, and two of his Assistant Maintenance Officers, along with other maintenance personnel and technical inspectors, flew out to "The Boony Bus" (452) to see what had to be done and to determine what parts and equipment would be needed to get her airborne again. They did not really think the repairs would happen, but they got all the stuff ready just in case. We all figured 452 would be destroyed by NVA mortars during the night. On the morning of 21 May, 452 was still there, less all the stuff the ARVN troops had stolen out of it. They took the seat cushions (backs and bottoms) out of both pilot seats, all the hand tools, and anything else that was not nailed down.

Our maintenance crew made all the necessary repairs in the field, including the removal and replacement of damaged rotor blades. Those blades are about thirty feet long and weigh several hundred pounds each. I did not know that changing the blades was possible without some type of power lift equipment. I learned that Boeing made a portable, hand operated, crane that fits into a slot in the Chinook frame for just that purpose. By the end of the day, 452 was flyable again. The million-dollar question was: Who would dare risk their lives to get 452 off that hilltop and maybe even make it back to Chu Lai? CPT Sines said he would do it, and he got volunteers to fly with him. He was that kind of leader. I'm not sure how smooth the flight was, but they made it back safely.

I served with Frank for five more months, before I completed my tour and rotated back to the States. He turned out to be a really great guy. He was constantly joking around and generating a lot of laughter. Frank was just a fun guy to hang out with. He would pick at me about the chip light that caused him to take our load and our spot in the rotation, and to get shot down on his very first flight. He always claimed that we probably faked it. My answer to him was always the same. I told him that God clearly had other plans for me, or HE would not have turned on that chip light. I suggested that Frank might want to give that idea some serious thought. Maybe God had other plans for him too. We both survived our tours and our time in the Army. We got back in touch in 2008, and we had a great reunion after 42 years in 2013.

VINCENT C. CORICA

US Army— Field Artillery Officer
Dates of military service: 1969 to 1978
Vietnam service unit: 3rd Brigade (Separate), 1st Cavalry Division (Airmobile)
Dates in Vietnam: Jul 1971 to May 1972
Highest Rank Held: Captain (O-3)
Place of Birth: Johnstown, PA 1947

"PROTECT THE INFANTRY"

I had three very different Field Artillery assignments as a US Army Captain during my 11 months in Vietnam with the 3rd Brigade (Separate) of the 1st Cavalry Division (Airmobile). I loved being a part of the 1st Cav! It was the only American division to fight in all four Corps tactical zones. The bulk of the division began departing Vietnam for Ft. Hood, Texas, in late April 1970, but the 3rd Brigade (Separate) remained until June 1972. I left Vietnam for a Battery Command assignment in the Panama Canal Zone at the end of May 1972, just about one month before the Brigade started their return to Ft. Hood. During my tour, the 3rd Brigade operated in the vicinity of Bien Hoa, in III Corps, roughly 25 miles northeast of Saigon.

ASSISTANT S-3, BRIGADE TOC

My first assignment, which this story is about, was three months long, from July to October 1971. I was one of two Assistant S-3s in the Brigade Tactical Operations Center (TOC). My other two assignments in RVN were roughly four months long each. I wrote about those assignments in two stories in our first AVVBA book, "I'm Ready to Talk."

The other two assignments sound way more exciting than this one. They were also actually much closer to the action. In fact, they were the two combat assignments a Field Artillery Captain dreams about: four months as Field Artillery Liaison Officer ("LNO") to LTC Charles

384 | ROBERT O. BABCOCK

Hodges, Commander of the 1st Battalion, 7th Cavalry (Airmobile); and four months as Commander of Bravo Battery, 1st of the 21st Field Artillery, reporting to LTC Jack Keaton, Battalion Commander.

Both LTC Hodges and LTC Keaton were extraordinary officers and decisive combat leaders. I was fortunate to report to them.

What I didn't understand at the time was this first assignment would become massively important to the learning and the instincts I needed to execute my other two assignments properly. Let me explain why.

I shared the Assistant S-3 position with another Field Artillery officer, Captain Gene Carroll. We were good friends, having served together as 1st Lieutenants in Charlie Battery, 1st of the 319th Artillery, in the 82d Airborne Division, before deploying to Vietnam. Gene and I worked our respective 12-hour shifts in the Brigade TOC, along with a dozen or more other officers, NCOs, and enlisted men. When things got hot for our troops, we'd ignore our 12-hour shift and gladly work around the clock. I have a candid photo someone took of me in front of a giant Plexiglass-covered map of the Brigade Area of Operations with two radio handsets, one to each ear. All of us in the TOC had one mission:

"Provide plans and support to defeat the enemy
and keep our troops safe."

Our Brigade Commander, BG James Hamlet, loved what his 105mm Field Artillery Battalion could do for his AO. When I had the chance to interact with him, he would always say the same thing to me, "Protect the Infantry." Many people have written that effective combat leaders understand the beauty of simplicity. BG Hamlet was just such a leader.

With guidance from the Brigade S-3, Gene Carroll and I would coordinate closely with the Infantry Operations team to plan artillery firepower in support of our troops. We had two kinds of missions, Planned Fire Support and Contact Fire Support, each with varying levels of urgency, of course.

PLANNED FIRE SUPPORT MISSIONS

Planned Fire Support Missions occurred around the clock, based on intel from the Brigade S-2 Intelligence Officer about where the enemy had recently been or might soon be again. The S-2 asked us every day to plan multiple Artillery Harassment and Interdiction ("H&I") fire at coordinates along suspected enemy supply and personnel movement routes, possibly in use at any time by the bad guys, especially at night.

The S-2 based his H&I missions for us on "URS intel" (Usually Reliable Source). URS intel came to us from farmers, loggers, and villagers who desperately wanted us to rid their peaceful country of the ruthless North Vietnamese Communist oppressors and their evil partners, the Viet Cong. Our troops also provided H&I target coordinates to the TOC as they encountered recently used enemy base camps, tunnel complexes, or ammo, supply, and food dumps. We coordinated all H&I missions with our S-3 to ensure no chance of friendly troops near our targets.

Landing Zone (LZ) Prep was another kind of Planned Fire Support Mission, but vitally more critical than H&I missions and about a million times more exciting and central to how we saw ourselves as "Redlegs." LZ Prep missions were so fulfilling to us! They gave us the chance to Protect the Infantry by demolishing the enemy on LZs where our troops were soon going to be inserted by UH-1 "Huey" helicopters. Saturating LZs with hot steel on the target immediately before the first Hueys touched down with US Infantry aboard was the best way to avoid hot LZs for our Infantry and our equally beloved Army Aviators.

We used Artillery "Time on Target" (TOT) Tactics in LZ Prep Missions. The most fearsome and effective of artillery tactics, Time on Target missions, called for multiple artillery units to compute their respective ordnance to hit the LZ simultaneously. When the tactical situation in the Brigade AO permitted, we would direct three batteries, 18 total 105mm howitzers, to bombard an LZ in a Time on Target LZ prep.

Well-trained 105mm howitzer crews can fire three rounds per minute. Each 33-pound 105mm round has a blast radius of 30 meters. We could have 54 rounds impact a target in one minute! We mixed airburst fuzes (in artillery, it's fuze, not fuse), with delayed fuzes for bunker-busting, with contact fuzes to destroy the enemy, dug in or otherwise. In the slight chance that any enemy could survive this tornado of hot steel, they would surely "di-di mau!"

COMBAT FIRE SUPPORT MISSIONS

Combat Fire Support was our second type of fire mission. Our boys were under fire! We had to be instantaneously accurate and devastating in our fire support. When our troops called for artillery while in enemy contact, we Assistant S-3s were responsible for providing in-depth command and control to get steel on the target where and when the Infantry needed it. Everyone in the TOC would pretty much "stop breathing" and listen intently to radio traffic from the ground commander about what he and his troops were seeing and doing. Individually and collectively, we jumped to fulfill every requirement from the ground commander. Combat Fire Support Missions were "what we're paid to do," as we would proudly declare to one another in the TOC. We whooped and hollered and cried like babies when our supported Infantry would radio us to say thank you for getting them out of the s — t. There's no feeling better than that for anyone working in a TOC.

THE LEARNING

So, why did I say earlier in this story that this Assistant S-3 position in a combat Brigade TOC was "massively important to the learning and the instincts I would need to execute my other two Field Artillery assignments effectively"?

Because this assignment required me to think, act, and take personal accountability on a gigantic stage for life-or-death support of our beloved troops. With at least a dozen senior officers rightfully overseeing every move, our fast, accurate actions were required to save American lives. This assignment is where I learned all I would ever need to know as a Field Artillery officer.

The learning came in just three words, taught by BG James Hamlet. Three words that resonated in my mind and heart multiple times a day for 11 months:

"PROTECT THE INFANTRY."

HUGH D. PENN

US Air Force—Personnel

Dates of Military Service (Active and Reserves): 1966 to 1972

Unit Served with in Vietnam: 633rd Combat Support Group

Dates in Vietnam: Feb 1969 to Jan 1970

Highest Rank Held: Staff Sergeant (E-6)

Place of Birth and Year: Birmingham, Alabama—1945

A LONG DAY AT PLEIKU

I can't remember the actual date or even the month that it happened. I do recall I was up earlier than usual and headed to the chow hall on Pleiku Air Base. The morning was overcast, and I was about halfway to breakfast when overhead I heard the distinct noise of a 122 mm rocket. Even though it had passed me, that's why I heard the scream, it still sent me running for a bunker because there may be more to follow. The base warning siren was by now blaring and the rocket had exploded in an officers' hootch, severely injuring one officer and leaving a crater in his floor and peppering the room with shrapnel every few inches. There were no more following then and the all-clear sounded. It looked like the day would be a normal day from then on out.

I worked in Personnel and, to be more specific, in what was called the machine room. We converted written paper records of airmen and officers onto IBM cards to be transmitted to Major Air Command to be stored on computers and conversely, when there were updates from MAC, the reverse took place. All this is to say the IBM cards and equipment had to be humidity and temperature controlled so as not to warp the cards and jam the equipment and keep the machines cool and not overheat. Okay, I'll say it, **AIR CONDITIONING,** I worked in an air-conditioned office in Vietnam.

Right at lunch time, I walked out of the office and found the rest of the CBPO (Personnel Office) deserted and the sirens wailing. We were under another rocket attack and I never even knew it. I ducked my head back into the office, sounded the alarm, and we all headed to the bunkers, getting there in time for the all-clear to be sounded. I can't even remember for sure how many rockets came at us then, but it was three, maybe four. However, we were lucky that none did any real damage to persons or property.

That evening the winds picked up and a tropical storm blew in and the force sent rain blowing in one side of the windows with the shutters closed and out the other side on a horizontal plane. I had experienced a hurricane once in Florida when I was growing up and the winds, rain, lighting, and experience was eerily similar. I can't remember exactly how long the storm lasted, it was well after dark when it subsided, and we had a chance to peek outside and assess the damage. Several people were injured, but none were killed. However, there was one hangar destroyed and the Headquarters' building all but destroyed.

It had been quite a day for Pleiku Air Base, from being targeted with a handful of rockets to suffering through a brutal storm, still only taking one serious injury. I often wondered if the NVA tuned into the weather report after that to determine when to or when not to attack.

DONALD H. NAU

U S Army — Armor/Infantry Officer

Time in Military (Active Duty and Reserves): 1967-1974

Unit Served with in Vietnam: HQ Co, 3rd Combat Brigade, 25th Infantry Division

Dates in Vietnam: Aug 1969 to Aug 1970

Highest Rank Held: 1LT

Place of Birth and Year: East Cleveland, Ohio — 1944

SUPER SENIORS

We called ourselves Super Seniors — The title was not afforded any University status. We just paid for an additional semester and graduated at the Mid-Year ceremony — which meant January in Northwest Ohio. This was a place where nobody wanted to be — except of course, parents. Even though indoors, it was a very fast-moving program.

All that was needed to be a "Super" was 1) work at a job for a semester or 2) change a major course of study. Then, you would have to go beyond at least one more semester than the originally planned four years. As in all life, time changes, the rest of your life goes a different direction — 'course you don't know that then. BUT, that single first domino has fallen in a new way and spells out a different picture or word or life.

This is NOT Yogi Berra's famous "When you come to a fork in the road — take it!"). This, at the University graduating level, begins a series of blind luck movements which are disguised as correct with proper planning — all guided by the incredible ability of beer or other such proven rational and legal means of dealing, or *not* dealing, with life.

All it really did, other than our own exalted honor, was, in the '60's, to postpone the inevitable. At some point, we were *all* going to Vietnam — and we were all going to die there.

Ironically, in 2018, I had a talk with a famous Vietnam decorated author. I mentioned that in a documentary, upon him preparing to go back to Vietnam — his wife said, "You know you're going to die there." His response, "I think, we're all supposed to die there." I then said to him,

"You know, we all died there in a way, didn't we?" He replied, "Yes—no one came back the same."

There it was—my future had been written. No matter where I am—or at what time of day—something would remind me of the War. Actually, it could be something somewhat funny. There were those moments, but of the "you had to be there" kind. Some were those I was just trying mostly to forget.

There I was a year later, tour over—August 1970—in San Francisco—in the front passenger seat of a taxi going from the Army Center in Oakland to the San Francisco Airport and ultimately to the VA Health System. Other soldiers were seated in the back—it was very, very quiet.

Finally, I said, "It's cold here." Driver: "57 degrees—always 57 degrees here." Silence returned.

I was not a Super Senior anymore—in fact he was right, I was not ever the same.

CLARENCE "CLYDE" ROMERO JR.

US Army, Scout Helicopter pilot, 1969-2005
Unit(s) served with in Vietnam: C troop 2/17 Cav 101st ABN Div AMBL
Dates served in Vietnam: April 1970 to April 1971
Highest rank held: Colonel (O-6)
Place and date of birth: Bronx, New York — 1950

THIS IS GOING TO LEAVE A MARK

Bob Pascoe and I were flying a white team, which consisted of two LOH-6 in support of Lam Son 719, on February 16, 1971, just north of Tchenpone, Laos. We were scouts from C troop 2/17 Cav looking for North Vietnamese follow-on forces attacking fire bases.

Operation Lam Son 719 was the unsuccessful South Vietnamese incursion into southeastern Laos with support of helicopters from the 101st Airborne Division and numerous other U.S. Army aviation units.

We had not taken much ground fire since we knew how to evade the enemy gunners by flying extremely low; the North Vietnamese were used to high-flying, fast-moving targets in this area. We were none of those.

The terrain made it easy to spot the large gun emplacements of anti-aircraft weapons, such as 23mm and 57mm guns, along with the .51 caliber machine guns. Too say that we were immune to them would be an understatement. We had been encountering these weapon systems since February 8.

We were well-seasoned with regards to the threat. While on this mission this day, we spotted a lonely fighter aircraft off in the distance. We then saw the guns open up on this aircraft. It was an F-4 and that's when I saw that aircraft take a hit and I said to Bob over the radio "That is going to leave a mark." Sure enough, the F-4 caught fire and the crew had to eject, right by where we were!

We saw both chutes and we knew where they were going to land. We then contacted an USAF FAC (Forward Air Controller) who was overhead and told him of the situation.

He responded that he had contacted King (they ran rescue for the USAF) and that Jolly Greens from Nakhon Phanom (NKP) were on the way. Now freeze frame here for a minute … Both Bob and I have a visual on the downed aircrew and can pick them up and fly them back to Khe Sanh, which was only 20 miles away!

In the meantime, these two aircrewmen were deep in enemy territory. We were told NOT to pick them up and let the USAF Jolly Green pick them up. We waited for them to show up, it felt like an hour, but it was most likely 30 minutes. For the guys on the ground seeing two helicopters flying around them, it must have felt like days.

But now it gets interesting. The Jolly Green helicopters show up; they are huge helicopters CH-53, big targets. We now are going to provide covering fire for the rescue of the two aircrew by drawing fire for them, how nice! The good news is that the aircrew are picked up, none the worse for wear.

They depart for NKP and we go back to Khe Sanh with this story to tell to the intelligence guys.

To this day Bob and I can't believe that the USAF let those guys wait around to be rescued. Every time we meet at one of our reunions we talk of this mission. I have subsequently found out the following about the F-4 that was shot down. It was from the 25TFS/8TFW Ubon F-4D Serial # 66-8787. Crew name LTC W R COX/ Maj W C Allen.

DAN HOLTZ

U.S. Air Force — Healthcare Administration
Dates of Military Service (Active Duty and Reserves): 25 years
Unit Served with in Vietnam: HQ MACV/CORDS, Military Health
Assistance Program, Ninh Thanh Province (Phan Rang, RVN)
Dates you were in Vietnam: Nov 1969 to Nov 1970
Highest Rank Held: Colonel (O-6)
Place of Birth and Year: Indianapolis, IN — 1943

SOME REFLECTIONS ON MY TOUR IN VIETNAM

Like most of the men who served during the Vietnam War, I was subject
to the military draft and made calculations about how I would serve,
which branch and doing what. I graduated from North Central High
School in Indianapolis, Indiana in the class of 1961 and was immediately subject to being drafted into the Army. However, I was accepted
to college at Ball State Teachers College (now Ball State University)
in Muncie, Indiana and received an educational deferment. I went to
Ball State thinking I would become a teacher; however, I decided after
my freshman year to change my major from education to business administration. Therein arose a problem, Ball State's business program was
geared to business education, and I had decided teaching was not what I
wanted to do with my life.

So, I applied for admission to Butler University in Indianapolis and
was accepted into the College of Business Administration. By changing
majors and schools, I lost a year and would graduate in 1966, instead
of 1965. I had been enrolled in the Air Force ROTC program at Ball
State and re-enrolled into the AFROTC program at Butler. When I
graduated, I had risen to the cadet rank of Lt Colonel and was the deputy commander of the cadet corps. In my final year at Butler, I was the
commander of the Arnold Air Society at the program.

One day in my senior year, I found a notice on the bulletin board in
the AFROTC area advertising for volunteers to apply for commissions
in the Air Force Medical Service Corps (MSC), as a medical adminis-

tration officer. Since my college major was business administration and I was not sure what my career goals would be following my military service, I felt medical administration was more in my line for a career in the service or following the service than was serving as an intelligence officer in the Air Force (which is what I would have been doing in the line) with no similar career ladder in civilian life. So, I applied and was accepted into the MSC, which then became my Air Force career for 25 years.

I went to the basic medical service administration course at Sheppard AFB in September 1966 and graduated in December. Following a leave, my wife, Linda, and I headed for Keesler AFB, Mississippi, where I became the plant manager at the *USAF Medical Center Keesler* for three years. In July 1969 all the MSC's at the medical center attended a "moon landing party" at the center administrator's home and watched history being made on the color TV at Colonel Bob Gaines house. Just a month later, Hurricane Camile came ashore on the gulf coast as the strongest storm of its kind recorded up to that date. Linda and our 9-month-old daughter hunkered down at the medical center's maintenance shop taking calls from the patient units upstairs and dispatching maintenance personnel to provide assistance and repairs. In my capacity as plant manager, I was roaming the halls looking for issues and assisting staff and patients dealing primarily with anxiety issues as the eye of the storm hit 14 miles to the west of the base.

It was just prior to the storm I was notified of my assignment to Vietnam to arrive in November 1969. In September, I was promoted to Captain and readied the family for my departure and their relocation to Muncie, Indiana, where Linda would enter graduate school in guidance and counseling at Ball State. We found an apartment for Linda and our daughter, Laura, in Muncie and they moved-in along with our dachshund and our three-legged cat. I departed Indiana for San Francisco and Travis AFB for the *World Airways* flight to Saigon.

I was met in San Francisco by one of my MSC buddies from Keesler, Don Dixon, a direct appointment MSC, who had gotten out of the Air Force and enrolled in a health administration graduate program at UC Berkley. On our way to Travis, he took me on a tour of the Berkley campus in his VW "bug." It was an interesting trip because I was in my Air Force "1505" uniform and blue windbreaker with nice shiny captain's bars on display for all to see. Fortunately, Don was able to keep the car moving and we did not draw attention to ourselves.

As I left Travis on November 2, 1969, *I'm Leaving on a Jet Plane* was playing on my radio as we boarded the plane—wonderful timing. The flight to Vietnam was long and uneventful. We stopped for refueling at Clark AB in the Philippines and for purchases at the duty-free-shop at the base terminal. Then we reboarded the plane for the final leg into Saigon's Tan Son Nhut Air Base.

Fortunately, when we arrived at "TSN" on November 4th, things were quiet. The weather was typical Vietnamese, hot and very humid, and it really hit us when we stepped from the plane onto the tarmac and walked about 100 yards to the reception center operated by the US Army in Vietnam (USARV). I checked in, was given a bunk assignment, issued an M-16 rifle (with some ammunition) and told to report to the 7th Air Force Command Surgeon's Office the next day for a briefing on what the Military Provincial Health Assistance Program (MILPHAP) was about from the Air Force perspective.

Since I was participating in a unique assignment, my transportation to my duty station at Phan Rang, Vietnam meant I had to take an *Air America* flight to Nha Trang, Vietnam to be briefed by the USAID/CORDS (United States Agency for International Development/Civil Operations and Revolutionary Development Support program) head-quarters downtown on the MILPHAP program in "II Corps." So, the night before departing TSN, I was able to attend a USO performance at an outdoor location by several performers, the most notable of which was *Kenny Rogers and the First Edition.*

Two days later I caught an *Air America* flight from Nha Trang to Phan Rang Air Base, which was located about six miles west of the city of Phan Rang. I was met at the base by the senior enlisted MILPHAP team member, USAF MSgt Clarence J. C. Coleman. "JC," as he was known to all the team members and the other U.S. advisors in Phan Rang. He was quite the character who knew how and where to get things and get things done. Like most NCO's I have known in my career, he was very reliable and the "go-to" guy in dealing with the Army advisors, the Air Force contacts at the base, and other people we needed to get things done from both the American forces and Vietnamese civilian and military personnel.

Apart from the MILPHAP team advisors in Phan Rang who were Air Force, all the military advisors were Army personnel, ranging from members of the infantry, armor, psychological warfare, and other specialties. They advised the Vietnamese military and police forces in all aspects of military operations and policing. The civilian advisors were all USAID personnel and civilian personnel contracted to USAID. They provided advice to the Vietnamese in areas such as agriculture, governmental services, policing, social services, etc.

The U.S. advisors in Phan Rang had three compounds where we lived. The Army compound known as the MACV compound, was the primary residence for the military advisors assigned to the Phan Rang operations. The civilian advisors resided in the CORDS compound that was about a quarter mile away from the MACV compound. The MACV compound was a typical Army compound, while the CORDS compound was outfitted for civilian "volunteer" advisors whose expectations were for more amenities, like privacy, air-conditioning, and grass growing around the buildings. Behind the CORDS compound was the compound for the "spooks." The "spooks" were the intelligence guys who officially were not there, but everybody, including the enemy, knew they were.

I mentioned earlier, Phan Rang Air Base was about six miles west of the city and because of the multiple missions and air frames (C-130's, F-4's, C-47's, and others) based there they were the target rich environment in the area for the enemy, the "VC." Unfortunately for the VC, Phan Rang was located on the coast of the South China Sea, far away from the Cambodian border and other more heavily fought for territories. That meant when the air base received in-coming mortar or artillery rounds they were not fired from weapons, but from bamboo tripods that were not exactly accurate. The rounds were launched in most cases from the surrounding hillsides, then the VC who launched them ran like h— —to get out of the launch area before return fire could reach them. The rounds landed often in open fields and not doing much harm to personnel, equipment, or aircraft. However, the VC kept trying. That left the nearby city and the advisors working and living there pretty much alone.

The Province Senior Advisor (PSA), a State Department Foreign Service Officer (FSO)-3 (O-6 equivalent) had decided prior to my arrival to have some medical capability reside in the CORDS compound because there had been an attack on the "spooks" compound next door and one of the rounds had hit inside the CORDS compound and injured one of the Vietnamese guards. So one of our team's surgeons (we had two), the internist, the nurse anesthetist and I became residents there.

All of this may make a reader think we were living a life of luxury. Compared to the soldiers, Marines, and others out in the field in direct combat with the enemy, there is some truth to that observation. By comparison, many of the other advisory missions, a total of about 27 around the country, were in areas more near to ongoing combat. Phan Rang because of its location on the South China Sea was more pacified than many other parts of the country.

The cultural adjustments for our team members were considerable due to the language barrier and the fact the history of the country with the extensive French influences were things that took getting used to. Fortunately, we had Vietnamese translators who worked with us and not only helped us to communicate to the locals, but kept us on track related to customs, courtesies, and expectations. Understanding these things was essential to advising and assisting the locals. We always wanted to be sure we were not offending the locals. We needed to be accepted by them, so they would be more willing to listen to us and accommodating to the advice we were providing.

As the MILPHAP team administrator (executive officer), there was not much work for me to do in the way of advising the Vietnamese on administrative topics. This was largely due to the fact administrative issues were guided and directed from the regional and national Vietnamese levels. So, most of what I was able to do in these areas was work around the margins and to tweak things to run a bit smoother. So to keep myself busy, "JC" and I found ourselves working MILPHAP team administrative issues, scrounging "stuff" from Phan Rang Air Base, Cam Ranh Bay Army and Air Base, bartering T-bone steaks for M-151 vehicle parts and some other things we needed to operate our mission better. In addition, we spent much of our time working with the two Team public health/ preventive medicine NCO's in helping the locals improve their water supplies.

On all our trips up Vietnamese Hwy-1 we always carried our M-16 rifles to provide personal protection in case we needed to defend ourselves from an attack. We marked our four M-151's with two red cross emblems painted on the front of the windscreens to identify us as non-combatant medical personnel. Our belief was this kept us from being targeted by the VC. However, just before I returned to the "world" some staffer at HQ/MACV determined those markings were being used as targets by the enemy and ordered all of them to be removed. We were also ordered to stop wearing distinctive clothing, such as red berets and red baseball caps and to wear camouflaged caps, so as not to stand out wherever we went. However, in the year I was there I never came under direct attack from the enemy; although, one of our team vehicles on a trip from Phan Rang to Cam Ranh Bay Air Base did come under fire by one or more rounds that were heard whizzing by. Fortunately, there were no injuries.

I found the Vietnamese people with whom I had contact to be very personable and wanting to see the war end and the northern invaders go back to where they were from. Unfortunately, in the end that did not happen. My tour of duty ended in November 1970, the Paris truce that ended U.S. forces involvement came in 1973 and the end to the conflict was in 1975.

I have often wondered what happened to all the good people in the Phan Rang area with whom I worked and, in many cases "broke bread." They were good people, most of whom just wanted to live in peace, raise families, earn a living, and do the things we Americans also want to do. While their style of living was not the same as ours, their desires, hopes, and dreams were just the same. They wanted freedom, they wanted peace in their time, they wanted love and families, as well as material things.

I believe our MILPHAP team was able to contribute to the betterment of the people of Phan Rang and Ninh Thanh province. Were our contributions sustained, or did they go away? It was probably the latter. However, I believe our MILPHAP team provided a glimmer of a better life for those with whom we connected. For that I am thankful.

JOHN FRASER

US Army—Chaplain

Dates served: 1953—1983 Texas National Guard (Enlisted) 1953-1956; Army Ready Reserve (Enlisted) 1956-1960; Army Active Duty (Commissioned) 1963-1983.

Units Served with in Vietnam: 2/14 Inf and 1/27 Inf, 25th Inf Div; 8 RRFS.

Dates Served in Vietnam: Apr 1966 to Apr 1967; Nov 1969 to Nov 1970

Highest Rank Held: Lt. Colonel (O-5)

Place of Birth and Year: Greenville, TX—1936

CHAPLAIN'S ADVICE TO A SOLDIER FLYING HOME FROM VIETNAM

I still kind of regret the advice that I gave to a young soldier who was on the "Freedom Bird" en route from Vietnam to San Francisco. What a happy plane load of soldiers that was! Our days in Vietnam were finished—at least for the year!

I had been chaplain for the 8th Radio Research Field Station (8RRFS) at Camp Eagle, near the town of Phu Bai, not far from the city of Hue, which was the big name in the 1968 Tet Offensive. I had missed the Tet excitement by nearly two years. I had arrived at the 8RRFS in late November 1969. And now it was late November 1970. What a different year 1969-1970 had been from my first tour in Vietnam. I had been with infantry at battalion level—lots of time in the field with the 25th Infantry Division.

At the 8RRFS we had lost only one man in a year, and only a few had been wounded. Instead of sometimes sleeping in a hole in the ground, I had slept in a room with a real bed and an air conditioner that worked most of the time. But the worst part of being in Vietnam either time was being separated from my wife and two little girls. How eager I was to get home!

I felt like I never quite let down my full weight on that C-130 from Phu Bai to DaNang for fear that in the last few hours in Vietnam something bad might happen. The one night that I spent at the airfield in DaNang, I listened carefully nearly all night because a mortar round or rocket might hit in just the wrong place during this last night in-country.

The next morning we were herded into lines to process out of Vietnam. I remember standing in ranks before boarding the "Freedom Bird" and thinking, "How dumb is this! Standing in ranks on a taxiway in a combat zone! What a target we are!" Then we got onto that big, beautiful civilian airliner with cooled cabin air, with several of the most beautiful young ladies with the most beautiful smiles I had seen in a year! And I was thinking, "Crank this thing up before the VC's drop a round on this big silver target!"

The flight attendants hurried through the usual briefing about seat belts and flotation devices, but no one listened. We were going home! Then we broke ground, and a cheer reverberated through the cabin! We were no longer in Vietnam! The flight attendants must have been told to just let us have the run of the airplane as long as we stay away from the pilots. They let us roam around the cabin—they even let us get our own coffee and soda pop. Those lovely round-eyed ladies were ready to spend time with us and talk with us, not just wait on us.

On one of my trips to the coffee pot, a young soldier walked up to me and asked a question—and he was really serious. "Chaplain, they have those hippies in San Francisco that don't like soldiers. They spit on you and no telling what else they might do! What are you going to do if someone spits on you?"

I thought about what I had seen on some of the news shows in Vietnam—hippies that jeered and spit on troops arriving back in the United States. I had already thought about that question, "What will I do if...." The word was out that San Francisco would not hire police officers that had not satisfied their two-year draft obligation because they didn't want to hire a police officer just to lose him to the draft. So many of the younger police had been in the military, and a good many of them had been in Vietnam. And the rumor was that police officers didn't like draft dodgers and hippies. And being spit on was a form of simple assault, and a person can defend himself against assault. So it was said that if you got into a fracas with a hippie who spit on you, the police would take you to a police station, give you all the coffee and soda pop you could drink, and escort you to your flight home.

So without really thinking about it, I answered, "If some hippie spits on me, I'm going to knock the hell out of him."

The soldier looked a little surprised, but asked, "What if it's a woman?"

Now I really wasn't expecting that, but thinking fast, I said, "Then I'll knock the hell out of the man standing closest to her."

The soldier looked at me a little wide-eyed, but then he grinned and said, "Yessir! That'll work!"

I've always been just a little ashamed that I've never been sorry I said that.

DAN BENNETT

US Air Force — Flight Engineer

Dates of military service (Active and Reserve): 1967 to 1975

Units served with in Vietnam: 4th Special Operations Squadron, Da Nang
AB and 18thSOS, Nha Trang AB

Dates in Vietnam: 1967 to 1968; 1972 to 1973

Highest Rank Held: Tech Sergeant (E-6)

Place of Birth: Atlanta, GA — 1947

VENGEANCE BY NIGHT

Motto of the famed 18th SOS — Hunter/Killers of the Ho Chi Minh Trail

A brief history of the AC-119 Gunship. After the AC-47 Gunship was retired, demands began pouring in from the field for gunship support. The Air Force did not want to bring back the C-47 since it didn't have the airspeed, payload capacity, or time on target that was needed. The Air Force wanted to equip the new gunships for a truck-hunting role, which meant heavier weapons and advanced electronics. The answer was the old Fairchild C-119 "Flying Boxcar."

The C-119 had the increased performance and it was readily available since many AF reserve units were using the C-119. Fifty-two C-119 airframes were turned into AC-119 Gunships; specifically for truck hunting with Infra-red night vision.

The Gunship had four miniguns firing 7.62 plus two 20mm multi-barrel Vulcan Gatlin-gun cannons. The aircraft was equipped with FLIR (Infrared Thermal Imaging) system. The aircraft had the state of the art, "forward looking" Infrared (FLIR) system. The aircraft also had a flare launching system that could launch a two million candle watt power — flare. Those things could really light up the night!

The AC-119's were assigned to the 18th SOS, headquartered at Nha Trang and so was I. Our purpose: truck hunting business along the Ho Chi Ming Trail. The AC-119 soon became the nightmare of North Vietnamese truckers on the trail in Laos. The OV-1 Mohawk crews worked in conjunction with the AC-119's and formed an ad-hoc hunter killer team. Enemy trucks quickly ran out of places to hide. The 18th SOS had some 2,206 confirmed truck kills by December 1972. It was about that same time when the war began winding down and the AC-119's were slowly being turned over to the VNAF (Vietnamese National Air Force).

The AC-119 had an empty weight of 80,000 pounds. It was powered by two Wright R-3350 reciprocating engines, 3,500 hp each and two GE J-85 tubojets, one on each wing that produced 2850 pounds of thrust. Duration time, approximately five hours plus 30 minutes of reserve fuel.

The AC-119 had a crew of 10. Pilot, Co-pilot, Flight Engineer, Navigator, night observer sight (NOS) operator, radar/FLIR operator, illuminator operator, and three gunners. I had the honor of being a Flight Engineer on the AC-119 Gunship.

December 1972, Ship # 584, had a controlled bailout of crew "except" for the pilot, copilot, and flight engineer (me)! This was due to a critical shortage of fuel. Why: AAA strike that opened a fuel tank. The aircraft commander made the call after three missed approaches to our home base (very heavy rain, strong winds, and dense fog) and after his third attempt, he decided to ascend to 3,000 ft. and have the crew jump. They were not thrilled with the idea, but that was the way it was going to be. The crew jumped and all were rescued within two hours, without injury. The three of us were alone in the aircraft and my **pucker factor** increased to a dimension I had never experienced before! We were flying on fumes and the weather was very bad. We could not see the field and yet we were going in one way or another!

The landing was made, and medals were eventually received for saving the aircraft. The best part of that evening was the amount of "ice cold beer" we consumed back in the Operations hut.

February 28, 1971, prior to my arrival, the 18th became known as the "famous tank killers." Eight Soviet/North Vietnamese PT-76 light tanks were destroyed that night near Hill 31 in Laos during Operation Lam Son 719. The 18th has the honor of being the first ever "fixed-wing" gunship to destroy eight enemy tanks.

I ended my Air Force career in mid-1973 and attended Embry Riddle Aeronautical University where I graduated with a BS degree. While there, I earned my fixed wing pilot licenses, Instrument rating, multi-engine rating, and an Airline Transport Pilot rating (ATP). After graduating, I worked for several fly by night airlines, becoming an airline gypsy going from one soon to fail airline to another. I applied and was hired by the Federal Aviation Administration, Flight Standards Division, and remained with the FAA until my retirement in 2004. Today, I am enjoying the good life of being a grandfather of three!

BILL MCRAE

US Army—Armor Officer, CH-47 Helicopter Pilot
Dates of Military Service: Aug 1969 thru Aug 1973
Unit Served with in Vietnam: 132nd ASHC, 14th CAB, 16th CAG, American
Division
Dates Served in Vietnam: Oct 1970 thru Oct 1971
Highest Rank Held: Captain (O-3)
Place of Birth: Gainesville, GA—1947

UNEVENTFUL TO UNFORGETTABLE

During my tour in Vietnam, I was a helicopter pilot assigned to the 132nd Assault Support Helicopter Company (ASHC) at Chu Lai, about 56 miles southeast of Da Nang. The 132nd was part of the 14th Combat Aviation Battalion (CAB), which was part of the 16th Combat Aviation Group (CAG). The 16th CAG controlled all the aviation assets of the 23rd Infantry Division (American), which covered the southern part of I Corps, from Da Nang south to the border with II Corps.

The 14th CAB was tasked to provide a CH-47 (Chinook) every day for emergency aircraft recovery. This mission was called "Gunsmoke", and it was shared by the 132nd "Hercules" and our sister unit the 178th "Boxcars." Both units operated off the same airfield called Chu Lai East. It was the first airstrip constructed by the Marines back in 1965. It was just off the beach, and it was made of interlocking metal panels, which provided a smooth solid surface for helicopters and for the Marine A-4's and the Air Force O-2's and OV-10's that were also stationed at Chu Lai East.

For the "Gunsmoke" mission we had to relocate an aircraft over to Chu Lai West and park next to the control tower. Chu Lai West was the main airport for the Chu Lai Combat Base. The runway was all concrete, and it was much larger in length and width. It could handle any type of fixed wing aircraft. The Marines operated two units of F-4's from Chu Lai West until they stood down in '70.

I was an Aircraft Commander (AC), and I drew the "Gunsmoke"

mission one day in mid-'71. My Pilot that day was an FNG, who worked in Admin in our Company Headquarters. He was new in country and had little flight time. I knew him, but that was about it. His name was Paul. We met at our Mess Hall early that morning for some breakfast, because lunch was going to be out of a C-ration box. Our Mess Hall sat on the beach, with a great view of some spectacular sunrises out over the South China Sea. That morning the skies were partly cloudy, and the sunrise was really nice.

We both had our weapons, so we headed straight to our Operations shack after breakfast, to get any last-minute instructions, pick up the SOI and KY-28 radio, grab our flight gear, and head on down to the flight line. The enlisted crew were already at the aircraft when we arrived. I explained what we were going to do and made sure we had a case of C's on board. I checked the logbook, while Paul started the pre-flight. Everything checked out OK, so we cranked the aircraft and repositioned the short distance over to Chu Lai West.

The day was a total bust. Next to the Control Tower was an empty hooch, with nothing but a table and some chairs in it. We killed some time quizzing each other on various systems on the aircraft, regarding what they do, how they work, and what happens if they don't work. I was surprised at how much the Crew Chief (CE) and Flight Engineer (FE) knew about the workings of the Chinook. I thought it was a good learning experience for all of us. At the end of the day, we were released to return to our home base. To get Paul a little more experience, I had him fly both legs of our short trips. After landing, we topped off the fuel tanks and proceeded to the nearest open revetment and shut it down for the night. I filled out the logbook. Paul and I grabbed our gear and the KY-28 and headed to Operations. The crew grabbed their stuff and the M-60's and headed toward the Flight Crew Shack.

Upon entering Operations, I heard the Operations Officer yelling instructions to a runner to go over to the Company Area and locate a flight crew for a recovery mission. I interrupted his instructions and said, "We're standing right here." I told him, "There is no need to try and find another crew when we can handle it. The aircraft is pre-flighted and ready to go." The Operations Officer accepted my offer, so we sent the runner down to the Flight Crew Shack to grab the crew before they got away. He did, so we were good to go.

The recovery mission was pretty simple: Go out to Tien Phuoc and pick up a 71st Assault Helicopter Company (AHC) Huey and the crew. They were sitting at the airfield with mechanical problems. We were told, "A team of Pathfinders will go with you to rig the aircraft and come back with you."

Tien Phuoc was a remote Special Forces camp about thirty miles northwest of Chu Lai. It had a short hard surface airstrip, with the camp sitting at the far end of the runway. At this time, I think it had been turned over to the Army of South Vietnam (ARVN). It had a refueling point for aircraft on the end next to the camp. It was not secure enough to leave an aircraft out there overnight. The main road cut right across the runway.

When the Pathfinders arrived at our Operations, I briefed them on our plan to recover the Huey. They grabbed their rigging gear, and we headed to the aircraft. By this time, it was after sunset, and it was beginning to get dark. During the day, the skies had become overcast with dark clouds out to the west. It was clear a storm was headed our way. I was beginning to wonder what I had volunteered us to do.

We cranked right away and took off from the revetment. We headed north for a straight-out departure, angling to the left toward Tam Ky, then west toward Tien Phuoc. I had Paul do the flying, as the weather became more of a problem. It was very obvious a big thunderstorm was developing out there in front of us with lots of lightning, and we were both converging on Tien Phuoc. So far, we were flying in some light rain, but the flashes of lightning would blind us each time, as the sky out in front of us was getting black. It was clear. We were now in a race to beat the storm to Tien Phuoc, and it was a race we could not lose. If we did not hustle, that storm looked big enough to trap us at the site right next to the Huey we were going to rescue.

Through the intercom, I advised the crew about the weather and that we needed to get in and get out as soon as possible. Otherwise, we might get trapped there for a long time and maybe overnight. I had the Flight Engineer (FE) pass that information along to the Pathfinders. They needed to do their job in a hurry, but still do it right. I had no intention of losing that aircraft on the way home.

Paul flew us out there and shot the approach in a light rain, landing next to the Huey. The Pathfinders got out with their straps and other gear, while the Huey crew got on board with their stuff. All of a sudden, the rain just stopped, and an eerie calm seemed to set in. That was great for the Pathfinders. They finished their tasks, and one got back on board. The other climbed on top of the Huey to slap the nylon doughnut on the hook. As soon as the FE told us that we were ready, I told Paul to pick it up to a high hover and rotate the aircraft, so he can see the Huey. We had parked with our backs to the west, so the flashes of lightning would not be in our eyes, and the Huey was to our right rear. As Paul lifted off the ground, the CE yelled, "Here it comes." At that moment the bottom fell out of the clouds. It was raining so hard we could not see anything. The wind from our rotor wash and the windshield wipers were no help. I popped open my side window to get a reference to the ground and grabbed the controls. We were moving slowly over the ground, which I stopped immediately. All I could see was to my left. I did not know for sure where we were in relationship to the Huey.

Paul opened his side window to see out the right. It was a team effort. I depended completely on the directions from the crew to keep us away from the Huey, until the rain eased up some, allowing us to see out the windshield. I eased over the Huey. The Pathfinder was ready and soaking wet. He slapped the doughnut on the hook, but in the process his hand contacted the hook, and a bolt of static electricity from the aircraft knocked him off the Huey. Luckily, he was not seriously injured. He had to climb back up on the Huey, so he could then climb in the hole next to the hook. He was scared, and it took a while for him to get enough courage to touch the aircraft again, but this was his ride home.

I managed to get close enough to the Huey for him to climb in, with a lot of help from those in the back. I think they basically grabbed him and pulled him up and on board.

With the Huey securely attached, I picked it up and departed to the east, heading toward Tam Ky. I climbed up to just below the lowest hanging clouds. It was plenty dark outside, but nothing like it was behind us. The lightning behind us gave us enough light to clearly see where we were going. There were no lights on the ground, except for those we could see up ahead at Tam Ky. I turned the controls over to Paul, thinking I might get a few minutes to relax a bit. That lasted for about five minutes. In that short time, the Huey started swinging wildly from left to right. I knew the Chinook was getting jerked around, as the hook moves from side to side on a beam in the floor opening. The CE said it was hitting the stops of both sides. I knew it was bad when I could see the Huey out to our left window.

So, I took over the controls, pulled in some more power, and lowered the nose to increase our speed. I was concerned about going into the clouds, but we had to get the load under control. In a short time, the load settled down, and I turned it back over to Paul for the flight back to Chu Lai. The weather closer to the beach was much better as we flew out of the rain.

We landed at Chu Lai East and deposited the Huey on the ramp at the 71st AHC Maintenance Hangar. Paul moved over to the side and landed so our passengers could get out, and the Pathfinders could retrieve their sling equipment. We then relocated to the "Hercules" ramp, topped off the fuel tanks, and parked in the same space we had before. What started out as a simple recovery mission, ended up as a real adventure, and an experience I'll never forget.

CHARLES SINGLETON

US Army—Combat Intelligence and Operations
Dates of Military Service (Active Duty and Reserves): 1969 to 1975
Unit Served with in Vietnam: 1st Cavalry Division, Airmobile, 2nd Battalion, 12th Cavalry
Dates you were in Vietnam: May 1970 to Apr 1971
Highest Rank Held: Sergeant (E-5)
Place of Birth: Summerville, SC—1947

FLASHBACKS OF VIETNAM: MY 15 LIFE AND DEATH EPISODES

During my tour of duty in South Vietnam, I survived several "firefights" and 3 ambushes. I was proud to fight and serve with combat-ready servicemen.

1. Bien Hoa Air Base Airport, South Vietnam: I saw piles of garbage bags: Cadaver Body Bags! Vietnam 1970.

2. "NCO Shake and Bake," Private Rios told me one day, shortly after arriving on Fire Base Nancy (southeast of Quang Tri and northwest of Hue, South Vietnam). On our first ground patrols he would repeatedly call me a "Shake and Bake Sergeant," Noncommissioned (NCO) Officer, who attended and graduated from Fort Benning, GA. However, Rios during this time, taught me so much about fighting in Vietnam. He would often remind me that some members in our combat intelligence and reconnaissance squad were not good at "walking point or leading us on the ground." His favorite quote was, "Shake and Bake, I am getting short; my time fighting in Vietnam is almost over!"

3. Montagnard or "GI's Mountain Yard," indigenous people, Central Highlands of Vietnam, "same, same me; same, same you; no same, same me; no same, same you, Intelligence Saved Our Lives One Day. They said, last night, near their mountainous village, "Beaucoup

Viet Cong and NVA (North Vietnamese Army soldiers) were traveling nearby, "no same, same me; no same, same you! We took their advice and were quickly evacuated back to a much safer areas of the jungle that day. Later, The U. S. Air Force, via the U. S. Army, used our report concerning Montagnard's observations to successfully bomb the suspected area, where a battalion of NVA was occupying.

4. Do Not Walk on Trails; Nor Cross Open Fields, Without Cover Fire. Well, on this September day of 1970, my combat intelligence infantry squad, 6-8 soldiers, walked out of the camouflaged jungle's dense foliage into an open field. And upon crossing this exposed area, we were fired on by AK-47s of the Viet Cong. Once we grounded ourselves, bullets continued to land all around us. During this sudden exchange of gunfire with our M16 rifles and M 60 machine gun, Private Eddie "Bulldog" Foster (Florida) avoided getting struck by enemy bullets while rolling on the ground from side-to-side and shooting his weapon lying on his back. Shortly, after this encounter, the Viet Cong attackers moved away from the area. From that day forward, we called Eddie Foster "Chuck Connors, The Rifleman." All throughout this encounter (enemies' ambush), I too rolled on the ground, and ducked the oncoming AK-47 bullets, to avoid being placed in a body bag and ending up at Bien Hoa Air Base Airport.

5. After this near-death experience, I kept saying to myself, "If I should die in Vietnam, the disappointing news would kill my mother (Catherine) and father (Clement A. Sr). Because, in the late 1940s, my mother was carrying me and suffering with a deadly case of asthmas. Then, at the Old Dorchester County Hospital (1937-1980s), Summerville, SC, the doctor attending to my mother told my father that he could not see how my mother was going to birth me with her failing lung condition. So, my father decided to bring my mother and me home, if we were going to die. If that was the case, my father said, "Let them die in our two-room house on the "Red Road,"

Orangeburg Road, SC (S-18-22). Considering therefore, in 1970, if I died in Vietnam, my father, a C-130 Hercules civilian-loadmaster employee, Charleston Air Force Base, would have been so disappointed that, "His Charles" was killed, and then placed in a garbage-like body bag on a C-130 Hercules! It would have been too much for my father to handle.

6.   Outdoor Pit Latrine Toilet-Ditch, Firebase Nancy, U.S. Army and Army of the Republic of Vietnam (ARVN) Base, Southeast of Quang Tri, Vietnam: Seemingly, days after the September 1970 firefight-open-field crossing, we were waiting for our next reconnaissance (recon) assignment, when suddenly, North Vietnam Army (NVA) and Viet Cong launched a surprise mortar attack. During this attack, I seriously thought about taking cover in the Outdoor Pit Latrine toilet-ditch. As the attack subsided, I decided that I did not have to jump into the septic ditch!

7.   October 7, 1970: Red Badge of Courage, Stephen Crane (1871–1900) and my Purple Heart Day. Author Crane's Henry Fleming, who earlier ran from the battlefield in shame, later regretting his cowardice, wanted desperately to be wounded, thus, receiving a "Red Badge of Courage." Unlike Henry Fleming, I Charles Louis Singleton did not want to be WOUNDED! However, on Wednesday, October 7, 1970, after receiving a shrapnel injury (burns and bruises), and concussion from a 'Chicom' grenade explosion, "Rigger, Demolition Genius" and I were injured, along with others, as we were protecting our bomb-crater position. The more seriously injured of our platoon members were medevacked by the U. S. Army UH-1 Huey helicopters.

     Shortly afterwards, a second lieutenant, U. S. Army forward observer, South Carolina State College, Orangeburg, SC, was called into battle, after my platoon (2 squads:15 soldiers) were pinned down for hours by Viet Cong snipers. During this firefight, we initially were supported by AH-1 Cobra gunships. However, the gunships were ineffective, because the enemy, after shooting at us from surrounding trees and tall canopy vegetation, would return to their underground bunkers. Realizing the continuous life-threatening dilemma, a second lieutenant, U. S. Army forward observer from South Carolina State College, Orangeburg, SC, was called into battle. This "Guy," the forward observer, coordinated a barrage of Army Cannons (Artillery at Firebase Nancy and Navy Artillery Long-range Guns (Central Coast of Vietnam).

Hallelujah Amen, It Worked! As the night came upon us, the firefight ceased; that was when The Big-Headed (BHA) ants took over in our perimeter: Pheidole Megacephala (Fabricius). Several of us, after being repeatedly bitten and stung by these big-headed ants, cried out in expletives, after expletives, profanities, four-letter words! Big-headed Fabricius kept us awake, and NVA and Vietnam Cong Sappers were not able to attack us while we were resting and sleeping.

8. Liquid Fire, Napalm, The Vietnam War: After almost losing my life on October 7, 1970, we were on patrol in early November 1970, when a call came in on the RTO (radiotelephone) that napalm bombs were going to be dropped possibly miles away from our position. Using "Silence and Stealth," we were motionless! Then ALL suddenly, the exploding Napalm bombs took the oxygen out of the air surrounding us! Thank goodness, we endured and got another chance to live one more day.

9. First Nighttime Ambush Reconnaissance: In late November 1970, as I recall, our recon platoon was given the mission of going on a nighttime patrol. Much to my surprise, when it was time for my squad (5 or 6 of us), to go on duty, my best friend, SSG Samuel "Sam" Houston, volunteered to go with us, although he was not assigned to do so. All throughout the night, Sam made sure that we always stayed alert. He kept reminding us that this was his 3rd tour in Vietnam: combat intelligence, learning is staying alive and living;

quiet stealth, camouflage, no cigarette smoking on the perimeter while on duty at night. As a result of his timely knowledge about fighting at night in Vietnam, we got to live and see another day!

10. Early December 1970, RPG (Rocket-Propelled Grenade) Ambush: This Soviet Union weapon, which was fired at us during a reconnaissance by a North Vietnamese Army, or Viet Cong soldier, came awfully close to killing us, when it was shot at my squad. Happenstance, the rocket-propelled grenade barely missed the head of a sergeant, who was walking point. Quickly, we pulled the sergeant to the ground, and gave him cover fire in the direction the RPG came from. Following that brief, but life-threatening encounter, we had to medivac the sergeant, who became a mental casualty, because of this near-death experience.

11. Christmas Eve December 1970, Black Virgin Mountain Cease-Fire Surprise: Seemingly, the week before the Thursday, December 24, 1970, Vietnam cease-fire, Tây Ninh Province, Vietnam, Nui Ba Den (Black Virgin Mountain), our platoon, 2nd Battalion, 12th Cavalry Air Mobility was on standby to support U.S. combat troops fighting in the area. Charlie Alpha: While we waited our turn on to be helicoptered or transported into combat that fatal day up the Black Virgin Mountain, much to our surprise, the heliborne assault was called off, because of the number of friendly casualties.

12. January 1971 Cambodia, "Presumption of Death Finding." In early January of 1971, my platoon was given new maps coordinates and helicoptered into Cambodia. Our combat assignment consisted of gathering information and looking for a U.S. Air Force Phantom Fighter Jet that was shot down by a North Vietnam Surface-to-Air Missile (SAM). After searching in the mountainous thick-vegetation and mosquito-infested jungle for several days and nights, we were unsuccessful in locating the fallen F-4 Fighter Jet and pilots (Missing in Action, Presumption of Death Finding).

13. January 1971 R&R (Rest and Recuperation), Taipei Taiwan, The Republic of China (ROC). During my 8th month in South Vietnam, I selected Taipei, Taiwan for my well-deserved rest, recovery, relaxation, recreation, and rehabilitation, et al. Upon arriving in Taipei, Taiwan, I quickly learned that the US dollars converted into Taiwanese dollars were outstanding currency swaps! I was able to eat in upscaled Chinese restaurants, buy men's tailored suits, "You draw, I make," said the Taiwanese Tailor. Other (ROC) R&R highlights were as follows: (A) Do not mention Chairman Mao Zedong's "The Little Red Book of China." (B) "The Catch-of-The-Day" included everything that was caught by Chinese fishermen that day (all types of Seaweeds and animals of the ocean: Octopuses, Snakes, Crabs). (C) "Gigantic Movie Theaters' Fried Chicken Feet Instead of Popcorn." (D) All of the young teenage children repeatedly defeated American R&R vacationers in table tennis for a $dollar. WOW Rich Kids! (E) Local Chinese Entertainers Stateside Perfectly Imitated Sounds were, "The Night Train," (James Brown), "Yesterday," English rock band, (The Beatles), and (Sittin' On The Dock of The Bay; Fa-Fa-Fa-Fa-Fa (Sad Song: Otis Redding).

14. January 1971—April 1971 Army Tactical Operation Center Brigade and Battalion (TOC) Assignment and Early Out. After I returned from R&R, I was then assigned to Army intelligence and operations until my "early out," the end of military duty in Vietnam ordered by US President Richard Milhous Nixon.

15. Fast Forward Today: "Singleton's PTSD-Related Insomnia, RVN 1970," Post-Traumatic Stress Disorder. "Here I am again. Back on the corner again. Back where I belong. Where I've always been. Everything the same. It don't ever change. I'm back on the corner again. In the healing game." So, "Don't look back to the days of yesteryear, you cannot live on in the past. Don't look back. And Live on in the future."—John Lee Hooker and Van Morrison, Fair Use Lyrics

BOB LANZOTTI

US Army Aviator
Total Time in Military: 1960 to 1985
Unit Served with in Vietnam: 1st Avn Bde; 1st Cav Div
Dates in Vietnam: 1967 to 1968; 1969 to 1970
Highest Rank Held: Lt. Colonel (O-5)
Place of Birth: Taylorville, IL — 1937

MY LONGEST DAY

The fatal crash of one of our CH-47s at Quan Loi on March 9, 1970, and the loss of the Chinook on the opening day of the Cambodian Incursion had brought us down to fourteen aircraft. We picked up a new CH-47B in early June and put it into service immediately. No other CH-47 before or since has likely beaten this bird to its first and second periodic inspection (one-hundred-hour inspection). The periodic inspection gets more involved and prolonged as the aircraft ages; but early on, the periodic maintenance inspection entails not much more than what is required during the intermediate inspection that is conducted at twenty-five-hour intervals.

By the last week in July, we were on track to set a CH-47 flying hour record for a single month. On July 30, the aircraft had 221 hours for the month and our goal was to reach 228 hours — the numerical designation for our battalion, the 228 ASHB. I was scheduled to fly the aircraft on the thirty-first and had no doubts about achieving our goal, since we were averaging about twelve hours of flying time per day on all of our aircraft.

The remarkable thing about setting a CH-47 monthly flying record had more to do with the endurance and performance of the flight crew than the aircraft's feat. The flight engineer, crew chief, and door gunner had been virtually living on the aircraft since it went into service. I had decided about mid-July that the entire flight crew should be awarded an Army Commendation Medal (ARCOM), to be presented as an impact award. Impact awards, or awards presented on the spot, require Assistant Division Commander approval. We not only got approval but were informed that one of the ADCs, BG Burton I believe, had indicated he would like to try to make the presentation. The 228th was indeed popular with the brass.

The presentation was scheduled for 1600 hours. The flight crew didn't have a clue about the awards. We would fly most of the day, then break away from the AO in time to taxi up to the front of our maintenance hangar where the ceremony would take place.

The day started out normally enough. My co-pilot for the day was Captain Bill Norton, a US Military Academy graduate. Bill was a fun guy to fly with and a good pilot. It was early in the morning, and we were hauling a sling load of bulldozer tracks at an altitude of about three thousand feet. We had just departed Phuoc Vinh and were about ten miles north, heading to the Song Be area. Bill and I were looking forward to our two milestones that day, the awards ceremony and getting 228 plus hours on the aircraft for the month. It started out to be one of those hours and hours of boredom days. We had flown most of the morning hauling ammunition, then about mid-day the boredom was interrupted with some of those moments of stark terror.

The Chinook has two hydraulic systems. The systems are interrelated, but one serves as a backup if the other fails. The Chinook has another small utility hydraulic system to operate such things as the engine auxiliary power unit, the ramp, the hook release mechanism, and the brakes. But the two main systems are the babies that enable the pilot to control the aircraft. Both gauges are positioned right in the middle of the instrument panel, one on top of the other, and each look real good when the needles are pointing to 3000 PSI.

I was well aware that there had been only one dual CH-47 dual hydraulic system failure on record, and it had taken the life of a friend in one of our sister CH-47 companies within the 228thASHB. I was first to notice the needle on the top gauge begin to fall. It dropped to 2,000 PSI fast. We had just passed over an occupied Fire Support Base (FSB), so I called our operations, reported our position, our problem, and where we were landing.

While I was transmitting, the needle on the instrument consul continued to fall. Then Bill and I really puckered when we saw the other needle start its downward movement. I transmitted an emergency mayday call, then reduced airspeed, leveled the rotors of aircraft, and set a low rate of descent, about 50 feet per minute or less. I knew if we lost both systems, we would be unable to maneuver the controls, so essentially the attitude and rate of descent that I was trimming up would hopefully be the one we would be in when we touched down. If we were lucky, we would maintain the level attitude and low rate of descent all the way down, but we had a lot of altitude to lose.

The dirt road running north from the FSB ran all the way up to An Loc. It was flat, straight, and clear of trees, thanks to the Army engineers. We needed a long runway, because our low rate of descent would likely take us almost to An Loc, some 10 miles to our north. Bill was busy on the radio, talking to our base operations and to other aircraft responding to our mayday call. I had told him to punch off the load as I was trimming up the aircraft.

What happened next was frightening. When the needle on the top gauge dropped below 1200 PSI, the bottom gauge needle would follow its downward path toward the same 1200 PSI mark, then as it met the 1200 PSI mark, the top needle would shoot back toward 3000 PSI. This exchange went back and forth several times, and each time the systems' needle indicators met at their respective 1200 PSI marks, the aircraft sort of shuddered and yawed to the right. I was making small adjustments with the cyclic trim button and to the collective as we continued to watch the needles seesaw back and forth. The aircraft responded well to each adjustment, and I began to gain confidence that we might be able to make a safe, controllable landing under power.

I did not want to autorotate because I was still afraid we might lose everything and the rate of descent would then be too great for survival. I finally decided to make a slow turn back to the FSB helipad and increased our rate of descent. As we approached the FSB helipad, I started to begin breathing normally again, but there was not a word being spoken inside the aircraft. As I started to flare and pull pitch to decelerate my approach, the flight engineer said over the intercom, "Sir, your load's one hundred feet off the ground!" "What frigging load?" Bill had never heard me tell him to release/punch off the bulldozer tracks! We did land safely and saved the load as well.

It was comforting to see two Cobra gunships overhead shortly after we landed safely. Less than an hour later, our unit's maintenance officer was standing next to us, together with his maintenance team. A pin-sized hole was found in one of the hydraulic lines. It was repaired or replaced, and we were flyable again within a couple of hours. The experience was only the second time in two tours that I feared for my life, but it would not be the last time. The next time would come sooner than I could imagine.

We flew sorties into and out of FSBs, in and around the Fishhook and Loc Ninh area until it was time to head south to Phuoc Vinh for the award ceremony. The monsoon season in Vietnam begins in April and lasts until October. Our flying had been hampered several days after the Cambodian Incursion with heavy rains and poor visibility. The weather in the morning of 31 July was good for the monsoon season but began to deteriorate in the afternoon.

About 20 miles north of Phuoc Vinh, I saw what appeared to be a meteorology textbook picture of a squall line. It extended across the horizon from east to west like a huge gray trough. It appeared to be moving north. I presumed it had just passed over Phuoc Vinh. I had encountered similar squall lines in Vietnam and usually punched through them in a matter of seconds.

When we broke off from our mission work, I noticed that the weather looked much worse in the direction of our destination, so I called Paris Control out of Saigon and requested a radar vector to Phuoc Vinh. While en route, I tried contacting Paris Control again to check the weather but could not raise them. As we got closer to the squall line, I could tell it was carrying an inordinate amount of rain. As we were about to enter the cloudbank, we passed directly over the same FSB where we made our forced landing earlier in the day. I had thought about landing there again and letting the squall line pass, but we were getting close to that 1600-hour ceremony time, and I did not want to keep a brigadier general waiting.

We entered the squall line and there was indeed lots of rain and excessive turbulence as well. We flew long enough to discourage my thinking that we could rapidly punch though it. I did a 180 degree turn with a new and more sensible plan that would fly us back to that FSB we had just flown over, land there, and wait out the weather. I was able to contact my base operations and apprise them of our intentions so they, in turn, could tell the general of our delay.

The squall line was moving fast, because when we broke out of it to the north, it had already passed the FSB. We likely overflew it, turned back to find it, but couldn't. In our frustration at not being able to find it, we found ourselves flying on the leading edge of the fast-moving squall line. We were still flying VFR, with our eyes out the cockpit, trying, in vain, to find that FSB. We spent about ten minutes looking, then decided that we would fly westward and attempt to fly around the squall line.

About ten minutes later, one of us noticed that there were no longer any bomb craters below us. This could mean only one thing. We had to be flying in Cambodia air space, because you couldn't find a square mile in the III Corps area without bomb craters. By now Bill and I started to realize that our problem was a little more serious than missing an award ceremony and keeping a general waiting. We were running low on fuel and realized that we had no idea where we were at the moment. Then I saw it! It was LZ East, the LZ in Cambodia where one of our pilots had clipped some trees, damaged his rotors, became unflyable, and had to remain over night until a recovery could be attempted. I was familiar with the LZ because I had orbited above it in a Huey long enough to see our CH-47 recovered.

I looked at my map and determined that the closest fuel to LZ East was a Special Forces site named Katum. It was located on the southwest border of Parrot's Beak, due north of Tay Ninh. It was a good forty nautical miles away on a westerly heading. I drew a line from LZ East to Katum on my 1:50,000 map, determined the azimuth, then set course for our quest for fuel. The ceiling and visibility deteriorated, and we dropped the aircraft down just above the trees.

I maintained my heading without a degree of deviation. When the fuel warning light came on, indicating we had twenty minutes of fuel remaining, it was déjà vu all over again. I was experiencing the same feeling I had just a few hours earlier while looking at hydraulic gauges. We were now going through a torrential rainstorm, reducing our visibility to about a quarter of a mile. The bright yellow of the warning light was disconcerting enough, but the jungle below us was even more worrisome.

I was sure that we were going to run out of fuel and that I would soon be flaring the aircraft out to kill off the forward airspeed, then falling downward through the triple canopy jungle. I also knew, by time and distance, that we had to be close to Katum. I also knew that we were in the vicinity of many NVA infiltration routes from Cambodia to South Vietnam. There was not a more dangerous place to be in Vietnam if one was forced to escape and evade.

I told the crew to strap themselves in because I thought we would soon be going down. I had no sooner said that when we broke out into a clearing of about a mile in diameter. It was Katum! Heaven couldn't be more beautiful as seeing those gun emplacements, bunkers, and vehicles below us. We had hit Katum right on the button after flying some forty miles of dead reckoning, mostly over jungle terrain, and in some of the worse weather I have ever flown in.

Fully fueled, a Chinook takes a little over one thousand gallons of JP4. We completely emptied two five-hundred-gallon rubber blivets. The squall had passed to the north and we had an uneventful thirty-minute flight back to Phuoc Vinh. The crewmen received their Army Commendation Medals, sans the general. When the green weenies were being pinned on the flight suits of our crewmen by our Group Commander, I was thinking that these guys sure deserved one hell of a lot more.

It was about 1800 hours, and we still had five birds out. The sorties remaining did not warrant our return to the AO. Bill and I felt pretty damn good and damn lucky as well. We had accomplished both our objectives. Although, in that achievement, we may have also accelerated our aging process. Our well deserving crewmen had been presented their duly earned awards and we had achieved a new monthly flying hour record for a Chinook helicopter. We had our 228 hours! Whoopie!

The sorties for our unit went much longer than we expected. I was in operations, monitoring the radio calls of our aircraft and waiting for their release. About 2100 hours we got a call from one of our pilots, who reported that he was having trouble finding Song Be, his destination. Song Be's ADF radio signal was inoperative, and he was having a problem visually finding the base. It can get mighty black at night in that area, and it was definitely overcast.

He also reported that he was shutting down one engine to conserve fuel. He was in communication with several of our aircraft working in the AO, but nobody had visual contact with him. It was apparent that he was about to run out of fuel.

I sympathized with the aircraft commander since I had been in his shoes just a few hours earlier. About the time he ran out of fuel, one of our aircraft spotted his grimes light as he was descending. Somehow, he autorotated into what we would call a tight confined area and had made a beautiful autorotative landing with minimal damage.

The aircraft who spotted our aircraft going down orbited above and reported that it appeared to have some rotor blade damage while coming through the trees. We thankfully learned that there were 1st Cavalry Infantry units nearby and that the area was considered relatively safe. When the gunships arrived in the area, we asked the orbiting aircraft if he could find a landing area nearby to rescue the crew of our downed aircraft. The crew took out the secure radio and everything else they could carry and climbed aboard their rescue bird. We planned and prepared for recovery of our downed bird the next day.

July 31, 1970, turned out to be the longest day of my life. Fifty years later, I still haven't experienced another day like it. When I pulled the poncho liner over me that night, I was both physically and mentally exhausted. But I fell asleep knowing that we had not lost anybody that day and we still had fourteen flyable aircraft to support our mission.

Bob Lanzotti
Tide 6

R. BRUCE AVERY

U.S. Navy – Communications Officer
Dates of military service (Active and Reserve): June 1, 1970 to June 1, 1976
Unit in Vietnam: USS Westchester County (LST 1167)
Dates served in Vietnam: August 1970 – October 1971
Highest rank: Lieutenant (O-3)
Place and date of birth: Tarrytown, NY, August 6, 1948

JUST ANOTHER DAY IN PARADISE

My first ship after being commissioned as an Ensign in the US Navy, in June 1970, was the Westchester County (LST 1167). LST's (Landing Ship, Tank) were originally designed to deliver fully loaded vehicles and tanks directly onto an invasion beach. In South Vietnam, the LST was ideal for going into the country's shallow rivers that were full of uncharted shoals because the ship could be easily extricated if it ran aground. The WESCO, as she was referred to by the crew, served as a base for brown water Navy boats and helicopters in South Vietnam.

We were anchored at the mouth of the Bo De River on Ca Mau peninsula in IV Corp (far south South Vietnam). We provided mooring for Swift (Patrol Craft, Fast) and PBR (Patrol Boat, River) patrol boats, utilizing the main deck as a flight deck for HAL (Helicopter Attack (Light)) 3 Seawolves gunships, and command facilities for US and South Vietnamese military. Key responsibilities included refueling and rearming boats and helicopters and offering "hotel" services (mess decks, sleeping quarters, ship's store, laundry, etc.) for their crews.

Several months after I had arrived on board the WESCO, my beauty sleep was rudely interrupted just after 6:00 AM when the 1MC (ship's public announcement system) clicked on with the command, "General Quarters, General Quarters, Fire, Fire, Fire." I grabbed a shirt, pulled on pants, walked into my shoes, and hurried up the ladder to the bridge to man my General Quarters station as the junior officer of the watch. As I arrived, all I could see was grey oily smoke rising from the engine room vents located just below the bridge.

As normal procedure, at about 6:00 AM, the ship's main diesel engines were started and allowed to warm up before being shut down for the day. Unfortunately, on this particular morning, there was a massive backfire that blew out the manifold covers and filled the engine room (located under the tank deck) with flame, hot gases, and plenty of smoke. Fire on a ship at sea is always serious, but we were particularly concerned because the tank deck under the main deck was loaded with over 50 tons of ammunition and explosives! Quick action by senior engineers shut down the engines and flames were contained before a cataclysmic explosion could occur. However, several watch standers, wearing only cut-off dungaree shorts and t-shirts in the heat, were badly burned.

Crisis averted, the regular anchor watch resumed, and I raced down to the Wardroom to grab a quick breakfast before starting my 7:30 AM to Noon stint on the bridge as officer of the deck at anchor. During the over four-hour watch, I expected our daily noontime visit from the CH-46 Admin helicopter. (This flight originated in Saigon and visited various positions in IV Corp to pick up mail and provide a "ferry service" for incoming and outgoing personnel.) I also awaited a middle-of-the-morning return of our own Seawolves detachment who had spent the night at Sea Float/Solid Anchor further up the river from us.

But now the Operations Officer called the bridge to inform me that a MEDEVAC (Medical Evacuation) helicopter flight had been arranged for early in the day to pick up our badly burned sailors. No problem says I, it will break up the monotony of the morning watch. Well…I had not considered the possibility that Murphy's Law would almost immediately come into play.

My well-ordered mental schedule was quickly disrupted when the MEDEVAC chopper and escort were nearly two hours late, finally calling via the air operations radio net around 10:00 AM to announce they were on their way in. I ordered, "Flight Stations to receive MEDEVAC helicopter" thereby initiating a standard fire safety procedure in which the deck force hauled out a couple of charged fire hoses and a very large foam fire extinguisher, followed by a shipmate wearing a heavily insulated silver fire suit. (The fire suit would allow this sailor to approach a crashed helo to extract survivors. However, the heavily insulated suit was no fun to wear in the Vietnamese heat.)

As we watched for the MEDEVAC, up came the anticipated radio call from our Seawolves helos saying they were in-bound with very little fuel on board. At this point my anticipated smooth timeline was shredding and my normally calm demeanor frazzling. I returned their radio call with the not-well-received information that they would have to hold off our starboard bow until we could clear the MEDEVAC flight.

With the clock ticking and fuel burning away on the Seawolves aircraft, the MEDEVAC flight, obviously not used to landing aboard a ship, very cautiously and s-l-o-w-l-y approached our cleared deck. Fortunately, our Chief Hospital Corpsman was his efficient self and had the wounded up on deck and strapped into stretchers. We started loading them on the helo as soon as the skids hit the deck. As the process was underway, the bridge radio speaker came alive once again, announcing the early arrival of the daily Admin helo!

With my morning schedule shot, anxiety peaking, I went into "air controller mode" and barked out instructions to the CH-46 copter to circle off our port side until we cleared the MEDEVAC flight. They acknowledged the call and the Seawolves again reminded me that they were low on fuel and complained that they might soon be going for a swim in the Bo De River rather than enjoying lunch in the air-conditioned Wardroom. (Sound logic dictated my decision: while the CH-46 had significant fuel, it still had a long flight ahead. It made no sense to bring the Seawolves aboard for a quick refueling because they were to remain onboard the WESCO for the rest of the day.) {Spoiler Alert—no one went swimming that day.}

Soon, we launched the MEDEVAC and cleared the Admin helo to land. They dropped the incoming mail and supplies, loaded outgoing mail and cargo, and the ship-prepared bag lunches and cold drinks (again, very much appreciated in the 'Nam heat) we always provided. As the Admin helo launched, I gave the permission for the Seawolves to come in.

After they landed and shut down, the senior Sea Wolf pilot proceeded to the bridge to deliver a blistering lesson on aero dynamics that explained in some graphic detail that helicopters without fuel cannot remain in the air and that young Ensigns should keep that in mind. I politely thanked him for the applied physics lecture and reminded him that the MEDEVAC and Admin flights had priority and I had to clear them first to leave the Seawolves an open deck. He scowled at me and tramped off the bridge, unimpressed by the issues and anxiety this wet-behind-the-ears Ensign had faced.

Of course, with the drama over, the watch returned to its normal monotonous course and eventually ended when my relief arrived. As I started to leave the bridge, my relief asked, innocently, how the day was going. I replied, "Oh, you know, just another day in paradise."

FRANK CRANFORD

US Army — Military Police

Dates of military service (Active and Reserve): 1970 — 1973

Unit(s) you served with in Vietnam: 188th MP CO, 504th MP BN

Dates served in Vietnam: Dec. 1970 to Dec. 1971

Highest rank held: SP4 (E-4)

Place and date born: Macon, GA — 1948

ONE UNUSUAL NIGHT ON THE PERIMETER

In December 1970, I was assigned to the 188th MP CO, 504th MP BN, 18th MP BDE. The company was based at Camp David Land near Danang, RVN from 1970 to 1972. The company's mission was maintaining law, order, and discipline in and around the City of Danang, in addition to convoy escorts and other special projects. The company consisted of two operational platoons plus various support personnel such as the cooks, clerks, armorers, and motor pool.

There were two shifts per day covering the area of operation, from 0600 hours until 1800 hours and from 1800 to 0600. Shifts were switched between the platoons every month or so.

The platoon assigned the night duty was also responsible for the perimeter security of Camp Land. Perimeter duty began at dusk and ended when relieved at sunrise. Most everybody disliked perimeter duty, mainly because most of the time it was excruciatingly boring and exposed to the weather, ranging from steaming hot and muggy to the horizontal rainfall and chill of the monsoons.

The northwestern perimeter of the camp looked out toward the southern side of Freedom Hill (Hill 327). Looking to the left was open ground stretching all the way to the foothills of a mountain range, twenty or more kilometers in the distance. It was from this direction that rockets often flew overhead toward the air base, which was about five kilometers to the east.

The perimeter was a curving line with about 12 bunkers spaced approximately 10 to 15 meters apart, each occupied by two men, the middle bunker equipped with the "Ma Deuce," an M-2 .50 caliber machine gun. Just in front of the bunkers was the wire. The "wire" was concertina barbed wire stretched from one end of the perimeter to the other, stacked about waist high, with soda and beer cans partially filled with gravel attached, designed to make noise if the wire was disturbed. There was no vegetation from the bunkers to the wire and beyond, it having been killed by defoliant. Other weapons used along the line were the M-16 rifle; the M-60 machine gun; and the M-79 grenade launcher. Starlight scopes and parachute flares were also provided.

The bunkers themselves were constructed of recycled CONEX containers with the top half of three of the sides cut out for viewing, and the fourth wall removed for ingress/egress. The containers were reinforced with sandbags on the sides and the top. Wooden benches were built in as well.

Perimeter duty began before dusk with an informal guard mount and roll call held by the duty NCO. At that time, Intel (if there was any) was reviewed as well as an inspection of weapons. Following this was a "mad minute" when all weapons were test fired at the base of a nearby hill. This of course generated a great deal of noise, but the noise from the "Ma Deuce" on Bunker 7 dominated the conversation of all the racket. The bright red tracer trails of the ammunition was an amazing sight to see, even at dusk, as it lit up the hill, sometimes causing small fires to break out. Then everyone went out to spend a night in a two-man bunker.

We passed time on the bunkers in conversation about all the topics young men talk about…family, friends, and our previous lives back in the "world" (the USA). Other subjects included girlfriends, wives, school, politics, religion, the Army, jobs, and future plans after returning home. In other words, most problems of the world were solved in those bunkers. Everyone was from diverse ethnic backgrounds and geographical locations, so this dialogue proved to be educational and enlightening for more than a few of us.

At this time, the Company was commanded by CPT Roy S. Moore from Alabama. CPT Moore went on to become the Chief Justice of the Alabama Supreme Court (twice) and ran for the U.S. Senate as well (he lost.). CPT Moore was a West Point graduate. His strict military manner annoyed some of the troops under his command as he rigidly enforced discipline and took a hard stand on drug use. Some people derisively called him "Captain America."

I would say most line MPs didn't use hard drugs regularly, but some did, and some of the support personnel used marijuana frequently, and hard drugs were available as well. Apart from the non-users, users and abusers were informally divided into three groups: Juicers (alcohol), heads (marijuana), and skag freaks (hard drugs). Pills were available as well. A certain part of the company did a lot of grumbling about CPT Moore and the First Sergeant, Paul Howard.

On one night, I was manning a bunker along with a partner, whose name I can't recall. We were watching the assigned area for movement and listening for any unusual noises. Nights were normally quiet, occasionally interrupted by a rocket passing overhead on its way toward the air base. We could also hear the aircraft at the base in the distance and watch the bright exhausts of the departing jets if the weather was good.

The weather this night was calm and clear, and visibility was virtually unlimited, with bright stars overhead. There was an outdoor movie scheduled for later in the evening after it was good and dark. If we looked behind us toward the company area, we could just see the flickering light of the movie at the top of the outdoor screen in the distance. Of course, it was too far away to hear any of the dialogue.

Shortly after sunset, we had settled in for a long night manning the bunker where the only breaks would come when you had to take a walk over to the relief tube, when you had your rations (either a sandwich made in the chow hall or the ever-popular C rations), or when the Officer of the Day or more likely an NCO came around to make sure everyone was awake. A snoozing troop would be in line to receive one of CPT Moore's favorite articles (15).

The night's quiet calm was suddenly broken by gunfire behind us, inside the company area, not from the direction you would expect to hear it. Immediately three or four parachute flares popped, and the area was lit by the yellowish twilight of the drifting flares, followed by their smoky trails. As everyone's attention was directed back toward the company area, you could hear excited shouts and weapons being charged and readied along the line. After the initial two or three shots, there was a pause of a few seconds, then a short burst of automatic weapons fire.

Shouting came from that direction as the company's alert siren began to wail, adding to the confusion on the perimeter. At this point, of course, everyone was on high alert, with weapons locked and loaded. Most of us had been on alert before, but never from behind. I looked through the starlight scope but was unable to see anything other than ghostly greenish images of a few men hurrying toward the NCO billets. We continued to hear activity from inside the company, but no more weapon fire. Word came down the line that there was no enemy attack, but there had been a shooting.

Accidental discharges happened sometimes, but this had definitely sounded like more than one weapon. The rumor mill churned out potential victims from the CO to one of the clerks, but nobody on the perimeter knew for sure. Flares continued to burn, and the pucker factor remained in effect. About half an hour later, we heard the sound of an incoming chopper that landed on our small LZ inside the compound. The helicopter stayed on the ground with its blades spinning for less than a minute, then lifted off into the clear night sky.

The rumors continued to circulate until the next morning when the preceding night's activities slowly came to light.

An enlisted soldier had recently gone on the Army's amnesty program that was offered to some individuals to deal with drug related issues. The soldier, whose name will go unmentioned, had acquired a .45 and held some kind of grudges against the CO and the First Sergeant. He went to the First Sergeant's hooch, entered, and fired a couple of shots at the First Sergeant (who had less than ten days left on his short timer's stick), striking him once in the upper leg, then ran away. Top kept a loaded .30 cal Thompson nearby, managed to grab it, and returned fire in the direction of the attack, which accounted for the automatic weapons fire we had heard on the previous night. He apparently did no damage to the intruder.

In the meantime, someone alerted the CO, telling him what had happened, and that the un-named soldier had threatened him as well as Sgt. Howard. He got on his boots and grabbed his weapon and headed outside toward his office. By the time he arrived, the shooter was in custody, restrained with hand irons, under guard, and seated on a bench in the company day room.

The First Sergeant was medevaced over to the 95th Evac Hospital at China Beach, and never came back to the 188th because of his approaching DEROS. I heard later, from someone who had run into him stateside, that he had remained in the Army. The shooter, of course, was gone, I assume eventually to the Disciplinary Barracks at Ft. Leavenworth.

As you can imagine, a night like this made me appreciate long quiet nights and a new appreciation for boredom.

This type of attack is technically not classified as a fragging, but as an assault on a superior since no explosive was used. Surprisingly, as responders, we worked only a few cases like this or fragging incidents, especially considering the availability of weapons and the deteriorating morale of some of the troops during this period of the war.

Thanks to my friends Ken Gould and William Gruendler of the 188th who helped me with some of the details of this account.

SUMNER "SKIP" J. DAVIS

U.S. Army — Aviator — Captain, Corps of Engineers

Dates of Military Service (Active and Reserve): 10 Nov 1966 to 1 Jun 2006

Units Served with In Vietnam: 213th Engineer Detachment (Construction); 508th Engineer Detachment; 510th Engineer Detachment; 187th Assault Helicopter Company.

Dates in Vietnam: 15 May 1966 – 25 Dec 1969 / 6 Jan 1971 – 18 Dec 1971

Highest Rank Held: Captain (O-3)

Place of Birth and Year: Melrose, Massachusetts – 1945

YOU HAVE TO SAY "OVER" MA'AM

After 19 exceedingly long, sometimes interesting, sometimes frightening, months in the Mekong Delta of the Republic of South Vietnam, I finally returned to the "World." I had returned from Vietnam on Christmas Day, 1969. Home was a suburb of Boston, Massachusetts. I was home with my family for the first time in six months. What I remember most was the cool weather. It was not hot. It was not humid. It did not smell like rotting vegetation.

On the New Year, I was informed I had been selected for the U.S. Army Officer Rotary Wing Primary Flight Course at Fort Wolters, Texas. I was to report on January 31, 1970. I was finally going to get to fly. I was going to be an Army Aviator. I was going to have to go back to Vietnam. All good things come with a price tag.

In the middle of my twenty-fifth year, I found myself an orphan. My father having passed five years earlier and my mother died in June 1970. I had just completed the "learning how to fly a helicopter" at Fort Wolters, Texas. Now I was at Fort Rucker, Alabama. From June through mid-August, I struggled with learning to fly under instrument. I made the grade, barely, and advanced into the Bell UH-1A/B/D model "Huey" Helicopter. We learned multi-ship combat assault tactics and emergency landing auto-rotations. We learned to fly at night and across country. We spent time flying in the Florida panhandle with Ranger trainees as our cargo. And we got paid to do all this stuff.

On Saturday, the 15th of August, two pilot friends from Vietnam invited me to go to Panama City, Florida for a brief weekend visit. One, a fellow New Englander from New Hampshire, had flown the twin rotor Chinook helicopter in Can Tho, RVN. He committed to the OV-1 Mohawk transition to be allowed to return to Southeast Asia for the 4th or 5th tour. An OH-6A Observation Pilot I had also served with was the second. I had originally declined the invitation, but they came to my home (a single wide trailer) and kidnapped me.

I had never visited the Sunny Mecca of Panama City Beach. Once there. we realized there were probably no hotel rooms available, and we would have to end up sleeping on the beach. Then my friends remembered a girl they knew from Georgia was staying at the family home there. They decided to impose on her good nature to allow us to sleep on the porch. We pulled into the driveway of a neat house back from the beach. A pert little Dodge Charger was in the driveway. I began to worry about whether this lady would call the local police as we invaded her space. My teammates bounded up the back steps and knocked on the door as I shied in the background. This could not end well.

I was stunned when this beautiful, wonderful, and forgiving lady answered the door with a smile. I did not know at the time that she had given my two friends specific instructions not to show up as she was recuperating from a recent illness. You would not have deduced this from the graciousness of her welcome. She invited us in and offered us each a beer. When she came to me, I stupidly said, "If you can spare it." If I had not ducked and caught the bottle it would have smashed into my head. Of course, she had no way of knowing I was embarrassed that I had been talked into this situation.

After some brief negotiations, we were allowed to stay on the couch and porch of her house. As it was dinner time, I suggested we should take the lady to dinner with us as a form of appreciation for the lodgings. We set out for a local steak house. After dinner we decided to go to the lounge at the Holiday Inn on the beach for a few drinks. I was still less then entertaining as I was uncomfortable in the lady's presence as she worked to be pleasant. A small band started playing in the lounge and my LOACH pilot buddy asked the lady to dance. As they left the table my other friend, the Mohawk pilot (nee the Chinook pilot) looked at me in agitation and demanded, "What in hell is wrong with you? You're acting like a fool to her, and she doesn't deserve it!" I sheepishly responded, "I am not going to try and intervene in a buddy's relationship with his girlfriend."

"Girlfriend!" He repeated. "Girlfriend! She doesn't even like the guy. She is only here because I am dating her roommate in Georgia, and she feels she needs to take care of me."

The world suddenly changed before I could respond. My second life had started. Katherine Diane Brown became the most important person in my world within the next 24 hours.

We danced. We talked. We walked the beach until sunrise. Starting on August 15, 1970, I spent every minute I could with her. We dated until my graduation at Fort Rucker. She even pinned my newly awarded aviator wings on my chest in October. We dated through the month of November while I attended the AH-1G Cobra Transition Course at Hunter Army Airfield in Savannah, Georgia. Finally, in the first week of January 1971 we said goodbye until...

In late May, we met in Connecticut for 10 days leave on Long Island Sound. In September, we met again in Hawaii for Rest & Recreation Leave. Neither visit went as well as I had hoped. I really loved this woman, but I was seriously concerned about leaving my unit to be with her. I tried to be as upbeat as possible, but I was not a raving success.

Back in Vietnam I tried to carry on our correspondence as though everything was great between us. Sometime during the first week of October 1971, I received a letter from Diane that ended with the classic "I think we should consider the possibility of dating other people." I was devastated. This was not happening to me. I could not imagine returning home to find she was gone. After an hour or two of feeling miserable, I rallied into rescue mode, and I decided to face the issue head on.

I had made friends at the local Air Force MARS Station. During the Vietnam War, the Military Affiliate Radio System (MARS) was most known for its handling of "Marsgram" written messages and providing "phone patches" to allow overseas servicemen to contact their families at home. I called the MARS local senior Non-Commissioned Officer and asked him to put through a call to Atlanta. I gave him the number and waited for him to do his magic.

His station would call a HAM radio operator in North America (amateur radio, or ham radio, is a popular hobby used to converse around the world, or even into space, all without the internet or cell phones. It can be a lifeline during times of need) and they in turn would place a collect telephone call to the number I had given him. The whole process usually went quickly from my duty station in Vietnam because there was a twelve-hour difference in time with the Eastern Time Zone in Atlanta. It was midday for me so early in the morning at home. Diane answered the telephone on the second or third ring on my end of the call and drowsily said, "Hello."

"Ma'am, this Air Force Communications Staff Sergeant Reilly in Di An, Vietnam" he introduced himself. "I have a call from Captain Davis for you. Will you take the call?" He followed this message with the usual instructions "You have to say 'Over' each time you finish speaking Ma'am. Over."

Diane came awake and answered quickly. "Of course, I'll take the call…."

There was a short pause until Sergeant Reilly injected "You have to say, 'Over' Ma'am."

"Over" came her slightly embarrassed response.

"Diane, I got your letter today," I stammered. "Over."

"Okay. I'm glad it got through all right," she replied.

"You have to say, 'Over' Ma'am."

"Over." This time she was laughing.

I immediately started into my rehearsed speech. "I have no interest in dating anyone else but you, over."

"Glad to hear it," she responded somewhat smugly.

"You have to say, 'Over' Ma'am."

"Over." This continuous interruption was making me nervous. Quickly, I just blurted out "Diane, will you please marry me? Over."

"Yes! Of course, I will marry you!" came her strong, unequivocal response.

"You have to say, 'Over' Ma'am."

"Over" she laughed. I was spent. I had been so concerned that she would say "no" that I was speechless. "Outstanding!" was the only thing I could think to say. I was ecstatic! No, the two remaining months until I got back to Atlanta seemed like forever. After further light conversation I let he go back to sleep with a ringing, "You have to say, 'Over' Ma'am," racing through my brain.

Now, almost fifty-one years later, Diane is still with me. We are still married, and still very much in love. We have survived Vietnam, four children, six grandchildren, COVID 19, and the ups and downs that accompany such a journey. It has been a blessed life which had seemed so far out of my reach back in Vietnam. For me, that MARS call was the beginning of the rest of my life. A happy life. A rewarding life. And it still goes on.

"You have to say, 'Over' Sir."

CARL H. "SKIP" BELL, III

U.S. Army—Armored Cavalry Officer, Aviator

Dates of Military Service (Active and Reserve): 1967 to 1998

Units Served with In Vietnam: A Troop, HHT, B Troop, 1st Squadron, 4th Cav,1st Inf Div (First Tour); C Troop, 3rd Squadron, 17th Air Cav; 18th Corps Avia -tion Co; G3, HQ 1st Aviation BDE (Second Tour)

Dates in Vietnam: Feb 1969 to Feb 1970; Feb 1972 to Feb 1973

Highest Rank Held: Colonel (O-6)

Place of Birth and Year: Decatur, GA—1945

THE MOST AFRAID I EVER WAS IN A HELICOPTER

In the spring of 1972, I was flying a UH-1H helicopter in the Mekong Delta. I was assigned to the 18th Corps Aviation Company, a General Support aviation company based at Can Tho. We were returning home from a mission on the Ca Mau peninsula in the southern part of the Delta. It was the rainy season, which meant generally low ceilings and thunderstorms, especially in the late afternoon, which was when we were flying home.

The ceiling was about 1,200' and I had my rotor disc in the base of the clouds above me (note that flying below 1,500' was called the "dead man's zone" because the tracer burn-out for an AK-47 rifle was 1,500'—that meant the enemy could engage an aircraft with reasonably accurate fire below 1,500'). My plan was that if I was shot at, I would check my compass heading, go up into the clouds, and fly on instruments in that same direction until I felt it was safe to descend below the clouds again. I felt reasonably confident in my ability to fly on instruments—I would practice doing that on the way home from missions.

We were flying over a landmark called the Vi Thanh Canal, which was a wide, straight canal, several miles long and was an easily identifiable landmark in an area where there were thousands of rice paddies, all of which looked a lot alike. The easily identifiable landmarks included certain bends in the rivers, certain wide canals (like the one we were following), and certain large villages with unique visual characteristics (a church with a steeple, an old French fort, etc.). The Vi Thanh Canal was a good landmark because it pointed toward Can Tho (our home airfield) at the northern end of the canal. The canal itself ended about 10 miles from Can Tho, but if you kept the compass heading you had when you were following the canal, you would reach Can Tho.

As luck would have it, we took fire from people in a couple of sampans in the canal and I did what I had planned to do—checked the compass heading and climbed up into the cloud. Bad move. We flew for several minutes and right into a thunderstorm. I was completely surrounded by clouds (no reference to the ground); it was like flying through the inside of a gray cotton ball. There were lightning flashes all around the aircraft, and we were being buffeted around like a cork on the ocean.

My airspeed indicator was going from 80 knots to 120 knots to 0 knots and I was not moving the cyclic control. We hit a thermal and began a climb (the vertical speed indicator was showing a 2,000 feet per minute rate of climb), and I had bottomed out the collective (which should have put us into autorotation—we should have been descending instead of climbing).

We continued to climb, bounced around like a cork, and the lightning continued to flash all around us. This went on for several minutes, which seemed like hours. We hit the top of the thermal at a little over 10,000' and began to drop like a rock. I tried to keep the aircraft as level as I could (using the attitude indicator). Of course, I had no idea where the cloud bottoms were (or how high they were), nor did I know where we were located.

This meant that if the clouds went all the way to the ground, we would slam into the ground before I could do anything about it. I added collective so we were not descending as fast as we had been but was still descending to find the bottom of the clouds.

We finally broke out at about 800' and we were tilted to the right. I righted the aircraft and got everything back under control by the time we had reached 400'. I had no idea where we were—all I could see were rice paddies, all of which looked alike, and no landmarks.

Then I did what I should have done immediately when I originally went up into the clouds—I called the USAF flight following radar people ("Paddy Control") and asked if they could vector me back to Can Tho. They had me transmit a code on the aircraft's transponder and once they identified me, they gave me a vector to Can Tho. We were pretty low (400'), but I didn't want to take my chances in the clouds again unless we got shot at. If that happened, I would have asked Paddy Control to vector me around any thunderstorms (which, again, is what I should have done to begin with). We made it back to Can Tho without further incidents.

Flying through a thunderstorm in a helicopter is a terrifying experience. I was the pilot and I knew that I had no control over that aircraft as long as we were in the thunderstorm. That was the most frightened I ever was in an aircraft (including times we were shot at). I was very fortunate to have lived through that experience, and I learned a valuable lesson about using the excellent resources provided by the USAF flight-following radar folks.

RUNO C. ANDERSON

US Army — Armor/Airborne/Psychological Operations Officer
Dates of Military Service: 1969-1972
Unit Served with in Vietnam: MACV -CORDS II Corp, Team 25 Ban Me Thuot
Dates in Vietnam: Dec 1970 to Dec 1971
Highest Held Rank: Captain (O-3)
Place and Year of Birth: Richmond, VA 1946

THE SAGA BEGINS

I arrived in the Republic of Vietnam around 1200 hours on Dec 31, 1970. It was quite a welcome. After landing at Bien Hoa and being sent over to Long Binh for billeting, we tried to go to sleep with the jet lag trying to take hold, but the adrenaline was flowing and it wasn't easy to sleep. At midnight, the whole perimeter let loose with gunfire, rockets, and any other explosive device that would make noise. A lot of us newbies who were trying to sleep hit the floor, and the old timers just laughed and took another swig of whatever they were imbibing. The reason I'm relating this is because the next day, New Year's Day, was sort of a holiday, but business still went on.

I was directed over to where I was supposed to report for my assignment and learned three surprising things. First of all, I was handed a pair of Captain's bars. The second fact was that I was not supposed to arrive for another two months according to the paperwork in front of the assignments officer, and thirdly he therefore had no assignment for me. He handed me a loose leaf binder about 4" thick with all of the available assignments for incoming MACV Advisors.

He told me to contact any friends or compatriots who had rotated out of Germany and the MATA Advisors course at Ft. Bragg and happened to be presently in country.

He said ask them for some input that might be able to give me (and him) some idea of where I might want to serve. I firmly believe not everybody got this special gift, but who was I to look a gift water buffalo in the mouth. I found that there was a MACV/CORDS province Psyop

Advisor due to rotate home. This was in Darlac Province, city of Ban Me Thout, in the Central Highlands of II Corps.

Arriving on a (Scare) Air America flight, I was greeted by my new boss who actually worked for the US Information Agency. We were all part of Team 25 that included American civilians from varied walks of life, Police advisor (ex LA Police), State Department (our second in command), Medical Surgeon (US Army), and the Commander of Team 25, a Special Forces Colonel. We had various other US Army Advisor officers on the Team for Supply, Intelligence, as well as Tactical Advisors to the Vietnamese local PF and regional RF defense forces as well as the ARVN Division stationed on Ban Me Thout.

HERE IS WHERE THE REAL STORY BEGINS.

It was around 1900 hours when we got a call that the regional forces had been attacked on the outskirts of one of the local villages. They were bringing in casualties to the local Vietnamese hospital. Our medical advisor/surgeon who had trained at the Mayo Clinic, frequently did surgery at the hospital. Usually, he was requested when one of the few local physicians could not make it in time. We were sitting in the Doc's house (he got better accommodations than we did) and he asked me if I wanted to go with him to help. I had started helping him in the operating room as an extra pair of hands. (Swatting flies was my first job, no AC). The Vietnamese nurses were sincere, but not able to pick up the language when he needed specific instruments quickly.

They brought in a young boy. He was maybe 15 or 16. He had been shot in the chest and the bullet had shattered his shoulder (AC joint). Doc immediately saw he had to open him up if we were to stop the bleeding. He couldn't do anything for the shoulder, but he thought he could save the boy's life. We had scrubbed in and gowned up. He took the scalpel, opened the chest, cut the sternum, put in the retractor. I cranked it and there was the bleeder. A nick on the aorta. The heart was pumping spurts. To stop the bleeding, he carefully took out the pumping heart, carefully handed it to me and said keep squeezing, but gently.

Within seconds he was able to put a suture stitch on the aorta and stop the bleeding. Irrigation…no more bleeding.

Close him up and pray for the best. We did and his brother took care of him in the hospital until we were told he had requested some ice cream. That was the last we heard. Doc asked me during the operation did I know I had passed up 11 years of medical training to be where I was, standing across from him holding a beating human heart. I could only nod and try to comprehend the enormity of what I had just been allowed to do. A living human heart.

Over the year we did a lot of assisting operations at the Vietnamese hospital. Unfortunately, many Typhoid cases did not result in successful outcomes. We always needed supplies for the hospital and especially the operating room. Eventually we worked up a system of getting oxygen cylinders, air conditioners, and other much needed medical supplies flown up to Ban Me Thuot, thanks to a number of military personnel who shall remain nameless. That was the price for a Martini Vasectomy. But that's another story.

BOB LANZOTTI

US Army Aviator
Total Time in Military: 1960 to 1985
Unit Served with in Vietnam: 1st Avn Bde, 1st Cav Div
Dates in Vietnam: 1967 to 1968; 1969 to 1970
Highest Rank Held: Lt. Colonel (O-5)
Place of Birth: Taylorville, IL — 1937

TIDE 6

Upon arriving in Vietnam in January of 1969 to begin my second tour, I was informed by the 11th Group Commander of the First Air Cavalry Division that I would take command of Charlie Company of the 228th Assault Support Helicopter Battalion. I was thrilled to get a command, but not so thrilled with Charlie Company's call sign, Crimson Tide. Being a member of the University of Illinois football squad from 1955-1960, I would have certainly preferred a different call sign, perhaps Fighting Illini!

I may have been troubled by the call sign, but nobody else was. And why should they be? The University of Alabama under Coach Paul "Bear" Bryant had eight National Championships to their credit, the most recent in 1961, 1964, and 1965. I admired Coach Bryant, not so much for his national titles, but more for his credo with respect to what he looked for in a football player. He was quoted as saying, "What matters most is not the size of the dog in the fight, but the size of the fight in the dog." Being an undersized linebacker for the Illini, that was my kind of philosophy.

I decided early on, since I was announcing to the world over FM and UHF radio waves that I was head coach of the Crimson Tide in Vietnam, I might as well communicate with the real head coach of the Crimson Tide back in Tuscaloosa, AL. So, with the help of First Sergeant Bob Bratton and XO Captain Rick Storm, we drafted a letter to Coach Bryant to inform him that there indeed was another Crimson Tide team on this planet. We told him we were proud of our name and he and his team would likewise be proud of our achievements. The letter included some details about what we did for a living and how we went about doing it. We also included a company guidon and a couple of action photos of our CH-47 Chinook aircraft supporting 1st Air Cav soldiers in the field.

About a month later, we received a letter from Coach Bryant along with a Crimson Tide football. One panel of the football was signed by Coach Bryant, his coaching staff, and the entire 1969 football squad. Because of Coach Bryant's popularity, Charlie Company gained a little notoriety as his gesture was written up in the Stars and Stripes.

When I left the unit, the officers and NCOs of Charlie Company signed the remaining two panels of the ball and gave it to me as a going away gift. Today that ball resides in my home as one of my most prized possessions.

Ironically, the last of Coach Bryant's twenty-four straight bowl appearances would be against the Fighting Illini in the Liberty Bowl on December 29, 1982. It was Coach Bryant's last game, and the outcome would advance his win column from 322 to 323. While my loyalty remained with the Fighting Illini during the entire game, the disappointment of the final score was certainly diminished by my affiliation with Crimson Tide of Vietnam.

Like the rest of the world, and certainly all the Vietnam Crimson Tide veterans, I was pleased that Coach Bryant improved his winning percentage in the very last game he would coach. Hell, I just wish his last game hadn't been against the Illini. Yeah, I just loved my call sign in Vietnam...Everyone loves a winner.

Bob Lanzotti
Tide 6

JOHN SOURS

Army — Judge Advocate General Corps (JAGC)

Dates of Military Service (Active Duty and Reserves): Sept 1966 to Oct 1978

Unit Served with in Vietnam: HQ USARV

Dates Served in Vietnam: 5 January 1971 to 1 December 1971

Highest Rank Held: Major (O-4)

Place and Year of Birth: Harrisburg, PA — 1944

THREE VIETNAM VIGNETTES

A Brief Background: I served in Vietnam between 5 January and 1 December 1971 as a Captain in the U.S. Army Judge Advocate General's Corps ("JAG"). Except for the initial five or six days of my tour, I was assigned to a small and relatively obscure staff activity known as the "U.S. Army Procurement Agency (USAPAV)," located in a dilapidated six-story building on Plantation Road, on the outskirts of Saigon. It was a small organization, led by a Colonel and reported directly to the USARV G-4, who at the time was LTG Walter Woolwine, located at Long Binh. USAPAV had a total complement of about 230, consisting of 35 or so officers, including five or six JAGs, about the same number of mostly senior enlisted personnel, 30-40 DACS (Department of the Army civilians) and around 120 Vietnamese nationals.

Though small, we were busy, especially in the Spring and early Summer months—back then the federal government's fiscal year ended June 30, meaning that the current year's appropriation had to be spent by then—and our annual budget was between $500 and $600 million which, as they say in government circles, was "real money" in those days. We procured a lot of different services and supplies, all for periods of one year or less. By law, we were required to negotiate, rather than invite bids for, all contracts. Naturally, since we were dealing with government funds and property, there were a lot of paperwork requirements to keep up with.

I. A FISHING TRIP

One steamy evening around mid-July, our Staff Duty Officer received a call from his Navy counterpart at Newport, a large supply offloading and storage facility along the Saigon River, reporting that one of our agency's contract tugs had run into and damaged an American ocean-going vessel, the S.S. Indiana, that was offloading a large shipment of artillery shells onto storage barges moored in the middle of the river a few miles downstream. Naturally, this incident required that two separate investigations be conducted by the Contracting Officer and his staff. As the JAG assigned to assist the agency's Transportation Section, I was therefore asked to accompany him, along with his Contracting Officer's Assistant (COA) on a trip to the scene the following morning. As a bonus, we were told that the ship's captain had extended an invitation to join him for lunch.

We set out shortly after dawn the next morning in a small riverine craft carrying a crew of four and proceeded at moderate speed down the serpentine channel toward the damaged vessel. As it was a very hot, but clear day, and having been assured that all had been quiet along that stretch of the river for some months, we three passengers decided to remove our fatigue shirts and lay face up to catch some rays on the raised deck running in front of the boat's cabin. The trip was almost blissful until just after we had reached what was said to be at the halfway point when, to our consternation, considerable firing began from the starboard side. Being without either a weapon or a flak jacket, each of us immediately rolled off the deck into the narrow walkway which surrounded the cabin.

On my part, all I could think of was that I was about to go on R & R in another week or so, and that this was a hell of a predicament! Then, it occurred to me that I really didn't have to have come along at all. I could have just read the reports back at the agency the next day. Fortunately, before I could do or think anything else, one of the sailors got up on top of the cabin from the port side, trained the .50 caliber mounted there on the shore, and cut loose. No further shots were heard from the shore;

however, just then the boat took another sharp turn in the river and, looking up now, all seven of us saw two Vietnamese men shooting at a school of fish near the shore.

Speculating about what it was that had just occurred, we gathered ourselves back into full attire, proceeded to the supposedly stricken ammo delivery ship, were warmly welcomed by its captain, conducted a rather speedy inspection, and found only very minor damage to both his ship and our contractor's tug, and repaired to the captain's cabin for a hearty lunch whose main dish was a huge helping of deep-fried — FISH!

2. THE FACE-SAVING LAUNDRY CONTRACT

Several weeks prior to my fish trip discussed above, I was summoned to meet with the General Services Section of the agency to discuss the forthcoming annual procurement of laundry services for each of the four corps operational areas of RVN. It was decided to first solicit quotes from interested parties for the five separate contracts to be entered into for the III Corps area, which included Saigon. All those contracts, as well as the majority of those for laundry services in I, II and IV Corps, were reserved — whether by formal agreement or otherwise was not clear — for South Korean contractors. Based on lists containing the names of both current year contactors and others who had been part of the procurement process in prior years, as supplemented by information furnished by the Economic Section of the ROK Embassy, we extended invitations to four to six prospects to compete for each of the III Corps laundry contracts.

The first group of four, who were thought to be interested in the forthcoming contract for the Gia Dinh Province area contract, came to the agency the following Monday. It became very clear very quickly that there was only one serious prospect, a firm which was the only one of the four accompanied by the Economic Attaché from the ROK Embassy, who introduced himself and the preferred contractor, then departed.

Discussions with the obvious select launderer proceeded for about an hour, then reached an apparent impasse as to price, both as to unit figures and the overall total estimate. The prospective contractor, who was also the only one that sent two representatives and produced at least a rudimentary written presentation, then asked for a recess of 15 minutes so that he and his assistant could "consult our superiors." The Contracting Officer, COA and I then withdrew from the conference room, which had only one door, no windows, and no telephone or other means of communication with the outside.

The three of us spent the entire 15-minute recess sitting at or on top of two desks located about five feet from the conference room door, from which no one emerged until the preferred contractor's "President" opened the door, invited us to return to the conference room, and proceeded to regale us with an elaborate oral presentation culminating in his dour formal announcement that, "having fully discussed the issue with our superiors" he and his colleague were prepared to lower their prices by "20% across the board." The Contracting Officer smilingly congratulated him on his generous price reduction, offered equally generous praise for his 'superiors' great sacrificial contribution to allied unity," and we all called it a day with bows and handshakes all around.

3. INTERESTING LATE-NIGHT READING NEAR TOUR'S END

November 12, 1971, was a momentous day. First, my orders for returning stateside three weeks hence arrived at the agency around midday, meaning that I was getting an unexpected but welcome 34-day drop as the holidays approached and force drawdowns were accelerating. Later, after a few celebratory drinks and a fine dinner at the Officers Club atop the Massachusetts BOQ where I had been living for the past four or so months, I went down to the ground floor to get some fresh(?) air before going back upstairs to my third-floor room for the evening.

As I was passing back through the lobby, another Captain—a Chaplain with whom I was barely acquainted—thrust a paperback book in my hand and said, "You might want to read this!" Turning the book over to examine its cover, I beheld "The Pentagon Papers." The book had been printed by or for the New York Times that previous summer and was a top-secret in-depth staff study that had been undertaken by various personnel and contract hires of the Department of Defense. It was said to be a comprehensive study of our nation's military involvement in Vietnam for the period 1945-1967. The Times had acquired a copy of the study from Daniel Ellsberg, a civilian who had worked on the study and secretly smuggled out of the Pentagon (i.e., stole) a copy of the finished product.

I was now too wide-awake to contemplate sleep, and so spent hours reading the book, sitting up on my cot while braced up against the wall behind it. My roommate asked to borrow the book next, then went off to sleep around 2300 while I kept reading. As I approached its midpoint nearing midnight—being a good deal faster as a reader then—a very loud explosion erupted at the ground floor front of the BOQ, lifting and throwing me off my bed onto the floor about three feet away, still in my original sitting position, book in hand. Naturally, my roommate awakened as well, also on the floor, and we both sat there expecting further action, lamenting the fact that neither of us had a weapon—nor did practically any other personnel living in the Headquarters Area Command (USAHAC) area. Fortunately, nothing else occurred that evening, other than development of a sudden lack of continuing interest in the book on my part, and a considerable loss of sleep at the Massachusetts BOQ.

M. JEROME "JAY" ELMORE

Navy — Disbursing Officer and Officer of the Deck aboard a destroyer escort
Years of Military Service: 1968-1974
Unit Served with in Vietnam: USS Roark DE-1053 — Two deployments. January 7 to August 10, 1971 and February 8 to August 31, 1972
Highest Rank Held: Lieutenant (O-3)
Place and Date of Birth: Eufaula, Alabama, 1948

FIRE

The hazards in a sailor's life do not begin when the ship enters a combat zone but commences shortly after the word is passed to single up all lines, set the sea and anchor detail, and prepare to get underway. The ship may experience storms, collisions, ordinance malfunctions, parting lines under stress during refueling, among many other things. One of the greatest risks, though, for any ship, is a major fire. The *USS Roark* (DE-1053) experienced just that on the way to Vietnam. I will tell the story from the beginning, or at least my beginning with the ship.

I reported aboard the *Roark* as a freshly minted ensign shortly after New Year's Day, 1971. The ship departed San Diego for Vietnam a few days later, January 7. We had barely passed the Point Loma lighthouse when the general quarters alarm sounded. This was a drill; the captain wasted no time ensuring that the crew was ready for action. The captain had the various damage control parties practice fighting imaginary fires, shoring pretend breaches in the bulkheads, and the like. These drills continued at various times during the five-day transit to Hawaii as the crew refined their skills.

We passed Diamond Head and entered the channel to Pearl Harbor. The ship rendered honors to the *USS Arizona* (BB-39) where over a thousand sailors and Marines have their final resting place. We refueled and a day later set course for Midway Island for our next refueling stop. The waters off the island were the site 29 years earlier of the pivotal carrier engagement of World War II — the Battle of Midway. When we visited the island, it was a sleepy refueling outpost where goony birds nesting on every available lawn space seemed to outnumber the inhabitants.

After refueling, we left on the 19th for Guam. Things were going smoothly until the middle of the night on January 20, when engineering performed a routine shift of a lube oil strainer, during which lube oil sprayed onto a hot steam line and ignited. As was reported in a message later that night: "ENTIRE ENGINEROOM ON FIRE WITHIN 60 SEC. AND SMOKE THROUGHOUT SYSTEM IN 90 SEC." Acrid smoke immediately filled the berthing compartments and passageways throughout the ship. An investigation later concluded that locating the lube oil strainer, which needed to be routinely changed, next to a hot steam line was a design flaw in this new class of ship.

Before retiring to bed the night of the fire, my roommate and I taped cardboard over the vents in the room because the air was cold. When the general quarters alarm went off, neither of us heard it initially since in our area it was muffled. What woke us was the stillness of the ship, no vibration from the engine or propellor. We then heard the muffled alarm. When we opened the door to our small "stateroom" the passageway outside was completely engulfed in thick black smoke. The battery powered battle lanterns were on but could barely penetrate the smoke.

Thankfully, because we had covered the vents the night before, the air in our room was clear. We quickly dressed, took a deep breath, and hustled to the weather deck and fresh air. Since general quarters had been set somewhat earlier, our progress was impeded by dogged down hatches and doors. The passageways were so filled with smoke you could see nothing, and the acrid smoke stung your eyes and made it impossible to open them anyway. We progressed blindly by memory only, which was limited by having been on the ship for such a short time. Eventually, after nearly running out of breath, we made it outside to clear air. I worried about the sailors in berthing compartments several decks lower.

Damage control parties had mustered and were gearing up to go below to fight the fire. This would require them to haul water hoses down several decks and through small hatches to get to the engine room and other areas on fire. Each sailor wore an Oxygen Breathing Apparatus or

OBA. The OBA was a rebreathing device with a cannister at the base filled with a dry chemical which when ignited (or heated to a high temperature) gave off oxygen. As the sailors began their decent, they would pull a chord which would ignite a "candle" or primer that began giving off oxygen immediately for approximately five minutes, by which time the primer was designed to heat the full cannister sufficiently, allowing it to give off oxygen for an hour. At least that was the theory.

As the sailors descended into decks filled with smoke, hauling their hoses through small hatches, the primer gave them air for the first deck or two. But in many situations the main cannisters were defective and never heated to a temperature to give off oxygen, leaving the sailors without air several decks below in smoke filled passages. When they tried to return, they were ascending against a tide of other sailors coming down, struggling to get their gear through the tight hatches. Some became overcome with the smoke and lack of oxygen and might have perished but for their crewmates physically hauling them up.

The earlier training paid off when most of the fire parties were able to get to the fire and begin pouring water on it. In addition to water, a firefighting foam solution was also used which was more effective than water alone. One of the major drawbacks of the foam was that it was made from organics which attracted sharks; and, as the foam washed overboard and surrounded the ship in a film, it did just that. Sharks were reported circling the ship. The possibility of abandoning ship into the water with the sharks was an unacceptable option in my mind; I was familiar with what had happened to the sailors on the *USS Indianapolis*.

Since my general quarters station located several decks below the bridge was engulfed in smoke, and encryption and secret battle codes kept there in safes were not needed, I went to the bridge to see where I could help. A concern was raised that the torpedo magazine located amidship could be heating up and the torpedoes might cook off. I volunteered to assemble a party to go into the magazine to fight any fire there since most of the damage control personnel were already employed fighting the fire below deck.

When the hatch to the magazine was opened, a blast of singeing air blew out. Things were worse than expected. We could see flames coming up from below through vents leading topside and the plastic cones on the heads of the torpedoes were beginning to melt off. The magazine had been transformed into a giant oven, cooking the torpedoes. The walls were too hot to touch and the air in the magazine was scorching. We moved into the magazine with a fire hose, using the spray of the nozzle to protect us. We directed our hose onto the several torpedoes stored in the magazine. We were aware if any one of the torpedoes exploded, all would go and the ship, or at least what would be left of it, would be severed in half, and sent to the ocean floor.

We stayed in the magazine until the flames subsided and the room, while hot, was cool enough, so that a threat of a cook off had subsided. I was informed later that the torpedoes were within a few degrees of exploding when we got there.

Because of the well trained, disciplined, and, I might add, brave damage control personnel, the fire was extinguished throughout the ship. The only serious injury was a back injury suffered by the Chief Engineer who fell down a ladder directing the firefighting. Although he was later medevacked by helicopter, to his credit he continued to direct his people until the fire was completely out. The engineers in the engine room when the fire started were able to scramble topside to safety by means of an escape ladder and hatch.

Although the fire was out, the ship was dead in the water in the middle of the Pacific. The emergency generators worked, but there was no ability to make fresh water and communications were limited. We were transiting with the *USS Towers* (DDG-9) at the time of the fire and after the fire was out, the deck crew rigged a hawser off the bow so that the Towers could commence towing us. They were relieved of that duty when a fleet tug, the *USS Quapaw* (ATF-110), arrived and towed us the rest of the way to Pearl.

Everything in the interior of the ship, if not actually burned, was covered in soot and ashes. During the seven days it took to be towed back to Pearl, the crew mostly slept on deck and the cooks did a yeoman's job of feeding the crew under challenging circumstances, especially in light of the limited water supply. During this time, the crew began the laborious clean-up process. To make an already difficult situation worse, a storm was developing south of us that if it hit would wreak havoc while we were under tow. Thankfully, it stayed away but added to our many concerns.

During the fire and afterwards during the cleanup and repair, the crew was exposed to a variety of chemicals and substances, which they might say today are "known to the State of California to be bad for you!" For example, many of the pipes and lines in the engine room as well as throughout the ship were insulated in asbestos. If the crew was not exposed to it during the fire, they certainly were when the insulation was torn out during the refurbishment. Another potential long-term legacy of the fire.

A little over a month later, after the crew worked 24/7, *Roark* steamed out of Pearl and pointed her bow toward Vietnam where she served as an escort for the *USS Midway* (CV-41), now a museum in San Diego, and as shotgun for *PIRAZ*. As we left Pearl, our flotilla admiral's parting words were, "YOU HAVE EARNED THE ADMIRATION OF THE FLOTILLA."

Roark was a new ship on its first deployment at the time of the fire; and much of the crew, like me, were new to the ship, having relieved the original commissioning crew. Like strengthening steel, the fire forged a new crew; one whose lives had depended upon and were preserved by their shipmates. A great bond and trust were created between and among the officers and men, a new esprit de corps.

Most of the crew remained aboard for this deployment as well as a second deployment to Vietnam in 1972. Together we weathered storms, combat on the gunline, and steaming almost into Haiphong Harbor to attempt the rescue of POWs. No matter what challenge we faced, we knew we could depend on our shipmates and had a great respect for them. Personally, I felt I had persevered through this test by fire and that my new ensign bars had developed a seasoned salty crust, better preparing me for whatever might lie ahead in Vietnam.

VINCENT C. CORICA

US Army— Field Artillery Officer
Dates of military service: 1969 to 1978
Vietnam service unit: 3rd Brigade (Separate), 1st Cavalry Division (Airmobile)
Dates in Vietnam: Jul 1971 to May 1972
Highest Rank Held: Captain (O-3)
Place of Birth: Johnstown, PA— 1947

"THE LAST RIDE WITH MY BEST FRIEND"
MAY IT BE SAID, "WELL DONE; BE THOU AT PEACE"

Excerpt from the book, *Six Silent Men, Book Three*, Gary A. Linderer, First Edition, November 1977: "A book covering Lima Company, 75th Rangers, 101st Airborne Division": "Besides this array of company commanders and first sergeants, the Rangers saw a number of outstanding junior officers and senior NCOs who earned their scrolls and the respect of those they led serving as executive officers, platoon leaders, and platoon sergeants in L Company. Lieutenants Owen Williams, John Gay, David Grange, Jim Montano, Jim Smith, and Paul Sawtelle were a group of real 'studs' who willingly put in their time in the bush, usually as the 'sixth' man without rank or position. But when called on to command 'heavy' teams or Ranger platoon-size operations, they led as well as they followed."

This the story of 1LT Paul C. Sawtelle, Killed in Action at age 24, leading his Ranger Platoon on an ambush of NVA Regulars in the A Shau Valley on April 16, 1971.

Paul Coburn Sawtelle was my best friend and roommate at West Point. He was tall and lean, a cross-country athlete. Handsome, charming, sincere, quick-witted, seemingly always smiling, full of life, hope, and his Christian faith. Everyone who knew Paul respected and admired him. He was unforgettable. In 1968 and 1969, as First Classmen, he and I commanded Second Regiment, one of four Cadet Regiments at West

Point. We had approximately 800 cadets in our Regiment. We were ecstatic to be granted the opportunity to serve our fellow cadets in this way.

Paul was XO; I was CO. We made our command decisions as a team. We worked out together. We played handball together. We studied together. We spent time with each other's families while on leave, his in Hicksville, NY, mine in Johnstown, PA. Our social lives were joyfully intertwined as well. I introduced him to his fiancée. He was working diligently on helping me find mine. We knew we didn't invent the phrase "brothers from other mothers," but we felt like we did. We knew we would be joined at the hip for life. We vowed to be each other's Best Man. To be godfather to each other's children when we had them. To care for the other's widow and family when the first of us died.

We never got to keep any of those vows.

When we graduated from West Point on June 4, 1969, Paul's dream as an Infantry officer was to lead a Ranger Platoon in Vietnam. As the tragic saying goes, "he died doing what he loved."

Here was the tactical situation on Paul's last day on this earth. I've collected these facts from some of Paul's counterpart Ranger leaders and the book I mentioned earlier, "Six Silent Men, Book Three."

"It was April 16, 1971. US war efforts in I Corps were centered around the US-supported invasion of Laos, Lam Son 719. The Operations Order for Lima Company, 75th Infantry Rangers that day called for five six-man Ranger teams to insert west of Route 547-A, which ran north and south the length of the A Shau Valley. The Rangers would go in with a company from the 1st Battalion, 502d Infantry. Their joint mission was to conduct sweep operations in the Valley. Later in the day, the Infantry would be extracted while the Rangers moved into cover to establish early warning and flank security positions and set up ambushes. 1LT Sawtelle was the overall commander of the Ranger contingent. He and his team established what would soon become the fateful ambush site.

The morning after the Rangers' ambush was set up, a 10-man NVA patrol moved down Route 547-A from the north, flanking the sides of the road. The NVA patrol slowly approached in the direction of the kill zone. The concealed Rangers were armed with their personal weapons, reinforced by two M-60s in elevated positions plus carefully placed Claymore mines. The enemy soldiers were alert and moving cautiously. Inexplicably, automatic weapons fire erupted from in front of the Rangers' position.

First Lieutenant Paul Coburn Sawtelle, courageously leading his beloved Rangers in a dangerous ambush patrol, was immediately hit in the forehead by a single round, killing him instantly. Paul's Rangers charged out of their hidden positions to fire up the enemy survivors and complete the ambush."

When I learned of Paul's death, I was stunned, crushed, disillusioned, and insanely angry with the enemy. My sense of loss was dark and infinite. But none of those emotions would help Paul. None of those emotions would help me. None would help his destroyed parents, siblings, fiancée, and his countless friends. Such emotions would accomplish nothing. I knew I had to redirect them into useful action.

At the time, I was a 1LT with Charlie Battery, 1st Battalion, 319 Artillery, in the 82d Airborne Division at Fort Bragg, NC. My RVN orders didn't have me reporting to Vietnam for another few months. I realized *exactly* how I had to use some of that time; I would oversee Paul's journey from Vietnam to the West Point Cemetery. I had orders cut, designating me the Escort Officer for Paul's body. I contacted Paul's parents, who were like parents to me as well. I promised them I would "take care of our boy" every step of the way.

When Paul's casket arrived at Dover Air Force Base, Delaware, one of my tragic official duties was to inspect his fully prepared, uniformed body in the Plexiglas-sealed coffin. Despite his fatal head wound, he was almost as beautiful in death as he was in life. I assured his family of this, but they told me in barely audible, heart-broken voices that they had decided on a closed coffin at Paul's Memorial Service. In a sad but sacred irony, I was the only person among Paul's loved ones to see him during this, his Final Salute chapter.

We made plans to hold Paul's Memorial Service in the majestic West Point Cadet Chapel, with burial in the West Point Cemetery. At Dover,

I supervised the placement of Paul's flag-draped coffin into the Army hearse, and the driver and I began our wordless, four-hour drive north to a mortuary near West Point designated by West Point Cemetery officials.

Paul's precious parents allowed me to grieve in my own way by permitting me to handle all military aspects of honoring his death. At Paul's graveside, I presented the beautifully folded American flag from the Army Honor Guard to Paul's devastated mother. Shortly later, I would write Paul's Memorial Article for the West Point "Taps" memorial magazine with help from his parents and some of our classmates.

My most enduring formal task in honoring Paul's memory was arranging to have his Class of 1969 West Point ring enshrined in the West Point Library. Each Class is permitted to have just one ring in the Library display case. I knew that Paul would be so proud of this distinction! Paul and I had identical rings, with a gray Linde Star Sapphire as the gem. Every day when I put my ring on or take it off, I pray for Paul, promoted to Captain posthumously, who died a valiant, soldier's death in battle, leading and protecting his beloved Rangers. Precious best friend and brother, Paul, as is written so profoundly in the West Point alma mater, "May it be said, 'Well Done; Be Thou at Peace.'"

You didn't get to be my Best Man. I didn't get to be yours. Nevertheless, you are the Best Man I have ever known.

MAX W. TORRENCE

Army — Skycrane Pilot

Dates of military service (Active and Reserve): 1966-1988

Unit(s) you served with in Vietnam: 273rd Aviation Co. (Skycranes), 12th
Aviation Group.

Dates served in Vietnam: May 1970 to May 1971

Highest rank held: Lt. Colonel (O-5)

Place and date born — Ohio — 1946

DAMN, THAT WAS CLOSE

I completed the US Army Rotary Wing Flight Course in January 1970 at Hunter AAF in Savanah, Georgia. My class of 48 officers, including seven Marines were mostly Lieutenants and a few Captains. Following graduation, several new pilots were selected for the AH-1 Cobra gunship transition and remained at Hunter AAF for a few extra weeks to attend the qualification course. The remainder of the pilots headed off for 30 days of leave and then on to Vietnam, except for me.

Through extra study during the course, I had managed to obtain my FAA instrument rating with the help of my Instrument Flight Instructor. Now my goal was to get a transition into the CH-54 Skycrane, the Army's most advanced heavy lift helicopter. To qualify for the Skycrane transition course at Ft. Rucker, pilots were required to have 500 hours of helicopter time and possess an Army helicopter instrument rating. I only had 211 hours of single engine helicopter time, but I did have a full Army instrument rating, not just the tactical instrument ticket! After several calls to the Aviation Assignments Officer in DC, I was finally approved to attend the Skycrane transition at Ft. Rucker in March 1970. I remained at Hunter AAF for the next eight weeks, waiting to go TDY to Rucker.

Fresh from the six-week CH-54 qualification course and a 30-day leave, I arrived in Vietnam the last week of May 1970 and reported to the 273rd Aviation Company (Superhooks) at Long Binh. It was one of only three Skycrane units in Vietnam and had the responsibility of providing heavy lift support in the III and IV Corps areas of operation. The unit had been heavily involved in supporting the incursion into Cambodia since May 1st. My first flights were into the Fish Hook region of Cambodia to continue moving captured NVA supplies and equipment back into South Vietnam. These missions continued daily until President Nixon directed all US Forces to leave Vietnam at the end of June.

By July, our primary mission had returned to providing heavy lift support to the 1st Cavalry Division, which was headquartered at Phuoc Vinh, about 50 miles north of Saigon. Our missions around III Corps regularly included relocating 155mm artillery howitzers, recovery of downed aircraft, moving bulldozers to create new LZs, and resupply of fire bases with ammunition and cargo nets full of whatever else they needed. During that time, I also flew one mission deep into IV Corps to Ca Mau to pull out a prime mover that was stuck in the mud. The Delta was a very bleak AO, and I was glad that I wasn't stationed there.

Our standard mission profile for sling loads was 12,000 to 17,000 pounds. The maximum load limit of 17,000 pounds would allow enough fuel on board to make the delivery and return to a base that had a refuel point. Our range at maximum gross weight was about 30 minutes, which allowed a 20-minute fuel reserve. It was critical to get the load into the LZ quickly and depart for a refuel point as the low fuel warning lights in the cockpit were most often blinking at that point.

A few weeks after pulling out of Cambodia, I was on a sling load mission to a fire base north of Xuan Loc when I learned all about the "low fuel pucker factor." We had hooked up a load that was heavier than expected but calculated that we could still get it to the fire base. About five miles out, we advised the unit that we were inbound with the load. The unit reported they had been receiving sporadic small arms fire and suggested we divert to another location. A quick calculation of our remaining fuel told us that we either had to deliver the load as planned or punch it off into the jungle. Punching off the load was not an option that we could live down.

The aircraft commander made a quick broadcast call for any gunships in the area. By good fortune, two Cobras from the 2/20 ARA were in the area and immediately headed our way. Quick coordination with the fire base and the Cobra team set us up on a direction to land with the Cobras providing suppressive fire along our flight path. I started the approach and on short final, I caught a glimpse of a burst of red smoke just out my cockpit door. As I turned to look, the Cobra was making a hard right break, and I saw a massive human that was packed into the front seat of the aircraft. I turned my focus back to delivering the sling load and then made a rapid vertical departure above 2000 feet and headed to our planned refuel point.

I called the Cobras to thank them for the support and couldn't resist asking if the massive human I saw in the lead bird was code name Cliff. The response was "Hell yes!" Cliff was in my flight class and went on to Cobra training after graduation. Now seven months later, he was flying gun cover for me in a combat zone!

The Cobras followed us to the refuel point and Cliff and I got to catch up and share a few laughs. I pointed out to him that the burst of red smoke from his flechette rocket was right outside my door and was damn close! He grinned and replied, "You wanted their heads down, didn't you?"

Looking back, I can't think of anyone that I would rather have flown gun cover for me that day than my friend and classmate Cliff.

SUMNER "SKIP" J. DAVIS

U.S. Army — Aviator — Captain, Corps of Engineers
Dates of Military Service (Active and Reserve): 10 Nov 1966 to 1 Jun 2006
Units Served with In Vietnam: 213th Engineer Detachment (Construction);
508th Engineer Detachment; 510th Engineer Detachment; 187th Assault
Helicopter Company.
Dates in Vietnam: 15 May 1966 — 25 Dec 1969 / 6 Jan 1971 — 18 Dec 1971
Highest Rank Held: Captain (O-3)
Place of Birth and Year: Melrose, Massachusetts — 1945

WELCOME TO VIETNAM

I enlisted in the United States Army in 1966. I had lost my college deferment in June and within two weeks the local draft board was chasing me. After 16 weeks of Basic and Advanced infantry training, I was selected for Officer Candidate School. This turned into a not-so-great 23-week experience of restricted living, learning, and running seven days a week, 24 hours a day. It all culminated with being commissioned as a Second Lieutenant in September 1967. After a short assignment in Texas, I received orders to the Republic of South Vietnam.

Vietnam has its own characteristics which make it unique. Sounds. Smells. Colors. It has a different energy, unique to the various areas one was assigned. I was ordered to the Mekong Delta known as the rice bowl of Southeast Asia. The heat could be overwhelming. Located to the south of Saigon, it was only slightly less foreboding than the other regions to the north. The geography was unvaried with little elevation change above sea level. But it is hot. And damp. And just a little threatening.

Starting my Vietnam service as a Second Lieutenant, I received annual promotions to First Lieutenant and then to Captain. I spent the better part of 19 months assigned to the Engineer Support Team in Can Tho. At last, on Christmas Day 1969, I returned to my home outside of Boston. I was free from the hostile environment of Southeast Asia and the threat of people wishing to kill me. I would have just nine more months to serve before my release from active duty.

And then things got interesting.

While still at home during Christmas, I received a change order to report to the Rotary Wing Officer Flight Training Course at Fort Walters, Texas. Flight School was something I had wanted to do from the time I graduated from high school seven years earlier, but I had failed to qualify due to near sighted vision. Throughout Basic and Advanced Infantry Training, Officer Candidate School, and 19 months assigned to the Military Assistance Command Vietnam (MACV) Engineer Support Team in Can Tho, I took Flight Physicals whenever I could convince someone to schedule me. I went from Second Lieutenant to Captain while "In-Country" Vietnam from May 1968 to December 1969. I covered just about every corner of the Mekong Delta building troop billets, mess halls, roads, and helipads. Often, I begged helicopter rides to get to the job sites as the Mekong Delta had a limited and primitive road network. And then I came home to a late Christmas present. My last, and first acceptable, flight physical had been approved.

The New Year found me at Fort Walters, Texas, just northwest of Dallas. After completing the Officer Rotary Wing Basic Flight Training Course, I was ordered to the Officer Rotary Wing Flight Course at Fort Rucker, Alabama. Upon graduation, I was sent to the AH-1G Cobra Attack Helicopter Course in Savannah, Georgia.

As a result of my successful completion of Flight School, I was awarded another tour in Vietnam.

While still at the 90th Replacement Battalion in Long Binh east of Saigon, Carl Key, a fellow Flight School graduate, and I were provided the courtesy of a personal interview at the 1st Aviation Brigade Headquarters due to our seniority as Captains. We were offered staff assignments with Brigade, and we stated appreciation for the offer but requested an assignment to a Cobra Unit in the field. This process was repeated at the 12th Group at Plantation Base Camp within the Long Binh Base and the 11th Combat Aviation Battalion in Phu Loi. Eventually, we arrived at the 187th Assault Helicopter Company (187th AHC) in Tay Ninh. I was finally a Combat Helicopter Pilot in Vietnam, and I was going to fly the AH-1G.

Well, not quite.

Captain Key and I reported to the unit commander, Major Joe D. Carothers. While welcoming enough, MAJ Carothers deflated my pipe dream of just flying quickly enough.

"Welcome to the Crusaders. As a new member of the Rat Pack Gun platoon, you are the senior aviator. As such, you will assume Command of the Platoon in two weeks. Get up to speed and complete your check ride. Handle the transition from Captain Siddons. And do not lose any aircraft or crews!"

Following our in-briefing from the Commander, we then had the pleasure of meeting Captain James Siddons, then the Platoon Commander. Jim said he was glad we were assigned to his Platoon. It was an informal meeting with Jim, Captains Tom Balfour, and Bernie Yeager, and First Lieutenant Rodney Woods in the "hootch" which served as Siddon's quarters.

"Welcome to the Rat Pack gentlemen. We have billets available for you and an aggressive in-country orientation program planned for you." Captain Siddons said. "We need to get you up to speed as quickly as possible because we are going to be busy soon enough." I looked at CPT Siddons for a moment trying to be respectful of the news of my orders from MAJ Carothers. I spoke for Carl and myself when I responded "We appreciate that very much, but…" I was quickly interrupted by Siddons.

"What is your Date of Rank?"

"September 7, 1969," I responded as gently as I could. Siddons face froze just for just an inkling and then he responded enthusiastically "I will be the best damn Assistant Platoon Leader you have ever seen!" At that moment, Captain Key cleared his throat. Siddons asked, "And yours?" After Carl responded, Siddons turned to me and said, "I will be the best damn Section Leader you have ever seen!"

And my introduction to Vietnam Aviation was complete. Captain Siddons had gone from Platoon Commander to line pilot with admiral style. He had also graciously defused a tricky situation with his officers and friends all present.

Just as I was taking command of the Rat Pack at the end of January 1971, we were conducting regular support for our UH-1H "Huey" Lift Platoons. Then the 7th Air Force Command came knocking on our door. As reported in the Unit History Files of the 187th AHC:

The enemy had been carrying the war to the Cambodians during the past few months, in an attempt to regain the lost sanctuaries and depot areas of pre-1970. Our own Air Force was providing the much-needed air power to support the allied effort against the enemy in Cambodia. But because the enemy hid himself too near to innocent villagers, the big bombs and napalm of the Air Force couldn't get close enough. A more surgical method of destruction was called for, it was decided to fill the gap with Cobra gunships.

Chosen for the job was the Cobra Gun Platoon of the 187th: "The Rat Pack" and "Stand Down" soon became a bad joke in "The Holy Land", in spite of the disappointing indications that the "Crusaders" would be among the last to leave the country, the "Rats" answered the call with typical professionalism and efficiency. With light fire teams consisting of two Cobra Gunships led by one Huey Command and Control ship, the "Crusaders" once more carried the flight "over the fence."

Since the incursion in 1970, the U. S. Air Force (USAF) had been in support of the Cambodian Military against the North Vietnam Regular Army. As such, the USAF wanted precision aerial interdiction fire along the Mekong River from the Cambodian Capital of Phnom Penh to the South Vietnam border. They called on the Rat Pack AH-1Gs.

From February 1, 1971, the Rat Pack became part of a multinational interdiction team. Along with the Rat Pack's two Cobras, a 187th AHC Command and Control UH-1H (C&C) which carried a USAF Officer, a Military Assistance Command—Vietnam (MACV) US Army Officer, and representatives from the Cambodian and Vietnamese Military flew missions into Cambodia several times a week. C&C would search areas along the Mekong River from Phnom Penh, the Capital City, south to the RSVN border for North Vietnamese (NVA) routes and storage areas. There were known locations of reported suspicious activity and the C&C Team would search along the Mekong River in attempts to uncover enemy operations. When they identified a target, they would call in our gunships and clear them to fire within an extremely specific area. We would shoot high explosive rockets, mostly at Sampan-type cargo boats or gun emplacements along the riverbanks. It was an interesting mission, vastly different from our usual support missions protecting our Huey Flights.

The Rats flew 306 sorties (aircraft missions) and logged 251 hours of blade time (actual flight time in the air).

During what had become a routine interdiction mission on the twelfth of February 1971, one of our Cobra Teams received ground-based rifle fire after completing a gun run. Against most odds of the time, the aircraft took bullets to the tail rotor which provides its directional control. As the aircraft began to rotate to the left, the pilot-in-control (PIC) began an exceedingly difficult emergency landing procedure which almost always resulted in a serious crash. However, this time, the PIC executed a near perfect landing. In the resulting landing of the aircraft skids, (Cobras were equipped with tubular landing "skids" rather than wheels), the aircraft ran upon a rice paddy dike and stopped leaning up and to the left. This caused the main rotor blades to hit the dike to the aircraft's left rear.

What happened next was a tragedy belying the amazing job of flying on the part of the PIC. As reported in the Unit After Actions Report for 12 February 1971:

12 Feb. 71 — Aircraft #297 (AH-1G) lost its tail rotor while on a special mission in Cambodia and the pilot AC/ 1LT. Rodney Woods performed a near perfect autorotation. The only damage to the aircraft was a broken left skid. After the aircraft came to rest very near to the enemy positions, the front seat pilot/gunner (**Cpt. James Garland Siddons**) jumped from the aircraft and ran for the C&C ship. Cpt. Siddons was struck by the rotor blade and killed instantly. The crew chief of the C&C ship (**SP5 William John Johnson**) in an effort to retrieve the body of Cpt. Siddons was also hit by the still spinning rotor blade and was also killed. The downed Cobra was later recovered.

From Official Report: Siddons, James Garland. Class 70-14, Cause: Ground Casualty. How Died: Shot down. Received ground fire after autorotation. Siddons ran upslope (sic) to suppress enemy fire with pistol, hit by rotor blade.

Jim Siddons, the man I had just replaced as Gun Platoon Leader 12 days earlier, was returned to his family and given a hero's welcome. He left behind a new wife, his parents and two brothers, Mark Siddons (five years junior to Jim) and John Siddons (nine years younger to Jim). He was dedicated to his family, the 187th AHC, and to our Nation. He was a young volunteer, just as Rodney Woods was a volunteer, and died serving his fellow aviators. I will cherish the memory of my experiences with these people for as long as I live.

Now, some 50 years later, Jim, Rodney, the entire 187th AHC personnel, and the men and women of the Vietnam War are with us every day. Some of them are old and gray. Some, as with Jim Siddons, are forever young.

RICK LESTER

US Army — Aviator, Armor Officer

Dates of Military Service: 1967 to 1994

Unit Served with in Vietnam: 10th Combat Aviation Battalion (1st tour); 48th Assault Helicopter Company (2nd tour)

Dates in Vietnam: 1969, 1970 to 1971

Highest Rank Held: Lt. Colonel (O-5)

Place of Birth and Year: Marietta, GA — 1948

A WARRIOR'S TRUE HEART

I arrived in Vietnam for my second tour as an Army helicopter pilot on 6 February 1970 and was assigned to the 48th Assault Helicopter Company. At that time the unit was co-located with the 9th "Whitehorse" Division of the Republic of Korea Army near the village of Ninh Hoa. While many of our missions were in support of this Division, our unit worked with units from the Armies of South Vietnam, Australia, and the United States all throughout the Central Highlands area of II Corps.

On 10 January 1971, I deployed a light fire team of two UH-1 C model gunships along with two UH-1 H model "Huey" lift ships in support of U. S. units deployed near Bao Loc and Gia Nia. This mission required us to mount specialized equipment manufactured by General Electric for the Army's Chemical Corps on one of our lift ships. This equipment was designed to detect the "scent" of humans based on secreted fluids. I had seen this equipment at 5th Special Forces Headquarters in Nha Trang in the "backpack" configuration designed to be carried by infantrymen on "search and destroy" missions.

I asked the 5th Group Operations Officer if the concept worked. He responded, "I guess so, it was sensitive enough to detect the perspiration of every one of my team members that accompanied me on the last mission!" He also said the Viet Cong had quickly adapted to the "people sniffer" equipment and would leave buckets of urine near potential ambush sites.

I wasn't very enthusiastic about allowing my slick crew to employ this equipment, flying at low altitude at reduced airspeed in the mountains in hopes that "Nguyen" had worked up a sweat carrying guns and ammo down from Hanoi! My copilot for the mission was my best friend, Lt Ed Bilbrey. (I wrote about his dedication in the AVVBA's first book, "I'm Ready To Talk"). He asked why, if we only had equipment for one Slick, were we having the second ship fly with us? He looked kind of surprised when I said, "To rescue the crew from the 'Sniffer Ship' after they get shot down."

Which brings any good gunship pilot to express what was coldly considered to be the only benefit from this mission, that any VC or NVA soldier would find such a vulnerable target hard to resist. It wouldn't be his bladder or armpits which would give his position away, it would be his eagerness to engage the crew of an American helicopter so stupid as to fly so low and slow over their position.

It was just that which enabled us to engage numerous targets of opportunity over the days of our deployment and place accurate fire into enemy positions throughout the designated area of operation and set off many secondary explosions. The equipment never actually detected and alerted us to the presence of any enemy troops, even as we were taking heavy fire.

We ended our mission in Lam Dong Province at Dalat/Cam Ly Airfield to refuel. After refueling, we were positioning our aircraft to park on the ramp near the tower. As we hovered across the ramp, the tower controller directed us to hold our positions clear of the runway saying that a USAF C-7 Caribou transport plane was inbound for a single engine approach. Immediately after the controller's call, we heard the pilot call that he was turning right base for a single engine landing. I alerted my crew to watch the approach and as we looked toward the approach end of the runway, we were distressed as we immediately noticed the rapid sink rate of the aircraft and then witnessed the aircraft hit the runway with tremendous impact.

The aircraft bounced back into the air and veered left as the pilot was apparently applying power to the still operating right engine. The continued application of power caused the aircraft to quickly "cork screw" farther left to the point where the left wing impacted the ground off the left, down sloping side of the runway. This contact immediately pivoted the nose of the aircraft into the ground, setting off a violent cartwheeling effect as the right wing, tail, left wing, and nose impacted the ground in sequence as the aircraft continued out of control down the runway. In this sequence both wings were sheared from the aircraft and bounced alongside until the aircraft slid to a stop off the left, far end of the runway. The fuselage was broken open on the right side with the nose and tail both pointed down the left slope of the terrain.

As the aircraft finally came to a stop, a large fire erupted. I immediately exited my aircraft and sprinted to the wreckage to assist the survivors. When I arrived at the right front of the aircraft, I noted movement in the cockpit and realized there were three crew members attempting to exit through the rescue hatch on top. The hatch had been freed but was jammed as the crew members were all pushing against it in their haste to clear the smoke-filled cockpit. I climbed onto the top of the cockpit and positioned myself by the rescue door and pushed down to get the door evenly back in the track and directed them to stop pushing against the door until I could jettison it. Once they backed away, I was able to lift the door and toss it clear to the left side of the fuselage. The three crew members excitedly climbed from the cockpit and as they rushed past me, knocked me into the fire on the left side of the fuselage.

I ran out of the fire around the front of the aircraft, shouting to ask them if there were other people onboard and someone shouted back saying, "Our NCO was in the back." I then entered the fractured fuselage through the jagged hole on the right side and worked my way to the back of the aircraft but didn't see anyone. I went back to the front and worked my way along the steps to again check the cockpit area. When I was certain the interior was clear, I turned to exit through the torn fuselage and noted the area was now filled with fire from the fuel-soaked grass burning around the aircraft. The fire and smoke were being drawn through the opening and filling the interior.

I was afraid of being trapped so I held my breath and ran through the opening. I heard people shouting for me to go right because I was running upslope toward the detached wing and engine. As I moved right, I saw someone wearing a flight suit run up the slope from the back of the aircraft and I shouted to ask if he was part of the crew and if anyone else was onboard. He shouted, "Two more!"

I quickly ran back through the opening in the fuselage to reenter the aircraft and ran through the interior again looking for any other survivors until I was finding it hard to breath. I ran back out of the aircraft and saw the man who had run from behind the aircraft running toward me with another crew member telling me everyone was accounted for.

I ran until I was free of the burning terrain. Since my helmet visor was down, it took me a few minutes to clear my eyes. I realized the fire was being fed by an arc of flames spewing from the right engine upslope from the aircraft and decided to attempt to extinguish this fire. I saw other personnel now running toward the aircraft and one was carrying a large fire extinguisher. I asked them to help me. They tossed me the fire extinguisher so I went back into the fire, ran toward the burning engine, and hurriedly put the extinguisher into action.

There was an immediate explosive burst of flame which launched me through the air to a point down slope below the nose of the aircraft. The next thing I was aware of was my Crew Chief, James Schaefer, hitting me with a seat cushion trying to extinguish the flames on my flight suit.

My eyes, mouth, and tongue were causing me a lot of pain and I quickly pulled off my helmet. Schaefer grabbed my arm and pulled me up the slope toward the runway. I checked with all the crew from the Caribou and, though two of them looked pretty bloody, they said they were okay. I offered to assist them if they wanted one of our aircraft to take them to the USAF hospital at Cam Ranh Bay.

They were obviously in shock but told me that the Tower operator had contacted their unit at Cam Ranh Bay and their unit was sending an aircraft with emergency personnel. I was having difficulty breathing and my eyes were causing a great deal of pain. A vehicle arrived at the scene and there were two MACV medics on board. One of the pilots from the Caribou crew brought the medics to me and they began to assess and treat my burns.

The weather began to deteriorate. I asked the lead pilot of our lift element if he wanted to depart. He didn't want to leave until he was certain I was going to be taken care of. Over the next hour or so the burns became extremely painful. My eyes were swollen shut and my tongue was swollen so badly, I wasn't able to speak and had great difficulty breathing. The MACV medics decided to take me to their compound where they were equipped to do a tracheotomy if my breathing didn't improve.

When they were treating me there, the swelling and burns caused my lips and nostrils to split open and the pain became even more intense. The medics said they had received a radio call that the USAF Caribou had arrived at the airfield and decided to return there so the USAF medical personnel could assist me. Prior to placing me in their vehicle, they gave me a shot of morphine and wrapped some sort of medically saturated gauze around my face. I was afraid the morphine would make me sleep and the swelling would get worse, and I would suffocate.

When I arrived back at the airfield, two of the pilots who had been in the crash took me to the USAF team. My copilot, Lt Ed Bilbrey, had checked our crews into a local hotel with the USAF personnel and the medical team helped me to my room. Ed was my roommate. The medical team briefed him about what to watch for and said they would be nearby if my breathing didn't improve, or if I went into greater distress.

Ed was very concerned about my condition. I heard him telling one of pilots how bad the burns were. When Ed came back into the room, I asked him to help me stay awake and he told me not to worry, he was going to take care of me. The pain became more unbearable and every time I took a breath I would have to fight to keep from panicking. Ed said the USAF doctor said if I continued to have trouble breathing, they would do a tracheotomy. I didn't want that.

We heard someone knocking loudly at the door, and I could hear the voices of Americans laughing and joking with Vietnamese women. When Ed opened the door, he saw two of the pilots from the Caribou, who sounded pretty intoxicated, saying they came to thank me for saving their lives. Standing next to them were two Vietnamese hookers, each carrying a bucket full of ice and beer. They had hired the girls to help thank us.

I asked Ed what was going on and he explained. At about the same time I heard one of the Caribou pilots tell the other one in a distressed voice, "Oh s**t! Look at his face! He's really F***ed up!" Then Ed pushed them all out of the doorway while he dressed them down. He eventually opened the door and explained what was going on.

I told Ed to respectfully decline but tell them to leave the beer. The pilots insisted we allow the girls to stay and said, "And when you're done, let us know and we'll bring you two more!" The next thing I was aware of was one of the girls sitting on the bed next to me "introducing" herself. I handed Ed my wallet and told him to give them some money and tell them to leave. Ed said, "Look I know you're not married, if you're feeling up to it, I'll leave both of them with you and wait outside with your wallet and pistol." I couldn't believe it, but then heard him laughing and scurrying the "ladies" away.

I told Ed that I would do the same for him and leave both the girls with him, but he declined. Finally, he sent the girls on their way with a hand full of MPC and closed the door. I told him I had heard that if for some reason one of your main senses is degraded, that the others become more acute. I realized that since I couldn't see or smell, my hearing was at its best. I told Ed about hearing every word the USAF pilots said and then joked that our reputation as Army Aviators would now certainly be ruined when the two hookers walked back into the bar after having only being in our room for ten minutes. Ed asked me if I wanted to try a beer and I told him it might help me clear my throat. He said, "Yeah, and it might kick start that morphine shot!" I was now in so much pain that I responded, "In that case, give me two!"

As I tried to drink the beer, I noticed I couldn't really taste anything. I could only sense that it was ice cold and soothing to my burned mouth. I laughed and told it him it was the first time that the infamous Vietnamese beer "Export 33" (commonly referred to by the troops as 'ba muoi ba), [i.e., Vietnamese language for the number 33]), ever seemed drinkable.

The "visit" provided a brief distraction, but soon the pain was really becoming intense. Ed used the ice from the beer buckets and made a compress that he placed on my neck to help counter the swelling. I could tell he was really worried. When some of my crew came to check on me, I heard him telling them to go get the Air Force Flight Surgeon. When he came back into the room, I joked and said I thought he had changed his mind and went to get the hookers. He laughed and then seemed to get very serious.

Ed told me he had only been married for a few months before he left for Vietnam. We had talked before about how he met his wife and how much she meant to him. He then asked me if I recalled the difficult trials from Survival, Evasion, Resistance and Escape, (SERE) training we had to go through before deploying to Vietnam? He talked about being captured in training and being made to strip down to his underwear and having a soiled sandbag tied around his head. He said that he gave a lot of thought to what POWs had to endure.

He talked about his standards saying, "I know in the days of hippies and free love this might sound old fashioned or 'corny', but I took a vow in marriage, and I don't ever intend to break that vow. A man's word is his bond, and you have to live by certain standards. I believe that any man who will violate his vow to his wife, would coldly throw his best friend under the bus. I made a decision in that mock POW camp in training. You might be able to take all my earthly possessions, but you can never take what's in my heart!"

I wasn't surprised; that's all I'd ever seen in Ed. He worked his tail off to be the best at everything. I talked in the first *I'm Ready to Talk* book about how he got stuck being the unit's Mess Officer and excelled. He always took care of our crews, and he was now nursing me through my injuries. Ed was worried about me and thinking about home, and it was getting a little melancholy in our, "No Tell, Motel" room. To bring us back with a little warrior bravado, I thrust my hand out and said, "Ed, I love you like a brother and want to shake your hand!"

As I felt him lock on to my hand, I said, "I have to tell you the truth, Ed. You're a better man than me. I'm not married, and I really wanted to partake of the grateful USAF pilot's offerings, but not being able to see, I knew that if I did, the next time we were in the Vill' in Dalat, you would point to some really old stooped over Mama San with teeth blackened by chewing beetle nut and point to her saying, 'Look! There's one of the girls you serviced in our room that night.'"

Ed hugged me and we both laughed our butts off until we heard someone banging at the door. Ed told me he thought that was probably the Air Force crew bringing "…our second 'thank you' gift."

Ed opened the door to find the USAF flight surgeon staring back and asking if he was interrupting anything. Ed explained we were just having a couple of beers and offered him one as he tried to remove the wrap from my face. That was all I needed for reality to come back in. The doctor didn't like what he saw and heard me straining to breath. He asked Ed how much beer I drank and then commented that the form-aldehyde the brewery induced into the brewing process to age their beer would only complement what he was giving me—a shot of Benadryl and more morphine.

I don't remember much after that, I just remember that when I woke up in the USAF hospital at Cam Ranh Bay, the first voice I heard was Ed's. He said the pilots from the Caribou unit had been coming by the room to check on me and they seemed to know all the nurses, so I was being well cared for. I stayed there until I could open my eyes and get examined by the flight surgeon and his crew. The flight surgeon from my unit stopped by the next morning after being flown to the hospital by my roommate from Ninh Hoa. He was briefed by the USAF team, and I was released back to my unit. I had to cope with wounds for a while and finally got cleared back to flying status.

I was the Officer-in-Charge of our advance party to relocate to Dong Ha in late January for the LAMSON 719 operation into Laos, but DER-OSED home on 8 February as the operation kicked off. On 11 March, my friend Ed Bilbrey was shot down in Laos near LZ Brown while providing cover for the lift ships extracting South Vietnamese soldiers.

Ed was killed instantly, and the aircraft crashed among the enemy anti-aircraft positions. His copilot and crew chief were able to carry the severely wounded door gunner to a point where they could be safely extracted. Ed's body had to be left in the aircraft until allied troops could fight their way in to effect recovery three days later. They found Ed's body removed from the aircraft and stripped of his helmet, flight suit, New Mexico Military Institute class ring, the Benrus Chronometer watch on a sterling silver and turquoise watch band that his dad had especially made for his college graduation, his Saint Christopher's medal, and his wedding band.

I think often of Ed and can't help but wonder what he would have accomplished in life. He was prepared to accept his fate in every way. He demonstrated courage, dedication, professionalism respect, commitment, and love for God and country in his every action

The North Vietnamese soldiers had taken all Ed's earthly possessions, but they couldn't take what was in his heart.

M. JEROME (JAY) ELMORE

Navy — Disbursing Officer and Officer of the Deck aboard a destroyer escort

Dates of Military Service: 1968-1974

Ship Served On: USS Roark DE-1053

Dates Served in Vietnam: Two deployments. Jan. 7 to Aug. 10 ,1971 and Feb. 8 to Aug. 31, 1972.

Highest Rank Held: Lieutenant (O-3)

Place and Date Born: Eufaula, Alabama — 1948

CYCLONE

No sea story is worth its weight in plunder without a description of a ship's weathering a gale. So here it is, except in our case it was a much more serious cyclone. (Hurricanes and typhoons in the Southern Pacific and Indian Ocean are referred to simply as cyclones)

After departing the Gulf of Tonkin in June 1971, the *USS Roark* DE-1053, rather than being sent directly to its home port in San Diego, was ordered "down under" to Australia and New Zealand on what might be referred to as a friendship visit. On the 26th of July, after a wonderful visit and R&R, we left New Zealand. Our navigator set a course north by northeast with planned stops at Pago Pago (American Samoa) and Hawaii for refueling. When we arrived at Pago Pago on the 29th the *USS Henderson* and the *USS Turner Joy* were there refueling. Since there were only two fueling berths, and because we were the junior ship, we stood off the island waiting for the two senior ships to leave.

Perhaps it was my imagination, but it seemed to me they were taking an unusually long time to refuel. More like they were enjoying the day on a tropical island as we steamed back and forth offshore! (Maybe if the commodore on the Turner Joy had known our captain would later become a four-star admiral, he would have been more accommodating.) We finally entered the harbor late in the day with instructions to refuel quickly and rendezvous with the other two ships already on their way to Hawaii, which we did. Unfortunately, the delay put us in the path of a growing tropical depression.

After we got underway, the winds increased, and the seas worsened as night fell. When I came to the bridge at midnight to relieve the Officer of the Deck for the midwatch (Midnight to 4AM) the wind was beginning to howl, and water was breaking over the bow. I relieved the watch and as the OOD for the next four hours knew I was the captain's eyes and ears on the bridge while he slept. The ship was fighting through the waves and a drenching rain. The ship's gyroscopic horizontal stabilizers could be felt working hard to reduce the ship's rolling. As the night progressed, the wind, rain, and waves increased. I brought all the lookouts inside except the after lookout who was moved to a secure nook. He was still needed to sound the alarm if someone were washed overboard, although there would have been little we could do other than deploy a raft and mark his position.

As things worsened, I kept an eye on the anemometer and saw the wind speeds increasing toward cyclone (hurricane) range. The seas were, as mariners call them, confused, but with monstrous swells. The ship was pounding into the waves and bucking and rolling violently. The helmsman had his legs spread wide as he fought to maintain heading. It was difficult to stand. I constantly checked the inclinometer to ensure our rolling motion was inside our design parameters. It was, but not by much. Too much roll and the ship would not be able to recover.

While we had two boilers, we only had one engine (a geared turbine) and one screw and shaft, so there was not a lot of room for error. We were the second of the Knox class destroyer escorts built and the first to be deployed with the new design. I called down to engineering to see how things were going. As always, these incredible sailors, or snipes as they were sometimes called, working several decks below, said they had things under control, somehow working miracles to keep the boiler feed water and steam under control in the most challenging of situations. But I still worried about possible shortcomings in the ship's untested new design. A fault in the ship's design had already resulted in a major engine room fire in January off Midway, requiring the ship to be towed back to Pearl Harbor and being out of commission for refurbishment for over a month, delaying our reporting to Vietnam.

Any incidence where we lost power or steerageway in these conditions would be fatal. I was concerned that loss of the stabilizers which countered the rolls might pose a serious threat to the ship as well. You could already feel the ship shudder throughout as the stabilizers fought the rolls. I kept an eye on the inclinometer, as the ship took a pounding.

As part of the night orders, the captain had directed that we maintain an aggressive speed to rendezvous with the other two ships. As the seas built and the ship beat into them, I called the captain, woke him up, and requested permission to reduce speed. To my surprise he said he would like to keep our present speed so we would reach our rendezvous point on time. So, I did.

The ship now would rise on a wave and plunge down into the next with water covering the entire fo'c'sle. Waves appeared to be approaching twenty feet in height and were beginning to break on themselves. The wind whipped over the crest of the white capped waves sending blinding spray across the ocean's surface. Even though the night was pitch black, one could see the ocean covered in white foam. Then, one rogue wave, much larger than the others, hit us, smashing into the bridge which was over thirty feet above the waterline and tearing the windshield wipers off our windows. Our heavy 5-inch 54 caliber gun on the forward deck was knocked partially off its mount! The whole ship shook from the impact. I heard the buzzer on the sound powered phone to the captain's cabin hum. I picked up the phone and he calmly said, "You can reduce speed now."

People unfamiliar with the sea have asked me "Oh, you were on a small ship, did it rock much?" I just smile and reply, "A little."

CARL H. "SKIP" BELL, III

U.S. Army—Armored Cavalry Officer, Aviator

Dates of Military Service (Active and Reserve): 1967 to 1998

Units Served with In Vietnam: A Troop, HHT, B Troop, 1st Squadron, 4th Cav, 1st Inf Div (First Tour); C Troop, 3rd Squadron, 17th Air Cav; 18th Corps Aviation Co; G3, HQ 1st Aviation BDE (Second Tour)

Dates in Vietnam: Feb 1969 to Feb 1970; Feb 1972 to Feb 1973

Highest Rank Held: Colonel (O-6)

Place of Birth and Year: Decatur, GA — 1945

RESUPPLY MISSION TO SURROUNDED FORT

In May 1972, I was pilot-in-command of a UH-1H helicopter belonging to one of the flight platoons of the 18th Corps Aviation Company (CAC), which was the General Support Aviation Company for Military Region IV (the Mekong Delta area of South Vietnam). The 18th CAC (Callsign: Green Delta) was based in at Can Tho Airfield; it was a composite unit that contained two platoons of UH-1H Iroquois ("Huey") helicopters, one platoon of CH-47 Chinook helicopters, and one platoon of OH-58 Kiowa helicopters.

That unit organization came about during the drawdown of U.S. Army aviation assets throughout South Vietnam — as units went home, portions were left in-country to provide ongoing aviation support and in the Delta, helicopters with a Combat Support mission went to the 18th CAC. There was also one Air Cavalry Troop (C/16 Cav, Callsign: Darkhorse) remaining in the Delta, and they were also based at Can Tho Airfield.

Most of our missions were single-ship province support missions, but we also had a VIP mission — we provided the Commanding General of Military Region IV with his daily Command and Control aircraft. Those of us given the province support missions would fly out to the appropriate province headquarters, report to the tactical operations center (TOC) and receive our missions for the day. Most of these involved flying advisors or local leaders from town to town, resupply of

Regional Forces/Popular Forces outposts, mail delivery, and the occasional medevac.

Medevac missions could be a bit "hairy" since we were usually single-ship (no gun cover other than the two M-60 machineguns on our aircraft). In the case of the medevac, we usually didn't know what the enemy situation was (other than someone on the ground was wounded) and it was very difficult to get a clear picture of the best routes of entry/ egress, actual number of wounded, cause(s) of the wounds, etc. Also, we had no medically trained personnel on-board the aircraft, so the only thing we could do was pick up the casualties and take them to the nearest hospital. Since we usually had a MACV (Military Assistance Command Vietnam) advisor and his Vietnamese counterpart in the back of the aircraft, they rendered first aid to the casualties and directed us to the nearest medical facility.

I had spent the first part of that tour of duty flying Cobra gunships with an Air Cavalry troop, so moving to a Combat Support aviation company was a bit of a culture shock at first. In the Air Cavalry troop, we rarely (if ever) went on single-ship missions. Due to the nature of our business (direct combat with the enemy), we always tried to send at least two aircraft on each mission; that way, if someone got shot down rescue was close by (or at least somebody else would know where you went down). In the Combat Support unit, the vast majority of our missions were single-ship. That meant that each aircraft was responsible for every aspect of the mission (artillery flight following, navigation, knowing where to find fuel, etc.—in the Air Cavalry troop, those duties were relegated to the Air Mission Commander; the rest of us just flew and did what we were told).

I think the biggest difference was the lonely feeling that came with single-ship missions. By that time in the war, it was not unusual to fly for 30 minutes or more without seeing another aircraft. For someone used to going out and back in a group, this was initially somewhat disconcerting. I came to enjoy it after a while, though. It was nice to be my own boss and to be totally responsible for the outcome of the mission.

My first tour of duty in Vietnam I had been an Armored Cavalry

Platoon Leader and later that tour an Armored Cavalry Troop Commander. The nature of our employment was such that we were given areas of operation (AO) for which we were responsible and how we patrolled those areas, kept our troops resupplied, maintained knowledge of platoon locations and situations, etc., was left up to the unit commander. Flying single-ship missions was a lot like that (there were fewer people involved, but every aspect of the mission was my responsibility).

On this particular day, we had been flying "ash and trash" missions for a province located in the northern Mekong Delta. When we landed at the province headquarters pad for the last mission of the day, the Senior Military Advisor (an Army Lieutenant Colonel) came out to the aircraft with a troubled look on his face. He said that there were a series of six triangular forts (two rows of three forts that were 2-3 kilometers apart) that had been manned by Regional Force/Popular Force (RF/PF) soldiers. Five of the six forts had been overrun and the final one was under siege. They were in desperate need of food and ammunition and the advisor asked if we could resupply them. He further stated that we could only make one pass over the place due to the large number of enemy soldiers in the area and the (strong) possibility that if we went in more than once we'd be shot down.

He said that we would have gunship cover (which told me how bad the situation was—we *never* had gun cover for any mission that I had ever heard of since I joined the 18th CAC). The guns were from the Air Cavalry Troop (C/16 Cav—callsign: Darkhorse) that was the other aviation unit at Can Tho airfield. I knew the lead gun pilot—CPT Tony Snow—he was a good guy and (as far as I knew) a competent gun pilot.

The plan was that we would fly at altitude (2,000') to the town nearest the area where the forts were located, drop out of the sky to treetop level, rendezvous with the guns (who would be flying at altitude) and be vectored into the fort under siege. We were not to land at the fort but were to do a 'quick stop' over it, toss out the supplies, and get out of there ASAP. The guns were cleared 'full suppression' in and out, which meant that they could engage anything outside the fort.

This was the first time I had worked with the Darkhorse guns, but the mission seemed to be pretty straightforward. We established radio contact with the gunships and flew the UH-1H at a pretty good clip (80-90 knots) away from the village and toward the forts. I had my co-pilot 'ride light' on the controls in case I got shot and switched the force trim on with the cyclic slightly aft so that if I went limp on the controls the aircraft would start up. I also instructed the door gunner and the crew chief to be ready to engage targets with the two M60 machineguns on the aircraft. In addition to the normal crew of the aircraft, we had a couple of Vietnamese soldiers in the back who were to kick out the supplies when we did the 'quick stop' over the fort.

Our flight path was to take us down the long axis of the forts (there were two rows of three forts running roughly east to west—we were flying west). Evidently there was some confusion with the gun pilots as to which fort we were to go to and we were initially vectored to the wrong one. As I was decelerating over the fort, the guys in the back started throwing out supplies—then one realized we were over the wrong fort and quit throwing out the supplies. I didn't notice us taking fire on the way in there, and that was probably why—the bad guys had already taken the fort and we were essentially resupplying them.

So now I had a half-loaded Huey and an un-accomplished mission. We had gone past the fort we were supposed to resupply, and we would need to turn around and move back through that area if we were to get any supplies to the beleaguered fort. I talked it over with the gun pilot and we decided that we'd try to hit the right one (even though the advisor had said not to make a second pass through the area).

As we started back toward the correct fort, we began to take a lot of small arms fire. I was trying to sound cool on the radio (I knew Tony Snow would be sure to 'razz' me about it later if I sounded panicky—assuming that we lived). I said, "We're taking fire, taking fire, taking fire" and unkeyed the radio. Snow came back with, "Which way, which way, which way?!"

Since most of the fire was from the three o'clock position of the aircraft, I wanted to say, "Three o'clock" but I could not remember the clock system for some reason, so I said, "From the right! From the right!"

We immediately had rockets landing under our aircraft and along our right flank. The Huey bounced like a car on a bumpy road as the rockets exploded, but the small-arms fire seemed to decrease a little.

I looked to the front and above the foliage I saw a South Vietnamese flag waving in the breeze about 150 meters ahead of us. I began to decelerate and pretty much stood the aircraft on its tail over the triangular fort. The remaining supplies were kicked out and we nosed the aircraft over and got out of there.

When I got back to the province headquarters pad, I told the senior advisor what had happened. He was disappointed that we hadn't gotten all the supplies where we were supposed to put them, but he appreciated what we had tried to do (especially when he saw the bullet holes and shrapnel holes in the aircraft).

Of course, when we got back to Can Tho and I got to the airfield officers club, I heard, "From the right! From the right!" in a loud squeaky high-pitched voice when I came in. It was Snow and I bought him a beer.

Approximately two years later, I was teaching Armor and Infantry Tactics at the U.S. Army Field Artillery School. As I was walking down the hall, I heard a loud, squeaky, high-pitched voice yelling, "From the right! From the right!" It was CPT Tony Snow and he was attending the Field Artillery Officers Advance Course (I didn't know that he was a Field Artilleryman — the guys in the Air Cavalry Troop usually wore crossed sabers on their uniform collar). It was good to see Tony again. I guess one never lives down some things that are done under duress. I certainly haven't.

SUMNER "SKIP" J. DAVIS

U.S. Army—Aviator—Captain, Corps of Engineers

Dates of Military Service (Active and Reserve): 10 Nov 1966 to 1 Jun 2006

Units Served with In Vietnam: 213th Engineer Detachment (Construction);
508th Engineer Detachment; 510th Engineer Detachment; 187th Assault
Helicopter Company.

Dates in Vietnam: 15 May 1966 – 25 Dec 1969 / 6 Jan 1971 – 18 Dec 1971

Highest Rank Held: Captain (O-3)

Place of Birth and Year: Melrose, Massachusetts – 1945

MEMORIES AND OTHER THOUGHTS OF A VIETNAM HELICOPTER PILOT

It has been almost 50 years since I last left the Republic of South Vietnam (now known officially as the Socialist Republic of Vietnam). Some of my memories are vivid while others I am not absolutely certain happened. That is what surviving in this life for more than seventy-five years does. Is it a memory? A recollection? A dream?

As an example, I honestly have no recollection of my return flight to California. It was one of eight round trips into the theater, into and from five different countries and three continents. I lost track of the actual flights themselves.

I do vividly remember my time with the 187th Assault Helicopter Company, both while it was assigned to Tay Ninh and later, Di An. Di An had been home to the 135th Assault Helicopter Company, the EMUs (EMU short for Experimental Military Unit I believe). It was a combined U.S. Army and Australian Military Unit utilizing the American Table of Organization and Equipment.

Earlier in my military service, I had the good fortune of not attending flight school until I had served time as an Engineer Construction Officer in the Mekong Delta. The 19 months I was there provided time for me to mature in such skills as leadership, personnel management, and tactical decision making. That might sound very mundane, but it truly was not. I had left a college campus in August 1966, entered the military, trained as an infantry squad member, attended Engineer Officer Candidate School, and was commissioned a Second Lieutenant in less than 10 months. Not exactly stellar leadership material at the time. My belabored point is I had not led the first squad maneuver by the time I was thrust into a combat zone. It was "On the Job Training" in its truest form. My responsibilities were not the same as the Infantry's, but it was to support the Infantry in their accomplishment of the mission.

In carrying out my responsibilities, I began to gain an appreciation of the importance of thorough mission planning. Not only the beans, bullets, and transportation of the action, but also the skills of each team member and how they could best meet the mission requirements. I had to learn how to communicate with the soldiers in such a way as to have them assume some ownership in their role personally.

Everyone involved had to understand the other members' responsibilities in the event they had to take over for them. Most importantly, I had to convince the soldiers of my own personal military competence, my confidence in our readiness to accomplish the assigned mission, my knowledge of each of their individual skills and abilities, and my commitment to provide for their welfare. Without these convictions, my soldiers would be less assured of the success of the mission and more reserved in their commitment.

Upon assignment to the 187th AHC, I immediately became the Platoon Leader for the "Rat Pack," the unit's Aerial Gun Platoon flying the AH-1G Cobra. It was the most thrilling flying job a person could hope to experience. As the "Old Man" of the platoon, I was more involved in management than flying. It was still amazing.

Then the reality of the war burst into my life.

I lost my first soldier after more the 19 months of service in a "Combat Zone." The world of a new Army Aviator in command of the sky returned to that of a combat leader sending men into harm's way.

As my tour moved into the spring and summer, I was assigned to a "Lift Platoon" of the UH-1H Huey Helicopter, again as the Platoon Leader. A utility style multi-role aircraft, the Huey was used by the 187th

AHC in the movement of ground troops into contact with the enemy, cargo hauling, and command and control of multi-ship missions. We flew mostly with the Army of Vietnam Infantry (ARVN) and special operations soldiers. We completed emergency evacuation of wounded when the Medevac Units were mission overloaded. And we hauled food.

During the late Summer of 1971, the 187th AHC moved to Di An, located just north of Saigon. We were co-located with the 135th AHC and shared the small airfield with that unit. I had begun to sense the completion of my combat tour and my return to the States. I believed the worst of this assignment was behind me.

Then the reality of the war returned.

I lost an entire crew of four on a mission that never got started. Bad weather had called it off and they were returning to Di An and safety. One of the flight of eight became disorientated and crashed, killing the entire crew. I was once again responsible for sending men into harm's way.

After the move to Di An, I assumed the position of the 187th AHC Operations Officer. In this role I was responsible for the assignment of missions to the three platoons. I would start my day between 5:30 and 6:00 in the morning distributing mission packets, aiding crews in getting ready to fly and coordinating maintenance. On the days I was not flying Command and Control for combat assaults, I would normally sneak out at 10:00 for a quick breakfast and then back to the office to check on the mission progress. Around 1:00 pm I would head to my quarters for a couple hours of rest and then back to Operations for the recovery of the day's flights. Around 6:00 pm I would head to dinner and then back to quarters for a little more rest. At 9:30 pm I was back in Operations to receive the next day's missions from our Battalion. Then my Operations Staff and the Unit Safety Office would break out the flying schedule and send the assignments to the Platoons. Around midnight, I would get to sleep to start all over again at 5:30 or 6:00.

I flew some missions and otherwise kept busy throughout October and November. Then I accepted a Command and Control Mission back up near Tay Ninh. It was an eight Ship Combat Assault near the Cambodian Border. We were supposed to conduct two lifts of ARVN Soldiers into a landing zone. As fortune would have it, the ARVN put too many soldiers on the first flight, and we really only required six aircraft to complete the second lift. I sent the last two aircraft in the flight back to the refuel point and planned to meet up with them there and return to Di An. I never thought. What if?

Then the reality of the war returned.

I lost an entire crew of four on a return from a completed mission. And another aircraft and crew of four had crashed but survived with life threatening injuries. I was once again responsible for sending men into harm's way.

I continued to fly for two more weeks, mostly support missions and VIP Flights. I stayed pretty much to myself, tending to administrative duties and writing recommendations for awards and completing soldier efficiency reports. I left Di An, physically, and returned to CONUS (Continental United States). I received a ground assignment, got married, left active duty, and raised a family. I subsequently served 33 more years in the Reserves and flew for a total of 35 years. I retired, had grandchildren, and had a great life.

In the recesses of my mind, though, there are those ten faces. These men present themselves to me almost every day. They are still young and full of themselves. They are doing what they wanted to do. They are flying helicopters in combat. They are the best our nation had. They are Heroes. I had sent them into harm's way, and they did not return.

It has been almost 50 years since I last left the Republic of South Vietnam. Not all of me came home. A part of me that reflects on those ten men is still in-country. I still see the crumpled and burned aircraft. I still see their faces on our flight line preparing for the day's missions. They have not aged as I have aged. They are not old as I am old. They smile at me as if to say, "We understand."

I wish I did.

DAN BENNETT

US Air Force—Flight Engineer

Dates of military service (Active and Reserve): 1967 to 1975

Units served with in Vietnam: 4th Special Operations Squadron, Da Nang
AB and 18thSOS, Nha Trang AB

Dates in Vietnam: 1967 to 1968; 1972 to 1973

Highest Rank Held: Tech Sergeant (E-6)

Place of Birth: Atlanta, GA—1947

A CHANCE R&R MEETING AND A HUEY RIDE

While going on R&R from my second tour of duty in Vietnam, I sat
next to an Army Captain (aviator) for the ride back to the States. We
talked and had a great time swapping stories. He was on his way to Texas, and I was on my way to Charleston, South Carolina. We parted ways
in LAX and agreed to meet at the same airport bar on our return trip.
He gave me his name and contact info and I put it in my wallet. I had a
wonderful 14 day stay at home, which I needed badly.

One day my wife asked me about the name she found in my wallet "Donald Nimblett." Apparently, she rummaged through my wallet,
looking for who knows what! I said he was a guy I rode with part of the
way out of Vietnam and agreed to meet up again on our way back. She
said, "I think I knew him." I was curious! She, being a military brat who
once lived in Germany, knew two boys named Donald and Ronald Nimblett and that Donald Nimblett dated her older sister, Shelia.

When I met Don at LAX airport, I asked if he knew the Griffin girls
when he was in high school in Germany. He said yes! Sure enough, he
was the same guy!

We arrived back in country and remained in touch. I mentioned to
Donald that my part in this war seems very minor compared to what
they do, and I had the desire to do more! I visited him at Long Binh and
in exchange I gave him a tour of our AC-119. He asked, "Where do you
put the key to start the engines?"

One evening over a beer, I asked if it would be possible for me to ride along in his UH-1. He was part of the 129th Assault Helicopter Company, supporting the 25th I.D. and I was looking for a little adventure. He said, "Sure" and he would arrange it.

My days off were few, but he sent for me on a day off and I was briefed on what to do and when to do it. I was given an M-16 and a side arm, chicken plate, and flak vest. It was suggested that I might want to sit on the chicken plate while we were airborne. Made sense to me!

I was armed with a Super 8MM movie camera and was able to get some very good footage of Special Forces Camps and other such exotic places like: Quan Loi, An Loc, Tay Ninh, Lai Khe, Cu Chi, Katum, Phouc Vinh, Moc Hoa, and I was afforded the luxury of a *two-night stay* on top of "Nui Ba Dinh" (Black Virgin Mountain) where I was quartered in a hole in the ground. Uncle Charlie sent several mortars in every night to remind us that he controlled the rest of that mountain.

I can't remember all the Fire Bases or Hamlets we visited, but it was a lot! All in all, I was having the time of my life! For the first time in my two tours of duty, I was able to shoot back. I probably never hit anything, but at least I was afforded the opportunity to try. On one of my adventures, while we were enjoying a cup of coffee at a Special Forces camp (Song Ba?), when a call came in saying two Armored Personnel Carriers had been ambushed. I was asked, "You want to stay here or come along?" That was my only ride out of that place, so I went along! A major from the Special Forces camp was on board, and we headed out to the ambush site. Everyone was locked and loaded. The pilot came to rest in the middle of a dirt road about 100 yards back from two burning APCs; he kept up the torque just in case.

It was very clear and ugly since there were multiple casualties scattered about. The major jumped out, hugging a ditch, and ran to where other troops were hunkered down. Small arms were popping everywhere. In a few minutes the major came back, and the UH-1 began a slow airborne spiral from the ambush site going out more with each rotation looking for the bad guys. We found them! That was my first experience with something other than small arms. A Chinese .51 caliber machine gun opened on us and the noise it made was heart stopping. Plus, the holes the rounds opened in the aircraft were amazing. Softball size holes! We had two casualties on board, and we quickly went back to Tay Ninh. That was probably one of the last trips I took with those guys. I have to admit, taking rounds from a .51 caliber gun was an eye-opening experience.

Captain Nimblett and I have remained friends until this very day. He retired from active duty as a Lt. Col. and lives in Austin, Texas. I intend to send my friend a copy of this book.

JON P. BIRD

US Army— Signal Corps Officer
Dates of Military Service (Active and Reserve): 1968 to 2000
Unit Served with in Vietnam: 221st Signal Company
Dates in Vietnam: Nov 1970 to Nov 1971
Highest Rank Held: Colonel (O-6)
Place of Birth and Year: Syracuse, NY—1944

In my second assignment while in Vietnam, I worked at two telecommunications centers at Long Binh, Russell Major Relay and the US Army Vietnam Telecommunications Center (USARV TCC). My overall mission was to come up with a plan to consolidate these centers, which I accomplished. While working at these TCCs, several incidents come to mind, here are two of them.

PRIOR PLANNING PREVENTS PEE-POOR PERFORMANCE

Working in any telecommunications center can be stressful, because of the 24/7 nature of operations. Personnel had to be 100% functional, which meant sober and drug-free. Any failures of these standards meant temporary removal of the individual's security clearance and removal from duty, too. This latter requirement meant periodic spot-checks for drug usage and there was only one way to test!

I found this out the hard way one morning. I had come into work for my 12-hour shift and like most days, had a cup or two of Army coffee, followed a bit later by a pit stop to relieve myself. I had barely sat down to do some work on my consolidation plan, when I received a phone call from headquarters telling me to assemble my men in front of the orderly room for a surprise Pee-Test.

While most of the Pee-Tests were going fine, I was in trouble, because I literally "gave at the office." So, I proceeded to drink what seemed like gallons of water and "bug juice (Kool-Aid)" and swore that my jungle fatigues were sloshing as I walked around, trying to loosen up and "answer the call." Perhaps an hour later, my prayers were answered. Oh, did I mention that a senior NCO was present to ensure that what you donated to the Pee Pool was yours and yours alone? Welcome to bureaucracy in Vietnam.

THE CASE OF THE PURLOINED MESSAGE

You'd think that moving "up the hill" to the USARV TCC near USARV headquarters would bring a better clientele. Not so. One day, I had a customer ring the service bell at our TCC and ask to speak to the OIC (Officer-In-Charge) That would be me! The officer, another Captain, represented an office that no longer wished to receive a classified multiple addressee message (one that went to many offices), because it had no further need. I politely explained that we could help him out, but it would take some time to contact the originator of the message and remove his office's name from this classified message. The Captain said his boss might be unhappy with my reply.

Later that day, there was another ring at the door asking for the OIC. When I showed up, a Lieutenant Colonel with fire in his eyes waved a message in my face and said, "Captain Bird, didn't my operations officer tell you that we no longer needed to receive this message?"

Knowing this wasn't going to go well, I reached behind me and rang the famous bell, asking quickly for my Senior NCOIC, Sergeant Rourke, a "lifer" who stood 5'8" tall and weighed about 260 pounds. I said to the Lieutenant Colonel, "I've called Sergeant Rourke here to witness my comments, in case I am making a mistake." When I said, "Is it true that it could take up to a couple of weeks to get the colonel's office removed from the classified message?" Rourke replied in the affirmative. "Then is it also true that TCCs only transmit and receive messages and are not required or allowed to store them, especially classified messages," I asked.

Again, Rourke replied, "Yes sir, you're right. We can't store messages, because we're required by regulations to deliver them in a timely manner."

I could see the colonel getting red around the collar, because it wasn't making sense to him and that I wasn't getting anywhere. Finally, out of desperation, I said: "OK, colonel, from today onward, you will no longer receive this message."

He replied, "That's more like it, Captain Bird."

Then I forcibly stated, "As a matter of fact, from today, your office will no longer receive ANY messages, no orders, no pay information, absolutely nothing." The colonel abruptly turned away, yelling over his shoulder, "We'll see about that, Captain Bird."

I went back in the TCC and told Sergeant Rourke to call Colonel Cassidy, the USARV G6 (communications-electronics officer), who may have been the most senior colonel in Vietnam. Yes, he was that old! When Colonel Cassidy came on the line, I said: "Sir, I need your help real bad!" Then I explained the entire situation and had Sergeant Rourke back me up on the facts. Cassidy said, "Don't worry, Captain Bird, I think I can take care of this problem for you."

Sure enough, about an hour later, the Captain came back, rang the famous bell and asked for the OIC. That would be me. When I opened the service window, he said, "OK, Captain Bird, where are those classified messages I have to pick up?" I never heard another word from this office again.

OVERAGE AT THE SUI CAT BEER & SODA DEPOT

As a young officer on a large base like Long Binh, your command may send you extra duties. For me, one such duty was that of being the Survey Officer for the Sui Cat Beer & Soda Depot, a warehouse where pallets of canned liquid refreshment were stored, located not too far from our compound. Clipboard in hand, I entered this hot building with my NCO and we began the laborious process of inventorying all the beer and soda at Long Binh. Hours passed, sweat poured down our brows, and at the end of the day, I somehow came up with what amounted to a $15,000 overage! Who knew?

I said to my NCO, "Holy sh_t, Sarge, what do we do now?"

My sergeant, an E-7, said, "Let me talk with Chief Kaui, our mess hall warrant officer, and see what he wants to do." Well, my day of duty was done, so I went back to my compound and joined my buddies in a few refreshments. I then went to my hootch for some much-deserved rest, but almost all might I heard what I thought were diesel truck noises.

The next morning, I joined Chief Kaui and my NCO back at the warehouse, where I asked them, "Did you hear those Deuce and a Halfs (two—and one-half ton cargo capacity trucks) running last night?" The chief looked at the NCO and then me, smiled and said, "I don't really know much about that, sir, but I can guarantee you that your inventory now balances perfectly." Problem solved.

LEAVING VIETNAM IN DISGUISE

Prior to my Vietnam tour, I was stationed in Japan. There, I met my wife to be, Yoshii, who worked for an insurance company. But we didn't get married then, because I wasn't sure how my Vietnam experience would turn out. When I switched jobs to become the OIC of two telecommunications centers, I decided life was a lot safer and so flew back to Japan, where we got married in two civil ceremonies, at the US Embassy and in a Tokyo Metropolitan Office.

Now back in Vietnam, with my new wife being command-sponsored, but in Japan, I had to figure out how to finish my tour, then get back to her, have a proper church wedding, and then get us both back to the US.

My military status was "voluntary indefinite (VI)," which meant I had no DEROS, ETS, or anything. When discussing my Army "future" with Army Personnel, it looked like three years for 50% of a maybe to meet my interests, so I decided to get out! Easier said than done.

I first had to apply for revocation from my VI status. But I couldn't wait for the approval, so referencing this request, I immediately sought release from active duty, because I would've then served over three years.

But my Release From Active Duty (REFRAD) would've been in the US, leaving my wife in Japan. So, referencing all my prior requests, I then decided to apply for separation in-country, meaning if everything worked out, I would be leaving Vietnam as a civilian! I think this entire process required five different applications.

The next step required obtaining a passport and then an exit visa from Vietnam, which was an expensive undertaking, because I had to bribe a few local Vietnamese officials. Obtaining these documents, I then requested travel to my home of record in the US, with a delay in route in Japan, then concurrent travel for my new wife! Oh, did I say I was also arranging for a wedding at a military chapel in Japan, using my old warrant officer friend and soon to be best man as my sponsor?

The day came when I was to leave Vietnam, so I dressed in my James S. Lee double knit suit, complete with combat boots (because they were easier to wear than pack) and headed to Tan Son Nhut Air Base for my flight to Japan. It was pouring down rain, and I recall seeing large rats scurrying around the terminal.

Some guy was looking at me and said something to me like, "I see they made you get a passport." I wasn't paying much attention, but replied, "Yes, and I have a visa, too," wondering what in the hell he was talking about.

Later, this same guy asked me if I had ever flown on the CIA's Air America. Well, their Turbo Porter STOL planes were perfect for photography, because they didn't oscillate like a helicopter, so combat photographers loved them. I replied in the affirmative, thinking of those Porters I had flown on in Can Tho, and started walking toward my Freedom Bird flight out of Vietnam. It was then that a big smile crossed my face, because I realized that in my civvies and combat boots, this guy probably thought I was a CIA agent, which wasn't a bad way to leave Vietnam!

But wait, there's more. Arriving in Japan and reporting into the US Army Japan G1 with all of my carefully crafted paperwork, I was told, "We're not sure all of this is correct, so please come back in a week and we'll tell you our answer." So, we got married for the third time in the base's chapel center attended by Chaplain Myer and Fr. Colligan, followed by a short honeymoon trip to southern Japan, all the while not knowing whether my wife and I would be able to travel back to the US together. But that's another story.

JOHN BUTLER

US Army— Field Artillery Officer

Dates of Military Service (Active Duty and Reserves): 1968 to 1974

Unit Served with in Vietnam: 11th Armored Cavalry Regiment, 2/94th Heavy Artillery

Dates in Vietnam: A Troop, 1st Battalion, 11th Armored Cavalry Regiment (11th ACR), Oct 1970 to Feb 1971; 2nd Battalion, 94th Heavy Artillery, Feb 1971 to Oct 1971

Highest Rank Held: 1LT

Place of Birth: Pittsburg, Kansas— 1945

WHERE TO, UNCLE SAM?

Looking back, it's kind of shocking that less than five of my high school class of over 100 served in the military. This is especially surprising since the draft was in full force when we graduated in 1963, and more and more guys our age were going to Vietnam.

I'm pretty sure that not one of my classmates served in Vietnam! On the other hand, I KNEW I was going to serve, and that I would be going to Vietnam! I just knew it!

To be clear, I didn't particularly WANT to go to Vietnam. I didn't know enough about why we were there, and I wasn't too keen on getting shot at, but I never questioned that I would do my duty to my country wherever and however I was called on to serve.

So, after I completed the then-mandatory two-year Army ROTC (Reserve Officer Training Corp) program at my college, I signed up for the Advanced ROTC program to become an officer when I graduated. I figured that since I was going to Vietnam, I might as well go as an officer.

I got through high school without really learning how to study, so my first semester in college was a real eye-opener! As a result, I managed to squeeze a "D" out of both Calculus and Inorganic Chemistry…not my proudest moment. Fortunately, I was given the option of taking both courses over and my new grade would be used in my grade point average rather than those D's.

Because of that shaky start, my graduation (and commissioning) was delayed by one semester. Fortunately, I had accumulated a few hours toward my master's degree when I received my bachelor's, so I requested and received permission from the Army to delay starting my active duty to allow me time to work on completing my master's.

When I finally received my orders to enter active duty, I was surprised to discover that I had received a delay of three semesters; far more time than I had anticipated. My orders were to report to Ft, Sill, OK, for Field Artillery Officer's Basic Course on 16 February 1970, nearly seven years after graduating from high school!

I took advantage of an opportunity to teach "related math and science" at a brand new Vocational-Technical school in Manhattan, KS, while I finished my master's degree. It was like a paid vacation after working full-time while taking a full load of college courses during my undergraduate years.

The only downside of that three-semester "paid vacation" was the constant nagging realization that I would be going to Vietnam, which churned just below the surface of my mind. It seemed to surface most powerfully when I was enjoying something like fishing with my brother-in-law.

Artillery school at Ft. Sill was a positive experience. I was pleasantly surprised at how technically challenging it was to properly calculate accurate firing data for field artillery batteries.

Our primary instructor was a Marine captain who seemed to me to be the perfect man and soldier. I often wonder what happened to him, and if that assignment at Ft. Sill hurt his career since it wasn't very glamorous.

As our class came to an end, we all received our orders. Like nearly every other 2d LT graduating Field Artillery School, I was going to Vietnam...wait, no...my orders were to go to Germany! I was shocked! Germany would be my first permanent duty assignment!

My wife and I had carefully and fully prepared for me to go to Vietnam, then have a stateside assignment. All our preparations would need to be undone, vehicles sold, etc. She was eight months' pregnant with our first child and wanted to deliver our daughter in the States, then fly to Germany to join me.

Early on a Wednesday morning, I put on my class-A uniform and took my first-ever commercial plane ride from Manhattan, Kansas to Kansas City on an old "tail-dragger" Douglas DC-3 piston-engine airplane. Then I flew on a Boeing 707 to New Jersey. Then after many hours of what seemed to be wasted time, I boarded another four-engine jet to Germany.

I was too wound up to sleep on the plane. We landed at Rhein-Main airbase near Frankfort early on Friday morning. I called the designated phone number of my "sponsor" at my new unit, and he headed over to pick me up. By the time we were on our way, it was nearly noon, and I was beginning to feel the weight of having been awake for nearly 48 hours.

My sponsor informed me that our battalion commander wanted to meet me as soon as we arrived. I objected since my uniform and I were both a mess, but I was assured that wouldn't be a problem.

We arrived at the battalion headquarters, and I met the CO. He welcomed me then told me to go get cleaned up, put on a fresh set of fatigues, and be back at 5:00 to participate in the Retreat ceremony. Then I was to attend "command beer call" at the officer's club.

I was running on fumes, but had no inclination to decline the invitations, especially since they did not seem optional! Retreat was impressive and meaningful. So far, so good. My first glass of German beer was amazingly smooth and went down like a glass of Kool Aid. So, I had another one!

When it was time to leave, I discovered I couldn't stand up! A couple of my fellow LTs helped me get to a car and to the apartment I was sharing until I got my own place. To say that I slept would be the biggest understatement since Noah said, "It looks like rain."

I was assigned to the 6/40 Heavy Artillery (8" self-propelled) Battalion as part of the Third Army. I would be the battalion's Recon and Survey platoon leader.

I found and leased a beautiful house on the side of a mountain overlooking the charming little town of Kleinaustime. The bedrooms opened onto a balcony with a stunning view of the picturesque town down below. A church bell tolled every hour. It was truly like living in a dream.

I attended a one-week CBR (chemical, biological, radiological) warfare school in Grafenwoehr. While I was at that school, our daughter Julie was born. When I returned to the battalion to sign in after the school, my battery commander informed me that I was "on a levy" which meant I had received orders for Vietnam. I had been in Germany for only 30 days of what was a "permanent assignment."

As I processed out and waited for transportation to fly back to the States, another 2nd LT arrived to take my place. He had just graduated from Officer Basic Course at Ft Sill.

It is traditional for a unit to have Hail and Farewell parties for officers—one when the officers join the unit and another one when they depart for their next assignment. My Hail and Farewell parties were combined into one event.

Welcome to the Army! Thanks a pants-load, Uncle Sam!

TERENCE H. "TERRY" WHITE

Army — Infantry
Dates of Military Service: January 1969 to August 1970
Unit Served with in Vietnam: Bravo Company, 2nd Battalion, 27th Infantry,
25th Infantry Division
Dates Served in Vietnam: June 1969 to August 1970
Highest Rank Held: SGT (E-5)
Place and Date of Birth: New York City — 1946

THERE BUT FOR THE GRACE OF GOD, GO I ...

My first of two R&R trips out of Vietnam was to Sydney, Australia, for a couple of weeks in April of 1970, springtime on Long Island where I grew up, but seasonally mid-fall in the land down under. Except for two whole Sundays spent at Bondi Beach, all my time was spent at the University of Sydney. On campus I was very warmly received by students, faculty, and staff in the math and philosophy departments. There were two Friday sessions, each lasting longer than two hours, when I was grilled by students, faculty (and even some staff people), about the war from the grunt perspective. Clearly, they wanted feedback from someone who had first-hand knowledge: were we winning or losing, anyone believe in the domino theory of communist aggression, how long did I think the war would last, etc.

They rewarded me with the opportunity to teach two classes (one in ethics and one in symbolic logic) and, in conclusion, to give one departmental-wide lecture on any topic of my choice. Also, and best of all, they gave me a very generous gift allowance to the campus bookstore as they did not want me to return to Vietnam without good reading material. R&R in Sydney was comfortable beyond belief for two whole weeks, especially when compared to my previous eleven months in the bush as an E4 11B grunt with the 2nd Battalion, 27th Infantry Regiment Wolfhounds.

Several times, restaurants refused my money for steak dinners, taxi drivers refused payments, and when I checked out of the Florida Motel in Kings Cross, Sydney, the manager cut my bill in half. Clearly, they wanted me to know their appreciation for what the US Army was doing. The whole time I was in Australia the weather was all sunshine and warmth. The flight back to Saigon was on-time and easy, but after that much changed.

I landed at Tan Son Nhut AFB and made my way over to Long Binh, where I was told I could hop on a courier flight back to Cu Chi, 25th Infantry Division Base Camp. I got over to Hotel 3 about 1330 hours and waited till 1800 hours for this last of the day "taxi" ride out into the hinterland. I was the first of at least a dozen or more people wanting to do the same thing. When everyone got on, we lifted off the concrete landing pad. When we were about six feet up, the pilot said we were too heavy, and a few would have to jump off. He settled back down on the ground, but no one got off. He attempted to lift off again, but at about six of seven feet up started to scream that the chopper was still too heavy and that some had better get off or "no one was going anywhere." Again, no one seemed to be volunteering.

Next thing I knew a boot was on my back and I was literally kicked off, along with two other E4's. We fell to the ground about five or six feet below, then our duffle bags landed on top of us. I thought my arm was broken at the elbow. The other two enlisted men fared no better. The three of us spent the night sleeping on the concrete floor inside the H3 terminal. The next morning, we were on the 0900 hours courier flight. After three stops, I got off in Cu Chi and walked to the 2nd Battalion, 27th Wolfhounds Regimental Headquarters.

After changing back into fatigues, I reported to Battalion Headquarters and was told I would return to my field unit on a resupply chopper around 1500 hrs. In the meantime, I volunteered to accompany the new battalion legal clerk to the 25th JAG office since he had no idea where it was. I had done some ad hoc legal beagle work for the Division JAG office several times due to my time in law school before being drafted.

When we arrived at the JAG office, I was surprised to see several attorneys putting up funeral bunting over their doorways. Immediately I asked what had happened only to learn that a Captain that I knew had died the day before. Shocked, I refused to believe it, saying that I had talked with him for almost two hours the previous afternoon while waiting for a courier ride. The Colonel explained to me the helicopter he was returning on had flown right into high tension wires going over the Saigon River, that it exploded upon getting tangled in the wires, fell straight down into the river, with no survivors.

I told the Colonel that the Captain and I had been admiring the magnificent sunset all the while we talked and that the Captain had told me all about his R&R in Hawaii with his wife and young daughter. The Captain and I knew each other a little bit because we went to the same law school. LBJ drafted me during my first year of law school in 1968, but the Captain was in his third year and thus not deprived of his deferment, he was able to graduate before going into the Army. I am sure in the official Army records it was noted there were no survivors to this horrible tragedy, but oddly, and perhaps unofficially, there were three: I was one of them!

This tragedy comes hauntingly into my thoughts every so often, always leaving me profoundly unsettled; it mentally stings me. For one who has been there, the realization how quickly human life can change, just how closely someone can come to death without actually dying, can trigger a brain freeze. If it is true that no sparrow can fall to the ground without our Father knowing of it, what about all those soldiers that went down into the Saigon River?

We are told to fear not, that we are worth more than many sparrows. For more than fifty years now this memory has made me more reliant on belief and prayer and hope. I find comfort in the words of Isaiah: "The work of righteousness will be peace, and the effect of righteousness, quietness and assurance forever." Yes, that's exactly what every grunt in my squad every night in the bush hoped for: PEACE and QUIET.

ED DEVOS

US Army— Infantry Officer

Dates of Military Service: 1969 to 1989

Unit Served with in Vietnam: Battalion Advisor, 21st ARVN Division

Dates Served in Vietnam: Dec 1971 to Dec 1972

Highest Rank Attained: Lt. Colonel (P) (O-5)

Place and Date of Birth: Grand Rapids, Michigan— 1947

THE FIRST FEW DAYS AS AN ADVISOR TO A VIETNAMESE INFANTRY BATTALION

On Christmas Day, 1971, Captain Ed DeVos was instructed to pack what little he had as he would be flying out later that day to be the battalion advisor to the 3rd Battalion of the 33rd Infantry Regiment, 21st Infantry Division, Army of the Republic of Vietnam (ARVN). That battalion had its own fire base and was located in the middle of the rice growing area nicknamed "The Rice Bowl," halfway between the Song Trem River and the Gulf of Thailand, seven kilometers (clicks) west of the regimental fire base in one direction and seven clicks east of the Gulf of Thailand in the other direction.

Major Chan was the battalion commander of 3-33 Infantry, and he also had one battery of 105mm howitzers to support the unit. The mission of 3-33 Infantry was to interdict all VC traffic through the Rice Bowl and keep the Vietnamese citizens who lived in that rice growing area free from VC interference. A Sergeant First Class (SFC) from the regimental team and an interpreter would accompany DeVos.

Later that afternoon the three men hopped off a Huey at the fire base and met Major Chan. This man was an average looking Vietnamese in stature — about five foot six and thin, but his eyes had the look of cold steel. In later conversations, DeVos learned that Chan, thirty-one years old, had been fighting the VC for over half his life. He spoke broken English, far better than the U.S. captain spoke Vietnamese, but through the interpreter, a young soldier who had learned English four years ago, they were able to communicate easily.

As he walked around the fire base, a place that would be his home for the next three months, DeVos noted that, like the regimental fire base, this one was in the shape of a square, and it sat next to a good size stream, its water flowing slowly west toward the Gulf of Thailand. There were numerous places on the dirt and mud-filled dike walls where the soldiers could shoot from if attacked. The base of the walls on the inner side was around eight feet wide because the soldiers' families had staked their claim to that ground as their home. Cooking fires were every fifteen, twenty feet along the inner walls. Small children and wives of the soldiers were everywhere. Most knew no other life.

In the center of the fire base were six 105mm howitzers, two guns facing due north, two guns facing southeast, and the other two facing southwest; rounds for each of these artillery pieces were stacked up next to each gun, ready to fire. The helicopter-pad where the Huey put DeVos down was in the center of the firebase. There was a large ammunition bunker also near the center which Major Chan offered as the captain's sleeping quarters. With no other options readily available, the young advisor dropped his rucksack off there while the more experienced SFC said he would find some place along the wall.

The evening meal that first night was like so many others that followed: some thin tea followed by a bowl of rice in which sat the meat of the day. Sometimes that was fish, sometimes chicken, sometimes dog, sometimes monkey, or sometimes other delicacies of unnamed origin. Major Chan and others watched with great interest to see if this U.S. advisor, "*Co Van My*" in Vietnamese, would eat, because if he did, he would be offered a second helping. The Co Van knew if he rejected the meal or any of its contents, this could put a damper on his relationship with his host.

Therefore, like it or not, eating whatever was put in front of him was part of the advisor's job. While he quickly became an expert at using chopsticks, some of these meals contributed to DeVos having diarrhea for long periods of time.

Over time, two things saved his dietary system from irreparable damage. First, every time he filled his canteen with water, he dropped in a few halazone tablets. These tablets were first used in World War II for the same purpose Ed was using them; to disinfect the water. Second, after every evening meal, Major Chan always had several shots of his favorite drink, Hennessey Cognac, and like any good advisor, the young captain used this opportunity to bond with his counterpart.

This nightly custom helped stave off the taste and contents of such epicurean delights such as duck blood soup, twelve-day-old turtle eggs, or the various parts of the chickens that were chopped and cooked after all the feathers of the bird had been plucked and what was left was thrown into a big pot to become the chicken stew for the evening meal. There was also ever-present dipping sauce known as *nuoc mam*, the Vietnamese fish sauce made from a combination of sugar, sweet and sour juices, garlic, and various parts of fish.

As the weeks passed, on every occasion when Ed had the opportunity to get back to Ca Mau to get a shower, he would go by the small post-exchange (PX) located there to purchase more "medicinal" liquids for him and Major Chan to share. It was, after all, in the spirit of maintaining good rapport and proper international relations between these two men from different cultures.

The first night in the ammunition bunker proved to be one this young infantryman would never repeat. No sooner had he gotten into the small entrance to lay out his camouflage sleeping blanket, which he still has in his possession fifty years later, and get his mosquito net strung up, he heard the scurry of small creatures in one of the corners of the ten-by-ten-foot space. Thinking he scared whatever it was away, the man was stretching back down on his poncho when he heard the noise again, this time in two corners, then three, and in short order, he realized all those noises came from rats of varying sizes up to that of a small cat.

After whacking a few of the invaders away with his entrenching tool, the racket grew worse as the creatures became bolder in their approach to this interloper who sought to occupy their space. Within thirty minutes, DeVos picked up his gear and found an open spot near one of the artillery pieces and tried to sleep, only to be interrupted in the middle of the night by a thunderous deluge from above.

The next morning, DeVos, after hardly sleeping a wink, was given a cup of thick, dark coffee by one of Major Chan's men, the coffee made according to French customs as their influence in Southwest Asia dated back to World War II and before. Feeling better with that hot liquid in his gut, this experienced battalion advisor of all of one day was about to take a "walk about" when Major Chan strolled over to him. With a big grin on his face, he told DeVos he found a spot where the American could bed down that evening which might be a little more comfortable.

In thinking about this as he walked around the fire base, Ed knew that, because he hadn't made a big deal of the previous night's experience with all the furry creatures visiting him, he had passed a vital test.

With every step around the perimeter, a new world opened to the American. Small children followed him around, touching the hair on his arms, smiling at him as they laughed back and forth with each other as this man tried his best to speak Vietnamese. The wives of the soldiers he encountered along his walk kept bowing to him even as he bowed back. He noted several soldiers and some women along the riverbank, the women washing their clothes while some of the soldiers were catching some fish ten or fifteen yards from those downstream from others who were using a cleared area along the bank as the camp latrine.

When his bouts with "Montezuma's Revenge" were at their peak, the picture became clear. Human waste was eaten by the fish. Men caught those same fish to eat. Then men deposited their waste back into the water so the fish could eat, and then the cycle repeated itself. Since infantrymen are not known to be too bright, it took DeVos some time to fully comprehend this sequence.

* * * * *

During the next few weeks, Ed went on several missions with Major Chan's men. The first tromp he made in the woods was with a rifle company which was given the task to move toward the Gulf of Thailand looking for any signs of enemy movement, circling back to the fire base by a different route. While the company did not find anything on this six-hour mission, it was instructive to the advisor to see how these men moved in the woods, how alert they seemed to be, and to see the state of their physical fitness.

In all these areas, the American felt good about what he saw. It was good to get out of the firebase and pick fresh bananas off the trees they passed by. More importantly, he realized that he needed to get in better shape because his size ten jungle boots got sucked down into the mud so far, he struggled to pull his feet up fast enough to keep up with the soldiers near him.

The second mission DeVos went on was a squad night ambush. This was with ten men going out to set up an ambush five hundred meters outside the firebase on a trail the VC had been known to frequent. While no contact was made with the enemy that night, the advisor learned that the men he was with were quiet and disciplined. While it was difficult to assess how effective their weapons covered the kill zone, upon his return to the firebase four hours later, he had a new-found respect for the size and stings of the mosquitoes that owned the night sky in the Rice Bowl. This one night reinforced the need to follow orders and once a week take those giant-size malaria pills he had been issued.

Occasionally, U.S. Navy helicopters would fly over the Rice Bowl on their way to some ship out in the gulf. On one occasion, one pilot flying overhead radioed DeVos, asking him if he needed anything, to which the advisor responded that he had not had any ice cream in months. Within an hour, this Navy helicopter landed in the center of the firebase with a gallon of chocolate ice cream from some Navy ship. It didn't take too long to consume this feast in the ninety-five-degree heat.

In the midst of all this, one nagging administrative issue kept raising its ugly head. Just before Ed flew to Vietnam, the Army had updated its pay system to automatic bank draft. Complying with instructions, before deploying, the young captain filled out the paperwork so that he would receive fifty dollars a month and all the rest of his money would directly to his wife's checking account in Florida. And you know the rest of the story. The Army reversed those instructions. It took several months of mailing money to Florida before all this got worked out.

SUSAN DEVOS
Wife of Ed DeVos

ONE WIFE'S PERSPECTIVE OF MEETING HER HUSBAND FOR R & R IN HAWAII

Editor's Note: Ed DeVos was pulled from several weeks of heavy combat as an advisor to a South Vietnamese Division during the Easter Offensive of 1972, where he earned two Silver Stars. He was pulled offline and sent on R&R. He returned to the ongoing fight—thus the background of the R&R story from his wife, Susan.

Yes, the anticipation grew as I was on my way to see Ed, but the reality of not seeing that strong, well fit soldier of a few months ago was a situation I was not sure how I would react to. It seemed to overshadow that first moment of our reunion so much so that I truly did not recognize him.

The embrace—the kiss—the moment of really having each other enveloped in a hug was something we did not want to let go of.

Looking at him face to face instantly showed the effects of war. The stress, the strain, the lack of sleep, and the guarded secrets that I knew would not be revealed, showed up in the silence and as we spoke to one another. It quickly became apparent that my many questions need not be asked and those that were may not be answered and maybe that was best, for I probably could not bear the fullness of what my husband was going through.

Was it a time of rest and relaxation? In some ways yes, and in some ways no. Many events and many offerings of entertainment were planned, but he could not fully engage into the transition of "our world" and the attention. It would take more than five days. He tried his best, but that switch could not be flicked on so easily because his mind was elsewhere. Thus, R & R was "bitter-sweet."

To say goodbye a second time, especially after seeing the deterioration physically and emotionally was very hard. The brave front on my side was camouflaged by all the courage I could pretend at that moment. Both of our "reassurances" were given as we held back many tears.

The flight back to Florida was lonely and somber. It was quiet; the joy suspended because all my questions came back again. Will I see him again? Will he come home whole? And when he gets home, will he be able to adjust easily as he integrates back into the household as husband and father? Will he carry memories deeply imbedded in his mind, not to be unearthed and allowed to be private, or will others try to pry too much information from him and hinder his adjustment to his next military assignment?

To try to be an encourager to family members was another challenge as the flight home continued. Gentle grace with not too many details seemed to be the best way to keep the picture of strength and not weakness in their mind, because that way hope stayed alive for us all. Only then could we face each day with much continued faith and prayer until he was back with us and away from the war zone.

M. JEROME (JAY) ELMORE

Navy — Disbursing Officer and Officer of the Deck aboard a destroyer escort

Dates of Military Service: 1968-1974

Ship Served On: USS Roark DE-1053

Two deployments. The first was from January 7 to August 10 ,1971.

The second from February 8 to August 31, 1972.

Highest Rank Held: Lieutenant (O-3)

Place and Date Born: Eufaula, Alabama — 1948

THE GUNLINE

The ship's bow sliced through the calm water sending up a spray of mist. The phosphorescence of the open ocean was now gone from the bow wave. If there had been light, an observer would have noticed that the clear blue water of the sea had changed to a brownish green, suggesting the approach of land. But one did not need light to know this, the gulf water had an earthy smell and the breeze brought with it a warning that land was rapidly approaching.

A hundred years earlier a skipper would have shortened sail and broken out a lead line or more likely stood off the coast until dawn. We did not have that option. It was April 1972, and we were headed to the waters off Quang Tri, Vietnam, which was just south of the so-called Demilitarized Zone (DMZ), referred to by the Army as Military Region I.

A massive North Vietnamese military force had surged across the DMZ and was headed south, decimating the defensive forces of South Vietnam. The surge would later be called the Easter Offensive and was more massive than the famous Tet Offensive of 1968. At the time of the Easter Offensive, most American forces had departed or were in the process of departing Vietnam, but there were still Americans present in harm's way as independent units or as "advisors" to the South Vietnamese. In any event, the South Vietnamese needed our help to prevent total annihilation.

There was very low cloud coverage which not only blocked out light from the moon and stars but also prevented effective air support. We were a small ship—the *USS Roark* DE-1053—a destroyer escort which was designed to escort larger ships like carriers and protect them from submarines or surface vessels. Our primary weapons were torpedoes and an ASROC—an anti-submarine rocket—capable of carrying a tactical nuclear warhead. Unlike the World War II torpedoes, if a hostile sub were detected miles away by our sonar, an ASROC missile could be fired in the sub's vicinity. A parachute would deploy, gently lowering the torpedo into the water where it would be released. The torpedo itself would search for and find the sub and destroy it. If a tactical nuclear warhead was involved it was like horseshoes, you only needed to be close. Unfortunately, neither of these primary weapons would be of any use on this mission. Instead, we would use our gun mounted on the forward deck.

The gun was a rapid fire 5-inch / 54 caliber which could send five-inch shells thirteen miles with great accuracy. There was, however, one serious drawback. The magazine for the gun was very limited, storing only enough shells to sink a sub that had been forced to the surface or to engage a threatening surface vessel. It was not designed for extended naval gunfire support. But help was needed quickly...so what to do? The ship had been designed to support a drone antisubmarine helicopter (DASH) which the Navy had found to be unreliable, so we had a helo hangar but no drone.

The decision was made to fill the helo hangar with shells for the mission, which we obtained in an underway replenishment from an ammunition ship off the coast. This was accomplished by traveling at 12 knots for about an hour a couple of yards from the ammo ship as crates of shells were passed by wire between the ships. The maneuver was as follows. The replenishment ship sets the course and speed. The ship being replenished approaches from the stern and slowly matches its speed to that of the ammo ship, just a couple of yards apart. Because the water passing between the two ships is funneled through at an increased speed, the venturi effect comes into play, tending to suck the two vessels together. Many collisions have occurred because of this. Overall, the procedure is a stressful and dangerous maneuver, particularly where explosives are involved.

Under normal circumstances, a helo hangar would never be used as an ammo magazine because it is part of the ship's exposed superstructure, with thin walls. A direct hit on the hangar would not be required to destroy the ship, any stray piece of shrapnel could penetrate the thin walls and ignite the stored shells. As we headed into the fray, the existence of this full hangar magazine could never entirely leave our minds.

This was all before the days of GPS, and it was imperative that we have an accurate fix of where WE were in order to accurately provide gunfire support since we would be shooting over a civilian population. A miscalculation could be deadly. While we had traversed the Pacific by means of celestial navigation — using a sextant to shoot the stars at dusk and dawn to determine our position — that option was not available to us and would not have been accurate enough for the precise gunfire support needed in any event. It being night, we were not able to get range and bearing on prominent landmarks on the beach. The only other option available to us was to obtain a fix using our radar. This was done by getting a range and bearing on various points along the coast.

The radar would give a range and bearing to a point on land from which a line would be drawn on the chart. If we could have "shot" several points simultaneously we could have easily calculated where we were on our chart. But we were moving forward, which required stepping each bearing line forward, considering the elapsed time and ship's speed, until the last "shot" was obtained and a fix determined. This required the ship to proceed at a constant speed and course in order to ensure accuracy. Unfortunately, this also made us a more vulnerable target for the enemy's shore batteries, especially since our radar itself could be homed in on.

I was the Officer of The Deck. The skipper, Commander A. S. Moreau Jr., had chosen to fight the ship from Combat Information Center (CIC or Combat)) one deck below and behind the bridge so he could monitor the fix calculation. This was my second cruise to Vietnam with Commander Moreau, and I had developed a good relationship with him. He was an incredible captain who ultimately rose to the rank of a full four-star Admiral and served as commander — in — chief United States Naval Forces Europe and later as commander-in — chief, Allied Forces

Southern Europe. It was a privilege and honor to serve with such a brilliant and knowledgeable officer.

I was a somewhat unusual choice for an officer of the deck in general, much less in combat, since I was a Supply Officer and not a Line Officer, due to my being partially color blind. Over the two voyages with Commander Moreau, however, I had fully qualified as what is termed a "Fleet Qualified OOD "and the captain seemed to want me on the bridge. And besides, all the ships were at "darken ship" with no running lights during combat so color vision was not an issue.

It was dark on the bridge except for the soft red glow of a few instruments. The ship was at General Quarters and fully battened down. The gun mount was manned and ready for action with damage control parties stationed to deal with any casualty. On the bridge with me was a Junior Officer of the Deck, helmsman, quartermaster, and various sailors with sound powered headphones connected to lookouts, damage control, and other areas of the ship. Everyone on the bridge wore helmets and flak jackets. We were steaming at about 12 knots on a straight course toward land. Lights, fires, and explosions were coming into view as we proceeded westward. We were asked to fire two star-shells to illuminate the landscape. These were shells which released very bright flares that floated down under parachutes and illuminated the battlefield. As the flares descended under the parachutes, they would rock back and forth casting an eerie light and causing shadows to swirl across the bridge as if we were part of a Grade B horror movie. Perhaps we were.

Combat, reported over the intercom or "squawk box" that they should have a fix in a couple of minutes. Shortly after that they reported their electronic equipment had detected a fire control radar from an enemy shore battery in what was referred to as a "scan sweep mode"...essentially searching the coastal water for a target. But no fix by us yet, so we continued on our constant bearing at our constant speed.

Shortly the intercom came alive with a voice announcing that the enemy's fire control radar was now locked on and tracking us. The sailor's voice was calm and professional as if he were merely announcing the evening movie rather than that a radar guided shore battery was seconds away from firing on us. But still no fix. Combat said they were just moments away from getting one.

The captain had three choices. We could fire now with a partial fix which would risk the lives of civilians if our fix were off by much. We could turn around and begin evasive maneuvers but that would mean precious time would pass before we could get back in the action. Or we could proceed as we were, recognizing there was a risk to the ship. The captain chose door three. (I am sometimes miffed when I hear people suggest Americans did not consider the welfare of civilians in Vietnam. I know our captain put his 245 crew members at risk to ensure, among other things, that civilians were kept out of harm's way).

So, we steamed on. American soldiers and Marines, along with our allies, needed us now, they were being overrun. The seconds seemed like hours. Everyone on the bridge had heard the last message from Combat and there was a deathly silence, almost as if no one were breathing as the seconds passed. The shifting shadows from the dying flares only added to the drama. Everyone knew that highly accurate rounds may already be on their way, but each sailor, some hardly over eighteen, manned his post without flinching. But no one could forget there was the hangar full of shells.

The intercom awoke with a jolt with a voice announcing we had a fix which, on previous orders from the captain, allowed me to commence evasive action. Our fire control computer, now that we had a fix, would keep an accurate plot as we took evasive maneuvers. We commenced firing immediately as I ordered the helm hard over to port, with our one engine ahead flank. The ship, designed for speed and maneuverability in chasing subs, responded immediately, turning like a ballerina performing a pirouette. From the last light of the flares, I could see plumes of water and spray from the enemy's shells hitting the water where we would have been. Only shrapnel hit us, but none pierced the skin of the ship, none hit the hangar, and no one was injured.

As we zig-zagged, we laid down protective fire for the infantry, but the shore battery kept firing at us. We had range and bearing to the battery based in part on its own radar, so the captain ordered our gun to target their shore battery. After a few rounds the battery went silent.

The above was just one night. We, along with several other ships, provided naval gunfire support during portions of April, May, July, and August 1972. Little sleep took place on the gunline since if we were not at general quarters shooting, we were replenishing food, oil, and ammunition.

I was a young Lieutenant (JG) who turned 24 during the middle of this. I aged many more years.

CARL H. "SKIP" BELL, III

U.S. Army—Armored Cavalry Officer, Aviator

Dates of Military Service (Active and Reserve): 1967 to 1998

Units Served with In Vietnam: A Troop, HHT, B Troop, 1st Squadron, 4th Cav, 1st Inf Div (First Tour); C Troop, 3rd Squadron, 17th Air Cav; 18th Corps Aviation Co; G3, HQ 1st Aviation BDE (Second Tour)

Dates in Vietnam: Feb 1969 to Feb 1970; Feb 1972 to Feb 1973

Highest Rank Held: Colonel (O-6)

Place of Birth and Year: Decatur, GA—1945

HOW I GOT MY VC FLAG

It was the spring of 1972, and I was flying a UH-1H helicopter for the 18th Corps Aviation Company, based in the Mekong Delta at Can Tho airfield. Our mission that day was a Province Support mission—we would fly to the Province HQ (in this case, Tra Vinh) and receive missions from the MACV Province Advisory Team.

The first mission of the day was to take the Province Senior Advisor (a high-ranking U.S. civilian) and his Vietnamese Counterpart (the Province Chief), along with their retinue, to a village that had been overrun by the Viet Cong several days before, but which had been recently re-captured by Province Militia units. In situations like this, the South Vietnamese government wanted to re-assert its influence in a re-captured village as soon as possible after the re-capture.

This influence reassertion usually involved visits by the ranking people in the province plus bringing in food, medical supplies (and medics), civil affairs people, etc. The plan was to drop off the VIPs at a triangular fort at one end of the village (which was a long, narrow village built along a road), and then fly to another village about six km away and pick up several pigs, chickens, bags of rice, medical supplies, and people and ferry them into the village, making as many trips as it took to get the job done.

When we were approaching the village, our flight path took us along its length until we sat down in the area between the end of the village and the triangular fort (probably about 50 meters). I noticed lots of Viet Cong flags flying in the village and thought to myself that they weren't kidding about recently re-capturing it. We landed and disgorged the passengers. I made a climbing turn as we departed and did not notice that there were mortar rounds impacting the area that we left. My co-pilot did notice them but didn't say anything—it was literally his first mission in Vietnam, and he didn't know what he was seeing (although the explosions should have gotten his attention). The door gunner on that side of the aircraft should have also noticed (and said something, but he didn't, either).

We went to the village about six kilometers away and got the first load of supplies and people that were to follow the visit by the VIPs and headed back to the village and the triangular fort. As we were making our approach to the fort, it seemed like the whole world opened up on us—small arms fire was coming out to the village and mortar rounds were landing outside the triangular fort (right where we were going to be landing). I aborted the approach and flew out of the area. On the way out, I asked the co-pilot if he thought the mortar rounds were 82mm, and he said he didn't know, but that he had seen explosions like that as we were leaving the area earlier. I asked why he had not mentioned that, and he apologized profusely.

I called the Province TOC (tactical operations center) and reported the situation—that we had a senior American advisor on the ground, along with his Vietnamese counterpart, and they were in an insecure area and might be captured. I was told to return to the Province Headquarters, which I did after taking our cargo and passengers back to the village where we had picked them up and shutting down the aircraft to check for bullet damage. We had a couple of bullet holes in the rotor blades, but not in critical places.

When we got back to the Province TOC, I asked the U.S. advisors how they planned to get the Province Senior Advisor out. They did not know at that point—they did know that he was in the triangular fort and was, for the moment, not in enemy hands. I suggested that they try to get me some gunship cover so we could go back in and get the VIPs out of there. They tried to get gunships for several hours but were unsuccessful. Meanwhile, we flew some other "ash and trash" missions for the Province while the advisory team tried to ascertain the situation on the ground and devise a plan to extract the Province Senior Advisor and the Province Chief.

Finally, late in the day, they told me that the VIPs had been spirited out of the fort and were in an area about one km away with a cohort of Regional Forces for security. I was to pick up an advisor (an Army Captain) and his interpreter/RTO (radio-telephone operator) who would have contact with the Province Senior Advisor's security force and they would identify the landing zone with a smoke grenade when we approached. The U.S. advisors were unable to get us gunship cover, so we were going to have to go in single ship and pluck the VIP's out.

We flew to the vicinity of the village (still had lots of Viet Cong flags flying) and saw a smoke grenade in a dry rice paddy about 500 meters from the village. When we started our approach, the field erupted in mortar rounds, and we could hear the pop of small arms fire. I continued the approach (didn't like the idea of leaving an American behind) and when we got to the smoke grenade at a hover, the advisor in the back was told that the VIPs were in an adjacent rice paddy. With the mortar rounds and small arms fire continuing, we hovered over to the next rice paddy, found the VIPs, and touched down so they could board.

The Viet Cong were continuing to walk the mortar rounds behind us and we continued to take small arms fire from the village. It was not accurate, but it was coming in and there was a lot of it. The VIP's got on the aircraft and their security detail (about 20 people) attempted to get on the aircraft with them. When I first attempted to pick the aircraft up to a hover, nothing happened—we were badly overloaded, and the aircraft would not leave the ground. The mortar rounds were coming closer. Several of us screamed to the crew and the advisor in the back to start throwing people off the aircraft.

I continued to try to pick up to a hover and was able to break ground and move forward for a few feet, then bounce down and up again for another few feet, then bounce down and move forward again for another few feet. The distances for each bounce were getting longer each time, and the folks in the back continued to throw the folks from the security team off. I was able to bounce the aircraft over a paddy dike and continue making longer and longer bounces until the aircraft stayed airborne and we were able to fly back to Province HQ. (Thank goodness for hard, dry rice paddies!).

We dropped off the Province Senior Advisor and the Province Chief. Neither one said a word to us. I guess they were somewhat traumatized by their experiences that day.

One week later, I drew the mission to support that same Province. I flew to Tra Vinh and landed the aircraft. One of the radio operators from the Province TOC came out with four VC Flags (taken from that village after they had finally re-captured it) and asked me if I knew who the crew was that had flown the mission for them last week. I told him that I did—that I was the pilot, and that I would see to it that each crewman received one of the VC flags.

So that's how I got my VC flag. I had the patches for the two units I flew with that tour (C Troop, 3/17 Cav, and the 18th Corps Aviation Company), along with the 1st Aviation Brigade patch and the patch for the 23rd Cambodian Infantry Brigade sewn onto the VC flag. (The Cambodian 23rd Infantry Brigade was a unit that we flew for on one of our missions into Cambodia—their operations officer gave me the patch).

JOHN BUTLER

US Army— Field Artillery Officer
Dates of Military Service (Active Duty and Reserves): 1968 to 1974
Unit Served with in Vietnam: 11th Armored Cavalry Regiment, 2/94th Heavy
Artillery
Dates in Vietnam: A Troop, 1st Battalion, 11th Armored Cavalry Regiment
(11th ACR), Oct 1970 to Feb 1971; 2nd Battalion, 94th Heavy Artillery, Feb 1971
to Oct 1971
Highest Rank Held: 1LT
Place of Birth: Pittsburg, Kansas— 1945

WELCOME TO VIETNAM

When I arrived in Vietnam, the scuttlebutt regarding duty assignments was two-fold: If you're a Field Artillery 2nd Lieutenant, you'll probably be assigned to be a Forward Observer. Any other assignment than that would be strongly preferred.

The 11th Armored Cavalry lived up to their motto, "Find the Bastards and Pile On" and was not only engaged in frequent contact with the enemy; they actually sought it out. Any other assignment than the 11th ACR would be strongly preferred.

I was assigned to A Troop, 1st Squadron, 11th Armored Cavalry Regiment as an artillery forward observer.

However, my first face-to-face encounter with the possibility of death in Vietnam had nothing to do with the enemy or combat. Shortly after landing in Vietnam, I arrived at our regimental headquarters near Saigon outside of Dĩ An (pronounced "Zee Ahn"). My troop was operating independently as a company-sized unit in the jungle.

As a forward observer with the 11th ACR, I would have a crew of four other guys and our own ACAV (Armored Cavalry Assault Vehicle) assigned to me. An ACAV is a glorified APC (Armored Personnel Vehicle) with two (extra) M60 machine guns & shields, and some additional armor plating.

My crew would be coming out of the jungle to rendezvous with me near a two-lane highway about 25 klicks (kilometers) north of Dĩ An. A Spec. 4 with a jeep was assigned to drive two other newbies and me and drop us off at pre-determined locations to meet up with our assigned units.

I would later learn that our Spec. 4 driver had never actually learned to drive before coming to Vietnam. That little nugget of information had slipped by the Army somehow.

Since the jeeps in those days were quite small and four people completely filled it up, we pulled a trailer with our gear. My duffle bag had my full Social Security number printed on the side of it along with my full name. We obviously had no concerns about identity theft in those days. I still have it, by the way. I'll have to have it shredded if I ever want to get rid of it!

Back to my story: We're heading north on a paved two-lane highway, following a deuce and a half (2 ½ ton truck) full of Korean soldiers (ROKs). Our driver decided to pass the truck. We're about half-way around the truck when the truck decides to pass the vehicle in front of it.

So rather than slowing down and getting back behind the truck, which is what any experienced driver would do, our guy decided to just pull over onto the shoulder to the left of the oncoming lane and maintain his speed. The shoulder is not a friendly place to be—our jeep and our trailer were bouncing around madly…but at least we were still attached.

We were speeding along on the shoulder with no apparent solution in sight as we saw a huge pile of rocks looming ahead of us in our newly acquired traffic lane! The deuce and a half was right beside us, so there was nowhere to go.

At this point, slowing down and stopping would have been a really wonderful idea. To be fair, it would have been embarrassing to have had to stop on the (wrong) shoulder, but we would have happily and gratefully endured the shame.

Our Spec. 4 had other ideas though. He decided to just pull back into the oncoming lane which was still quite full of the deuce and half. I was in the back seat on the right side, so I got to see "up close and personal" when the flimsy top brace of our jeep and the rear wheels of the truck "kissed" violently!

Our driver was still not using the brakes! Instead, he was jerking the wheel to the left, then to the right, then to the left (you get the idea), always reacting in the exact opposite way he should have. Our gear was being launched onto the highway behind us, making quite a trail. Our trailer had finally had enough and decided to go solo, tearing itself off the hitch of the jeep.

The jeep was now spinning around and heading for the ditch next to the oncoming traffic lane, pointing in the opposite direction than we are moving. The driver bailed out as we slid down the embankment and finally came to rest after slamming into the ditch on our side (my side, by the way).

Miraculously, we were alive! The driver was the only one who was actually injured, amazingly enough.

I'm thinking, "If I'm going to die in Vietnam, shouldn't I at least get shot at first?"

ALAN C. GRAVEL
US Air Force— Pilot
Dates of Military Service: 1969 to 1974
Unit Served with in Vietnam: 536th Tactical Airlift Squadron of the
483rd Tactical Airlift Wing; 4102nd Aerial Refueling Squadron
Dates in Vietnam: Sep 1970 to Sep 1971; May 1972 to Dec 1972
Highest Rank Held: Captain (O-3)
Place of Birth: Alexandria, LA— 1945

BULLSHIT DISAPPROVED

When we finished tanker school at Castle AFB in Merced, CA, we reported to Barksdale AFB in Bossier City, LA. We moved our mobile home from Alexandria, LA, where Sheri and Alan W. had lived while I was in Vietnam in Caribous to a nice mobile home park in Princeton, LA, a few miles east of Barksdale. We settled in and started training flights around the first of March 1972.

I was a senior 1st Lieutenant with almost 1,000 hours of combat time in Caribous in Vietnam, but I had only the upgrade training hours in the tanker, so I started out as a co-pilot. I was assigned to a crew led by an Aircraft Commander who had come to tankers right out of pilot training, accumulated the minimum required 500 hours in the tanker, and had just recently been upgraded to Aircraft Commander.

Early in May, the entire squadron was deployed to Clark AB in the Philippines to fly missions into Vietnam as part of the US response to the 1972 Easter offensive when the North Vietnamese tried to overrun South Vietnam. Unlike my other experience in Caribous, we deployed as a unit. The morning we left Barksdale was a very dramatic scene, with wives and children crying and saying their goodbyes and the aircrew and support personnel preparing to embark on a long flight across the Pacific while at the same time bidding farewell to their families and having no idea how long they would be gone.

We crossed the Pacific in two legs: Barksdale to Hickam in Hawaii and Hickam to Clark in the PI (Philippine Islands). We flew three-ship trail formation, with each aircraft a mile behind and 1,000 feet above the aircraft ahead. As a junior crew, we were third on both legs. In and out of the weather, this arrangement concerned me enough that I never left my seat for 16 hours on the Hickam to Clark leg. I remember we arrived at Clark with 12,000 pounds of fuel remaining, likely not enough to make any reasonable alternate landing site.

While at Clark, we lived in small mobile homes, one crew to each trailer. Something like 60-80 of these were arranged in a grid with asphalt streets between them. We had a kitchen and ate lots of TV dinners. On days off we could play tennis, go to the library, take in a movie, and visit the BX or Commissary.

On that initial deployment, we took 11 airplanes and 14 crews. The whole operation was commanded by a major. Before we left Clark in late summer, there were something like 40 airplanes, 60 crews, and we had three or four full bird colonels running the operation. It was much more enjoyable at the outset when we were flying more and had fewer people telling us when to go to the latrine.

At that point we were launching an airplane every hour, 24 hours a day. We took off at 255,000 pounds, which was considerably lighter than our nuclear war (Emergency War Order) weight back in the States, but Clark had a pressure altitude around 1,400 feet so the KC-135 seemed over-loaded and under-powered, a lot like they did on EWO launches in the States.

Toward the end of the summer, "Notices" and "Directives" were appearing on the bulletin boards at an unbelievable pace. Most crews resented this micro-management as most of these directives were conceived and promulgated by senior officers who were not actually flying the missions. Someone (I never knew who and didn't want to know) started stamping these documents with a "Bullshit Disapproved" rubber stamp that had, in addition to the words, the image of a bull defecating.

Several notices appeared warning that person to cease and desist but, predictably, those got promptly stamped as well.

Note: This story originally appeared in the book Haulin' Trash & Passin' Gas.

HAM HENSON

US Army — Infantry Officer
Dates of Service: 1969 to 1978
Unit in Vietnam: Charlie Company 1/502 Infantry 101st Airborne (Airmobile);
8th Radio Research Phu Bai
Dates served in Vietnam: May 1971 to May 1972
Highest rank held: Captain (O-3)
Place of Birth: Savannah, GA

FEAR UNDER A PONCHO

When the 101st was preparing to exit Vietnam, I was the XO (Executive Officer) of C/1/502 Infantry, having served several months as a platoon leader before that. I was looking forward to packing up our gear and moving to Ft. Campbell, KY. That was not to be. I was called to Brigade Headquarters to meet LTC Wesley Loeffert who had just been tasked to command a group remaining behind to protect the 8th RRG. This organization was housed in an old concrete French fort surrounded by the 101st Airborne and supporting elements. I had been in the 101st for several months and had no idea this place existed. Anyway, I was told I was reassigned (with no option) since they needed people with combat time.

So, I packed my gear and moved to my new quarters. In a concrete building with my own room with a window, no less, and a shower stall at the end of the hall. I don't honestly remember if there was also a flush latrine, but I do remember the shower as a HUGE luxury! This was big for a grunt.

We had a large multi-room bunker outside the entrance to the 8th RRG to serve as our TOC (Tactical Operations Center). Most of the 101st area was demolished and bulldozed after they left. The airfield at Phu Bai remained. There was a large antenna field full of large antennas attached to the 8th RR on the other side. It was guarded by a group of Vietnamese veterans under the command of a 1LT Campbell as I recall. He was the only US guy there. He was quite experienced in my mind, based on his knowledge level, but I never had much interface with him. Regardless, I felt the antenna field was well guarded.

My job as a junior TOC officer was to be a glorified RTO and relay information to FRAC in Da Nang. As part of my duties, I was also assigned to conduct routine inspections of the bunker positions along our perimeter to assess their readiness. I had my own jeep so I would grab my gear at night and drive around. I had a backpack radio to stay in touch with the TOC and my web gear and weapons. I had an M-79 grenade launcher I had appropriated along with an assortment of ammunition in a vest, plus my pistol. I figured I could use the CS or illumination rounds if there was movement while I was checking a bunker. I never did.

Not long after starting this activity, I drove up behind a bunker and announced myself, even though they knew I was making the rounds. Many of the soldiers manning the bunkers were from 8th RR and I found them to be quite intelligent and engaging. On this particular night, I announced we were going to engage a fixed target aligned with an avenue of approach that had been pre-plotted. I told the M-60 gunner to set up on the aiming stakes for the designated target. After he engaged, we would call in illumination and see how he did.

He did as instructed and "CLUNK" was the sound—not automatic weapons fire. I asked what he should do now, and he said he had no idea, as he had not been trained on this weapon in basic. (My first clue). I asked him his MOS, which I had never heard of (my second clue), and he said he was assigned here because he was fluent in Chinese (my third clue). I explained he should declare a misfire so we did, and I got out my poncho and red lens flashlight so we could look at the malfunction without violating light discipline. When I turned on the light, I saw that the belt of ammunition had been loaded in backwards! We were fortunate it had not detonated. I cleared the bunker and called for an armorer who came and took the M-60 with him.

Reflecting on this a few hours later, I decided I had been safer in the field in an NDP (Night Defensive Position) with my platoon of experienced infantrymen than I was in this rear area. So, I started sleeping with my M-16 again. When I left RVN, 8th RR was still there, but we were seeing tracked vehicle trails on aerial recon flights to the west and were flying last light recons to the east along the land evacuation route (as in we will walk out) to meet the Navy if we couldn't be air lifted.

I recently read an article where LTC Loeffert was quoted as saying "If 8th RR had been captured, it would have been worse than 10 Pueblos" (the USS Pueblo had been captured earlier by the North Koreans). That confirmed my understanding that it wasn't the NVA they were listening to.

TWO SOLDIERS IN A JEEP

This is a story about two men in a jeep. I want to go backwards in time. On 8 October 2010 Stewart (Moose) Davis died at 66 years of age. This story came up during our talks while he was in chemotherapy at Northside Hospital in Atlanta. I was one of the volunteers who drove him to and from chemo. We talked a lot about his career (after retiring as a full Colonel) at Fort McPherson, especially during Hurricane Katrina. Moose had two tours — the first was much more intense, but I knew him on the second tour where the jeep ride took place.

Several years before, I was looking at the items in a garage sale a few houses down from mine. I saw a guy who looked familiar, and we started "the conversation." "Were you in the service?" "Yes — Army." "Wait — is that you Ham?" "Wow — it's Moose!"

Turned out he lived two houses away from the garage sale. He moved to Roswell, GA a few years later when his wife died. After some banter, he invited me to my first AVVBA meeting at the 57th Fighter Group restaurant at Peachtree DeKalb Airport, saying it was a great group. I had not joined any veteran's groups since I left service in 1978. He was right — I joined on the spot and have served in that organization for a long time.

Moose and I were assigned as TOC (Tactical Operations Center) officers at 8th Radio Research Group in Phu Bai just down the road from Hue in I Corps RVN. The 8th RRG was inside an old concrete French fort that had been surrounded by the 101st Airborne and support elements. Just across the highway was the Phu Bai airport. There was a LARGE antenna field attached to the fort. Its operation was Top Secret. I never made it past the entrance gate to the fort. I was the junior TOC officer (actually a glorified RTO) with a captain as senior TOC officer on each shift. Moose was one and the other was CPT Robert (Bob) Rosa who I knew previously from our attendance at a Ground Sensor School at Ft Huachuca AZ on our way to Vietnam.

Now to the jeep ride. In March 1972, the NVA (North Vietnamese Army) came across the DMZ in what came to be known as The Easter Offensive. Firebases along the DMZ fell rapidly and the NVA kept moving south. Our facility quickly became the northernmost US facility in RVN. As a demonstration of how rapid and massive the attack was, I offer this story. We were sitting in the TOC trying to monitor and relay messages from the MACV advisors when a group came in. They were advisors who had made it on the last Huey out of Quang Tri. One of them was clad in helmet, web gear, weapon, boots, and undershorts and a t shirt. He didn't have time to get dressed. He asked if someone could get him a uniform. I volunteered since we were about the same size. His name was Jim Avery. A couple of years later we met again when he was assigned to Ground Committee of the Airborne Department at Ft. Benning. I heard he died several years ago from leukemia.

Just after this visit, Moose asked me if I would ride shotgun for him on a jeep ride. I agreed and he drove to the gate on Highway 1 and turned north. We were met by a constant stream of people going south. People walking, riding bikes, pushing bikes with all their possessions loaded, mopeds, little trucks and military trucks with solders loaded on board. After a couple of miles, he said, "I'm turning around." I did not complain! I was thinking we would see NVA tanks around the next bend in the road.

Moose shared that day in Chemo that that moment was the most scared he had been in two tours. Remember his first tour was when things were in full mode. Moose said, "As we were riding along, I had the thought that all those people in the trucks could be NVA in borrowed equipment and uniforms, infiltrating to the south, and we two loners were behind enemy lines and didn't know it." That never occurred to me at the time, but it did to him. We made it back and told those who asked, "We just went outside the gate to observe."

A good friend—gone—but not forgotten.

CARL H. "SKIP" BELL, III

U.S. Army—Armored Cavalry Officer, Aviator

Dates of Military Service (Active and Reserve): 1967 to 1998

Units Served with In Vietnam: A Troop, HHT, B Troop, 1st Squadron, 4th Cav,
1st Inf Div (First Tour); C Troop, 3rd Squadron, 17th Air Cav; 18th Corps Aviation Co; G3, HQ 1st Aviation BDE (Second Tour)

Dates in Vietnam: Feb 1969 to Feb 1970; Feb 1972 to Feb 1973

Highest Rank Held: Colonel (O-6)

Place of Birth and Year: Decatur, GA—1945

"TANK" HUNT IN CAMBODIA

In March 1972, C Troop, 3/17 Air Cavalry (Callsign: Lighthorse) was attached to 7/1 Cavalry and was flying out of Vinh Long Airfield in the Mekong Delta of South Vietnam. I was assigned to the gun platoon (Callsign: Crusaders). When we had missions in the western Mekong Delta, we staged out of an airfield at a place called Chi Lang (about one kilometer from the Cambodian border near a prominent terrain feature called the Seven Sisters Mountains (yes, there were mountains in the Delta—not many, but they were there). Chi Lang was an interesting place to stage out of; it was the headquarters for the 44th Special Tactical Zone (an organization whose mission I wasn't sure of, but I suspect it had something to do with cross-border operations since their troops were ARVN Rangers and Special Forces units).

Another organization at Chi Lang was the New Zealand Army's contribution to the Vietnam War (at that time)—a school for mid-level Vietnamese officers (roughly equivalent to our Command and General Staff School). There was a total of 50 people assigned to that school—49 of them were New Zealand Army officers, and the 50th member of the group was the cook (the sole enlisted man). He was an excellent cook (he had trained in civilian hotels and restaurants in New Zealand), and we took our meals in their mess hall whenever the OPTEMPO would permit it. In addition, he would bring us out cookies and lemonade when we were on strip alert at the Chi Lang airfield. The New Zealanders are really great people, and it was a pleasure to get to know them.

One day when we were working out of Chi Lang, we got scrambled to go into Cambodia and look for a North Vietnamese tank that had been reported by a VNAF (South Vietnamese Air Force) FAC (Forward Air Controller). We had been hearing rumors that Russian—or Chinese-made PT-76 tanks had been seen in southern Cambodia and we jumped at the chance to go get one.

Operating policy at that time stated that we could not take Scout aircraft (OH-6) into Cambodia, so we went in with two Cobras and a UH-1H that was acting as both Command & Control (C&C) aircraft for the mission and as our "scout." The Huey was flying low (20' AGL) and the two Cobras were high (at approximately 1,500' AGL). (The SA-7 "Strella" shoulder-fired anti-aircraft missile had not been introduced into South Vietnam-Cambodia at that time so the guns still flew high—this would change later on).

The lead gunship pilot did the map reading and guided the UH-1 while it was flying low. The Air Mission Commander (flying the UH-1) was the Gun Platoon Leader, CPT George Anderson. George was on his second tour of duty in Vietnam (his first had been as an infantry officer in the 101st Airborne Division where he was awarded the Silver Star). George was a good Platoon Leader—he led from the front, was cool under pressure, and his laconic Arkansas accent rarely reflected any sense of stress when he talked on the radio.

As we began to search the area where the tank had been reported, the UH-1 dropped out of the sky and began to fly low and fast over the terrain (which was a flood plain, flat and dotted with trees with long bare trunks and foliage on the top except for the occasional piece of higher ground that had scrub bushes in addition to the tall trees). In order to be as fleeting a target as possible, the UH-1 was jinking and alternating its airspeed between 20 knots and 80 knots and varying its direction of flight. The Cobra's were flying a "racetrack" pattern over the UH-1, with the inbound aircraft ready to dive in and cover him when/if he took fire.

Suddenly we heard George's voice on the radio, and he clearly was excited and concerned. He said, "We just took a hit, and I don't know what it was, but it busted out the chin bubble!" We (in the Cobras) had not seen any indication of enemy fire (no flash, no smoke, etc.). The UH-1 continued to jink along the ground and after a few more seconds, George's voice came over the radio again and said, "There's blood all over the place!" The lead gunship pilot asked who was hit. After a few more seconds, George answered by saying that they had a bird strike—he said that there was blood and feathers all over the place inside the aircraft and that his chin bubble had a big hole in it. He said we should call in one VC bee-one-are-dee KIA.

There was some discussion about aborting the mission and going back to Chi Lang when suddenly George reported seeing some wide tracks heading into one of the bushy areas. He said that he would go check out the area where the tracks led and for us (the guns) to be ready to cover him if he ran into anything. The UH-1 moved slowly toward the patch of jungle in which the tracks disappeared.

After a couple of minutes, George came back on the radio and said that the "tank" was actually a large green John Deere tractor! Of course, nobody had a clue how it got there and there did not appear to be anyone around it. We reported our find back to our Troop Operations section and were instructed to return to South Vietnam, which we did. We never did find out how that tractor got to southern Cambodia.

VIETNAMIZATION
ADVISORY PHASE

(1973 TO 1975)

January 27, 1973 — Draft comes to an end.

February 12, 1973 — POWs return to United States. First C-141 flight returns first American POWs to US as part of Operation Homecoming; an additional 53 flights returned over 2,000 servicemen by April 4, 1975.

March 29, 1973 — Last combat troops leave Vietnam.

August 8, 1974 — President Nixon resigns as President of the US In the wake of the Watergate scandal. Gerald Ford sworn in as 39th President.

April 30, 1975 — North Vietnamese troops enter Saigon, ending the Vietnam war.

Source: www.vvmf.org/VietnamWar/Timeline

Unfortunately, we have no stories from the last years of the Vietnam War. However, there are several stories, including two about the fall of Saigon, in our first *I'm Ready to Talk* book. I am including three of those stories here to get three different perspectives from this final phase of the war.

DAN HOLTZ

U.S. Air Force— Healthcare Administration
Dates of Military Service (Active Duty and Reserves Combined): 25 years
Unit Served with in Vietnam: HQ MACV/CORDS, Military Provincial Health
Assistance Program, Ninh Thanh Province (Phan Rang, RVN)
Dates you were in Vietnam: Nov 1969 to Nov 1970
Highest Rank Held: Colonel (O-6)
Place of Birth and Year: Indianapolis, IN—1943

ESCORT OFFICER FOR A PRISONER OF WAR RETURNEE

In March of 1973, I had the honor and privilege to serve as an escort officer for a newly promoted Air Force major, James Cutter. Jim had been an F-105 pilot who was shot down over North Vietnam in late December 1971. He was taken to the Hanoi Hilton and released as one of the last POW's to come back to the States following the end of hostilities.

Jim was originally from Oklahoma and his father was a coach at Oklahoma State University. Jim and I were matched up for the "home—coming" at Sheppard Air Force Base (SAFB) in Wichita Falls, Texas. SAFB was the closest Air Force base with a regional hospital that was a designated site for POW returnees to meet with their families. I was stationed at SAFB at the School of Health Care Sciences, which is how our paths crossed. However, the first question Jim and I had was, how did a non-combatant medical service corps officer get matched to an F-105 pilot, more later.

My wife Linda and our two children, Laura (then four years old) and Jack (then a year and a half) lived in base housing. Jim's wife, Ginny, her two sons, and Jim's parents all came to our house the morning of Jim's return so we could get acquainted and ready for Jim's arrival that afternoon. The bottom line is, we made lasting friendships with them that have lasted to this day.

When it came time to go to Base Operations, all of us piled into three cars and drove across the base and parked in the reserved lot. We went into the operations center lobby, where we joined about five to seven other families and escort officers who were there waiting for the landing of the airplane carrying the precious cargo. After wonderful and in many cases tearful reunions, the returnees were taken to the USAF Regional Hospital Sheppard for medical examinations and debriefings, which lasted three to five days, depending on each returnee's needs. During this period, family members were permitted to visit with their loved ones each day.

Following the debriefings, the returnees were permitted to do interviews with the news media and then released to their families to go on leave before returning to duty. The media interviews were mandatory if the returnees wanted to do later interviews with local press in their hometowns. Jim and Ginny decided to stay at SAFB for the weekend and depart for Oklahoma on Monday, so Linda and I invited them to go to church with us Sunday morning at our church, Christ United Presbyterian Church on the Northside of Wichita Falls. It was at this point we figured out how Jim and I were matched, he too was a Presbyterian. That seemed to be the common thread.

We got to the church in time for the 11:00 AM worship service. Linda and I were adult leaders for the youth group, so I asked Jim if he would be willing to speak with our youth group about his experiences as a POW and he said he would. I then told our pastor, Rev. Herman Boles, about what was going to be our activity at the youth group meeting that evening. Herman was an old radio preacher from west Texas and took it upon himself to announce to the congregation about the special guest who was with us at the worship service and who had graciously agreed to speak at the youth group meeting that evening. The congregation gave a standing ovation to Jim and a special prayer was offered for his wellbeing and thanks for his safe return to the States. Following the worship service, the members of the congregation were all taking the opportunity to meet Jim and Ginny and welcome Jim back home.

That evening was an even bigger surprise for everyone. The youth group usually met in the small fellowship hall of the church, or sometimes in the front pews of the sanctuary. Well, that evening we decided to meet in the sanctuary, since Rev. Boles had invited anyone interested to come to the youth group meeting that evening. That decision was a great one because we had not only the youth group members attending the gathering, but I believe most of the entire congregation, largely made up of local Texans with some members from the base, who showedup. The sanctuary was filled with every seat taken and quite a few folks standing. Jim did an informal opening with a few remarks and then spent almost two hours answering questions about who, what, when, where, how, why, etc. The kids in the youth group were thrilled, with many asking questions. The adults probably learned more about what had happened during the war and especially during Jim's imprisonmentthan they had ever expected to learn.

Looking back on the evening and subsequent events over the years, I believe this gathering was the first of the telling of the truth about the Vietnam War by someone who had actually been there and seen a side of it, thankfully, few others had seen.

Jim went back to flying for the Air Force and was stationed in Germany. One day while on a routine mission over the Black Forest, his aircraft experienced a malfunction and he had to eject from the plane. Fortunately, he was not injured, his plane was destroyed and the U.S. government had to pay the German government money for the destruction to the forest caused by the plane. Following that incident, Jim decided he had enough of piloting for the Air Force and that flying a desk was the better part of continuing a long and healthy life. He subsequently retired from the Air Force and settled in the western part of the U.S., where he and Ginny lived most of the time until his death about five years ago in 2014—2015. Ginny still lives there, and the boys have gone on to have families of their own.

Our contact with Ginny today is limited to exchanging Christmas cards every year. However, we look forward to them and are thankful each year when we get them. This experience for me started out as a challenge and became a labor of love for which I am most thankful.

BILL HACKETT

USMC—Combat Engineer Officer

Dates of Military Service (Active and Reserve): 1968 to 1988

Units Served with in Vietnam: 1st Engineer Bn, 1st Marine Div; 9th MAB, 1st Marine Div.

Date in Vietnam: Apr 1969 to May 1970; April to May 1975

Highest Rank Held: Lt. Colonel (O-6)

Place of Birth and Year: Griffin, GA—1946

OPERATION FREQUENT WIND—THE END

I reported to RVN in April 1969. My tour was as a Combat Engineer Officer with 1st Marine Division south of DaNang. As you know, Marines spent 13 months of duty. About 30 days before my RTD, my unit transferred me to a unit being sent home. My job was commanding officer of a medical unit. Eighteen long days on a big grey boat on the high seas...Coming home by ship did give us time to decompress and had a nice welcome at San Diego.

Forty-eight months later, I found myself back overseas in Okinawa. Things were heating up in Vietnam in April 1975. My Battalion was tasked to provide a 72-man Ships Detachment for deployment aboard Merchant shipping tasked to assist picking up boat people/refugees leaving country. The specific reason I was given command of the Detachment Hotel (one of ten our Division provided) was I was the only Captain who had a previous RVN tour.

We boarded a C-130 and flew to Cubi Point in the Philippines and boarded the USS Dubuque, an amphib with five helo spots and a ramp for amphibs. Our unit was designated the 9th Marine Amphibious Brigade (9th MAB).

We sailed up and down the coast of RVN, preparing and planning for the evacuation of Saigon. This became known as Operation FREQUENT WIND. I will never forget being in the CIC of the Dubuque on April 30, 1975 and observing the SAM missile sites plotted along the helo evac routes. CH 46's flying almost 24 hours straight picking up ref ugees. I observed many helo's tossed overboard with no space for them. Later we debarked the Dubuque and boarded USNS merchant ship TRANSCOLORADO and gathered off coast and transported 4,250 refuges and families to ANDERSON AFB in Guam.

We prepared for numerous operational exigencies such as sailing in a Mike Boat up the Vung Tau river to bring refuges out, but never had to actually set foot back in country. This phase of my RVN experience will never be forgotten.

Semper Fi, Bill Hackett

JOHN W. PATTON

USAF -C-130E pilot

Dates of Military Service: 1973 to 2003

Unit Served with in Vietnam: 21st Tactical Airlift Squadron

Dates in Vietnam: Jun 1974 to Apr 1975

Highest Rank Held: Colonel (O-6)

Place of Birth and Year: Shreveport, LA 1950

THE EVACUATION OF SAIGON—A PERSONAL REMEMBRANCE

None of us knew quite what to expect. We knew what was happening, but we still did not know how we would fit into the puzzle. We had been told to report to the wing theater at Clark AB, Republic of the Philippines, for our briefing. My crew consisted of Capt. Bill Lundberg, Aircraft Commander; 1Lt. Paul Boudreau, Navigator; MSgt. John Kays, Flight Engineer; TSgt Steve Tkach, Loadmaster; and 1Lt. Frank Jershe, Scanner and relief pilot. I was the Co-Pilot. There were many other crews similar to ours at the briefing, all wondering the same things. When were we going? Where exactly were we going? How were we going? What were we going to do?

All this happened over forty-six years ago but much of it is still fresh and clear in my mind. I guess that is how fear and apprehension can affect a person. I know that there was plenty of fear and apprehension in this 24-year-old First Lieutenant.

South Vietnam was collapsing. The North Vietnamese Army was moving through the countryside just like the tide rolling over a beach. And it was all happening so fast! I could hardly believe that as recently as March 21st I had been in Hanoi. Each week we had a mission to transport the different parties in the peace talks back and forth between Saigon and Hanoi. Only a month ago I had been on one of these trips and now in April, just a month later, it looked as if Saigon would be overrun at any time. Ban Me Thout had fallen on March 10 and the South Vietnamese government by mid—March had abandoned Pleiku. When would Saigon take its turn?

"Room Attention" came the command. As we all got to our feet, the 374th Tactical Airlift Wing Commander, Colonel James Baginski, entered the theater for the briefing. Now perhaps some of our questions would be answered.

It was called Operation Frequent Wind. We would be flying into Tan Son Nhut AB at Saigon to evacuate Americans, their dependents, and those South Vietnamese people who would be in grave danger after the communists took over. We were to load these people into our aircraft and fly them to safety back at Clark AB.

Once the details of the briefing were completed, we were released to crew rest until we were needed. As the operation called for flights to eepart every thirty minutes, some crews left immediately while others would see a couple of days pass before they got the call.

When our turn to fly came, we once again had a briefing to update us on the latest developments. This done, we set about to flight plan, draw our weapons, ammunition, survival vests, and flak jackets before proceeding to our aircraft. Normally we weren't issued weapons, much less survival vests and flak jackets for our flights, so this was a little unnerving. By the time we made all the necessary stops to pick up equipment and arrived at the aircraft, I felt like I was carrying an extra fifty pounds of gear.

Once our pre-flight checks were done, we were finally ready to go. The missions were initially set up so that the C-141s flew by day and the C-130s at night. But now that things had begun to heat up, only the C-130s were allowed to fly into Tan Son Nhut. We began our take-off roll just as the sun was going down. In about four hours we would be in Saigon.

A four-hour flight over water at night gives one a lot of time to think. I do not remember much conversation inbound to Vietnam; we each had too much to think about. Our Flight Engineer, John Kays, and our Loadmaster, Steve Tkach, had each served in Vietnam before, when the war was really hot. They knew what to expect. Our Aircraft Commander, Bill Lundberg, had flown EC-47s earlier over Vietnam and knew what was ahead. The rest of us, all first lieutenants, were rookies. We had no way of knowing what to expect and we had no way of knowing how we would react. But old hands or rookies, we all had our thoughts and emotions to deal with.

Somewhere inbound to Saigon I began to ponder all the equipment I had been issued—flak jacket, survival vest, and .38 pistol and ammunition. Our C-130s had armored seats—panels of thick material on all sides of the crew seats—all sides except the bottom, that is. I decided that this would be a very good place for all that equipment I had been issued. So, I wore the survival vest and .38 pistol, and slid the flak jacket under my seat in the probably foolish notion that it afforded me some degree of protection. It was well that I did all this over the water because I got so busy later that I never thought about any personal preparation.

Eventually the coastline of Vietnam began to show up, first on radar, then after a while we could see the lights from the villages along the coast. I still remember the taste in my mouth. Now there was no more time for private thoughts; we began to get busy. There were many radio calls to make and answer. Often I was listening to three radio frequencies at the same time. Frank Jershe, the other co-pilot, assigned as a scanner for our flight was able to help with the radios until we got overhead Saigon, but then he had to return to his duties in the cargo compartment with the loadmaster. As busy as I was, Bill Lundberg, our aircraft commander, clearly had the most difficult job. In addition to flying the plane, he had to coordinate with each one of us to make sure that things went as smoothly as possible.

We had been briefed to fly overhead Saigon—right over the city at twenty-thousand feet. We were all wearing parachutes and our flight helmets and oxygen, and we were to depressurize the aircraft and open the paratroop doors on each side in the back of the cargo compartment as we descended in circles. The loadmaster and the scanner each hooked up safety harnesses and stood in the open doors with flare pistols loaded with phosphorus flares. If they saw SA-7 shoulder fired missile launches, they were to fire these flares at the oncoming missiles in the hope that the heat from the flares would decoy the missiles away from us. Just off-shore we had turned off all our navigation and position lights and our red rotating beacon so that we were completely dark.

Now we were over the city, flying blacked out, depressurized, with two crewmembers strapped at the open doors ready to launch flares at any missiles as we spiraled down in the dark. All the way down we had to look out for missiles and small arms fire, find Tan Son Nhut AB (it was blacked out too), and hope to avoid any other aircraft in the area. We could hear other crews calling out their altitudes over the radio as they spiraled up or down over the city just like we were doing. We all hoped that they were not too near. I remember straining my eyes looking through the dark at the ground as we descended, trying to look out for shoulder fired missiles, and wondering if the twinkling lights I saw below were the result of ground lights shining and flickering through the trees in the city or small arms fire.

Finally, as we got lower and flew more towards the northwest part of the city, we located the blacked-out patch of ground called Tan Son Nhut AB. Our final spirals in the dark brought us in for a landing over the dark runway. All the lights on the runways and taxiways had been turned off lest they provide illumination and range for any enemy soldiers in the area. We made our final approach as steep as possible, completely blacked out onto a blacked out runway. I let out an audible sigh of relief as the landing gear made contact with the pavement and Bill threw the propellers into reverse. We had made it!

It only took a few minutes to taxi to the part of the ramp where we were to load our passengers; by the time we got there I realized how tired and drained I was. But we weren't through. We had to run this gauntlet again on our way out of Vietnam!

Some crews experienced lengthy delays on the ground at Tan Son Nhut waiting for their passengers. This never happened to us. Both times we went into Saigon our passengers were ready and we loaded them immediately. Certainly on one occasion we left the engines running, loaded our people and took off again, all in the space of a few minutes. I do not remember much from our ground time in Saigon. I guess we filed a "round-robin" flight plan before we left Clark AB, because I do not remember filing one or even leaving the aircraft in Saigon.

The C-130 is designed to hold about 75 troops in full combat gear or about 90 regular passengers. Normal maximum take-off weight is 155,000 pounds. I have no idea how much we weighed on these flights — none of us knew. I am sure that we did not weigh more than the limit, but we sure carried a lot more than 90 people. We loaded our passengers from the ramp door at the tail of the aircraft and just kept putting them on until the airplane would not hold any more. I can remember our loadmaster losing count after 200. This was not anything unusual or isolated; all the other crews were doing the same things. We had been given a job to do and we were going to do it.

Finally, we took off and climbed up over the city. Once again, we were totally blacked out, spiraling up, calling out altitudes, hearing altitude calls in reply, and looking out for small arms fire and missiles. I prayed that we wouldn't see any, but I prayed even harder that if we did see missiles we would see them in time.

All the way from take-off to coast out, really all the way from coast in to coast out, I was filled with both apprehension and uncertainty. What a sense of relief when we were safely off the coast of South Vietnam headed back to the Philippines!

Once we were over the water and safely on our way back to Clark AB, I got out of my seat and went to the steps leading to the cargo compartment. I guess I felt that I had to see what it was like in the back. The cargo space was packed with people, all of them sitting on empty cargo pallets on the aircraft floor. It was so crowded that no one could move anywhere. None of us in the cockpit could go to the back, and neither our loadmaster nor our scanner could come up front. This airborne sea of humanity was very subdued. There were no smiling faces in spite of being airlifted out of a war, only faces that reflected fear and uncertainty. These people were leaving behind their homes and in many cases, their families. What they must have been feeling, I can only imagine. It was a pretty quiet flight home, as we each had a lot to think about on our way out of Vietnam.

While my flights evacuating Saigon were uneventful, some of my fellow crews from the 21st Tactical Airlift Squadron had different experiences. Our ground times were very short, but some of the other crews spent many hours waiting for their passengers to be processed before they could be boarded onto the airplanes. I can only imagine what that must have felt like, spending hours in the dark on the ramp at Tan Son Nhut, wondering when the airfield would be attacked.

Tan Son Nhut was attacked at least twice while C-130 crews were on the ground. One attack came from South Vietnamese A-37 aircraft either captured in the fall of Pleiku or flown by disgruntled South Viet namese airmen. One of my friends, First Lieutenant Fritz Pingel, was the aircraft commander of a C-130 on the ground when the field was bombed by these A-37s. He took off as quickly as he could, only to be chased by one of the A-37s. Fritz did about the only thing you can do in a C-130 in a situation like this; he flew as fast and as low as he could and headed for the coast. He also tried to fly into any cloud he could find in the hopes of losing his pursuer. Only when he got to the coast did the A-37 turn away. He told me later that he could never figure out why they did not get shot up that day unless the A-37 was out of ammunition.

Shortly after this incident, on April 29, the field came under rocket attack. One of the rockets hit the wing of a parked C-130 and it immediately burst into flames. Captain Greg Chase and his crew were parked nearby and watched in horror as the airplane burned. Fortunately, the plane had not yet been loaded with passengers and all the crew members managed to escape the wreckage and scramble into Greg's airplane. They immediately took off for Clark AB. I believe that this was the last Amer ican C-130 to leave Tan Son Nhut.

My crew made two trips in and out of Saigon that April. On April 29th, about the time Tan Son Nhut was under rocket attack, we were inbound to Saigon for our third time when we got the call from the Command Post. "Come on back to Clark, it's over." The following day, April 30, 1975, Saigon fell to the North Vietnamese Army. The war was truly over.

Over forty-six years have passed since then, and while I am sure that I have forgotten or confused some of the details of those trips, onething is sure. I will never forget the faces of those people, mostly women and children, on my airplane that April in 1975.

POST-VIETNAM MEMORIES

STEVE MOSIER

USAF: Fighter Pilot, Squadron Commander, Chief Checkmate Group, HQ
USAF

Dates of Military Service — Active Duty: September 1966 to July 1993

Unit Served with in Vietnam: 433rd Tactical Fighter Squadron, 8th Tactical
Fighter Wing, Ubon Royal Thai Air Base, Thailand

Dates you were in Vietnam: August 1968 — August 1969

Highest Rank Held: Colonel (O-6)

Place of Birth and Year: Kansas City, Missouri — 1943

THE WALL

I completed my one tour in the 433rd Tactical Fighter Squadron at
Ubon Royal Thai Air Base in late August of 1969. My next assignment
was Bitburg, Germany where, after about a month in the States visiting
family and friends, we'd spend the next four years. I had been warned the
environment outside Travis Air Force Base, a couple of hours east of San
Francisco was not particularly hospitable to men in uniform, especially
those returning from the Southeast Asia "war games." Funny, since I was
there on in the summer of '67 and anyone with a buck and a hankering
to go to the Condor Club was welcome, pretty much the same when
my best friend from pilot training and I met there in August before our
MAC flight to Clark AB and on to Ubon. San Francisco was ringed
with Army, Air Force, Marine, and Navy facilities.

San Francisco was a military friendly town. Not so a year later. On
the bus to the Airport in civilian clothes and on to meet Pat and spend
our vacation in mid-America. Not hostile territory, but not much discussion about Vietnam. Nixon was the president, LBJ was back in Texas on
the ranch, and there was unrest in many parts of the country. We headed
to Germany, except for only two occasions not to return to the States for
four years.

We were back in fall of 1973 — Nixon, was gone, we were out of
Vietnam for the most part, we were working our way back to the California Kool and the society of our country after a long time having only

AFFN radio, black and white TV a few hours a day, and irregular access to Stars and Stripes. In some ways it was overload. Twelve years and four assignments later, we were living in West Springfield, Virginia, and I was on duty in BF940, a subbasement of the Pentagon. At that time, the Vietnam Memorial Wall had been constructed and was a well trafficked site for tourists in our nation's capital.

I'd heard about the Wall, and much of the controversy of the symbolism and choice of material used in its construction. Indian marble was chosen for its reflectivity and similar material from Canada and Sweden because of their harboring of Americans avoiding military service in Vietnam. I couldn't visualize the design by Maya Lin as being what my mind's eye had for any monument honoring the over fifty thousand dying in what at the time was our nation's longest and costliest war. I'd seen it a few times, but then came Memorial Day of 1988 when my family made the trip to the Wall.

Driving by the Wall you don't notice it, but you almost always see people visiting—in small groups—moving quietly in the area. We parked and headed to where the people were—quietly and with some wonder. Then we got there—it is semi-recessed and long, fifty thousand names long. It is arranged, left to right, with the first losses moving to the last. Along the Wall are mementos—artifacts actually—people leave near the names they came to see. Jungle boots, some worn, some pristine, flowers, medals, ribbons, and sometimes a helmet or some other item of significance to a friend, relative, family, or loved one.

Pat and Megan and I walked the line. I was looking for names. Two were fraternity brothers from Mizzou, one a Riverine commander, the other a Navy Intruder pilot. Both lost while I was in college. There were five names from my squadron, Satan's Angels. Two were lost on a night mission—ground fire, weather, or just a karst in the wrong place, we never knew. One was prematurely ejected from his Phantom after hits by ground fire while dropping high drag weapons in Mu Gia Pass, a mouth of Hell on the Laotian-North Vietnam border—his wife and my wife had met us for R&R in Honolulu only weeks before he died on the side of a mountain while PJs unsuccessfully tried to pull him out.

Two more were lost—I mean lost—never found—never any evidence found—on a Wolf FAC mission in their Phantom. One wasn't supposed to be there—he was a fill-in for a buddy too sick to make the mission.

Later that day, I was interviewed by a reporter from the *Baltimore Sun*. She wrote a story that was front page with pictures the next day, the headline was, "You think of your brothers who never made it back." She interviewed many vets. My coverage by Lyndia Robinson went, " .... In Dockers and polo shirt, looking little like the motorcycle veterans .... Living in northern Virginia, he shed tears as he read a letter one veteran left to a friend .... "Most of us were young when we went ... they did their best ... and there is value in that ..." The Wall is just right.

If you've seen it, you may have notions about what it could have been, but you will probably say, at least to yourself, it is right—it says it. If you haven't been, go. You may quibble about the location and the design, but I'll bet you'll never be the same again. Go. It will take your mind off the physical and mental fence that surrounds the building and the minds on the east end of the Mall. And never forget, those are the men and women you elect, and allow young people to be sent to places like Vietnam.

DONALD H. NAU

U S Army — Armor/Infantry Officer

Dates of Military Service (Active and Reserve): 1967-1974

Unit Served with in Vietnam: HQ Co, 3rd Combat Brigade, 25th Infantry Division

Dates in Vietnam: Aug 1969 to Aug 1970

Highest Rank Held: 1LT (O-2)

Place of Birth and Year: East Cleveland, Ohio — 1944

DID YOU KILL ANYONE?

Pensacola Florida has a 1/2 size Vietnam Veterans "Wall" located at the Veterans Memorial Park a few blocks from downtown. Every Ceremonial Day, an event would take place with the music, speakers, veterans' families, and — politicians. My wife, Elaine, and I went once and, because of the "vote for me" politicians, decided to never attend any more. Instead, we would go the following day. If anyone was there, it would be park workers, who would leave everyone alone and veterans/families that did not want to be disturbed.

As I have many, many buddies on that Wall, I would wear my Army dress green uniform complete with patches and medals. No one bothered me — until ...

One day, as we were walking down the sidewalk to leave, a school van pulled up and outflowed Cub Scouts — all in uniform. After what seemed like a short lesson to them from their Den Mother, she stopped to ask if I would speak to the Scouts — How could I not?

She introduced me as a Veteran and told them they could ask me questions. A short silence followed and then the first Cub Scout asked, "What is a Veteran?" I thought for a bit and began trying to answer in a coherent way to these youngsters. I got as far as Service to the Country when it happened — In mini-gun rapidity, the questions came: How long have you been a Veteran? Did you fire guns? Did you sleep outside? What are your medals? Were you shot? Did you shoot anybody? Did you kill anybody?

With the quickness and kindness of a mother protecting her sons, the Den Mother stepped in and told the children to thank me and re-directed them to the helicopter on display. Soon they were gone—as fast as they arrived. I stood there with every Vietnam memory blazing through my mind.

We left and I have since tried to come up with an answer for them—I was saved by the Den Mother, but I still haven't settled on any response—the Den Mother probably knew that. After all, these were children earning project badges and pins to wear, going to pack meetings, hiking, camping, community projects, playing games, and enjoying Scout Night at a ballgame.

I have still never answered that last question to anyone.

Regrettably—I never got to tell them I was a Cub Scout once.

CARY KING

US Army—Artillery and Infantry Officer

Dates of Military Service (Active and Reserve): 1963 to 1987

Unit Served with in Vietnam: 2nd Bn, 28th Infantry Regt, 2nd Bde, 1st Inf. Div.;1st Bn, 7th Field Artillery Bn; HHB, Division Artillery

Dates in Vietnam: Apr 1967 to Oct 1968

Highest Rank Held: Lt. Colonel (O-5)

Place of Birth and Year: Atlanta, GA—1941

LESSONS LEARNED

Before I started trying to compose my thoughts for this article to be included in the sequel to *I'm Ready to Talk*, I decided to re-read the first article I wrote. As I read it, hopefully with some objectivity, I realized that while the details of most of the things that I did or experienced were there, the impact of those things in the long run on my life were not there or were very difficult for me to convey. The pain from the loss of comrades, friends, bosses, and sometimes service members lost in combat whom I barely knew, was sorely missing in that article. The pain remains with me, 53 years after I returned home. It is mostly at night when I am trying to sleep, and my defenses are down. My Vietnam experiences were key factors in how I live my life and what decisions I have made, personally and professionally. What I learned there, for better or worse, shaped everything in my life that I have done since the Vietnam War. Because of that, I have titled this second writing, **Lessons Learned: Post War Veterans Support**.

POST WAR VETERANS SUPPORT

I returned from Vietnam in November 1968, having served as an Officer with the 1st Infantry Division in both Infantry and Artillery units during 1967 and later leading to the 1968 Tet Offensive, probably one of the worst two years of the War. I remained on active duty until January 1970 when I left active duty after seven years' total active service.

At first, I didn't discuss the War, or anything about what was on my mind (or in my heart), with anyone. After I left active duty, it would be a period of several years until I re-affiliated and joined the Army Reserves and later the National Guard. I didn't discuss my feelings or my experiences in Vietnam for many more years, really until 1979 or 1980. I often would not respond to inquiries about "what was the war like" until the AVVBA was formed; and I joined in 1985 or 1986.

In 1980, my first wife and I divorced, and I decided to return to Law School (at night), a goal I had set for myself in college but one that was very much interrupted by the War. In 1983, I graduated from Law School, passed the Bar Exam, and opened a law practice at age 40, where I still practice law today with my son.

I married one of my closest girlfriends (and crushes) from High School in 1984. It is to her I owe my sanity and whatever small successes I may have had since 1981. She has been my gyroscope and is the person who helped me talk about and deal with that War.

THE LESSONS I LEARNED

I don't pretend that anything I experienced is any different, any better, any worse, or any more dangerous than that of any other Vietnam Veteran, or any other combat veteran. I also don't claim that my lessons learned are some new or revolutionary deep thoughts or that I have some words worthy of publication to the world. My lessons learned are *purely personal observations* as are all lessons learned by someone. I was a young naïve guy when I arrived at my War, but most of us never can or will return to that simplicity again after our individual Wars were over.

We are all fragile physical beings, and our existence, which may seem permanent, but our existence, and our very life, can be gone in a split second. It doesn't make any difference how young, how strong, or how smart you are, every second you are alive, you must value that alone above all else. Human life is the most precious gift we have. The ability to change things that make you unhappy or that hurts someone else or that may make things better for you or them, is always available if you just act to overcome your fears and you have life.

In war, as in life, it's other people that we are here for, not just for our own aggrandizement or gratification. During my War, I saw people sacrifice everything they had, including their lives, for another person. I have heard numerous speeches by veterans, even Medal of Honor recipients, and this much I have learned and have had confirmed by others who served. In combat, your first thought and priority in the worst possible situations, is first to protect your comrades, secondly, to not dishonor your family, thirdly, not to dishonor your Country and then, not to dishonor your branch of the service. It is usually your own welfare that comes last.

We are all spiritual beings on some level. I am not speaking of an organized religious group necessarily, although many of us do belong to one religion or another. I learned that actions in combat are often propelled by the spiritual strength given to us that we may not know we have until the crisis presents itself. It is that spiritual connection and spiritual paternalism, in my opinion, that makes us care more for one of our soldiers than we do for own existence.

As a soldier, I learned that night could be my enemy. We somehow felt that when we were toddlers. I had to learn that the night was not my enemy if I could overcome that fear. I see it as a kind of a metaphor to living your life — if something scares you, face it directly and deal with it.

Connected to any medals or awards for valor/bravery that any combat veteran has received, someone has been badly wounded or killed in action. That is a fact and a painful reminder for all combat veterans, about those who we lost. The greatest majority of combat veterans, including me, wear our decorations proudly, none of us ever forget that those medals or ribbons are a constant symbol and reminder of those we lost.

What Vietnam Veterans want people to do for us is to *Welcome Us Home*, because when we returned, we were either treated with disdain or scorn, or worse yet, were treated with apathy. While I have long ago made peace with my bitterness at that treatment, I can't forget it. To quote Lt. General Harold Moore, Jr., the hero of the 7th Cavalry action in 1965 and the co-author of the book and movie, *We Were Soldiers Once… and Young,* "Hate War, love the warriors."

We all, as human beings, are capable of the greatest acts of bravery, kindness, and empathy, or the worst acts imaginable, to each other. War is witness to both. We have choices in War as in everyday life as to which path we take.

THE 2002 DÉJÀ VU TRIP

In 2001, my next-door neighbor and good friend, Rick Columbia, a Navy Fighter pilot instructor and later a Delta Airlines pilot, convinced me that he and I should plan a trip to Vietnam and, since he was never on the ground there, that I should plan the agenda. I repeatedly said no because the prospect of going back, even to the now Post-War Vietnam, was confusing and a scary prospect to me. I decided that this was one of the fears I needed to face and resolve or, at least not run from it.

In spite of that, by 2002, I had decided that the best way to deal with my fears and my trepidations about *MY War* was to face them head on. After lots of stalling, I planned the trip with an agency called *Nine Dragons Tours*, only this time, I took a blank journal to record what each day was like for me — not just a travelogue.

While going back to Vietnam was very rewarding in many ways, it was also deeply spiritual for me, which was not always easy to handle then, or even now as I write about it. Simply put, I planned the trip as a return to the 1st Infantry Division Area of Operations (AO) and retraced my steps and my memories, as best I could[2].

During my déjà vu trip, I think the most difficult days were the trip to a Viet Cong/NVA Military Cemetery near Bien Hoa, slightly north of Saigon (Ho Chi Minh City) and a visit the same day to a Buddhist

---

2. For many of the base camps I had been in, or areas where there had been heavy fighting such as the airstrip at Loc Ninh, we were barred from entry or even taking photographs, probably from a military security standpoint. I was unable to find the jungle position where I lost three of my men on June 22, 1968.

shrine. I asked our guide, driver, and interpreter, if it would be considered disrespectful if l went into the military cemetery. He said it would not be considered disrespectful, but that we would have to go to the main building and then we would be escorted by the caretaker. When we entered the building, the guide explained to the caretaker that we wanted to pay our respects and that I had been there during the War as a soldier.

He did not tell the caretaker that I served there with the 1st Infantry Division, so the caretaker asked me himself through the interpreter. When he found out that I had been with the 2/28th Infantry at Loc Ninh and later was heavily involved in the Tet Offensive of 1968 as S-2 of 2nd Brigade, where we were tasked with defending an attack on the Thu Duc water purification plant which serviced the Saigon area, the caretaker shook my hand, bowed, and asked us to follow him.

He escorted us to a section of the cemetery where there was a series of head stones bunched together. He explained through the interpreter that all the graves there were members of the same squad from the Viet Cong 273d VC Regiment and that they had all been killed during the 1968 Tet Offensive or immediately after, probably by units with whom I was involved. Part of me felt physically ill to hear this so many years later, while part of me wondered why he was showing me this. We all stood in silence for what seemed like ten minutes, but I'm sure it was a shorter time.

The caretaker then turned to me and, in Vietnamese he said that he had been with this V.C. unit, that he and I were all fellow veterans and comrades (not in the communist sense), and that now it was like "Karma" (not his word) for us to meet again and honor each other. At that point he embraced me. I do not have the writing skills to express the feelings from that meeting.

The next day, I went to a Buddhist shrine in Saigon, near the Cholon Market (the Chinese area) and lit three sticks resembling the old sparklers we used to have on July 4th. We let the smoke rise through the ceiling as a Monk had told me to do, to allow the souls of the three men I lost on June 22, 1968, to reach the heavens. I experienced some sort of release that day, but there can never be "closure", a term I hate.

Nor should there be closure to a split second in time that destroyed the lives and the futures of three young men. I will never shake the feeling as their CO that I was accountable for their safety, so why couldn't I protect them?

POST WAR VETERANS SUPPORT

On June 22,1968 as Battery Commander of "C" Battery, 1st Battalion, 7th Artillery, I made a pact with myself and with three men who died that night under a ground and mortar attack. Something or someone greater than me allowed me to survive, maybe for some purpose. I promised silently that night that If I survived, I would find a way to honor those men and others by finding a way to give back somehow. I had no idea at the time what form that giving back might take or, what promises I could fulfill, but I didn't forget it. I believe that all of us who survive made that promise, even if we aren't consciously aware of it.

THE VA LEGAL CLINIC

As the years went by after my return home and I left active duty with the Army, I kept trying to find the place where I might be able to fulfill the promise I made that night.

In 1998, 30 years after I had returned, my question was answered. As a member of the State Bar of Georgia, I belong to many groups of law professionals. During a luncheon for one of those groups, a retired lawyer, World War II veteran and former POW, approached me and another ex-infantry officer who was now a lawyer. He asked us if we would be interested in starting a *pro bono* (free) legal clinic at the Veterans Administration Medical Center (VAMC) at Clairmont Road, in Decatur, Georgia, and giving a day or so per month to help veterans with legal problems.

I knew at that moment that this was the way I was going to fulfill that promise I made 30 years before. Since that day. I remain a permanent member of the clinic and that legal team. In 2002, I became the co-director of the clinic with Greg Studdard, the other infantry officer / lawyer and numerous other lawyers who have volunteered and worked with veterans through that clinic and other clinics which now have been formed around the state. That original clinic has provided more than 15,000 free legal hours for veterans and has now been in existence for 23 years.

For me, there has never been a more rewarding way to use my legal knowledge than the work we all do through the clinic. I continue to work to try and expand our clinics to every major area of Georgia where veterans need legal help.

THE STATE BAR OF GEORGIA

Realizing how much the VAMC Clinic helped me to find my path to contribute, I joined the Military and Veterans Law Section of the State Bar in 2010 and became involved with the Military Legal Assistance Program (MLAP) managed and led by Norman Zoller, a two-tour Vietnam Veteran and the MLAP Executive Director. I connected with many others in the section and the MLAP who shared our goals of providing legal advice to veterans. I served as Chairman of that committee for two years and remain active on the MLAP Board. The State Bar is continually working on forming new veterans' clinics and starting other projects aimed at helping veterans of all services and all wars. In January 2013, I was awarded the Marshall-Tuttle Award by the Military Legal Assistance Program for work with veterans and recognition by the VA General Counsel of the United States Department of Veterans Affairs in the same year. It was that same committee that helped create the Veterans Courts which now are conducted in over 50% of the State of Georgia's 49 judicial circuits.

THE AVVBA

The Atlanta Vietnam Veterans Business Association (the AVVBA) is an organization that never loses sight of the objective to help Vietnam and other veterans and to demonstrate to the world that Vietnam veterans have contributed greatly in every way to this country since our return. That organization and its members have been the catalyst for almost everything I have been able to do for veterans, outside of the VAMC clinic. I am a Past President and Chairman of the AVVBA and currently serve on the AVVBA Board of Directors. I am a Vice President of the AVVBA Foundation, our 501(c)(3) charitable entity that provides, among its accomplishments, scholarships to educational institutions for qualified veterans and relatives of veterans.

Knowing how much the VAMC Clinic has enriched my life, I have continued to try and find places where I could serve. It is the AVVBA that has always provided those additional avenues. The USO at the Airport, the Atlanta History Center Legacy Project, and oral interviews of veterans for the Library of Congress have provided wonderful opportunities for many of us to "give back" and for that, I thank the AVVBA, a great organization composed of people who care.

I am now 80 years old at this writing and have been practicing law in State and Federal Courts for almost 40 years. I mention this in closing because when I look back over the hundreds of private cases, some involving large amounts of money and others involving someone's freedom, the cases that stand out to me and loom largest when I wonder if I have made a difference in the world, are almost always the *pro bono* cases I have handled for veterans.

And that may be the largest lesson I have learned, that when you look after your troops, it is its own reward.

EDWARD ETTEL

U.S. Navy

Dates of Military Service (Active and Reserve): 1963 to 1989

Unit Served with in Vietnam: USS Hollister (DD-788)

Dates you were in Vietnam: 1964

Highest Rank Held: Navy Captain (O-6)

Place of Birth and Year: Corpus Christi, TX—1940

SUPPORTING DEPLOYED MILITARY PERSONNEL

Did you ever receive letters or packages from home when you were deployed? If so, you know how much it meant to you. If you never received anything, you also know how that felt. Except for five weeks, I served overseas continuously for three years, from 1964 through 1967, so I know the "Drill." I was in the Pacific waters when the Gulf of Tonkin event happened, starting the buildup in the Vietnam War. By the time I left, the U.S. had over 300,000 military in Vietnam and the waters and airspace around it. I was fortunate that my family seldom let a mail call go by without me receiving a letter or package or both.

From that background and knowing deployment environments and needs of the troops haven't changed, when the War on Terror continued to grow, my wife, Mary, and I founded the Project Mail Call mission in 2005. Our objective was, and is, to help ensure that our current deployed military know we appreciate and support them.

While this is not the typical story you will read in this book, it shows how our experiences in the Pacific Theater during the Vietnam War made a change in our lives that we will cherish forever.

Mary and I ensure that customized care-packages and letters of encouragement provide a personal touch, supporting and increasing morale by mailing merchandise the troops specifically request or need. You say, "What about the USO?" There are many organizations that support the US military, but Project Mail Call is unusual in that it brings volunteers together to pack customized and personalized care-packages, providing a more meaningful experience for themselves and the troops they are supporting.

Now in our 17th year, the mission has packed and mailed over 10,000 customized care-packages weighing over 160,000 pounds. The boxes were mailed to over 7,500 military units representing over 190,000 military personnel in 64 countries and many ships at sea. Over 48,000 volunteers have packed care-boxes or written letters of support that were enclosed in the boxes. Volunteers from civic organizations, corporations, all denominations of churches, clubs, schools, and other groups attend regularly scheduled care-box packing sessions in our home basement, 45 sessions a year on average. We have also hosted *Bar Mitzvah* events, birthday parties, family reunions, catered club meetings, and corporate team-building exercises. No weddings yet!

Project Mail Call serves U.S. deployed military, but it is also a mission that gives the American people an opportunity to say, "thank you for your service" in a very personal way. The volunteers know they are doing something of value, and something that supports our military serving overseas. Particular attention is given to service personnel who are in remote locations, do not receive mail from home, do not have a BX/PX, or who provide humanitarian aid to locals at their deployment location. Many military families do not have the funds or time to purchase merchandise and mail care-packages, or they are unfamiliar with the process. Individuals and organizations also want to support our deployed military, but don't know how to do it. We make it easy for them to do so.

We maintain a large inventory of several hundred item categories that are requested most often. This includes snacks, food staples, toiletries, household items, medical supplies, paperback books, magazines, stationery, blank greeting cards, batteries, flashlights/headlamps, hand/foot warmers, sports equipment, gloves, woolen caps, bedding, and towels. Several months ahead of holidays we mail holiday decorations and blank holiday greeting cards for the troops to send home. If a military unit requests an item that is not in our inventory, we try to purchase that item for that unit.

In many cases the unit or service member asks for a specific brand or flavor, so we shop for that specific item, knowing it will have deeper meaning for them. For those military units that are voluntarily supporting schools, clinics, orphanages, or villages in other countries, we mail tons of school supplies, clothes, shoes, toys, blankets, sports equipment, and other merchandise to the units so the units can give to the locals themselves. Schools and organizations create seasonal cards, such as Valentine's Day, Easter, 4th of July, Veterans' Day, Thanksgiving, and Christmas, which we mail with sufficient lead time. Besides inserting their own personal support letter, the packers also sign information sheets that describe the packing process, and if they desire, include their email and mailing addresses so the military units can respond. When the units respond, it further enhances the personal nature of the mission for the volunteers.

We use a combination of sources to obtain information about military units and individual military personnel that need support. We encourage churches or other organizations to identify families of deployed military personnel so we can mail care packages. However, we predominately use the AnySoldier.com® website, which manages a list of deployed personnel who are single points-of-contact who have volunteered to represent their unit. The list is continuously maintained to reflect the unit's situation, environment, and their specific requests. The points-of-contact also provide the number of men and women, whether they have access to a microwave, refrigerator, or laundry service. We then select the military units we determine need the most support.

We prepare paperwork several days before each packing event. The U.S. Postal Service provides an on-line application for users to process Customs Forms, mailing forms, and options for paying for the postage ahead of time. The post office then picks up the Priority Boxes, which is overwhelmingly our primary mailing method. Our volunteers write their own letters of encouragement and insert other pre-written letters from schoolchildren and other supporters. We also include group photographs of the volunteers in each box.

The troops tell us that the letters from children and the photographs are more important to them than any merchandise in the boxes. We have also found that it is a special moment for them when they receive specific items that they are fond of, because they know we are attentive to their needs, and it brings them closer to home. They tell us that when they open their boxes, their comrades are right there, watching each item that is revealed. They say it is "just like Christmas," and they also say it means a lot to them that someone they don't know has taken the time to remember and support them in a very personal way.

Many families or relatives of military personnel serving overseas have come to our basement to pack for their loved ones. Soldiers returning from Iraq, Afghanistan, and other theaters have come to "see where the boxes came from" and as they put it, "give back", by supporting us and packing boxes for others. Mothers and fathers who have lost family members in Iraq and Afghanistan have also come to pack boxes for other troops.

To show his thanks after returning from deployment, an Army sergeant diverted a Boston-to-Florida family trip to Atlanta to stop by our home and thank us. Being a Sunday, we were at church, but he found our church, left his wife and kids in his van, located where we were in our Sunday School Class, and presented a certificate and flag from his unit.

We also give presentations to civic organizations, corporations, church groups, and schools of all kinds, from elementary schools to high schools. These presentations make them aware of what the military is doing, what their environment is like, and why they need our support. I always give the presentation in uniform to add emphasis to the mission, using professional PowerPoint presentations, customized to each audience. It is meaningful to volunteers and donors when they are more personally involved in the process.

For example, after hearing presentations, they conduct merchandise drives, shop for items they know the troops have asked for, write letters, and attend care-box packing sessions. They are also excited when they receive thank-you letters from the deployed military. In short, they are more engaged when they understand why the troops need their support and are directly involved in providing such personal support.

It is inspiring to us that many young people have gone out of their way to support the troops. Besides the many schools that have conducted merchandise collection drives, a young brother and sister opened a lemonade stand to raise money for the mission, and then opened a hot chocolate stand in the Fall. Another high school student wrote and conducted a play at his high school and raised $500 for Project Mail Call. A high school girl packed boxes with us, then later brought a group from Georgia Tech, and after graduation scheduled a packing session for her company.

To advance to the highest rank of Eagle Scout, scouts are required to perform an Eagle Scout Service Project, and one young man planned, developed, and executed "You are Not Forgotten," a project focused on Project Mail Call. He coordinated merchandise drives at several schools, his neighborhood, and from Cub Scout families who attended the Boy Scouts Atlanta Area Council (AAC) Cub Scout Summer Day Camp. He also oversaw letter-writing campaigns at schools and the camp, and with his mom, delivered and restocked several large amounts of merchandise and thousands of "letters for the Troops." These are just a fraction of the many young people who go to great lengths to support the troops and Project Mail Call.

The mission is an official mission of Mount Bethel United Methodist Church in Marietta, Georgia, so donors can donate through the church or directly to Project Mail Call, which also has 501(c)(3) status. Approximately 32% of our costs are mailing costs. We purchase approximately 85% of our merchandise at retail stores, whereas the rest of the merchandise is donated directly to Project Mail Call. We have no salaried personnel and 94% of the costs are merchandise and mailing costs.

Project Mail Call has received numerous honors and recognition from local, state, and federal organizations, including from three U.S. Presidents, and in-chamber recognition from State Senate/House of Representatives, and the U.S. Senate. But the most treasured are the thousands of letters and certificates we have received from the deployed military. The best part of the process is something we don't see…the moment when the military units receive and open the boxes.

When serving overseas in the military, doing the work of our country, one of the most exciting times is Mail Call, when mail is distributed to the troops. That is why we named our mission **Project Mail Call**. See more details at www.projectmailcall.com. If you would like to help us, or maybe even start a similar mission wherever you live in this great country of ours, we'll be happy to help you in any way we can. You can contact us at info@projectmailcall.com.

DONALD H. NAU

U S Army — Armor/Infantry Officer

Dates of Military Service (Active and Reserve): 1967-1974

Unit Served with in Vietnam: HQ Co, 3rd Combat Brigade, 25th Infantry Division

Dates in Vietnam: Aug 1969 to Aug 1970

Highest Rank Held: 1LT (O-3)

Place of Birth and Year: East Cleveland, Ohio — 1944

IN TWO PLACES AT THE SAME TIME

18 miles…That is the drive from our family's old farmhouse on River Road to the center of the Kent State University Ohio campus — known as the Commons…18 miles.

Now, I would occasionally go to Kent as friends lived there and, back then, Ohio allowed 3.2% beer. The friends and beer would both be there. I chose not to attend KSU as it was just too close to home…18 miles. Instead, I went to another State University 140 miles away — just right.

KSU was started as a "Normal" school in 1910. The term "normal" refers to the goal of these institutions to instill and reinforce particular *norms* within students — they became also known as "Teacher's Colleges.» Through the 1960s, Kent was still a normal school to us. My neighbor on River Road, in fact, commuted to Kent for her education degree. Kent, Ohio was a peaceful small town. Very quickly one is in open land when leaving in any direction.

May 4, 1970, changed it all. No more 18 miles; I was 8,800 miles from the Kent State University Commons. On that day, I was now in places called The Hobo Woods, Parrot's Beak, Angels Wing, rice paddies, and the tunnels of Cu Chi. This was not Portage or Summit County Ohio — rather, Hau Nghia Province, Republic of South Vietnam. My friends were now Army buddies of the U S Army's 25th Infantry Division and beer was rare. But Kent State University — Kent Normal was, this day, a War Zone!

Not Kent State — Not Middle Ohio! This cannot be one of the

hundreds of colleges and universities student assemblies and protests of the military move into Cambodia. NOT Kent State! But there it was—Ohio Army National Guard, with fixed bayonets, firing on students who were participating or watching in a demonstration. We later learned the old, unused, and soon to be demolished WWII building being used for ROTC storage, had been burned the night before. Word also was that outside violent activists had arrived at Kent. Either way, only a few protestors were "armed" with small stones.

In 13 seconds, it was over: 13 casualties: 4 dead & 9 injured—all students. Officially, the Guard had fired 67 rounds—67—many would have had to go up into the air—just not all. I have not been back. Friend Kathy has remarried after her then husband Larry, a best high school buddy, died from cancer at the age of 38. He had been in Vietnam as a Navy Huey door-gunner and served on a Navy Brown Water Swift Boat. He was exposed to Agent Orange.

Today stands a Memorial on the Commons and a nearby Museum. On the next visit to see family, I have thought about going to the Commons. But, then to do what? Respect—sure, Closure?—no such thing. Curious—it won't be the same. I was in fact the real enemy in the minds of the students. The 25th did go into Cambodia. I did fly to Cambodia only to have the chopper hit by small ground fire and force the pilot to return us to Cu Chi.

Irony: The Kent students were killed by the National Guard for protesting against me who was defending the US Constitution which guaranteed their right of protest so they would never be killed by an enemy—foreign or domestic. A circuitous Catch-22. 18 miles is a lifetime.

UPDATE: During a family visit to Ohio, on August 27, 2021, my wife and I visited Kent State, the Commons, and the killing zone known as Prentice Hall Parking Lot. We, in fact, parked there—it is still used with enforced (?) window stickers for those privileged—$225.00 per school year. We parked there—used to be a saying, "What are they going to do—send me to Vietnam?"

Classes had officially started the day before, but the campus was very quiet. A few students walked around the Commons grass staring at their phone. A "Normal" day. Signs were mounted as one could take the walking tour of That Day. The museum was closed—would not have gone in—Hell, I am in there anyway.

A Parking Lot!! The students were killed or wounded in a Parking Lot!! A Parking Lot that was over *300 feet* away from the Ohio Guard soldiers. More than a football field length!

A small tablet with the names of the four killed is at an end of the Parking Lot. Small stones are placed on top of the marker—unused student weapons.

The 50+ year weight was lifted—though not about me. I prayed a silent prayer—actually, four. Prayers are never too late—are they?

ROBERT O. "BOB" BABCOCK

US Army— Infantry Officer

Dates of Military Service (Active Duty and Reserves): 1965 to 1974

Unit Served with in Vietnam: Bravo Company, 1st Bn, 22nd Inf Regt, 4th Inf. Div.

Dates Served in Vietnam: Jul 1966 to Jul 1967

Highest Rank Held: Captain (O-3)

Place of Birth: Heavener, OK—1943

AFTER THOUGHTS

Today is August 30, 1993. Less than a month after I arrived in Vietnam, I reached the ripe old age of twenty-three. Today, I am celebrating my 50th birthday with friends and family. Little did I realize back then that twenty-seven years later, those twelve months in Vietnam would loom so large and important in my life's memories. (And as I review my thoughts written in 1993, they are still the same today in 2021, or stronger, at age 78, as they were when I wrote them on my 50th birthday).

Lee Sherman Dreyfuss, past president of Sentry Insurance Company, former governor of Wisconsin, chancellor of the University of Wisconsin at Stevens Point, and renowned motivational speaker, described his World War II experiences far better than I could, therefore I quote: "With the Battle of Okinawa rated as a ten on my life scale, everything else I have done before or since then, is no more than a two." Vietnam had the same profound impact on my life.

As I wind down the odyssey back into my Vietnam experiences and wrap up this *What Now, Lieutenant?* book, a number of thoughts that have not been covered still churn through my mind. I will conclude with some random thoughts that I wrote in 1993 and are still as true today as they were then.

WHY DID I GO TO VIETNAM? WHY DIDN'T I TURN AGAINST THE WAR AS IT DRAGGED ON AND ON? WHY WOULD I DO IT AGAIN IF I WAS CALLED ON?

I guess the answer is very simple—patriotism and love of my country. I grew up in a protected small-town environment where I learned simple values—the American flag, motherhood, and apple pie. I was young and naive. In a way I did not understand at the time, I believed in what President John F. Kennedy had said my senior year in high school, "Ask not what your country can do for you, ask what you can do for your country."

I was also influenced by World War II, the Korean War, and the Cold War. Communism was a real threat in our world in 1966 and I was going to do my part to help stop it before it hit the shores of America. Again, it may sound idealistic, trite, or naive, but I never once considered not serving my country. In fact, I would be very upset today if I had not answered my country's call to duty. I have zero regrets about serving my country in Vietnam.

It should also be noted I was in the Vietnam War during its early troop buildup stage. Grace Coggins Kidwell, a lifelong friend who lived through two tours when her first husband flew bombing missions over North Vietnam from the aircraft carrier *Kitty Hawk,* explained it this way: "We are the in-between generation. Even though the Vietnam War was never popular, we were in it before it became unpopular. The general public thinks of it in its later stages when it got such bad publicity and had so many protestors and dope users."

Marian Faye Novak, in her book *"Lonely Girls with Burning Eyes,"* stated it a little differently. "We faced the future in those days of 1967 with what I think must be called courage. It's true that we were too inexperienced to feel particular fear and too unwise to be afraid of the abstract. But we knew something; I see it in the pictures of the wives. And yet we smiled and danced, and I remember laughter, too. I call that courage. And we had it."

In summary, we were a trusting, idealistic, young generation. We had not, at that time, lived through the Vietnam War, Watergate, nor experienced a press corps obsessed with sensationalism and digging up dirt on public figures. We were fresh off the assassination of JFK and still believed in Camelot. We, the young and naive, were led to war by leaders we had never had a reason to distrust. Oh, to return to such simple times.

WHY IS THE VIETNAM EXPERIENCE SUCH A POWERFUL FORCE IN MY LIFE?

That question has gnawed at me for years, and I think I understand it much better today than I did when I started writing my *What Now, Lieutenant?* book. And the answer is complex, not simple. Probably the most important factors are the intense individual experiences and friendships I developed. I had experiences, almost daily, which stand out above most others in my life.

No other bond measures up to those forged when operating at the most basic of levels. Mutual trust and support of the men you worked with became primary considerations over everything. All else became secondary in importance.

Again, a quote from Marian Faye Novak (I really enjoyed her book), "I watched Bob and Dave together, and I began to see the love that men can have for one another that has nothing to do with sex or romance. It is a kind of love that has to do with caring, and loyalty, and even the special sharing of knowledge about certain things." Never have I developed a bond and respect like I did with the men I served with in Vietnam.

At the age of twenty-three, I had to make more important decisions than any I have ever made in my life, before or since. Much of what we did was potentially a life-or-death situation. It is an awesome responsibility to be in charge of the lives of so many young American men. It is a great source of pride that I did my job...and did it well. That is not unique to Vietnam; it is true of all wars and all veterans.

It makes a lasting impression on you—and puts other decisions in your life in a different perspective. When making tough decisions even today in my IBM career, the question often comes to mind, "What are they going to do: send me to Vietnam?" That helps to put things into proper perspective.

There is a great deal of pride in answering the call as a soldier and living to tell about it. I have always liked the comment George C. Scott, in the title role of the movie "Patton", made as he was talking to his men prior to their going into battle. "When your grandson sits on your knee and asks, 'What did you do in the great World War II, Granddad', you won't have to say, 'Well, I shoveled sh*t in Louisiana.'"

We Vietnam vets will not have to tell our grandsons that we fled to Canada or sat the war out on a draft deferment or missed it for some other reason. We can point with pride at our service to our country. I'm sure there are other factors I have not yet found. I definitely recognize the impact Vietnam has had on me, even if I cannot eloquently explain why.

HOW ABOUT THOSE WHO DID NOT SERVE? WHAT DO YOU THINK ABOUT THEM?

I have never had a big problem with people who did not serve in the Vietnam War. Our national leaders did not mobilize the country, and I cannot expect everyone to have the same streak of patriotism I have. The Vietnam period was a time in America where we lacked strong leadership and national purpose. I cannot fault others of my generation for doing what their conscience dictated.

Those who flocked to the National Guard and Reserves took a legal and logical, for them, approach to service. I served in an Army Reserve unit for several years after my return from Vietnam and worked with some outstanding individuals.

I never did agree with some of their philosophies. Neither did I ever get overly worked up with those who protested the war. What they did was detrimental to our fighting men but part of what we were fighting for was to preserve that very right to dissent. Even Jane Fonda did what she thought was right, and the Constitution I was fighting for gives every living American that right.

576 | ROBERT O. BABCOCK

However, I have no respect for those who overtly and openly avoided service to their country. Those who went to Canada to avoid the draft and those who did other less than honorable things to avoid service, in my opinion, let themselves and their country down. But I can overlook that by attributing it to their youth and inexperience (or their cowardice) at the time. They are the ones who must live with their decisions, not me.

Again, a quote from Marian Faye Novak's book sums up my feelings. "I see the lines of people when we go to the Wall; some are veterans or the friends and relatives of veterans, some are too young to remember the war. But many are not, and I wonder at all these others. Where were you, I think, when these men needed you? When we all needed you? How can you look so long and lovingly on the silent names of these dead when you were so quick to turn your backs on their living faces?"

I think many people may be silently living with the ghosts of decisions made so long ago in their late teens or early twenties.

This story comes from *What Now, Lieutenant?* by Robert O. Babcock, available from Amazon.com or an autographed copy from my web page at www.deedspublishing.com

ATLANTA VIETNAM VETERANS BUSINESS ASSOCIATION (AVVBA) 40 YEARS OF HISTORY

1981 TO 2021

On Veterans Day 2021, the members and wives of the Atlanta Vietnam Veterans Business Association (AVVBA), along with invited guests, celebrated 40 years that our organization has been in existence. The gala event was held at the Atlanta History Center, a place we have supported for many years, thanks to former president Rick Lester getting us established with them. We celebrated our accomplishments over the past 40 years with a slide show and static exhibits.

Read on to see a summary of our accomplishments we as an organization have done to move the 1970s stereotype of the Vietnam veteran from a negative one to what most Vietnam veterans became after their return from Vietnam—hard working and proud American citizens. Since 1981, we have lived our motto—Proud, Professional, Patriotic.

WHAT WE'VE DONE OVER THE PAST 40 YEARS

Promoted the positive image of the Vietnam Veteran—proud of our service and professional appearance—honored our fallen brothers.

Dedicated 26 Memorials honoring Vietnam War KIA and their Families.

Partnered with the USO since 2005 supporting the troops transiting the Atlanta Airport

Established a Veteran Scholarship Program in 2015

Developed a partnership with the Atlanta History Center that helped to capture the true experience of our service in Vietnam, including a 4-hour Vietnam War Symposium and an extensive Vietnam War exhibit, plus other Vietnam War-related events and participation in the Veterans Oral History Program.

Marched each year in the Atlanta Veterans Day Parade (and won recognition as the Best Marching Unit several times).

Participated in the GA Vietnam Veterans Day ceremonies at the Georgia State Capitol in 2014.

Published two books of Vietnam War experiences written by AV-VBA Members.

Operated a Speakers Bureau that sends members out to high schools, colleges, and civic groups to discuss our experiences during the Vietnam War.

Participated in numerous civic projects and activities to honor Veterans and raise money for Veterans causes.

WHERE IT BEGAN...

Veterans Day 1981

Joe Harrison, Mike Turner, Don Pardue, Don Plunkett, Mal Garland, Walter Strohman, and Al Roberts met at Penrod's.

First of many Vietnam Vet gatherings at various bars and restaurants on Veterans Day and Memorial Day and other occasions.

In 1984 Mal Garland and Walter Strohman organized a meeting at the Marietta Holiday Inn to get as many Vietnam Vets as possible together and to establish a formal organization (Rick Lester and Duke Doubleday were there).

Walter Strohman formalized the group by drafting a charter as a 501(c)19 organization.

Steve Martin filed the charter through his law firm.

Mal Garland was elected first President.

First monthly luncheon held in November 1984 at the Cha Gio Vietnamese Restaurant—12 attendees at the first luncheon, 9 at the second, 17 at the third, and it continued to grow.

Eventually outgrew the Cha Gio Restaurant and moved to the 57th Fighter Group Restaurant at PDK Airport, then to the Happy Valley Asian Restaurant, then to the Retreat at Dunwoody, and finally to our current luncheon location at Dunwoody United Methodist Church.

The monthly luncheons helped us to develop an organization.

MEMORIALS

Our first Memorial was in 1987, at the Galleria Complex to Marine LT John Fuller, a classmate at The Citadel of Walter Strohman. (Note that this was one of the few Memorials in which the Honoree was known to an AVVBA Member—the majority of the Memorials were done simply to honor a fallen brother—"There but for fortune go I.")

This became an annual tradition of the AVVBA and was the major annual project for many years. It was done 27 times for 26 honorees (the one at the Atlanta Airport for WO Francis McDowall, Jr., had to be moved from Concourse A to the main atrium after 9/11).

Memorials were placed throughout the metropolitan Atlanta area, and other locations as far away as Dahlonega, Cartersville, and Jonesboro.

Memorial speakers have included such luminaries as Senator Max Cleland, MG George Patton, and MOH Recipients Gen Ray Davis, Maj Gen James Livingston, and Col Barney Barnum.

> *Our Charter: "To promote a positive image of the Vietnam Veteran through our actions in the community and to honor those from the Atlanta area lost in Vietnam."*

We strived to live up to that Charter with these Memorials and with other community service activities.

Photographs of Memorials can be found on the AVVBA web site—www. avvba.org—as is a list of AVVBA Members who passed away after joining the AVVBA.

USO PARTICIPATION

The AVVBA began its affiliation with the USO in 2005.

The Atlanta Airport USO became the assembly area for troops transiting from CONUS to Afghanistan and Iraq after the 9/11 attacks.

It was a very busy place; several hundred troops per day utilized the USO facility and Mary Lou Austin and her staff performed yeoman service caring for those troops.

They were augmented by volunteers from numerous churches and civic organizations throughout the Atlanta area, including the AVVBA.

Max Torrence was the prime mover for the initial AVVBA efforts at the USO; he was followed in that role by Bob Babcock, John Vail, and Bob Hopkins.

AVVBA sent 6-8 volunteers twice monthly for 15 years (until March 2020 when the COVID-19 situation started). We started again in April 2021 and continue to do that every month.

Duties of the volunteers include cooking and serving hot dogs and chili, keeping the snack counter stocked, greeting military personnel as they come up the escalator from the arrival gates, keeping the USO common areas clean, and going to Costco and Publix to pick up needed food and snacks for the upcoming day.

We also have a raffle at our monthly meetings with prizes donated by members; the proceeds of that raffle are donated to the USO.

In 2007 AVVBA members parked cars for Atlanta Braves games in partnership with the local IBEW union—over $40,000 was raised in that effort.

In 2007 AVVBA members Bill Stanley and Tom Owens served at the USO Center in Bagram Air Base, Afghanistan and Larry Taylor served at the Camp Buehring, Kuwait USO.

In 2005, 8 AVVBA volunteers (Max Torrence, Rick Lester, Dough Handley, Chuck Leisure, Ron Miller, Tom Williams, and Steve and Mary Bolen) deployed to Gulfport/Biloxi, MS, as USO volunteers in support of the Hurricane Katrina recovery.

AVVBA volunteers also supported Hire Heroes USA Warrior Transition Workshops at Forts Benning, Gordon, and Stewart.

USO STATISTICS:

Over $149,623 has been raised by the AVVBA and given to the USO.

Over 15,000 man-hours of volunteer time at the USO by AVVBA Volunteers.

VETERANS DAY PARADES

AVVBA marched in its first Atlanta Veterans Day Parade in 1991 and has marched in every Veterans Day Parade since.

AVVBA has **won several awards** for its sharp appearance marching in these parades.

During the COVID-19 shut-down we participated in a "virtual" Veterans Day Parade by videotaping our group marching past "The Wall That Heals" in John's Creek and submitting that video to be part of the Georgia Veterans Day activities which were held at The Battery in Smyrna. We received an award for that effort.

ATLANTA HISTORY CENTER

AVVBA has partnered with the Atlanta History Center for numerous events:

The Veterans Oral History Program
The Vietnam War Exhibit
Veterans Day Programs and Exhibitions
The Veterans Park outside the main building
The Vietnam War Symposium
Social events honoring Medal of Honor recipients

OTHER ACTIVITIES

Live Fire Exercises and Ranger Graduations at Fort Benning.

Trips to the Currahee Museum in Toccoa, the King's Bay Navy Base, Pensacola NAS, Charleston, SC, and Washington, DC.

Participation in and providing support for numerous charity Golf Tournaments.

Assistance with the setup and display of the moving "Wall that Heals" (now located at New Town Park in John's Creek).

Participation in the Vietnam War 50th Anniversary Commemoration at the State Capitol.

AVVBA members have written two books about their personal experiences in Vietnam, 167 stories by 111 members in the first book and 141 stories by 70 members in the second book. These books "*I'm Ready to Talk*" and "*I'm Ready to Talk Two*" are our gift to future generations of our Families and all Americans. Never forget—Freedom Is Not Free.

CONCLUSION

Article I, Section 2 of the AVVBA By-Laws states:

> "The purpose of the Association is to promote patriotism and sponsor activities of a patriotic nature among the business community; to recognize those who served and honor those who gave their lives in the Vietnam War; to promote a positive image of the Vietnam Veteran, their dependents and the widows and orphans of deceased Vietnam Veterans. "

OVER THE LAST 40 YEARS, WE HAVE LIVED UP TO THOSE WORDS AND HONORED THOSE COMMITMENTS. FOR MORE INFORMATION ON AVVBA, VISIT OUR WEBSITE AT: WWW.AVVBA.ORG

FINAL WORDS

It has been my honor that my fellow Vietnam Veterans have entrusted me to publish their most important stories and for many, the most memorable time in our lives. The reception of our first *I'm Ready to Talk* book confirmed that our Family members and the American public want to hear about the Vietnam War directly from those of us who served there, not from the ones who twist things to meet their own agenda. This book tells more compelling stories straight from veterans.

Over the past months as I've accepted, edited, and communicated with the authors who have contributed to *I'm Ready to Talk Two,* I have enjoyed reading and talking to each author about their experiences—some made me laugh or smile, others caused tears to roll down my cheeks. Each story helps portray the picture of what those of us who participated in the Vietnam War experienced—and helps others appreciate things only those who experienced it can explain. I also had the privilege of hearing intimate stories that they tell only to few people—stories that aren't in this book. Your favorite veteran most likely has stories to tell those who are closest to him/her but will only do so if you show interest.

I encourage Family members and friends to ask the veterans in your Family about their experiences in the military. Most of our WWII veterans are gone now, but those who are still around have lots of stories to preserve for future generations, as do those from the Cold War, Korean War, Vietnam, and the ongoing War on Terror. Every one of those veterans, and those who lived with them as spouses and Family members, had unique experiences that deserve to be preserved for your Family, for their unit, and for American history. Encourage your veteran to preserve and record their stories in some form—while they are still physically and mentally able to do so.

Will there be a third *I'm Ready to Talk* book? I don't know. We Vietnam veterans are all in our 70s and above, so it needs to be done sooner rather than later if it is going to happen. Stay tuned and we'll see if our AV-VBA members want and decide that more stories need and should be told.

Hopefully you've learned a great deal about the Vietnam War while reading this book and learned about the veterans who sacrificed and contributed. We are a cross-section of Vietnam veterans: all branches of service, all types of jobs, and all ranks. We've done our best to tell the Vietnam story as we lived it.

I remain—Steadfast and Loyal—Deeds not Words!
Proud—Professional—Patriotic

Bob Babcock, Rifle Platoon Leader and XO
Bravo Company, 1-22 Infantry, 4th Infantry Division
Vietnam—July 1966 to July 1967
Founder and CEO—Deeds Publishing LLC
www.deedspublishing.com
www.avvba.org

ROBERT O. "BOB" BABCOCK

Bob grew up in the small railroad town of Heavener, Oklahoma. He served in Vietnam with B/1-22 Infantry, 4th Infantry Division as an Infantry officer in 1966-1967. From 1968 to 2002, Bob was a Sales/Marketing Executive with IBM.

Bob is a founding official partner of the Veterans History Project, part of the Library of Congress, preserving memories of America's veterans. Bob recently has been elected for his ninth and tenth years as president of the National 4th Infantry Division Association. He continues as their historian. He previously served for ten years as president of the 22nd Infantry Regiment Society.

Bob is author of eleven books and is founder/CEO of Deeds Publishing LLC and of Americans Remembered Inc. Bob has published over 400 books for established and aspiring authors.

Bob is a member of multiple national and local veterans' organizations, including Atlanta Vietnam Veterans Business Association, National 4th Infantry Division Association, 22nd Infantry Regiment Society, American Legion, Veterans of Foreign Wars, and leads the Veterans ministry at Mt. Bethel United Methodist Church. Bob and his wife, Jan, have four grown children and five grandchildren.

BOOKS BY ROBERT O. BABCOCK

War Stories: Utah Beach to the Liberation of Paris
War Stories: Paris to VE Day
War Stories: Vietnam 1966 to 1970
What Now, Lieutenant?
You Don't Know Jack…or Jerry
Operation Iraqi Freedom I: A Year in the Sunni Triangle
Operation Iraqi Freedom 07-09: Dispatches from Baghdad
World War II WAC—Helen Denton as told to Bob Babcock
With Honor We Served—Veterans of Mt. Bethel UMC
I'm Ready to Talk—Vietnam Veterans Preserve Their Stories
I'm Ready to Talk Two—Vietnam Veterans Preserve Their Stories

These and many other military books published by Deeds Publishing can be found at **www.deedspublishing.com** or at **www.amazon.com** and other book retailers.

INDEX OF AUTHORS

CPSIA information can be obtained
at www.ICGtesting.com
Printed in the USA
LVHW061710141221
R17069800001B/R170698PG705971LVX00001B/1